FTCE SOCIAL SCIENCE 6–12

FLORIDA TEACHER CERTIFICATION EXAMINATIONS

 TestWare® Edition

Cynthia Metcalf, Ph.D.
Visiting Assistant Professor
Manhattanville College
Purchase, New York

 Research & Education Association
www.rea.com

Research & Education Association
61 Ethel Road West
Piscataway, New Jersey 08854
E-mail: info@rea.com

**Florida FTCE Social Science 6–12 Test
with TestWare® on CD-ROM**

Published 2016

Printed in the United States of America

Library of Congress Control Number 2010931596

ISBN-13: 978-0-7386-0808-2
ISBN-10: 0-7386-0808-4

The competencies presented in this book were created and implemented by the Florida
Department of Education in conjunction with the Evaluation Systems group of Pearson
Education, Inc. For further information visit the Florida DOE website at *www.fldoe.org/*.

Cover image: Jose Luis Pelaez Inc./Blend Images/Getty Images

About Research & Education Association

Founded in 1959, Research & Education Association (REA) is dedicated to publishing the finest and most effective educational materials—including study guides and test preps—for students in middle school, high school, college, graduate school, and beyond.

Today, REA's wide-ranging catalog is a leading resource for teachers, students, and professionals. Visit *www.rea.com* to see a complete listing of all our titles.

About the Author

Dr. Cynthia Metcalf is Visiting Assistant Professor in the History Department at Manhattanville College in Purchase, N.Y., where she teaches both graduate and undergraduate courses in Middle Eastern history, South Asian history, and World History. She also serves as a senior thesis advisor for history majors and as a freshman advisor and freshman seminar instructor for incoming students. In addition to teaching in a brick and mortar institution, Dr. Metcalf also teaches online as an Adjunct Instructor in History for Baker College Online. She received her Ph.D. in history from the University of Virginia. She received several major fellowships to conduct her research from the Social Science Research Council, American Research Center in Egypt, American Institute of Maghrebi Studies, and the United States Information Agency Documentation of Cultural Properties Program. Dr. Metcalf received her M.A. in South Asian History and her B.A. in Slavic Languages and Literature from the University of Virginia. Currently Dr. Metcalf is revising her dissertation manuscript and contributing entries to the *Dictionary of African Bibliography*.

Acknowledgments

We would like to thank Larry Kling, Vice President, Editorial, for his editorial direction; Pam Weston, Publisher, for setting the quality standards for production integrity; Kathleen Casey, Senior Editor, for project management and preflight editorial review; Diane Goldschmidt, Senior Editor, for post-production quality assurance; Wallie Hammond, for her expertise in modeling test items; Christine Saul, Senior Graphic Artist, for cover design; and Rachel DiMatteo, Graphic Artist, for test design.

We also gratefully acknowledge Farah Lipitz for copyediting, CaraGraphics for typesetting, the Editors of REA for proofreading, and Terry Casey for indexing the manuscript.

Contents

Introduction

About This Book and TestWare®

REA's *Florida FTCE Social Science 6–12 Test* is designed to help you pass the content exam that certifies prospective 6–12 social studies teachers in the Sunshine State. To enhance your chances of success in this important step toward your career as a teacher in Florida schools, this comprehensive test guide, along with REA's exclusive TestWare® software:

- Presents an accurate and complete overview of the FTCE Social Science 6–12 Test;

- Identifies all of the important information and how it's represented on the exam;

- Provides a thorough review of every competency and skill;

- Presents sample questions in the actual test format;

- Offers tips and strategies for successfully completing this exam;

- Includes computerized diagnostic tools to pinpoint areas of strength and weakness;

- Provides two full-length practice tests based on the most recently administered FTCE;

- Replicates the format of the official exam, including levels of difficulty;

- Provides the correct answer and detailed explanations for each question on the practice tests, which enables you to identify correct answers and understand why they are correct.

This guide is based on the best research and resources. The editors considered the most recent test administrations and professional standards. They also researched information from the Florida Department of Education, professional journals, textbooks, and educators in the field. This guide includes the best test-preparation materials based on the latest information available. Nonetheless, it is always wise to check for any late updates from the test administrator.

Practice Tests 1 and 2 are included in two formats: in printed form in this book and in TestWare® format on the enclosed CD. We recommend that you begin your preparation by first taking the computerized version of your test since the only format for Florida's entire series of teacher certification exams is computerized. The software provides the added benefits of enforced timed conditions and instantaneous, accurate scoring, making it easier to identify where you need to focus your study.

About the Test

Since 1980, the state of Florida has used the Florida Teacher Certification Examinations as a requirement for teacher certification. In 1986, the legislature added the requirement to pass a test in the content area in which the teacher desires to be certified. The purpose of this preparation guide is to help you successfully prepare for the test by providing you with a clear overview of what content is considered essential in the social science curricula for grades 6–12. The guide is not designed to be an all-inclusive source for social science content. The practice tests assume that you have some foundation of knowledge in social science; therefore, not all questions have been drawn from the review section.

There are two versions of the social science test in Florida. Be sure you are registered for the proper test. The version for grades 5–9 is what you should take if you want to be a middle school teacher. The version for grades 6–12 requires greater depth of knowledge. This guide is designed to prepare you for the grades 6–12 test.

All FTCE/FELE tests are given on computer. A list of computer-based tests and test sites is posted on the FTCE/FELE contractor website at *www.fl.nesinc.com*.

Below are the competencies used as the basis for the FTCE Social Science 6–12 examination, as well as the approximate percentage of the total test that each competency accounts for. These competencies represent the knowledge that teams of teachers, subject area specialists, and district-level educators have determined to be important for beginning teachers. This book contains a focused review of these competencies, as well as the specific skills that demonstrate mastery of each area.

Competencies	Questions	Percentage
1. Knowledge of Geography	12	10%
2. Knowledge of Economics	18	15%
3. Knowledge of Political Science	18	15%
4. Knowledge of World History	30	25%
5. Knowledge of U.S. History	30	25%
6. Knowledge of Social Science and its Methodology	12	10%

The test has approximately 120 questions and you will have 2.5 hours to take it.

Who Administers the Test?

The Florida Department of Education develops this test. Subject area knowledge tested on the FTCE Social Science 6–12 examination was identified and validated by committees of content specialists from the state of Florida. Public school teachers made up the majority of the committee members, but the committees also included district supervisors and college faculty. Selection of committee members was based on recommendations by professional associations, experts, and teachers' unions. Development of the appropriate content and difficulty levels of the exam involved literature review, teacher interviews, beta tests, and professional judgment. Testing services, including test administrations, for the FTCE are provided by the Evaluation Systems group of Pearson Education, Inc.

Can I Retake the Test?

If you do not achieve a passing grade on the FTCE, don't panic. The test can be taken again after 31 days, so you can seriously work on improving your score in preparation for your next FTCE. A score on the FTCE that does not match your expectations does not mean that you should change your plans about teaching.

When Should the FTCE Be Taken?

Florida law requires that teachers demonstrate mastery of basic skills, professional knowledge, and the content area in which they choose to specialize. If you've graduated from a Florida state-approved teacher preparation program and made the decision to teach Social Science 6–12, you need to begin the process by applying for a Florida Temporary Certificate in that subject. The Bureau of Educator Certification will evaluate your eligibility only in the subject(s) you request on your application form. The Temporary Certificate is valid for three school years, which allows you time to complete the certification tests while teaching full-time.

For high school graduates and out-of-state educators, the Bureau of Educator Certification will provide you with official information about which test(s) to take to complete requirements for the professional certificate. The FTCE is usually administered four times a year in several locations throughout Florida. The usual testing day is Saturday, but the test may be taken on an alternate day if a conflict exists, such as a religious obligation. Special accommodations also can be made for applicants who are visually impaired, hearing impaired, physically disabled, or specific learning disabled.

To receive information on upcoming administrations of the FTCE, you should consult the FTCE Registration Bulletin, which can be obtained by contacting:

Florida Department of Education
325 West Gaines Street, Suite 414
Tallahassee, FL 32399-0400
Phone: (413) 256-2893
Website: *www.fldoe.org/asp/ftce or www.fl.nesinc.com*
Bureau of Educator Certification: *www.fl doe.org/edcert*

The FTCE Registration Bulletin also includes information regarding test retakes and score reports.

Is There a Registration Fee?

To take the FTCE, you must pay a registration fee. You may pay by personal check, money order, cashier's check, or Visa or MasterCard. Cash is not accepted. Utilize the contact information above for any questions.

How To Use This Book and Testware®

How Do I Begin Studying?

1. Review the organization of this test preparation guide.

2. To best utilize your study time, follow our FTCE Independent Study Schedule. The schedule is based on a six-week program but can be condensed to four weeks if necessary by combining a few weekly periods.

3. Take the first Practice Test on CD-ROM and study the competencies that your scores indicate need further review.

4. Review the format of the FTCE.

5. Review the test-taking advice and suggestions presented later in this chapter.

6. Pay attention to the information about competencies and skills, content, and topics on the test.

7. Spend time reviewing topics that stand out as needing more study.

8. Take the second Practice Test on CD-ROM, review the explanations to your answers carefully, and study the competencies that your scores indicate need further review.

9. Follow the suggestions at the end of this chapter for the day before and the day of the test.

When Should I Start Studying?

It is never too early to start studying for the FTCE. The earlier you begin, the more time you will have to sharpen your skills. Do not procrastinate! Cramming is not an effective way to study, since it does not allow you the time to think about the content, review the competencies, and take the practice tests. It is important, however, to review the material one last time on the night before the test administration.

It is very important for you to choose the time and place for studying that works best for you. Some individuals may set aside a certain number of hours every morning to study, while others may choose to study at night before going to sleep. Other people may study during the day, while waiting in line, or even while eating lunch. Only you can determine when and where your study time will be most effective. Be consistent and use your time wisely. Work out a study routine and stick to it.

FTCE Social Science 6–12 Study Schedule

The following study schedule allows for thorough preparation for the FTCE. The course of study here is six weeks, but you can condense or expand the timeline to suit your personal schedule. It is vital that you adhere to a structured plan and set aside ample time each day to study. The more time you devote to studying, the more confident you will be on the day of the test.

Week	Activity
1	Take the first Practice Test on CD-ROM. The score will indicate your strengths and weaknesses. Make sure that you simulate real exam conditions when you take the test. Afterwards, score it and review the explanations, especially for questions you answered incorrectly.
2	Return to the review chapters and go through the appropriate chapter sections for material you missed. Useful study techniques include highlighting key terms and information, taking notes as you review the book's sections, and putting new terms and information on note cards to help retain the information.
3 and 4	Reread all your note cards, refresh your understanding of the exam's competencies and skills, review your college textbooks, and read over class notes you've previously taken. This is also the time to consider any other supplementary materials that your counselor or the Florida State Department of Education suggests. Review the department's website at *www.fldoe.org*.
5	Have someone quiz you using the index cards you created. Take the second Practice Test on CD-ROM, adhering to the time limits that will be automatically incorporated in the TestWare® program. Be sure to simulate other test-day conditions.
6	Review your areas of weakness using all study materials. This is a good time to re-take both practice tests printed in this book.

What is Geography?

Geography is the study of the earth's surface, including such aspects as its climate, topography, vegetation, and population.

Geography is a spatial discipline—one in which geographers preoccupy themselves with how to organize space. It is much more than just memorizing names and places and just studying the physical features of the earth. While geography requires an understanding of the earth's surface itself, it also is concerned with how living things and earth's features are distributed around the earth. It seeks to ask three questions: Where? Why there? What are the consequences of it being there? Geographers look at the earth's physical space and investigate patterns—a geographer might look at the space of your bedroom and ask several questions: How are things distributed? What processes operate in that space? How does this space relate to other nearby spaces? Such a way of identifying, explaining, and predicting the human and physical patterns in space and the interconnectedness of various spaces is known to geographers as the **spatial perspective**. The key to geography is that it views the earth through a lens of location and space and seeks to find patterns of place or interactions between places and people. So, essentially, geography is the science of space and place.

Branches of Geography

Generally, geography can be divided into four main branches:

Human Geography takes as its subject humans and the cultures they create relative to their space and encompasses areas like population geography, economic, and political geography and looks at how people's activities relate to the environment politically, culturally, historically, and socially.

Physical Geography focuses on the physical environment of Earth—its water, air, animals, and land (i.e., all that is part of the four spheres—the atmosphere, biosphere, hydrosphere, and lithosphere). It looks at land formation, water, weather, and climate, but also includes such areas as geomorphology, biogeography, and environmental geography.

Regional Geography focuses on areas of Earth that have some degree of similarity and divides the world into different **realms**.

Topical/Systemic Geography considers systematic studies of climate, landforms, economics, and culture.

Geographers may specialize in a variety of subfields that break off of the four branches of geography, but all of them have as their main focus the spatial perspective. **Population geography** is a form of geography that deals with the relationships between geography and population patterns, including birth and death rates. **Political geography** deals with the effect of geography on politics, especially on national boundaries and relations between states. **Economic geography** is a study of the interaction between the Earth's landscape and the economic activity of the human population.

COMPETENCY 1.1
Apply the six essential elements of geography.

There are five themes and six essential elements of geography that represent the fundamentals of the study of geography. In 1984, the National Council for Geographic Education and the Association of American Geographers came up with the five themes of geography to help facilitate and organize the teaching of geography in the K–12 classroom. Since then, these themes have been supplanted by the National Geography Standards, which we will discuss, but the original five continue to provide an effective way of organizing your understanding of the field of geography.

The Five Themes are:

1) Location

2) Places

3) Human/Environment Interaction

4) Movement

5) Regions

Location: (World in Spatial Terms—Position on the Earth's Surface)

One of the first things geographers do when they begin a study is to describe the location of a place. Geographers approach describing the positions and distribution of people and places on the earth's surface by looking at location in two different ways: **absolute** and **relative** location.

Absolute Location: This is the exact whereabouts of a place, person, or thing. Every point on Earth has a specific location that is determined by an imaginary grid of lines denoting **latitude** and **longitude**. Technically, a location is absolute when it has only one possible reference point. That is why latitude and longitude work; only one place on the planet is 85 degrees north, 37 degrees west. Parallels of latitude measure distances north and south of the line called the **equator**. Meridians of longitude measure distances east and west of another imaginary line called the prime meridian. Geographers use latitude and longitude to pinpoint a place's absolute, or exact, location. When we refer to the absolute location of a place, it could be as simple as a street address. Finding absolute location is the starting point for geographic research. For example, the absolute location of Miami, Florida, is 25.92 degrees north and 80.28 degrees west. In everyday life, absolute location is not really practical to use (Do you use longitude and latitude for directions in the same town, for instance?). However, some people do use it (e.g., cartographers, pilots, naval personnel, meteorologists, geologists, and geographers), because they need a specific place for a specific task—like identifying where an earthquake has hit.

Relative Location: This is the type of description of location that is most commonly used, as it is a description of the relationship of a place between and among other places. It is usually described by landmarks, time, direction, or distances from one thing to another. When using relative location, a point is usually described by focusing on the things around it. That point could be your home address—an absolute location because there is only one "28 North Main Street" in Williamsport, Pennsylvania. Its relative location takes into account its location as described in relation to places around it. Thus, the relative location of Nashville, Tennessee, could be described as being "south of Louisville, Kentucky," for example. "Hillsboro High School is located 9 miles southwest of McGavock High School" is another example of a relative location. While a site's absolute location will not vary (28 North Main Street in Williamsport, Pennsylvania will always be 28 North Main Street in Williamsport), the site relative to the Joe's Corner Grocery store may change, if, for example, Joe's Corner Grocery becomes Slidell's Barber Shop.

Places and Regions (Physical and Human Characteristics)

The theme of place addresses this question: What's it like there? This element of geography addresses the issue that all places have meaning and characteristics that make them unique from all other places on Earth. **Place** is a unique combination of physical and cultural attributes that give each location on the earth its individual "stamp." Geographers describe places by two kinds of characteristics and images: physical and human. Studying a place's physical and human characteristics help us understand its nature.

A place's **physical characteristics** comprise its natural environment and emanate from geological, hydrological, atmospheric, and biological processes present in that location. Some physical characteristics of a place include mountains, rivers, beaches, topography, flora (plant life), fauna (animal life), resources (trees, oil, petroleum, and diamonds), land forms (rivers, plateaus, plains), bodies of water, climate, soils, and natural vegetation.

The **human characteristics** of a place are derived from the changes to an environment as a result of human ideas and actions. Such characteristics include man-made designed features of places like architecture, religion, food, and transportation and communication networks.

The combination of these two parts of place, the human and physical, helps differentiate locations from each other, almost like fingerprints, and provides a starting point for geographers to begin to make observations about a place. By looking at the physical and human characteristics of a place, we can begin to answer two major questions that geographers ask: "Where is it?" and "Why is it there?"

Human-Environmental Interaction

Geographers look at both the positive and negative effects that result from human interaction with the environment: how humans rely on it, alter it, and adapt to it—and how the environment may limit what people are able to do. Much of the way that people relate to the environment reflects their economic and political circumstances as well as their culture and their technological capabilities. One significant issue with this geographical theme is that the interaction between humans and the environment can change quickly, and such change might be temporary. For instance, we might change the environment by building a dam, but then floods, earthquakes, drought, or mudslides could destroy the dam and change the environment again.

Movement

Not only do humans move, but their ideas, fads, goods, resources, and communication all travel distances as well. The theme of movement answers the question of how and why places, people, and things are connected to, and dependent upon, one another. It examines how relationships are shaped by the movement of transportation (imports and exports), flow of people (immigration and migration), and ideas and resources over time within a geographical area. This movement happens as people interact with other people, places, and things almost every day of their lives. Movement examines **cultural diffusion**, i.e., how ideas, innovation, and ideology spread from one area to another.

So, geographers analyze the movement occurring in a space—movement of information, people, goods, and other phenomena. Geographers also evaluate how places interact through movement, a process known as **spatial interaction**. Although everything is theoretically linked to everything else, nearer things are usually related more to each other than to faraway things. Thus, the extent of spatial interaction often depends on distance.

In evaluating movement and spatial interaction, geographers often evaluate the **friction of distance**, which is the degree to which distance interferes with some interaction. For example, the friction of distance for a working-class Ohio man wanting to visit a dentist in Ethiopia is quite high, meaning that the distance gets in the way of this interaction occurring. However, the friction of distance has been reduced in many aspects of life with improved transportation and communication infrastructures.

Today, the friction of distance is not as much of a problem for a business in Florida to sell something to a business in Taiwan, for example. Businesses can now communicate over the Internet, buying and selling their goods in transactions that would have taken months to complete just 30 years ago. This increasing sense of accessibility and connectivity seems to bring humans in distant places closer together, a phenomenon known as **space–time compression**. Note that space–time compression is reducing perceived distance, which is the friction of distance thought by humans, not the actual distance on the land.

Related to space–time compression is the effect of **distance decay**, in which the interaction between two places declines as the distance between the two places increases. Imagine putting a magnet on your desk and putting an iron nail on it. The farther you pull the iron nail away from the magnet, the less of a pull effect the magnet has on the nail—right? It is the same with distance decay; as the distance between two entities increases, the effect of their interaction decreases.

However, improved transportation and communication technologies have reduced the effect of distance decay on most human interactions. In 1850 on any given day, a person living in Atlanta probably never interacted with someone from 30 miles outside the city. Now a person in Atlanta can interact with people from all over the world via the Internet and improved transportation.

Regions

Geographers divide the world into more manageable units called **regions**. Regions have unifying characteristics that may be physical, cultural, or human-based—they may occur over large spaces and can be found across great distances. Physical characteristics of an area include land forms, climate, soil, and natural vegetation, like a mountain range. Regions may also be distinguished by human characteristics, like similar language, and economic, social, political, and cultural similarities.

There are three basic types of regions:

- **Formal regions** (sometimes referred to as uniform regions) are areas that have common (or uniform) cultural or physical features and are often defined by governmental or administrative boundaries (i.e., United States, Birmingham, Brazil). A climate region is a formal region because it links places that share a climate. A map showing where Christianity is practiced is showing a formal region, or a group of places sharing that region.

- **Functional regions** (sometimes referred to as nodal regions) are linked together by some function's influence on them. However, if the function ceases to exists, the region no longer exists. Functional regions are created through the movement of some phenomenon, like a disease, or a perceived interaction among places, like pizza delivery routes. For example, a functional region might appear on a map of Delta Airlines' flights from Atlanta, Georgia. A mapmaker would plot all the places to which Delta travels from its hub in Atlanta— the node. Then the mapmaker would draw a boundary enclosing all of those places into one functional region. The area affected by the spread of a flu epidemic is a functional region. A functional region could even show the transmission of a rumor from its source to all the people who hear it. Remember, functional regions are defined by the places affected by the movement of some phenomenon from its source or node of other places.

- **Vernacular regions** are those loosely defined by people's perception (e.g., the South, the Middle East). The boundaries of a perceptual region are determined by people's beliefs, not a scientifically measurable process. For example, the space in which the "cool kids" sit at lunch would be a perceptual region because its boundaries are totally determined by the region maker's perception of who is cool and who is not—something that could be debated by any other person in the room. Another example of a perceptual region is the South in the United States. People differ in their perceptions of which places are considered part of the South.

New Standards of Geographic Education

The National Geography Standards were published in 1994 to guide geographic education in the United States. The 18 standards are organized under *six essential elements* that shed light on what the geographically informed person should know and understand. The prime objective is for every student in America to become a geographically informed person through implementation of these standards in the classroom. Below you will find how the 18 standards are distributed among the six essential elements. We will go into further detail about each of these elements below.

The World in Spatial Terms

Geography maps the relationships between people, places, and environments by structuring the knowledge of them into real and mental maps and then conducting a spatial analysis of that information. So, maps become a primary tool that geographers use in order to present, acquire, process, and decipher information in spatial terms. Students are taught:

1. how to use maps and other geographic representations, tools, and technologies to acquire, process, and report information;

2. how to use mental maps (a person's internalized picture of a part of Earth's surface) to organize information about people places, and environments;

3. how to analyze the spatial organization of people, places, and environments on Earth's surface.

Places and Regions

Place and region are basic units of geography, and geographers examine the physical and human characteristics of places to understand how places work. They also trace people's perceptions of areas, how people create their own mental regions that come from their own view of the world, and how these perceptions or biases are created and organized. This element asks the student to understand:

4. the physical and human characteristics of places;

5. that people create regions to interpret Earth's complexity;

6. how culture and experience influence people's perceptions of places and regions.

Physical Systems

Physical processes shape Earth's surface and interact with plant and animal life to create, sustain, and modify ecosystems. This element of geography looks at environmental phenomena and their interaction through ecosystems, renewable resources, and the water cycle. Students should understand:

7. the physical processes that shape the patterns of Earth's surface;

8. the characteristics and distribution of ecosystems on Earth's surface.

Human Systems

People are central to geography in that human activities help shape Earth's surface. Human settlements and structures are part of Earth's surface, and humans compete for control of Earth's surface. This element looks at characteristics, distribution, and migration of human populations. It also tries to find patterns—in culture, economic interdependence, human settlement, conflict and cooperation—and how these influence people's relationship with each other and the Earth. This element asks geography students to understand:

9. the characteristics, distribution, and migration of human populations;

10. the characteristics, distribution, and complexity of Earth's cultural mosaics;

11. the patterns and networks of economic interdependence;

12. the processes, patterns, and functions of human settlement;

13. how the forces of cooperation and conflict among people influence the division and control of Earth's surface.

Environment and Society

Humans modify the earth's environment through their actions. Such actions happen largely as a consequence of the way people value or devalue the earth's resources. The geographically informed person knows and understands:

14. how human actions modify the physical environment;

15. how physical systems affect human systems;

16. the changes that occur in the meaning, use, distribution, and importance of resources.

The Uses of Geography

Geography informs people about the relationships they have between place and environment over time. This element explores how humans modify the physical environment, how physical systems affect human systems, and how the changes occur in the meaning, use, distribution, and importance of resources. The geographically informed person knows and understands:

17. how to apply geography to interpret the past;

18. how to apply geography to interpret the present and plan for the future.

COMPETENCY 1.2
Identify the ways natural processes and human-environment interactions shape the Earth's physical systems and features.

The Earth's physical systems and features are shaped and reshaped by a combined effort from natural processes and human interactions with it. Physical processes are nature's way of producing, maintaining, or altering the physical systems of the Earth. Physical processes can be categorized into four areas:

- Air—this is referred to as **atmospheric** and includes examinations of climate and meteorology.

- Land—this is referred to as **lithospheric** and can examine plate tectonics, erosion, and soil formation.

- Water—this is referred to as **hydrospheric** and examines things like the circulation of the oceans and the hydrologic cycle.

- Animals—this is referred to as **biospheric** and examines plant and animal communities and ecosystems.

There are seven main natural processes that have shaped the Earth's landforms and physical systems and features: plate tectonics, weathering, transportation, erosion, freezing and thawing, gravity, and deposition. Much of the **landforms** that the Earth has were the byproducts of interaction between these natural processes that interacted to produce sediments, which then got deposited together to form sand dunes, deltas, and glacial moraines. Some of the natural processes, like earthquakes and volcanic eruptions, produce dramatic alterations of the Earth's surface. Others, like weathering and erosion, take longer to happen.

Studying the interaction within and between these categories of physical processes and the natural cycles that water, rocks, and atmospheric gasses play allows us to see how the Earth functions. Natural Earth's processes shape the land and environment by reworking, conserving, and renewing its materials. For instance, the interaction between the hydrosphere and the atmosphere might produce floods, hurricanes, and cyclones that in turn reshape the Earth where they land. Plants alter the Earth's atmosphere in multiple ways—first, they remove the carbon dioxide, then they transform the carbon into sugar, and then they release the oxygen. Earthquakes and volcanic eruptions reflect internal earth processes as well. Earthquakes occur along the boundaries between colliding tectonic plates; sometimes the molten rock below creates so much pressure that it gets released by volcanoes and then these help to construct mountains. Under the ocean, volcanic activity along the ocean floor may form undersea mountains that can thrust above the Earth's surface and become islands.

Weathering is the physical and chemical breakdown of rocks at or near the Earth's surface. As rocks fragment, crack, and crumble, due to physical, chemical, or biological interactions, they become soil. As that soil and rock debris loosen and get carried away, **erosion** happens—without it, rock debris would just stay where it was formed, and we would have a rather rocky earth's surface to contend with. Erosion can happen for a variety of reasons and through a variety of natural agents, each producing distinctive changes both in the material that it transports and creating distinctive characteristics in the surface and landscape. There are various agents of erosion:

- Streams (running water): Sediments get transported by streams and shape the Earth as a result.

- Glaciers (moving ice): Glacial erosion can cause the formation of glacial moraines (material transported by a glacier and then deposited somewhere else), drumlins (streamlined long hills that are composed of sediment from glacial drift), and finger lakes (caused by glaciers advancing and retreating and dragging sediment along with them). Obviously, the **Ice Age** was an age where a significant amount of glacier formation and erosion happened during its waning and waxing.

- Wave Action: Erosion and deposition by waves cause changes in shoreline features, including beaches, sandbars, and barrier islands. Wave action is the most potent erosive force on Earth as it is powered by the force of gravity, and the worlds rivers alone move about 20 billion tons of rock and sediment to the oceans each year.

- Wind: Wind can aid the erosion of sediments and create dunes and sand-blasted bedrock.

- Mass Movement: This can cause Earth materials to move downslope under the influence of gravity.

Plate tectonics is concerned with the movement in the Earth and the forces that produce movement. Basically, it is the theory that Earth's lithosphere is broken down into a dozen plates that float. We look at plate tectonics to understand how volcanoes and earthquakes form. When forces deep in the earth make pieces of the Earth's crust separate, collide, and slide past each other, we get a variety of new forms—like mountains, islands, trenches, and valleys.

COMPETENCY 1.3
Identify the ways natural processes and human—environment interactions shape cultural features (e.g., communities, language, technology, and political and economic institutions).

Geographers look at not just the physical aspects of Earth but also the impact of humans on it. Culture is the way of life that characterizes a certain people. Culture consists of many components, like language, technology, political and economic institutions, religion, work ethics, values, education, dress, technology usage, and religion. Through people's culture, we see an interaction with the Earth—this is the study of **cultural ecology**.

Humans depend on the environment to provide them with their basic needs: food, shelter, and clothing. Humans also modify that same environment in order to meet their needs. For instance, people build dams to change the way water flows, plow and irrigate fields, clear forests to build houses, and dig mines. Humans also adapt to their environment if they cannot change it. For instance, people put on warm coats and use heaters when they live in cold climes. How people adapt to their environment depends to a large extent on their ability to do so—and it reflects their economic and political circumstances and their technological abilities.

Human–environment interaction has also shaped Earth's physical systems and features. Building on ocean fronts may increase erosion and alter the landscape. Clearing forests changes the appearance of the landscape, and making dams will change the way water flows. Clearing land to make room for cities changes the landscape of the land.

Geographers approach the study of human–environment interaction in a variety of ways:

Environmental determinism: This is the view that the environment can overpower people and determine their culture and the direction and extent of their development. This is widely considered a rather "not politically correct" belief in geography. The main train of thought in environmental determinism is that an area's physical characteristics, like climate, impact how people develop over time. For instance, a widely held idea was that "the higher the civilization, the higher the latitude," as it was believed that people in hot climates had to rest a lot in order to keep their body temperature cool—so, over time, they became lazy and did not work very hard.

Human—cultural determinism: This is the view that culture overpowers and shapes the environment. This informs the view of many environmentalists that people are destroying the environment. The problem with this way of thinking is that it is an inadequate way to consider the relationship between humans and the environment because indeed the environment does much to shape our cultural activities.

Human—environment interaction: This is the idea that there is a cycle of interaction between humans and the environment that is complex and tautological—the environment shapes people and people shape the environment. We can look at this interaction through a variety of lenses:

- Impact of climate on the interaction: Climate influences humans and cultures, as people avoid places that are too hot, cold, wet, or dry. It also influences what kind of agriculture can be produced. But, on the other hand, people have learned to adapt to the environment—they developed air conditioning and heating and have used trade to get the goods they need if they cannot be produced where they live.

- Impact of vegetation on the interaction: The quality of soil and vegetation and access to irrigation can affect how people interact with the environment—they can either leave an area, develop it and find another use for it, use technology to provide an area for water, etc.

- Impact of landforms on the interaction: Landforms can shape human and cultural activities, like hunting. But also, humans and cultures can adapt and change landforms to meet their needs, like building highways through mountains to make communication and transportation easier.

Political ecology is a multi-disciplinary study of how social and environmental change occurs in the context of power relations, social structures, economic issues, and human–environment interactions.

COMPETENCY 1.4
Analyze geographic information from maps, charts, and graphs.

Maps

What is a map? A map shows a view of an area. Maps are made for a variety of reasons: to represent an area that we cannot see, to show a phenomenon or process that we cannot see with our eyes, to present information concisely, or to show spatial relationships. They are one of the basic tools of geography as they enable us to depict spatial information on paper so that the geographer can read and use information effectively.

A **map** is a two-dimensional model of the earth or a portion of its surface. The process of mapmaking is called **cartography**. All maps include a somewhat simplified view of the earth's surface. Simplification is what a cartographer does to get rid of unnecessary details and focuses on the information needed to be displayed on the map. When designing a map of Europe for high school students to use to help them memorize the names of countries and capitals, a mapmaker would present a simplified map of Europe's political states and boundaries, eliminating details such as vegetation or climate. Another example of simplification involves a cartographer designing a map of London's Underground subway for tourists. Such a cartographer might eliminate unnecessary details such as unrelated buildings and streets from their maps because tourists do not need these details to understand London's subway tracks. Tourists are simply interested in getting on and off at the correct subway stops.

You might encounter a variety of maps on the test—not only a directional map but perhaps a **political map**, which shows political boundaries, states, cities, capitals, countries, a **physical map,** which shows landforms and bodies of water found in an area, or a **thematic map,** which features a variety of subjects, like climate, vegetation, population density, historical trends, etc.

Map Properties

Every map has four main map properties: shape, size (area), distance, and direction. **Shape** refers to the geometric shapes of the objects on the map. **Size** (**area**) refers to the relative amount of space taken up on the map by the landforms or objects on the map. **Distance** refers to the represented distance between objects on the map. **Direction** refers to the degree of accuracy representing the cardinal directions—north, south, east, and west—and their intermediate directions—northwest, northeast, southwest, and southeast. Less accurate are the relative directions that people commonly use to describe a location, such as right, left, up, and down, among many others.

All four properties cannot be accurately represented, so a cartographer must choose which of the properties to distort. Cartographers make this decision by considering the map's purpose. When designing a map for navigational purposes, the cartographer would keep direction and distance accurate; size (area) and shape are not as important. It is impossible to take the Earth's round surface and put it onto a flat surface without some form of distortion, or error, resulting from the "flattening" process. Think of distortion as being caused by a process similar to trying to flatten an orange peel. Sorry to inform you of this, but all of the maps that you have memorized are wrong. As it is often said, "All maps lie flat, and all flat maps lie." Yes, that's right: every map is, in some way, wrong. The globe is the most accurate representation of the Earth.

Every map has six parts, and these parts often provide great clues to help you read and understand the map. The **title** reveals the subject of a map and gives you an idea about what information the map conveys. A **compass** (or a **compass rose**) helps you orient a map—look carefully on the maps in the test to make sure you can identify north—sometimes it just has an N with an arrow. A **scale** tells you how much smaller the distance is on a map compared to the actual distance. The smaller the scale, the more detailed the map. **Labels** are words or phrases that explain features on a map. A **key (legend)** will explain or show what the symbols or colors on a map mean. Most maps use a longitude and latitude grid. In your exam, you may come across an example of a **contour** map that depicts elevation. You should know that **contour lines** that are closer together mean that the elevation is steeper. During the FTCE Social Science 6–12 Test, you will have to use maps, charts, and graphs. Familiarize yourself with the information provided before reading the questions. Typically, a map, chart, or graph will be displayed with a set of questions following it. Be sure you understand what the data reveal before proceeding to the questions. The practice tests in this guide will give you the opportunity to use some of these items.

Graphs and Charts

Graphs and **charts** are graphical representations usually of a large amount of numeric data and also detail the relationships between the parts of data. Sometimes the use of images helps convey information with much more impact than just a bunch of numbers. Graphs and charts have the capability of strengthening the implications about data through the use of visual images, colors used, and other tools. There are a few key elements that you will find on every graph. Each graph contains an *x*-axis and *y*-axis. The *x*-axis goes along the horizontal border of a chart and the *y*-axis is the vertical.

Features of Graphs and Charts

Title: The **title** usually appears above the main graphic and provides a description of the information contained in the chart or graph.

Diagram: A **diagram** represents the visualization of the underlying data.

Dimensions: **Dimensions** in the data are expressed along **axes.** All charts, with the exception of pie charts (circle graphs), have one or more axis—usually an *x*-axis and a *y*-axis.

Scale: Each chart or graph will have a scale marked by periodic gradations and accompanied by numerical or categorical indications.

Labels: Each axis will have a label displayed outside or beside it that describes what sort of dimensions it represents.

Data: All charts and graphs represent data of some sort. The data can appear in a variety of formats, some of which are mentioned below. It can also appear as dots or shapes, connected or unconnected, and in any combination of colors and patterns.

Legend: When the chart or graph represents multiple variables, a legend is usually included that lists the variables in the chart and an example of their appearance.

Types of Charts and Graphs

There are a number of different types of charts with which you should be familiar:

- **Area Chart**: An area chart (**area graph**) is used to show how something changes with respect to time. It shows the contribution, over time, of each type of data in a series, in the form of a whole picture.

- **Bar Chart**: A bar chart (also referred to as **a bar graph**) uses horizontal or vertical blocks or bars to compare the amounts or frequency of distinct items or shows single items at distinct intervals. Bar charts are useful for comparing groups of data that are in competition with one another. Usually, a bar chart is laid out with categories along the vertical axis and values along the horizontal axis.

- **Column Chart**: Column charts are similar to bar charts because they compare items at distinct intervals. However, they differ from bar charts in that they arrange the categories along the horizontal axis and place the values along the vertical axis. As a result, the bars are vertical on the chart. Column charts are often used to show how values can change over a certain period of time.

- **Line Chart**: A line chart (also referred to as a **line graph**) allows you to look at two pieces of information, which have both similarities and dissimilarities with one another. A line chart plots the value of data in a **data point** and then "connects the dots" in order to illustrate the relationship of consecutive points. Line charts are usually used to show how something changes over time. Unlike bar and column charts, which show change over a small amount of time, line charts imply continuous change.

- **Pie Chart**: A pie chart (also referred to as a **circle graph**) is used to represent a part-to-whole relationship between data groups. In these charts, the circle represents the whole and the pie is split into parts called **sectors** that represent a part of the whole. Each sector typically is in proportion in size to the amount each sector represents. **Sector labels** indicate the category of information the sector relates to and may also give numeric data, like percentages. Pie charts enable one to understand the relationship between component values. Importantly, though, these types of charts only reflect a snapshot of *one* moment in time.

- **Scatter Plot**: A scatter plot or **scattergraph** is the simplest type of graph. The data are displayed as a collection of points that simply plots the data points against their values, without making any connection lines, columns, or bars. It does usually have one variable on the horizontal axis and another value on the vertical axis.

CHAPTER 3

What Is Economics?

Studying economics requires a specific way of looking at how things work in the world. The approach has three main components: economic methods, macroeconomics, and microeconomics. Adam Smith (1723–1790) is widely considered to be the founder of the field of economics. Smith was a Scottish economist whose writings can be said to have inaugurated the modern era of economic analysis. His *Wealth of Nations,* published in 1776, can be read as an analysis of a market economy. It was Smith's belief that a market economy was a superior form of organization from the standpoint of both economic progress and human liberty. Smith acknowledged that self-interest was a dominant motivating force in a market economy, yet this self-interest was ultimately consistent with the public interest. In Smith's view, market participants were guided by an invisible hand to act in ways that promoted the public interest. Firms may only be concerned with profits, he said, but profits are only earned by firms that satisfy consumer demand and keep costs down. Since his work was published, many others have furthered the study of economics, though they certainly have not always agreed with Smith. In fact, four general—and differing—viewpoints have evolved regarding the workings of markets: Classical, Keynesian, Monetary, and Neoclassical.

Most contemporary definitions of economics involve the notions of choice and scarcity and their relationship to one another. Perhaps the earliest of these is by Lionel Robbins in 1935: "Economics is a science which studies human behavior as a relationship between ends and scarce means which have alternative uses." Virtually all textbooks have definitions that are derived from this definition, though the exact wording differs from author to author. The standard definition is something like this: "**Economics** is the social science that examines how people choose to use limited or scarce resources to obtain maximum satisfaction of unlimited wants."

Macroeconomics is the study of the economy as a whole. Some of the topics considered include inflation, unemployment, and economic growth. **Microeconomics** is the study of the individual parts, like households, business firms, and government agencies, that make up the economy and particularly emphasizes both how these units make decisions and the consequences of these decisions.

COMPETENCY 2.1
Analyze how scarcity and opportunity cost influence choices about how to allocate resources.

Economists believe that human wants are unlimited while the resources to satisfy those needs are limited. Consequently, society is never able to produce enough goods and services to satisfy everybody, or almost anyone, completely. Alternatively, resources are scarce relative to human needs and desires. When resources are limited, the limitation affects prices (the amount of money needed to buy goods, services, or resources). **Scarcity** means that choices have to be made when either purchasing or producing goods. Theoretically, a society that does not have scarcity is a lucky society that has no problems and, thus, never has to make any decisions. In the real world, all societies must make three crucial decisions:

1. which and how many goods and services it should produce;

2. how it should produce these goods and services;

3. how the goods and services should then be distributed among the people.

If a society chooses to produce more of some goods, then there are fewer resources available to produce other goods. These seemingly local decisions may affect other people and even other nations.

There are two important components of the idea of scarcity: a good has to be limited AND people have to want it. If no one wants a good, no matter how limited it is, it is not scarce.

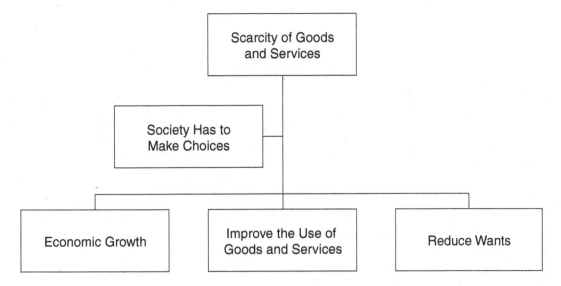

Economic Growth: One way to deal with scarcity is to grow the economy to produce more of the goods and services that people want so that whatever is wanted is in abundant supply. In order to accomplish this, you would need more resources, better resources, and better technology to get those resources.

Improve the Use of Goods and Services: If society uses its resources wisely, then scarcity is less likely to be an issue.

Reduce Wants: Another way to deal with scarcity is to get a society not to want so much of an item. If people did not want so much, then an item would not be scarce. In the long term, however, this is difficult to do.

There are four ways that society can use its existing resources to reduce scarcity and obtain the maximum satisfaction possible—we refer to these as the universal economic goals, but as a handy mnemonic device, we can also refer to them as the 4 E's:

- Allocative **E**fficiency

- Productive **E**fficiency

- Full **E**mployment

- **E**quity

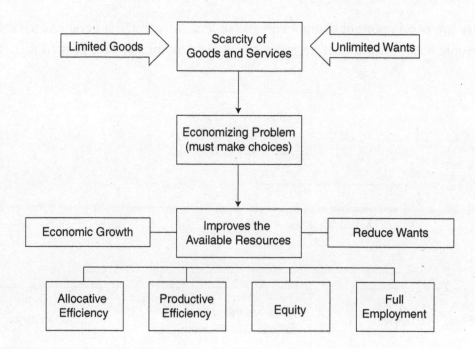

Universal Economic Goals

Allocative (Economic) Efficiency—A society achieves allocative efficiency if it produces the types and quantities of goods and services that most satisfy its people. Allocative efficiency is using our limited resources to produce the right mix of goods, so that society makes more of what people want, and less of what people do not want. Failure to do so wastes resources by producing a lot of things people do not want and few things that people want.

Productive Efficiency (Technical Efficiency)—A society achieves productive/technical efficiency when it is producing the greatest quantity of goods and services possible from its resources at a minimum cost, thus using fewer resources and increasing production quantities. In turn, scarcity is reduced. Failure to do so is also a waste of resources. There are three methods that can be used to achieve productive efficiency:

- not using more resources than necessary;

- using resources where they are best suited;

- using technology that minimizes costs.

Equity—A society wants the distribution of goods and services to conform with its notions of "fairness." Equity is not necessarily synonymous with equality. There is no objective standard of equity, and all societies have different notions of what constitutes equity. Three widely held **Standards of Equity** are as follows:

1. **Contributory standard**—Under a contributory standard, people are entitled to a share of goods and services based on what they contribute to society. Those making larger contributions receive correspondingly larger shares. The measurement of contribution and what to do about those who contribute very little or are unable to contribute (i.e., the disabled) are continuing issues.

2. **Needs standard**—Under a needs standard, a person's contribution to society is irrelevant. Goods and services are distributed based on the needs of different households. Measuring need and inducing people to contribute to society when goods and services are guaranteed are continuing issues.

3. **Equality standard**—Under an equality standard, every person is entitled to an equal share of goods and services, simply because he or she is a human being. Some of the ongoing issues with this theory are how to allow for needs and how to induce individuals to maximize their productivity when the reward is the same for everyone. Economists remain divided over whether the goals of equity and efficiency (allocative and technical) are complementary or in conflict.

Full Employment—Full employment means using all available resources, not just labor. If an economy has full employment, it produces more; if all resources are not employed, it produces less.

Trade-Offs and Opportunity Cost

Another basic observation of economics is that the economic choices we make result in trade-offs that can be measured. As those trade-offs are measured, we realize that various combinations of goods and services can be produced. However, as we produce more of one good, we incur a cost in the form of lost production of an alternative good or service. The **Production Possibilities Frontier Curve**, the **Law of Diminishing Marginal Returns**, and the **Law of Increasing Opportunity Cost** help us to understand this axiom. Together, these realities govern the behavior of the supplier in the free market system.

Production Possibilities Frontier Curve

The **Production Possibilities Frontier Curve** is a model of the economy used to illustrate the problems associated with scarcity. It shows the maximum feasible combinations of two goods or services that society can produce, assuming all resources are used in their most productive manner.

Assumptions of the Model

1. Society is capable of producing only two goods (guns and butter).

2. At a given point in time, society has a fixed quantity of resources.

3. All resources are used in their most productive manner.

Table 3.1 shows selected combinations of the two goods that can be produced given the assumptions.

Table 3.1
Selected Combinations of Guns and Butter

Point	Guns	Butter
A	0	16
B	4	14
C	7	12
D	9	9
E	10	5
F	11	0

Figure 3.1, below, is a graphical depiction of the Production Possibilities Curve (curve FA)

Figure 3.1
Production Probabilities Curve
Opportunity Costs

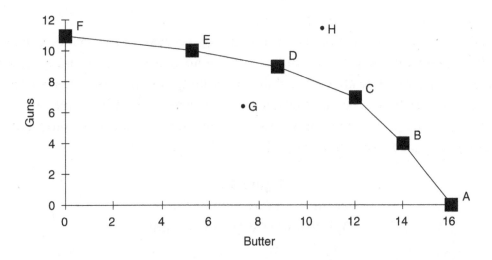

Technical Efficiency—All points on the curve are points of technical efficiency. By definition, **technical efficiency** is achieved when more of one good cannot be produced without producing less of the other good. Find point D on the curve. Any move to a point with more guns (i.e., point E) will necessitate a reduction in butter production. Any move to a point with more butter (such as point C) will necessitate a reduction in gun production. Any point inside the curve (such as point G) represents technical inefficiency. Either inefficient production methods are being used or resources are not fully employed. A movement from G to the curve will allow more of one or both goods to be produced without any reduction in the quantity of the other good. Points outside the curve (such as H) are technically infeasible given society's current stock of resources and technological knowledge.

Opportunity Cost—Consider a move from D to E. Society gets one more unit of guns but must sacrifice four units of butter. The four units of butter is the opportunity cost of the gun. One gun costs four butters.

Law of Increasing Costs—starting from point A and moving up along the curve, note that the opportunity cost of guns increases. From point A to B, two butter are sacrificed to get four guns (one gun costs one-half butter); from point B to C, two butters are sacrificed to get three guns (one gun costs two-thirds butter); from C to D, three butters are sacrificed for two guns (one gun costs one- and one-half butter); from D to E, one gun costs four butters; and from E to F, one gun cost five butters. The law of increasing costs says that as more of a good or service is produced, its opportunity cost will rise. It is a consequence of resources being specialized in particular uses. Some resources are particularly good in gun production and not so good for butter production, and vice versa.

At the commencement of gun production, the resources shifted out of butter will be those least productive in butter (and most productive in guns). Consequently, gun production will rise with little cost in terms of butter. As more resources are diverted, those more productive in butter will be affected, and the opportunity cost will rise. This is what gives the production possibilities curve its characteristic convex shape. If resources are not specialized in particular uses, opportunity costs will remain constant and the production possibilities curve will be a straight line (see Figure 3.2 below).

Figure 3.2
Production Possibilities Curve
Opportunity Costs as Constant

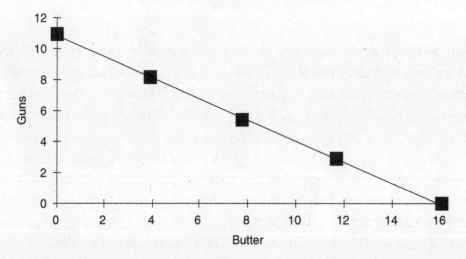

Allocative Efficiency—Allocative efficiency will be presented by the point on the curve that best satisfies society's needs and wants. It cannot be located without additional knowledge of society's likes and dislikes. A complicating factor is that the allocative efficient point is not independent of society's distribution of income and wealth.

Economic Growth—Society's production of goods and services is limited by its resources. Economic growth, then, requires that society increase the amount of resources it has or make those resources more productive through the application of technology. Graphically, economic growth is represented by an outward shift of the curve to IJ (see Figure 3.3). Economic growth will make more combinations of goods and services feasible but will not end the problem of scarcity.

Figure 3.3
Production Possibilities Curve
Economic Growth

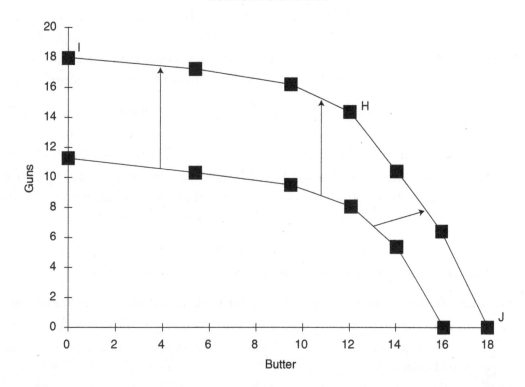

COMPETENCY 2.2

Identify how economic systems (e.g., market, command, traditional) answer the three basic economic questions.

An economic system of a country manages goods and services. All economic systems must answer the same basic economic questions of: What to produce? How to produce it? For whom to produce? Different economic systems answer these questions in different ways.

Traditional Economies—Traditional systems usually rely on custom/tradition to determine production and distribution questions. While not static, traditional systems tend to be reticent to change and ill-equipped to propel a society into sustained growth. Today we find many traditional systems in many of the poorer third-world countries.

Command—Command economies rely on a central authority, be it a dictator or democratically constituted government, to make all decisions about the economy.

Market—In a pure market system, there is no central authority, and custom plays very little role in this rather competitive market. Buyers and sellers decide what goods and services will be produced. Every consumer makes buying decisions based on his or her own needs and desires and income. Individual self-interest rules over the good of others. Every producer decides for himself or herself what goods or services to produce, what the prices will be, which resources are used, and what production methods to use. Producers tend to be solely motivated by a desire for profit.

Mixed—A mixed economy contains elements of each of the three systems defined above. All real-world economies are mixed economies, although the mixture of tradition, command, and market differs greatly. The U.S. economy has traditionally placed great emphasis on the market, although there is a large and active government (command) sector. The Soviet economy places main reliance on government to direct economic activity, but there is a small market sector.

Capitalism—The key characteristic of a capitalistic economy is that productive resources are owned by private individuals.

Socialism—This is a mixed economic system in which productive resources are all owned collectively by society, and thus, the allocation of them remains under the control of the government. Markets are used, however, to determine the price of goods and wages.

Planned—In a planned economy, the means of production are publicly owned with little to no private ownership. In these economies, instead of markets solving the basic economic questions, a central planning authority makes the decisions and decides what will be produced and how such production will occur.

COMPETENCY 2.3:
Analyze the interaction of supply and demand in determining production, distribution, and consumption.

Sellers are on the supply side of a market, and buyers are on the demand side of a market. Both supply and demand reveal the interaction between the buyer, seller, and price. **Demand** is the relationship that shows how much someone will pay for something. Economists examine the demand relationship through the lens of prices and corresponding quantities that are demanded. **Supply** too may be framed in terms of a relationship between price and corresponding quantities that are produced.

A **demand relation** shows the quantity demanded at a particular price. Economists have a unique way of graphing demand relation. The supply and demand diagrams are done sideways, with the price put on the *y-axis* and the quantity on the *x-axis*. Demand graphs usually slope downward because people buy less when the price is high and more with the price is low. Supply graphs, on the other hand, usually slope up from left to right, as the higher a price is, the easier it is to make a profit selling a good on the market. High prices attract more sellers and induce an expansion of production.

Figure 3.4
Supply and Demand Relationships

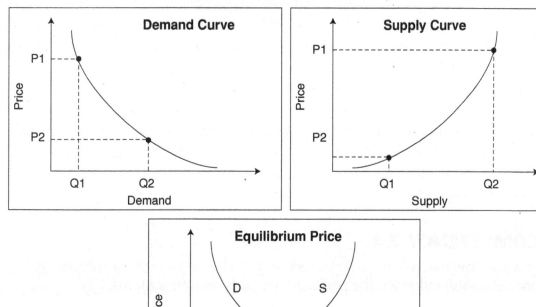

The intersection of the supply and demand curves is referred to as the **equilibrium**. The word equilibrium is synonymous with stable. The price and quantity in a market will frequently not be equal to the equilibrium, but if that is the case, then the market will be adjusting and, hence, not stable.

Market competition usually makes prices shift toward the equilibrium price. In turn, quantities supplied and demanded meet together at the equilibrium quantity. Both excess demand and excess supply put pressure on prices. Economists call the measure of the market's responsiveness of quantity to price as **elasticity**. If the quantity produced responds to changes in price, then demand is **elastic**; if quantity fails to respond to price change, then the demand is said to be **inelastic**. If the price is above or below the equilibrium price, it reveals a difference in quantity supplied versus quantity demanded. Such difference is termed "**excess demand**." If prices rise above equilibrium, there is "excess supply." An important caveat to consider is that when the price is low and there is excess demand, buyers cannot buy all that they want at the current price. Buyers begin to compete to buy more of these good deal products by offering higher prices that might chip away at their good-deal, but they may still be considered bargains. But sellers could respond to that as well and realize that there is a lot of interest in their product and, so, could raise prices. For the buyer, this is not a good thing at all, as all it takes is a little competition among buyers to raise the market price.

When there is no excess demand or supply, the price stays stable. As such, markets usually do trend toward equilibrium. As supply goes up, the price goes down. When demand goes up, both the equilibrium price and quantity rise, too.

COMPETENCY 2.4
Analyze how macroeconomic factors (e.g., national income, employment, price stability) influence the performance of economic systems.

Macroeconomics is the study of the economy as a whole. Macroeconomists try to figure out how aggregate units affect a national economy. In an effort to forecast economic conditions and ascertain the health of an economy, macroeconomists focus on three things: national output (measured by the **GDP—Gross Domestic Product**), the role of inflation, and unemployment.

National Output: GDP

GDP is the most important and comprehensive economic indicator that macroeconomists look to in order to ascertain the well-being of an economy. **GDP** is defined as the total money value of final goods and services that a country produces over a given period of time, usually one year. The number is like a snapshot of the economy at a certain point in time. Since almost all that is produced in an economy gets bought and turned into income, economists also use GDP to measure a country's income.

One way of measuring GDP, and perhaps the most common way, is the **expenditures approach**. The expenditure approach looks at the amount of new goods and services purchased in a country for a given year. The idea is simply that what each sector in the country spends is equal to what they earn producing it.

A simple equation is used in the expenditure approach: **GDP = C + I + G + NX.** This means that the total GDP is equal to the total amount of goods and services in one year (**consumption** = C), plus the total amount of investment items bought by businesses and individuals (**investment** = I), plus the amount of new goods and services bought by the government (government **goods** = G), plus (NX = net exports) is the difference between the goods bought by people outside of the country and the goods people in the country bought from outside of the country.

When an economy is functioning smoothly, the amount of national output produced (**aggregate supply**) is equal to the amount of national output purchased (**aggregate demand**). However, we know that economies have different cycles—sometimes things are good and sometimes not so good. Market economies experience fluctuations of aggregate economic activity. There are four phases to this economic cycle:

1. **Boom**—an expansion of the economy that brings prosperity;

2. **Recession**—a contraction of the economy with a decline in GDP and a rise in unemployment;

3. **Trough**—a turning point in an economic cycle, a period in which there is a slide from the mean to the lowest point in a recession;

4. **Recovery**—a period in which there is a rise from the trough back to the mean and during which there is lessening unemployment and rising prices.

Unemployment and Inflation

Two other indicators that macroeconomists look to when trying to figure out the health of an economy are unemployment and inflation. Particularly during periods of trough and recovery, these two indicators become quite important and they both have to do with spending. Inflation results from too much spending in an economy—this is when buyers want to buy more than sellers can produce and they bid up prices. Unemployment occurs when there is not enough spending in an economy. When sellers make too many goods and there are not enough buyers for those goods, there is a **surplus** situation that results in unemployment as sellers have to lower their production and do so by laying off workers.

Essentially, unemployment and inflation are indicators of an economy's instability and result when there is an inequality between aggregate demand and aggregate supply. Unemployment tells macroeconomists how many people from the labor pool are unable to find work. When economies grow, the unemployment figures are low as businesses need more people to work to keep up with the demand for goods and services.

Macroeconomists look at the **inflation rate**, or the rate at which prices rise, to determine whether the economy is growing at a healthy rate. An economy that grows too quickly and whose spending is too high has inflation—a period in which the prices rise too quickly because a monetary units' value has decreased and the purchasing power of that monetary unit has lessened. In these cases, governmental intervention should happen to try to slow the economy and encourage less spending. Conversely, governmental action is also required when there is not enough spending in an economy, production slows, and unemployment rises. During these periods, governments try to stimulate the economy and encourage higher levels of spending. The result of that sort of intervention usually leads to higher levels of employment.

Governments have a few tools that they can use in order to stabilize their economies. One method is to try to control spending and unemployment by manipulating the levels of spending and taxes through two types of fiscal policies: expansionary fiscal policies or contractionary fiscal policies. **Expansionary fiscal policy** raises government spending and/or decreases taxes in order to increase spending. **Contractionary fiscal policy** decreases government spending and increases taxes in order to decrease spending in the economy.

The other tool that the governments can use to stabilize the economy is monetary policy. In the United States, the **Federal Reserve System** (the Fed) implements monetary policy by changing the level of money in the banking system. The monetary policy actions of the Fed influence the availability and cost of both money and credit in the economy, and thus, they have a direct effect on prices, employment, and economic growth. As a result, Fed decisions wind up directly bearing upon the willingness of consumers and businesses to spend money on goods and services. So, Fed decisions can influence, either directly or indirectly, all levels of the economy. In order to influence the availability and cost of money and credit, the Fed uses three monetary policy tools: open-market operations, reserve requirements, and the discount rate.

Open-Market Operations

The Fed's most flexible and often-used tool of monetary policy is its **open-market operations** for buying or selling government securities. Open-market operations refer to the Fed's buying or selling of U.S. Government bonds in the open market. The purpose is to influence the amount of reserves in the banking system and, consequently, the banking system's ability to extend credit and create money.

a. **To expand the economy**—The Fed would buy bonds in the open market. For instance, if $50 million in bonds were purchased directly from commercial banks, the banks' balance sheet would look like this:

All Commercial Banks

R + 50 million	
Bonds – 50 million	

Banks are now holding an additional $50 million in excess reserves that they can use to extend additional credit. To induce borrowers, banks are likely to lower interest rates and credit standards. As loans are made, the money supply will expand. The additional credit will stimulate additional spending, primarily for investment goods.

Alternatively, the $50 million in bonds could be purchased directly from private individuals. The private individuals would then deposit the proceeds in their bank accounts. After the money was deposited, the balance sheet of all commercial banks would look as follows:

All Commercial Banks

R + 50 million	DD + 50 million

As above, the banks are now holding excess reserves they can use to extend credit. Lower interest rates, a greater money supply, and a higher level of total expenditure will result.

b. **To contract the economy**—The Fed would sell bonds in the open market. If it sold $20 million in bonds directly to the commercial banks, the banks' balance sheet would change as follows:

All Commercial Banks	
R + 20 million	
Bonds – 20 million	

In our example, the banks are now deficient in reserves. They need to reduce their demand deposit liabilities, and they will do so by calling in loans and making new credit more difficult to obtain. Interest rates will rise, credit requirements will be tightened, and the money supply will fall. Total spending in the economy will be reduced.

If the Fed sells the $20 million in bonds directly to private individuals, payment will be made with checks drawn against the private individuals' bank accounts. The banks' balance sheet will change as follows:

All Commercial Banks	
R – 20 million	DD – 20 million

Again, in our example, banks are deficient in reserves. They are forced to reduce credit availability, which will raise interest rates, reduce the money supply, and lead to a drop in total spending.

Bonds are a financial instrument frequently used by government and business as a way to borrow money. Every bond comes with a par value, a date to maturity (ranging from 90 days to 30 years), a coupon (a promise to pay a certain amount of money each year to the bondholder until maturity), and a promise to repay the par value on the maturity date. The issuing government or business sells the bonds in the bond market for a price determined by supply and demand. The money received from the sale represents the principal of the loan, the annual coupon payment is the interest on the loan, and the principal is repaid at the date of maturity. There is also a secondary market in bonds.

Reserve Ratio

Reserve ratio ia another type of policy that the Fed can use is to manipulate the banks' reserve ratio. The Fed can set the legal reserve ratio for both member and non-member banks. The purpose is to influence the level of excess reserves in the banking system and, consequently, the banking system's ability to extend credit and create money.

a. **To expand the economy**—The Fed would reduce the reserve requirement. Assume that the reserve requirement is 8%, and all banks are "all loaned up" at $500 million in loans. If the Fed reduces the reserve requirement to 6%, required reserves fall to $30 million, and there are immediately $10 million in excess reserves. Banks will lower the interest rates they charge and credit requirements in an attempt to make more loans. As the loans are granted, the economy's money supply and total spending will rise.

All Commercial Banks	
R 30 million	DD 40 million

b. **To contract the economy**—The Fed would raise the reserve requirement. Assume that the reserve requirement is 8%, and all banks are "all loaned up" at $500 million in loans.

All Commercial Banks	
R 50 million	DD 40 million

If the Fed raises the reserve requirement to 10%, required reserves rise to $50 million, and banks are immediately $10 million deficient in reserves. Banks will raise the interest rates they charge and credit requirements to reduce the amount of money borrowed. They may also call in loans. As the loans are reduced, the economy's money supply and total spending will fall.

Discount Rate

The third type of policy that the Fed can use is to control the discount rate. One of the responsibilities of the Fed is to act as a "lender of last resort" to banks. Member banks needing reserves can borrow from the Fed. The interest rate that the Fed charges on these loans is called the discount rate. By changing the discount rate, the Fed can influence the amount member banks try to borrow and, consequently, the banking system's ability to extend credit and create money.

a. **To expand the economy**—The Fed would lower the discount rate. A lower discount rate would make it less "painful" for member banks to borrow from the Fed. Consequently, they will be more willing to lend money and hold a low level of excess reserves. A lower discount rate would lead to lower interest rates and credit requirements, a higher money supply, and greater total spending in the economy.

b. **To contract the economy**—The Fed would raise the discount rate. A higher discount rate would make it more "painful" for member banks to borrow from the Fed. Consequently, they will be less willing to lend money and more likely to hold a high level of excess reserves. A higher discount rate would lead to higher interest rates and more stringent credit requirements, a lower money supply, and lower total spending in the economy.

Table 3.2
Monetary Policy Summary Table

Tool	Action	Effect on Interest Rates	Effect on Money Supply	Effect on Total Spending	Effect On GNP
Open Market	buy	lower	raise	raise	raise
Operations	sell	raise	lower	lower	lower
Reserve	raise	raise	lower	lower	lower
Ratio	lower	lower	raise	raise	raise
Discount	raise	raise	lower	lower	lower
Rate	lower	lower	raise	raise	raise

COMPETENCY 2.5

Evaluate the roles of government, central banking systems, and specialized institutions (e.g., corporations, labor unions, banks, stock markets) in market and command economies.

Government

Market Economy

Governments have five functions in a market economy:

1. Provide the economy with a legal structure and social framework: Without a legal structure in place, an economy may collapse. Governments must ensure property rights, provide enforcement of contracts, furnish regulations, legislations, and means to ensure product quality, define ownership rights, and enforce contracts. In the United States, several institutions combine to tackle this responsibility: the FDA, the Fed, and SEC.

2. Maintain competition: Because in market economies there is the potential for large firms to achieve monopolies, which actually limit competition and make the market inefficient, the government needs to develop laws and regulations to maintain competition. Competition persuades producers and suppliers to react to price and consumer choice.

3. Redistribution of income and social welfare: The government should provide protections for the people who do not have the skills or resources to earn a living in a market economy. Unfortunately, market economies leave many people vulnerable, and in order for society to function, market economies need to provide for those who cannot take care of themselves, so they need to provide relief to the poor, dependent, handicapped, and unemployed. In the United States, Welfare, Social Security, Medicaid, and Medicare programs are examples of such programs. These programs are built on taxing those with larger incomes to help those in need through progressive taxes in an effort to make tax policies and the after-tax distribution of income more fair. The United States employs other methods of redistribution, such as farm subsidies and low-interest college loans.

4. Provide public goods and services that the markets do not: The government must step in when markets cannot or will not provide the needed goods or the right quantity of goods and services. There are many types of goods and services that the markets do not provide and government picks up, like defense, security, police protection, judicial system, and sometimes education and health services if the market does not provide enough of them.

5. Correct any market failures and promoting growth and stability: Governments employ as their arsenal various budget, fiscal, and monetary policies to promote macroeconomic growth and stability (e.g., increasing the GDP, fighting inflation and unemployment) and provide the economic conditions through which the marketplace of private enterprise can function efficiently. In the United States, the executive branch of government's Treasury Department covers both taxing and spending through the Treasury Department, and the Federal Reserve System controls interest rates, money supply, and reserve requirements.

Command Economy

In a command economy, the government regulates production. The economy is centrally planned, and the government controls all economic decisions. The government has the final authority on which goods and services are produced, how the finished products will be utilized, and who buys which goods and services as well as the allocation of the revenues earned from their distribution. It sets actual wages and prices. The effort to control the many decisions that are needed to be made to control the economic activity of a country may be too complex to actually be effective in all areas. However, in most command economies, control revolves around the manufacture of the country's industrial goods. In these economies, the government usually owns and operates the production facilities and thus can regulate how much and what type of goods are produced. By controlling all elements of supply, the government in a command economy can ensure that their population has the goods it needs. Often the prices of the goods produced are regulated by the government in order to maintain balance in the economy. In addition, in command economies, the government makes sure that sufficient jobs exist and sets and enforces quality standards.

Command economies typically can boast of an efficient use of resources. Because they can control the rate of production, they also have the ability to adjust supply if it exceeds demand. As a result, inventories of finished goods are smaller, thus ensuring that the right number of goods is bought and sold and that products do not sell at a loss.

Although it might seem that command economies control the entire consumer market, that is not so, as not every type of consumer product is owned or heavily regulated by the central government. Some areas remain outside government regulation. For instance, usually command economies steer clear of markets like agriculture, much in the same way that the free enterprise systems do.

Characteristic features of Command Economy:

- Traditionally rather stable and relatively immune to financial downturn and inflation

- Surplus production and unemployment rates remain relatively level

- Encourages investments in long-standing project-related infrastructures with promise of no recession threats

- Deliberate and planned approach to money making usually improves a country's economic conditions

- Emphasizes collective benefit, rather than the requirements of a single individual, through distribution of wages and bonuses on the basis of collective contribution

Command Economy: Specialized Institutions

In a command economy, the government sends directives to both state-owned and private enterprises with regard to production capacity, volume, and modes of production.

Market Economy

Central Bank: The role of the central bank in a market economy is to oversee the stability of the banking system and conduct monetary policy in order to control inflation, unemployment, and to stimulate economic growth and function as a bank of last resort. In the United States, the Fed is the central bank.

Corporations: To a large degree, market economies are based on corporations, legal entities that have as their goal production of specific goods and services to make a profit. It is a major use of labor and resources. Corporations in a market economy compete with each other for profit. To get more investors in their company, owners of corporations sell pieces of ownership called **stock**. The people who own stock are called **shareholders** or **stockholders.** The size of their ownership is determined by the amount of stock in a company that they own. As part owners of a company, shareholders receive some of the profits from a company in the form of payments called **dividends**.

There are two types of stocks that are issued by corporations: private and public. Public stocks are traded freely in an open market called a **stock exchange**. With public stocks, anyone, if they have the money to invest, can own a part of these corporations. Private corporations can issue stock and have shareholders. However, their shares are not traded in public stock exchanges.

The **stock market** is the epitome of the market economy, where transactions take place exclusively for the purpose of making money. A stock exchange is a place where stocks are traded. As more people buy a stock, its value increases. The primary goal of a buyer is to buy the stock at a low price and sell it at a high price. When a stock is sold at a price higher than when they bought it, the profit is called a **capital gain**.

COMPETENCY 2.6

Analyze the features of global economics (e.g., exchange rates, terms of trade, comparative advantage, less developed countries) in terms of their impact on national and international economic systems.

World trade has increased globally and is an increasingly significant portion of the U.S. economy. The volume of world trade has increased tremendously since the end of World War II. The United States plays a major role in shaping this trade. Adam Smith's book *The Wealth of Nations* points out the advantages of specialization and international trade. They both increase productive efficiency and allow greater total output than would otherwise be possible. Production possibilities tables allow us to quantify the efficiency gains of specialization. This is known as the principle of comparative advantage.

Comparative Advantage

The **principle of comparative advantage** says that trade should be based on the comparative opportunity costs between two countries. It basically states that whichever country can produce a good more cheaply should produce that good and should trade for the good in which the country cannot produce as cheaply. Even though one nation may enjoy absolute advantage over another in the production of goods, it serves both nations' best interests to seek the lower domestic opportunity cost for the less productive nation. So, with comparative advantage, theoretically at least, both nations gain from trading and there is a more efficient allocation of the world's resources as well as larger outputs.

Financing International Trade—Exchange Rates

When nations engage in trade with one another, they have to pay for the items. But the question is, how to pay for these items when there are different national currencies involved. So, two nations have to exchange their currencies following an **exchange rate** rooted in the international currency market. For instance, an American firm that wants to export something to Brazil does not want to be paid in *riales*, because that currency cannot be used in the United States. So, the importer must exchange its currency for U.S. dollars. This service is provided (for a fee) by major banks that have created currency exchanges.

In our example, over time, we might see that the U.S. exports cause an increased demand by Brazilians for U.S. dollars. The increased foreign demand for the U.S. dollar increases the supply of the foreign currency in exchange markets and the dollar appreciates. U.S. imports would increase the demand for the foreign currency and would increase the supply of U.S. dollars in exchange markets. So, the international exchange rates work much like the law of supply and demand as the exchange rates float.

There are two major types of currency exchange formats: floating and fixed—although a managed float is also an available option. At the end of World War II, 44 nations met and created the **Bretton Woods system**. The U.S. dollar served as the focal point of this system because the U.S. dollar became the reserve currency of the system. Countries bought and sold dollars to maintain their exchange rates. The value of the U.S. dollar was fixed at $35 per ounce of gold and was convertible on demand for foreigners holding U.S. dollars. The dollar became "as good as gold."

Two new organizations were also created at the Bretton Woods Conference: the **International Monetary Fund (IMF)** and the **World Bank**. The IMF was created to supervise the exchange-rate practices of member nations. It also was intended to lend money to nations that were unable to meet their payment obligations (that is, to do "bailouts"). IMF funds come from fees charged to the 178 member nations. The World Bank, funded through the sale of bonds, loans money to developing nations for economic development.

The Bretton Woods system dissolved in 1971 as the U.S. dollar came under devaluation pressure and gold drained from the nation's reserves.

In March 1973, a managed, floating exchange rate was established by the major industrial countries. Central banks of various nations have at times intervened to alter their nation's currency value. An example of this occurred in 1995 when the Fed and U.S. Treasury sold German *marks* and Japanese *yen* to increase the value of the dollar, which they believed had fallen excessively. The managed float has withstood severe economic upheavals, such as the OPEC oil crisis in 1973. Some nations, to maintain a more stable domestic currency, have "pegged" the value of their currency to a fixed rate with the U.S. dollar or another industrial nation's currency. An independent floating exchange rate would be subject to the laws of supply and demand in the currency marketplace

Balance of Payments

The **balance of payments** account refers to the sum of a country's transactions with other countries and is summarized in three main accounts: current, capital, and financial account balances. Today, most economists combine the capital and financial accounts (as they are similar in content) into the financial account.

The **current account** primarily tracks the import and export of goods and services but also includes net international transfer payments and net international factor income. If a nation imports more than it exports, it has an unfavorable balance of trade/current account deficit. If a nation exports more than it imports, it has a favorable balance of trade/current account surplus. The current account is as diagrammed here

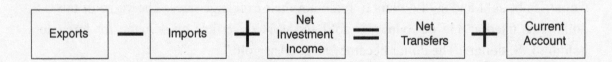

Net investment income is net interest and dividends paid by foreigners to Americans, and **net transfers** is foreign aid, money sent to Americans or their families living overseas. The current account is often termed the "balance of trade" and the United States has run deficits in this account for decades. This trade deficit results because the United States imports more than it exports. The economic impact of trade deficits is an oft-debated topic. Is it good or bad for an economy? If a nation imports more than it exports, a net job increase in the foreign nation is created. If there is unemployment at home, it is difficult to justify this "exporting of jobs." If the demand for foreign goods and services must be paid for in the foreign currency, this causes a depreciation of the net importer's currency that at some point may reverse the trade imbalance. Also, if the foreign workers' wages are lower, this represents a deflationary effect.

The financial account records trade in assets such as gold, government securities, banking liabilities (deposits/loans), corporate securities, and fixed assets such as real estate. The official reserves account consists of the foreign currencies held by a nation's central bank. These reserves are increased or decreased in reaction to the balance of the current and capital account. If the balance is negative, a deficit is noted; if the balance is positive, a benefit is noted. Whether a deficit or surplus is good or bad depends on how the issue is resolved. The implications of trade deficits or surpluses can be complicated.

Developing Nations' Economies

Many economists will tell you that for the economy to work for one country, it must work (somewhat) well for all countries. Economic growth in developing nations is confronted with four entrenched obstacles:

- traditional attitudes and beliefs;

- continued rapid population growth;

- a misuse of resources (including capital flight—the legal or illegal export of currency or money capital from a nation by that nation's leaders);

- trade restrictions.

COMPETENCY 2.7
Evaluate the functions of budgeting, saving, and credit in a consumer economy.

A **consumer economy** is the part of the economy that is centered on the consumer, rather than on the relationship between businesses. This is the part of the economy where we analyze individuals buying goods and services for their own use. The biggest drive in the consumer economy is urging the consumer to buy, buy, buy. But, an individual only has so much wealth. So, the consumer economy is driven by the availability of cheap credit. **Credit** is simply a promise to pay for goods or services that have already been provided. Individuals obtain this credit from banks and credit card companies who allow borrowers to pay back their loans over time. For giving people the privilege of credit, banks charge the consumer bank fees and interest on the balance of the loan. Banks use the money that they gain from lending out money to one person to finance their lending to another person.

There are positive and negative effects of credit. On the positive side, credit allows individuals to purchase really expensive items that they otherwise would never be able to afford if they had to pay outright, like homes and cars. On the negative side, credit creates debt. Consumers could use credit too much and wind up unable to make their payments. Moreover, with the addition of interest to the principle of the loan, consumers pay significantly more for these goods and services that they otherwise would have had they purchased it outright. Consumer debt becomes a problem for a larger economy when so many people are unable to pay their debt payments. Sometimes these loans are guaranteed by the U.S. government—in effect the public pays for it—and creditors can be paid if someone defaults on a loan; however, in some cases, consumers see legal help for their overabundance of debt and file for bankruptcy. If too many consumers file for bankruptcy, then many creditors never get paid.

What Is Political Science?

4

Political science is the organized study of government and politics. It borrows from the related disciplines of history, philosophy, sociology, economics, and law. Political scientists explore such fundamental questions as: What are the philosophical foundations of modern political systems? What makes a government legitimate? What are the duties and responsibilities of those who govern? Who participates in the political process and why? What is the nature of relations among nations? Political scientists use a wide variety of methods of investigation: qualitative, quantitative, historical comparative, interpretive, and critical lines of inquiry.

Principal Subfields of Political Science

At the present time, the study of political science in the United States is concerned with the following broad subtopics or subfields:

Political theory is an historical exploration of the major contributions to political thought from the ancient Greeks to the contemporary theorists. These theorists raise fundamental questions about the individual's existence and his or her relationship to the political community. **Political theory** also involves the philosophical and speculative consideration of the political world.

American government and politics is a survey of the origins and development of the political system in the United States from the colonial days to modern times, with an emphasis on the Constitution, various political structures such as the legislative, executive, and judicial branches, the federal system, political parties, voter behavior, and fundamental freedoms.

Comparative government and politics is a systematic study of the structures of two or more political systems (such as those of Britain and the People's Republic of China) to achieve an understanding of how different societies manage the realities of governing. Also considered are political processes and behavior and the ideological foundations of various systems.

International relations is a consideration of how nations interact with each other within the frameworks of law, diplomacy, and international organizations, such as the United Nations.

The Development of the Discipline of Political Science

Early History

Political science as a systematic study of government developed in the United States and in Western Europe during the nineteenth century as new political institutions evolved. Prior to 1850, during its classical phase, political science relied heavily on philosophy and utilized the deductive method of research.

Post–Civil War Period

The political science curriculum was formalized in the United States by faculty at Columbia and Johns Hopkins, who were deeply influenced by German scholarship on the nation-state and the formation of democratic institutions. Historical and comparative approaches to analysis of institutions were predominant. Emphasis was on constitutional and legal issues, and political institutions were widely regarded as factors in motivating the actions of individuals.

Twentieth Century Trends

Political scientists worked to strengthen their research base, to integrate quantitative data, and to incorporate comparative studies of governmental structures in developing countries into the discipline.

American Political Science Association (APSA)

The APSA was founded in 1903 to promote the organized study of politics and to distinguish it as a field separate from history.

The Behavioral Period

From the early 1920s to the present, political science has focused on psychological interpretations and the analysis of the behavior of individuals and groups in a political context. Research has been theory based, values neutral, and concerned with predicting and explaining political behavior.

Contemporary Developments

Since the 1960s, interest has focused on such subtopics as African-American politics, public policy, urban and ethnic politics, and women in politics. Influenced by the leadership of Harold Lasswell, political scientists showed greater concern for using their discipline to solve social problems.

COMPETENCY 3.1
Identify the features and principles of the U.S. Constitution, including its amendments, the separation of powers, checks and balances, and federalism.

Features of the U.S. Constitution

Constitutional Foundations

The government of the United States rests on a written framework created to strengthen a loose confederation that was in crisis in the 1780s. The **Constitution** is a basic plan that outlines the structure and functions of the national government. Clearly rooted in Western political thought, it sets limits on government and protects both property and individual rights.

Historical Background

Following the successful revolt of the British colonies in North America against imperial rule, a plan of government was implemented that was consciously weak and ultimately ineffective, the **Articles of Confederation**. The Articles served as the national government from 1781–1787. The government under the Articles consisted of a **unicameral** (one house) legislature that was clearly subordinate to the states. Representatives to the Congress were appointed and paid by their respective state legislatures, and their mission was to protect the interests of their home states. Each state, regardless of size, had one vote in Congress, as had been the case in the Continental Congress, which could request, but not require, states to provide financial and military support. Under the Articles of Confederation, the national government had the authority and responsibility to control foreign policy such as declaring war or making treaties, assess state contributions to the war effort, borrow and issue money, settle disputes between states, and admit new states to the Union.

Key weaknesses of the Articles included: its inability to levy taxes, draft troops, regulate interstate and foreign trade, its lack of a powerful or effective chief executive and a national court system, its rule that amendments must be approved by unanimous consent, and the inability of the government to make the states enforce legislation that they did not support. As a result, the government was rather weak and ineffective and seemed more like a confederation of sovereign states, rather than a united country.

Without a strong central government to reign these sovereign states in, the 1780s was a decade racked by internal conflict. The economy deteriorated as individual states printed their own currencies, taxed the products of their neighbors, and ignored foreign trade agreements. Inflation soared, small farmers lost their property, and states engaged in petty squabbles with one another. The discontent of the agrarian population reached crisis proportions in 1786 in rural Massachusetts when Revolutionary War veteran **Daniel Shays** led a rebellion of farmers against the tax collectors and the banks that were seizing their property. **Shays' Rebellion** symbolized the inability of the government under the Articles to maintain order. People began to realize that there was a need to create a national government that could replace the confederation of sovereign states. In response to the economic and social disorder and the dangers of foreign intervention, a series of meetings to consider reform and revision of the Articles of Confederation was held.

In 1787, the **Constitutional Convention** was convened in **Philadelphia** ostensibly to revise the ineffective Articles. Under the presidency of George Washington, representatives from every state except Rhode Island met and over four months drafted the **Constitution** that forms the foundation of our government today.

Philosophy and Ideology of the Founders

Among the 55 state representatives assembled at the 1787 Constitutional Convention were **James Madison**, who recorded the debate proceedings; **George Washington**, president of the body; **Gouverneur Morris**, who wrote the final version of the document and its famed preamble, "We the People of the United States, in order to form a more perfect union . . ."; and **Alexander Hamilton**, one of the authors of the *Federalist Papers* (1787–1788). This collection of essays, to which **Madison** and **John Jay** also contributed, expresses the political philosophy of the Founders and was instrumental in bringing about the ratification of the Constitution.

The **Founders** drew upon three important British documents as well as Enlightenment ideas gleaned from the *philosophes* of the seventeenth and eighteenth centuries in Western Europe. The **Magna Carta (1215)**, the **Petition of Right (1628)**, and the **Bill of Rights (1689)** promoted the principle of a limited government that resonated in the interests of the Founders. The framers of the constitution also drew upon the ideas of Thomas Hobbes and John Locke who stressed that government had a social contract with the people it represented—if the government did not protect their interests, the people had a right to alter or abolish it. **Thomas Jefferson** incorporated Locke's doctrines in his **Declaration of Independence** (1776), with respect to a government's responsibility to protect the life, liberty, and property of its constituency. The Founders also drew upon **Montesquieu's** ideas about the necessity of separation of powers and checks and balances.

Debates and Compromises Among the Founders Regarding the U.S. Constitution

The Founders did not have an easy time agreeing on the nature of the new government, and much of the resulting Constitution actually comes out of the necessity of having to compromise interests. The first point of disagreement centered on the role of the executive. As many had experienced the problems associated with an authoritative monarchy, they were concerned about the problems caused by a strong and unchecked chief executive. Others argued that the weak Presidency of the Articles of Confederation also led to problems, and this group wanted a strong central government. The compromise introduced the concept of **checks and balances** that would permeate the government, making sure that no one branch had unlimited or unchecked power. The compromise dictated that a president could have broad powers, but also his term in office would be limited to a term of four years. The president would have the ability to control foreign policy and could veto Congressional legislations. Should the president commit and be convicted of a crime, Congress would have the power to impeach him. The power to make appointments to offices and to conclude treaties was also tempered as Congress was required to provide its consent.

Another major conflict occurred between the large and small states over the matter of representation. Small states did not accept the argument from large states that they should have more of a voice in government because they represented more people. The large states, led by Virginia, presented a plan calling for a strong national government with representation favoring the larger states (**Virginia Plan**) and the smaller states, which countered with the **New Jersey Plan**. The latter would have retained much of the structure of the Articles of Confederation including equal representation of the states in Congress. Connecticut offered a solution in the form of the **Great Compromise**. The compromise resulted in the division of Congress into two parts—the **Senate,** where all states would have equal voting power, and the **House of Representatives,** which would be determined in proportion to a state's population.

Another matter of contention arose that pit the interests of northern states against those of southern states over the matter of slavery. Delegates decided on the **Three-Fifths Compromise,** which decided that each slave was to count as three-fifths of a person for purposes of determining population count and with regard to direct taxation on states. Representatives also disagreed about the role of slavery in the new nation. The compromise was that slaves remained the property of their owners, whether or not they had fled to states where slavery was illegal. In a nod to the emergent abolitionist movement of the period as well as to the realization of how much the south thought it needed slavery for its economic survival, it was decided that for at least 20 years, no law that prohibited the importation of slavery could be passed.

The method to be used for the selection of a president was one more area of conflict. Many of the Founders expressed concern over whether or not common people actually knew enough to vote for their leaders and feared that democracy might usher in a popular, but unqualified, ruler. So, the compromise introduced the idea of an **Electoral College** that actually elected the president. The framers of the Constitution decided that each state would have the same number of electors as it did senators and representatives.

Another concern remained about the limits of state power and the extent of control that the federal government had on the states. The compromise worked out determined that all laws must conform to the Federal Constitution; however, all power not explicitly given to the federal government belonged to the states.

Washington, Franklin, and others who supported the adoption of the new constitution began to call themselves **Federalists** while their opponents were named the **Anti-Federalists**. The Federalists, supported by the likes of **James Madison**, argued eloquently for the adoption of the Constitution. The Anti-Federalists, like **Henry** and **Sam Adams**, argued that the Constitution failed to uphold some of the basic rights for which the revolution had been fought. The Anti-Federalists believed that the Constitution would weaken the states, favor the wealthy, increase taxes, and diminish individual liberty. They objected in particular to the absence of a **Bill of Rights** or any written guarantee of certain basic rights and freedoms for all citizens. The voices of the anti-Federalists were heard as New York and Virginian were hesitant to ratify the new Constitution until the promise of a Bill of Rights convinced them to approve of it.

Basic Principles of the Constitution

The authors of the Constitution sought to establish a government free from the tyrannies of both monarchs and mobs. Two of the critical principles embedded in the final document, **federalism** and **separation of powers**, address this concern. The federal system established by the Founders divides the powers of government between the states and the national government. Local matters, such as zoning issues, are handled by local governments; however, those issues that affect the general populace are the responsibility of the federal government. American federalism is defined in the **Tenth Amendment,** which declares: "those powers not delegated to the United States by the Constitution, nor prohibited by it to the States, are reserved to the States respectively, or to the people." In practice, the system may be confusing in that powers overlap (e.g., welfare) and, in those cases where there is a conflict, the federal government is supreme.

The principle of separation of powers is codified in **Articles I**, **II**, and **III** of the main body of the Constitution. The national government is divided into three branches that have separate functions (**legislative, executive**, and **judicial**). Not entirely independent, each of these branches can check or limit in some way the power of one or both of the others (**checks and balances**). This system of dividing and checking powers is a vehicle for guarding against the extremes the Founders feared. Following are some examples of checks and balances:

- The legislative branch can check the executive by refusing to confirm appointments.

- The executive can check the legislature by vetoing its bills.

- The judiciary can check the legislature and the executive by declaring laws unconstitutional.

Additional basic principles embodied in the Constitution include:

- the establishment of a representative government (**republic**). **Popular sovereignty** or the idea that government derives its power from the people. This concept is expressed in the **Preamble** which opens with the words, "**We the People**";

- the enforcement of government with limits ("**rule of law**").

Overview of the Articles in the Constitution and the Amendments

Preamble:

"We the People of the United States, in Order to form a more perfect Union, establish Justice, insure domestic Tranquility, provide for the common defense, promote the general Welfare, and secure the Blessings of Liberty to ourselves and our Posterity, do ordain and establish this Constitution for the United States of America."

Basically, the Preamble lists the reasons that the 13 colonies sought independence from England and establishes why this newly independent group of people believed they needed to have a Constitution in order to correct problems with the Articles of Confederation and to set up a strong government that would protect and defend its people.

Article 1: This article establishes the Legislative Branch, the Congress, as a two-bodied entity comprised of the House of Representatives and the Senate that makes the laws for the United States.

Article 2: This article establishes the Executive Branch comprised of a president, vice-president, cabinet, and departments that serve under each cabinet member.

Article 3: This article sets up the Judicial Branch. It comprises the Supreme Court and the lower courts. The courts decide criminal and civil cases according to federal, state, and local laws.

Article 4: This article lists the states' powers to make and carry out their own laws. It also obligates states to respect the laws of other states and that "full faith and credit" shall be given to each state, which means that legal documents that are valid in one state must also be valid in others. It requires states to work together in terms of extraditing suspects. It also sets up how new states may be admitted to the Union and that these new states may not trample over another states' borders. It also states that the Federal Government must make sure that each state has a republican or constitutional government. The Federal Government must also provide for the defense of each state against invasion or domestic unrest.

Article 5: This article lays out how the Constitution may be amended—with the approval of two-thirds vote of each house of Congress AND three-fourths vote of the state legislatures. It also states that no state can be denied equal representation in the Senate without its consent.

Article 6: This article establishes that the Constitution and federal laws are the supreme laws of the land and are higher than state or local laws. Thus, if a state law and federal law come into conflict with one another, the state law must yield to the federal law.

Article 7: This article states that 9 of the 13 states needed to ratify it in order for it to go into effect. The Constitution was presented to the Constitutional Convention on September 17, 1787 and 12 out of the 13 states approved it.

There are currently **27 Amendments to the Constitution.** The first 10 amendments are listed as articles and were voted on and ratified together. These articles were a necessary addition to the Constitution in order to gain support for it among those who feared that the Constitution gave the Federal Government too much power. These first 10 articles are known as the **Bill of Rights,** and they deal primarily with civil liberties and civil rights. James Madison is credited with writing a majority of them.

Amendment 1: This amendment guarantees freedom of religion, speech, the press, and assembly and the right of individuals to petition the government to respond to grievances. (1791)

Amendment 2: This amendment provides for the peoples' right to keep and bear arms in a regulated militia and states that this right cannot be infringed upon by the government. (1791) (There is considerable debate here about whether this right allows any-one to possess a weapon to protect themselves, or only those in the militia.) (1791)

Amendment 3: This amendment gives people security from quartering troops in their homes during either war or peace without the consent of the owner. (1791)

Amendment 4: This amendment protects the rights of an individual against unrea-sonable searches and seizures and states that the government must have probable cause and a search warrant must be issued before a legal search can commence. (1791)

Amendment 5: This amendment states that the government must provide **due process** before punishing a person. It states that a person may not be held for a crime without being indicted; a person has the **right against self-incrimination**; it guarantees a person's right against double jeopardy (so, no one may be tried twice for the same crime; however, they may be tried separately on criminal and civil charges). (1791)

Amendment 6: This amendment provides, in criminal cases, for a person's right to a speedy and public trial and a trial by an impartial jury. It also establishes a right to legal council, that those accused be informed of the charges against them, be able to confront the witnesses against them, and be able to call witnesses on their behalf. (1791)

Amendment 7: This amendment provides for the right of a jury trial of civil cases in federal court (where the amount is in excess of $20 (these types of trials are no longer heard in Federal Courts); and that no decision of a jury shall be overturned by any court in the United States except according to the rules of common law. (1791)

Amendment 8: This amendment states that excessive bails or fines cannot be imposed upon individuals and that **cruel and unusual** punishments cannot be imposed. It is under this amendment that there are challenges to **death penalty laws**. (1791)

Amendment 9: This amendment indicates that citizens and states have rights beyond those stated in the Constitution. Even if not listed in the Constitution these rights cannot be violated or abridged. (1791)

Amendment 10: This amendment states that powers not delegated to the United States by the Constitution shall be reserved for the states, or the people. (1791)

Amendment 11: This amendment holds that states have a certain degree of sovereign immunity and that individuals may not sue states in federal courts. (1795)

Amendment 12: This amendment redefines how the president and vice-president will be elected. The two are chosen by the Electoral College and must be on a ballot together, rather than as it was previously, those with the highest votes. It also insures that whoever runs as vice-president must also be eligible to be president. (1804)

Amendments 13 and 14 are often referred to as the "Reconstruction" or Civil War Amendments, as they passed in quick succession following the end of the Civil War and they primarily deal with issues regarding newly freed slaves.

Amendment 13: This amendment bans slavery and involuntary servitude except as punishment for a crime in which one has been convicted. (1865)

Amendment 14: This amendment is the first one that addresses questions of citizenship. It states that "All persons born or naturalized in the United States, and subject to the jurisdiction thereof are citizens of the United States and of the State wherein they reside." This amendment confers state citizenship as well as national citizenship as some Southern states were reluctant to confer all rights and privileges to recently freed slaves. It also states that the Fifth Amendment's protection of due process for individuals also extends to states rather than just the federal government. It also applies the idea of **"equal protection of laws"** which would become one of the focal points of the modern civil rights movements. The amendment allows for the reapportionment of the seats in the house of Representatives following a census and counts all persons, except for untaxed Native Americans. It voids the three-fifths clause in Article 1 regarding population counts. (1868)

Amendment 15: This amendment states that all U.S. citizens shall not be denied the right to vote, regardless of race, color, or previous condition of servitude. This cleared the way for male African-American former slaves to vote. Many Southern states searched for ways to get around this amendment by trying to use literacy tests, poll taxes, and grandfather clauses to avoid letting former male slaves vote. (1870)

Amendment 16: This amendment allows the Congress to tax income (until this time, it was unconstitutional to do so). (1913)

Amendment 17: This amendment came about as part of the Progressive Movement in America and shifted the election of senators away from state legislators and to the people in a direct, popular election. (1913)

Amendment 18: This amendment, otherwise known as Prohibition, marked the sale or manufacture and transport of alcohol as illegal. This Amendment was repealed by the Twenty-First Amendment in 1933. (1913)

Amendment 19: This amendment gave women the right to vote as it stated that a citizen shall not be denied the right to vote on account of sex. (1920)

Amendment 20: This amendment changed the inauguration date of the President from March 4 to January 20 and the new terms of Senators and Representatives to January 3 in order to shorten the "lame-duck" session of Congress which was the session just after the November election and before the new president assumed office. It also establishes how the death of a president before a swearing-in would be handled. (1933)

Amendment 21: This amendment repealed the Eighteenth Amendment, making alcohol legal again. It is the only time an amendment has been repealed. It also gave states the power to make laws about making, selling, and drinking alcohol. (1933)

Amendment 22: This amendment limited the president to serve two terms, or ten years in the case of a vice-president who became president due to the death or removal of a president. (1951)

Amendment 23: This amendment gave U.S. citizens who live in the District of Columbia the right to vote for president, as it gave the District three electoral votes. (1961)

Amendment 24: This amendment made it illegal to use poll taxes as a way to deny the right of a citizen to vote. (1964)

Amendment 25: This amendment outlines the order of succession to the presidency and provides guidelines for presidential disability. So, if the president dies or cannot serve, the vice-president comes into office; if both the president and vice-president die or cannot serve, the Speaker of the House assumes the presidency. (1967)

Amendment 26: This amendment extends the right to vote to individuals who are 18 years of age (previously the age requirement was 21). (1971)

Amendment 27: This amendment establishes the procedures for Congressional pay increases—essentially they cannot give themselves a pay increase that would take effect immediately. Increases must wait until after the next election to go into effect. (1992).

Powers Reserved for the Federal Government

- Regulate foreign commerce

- Regulate interstate commerce

- Mint money

- Regulate naturalization and immigration

- Grant copyrights and patents

- Declare and wage war and declare peace

- Admit new states

- Fix standards for weights and measures

- Raise and maintain an army and a navy

- Govern Washington, DC

- Conduct relations with foreign powers

- Universalize bankruptcy laws

Powers Reserved for the State Government

- Conduct and monitor elections

- Establish voter qualifications within the guidelines established by the Constitution

- Provide for local governments

- Ratify proposed amendments to the Constitution

- Regulate contracts and wills

- Regulate intrastate commerce

- Provide for education for its citizens

- Levy direct taxes

- Maintain police power over public health and safety

- Maintain integrity of state borders

Powers Shared by State and Federal Governments (The Concurrent Powers)

- Taxing, borrowing, and spending money

- Controlling the militia

- Acting directly on individuals

COMPETENCY 3.2

Identify the functions of U.S. political institutions, including the executive, legislative, and judicial branches.

Structure and Functions of the National Government

The national government consists of the three branches—the legislative, executive, and judicial branches as outlined in the Constitution as well as a huge bureaucracy comprised of departments, agencies, and commissions.

The Legislative Branch

Legislative power is vested in a **bicameral** (two-house) Congress which is the subject of Article I of the Constitution.

The **expressed** or **delegated powers** of Congress are set forth in **Section 8 of Article I of the Constitution**. They can be divided into several broad categories including economic, judicial, war, and general peace powers.

Economic powers include:

- to lay and collect taxes;

- to borrow money;

- to regulate foreign and interstate commerce;

- to coin money and regulate its value;

- to establish rules concerning bankruptcy.

Judicial powers include the powers:

- to establish courts inferior to the Supreme Court;

- to provide punishment for counterfeiting;

- to define and punish piracies and felonies committed on the high seas.

War powers of Congress include:

- to declare war;

- to raise and support armies;

- to provide and maintain a navy;

- to provide for organizing, arming, and calling forth the militia.

Peace powers include:

- to establish rules on naturalization;

- to establish post offices and post roads;

- to promote science and the arts by granting patents and copyrights;

- to exercise jurisdiction over the seat of the federal government (**District of Columbia**).

The Constitution includes the so-called "**elastic clause**" which grants Congress **implied powers** to implement the delegated powers. In addition, Congress maintains the power to discipline federal officials through **impeachment** (formal accusation of wrongdoing) and removal from office. The House of Representatives has the power to charge officials (to impeach) and the Senate has the power to conduct the trials. The first impeachment of a president was that of Andrew Johnson. **Article V** empowers Congress to propose **amendments** (changes or additions) to the Constitution. A two-thirds majority in both houses is necessary for passage. An alternate method is to have amendments proposed by the legislatures of two-thirds of the states. In order for an amendment to become part of the Constitution it must be **ratified** (formally approved) by three-fourths of the states (through their legislatures or by way of special conventions as in the case of the repeal of Prohibition).

The Senate also has the power to confirm presidential appointments (to the cabinet, federal judiciary, and major bureaucracies) and to ratify treaties.

Both houses of Congress are involved in choosing a president and vice-president if there is no majority in the Electoral College. The House of Representatives votes for the president from among the top three electoral candidates, with each state delegation casting only one vote. The Senate votes for the vice-president. The Senate has exercised this power only twice, in the disputed elections of 1800 and 1824.

Article I, **Section 9** specifically denies certain powers to the national legislature. Congress is prohibited from suspending the right of **habeas corpus** (writ calling for a party under arrest to be brought before the court where authorities must show cause for detainment), except during war or rebellion. Other prohibitions include: the passage of export taxes, the withdrawal of funds from the treasury without an appropriations law, the passage of **ex post facto** laws (make past actions punishable that were legal when they occurred), and favored treatment of one state over another with respect to commerce.

The work of the Congress is organized around a committee system. The **standing committees** are permanent and deal with such matters as agriculture, the armed services, the budget, energy, finance, and foreign policy. Special or **select committees** are established to deal with specific issues and usually have a limited duration. **Conference committees** iron out differences between the House and the Senate versions of a bill before it is sent on to the president. One committee unique to the House of Representatives is the powerful **Rules Committee**. Thousands of bills are introduced each term, and the Rules Committee acts as a clearing house to weed out those that are unworthy of consideration before the full House. Constitutionally, all revenue-raising bills must originate in the House of Representatives. They are scrutinized by the powerful House **Ways and Means Committee**. Committee membership is organized on party lines with **seniority** being a key factor, although in recent years, length of service has diminished in importance in the determination of chairmanships. The composition of each committee is largely based on the ratio of each party in the Congress as a whole. The party that has a **majority** is allotted a greater number of members on each committee. The chairmen of the standing committees are selected by the leaders of the majority party.

The legislative process is at once cumbersome and time consuming (see the chart entitled **How a Bill Becomes a Law**). A **bill** (proposed law) can be introduced in either house (with the exception of **revenue bills**, which must originate in the House of Representatives). It is referred to the appropriate **committee** and then to a **subcommittee**, which will hold **hearings** if the members agree that it has merit. The bill is reported back to the **full committee**, which must decide whether or not to send it to the **full chamber** to be debated. If the bill passes in the full chamber, it is then sent to the **other chamber** to begin the process all over again. Any differences between the House and Senate versions of the bill must be resolved in a **conference committee** before it is sent to the **president** for consideration. Most of the thousands of bills introduced in Congress die in committee with only a small percentage becoming law.

Debate on major bills is a key step in the legislative process because of the tradition of attaching **amendments** at this stage. In the House, the rules of debate are designed to enforce limits necessitated by the size of the body (435 members). In the smaller Senate (100 members), unlimited debate (**filibuster**) is allowed. Filibustering is a delaying tactic that can postpone action indefinitely. **Cloture** is a parliamentary procedure that can limit debate and bring a filibuster to an end.

Constitutional qualifications for the House of Representatives state that members must be at least **25** years of age, must have been **U.S. citizens for at least seven years**, and must be **residents of the state** that sends them to Congress. According to the **Reapportionment Act of 1929**, the size of the House is fixed at **435** members. They serve terms of **two years** in length. The presiding officer and generally the most powerful member is the **Speaker of the House**, who is the leader of the political party that has a majority in a given term.

Constitutional qualifications for the Senate state that members must be at least **30** years of age, must have been **U.S. citizens for at least nine years**, and must be **inhabitants of the state** that they represent. Senators are elected for terms of **six years** in length on a staggered basis so that one-third of the body is up for re-election in each national election. The president of the Senate is the **vice-president**. This role is largely symbolic, with the vice-president casting a vote only in the case of a tie. There is no position in the

Senate comparable to that of the Speaker of the House, although the **majority leader** is generally recognized as the most powerful member.

The Executive Branch

The **president** is the head of the executive branch of the federal government. **Article II** of the Constitution deals with the powers and duties of the President or chief executive. Following are the president's principal **constitutional responsibilities**:

- serves as **Commander-in-Chief** of the armed forces;

- negotiates treaties (with the approval of two-thirds of the Senate);

- appoints ambassadors, judges, and other high officials (with the consent of the Senate);

- grants pardons and reprieves for those convicted of federal crimes (except in impeachment cases);

- seeks counsel of department heads (Cabinet members);

- recommends legislation;

- meets with representatives of foreign states;

- sees that the laws are faithfully executed.

Despite the attempts by the Founders to set clear limits on the power of the chief executive, the importance of the presidency has grown dramatically over the years. Recent trends to reassert the pre-eminence of the Congress notwithstanding, the president remains the most visible and powerful single member of the federal government and the only one (with the exception of the vice-president) elected to represent all of the people. The president's powers with respect to foreign policy are paramount. The president, as the commander-in-chief of the armed forces, can make battlefield decisions and shape military policy.

The most significant domestic tool that the president has is the budget, which the president must submit to Congress. Though Congress must approve all spending, the president has a great deal of power in budget negotiations. The president can use considerable resources in persuading Congress to enact legislation and the president also has opportunities, such as in the annual State of the Union address, to reach out directly to the American people to convince them to support presidential policies.

Presidents also possess the power to **veto** legislation. A presidential veto may be over-ridden by a two-thirds vote in both houses, but such a majority is not easy to build, particularly in the face of the chief executive's opposition. A **pocket veto** occurs when the president neither signs nor rejects a bill, and the Congress adjourns within ten days of his receipt of the legislation.

The fact that the president is the head of a vast federal bureaucracy is another indication of the power of the office. Although the Constitution makes no mention of a formal **Cabinet** as such, since the days of George Washington, chief executives have relied on department heads to aid in the decision-making process. Washington's Cabinet was comprised of the secretaries of **state**, **war**, **treasury**, and an **attorney general**. Today there are 15 Cabinet departments, with **Homeland Security** being the most recently created post. The **Executive Office of the President** is made up of agencies that supervise the daily work of the government. The **White House Staff** manages the president's schedule and is usually headed by a powerful **chief of staff**. Arguably the most critical agency of the Executive Office is the **Office of Management and Budget**, which controls the budget process for the national government. Other key executive agencies include the **Council of Economic Advisors** and the **National Security Council**, which advises the president on matters that threaten the safety of the nation and directs the **Central Intelligence Agency**.

The **Constitutional Requirements** for the office of president and vice-president are as follows: candidates must be at least **35** years of age, must be **natural born** citizens, and must have **resided in the United States for a minimum of 14 years**.

Article II provides for an **Electoral College** to elect the president and vice-president. Each state has as many votes in the Electoral College as it has members of Congress plus three additional electors from the District of Columbia—making a grand total of 538 electors. The Founders established the Electoral College to provide an **indirect** method of choosing the chief executive.

The Judicial Branch

Article III of the Constitution establishes the **Supreme Court** but does not define the role of this branch as clearly as it does the legislative and executive branches. Yet our contemporary judicial branch consists of thousands of courts and is in essence a dual system with each state having its own judiciary functioning simultaneously with a complete set of federal courts. The most significant piece of legislation with respect to establishing a network of federal courts was the **Judiciary Act of 1789**. This law organized the Supreme Court and set up the 13 **federal district courts**. The district courts have **original jurisdiction** (to hear cases in the first instance) for federal cases involving both civil and criminal law. Federal cases on appeal are heard in the **Courts of Appeal**. The decisions of these courts are final, except for those cases that are accepted for review by the Supreme Court.

The **Supreme Court** today is made of a **chief justice** and eight **associate justices**. They are appointed for life by the president with the approval of the Senate. In the early history of the United States, the Supreme Court was largely preoccupied with the relationship between the federal government and those of the states. In 1803, the process of **judicial review** (power to determine the constitutionality of laws and actions of the legislative and executive branches) was established under **Chief Justice John Marshall** in the case of *Marbury v. Madison*. This power has become the foundation of the American judicial system and underscores the deep significance of the courts in determining the course of U.S. history.

The Supreme Court chooses cases for review based on whether or not they address substantial federal issues. If four of the nine justices vote to consider a case, then it will be added to the agenda. In such cases, **writs of certiorari** (orders calling up the records from a lower court) are issued. The justices are given detailed briefs and hear oral arguments. Reaching a decision is a complicated process. The justices scrutinize the case with reference to the Constitution and also consider previous decisions in similar cases (**precedent**). When all of the justices agree, the opinion issued is **unanimous**. In the case of a split decision, a **majority opinion** is written by one of the justices in agreement. Sometimes a justice will agree with the majority but for a different principle, in which case he/she can write a **concurring opinion** explaining the different point of view. Justices who do not vote with the majority may choose to write **dissenting opinions** to air their conflicting arguments.

In addition to the Supreme Court, the federal District Courts, and the Courts of Appeal, several special courts at the federal level have been created by Congress. The **U.S. Tax Court** handles conflicts between citizens and the Internal Revenue Service. The **Court of Claims** was designed to hear cases in which citizens bring suit against the U.S. government. Other special courts include the **Court of International Trade**, the **Court of Customs**, and the **Court of Military Appeals**.

The Federal Bureaucracy

In addition to the President's Cabinet and the Executive Office, a series of independent agencies makes up the federal bureaucracy, the so-called "**fourth branch**" of the national government. Most of these agencies were established to protect consumers and to regulate industries engaged in interstate trade. Others were set up to oversee government programs. From the time of the establishment of the Interstate Commerce Commission in 1887, these departments grew in number and influence. Late in the 1970s, the trend began to reverse, as some agencies were cut back and others eliminated altogether.

Among the most important of these powerful agencies are the **regulatory commissions**. The president appoints their administrators with the approval of the Senate. Unlike Cabinet secretaries and other high appointees, they cannot be dismissed by the chief executive. This system protects the independent status of the agencies.

Following are examples of some of the major regulatory agencies and their functions.

- **Interstate Commerce Commission:** Monitors surface transportation and some pipelines

- **Federal Reserve Board:** Supervises the banking system, sets interest rates, and controls the money supply

- **Federal Trade Commission:** Protects consumers by looking into false advertising and antitrust violations

- **Federal Communications Commission:** Polices the airwaves by licensing radio and television stations and regulating cable and telephone companies

- **Securities and Exchange Commission:** Protects investors by monitoring the sale of stocks and bonds

- **National Labor Relations Board:** Oversees labor and management practices

- **Consumer Product Safety Commission:** Sets standards of safety for manufactured products

- **Nuclear Regulatory Commission:** Licenses and inspects nuclear power plants

Another category of the "fourth branch" of government is made up of the **independent executive agencies**. These were created by Congress and resemble Cabinet departments, but they do not enjoy Cabinet status. Nonetheless they are powerful entities. Some of the key executive agencies include the Civil Rights Commission, the Environmental Protection Agency, and the National Aeronautics and Space Administration. Their names are indicative of their functions. The top level executives of these agencies are appointed by the president with the approval of the Senate.

Some of the independent agencies are actually **government corporations**. These are commercial enterprises created by Congress to perform a variety of necessary services. Their roots can be traced back to the **First Bank of the United States** established in 1791 by Secretary of the Treasury **Alexander Hamilton**. The **Federal Deposit Insurance Corporation** (FDIC), which insures bank deposits, is a more recent example. Under **Franklin Roosevelt's New Deal**, the **Tennessee Valley Authority** (TVA) was authorized to revive a depressed region of the nation. Today it oversees the generation of electric power throughout a vast region and maintains flood control programs as well. The largest of the government corporations and the most familiar to the general public is the **United States Postal Service**.

The large and powerful federal bureaucracy shapes and administers government policy. It is inherently political despite sporadic efforts throughout the years to maintain the integrity of the bureaucratic staff. Dating back to the administrations of **Andrew Jackson**, the practice of handing out government jobs in return for political favors (**spoils system**) had been the rule. The **Civil Service Act** (the **Pendleton Act**) was passed in 1883 in an attempt to reform the spoils system. Federal workers were to be recruited on the basis of merit determined by a competitive examination. Veterans were given preferential status. The Civil Service system was reorganized in the 1970s with the creation of the **Office of Personnel Management (OPM)**. The OPM is charged with recruiting, training, and promoting government workers. Merit is the stated objective when hiring federal employees. A controversial policy of the OPM is **affirmative action,** a program to help groups discriminated against in the job market to find employment.

COMPETENCY 3.3
Identify the effects of voter behavior, political parties, interest groups, public opinion, and mass media on the electoral process in the United States.

Civic culture in the United States is dominated by the two major political parties and is heavily influenced by the activities of interest groups and the mass media. These latter forces, both directly and indirectly, are largely responsible for molding and swaying public opinion.

Political Parties

A **political party** is an organization comprised of people who hold similar ideas about government who seek to influence government by electing its members to public office. Political parties serve multiple functions:

- To recruit political leaders, provide a label for its candidates, and train them

- To integrate and mobilize citizens by organizing societal interests and providing voters with choices

- To articulate and aggregate interests and communicate popular preferences by building and aggregating support among broad coalitions of citizen interest groups

- To formulate public policy and structure public debate

- To structure political conflict and competition by integrating multiple conflicting demands into coherent policy

- To organize the process of government

- To link state governments to the national government

Political parties have three distinct elements:

- The party-in-the-electorate

- The party organization

- The party-in government (public officials and those who seek to be)

While certainly parties attract people with similar views, they also have a presence in the electorate that, over time, can alter people's beliefs and behaviors, so much so that political parties become defined by the ideas and behaviors of their members. As an organization, political parties have formal roles and structures that they follow in order to manage party affairs. As a government quasi-entity, political parties help shape institutions of government. Members of political parties elected to positions in state and federal executive and legislative branches tend to appoint members from their own political party to government positions.

While political parties today form a cornerstone of our civic society, this was not always the case. The Constitution does not mention political parties, and the Founders in general were opposed to them. Madison viewed political parties as "sinister interests" prone to undermining, perverting, or usurping the will of the majority; in 1796, George Washington warned in his *Farewell Address* of the "baneful effect" of the political party which "agitates the Community with ill-founded jealousies and false alarms." Political parties were thought of as searching for profit, not providing for the common good.

Despite early concerns about the evil of political parties, two of President Washington's chief advisors, Thomas Jefferson and Alexander Hamilton, formed the first two parties. It is interesting to remember the Founders' fears in the light of politics today. Yet they developed simultaneously with the organization of the new government in 1789. It was the initial conflict over the interpretation of the powers assigned to the new government by the Constitution that gave rise to the first organized American political parties. The **Federalist Party** evolved around the policies of Washington's Secretary of the Treasury, **Alexander Hamilton**. He and his supporters favored a "**loose construction**" approach to the interpretation of the Constitution. They advocated a strong federal government with the power to assume any duties and responsibilities not prohibited to it by the text of the document. They generally supported programs designed to benefit banking and commercial interests, and in foreign policy, the Federalists were **pro-British**. The **Democratic** or **Jeffersonian Republicans** formed in opposition to the Federalists. They rallied around Washington's Secretary of State, **Thomas Jefferson**. The Jeffersonians took a "**strict constructionist**" approach, interpreting the Constitution in a narrow, limited sense. Sympathetic to the needs of the "common man," the Democratic-Republicans were mistrustful of powerful centralized government.

By Washington's *Farewell Address* in 1796, the new political parties began to play an essential role in the Presidential Election. The election of 1796 was actually the first election in which political parties played such a central role. Both the Federalists and the Democratic-Republicans put up candidates for the office. Shortly thereafter, however, the Federalist party began to lose steam, first with the 1800 election of Thomas Jefferson, then the 1804 death of the Federalist leader Alexander Hamilton following the famous duel with Aaron Burr. Jefferson's re-election in 1804, followed by another Democratic-Republic win with James Madison in 1808, caused the Federalist Party to wither away.

By the 1820s, the Democrats had splintered into factions led by **Andrew Jackson** (the Democrats) and **John Quincy Adams** (National Republicans). The Jacksonians continued with Jefferson's tradition of supporting policies designed to enhance the power of the common man. Their support was largely agrarian. The National Republicans, like their Federalist predecessors, represented the interests of bankers, merchants, and some large planters. Eventually a new party, the **Whigs**, was organized from the remnants of the old Federalists and the National Republicans. The Whigs were prominent during the 1840s, but like their Democratic rivals, they fragmented during the 1850s over the divisive slavery issue. The modern **Republican Party** was born in 1854 as Whigs and anti-slavery Democrats came together to halt the spread of slavery. The Republicans built a constituency around the interests of business, farmers, workers, and the newly emancipated slaves in the post-Civil War era.

Although the two-party system is firmly established in the United States, over the years, "**third parties**" have left their marks. The national nominating conventions were introduced in the 1830s by the **Anti-Masonic Party** and were soon adopted by the Democrats and the Whigs. The **Prohibition Party** opposed the use of alcohol and worked for the adoption of the **Eighteenth Amendment**. In the 1890s, the **Populist Party** championed the causes of the farmers and workers and impacted the mainstream parties with its reform agenda. Among the Populist innovations were the **initiative petition** (a mechanism allowing voters to put proposed legislation on the ballot) and the **referendum** (allowing voters to approve or reject laws passed by their legislatures). The **Progressive** or **Bull Moose Party** was a **splinter party** (one that breaks away from an established party, in this case the Republican Party) built around the personality of Theodore Roosevelt. Another party formed around the personality of a forceful individual was the 1992 **Reform Party** of **H. Ross Perot**. Perot did not capture any electoral votes but garnered 19 percent of the popular tally.

Today, political parties exert a variety of functions essential to the democratic tradition in the United States. Nominating candidates for local, state, and national office is their most visible activity. At the national level, this function has been diluted somewhat by the popularity of **primary elections** allowing voters to express their preference for candidates. Raucous conventions where party bosses chose obscure "**dark horse**" candidates in "smoke-filled rooms" are largely a thing of the past.

Political parties stimulate interest in public issues by highlighting their own strengths and maximizing the flaws of the opposition. They also provide a framework for keeping the machinery of government operating, most notably in their control of Congress and its organization, which is strictly along party lines. American political parties appear in theory to be highly organized. The geographic size of the country coupled with the federal system of government keep the parties in a state of relative decentralization. At the local level, the fundamental unit of organization is the **precinct**. At this level, there is usually a captain or committee to handle such routine chores as registering voters, distributing party literature, organizing "**grass-roots**" meetings, and getting out the vote on election day. **State central committees** are critical to the parties' fundraising activities. They also organize the state party conventions. There is great variety from state to state regarding the composition and selection of the state committees, which often formulate policies independent from those of the national committee. In presidential election years, the **national party committees** are most visible.

They plan the **national nominating convention**, write the party **platforms** (summaries of positions on major issues), raise money to finance political activities, and carry out the election campaigns. Representatives from each state serve on the national committees, and the **presidential nominee** chooses the individual to serve as the **party chairperson**.

Political Beliefs and Characteristics of Citizens

The population of the United States, with its diverse components, is difficult to characterize with respect to political beliefs and attitudes, and indeed individual citizens tend to hold a variety, and often contradictory, set of beliefs about their government, leaders, and the political system. The process by which individuals form their political allegiances is called **political socialization,** and the culture that develops as a result of this is called **political culture.** Several factors (**cleavages**) are relevant to the formation of political opinions, including family, race, gender, class, religion, education, region, and media exposure. Following are some gross generalizations as to the impact of these cleavages on an individual's political identification and activity.

- **Family**—affiliation with a political party is commonly passed from one generation to another.

- **Race**—African-Americans tend to be more liberal than whites on economic, social, and public policy issues.

- **Gender**—women tend to be more liberal than men.

- **Class**—citizens from the middle and upper classes tend to be more politically active than those from the lower socioeconomic brackets. Low-income voters tend to identify more with the liberal agenda.

- **Religion**—Protestants tend to be more conservative than Catholics and Jews. Evangelical Protestants seem to be most conservative on ethical and moral issues. Recently, however, these divisions are not quite so easily made, as debate over abortion has led many Catholics to move more decidedly to the right of the political continuum.

- **Education**--graduate-level education seems to have a liberalizing effect that remains potent after schooling is completed.

- **Region**—Southerners tend to be most conservative, mid-westerners more liberal, and those living on the East and West coasts the most liberal of all.

- **Media**—The influence of the media—radio, TV, movies, news-papers, blogs, social networking sites, etc.—have all been used to influence political opinion by a variety of political parties and lobbyists. The effect of the media to sway public opinion should not be discounted.

Despite the categorization of Americans as either **liberals** or **conservatives**, most studies indicate that they do not follow clearly delineated **ideologies** (firm and consistent beliefs with respect to political, economic, and social issues). The terms liberal and conservative with reference to the political beliefs of Americans are difficult to define in precise terms. Liberals tend to favor change and to view government as a tool for improving the quality of life. Conservatives, on the other hand, are more inclined to view both change and government with suspicion. They emphasize individual initiative and local solutions to problems. A puzzling reversal is seen in the attitudes of liberals and conservatives when confronting moral issues such as abortion and school prayer. Here conservatives see a role for government in ensuring the moral climate of the nation while liberals stress the importance of individual choice.

The most basic way that citizens influence the electoral process in the United States is **voting**. Since the passage of the Twenty-Third Amendment in 1965, U.S. citizens, both male and female, who are 18 years old, are eligible to vote. The number of people, however, who actually choose to use their right to vote, is surprisingly few. Reasons for not voting range from belief that an individual really cannot change anything, votes are not counted properly, difficulty among certain racial or ethnic groups in being able to cast their votes due to voter intimidation, lack of adequate numbers of voting machines, limited hours to vote, and misunderstandings about the voter registration process. Only about

57% of eligible voters actually voted in the 2008 Presidential Election. In Florida, for example, that number was only slightly higher, at 58% of eligible voters cast ballots.

Political Institutions and Special Interests

Interest groups

Interest groups have a strong hold on politics today. Lobbyists are an ever-growing part of today's politics. Interest groups are not exclusively found in the Senate, but since each state has only two senators, it is the place where lobbyists spend a lot of time and money when a bill needs to be defeated. American officials and political leaders are continually subjected to pressure from a variety of interest groups seeking to influence their actions. Such groups arise from bonds among individuals who share common concerns. Interest groups may be loosely organized (**informal**), with no clear structure or regulations. A good example of such an informal or ad hoc interest group was the "March of the Poor" on Washington, DC, in 1963 to focus Congress's attention on the needs of the "underclass" in America. A group of neighbors united in opposition to a new shopping mall that threatens a wetland is an example of this type of group. Other interest groups are much more **formal** and permanent in nature. They may have suites of offices and large numbers of employees. Their political objectives are usually clearly defined. Labor unions, professional and public-interest groups, and **single-issue** organizations fall into this category. The National Rifle Association and the National Right to Life Organization are examples of single issue pressure groups. Interest groups employ a variety of tactics to accomplish their goals. Most commonly, they **lobby** (influence the passage or defeat of legislation) elected officials, particularly members of Congress. Lobbyists provide legislators with reports and statistics to persuade them of the legitimacy of their respective positions. They may present expert testimony at public hearings and influence the media to portray their causes in a favorable light. Lobbyists are required to register in Washington and to make their positions public. They are barred from presenting false and misleading information and from bribing public officials. Regulatory legislation cannot, however, curb all the abuses inherent to a system of organized persuasion.

One particularly controversial brand of pressure group is the **Political Action Committee** (PAC). PACs were formed in the 1970s in an attempt to circumvent legislation limiting contributions to political campaigns. Critics see these interest groups as another means of diluting the influence individual voters may have on their elected officials. Some politicians refuse to accept PAC money.

Media and Public Opinion

Public opinion refers to the attitudes and preferences expressed by a significant number of individuals about an issue that involves the government or the society at large. It does not necessarily represent the sentiments of all or even most of the citizenry. Nonetheless, it is an important component of a democratic society.

The **media** is another element of political science in which influence has exploded with the appearance of the Internet. A large segment of our society, our oldest citizens, grew up without television and depended instead on newspapers and radio for information on current events. Now cable television's 24-hour news channels and the Internet with YouTube and blogs (many offering opinions disguised as news) have changed our perception of media's reach. In today's technological society, the influence of the **mass media** on public opinion cannot be over-emphasized. The print and broadcast media can reach large numbers of people cheaply and efficiently, and now the electronic media joins the ranks of these opinion-shapers who serve as not only watchdogs over governmental, business, and society's actions as they scrutinize questionable actions or behaviors, but also have been accused of creating and manufacturing public opinion. In recent elections, the electronic media in particular have been criticized for over-simplifying complicated issues and reducing coverage of major events to brief sound bites. Both the print and broadcast media claim to present news in a fair and objective format, but both conservatives and liberals claim that coverage is slanted. **Paid political advertising** is another vehicle for molding public opinion. In this case, objectivity is neither expected nor attempted, as candidates and interest groups employ "hard-sell" techniques to persuade voters to support their causes.

Measuring the effects of the media on public opinion is difficult, as is gauging where the public stands on a given issue at a particular point in time. **Public opinion polls** have been designed to these ends. Pollsters usually address a **random sample** and try to capture a **cross-section** of the population. Their questions are designed to elicit responses that do not mirror the biases of the interviewer or the polling organization. Results are tabulated and analyzed, and generalizations are presented to the media.

Although polls are more accurate today than in the past, they are still subject to criticism for oversimplifying complicated issues and encouraging pat answers to complex problems. Public opinion is constantly in a state of flux, and what may be a valid report today is passé tomorrow. Another criticism is that interviewees may not be entirely candid, particularly with respect to sensitive issues. They may answer as they think they should but not necessarily with full honesty.

A type of election poll that has been the target of sharp criticism is the **exit poll** in which interviewers question subjects about their votes as they leave the polling places. These polls may be accurate, but if the media present the results while voting is still in progress, the outcome may be affected. Predicting the winners before voters throughout the country have had the opportunity to cast their ballots in a national election robs a segment of the electorate of the sense that its participation is of any consequence. In the 2000 election, exit polls led to confusion as Florida results were projected prematurely; the television networks vowed to be more careful.

Voter Apathy

In recent years, attention has focused on the problem of voter apathy. Despite efforts to extend suffrage to all segments of the adult population, participation in the electoral process has been on the decline. Several theories have been advanced to explain this trend. There is widespread belief that Americans are dissatisfied with their government and mistrust all elected officials. Therefore, they refuse to participate in the electoral process. Some citizens do not vote in a given election, not because they are "turned-off" to the system, but because they are ill, homeless, away on business, or otherwise preoccupied on election day. College students and others away from their legal residences find registration and the use of **absentee ballots** cumbersome and inconvenient. Efforts have been made in the 1990s to streamline the registration process with such legislation as the **"motor-voter" bill** that makes it possible for citizens to register at their local registries of motor vehicles.

While most attempts to explain voter apathy focus on negatives such as citizen apathy, some analysts disagree. They see disinterest in the ballot as a sign that the majority of Americans are happy with the system and feel no sense of urgency to participate in the political process.

Political participation is not limited to voting in elections. Working for candidates, attending rallies, contacting elected officials and sharing opinions about issues, writing letters to newspapers, marching in protest, and joining in community activities are all forms of political participation. While voter turnout has decreased in recent years, other forms of participation seem to be on the increase.

COMPETENCY 3.4

Identify the elements and functions of state and local governments in the United States.

The United States' government is a federal one, meaning that authority and jurisdiction is split among national, state, and local governments. It comprises one national (federal) government, 50 state governments, more than 3,000 county governments, and over 85,000 local government units comprising over 19,000 municipalities, 16,000 township governments, 15,000 school districts, and 31,000 special districts.

The federal government is the largest body of government, and it makes, enforces, and explains laws for the entire country. The Constitution functions as the foundation of all law for U.S. citizens and lays out the responsibility and structure of the federal government. The following are the specific powers that the Constitution delegates to the federal government:

- To regulate foreign commerce and interstate commerce

- To tax, borrow and coin money; universalize bankruptcy laws

- To regulate naturalization and immigration

- To establish a postal service

- To grant patents and copyrights

- To establish courts

- To declare and wage war and to declare peace, and conduct relations with foreign powers

- To govern territories, admit new states, and govern Washington, D.C.

- To raise and maintain an army and a navy, and to define and punish felonies and piracy on the high seas

- To fix standards for weights and measures

There are some powers that the federal and state governments share: Both Congress and the states may levy taxes, borrow money, and charter banks and corporations. Both the state and federal governments may establish courts, make and enforce laws, and take private property for public purposes, as well as spend money to provide for the public welfare.

The **Tenth Amendment to the U.S. Constitution** reserves to the states **any power that the constitution does not give to the federal government and does not deny to the states.** In situations where both the states and Congress claim jurisdiction over an issue, the federal courts decide which claim is more valid. State governments have the following powers:

- To conduct and monitor elections

- To establish voter qualifications within the guidelines established by the Constitution

- To provide for local governments

- To ratify proposed amendments to the Constitution

- To regulate contracts and wills

- To regulate intrastate commerce

- To provide education for its citizens

- To levy direct taxes

States may NOT:

- issue paper money;

- conduct foreign relations;

- impair the obligations of contracts;

- establish a government that is not republican in form – although the three-branch structure is not required;

- legalize the ownership of one person by another (slavery) (Thirteenth Amendment);

- determine qualifications for citizenship (Fourteenth Amendment);

- deny the right to vote because of race, color, or previous condition of servitude (Fifteenth Amendment);

- deny the vote to women (Nineteenth Amendment).

Today there are 50 states in the United States. Every state government is almost a mirror of the federal government in which each state has a constitution, elected officials, and governmental organization. The state constitutions may not disagree with the Constitution of the United States. Every state government also has three **branches**: the executive, the legislative, and the judicial. Laws passed by states cannot disagree with the federal Constitution. State laws apply only to the people that live in that state.

Every state has the responsibility to protect the lives of the people in that state. The state is responsible for transportation, education, and the laws of business in that state. State and local governments share responsibility for providing many important services that directly affect the daily lives of their residents. These include the following:

- Setting educational standards and establishing methods for funding public education

- Building and maintaining transportation networks

- Establishing state-sponsored colleges and universities

- Licensing and regulating businesses and professions

- Creating and overseeing nonfederal courts and the criminal justice system

- Issuing marriage licenses and driver's licenses

- Issuing and recording birth and death certificates

- Administering publicly funded health, housing, and nutrition programs for low-income and disabled residents

- Managing state parks and other lands for recreation and environmental conservation purposes

- Administering and certifying elections, including elections for federal officials

- Commanding the state National Guard, except when it is called to national service

- Regulating employment of children and women in industry

- Enacting safety laws to prevent industrial accidents

- Handling unemployment insurance

- Operating a state highway patrol

In the early nineteeth century, state governments were new and relatively weak entities. Their size alone made it rather difficult for them to adequately serve the needs of their largely rural populations, who tended to live further apart from one another. As the states strove to provide adequate transportation for its citizens and communication was rather difficult, it turned to local governments to manage local needs more carefully. County governments began to spring up and became important sources of information and administration. In many rural towns, then, as now, the county courthouse was the most prominent public building in the area. Because of this history of local governments acting as a liaison or even arm of the state government, we see that both state and local governments have overlapping duties and responsibilities and they cooperate in some of the above services that they provide for their residents, from welfare to transportation.

Local governments then may be considered creatures of state governments as they function as subordinate governmental bodies that exist in two tiers: counties, also known as boroughs in Alaska and parishes in Louisiana, and municipalities, or cities/towns. State governments have power over these local authorities as states can abolish a local government, merge it with another, or give it additional authority if they so choose. Local authority in counties, for instance, comes from state-approved charters that set up their county governments and state how they will function. County charters cannot disagree with their state's constitutions or the U.S. Constitution. Counties have a variety of powers. They determine the location of highways, are responsible for highway repair, provide relief for their poor, determine voting precincts and polling places, and organize school and road districts. In some states, counties are divided into townships.

Municipal governments, also called townships, boroughs, villages, cities, and townships and usually headed by a mayor or city manager, are one of the smallest bodies of government. There are usually many cities in a county. Municipal governments have the power to levy taxes; to borrow; to pass, amend, and repeal local ordinances; and to grant franchises for public service corporations. The taxes collected pay for police, fire departments, parks, and other services. Like counties, municipal governments have charters that must be approved by the state government. City government is the closest form of government to the people. In some areas, there are even smaller township governments.

Municipalities generally take responsibility for parks and recreation services, police and fire departments, housing services, emergency medical services, municipal courts, transportation services (including public transportation), and public works (streets, sewers, snow removal, signage, and so forth). Whereas the federal government and state governments share power in countless ways, a local government must be granted power by the state. In general, mayors, city councils, and other governing bodies are directly elected by the people.

COMPETENCY 3.5
Analyze the guiding concepts, principles, and effects of U.S. foreign policy.

The Constitutional Framework for Foreign Policy

The Constitution lays out the institutional framework for foreign policy that places it under control of the federal government. The Founders divided responsibility for foreign affairs between the president and the Congress. The president, as the head of state, could appoint and receive ambassadors, sign treaties, and represent the United States abroad. Congress could declare war, but the president, as commander in chief, could actually wage the war. The president also had the authority to negotiate treaties that are then subject to the advice and consent of the Senate (two-thirds vote needed for approval). The president appoints key foreign policy and military officials as well as ambassadors, but the Senate must consent.

The Theoretical Framework of International Relations

The study of how nations interact with one another can be approached from a variety of perspectives, including the following:

- A **traditional analysis** uses the descriptive process and focuses on such topics as global issues, international institutions, and the foreign policies of individual nation-states.

- The **strategists' approach** zeroes in on war and deterrence. Scholars in this camp may employ game theory to analyze negotiations, the effectiveness of weapons systems, and the likelihood of limited versus all-out war in a given crisis situation.

- The **middle range theorists** analyze specific components of international relations, such as the politics of arms races, the escalation of international crises, and the role of prejudice and attitudes toward other cultures in precipitating war and peace.

- A **world politics approach** takes into consideration such factors as economics, ethics, law, and trade agreements and stresses the significance of international organizations and the complexities of interactions among nations.

The grand theory of international relations is presented by Hans J. Morgenthau in *Politics Among Nations* (1948). He argues for realism in the study of interactions on the international stage. Morgenthau suggests that an analysis of relations among nations reveals such recurring themes as "interest defined as power" and striving for equilibrium/balance of power as a means of maintaining peace The idealists assume that human nature is essentially good; hence, people and nations are capable of cooperation and avoiding armed conflict. They highlight global organizations, international law, disarmament, and the reform of institutions that lead to war.

An analysis of international politics can be conducted at various levels by looking at the actions of individual statesmen, the interests of individual nations, and/or the mechanics of a whole system of international players. In studying the rise of Nazism and its role in precipitating World War II, the individual approach would focus on Hitler, the state approach would treat the German preoccupation with racial superiority and the need for expansion, and the systemic approach would highlight how German military campaigns upset the balance of power and triggered unlikely alliances, such as the linking of the democratic Britain and the United States with the totalitarian Soviet Union in a common effort to restore equilibrium.

During the Revolutionary War, John Adams was directed by the Continental Congress to outline a plan for the new country's foreign policy. Adams, like many of the Founders, advocated free trade and the avoidance of political ties. The demands of war, however, made military aid from foreign states a necessity. France, who had struggled with Britain, gave aid to the Americans. In 1778, France and the North American colonies signed a military alliance, the first and only military alliance until the twentieth century. The nation's early leaders, having led a revolution against Great Britain, were generally opposed to alliances with European powers, having known and seen the effects of alliances in Europe that led to war for the last few hundred years.

When the first Congress met in 1789, foreign policy was not a primary concern of theirs. They felt that they did not need a big army to protect the new country, and they authorized an army to have only a maximum strength of 840 men. Most of the nation's military strength came from state militias. Their concerns with trade were also relatively mild, and early tariff laws kept tariffs low to keep trade free from government interference.

Isolationism and Non-Interventionism

One of the earliest guiding concepts and principles of U.S. foreign policy was that of **isolationism**. Isolationism is basically a policy of non-interventionist policy in terms of military intervention combined with a political policy of protectionism, which states that there should be legal barriers to control trade with other nation-states. **Non-interventionism** is a diplomatic policy, whereby a nation seeks to avoid alliances with other nations in order to avoid being drawn into a war that is not related to their own territorial defense. The difference between ideas of isolationism and non-interventionism is that isolationism includes isolating oneself from immigration and trade, and non-interventionism refers solely to military alliances and policies.

America has a long history of non-interventionism. In George Washington's 1796 *Farewell Address*, he laid the foundations for a non-interventionist policy when he cautioned that the United States should "steer clear of permanent alliances with any portion of the foreign world." With regard to Europe in particular, he stated that

> "the great rule of conduct for us, in regard to foreign nations, is in extending our commercial relations, to have with them as little political connection as possible. Europe has a set of primary interests, which to us have none, or a very remote relation. Hence she must be engaged in frequent controversies the causes of which are essentially foreign to our concerns. Hence, therefore, it must be unwise in us to implicate ourselves, by artificial ties, in the ordinary vicissitudes of her politics, or the ordinary combinations and collisions of her friendships or enmities."

Both Adams and Jefferson followed Washington's advice, with John Adams avoiding a war with France and Jefferson including in his inaugural address in 1801, stating that the United States should practice "peace, commerce, and honest friendship with all nations, entangling alliances with none." This idea was elaborated upon during James Monroe's administration in response to the new independence of the Spanish colonies in

Latin America in the early 1800s with his **Monroe Doctrine** in 1823, which stated that the United States would not interfere in European affairs and it would oppose any European attempt to colonize the Americas. He stated that

> "In the wars of the European powers, in matters relating to themselves, we have never taken part, nor does it comport with our policy, so to do. It is only when our rights are invaded, or seriously menaced that we resent injuries, or make preparations for our defense."

Monroe elaborated saying that if any country attempted to re-colonize Latin America, or if Russia attempted to move on the western coast of America, the United States would respond with force.

While Americans sought non-interventionist policies with regard to military intervention, it had a bit of a different attitude with regard to trade. Beginning in 1776, John Adams recommended the idea of **trade reciprocity,** which simply stated that the United States would treat foreign countries the same way that it was treated. Tariffs became one measure that the United States would reciprocate with and tariffs became a standard trade policy until the twentieth century.

American interests became more concerned with the doctrine of **Manifest Destiny** which sought to settle the continent coast to coast, arguing that the United States had a divine obligation to civilize the continent and control its riches. Some political scientists today assert that the policy the US held against the Native Americans and the idea of Manifest Destiny were actually interventionist policies, and treatment toward the Native Americans and wars with them should be regarded as "foreign policy." It should be noted that while European states became reoccupied in the nineteenth century with grabbing territory overseas, the United States became more focused on expanding its territory in contiguous areas.

Throughout most of the nineteenth century, the United States did practice the idea of non-interventionism in global affairs. Toward the end of the nineteenth century, its involvement in world politics became more substantive as it sought to protect its imperialist and trade interests.

Expansionism and Unilateralism

The first significant foreign military intervention occurred in the **Spanish-American War** in which America occupied and controlled the Philippines. As a result of the war, the

Philippines, Guam, American Samoa, and Puerto Rico became American territories, and the United States gained hegemony over Cuba. In 1899, Filipinos revolted over American rule and the three-year-long war left nearly 4,500 American combat deaths, 16,000 Filipino combat deaths, and estimates of between 250,000 and one million Filipinos killed or dead of disease or starvation during the long war.

With the Philippines as a U.S. territory, the United States became embroiled in conflict in Asia. The United States began to claim, what was referred to by John Hay, McKinley's Secretary of State, as **spheres of influence** in which the United States had to protect its interests. But, with the European powers carving out spheres of influence for themselves in China, the United States called for an **Open Door Policy** that would allow all nations equal trading access in China.

In 1904, after Teddy Roosevelt sent the U.S. navy to Panama to help it throw off the yoke of Colombian rule and the United States started building the Panama Canal, Roosevelt issued his **Roosevelt Corollary** to the Monroe Doctrine. It stated that the United States would intervene in the domestic affairs of any weak or negligent state in the Caribbean or Central America to keep them free from outside forces who might seek to take them over. Under the Roosevelt Corollary, the United States sent military forces to Nicaragua, Haiti, the Dominican Republic, Cuba, Panama, and Mexico.

World War I and a Return to Isolationism from 1920–1941

Although World War I broke out in Europe in 1914, United States efforts to remain neutral succeeded for three years until it was forced into the war in April 1917 by the German policy of unrestricted submarine warfare. It entered the war in an effort to insure freedom of trade routes with Europe. During the war, the United States was not officially tied to the Allies by treaty but instead by military cooperation. By the end of the war, the United States had sent over five million men to serve in the aid of the Allies. By the end of the war, President Woodrow Wilson sought to enact his policy of **Fourteen Points** at the Versailles Peace Conference, and indeed, it did become the basis for postwar settlement. One of the goals that Wilson advocated was the establishment of a **League of Nations** that would hopefully resolve all future conflicts before they caused another war. Unfortunately for Wilson, the Republican-controlled U.S. Senate refused to ratify the Treaty of Versailles which had provided for the creation of a League of a Nations, and afterwards, the United States returned to an isolationist stance during the interwar period. The United States chose instead to make separate peace treaties with different European nations. While Wilson's 14 Points failed to gain support in the United States, his idea that people had the right to **self-determination** became a rallying cry for many under the thumb of British and French colonial rule in the Middle East and South Asia. Moreover, what is called **Wilsonianism**, the idea of spreading democracy and peace under American auspices, had a tremendous effect on American foreign policy. These efforts continued even with the 1928 passage of the **Kellogg-Briand Pact** which was designed to outlaw war.

The United States returned to a policy of high tariffs and isolationism. Despite having such a mindset, the United States continued to develop economic ties with Europe, so much so that the Great Depression of 1929 had a direct effect on all of the key European economies. The United States was keenly aware of growing tensions in Europe and in vain strove to keep out of it. In response to the growing threat from Nazi Germany, Congress passed a series of neutrality acts from 1935-1937 that sought to keep the United States out of a European conflict. It was only after the outbreak of World War II (September 1939) that President Franklin Roosevelt was able to shift American foreign policy to aid the Allies.

On June 10, 1940, President Roosevelt spoke at the University of Virginia in Charlottesville and outlined a shift in U.S. foreign policy from that of neutrality to **non-belligerency**. He stated that the United States would pursue "two obvious and simultaneous courses: we will extend to the opponents of force the material resource of this nation; and at the same time, we will harness and speed up the use of those resources in order that we ourselves in the Americas may have the equipment and training equal to the task of any emergency and every defense" and that the United States would gear up to be ready for war, should the need arise. In his State of the Union address in January 1941, Roosevelt spoke of the Four Freedoms that should be enjoyed by people everywhere in the world: the freedom of speech, religion, and freedom from want and fear. The passage of the **Lend-Lease Act** allowed the United States to assist countries whose defense was seen as vital to the United States by lending or leasing them war supplies, materials, or equipment.

World War II and the End of Isolationism, Unilateralism, and Strict Neutrality

With the Japanese attack on Pearl Harbor on December 7, 1941, the United States formally joined the war. The United States learned just how untenable the policy of isolationism was in modern world politics. The war created interesting alliances when the United States, Britain, and France joined with the Soviet Union—an alliance that lasted throughout the war but broke apart after Germany was defeated. The use of the atomic bomb to end the war changed the way that war was fought and set the stage for the Cold War that would follow.

Roosevelt was determined, even before war began, to help craft a peace that would best benefit the United States as a world power. FDR and the allies created the United Nations to guarantee the security of member nations and promote economic prosperity around the globe. The idea was to have an organization that would promote peace through understanding among nations. The agreement was the that five great powers—the United States , Great Britain, China, France, and the Soviet Union—would have permanent seats on the Security Council and could veto any action by the UN. They also created new economic organizations that would promote trade, and economic growth and would avert a repeat of the disastrous economic policies after WWI that led to yet another world war. Some of the institutions they created were the International Monetary Fund, the World Bank, and the General Agreement on Tariffs and Trade in an effort to regulate exchange rates, rebuild war torn economies, and lower trade barriers. These new institutions represented a shift in American strategy from isolation and unilateral action to engagement and multilateral action.

By the end of the war, the international order had changed and the United States rose to become the dominant economic power because it was unencumbered by the rebuilding efforts in Europe. The U.S. had an intact industrial base, a thriving economy, a military power made stronger by its relationship with business in what Eisenhower would refer to as the "military-industrial complex. "

Cold War (1945–1991)

U.S. foreign policy during this period can be broken into three parts: containment, détente, and unrestricted competition. Fissures in ideological stances among the allies increased steadily as the leader of the Soviet Union, Joseph Stalin, encouraged the spread of communism through eastern and central Europe. As this influence spread through eastern and central Europe after the Red Army liberated Eastern Europe, the British became a little concerned but could do nothing. When Stalin sought to gain influence in Greece and Turkey, the United States responded with its idea of **containment policy**, a term coined by State Department staffer George Kennan and based on the premise that the United States must apply counterforce to any aggressive moves by the Soviet Union, and implemented in the **Truman Doctrine**. This began an attempt by the United States to craft its foreign affairs around the idea to resist communism and oppose the Soviet Union. The world became divided into two camps, one side led by the United States and the other by the Soviet Union;

a third group also emerged, led by the efforts of the Indian Prime Minister Jawaharlal Nehru and the **Non-Aligned Movement**. One of Truman's main initiatives was to get Congress to pass the **Marshall Plan**, basically a plan to pump billions of dollars into Western Europe to help rebuild it and its economies to make it strong enough to prevent communism. The Marshall Plan set up a new guiding principle for U.S. foreign aid to be used as a key element of American diplomacy. For the first time, the United States joined a military and political alliance in peacetime: the **North Atlantic Treaty Organization (NATO)**.

Another guiding principle that emerged during the Cold War was the **domino theory,** in which it was believed that if one region came under communist influence, then other nations in the area would follow. In an effort to prevent this, the United States limited trade and technology transfer and surrounded the Soviet Union and its allies with military forces and American allies.

Nuclear and military tensions continued to escalate with the Cuban Missile Crisis in 1962 when the USSR tried to put nuclear missiles in Cuba, merely 90 miles from U.S. soil. The confrontation between the two super powers nearly brought the world to the brink of nuclear war. Shortly after, both the USSR and the United States sought to find ways to limit the nuclear and military tensions between the two. The United States began to seek ways to limit the growth of nuclear weapons through test bans and nonproliferation treaties. Both sides also began to limit their own arsenals, and eventually arms control became arms reduction in the 1980s.

One of the most striking applications of the domino theory was the U.S. intervention in Vietnam where nationalist forces from the north, led by Ho Chi Minh, defeated French colonial forces at Dien Bien Phu in 1954. Vietnam was divided into a communist north and a capitalist south, with the promise of elections in two years that could unify the country. The elections never materialized, as the struggle between the two Vietnams intensified. Determined to halt the spread of communism, the United States supported the corrupt capitalist regime in the south. Beginning early in the Kennedy administration, first hundreds and then thousands of U.S. military "advisors" were sent to South Vietnam.

Within a few weeks of each other in November 1963, both South Vietnamese Prime Minister Ngo Dinh Diem and President Kennedy were assassinated. Lyndon Johnson assumed the presidency with public declarations of no desire to "widen" the war in Vietnam. Yet he convinced Congress to support a massive military buildup in Southeast Asia and the **Gulf of Tonkin Resolution,** passed by Congress in August 1964, provided President Johnson with broad legal authority to combat North Vietnamese aggression. In July 1965, Lyndon Johnson chose to Americanize the war by increasing U.S. combat strength in Vietnam from 75,000 to 125,000, with additional U.S. forces to be sent when requested by field commander General William Westmoreland. As Johnson wrote in his memoirs, "now we are committed to major combat in Vietnam. We had determined not to let that country fall under Communist rule as long as we could prevent it."

By the early 1970s, the American military was mired in the Asian jungles, at a cost of billions of dollars and tens of thousands of lives. The U.S. national interest in the region was no longer clear, and the antiwar movement grew until the United States was completely split on the issue. Finally, a treaty with the North Vietnamese government allowed the United States to withdraw in 1973. The United States got involved in Vietnam for several reasons: to bailout the French colonial power, to promote "democracy," and most of all to contain communism. However, the U.S. understanding of the conflict was highly flawed. The South Vietnamese were not "democrats," the North Vietnamese were not controlled from Moscow and Beijing, and the war was mostly about nationalism and independence. By the time the United States extracted itself from Vietnam in 1973, there were 57,000 American dead and 300,000 casualties. The lying and deceit of the military and the Johnson administration had eroded trust in government. The war, and wars in general, became hugely unpopular, and many began to see the limits to the United States projecting its power over the rest of the world. The experience had a huge impact and continues to have an impact today. The credibility of much of the United States' foreign policy apparatus was undercut. The fiasco also led many citizens and leaders to question the role and effectiveness of U.S. foreign intervention. This debate continues today.

Détente and the End of the Cold War

In the 1969, President Nixon announced that the time for confrontation was over, a new era of negotiation was in order, and American foreign policy began to take a new direction. The United States realized that it needed a new direction as the toll of continued competition with the Soviet Union and an escalating nuclear arms race that had intensified since 1949, when the Soviet Union exploded their bomb, was not in the best interests of the United States. Under President Richard Nixon, détente, an easing of tensions between the United States and the Soviet Union, led to increased trade and cultural exchanges and, most importantly, to an agreement to limit nuclear weapons—the 1972 **Strategic Arms Limitation Treaty** (SALT I). In the same year, Nixon also began the process of normalizing relations with the People's Republic of China.

The culmination of détente was the achievement of the **Helsinki Accords** in 1975. The heads of government of virtually every European state, Canada, and the United States met in Finland. The Soviets hoped that the group in Helsinki would recognize their control of Eastern Europe and other conquered territories, and the western powers wanted the USSR to agree to human rights and other protections for all citizens. Both got what they wanted. The inviolability of borders was made an important point in international law and human rights. Until the fall of the Berlin Wall and the reunification agreement in Germany, the Helsinki Accords were as close as we came to a European peace since the end of WWII.

In 1977, President Jimmy Carter expressed his desire to make human rights the cornerstone of his foreign policy. In 1979, the Iranian hostage crisis erupted and undermined Carter's domestic support. The Republicans charged that Carter and the Democrats had made America weak. Détente finally died when the Soviets invaded Afghanistan in 1979. Carter also promulgated the **Carter Doctrine**—that the Persian Gulf was an area of vital U.S. interest and the United States would fight to maintain its interests there.

The Soviet Union's invasion of Afghanistan resulted in an American-led boycott of the 1980 Summer Olympics in Moscow. Superpower rivalry continued for a time, however, and particularly escalated with the election of Ronald Reagan to the presidency. When Ronald Reagan was elected, U.S.-Soviet relations deteriorated rapidly. He called the USSR an evil empire, stepped up defense spending, announced an activist foreign policy to be designed, once again, to contain Soviet expansion, and began funding the Afghan opposition. President Reagan actively supported anti-communist, anti-left-wing forces in both Nicaragua and El Salvador, which he considered client states of the "evil" Soviet Union. He increased American defense spending significantly during his first term. The Soviet Union simply could not match these expenditures. Faced with a serious economic crisis, in 1985, Soviet leader Mikhail Gorbachev instituted new policies called **glasnost** (openness) and **perestroika** (economic restructuring) that eased tensions with the United States. He announced a new way of thinking in foreign policy that renounced class struggle and the idea of confrontation as the sole way of dealing with other countries. Gorbachev and Reagan met at several summits. Gorbachev, in desperate need to reallocate his country's resources from military to domestic uses, kept up his spate of reforms and attempts at reducing tension. By the third summit meeting, the leaders seemed to have found a recipe for dealing with each other, and they signed an agreement to eliminate of all intermediate-range nuclear forces in Europe. By the early 1990s, the Cold War had effectively come to an end. The Soviet Union ceased to exist with the independence of the

Baltic States (Estonia, Latvia, and Lithuania), Ukraine, Belarus, Armenia, Georgia, and the Central Asian republics.

Searching for a New World Order

The collapse of the Soviet Union did not mean an end to conflict around the world. The Iron Curtain fell when Eastern Europe rebelled in 1989, and the USSR let them go. Communism was also rapidly collapsing in the Soviet Union itself. The Iraqi invasion of Kuwait in 1990 prompted the United States to put together an international coalition under the auspices of the UN that culminated in the brief Persian Gulf War in 1991. Both the UN and NATO were involved in seeking a resolution to the ethnic conflict in the former Yugoslavia. While the United States arranged a settlement in the region known as the **Dayton Accords** (1995), it did not prevent a new outbreak of fighting between Serbs and ethnic Albanians in the province of Kosovo. NATO aircraft bombed targets in Serbia, including the capital Belgrade, in response. This was the first time that NATO forces conducted combat operations in Europe.

Efforts of the United States to be the "world's policeman" led to the U.S. invasion of Kuwait and its war with Iraq under President George H. W. Bush. In 1990, when Iraq invaded Kuwait, the United States led a UN-approved operation to expel Iraqi troops from Kuwait. The operation was lauded as a great success and President Bush's approval ratings skyrocketed. Shortly thereafter, the Soviet Union was wracked by a coup in August 1991, and then, the collapse of the USSR. The Cold War and Communism were gone.

War on Terrorism, 2001 to Present

After September 11, 2001, when over 3,000 people were killed in terrorist attacks on New York City's World Trade Center, the Pentagon, and a related plane crash in Pennsylvania that did not reach its intended target, the United States responded by declaring a **"war on terrorism."** Part of President George W. Bush's approach was to create a new **Office of Homeland Security** that had Cabinet status. He declared war against the Taliban regime in Afghanistan, not because they had anything to do with the war but because they had harbored al-Qaeda, a terrorist organization claiming responsibility for the attacks. By the end of 2001, the Taliban regime was overthrown and over 17 countries had troops in Afghanistan.

The policies of the United States began to change from reactive strategies of containment and deterrence to a more proactive policy of preemptive military action under the

Bush Doctrine. The United States found itself having to deal with new threats to U.S. security: terrorism, anti-Americanism, and the clash of civilizations. In March 2003, Bush launched a war in Iraq arguing that Iraq was developing weapons of mass destruction, contrary to evidence from weapons inspectors and scholars of the region. The administration argued that Iraq was a safe haven for terrorists and asserted that the Iraq regime was connected to al-Qaeda without any direct evidence from intelligence or scholarly sources. While the UN did not approve of the invasion, a comparatively small coalition of countries launched an invasion, and Saddam Hussein was quickly overthrown. Coalition forces found no evidence of weapons of mass destruction. The Bush administration changed its justification for the war to the goal of promoting democracy in the Middle East. After Bush declared his "mission accomplished" and challenged Iraqi troops to "bring it on," violence escalated. By the end of June 2007, more than 3,585 American soldiers had died, and civil war broke out in Iraq.

The 2008 election of Barack Obama to the U.S. presidency signaled that the feeling in the country had turned from praising the goals of the Bush Doctrine to looking for a new way. President Obama's unofficially named **Obama Doctrine** places negotiation and collaboration over confrontation and unilateralism. Critics of the U.S. position in the world assert that "with power comes responsibility" and that the United States needs to deal more with some of the environmental and human disasters that happen on a global scale.

Overview of International Relations

International relations is a discipline inextricably linked to the field of foreign policy. **Foreign policy** involves the objectives nations seek to gain with reference to other nations, and the procedures they employ in order to achieve their objectives. The principal foreign policy goals of sovereign states or other political entities may include some or all of the following: independence, national security, economic advancement, encouraging their political values beyond their own borders, gaining respect and prestige, and promoting stability and international peace.

The foreign policy process are the stages a government goes through to formulate policy and arrive at decisions with respect to courses of action. A variety of models have been identified the process of creating foreign policy. The primary players (nations, world organizations, multinational corporations, and non-state ethnic entities such as the Palestine Liberation Organization) are often referred to as *actors*.

The **unitary/rational actor model** assumes that all nations or primary players share similar goals and approach foreign policy issues in like fashion. The actions players take, according to this theory, are influenced by the actions of other players rather than by what may be taking place internally. The rational component in this model is based on the assumption that actors will respond on the world stage by making the best choice after measured consideration of possible alternatives.

Maximizing goals and achieving specific objectives motivate the rational actor's course of action. The **bureaucratic model** assumes that, due to the many large organizations involved in formulating foreign policy, particularly in powerful nation-states, final decisions are the result of struggle among the bureaucratic actors. In the United States, the bureaucratic actors include the Departments of State and Defense, as well as the National Security Council, the Central Intelligence Agency, the Environmental Protection Agency, the Department of Commerce, and/or any other agencies and departments whose agendas might be impacted by a foreign policy decision. While the bureaucratic model is beneficial in that it assumes the consideration of multiple points of view, the downside is that inter-agency competition and compromise often drive the final decision.

A third model assumes that foreign policy results from the intermingling of a variety of political factors, including national leaders, bureaucratic organizations, legislative bodies, political parties, interest groups, and public opinion. The implementation of foreign policy depends upon the tools that a nation or primary player has at its disposal. The major instruments of foreign policy include diplomacy, military strength/actions, and economic initiatives.

Diplomacy involves communicating with other primary players through official representatives. It might include participation in conferences and summit meetings, negotiation of treaties and settlements, and the exchange of official communications. Diplomacy is an indispensable tool in the successful conduct of an entity's foreign policy.

The extent to which a player may rely on the military tool depends upon its technological strength, its readiness, and the support of both its domestic population and the international community. President George H. W. Bush's decision to engage in a military conflict with Iraq's Saddam Hussein in 1991, after Iraq's invasion of Kuwait, largely rested on positive assessments of those factors. Sometimes the buildup of military capabilities is in itself a powerful foreign policy tool and thus a deterrent to armed conflict—as was the case in the Cold War between the United States and the Soviet Union.

Economic development and the ability to employ economic initiatives to achieve foreign policy objectives are effective means by which a principal player can interact on the international scene. The Marshall Plan, through which the United States provided economic aid to a ravaged Europe after World War II, could be viewed as a tool to block Soviet expansion as well as a humanitarian gesture. It was a tool to resurrect the devastated economies of Europe which had been major trading partners and purchasers of U.S. exports before the war. Membership in an economic community such as Organization of Petroleum Exporting Countries (OPEC) or the European Community (EC) can drive the foreign policy of both member nations and those impacted by their decisions.

The Modern Global System

International systems today evidence many of the global forces and foreign policy mechanisms formulated in Western Europe in the eighteenth and nineteenth centuries. Largely due to the influence of Western imperialism and colonialism, the less developed countries of modern times have, to a great extent, embraced ideological and foreign policy values that originated in Europe during the formative centuries. Such concepts as political autonomy, nationalism, economic advancement through technology and industrialization, and gaining respect and prestige in the international community move the foreign policies of major powers and many less developed countries as well.

Historical Context of the Modern Global System

The modern global system or network of relationships among nations owes its origins to the emergence of the nation-state. It is generally recognized that the **Peace of Westphalia** (1648), which concluded the Thirty Years War in Europe and ended the authority of the Roman Catholic popes to exert their political dominance over secular leaders, gave birth to the concept of the modern nation-state. The old feudal order in Europe that allowed the Holy Roman Emperor to extend his influence over the territories governed by local princes was replaced by a new one in which distinct geographic and political entities interacted under a new set of principles. These allowed the nation-states to conduct business with each other, such as negotiating treaties and settling border disputes, without interference from a higher authority. Hence, the concept of sovereignty evolved.

The eighteenth century in Europe was notable for its relatively even distribution of power among the nation-states. With respect to military strength and international prestige, nations such as England, France, Austria, Prussia, and Russia were on the same scale. Some of the former major powers, such as Spain, the Netherlands, and Portugal, occupied a secondary status. Both the major and secondary players created alliances and competed with each other for control of territories beyond their borders. Alignments, based primarily on economic and colonial considerations, shifted without upsetting the global system. Royal families intermarried, and professional soldiers worked for the states that gave them the best benefits without great regard for political allegiances. The nation-state of the eighteenth century was a relatively new phenomenon.

Military conflicts in the eighteenth century tended to be conservative with the concept of the **balance of power** at play. Mercenaries and professionals controlled the action mindful of strategic maneuvers to bring about victory. Wiping out the enemy was not the principal goal. Major upheavals were avoided through the formation of alliances and a high regard for the authority of monarchs and the Christian Church. The eighteenth century has been dubbed the "**golden age of diplomacy**" because it was an era of relative stability in which moderation and shared cultural values on the part of the decision-makers were the rule.

Statesmen of the era traded territory with little consideration of ethnic loyalties. This style of diplomacy was irrevocably altered by the French Revolution and the Napoleonic Wars that saw **nationality** emerge as a rallying point for conducting wars and for raising the citizen armies necessary to succeed in military conflicts.

The trend was exacerbated in the mid-nineteenth century by the European drive for unification of distinct ethnic groups and the creation of the Italian and German nation-states. Structural changes in the process and implementation of international relations occurred in the nineteenth and twentieth centuries due to major political, technological, and ideological developments.

The twentieth century has seen a particularly impassioned link between nationalism and war. The scientific and industrial revolutions of the eighteenth century gave rise to advancements in **military technology** that in the nineteenth and twentieth centuries dramatically altered the concept and the conduct of war. Replacing the eighteenth century conservative, play-by-the-rules approach, was a new, fiercely violent brand of warfare that increasingly involved civilian casualties and aimed at utter destruction of the enemy. The World Wars of the twentieth century called for mass mobilization of civilians as well as of the military, prompting leaders to stir up nationalistic sentiments. The development of nuclear weapons in the mid-twentieth century rendered total war largely unfeasible. Nuclear arms buildup, with the goal of **deterrent capabilities** (the means to retaliate so swiftly and effectively that an enemy will avoid conflict), was viewed by the superpowers as the only safety net.

Another factor molding the structural changes in international relations that surfaced in the nineteenth and twentieth-centuries was the **ideological component**. Again the French Revolution, anchored in the ideology of "liberty, equality, and fraternity," is viewed as the harbinger of future trends. Those conservative forces valuing legitimacy and monarchy fought the forces of the Revolution and Napoleon to preserve tradition against the rising tide of republican nationalism. In the twentieth century, with its binding "isms"—Communism, democratic republicanism, liberalism, Nazism, socialism—competing for dominance, ideological conflicts became more pronounced.

The Contemporary Global System

The values of the contemporary system are rooted in the currents of eighteenth- and nineteenth century Europe, transplanted to the rest of the world through colonialism and imperialism. The forces of nationalism, belief in technological progress, and ideological motivations, as well as the desire for international respect and prestige, are evident worldwide. Principal players in Africa, Asia, Latin America, and the Middle East as often as not, dominate the diplomatic arena. The contemporary scene in international relations is comprised of a number of entities beyond the **nation-state**. These include: **non-state actors** or **principal players**, **non-territorial transnational organizations**, and **non-territorial intergovernmental** or **multinational organizations**.

Contemporary **nation-states** are legal entities occupying well-defined geographic areas and organized under a common set of governmental institutions. They are recognized by other members of the international community as sovereign and independent states. **Non-state actors** or **principal players** are movements or parties that function as independent states. They lack sovereignty, but they may actually wield more power than some less developed nation-states. The **Palestine Liberation Organization (PLO)** is an example of a non-state actor that conducts its own foreign policy, purchases armaments, and has committed acts of terror with grave consequences for the contemporary international community. The **Irish Republican Army (IRA)** is another example of a non-state actor that has employed systematic acts of terror to achieve political ends.

Non-territorial transnational organizations are institutions such as the Catholic Church that conduct activities throughout the world but whose aims are largely nonpolitical. A relatively new non-territorial transnational organization is the **multi-national corporation (MNC)**, such as General Motors, Hitachi, or British Petroleum. These giant business entities have bases in a number of countries and exist primarily for economic profit. Despite their apparent nonpolitical agendas, multinational corporations can greatly impact foreign policy, as in the case of the United Fruit Company's suspect complicity in the overthrow of the government of Guatemala in the 1950s. Initially, the MNC was largely an American innovation, but in recent years, Asian players, particularly the Japanese, have proliferated, changing the makeup of the scene. An **intergovernmental organization**, such as the United Nations, NATO, or the EC, is made up of nation-states and can wield significant power on the international scene. While NATO is primarily a military intergovernmental organization and the EC is mainly economic, the UN is really a multipurpose entity. While its primary mission is to promote world peace, the UN engages in a variety of social, cultural, economic, health, and humanitarian activities.

The contemporary global system tends to classify nation-states based on power, wealth, and prestige in the international community. Such labels as **superpower**, **secondary power**, **middle power**, **small power**, and the like tend to be confusing because they are not based on a single set of criteria or a shared set of standards. Some countries may be strong militarily, as was Iraq prior to the Persian Gulf War, yet lack the wealth and prestige in the international community to classify them as super or secondary powers. Others like Japan may have little in the way of military capabilities but have wide influence due to economic preeminence.

The **structure** of the contemporary global system during the Cold War was distinctly **bipolar**, with the United States and the Soviet Union assuming diplomatic, ideological, and military leadership for the international community. With the breakup of the Soviet Union and the reorganization of the Eastern bloc countries has come the disintegration of the bipolar system. Since the 1970s, when tensions between the United States and the Soviet Union eased, a **multi-polar system**, in which new alignments are flexible and more easily drawn, has been emerging.

President George H. W. Bush spoke of the **New World Order** at the end of the Cold War. This concept involves alliances that transcend the old bipolar scheme with its emphasis on ideology and military superiority and calls for multinational cooperation as seen in the Persian Gulf War. It also assumes greater non-military, transnational cooperation in scientific research and humanitarian projects. The multi-polar system is less cohesive than the bipolar system of the recent past and the orders of the distant past, such as the **hierarchical system** (one unit dominates) of the Holy Roman Empire or the **diffuse system** (power and influence are distributed among a large number of units) of eighteenth century Europe. A set of fundamental rules has long governed international relations and, though often ignored, is still held as the standard today. These rules include **territorial integrity**, **sovereignty**, and the **legal equality of nation-states**. However, in an age of covert operations, mass media, multinational corporations, and shifting territorial boundaries, these traditional rules of international conduct are subject to both violation and revision.

International Law

The present system of international law is rooted in the fundamental rules of global relations: territorial integrity, sovereignty, and legal equality of nation-states. It embodies a set of basic principles mandating what countries may or may not do and under what conditions the rules should be applied.

Historical Context

Despite evidence that the legal and ethical norms of modern international law may have guided interactions among political entities in non-Western pre-industrial systems, contemporary international law emanates from the Western legal traditions of Greece, Rome, and modern Europe. The development of the European nation-state gave rise to a system of legal rights and responsibilities in the international sphere that enlarged upon the religious-based code of the feudal era. In medieval Europe, the church's emphasis on hierarchical obligations, duty, and obedience to authority helped shape the notion of the "**just war**." **Hugo Grotius** (1583–1645), Dutch scholar and statesman, codified the laws of war and peace and has been called the "**father of international law**."

A new era was launched in 1648, with the **Peace of Westphalia**, that promulgated the idea of the treaty as the basis of international law. Multilateral treaties dominated the eighteenth century, while Britain, with its unparalleled sea power, established and enforced maritime law. By the nineteenth century, advances in military technology rendered the old standard of the "just war" obsolete. Deterrents, rather than legal and ethical principles, provided the means to a relatively stable world order. The concept of **neutrality** evolved during this period, defining the rights and responsibilities of both warring and neutral nations. These restraints helped prevent smaller conflicts from erupting into world wars.

Contemporary International Law

In the twentieth century, international law has retreated theoretically from the tradition of using force as a legitimate tool for settling international conflicts. The **Covenant of the League of Nations** (1920), the **Kellogg-Briand Pact** (1929), and the **United Nations Charter** (1945) all emphasize peaceful relations, among nations, but the use of force continues to be employed to achieve political ends. The **International Court of Justice**, the judicial arm of the United Nations, and its predecessor, the **Permanent Court of International Justice,** represent concerted efforts to replace armed conflict with the rule of law. Unfortunately, the World Court has proven to be an ineffective organ. Nation-states are reluctant to submit vital questions to the Court, and there is a lack of consensus as to the norms to be applied. Members of the United Nations are members of the Court, but they are not compelled to submit their international disputes for consideration.

The UN Charter seeks to humanize the international scene in its admonition that all member nations assist victims of aggression. This approach negates the old idea of neutrality. It further dismisses the tradition of war as a legitimate tool for resolution of disputes between nation-states of equal legal status. Aggressive conflicts can be categorized as crimes against humanity, and individuals may be held personally accountable for launching them.

The concept of international law has been criticized on several fronts. The rise of **multiculturalism**, with its emphasis on multiple perspectives, has called into question the relevance of applying Western legal traditions to the global community. International law has been seen as an instrument of the powerful nations in pursuit of their aims at the expense of weaker nations. Strong nation-states are in a position to both enforce international law and to violate it without fear of reprisal. These observations have led some to conclude that international law is primarily an instrument to maintain the **status quo**.

International law can be effective if parties involved see some **mutual self-advantage** in compliance. **Fear of reprisal** is another factor influencing nations to observe the tenets of international law. **Diplomatic advantage** and **enhanced global prestige** may follow a nation's decisions to abide by international law. It can be argued that international law is valuable in that it seeks to impose **order** on a potentially chaotic system and sets expectations that, while not always met, are positive, and affirming.

COMPETENCY 3.6
Compare various political systems in terms of elements, structures, and functions.

There are many forms of government and ways we could go about categorizing them, and political scientists tend to classify government based upon how power is distributed geographically, how and to what extent the legislative and executive branches of government interact with one another, and the size of the body that is governed.

One method of describing government is based on where supreme governmental authority lies—if it is centralized, de-centralized, or shared. Each way has its benefits and tradeoffs. In centralized systems, government can have more uniform policy, equity, and less conflict; however, de-centralized systems are considered closer to the people, more responsive and flexible to meeting their citizen's needs, and open to innovation. There are three types of systems that fall under this category: unitary, con-federal, and federal systems of government. If all of the authority lies in a sole, central organization, it is called a **unitary** form of government. In unitary systems, because every citizen is entitled to the same rights and benefits, it is easier to maintain unity and to form a common national identity. These systems tend to run more smoothly because policy is easier to implement, and less effort is spent sorting out who should do what. They also have economic benefits because regulations seem to be more consistent, one product can be sold across a whole nation, and efficiencies of scale can be more easily capitalized upon.

In the **confederation (con-federal)** form of government, most of the power is allocated to regional governments who can defy the national government to whom they allow only a limited amount of power. The regional states therefore retain a significant amount of sovereignty and can veto any national-level policy. Before the Constitution, the United States had a con-federal system of government in which the states had significant powers. During the Civil War, the South also was a confederacy. Today, the only remaining confederacy is the Commonwealth of Independent States, a coalition of the 15 republics of the former Soviet Union.

A **federal** government is the opposite of a confederation, as member states give up most of their power to a central government but retain some power as well. Power in this structure is viewed as being shared. Federal systems of government tend to work well in countries where variations in local conditions, economies, or cultures make it difficult to try to impose a single system. These systems also work with countries that have geographically diverse populations that make it difficult to impose rule from a single location as well as in capitalist countries where both people and businesses have the capacity to move if conditions do not favor them. Local governments must compete to keep people and jobs within their borders. The United States has a federal form of government where sovereignty is shared by the national government and the state governments.

Another way to define government is how the executive (law enforcing) and legislative (law making) branches interact. A **parliamentary** system of government is a fusion of the executive and legislative branches. In this system, the executive leader is referred to as the **prime minister** or **premier**. The executive in this form of government is not separated from the legislative branch but rather is a member of it who is elected by other members of the legislative branch to preside over it. Since the executive, or prime minister, is selected by Parliament, he or she is accountable to it. In these systems, if prime ministers lose a vote of confidence, they must resign and forfeit their positions so a new government can be formed. A strength of these systems is the idea that they deliver effective but responsible government. Because the prime minister has the confidence of the parliament, his or her legislative agenda can be more easily implemented. One problem with a parliamentary system is that it must rely upon catering to minority parties in order to gain power, and so many coalitions break down when only a handful of members disagree with an agenda.

Presidential systems of government are based on the strict application of the idea of *separation of powers*. In these systems, the executive, legislative, and judicial functions are divided into separate branches that retain equal amounts of power, and have a set of checks and balances that give each branch their own jurisdiction of power and limit the power of each. The United States has a presidential system as the Founders were quite anxious to avoid having a government that would give too much power to an executive branch. The executive branch in this form of government is, as the name suggests, a president. A weakness of the system is that because power is shared, if the parties in power in the executive and legislative branches are different, legislative agendas may be stymied by one party or another refusing to negotiate with the other.

Another way to define government is based on the number of decision makers who participate in government operations. If no one is making the decisions in government (everyone is free to do as he or she pleases), it is called **anarchy**. This political movement, often symbolized by a big, black flag, believes in the elimination of the state, and instead advocates self-rule by free individuals in autonomous communities. If only one person has dominant power and makes all the decisions in government, it is called an

autocracy. Usually autocracy refers to a government where power is controlled by a monarch, a political dictator, or a religious leader.

In an **oligarchy**, political power rests with a small, elite group that makes all of the decisions in government. These systems tend to be exclusionary and do not allow new groups into it. An oligarchy may be a **competitive oligarchy,** and some have accused the United States of promoting an oligarchy. While oligarchies do share power, unlike a dictatorship, they actually have tended to arise almost as transitional governments that have come out of a dictatorship.

A **plutocracy** is a type of oligarchy that has rule by only a few, super-wealthy individuals. A practical application of an autocracy and oligarchy occurs when autocrats need to surround themselves with loyal followers who will do their bidding, and so they must turn to an elite group of individuals to carry out their agenda. Autocrats have to be careful, however, that their enforcers do not decide that they want more power and depose (i.e., murder) the autocrat.

A **polyarchy** is rule by many. Both oligarchies and polyarchies hold elections, contrary to autocracies, which do not. However, polyarchies tend to have more fair elections, but oligarchies tend to engage in a number of practices to limit their political opponents. Polyarchies have problems because they consist of a rule by a group with mass participation that must rely, however, on a leadership that is managed by competing elites. This means that, on the one hand, it is democratic, in that there is some choice and competition for power, but undemocratic in that mass participation is limited to only what the wealthy elites permit.

When everyone is given the opportunity to participate in government and power is distributed evenly and more widely diffused, it is called a **democracy**. There are two forms of democracy: indirect and direct. In a direct democracy, referred to also as a pure or true democracy, everyone participates in the decision-making process and so each person votes on every issue. Direct democracies are rather difficult to have in countries with millions of people spread out over many miles. Today there are no direct democracies.

In an indirect democracy, otherwise known as a **representative democracy**, people choose individuals to run the government and to make decisions for them. Voters indicate their approval or disapproval of their representatives through elections that are held for a set number of years, depending on the position. The United States is a representative democracy.

In a **communist** form of government, all goods and production are owned equally, and commonly under this form of government; there is no individual ownership.

A **socialist** form of government operates under the belief that the inequalities that exist in society are unjust and the government provides extensive social services to its citizens.

A fourth way to define government is how the leaders get their positions. If the leader obtains his or her position by hereditary means, it is called a **monarchy**. A **constitutional monarchy,** such as exists in Great Britain today, has a monarch but also a government that is elected and a constitution that sets out how the government should function. If the leaders are elected as they are in the United States, it is called a **republic**.

A final method of defining government is based on whether there are effective constraints on the government. If there are effective constraints on the government, it is called a **constitutional** form of government. If there are no effective constraints on government, it is called a **dictatorship**. A dictatorship type of government actually is the oldest form of government as it does not require the permission of the people for an individual to take hold of the government. A dictator has absolute control over a government and is authoritarian in nature. Dictators often have complete control over their citizens' lives and can wield their power completely in order to enforce their will. While dictatorships often have a military and bureaucracy, and sometimes a legislature, a dictator usually has complete discretion to direct and overrule their efforts. In dictator systems that are based on military power, the term *military dictatorship* is used.

An **authoritarian** government is one in which rulers can make decisions without consent of those they are governing. Many systems of government have provisions that allow, in times of national emergencies, for an executive to make decisions without consulting others. Sometimes martial law can be declared, national security decisions can be made, and emergency powers may be used. A **totalitarian** government is an extreme form of authoritarian government in which it endeavors to achieve complete conformity by all to the ideals of the state with no dissension tolerated.

Another way of looking at government is to examine what the rights of its citizens are. Historically, in **monarchies**, a majority of citizens did not have a voice in public life. Because citizens are not agents in public life, their main contribution is as a subject, not a citizen. Historically, political power was reserved to be the domain of a few aristocrats who controlled most of the land and the wealth. The hierarchical structure of the society mandated a system of authority and obedience to those in highest authority. Over time, nobles began to demand a greater role in society and eventually, in many monarchies, the king's power became restricted and political rights became extended to a greater number of people in a society. In a **Marxist** state, the citizen sacrifices the expense of the individual and his or her family for the greater good of the state. In a **democracy,** because everyone is involved in the political process, a citizen has the responsibility to pay attention to public issues, become involved in public life, vote, support public institutions that serve the common good, and obey the laws of the land.

Table 4.1
Types of Governments

Defining Characteristics	Direct Democracy	Representative Democracy	Constitutional Monarchy	Absolute Monarchy	Dicta-torship	Oligarchy
Universal suffrage	+	–	–	–	–	–
Free and open elections	+	+	+	–	–	–
Tightly controlled elections	–	–	–	+	+	+
Leaders seize power	–	–	–	+/–	+	+
Inherited leadership positions	–	–	+	+	–	–
"Divine Right" rule	–	–	–	+	–	–
Elected representatives	–	+	+	–	–	–
Citizens are soverign power	+	+	+/–	–	–	–
National leadership is the sovereign power	–	–	+/–	+	+	+
Liberties and rights protected by a constitution	+/–	+	+	–	–	–
Commoners petition monarchy	–	–	+	–	–	–
Nobles serve and advise monarchy	–	–	+	+	–	–

Defining Characteristics	Direct Democracy	Representative Democracy	Constitutional Monarchy	Absolute Monarchy	Dictatorship	Oligarchy
National leader(s) grant liberties and rights	–	–	–	+	+	+
Multiple party system	–/+	+	+	–	–	–
One party system	–	–	–	–	+	+
Encourages citizen participation	+	+	+	–	–	–
Limited citizen participation	–	–	–	+	+	+

* NOTE: A "+/–," means that it can go either way, because there are examples of countries and governments that have used these defining characteristics in different ways.

COMPETENCY 3.7
Analyze the key elements of U.S. citizenship, including rights, privileges, and responsibilities

Civil Rights and Individual Liberties

Civil rights are those legal claims that individuals have to protect themselves from discrimination at the hands of both the government and other citizens. They include the right to vote, equality before the law, and access to public facilities. **Individual** or **civil liberties** protect the sanctity of the person from arbitrary governmental interference. In this category belong the fundamental freedoms of speech, religion, press, and rights such as **due process** (government must act fairly and follow established procedures, as in legal proceedings). The origin of the concept of fundamental rights and freedoms can be traced to the British constitutional heritage and to the theorists of the Enlightenment. Jefferson's **Declaration of Independence** contains several references to the crown's failure to uphold the civil rights that British subjects had come to value and expect.

When fashioning the Constitution, the Founders included passages regarding the protection of civil liberties, such as the provision in Article I for maintaining the right of *habeas corpus*. One of the criticisms of the Constitution lodged by its opponents was that it did not go far enough in safeguarding individual rights. During the first session of

Congress in 1789, the first ten amendments (the **Bill of Rights**) were adopted and sent to the states for ratification. These amendments contain many of the protections that define the ideals of American life. The Bill of Rights was meant to limit the power of the federal government to restrict the freedom of individual citizens.

The **Fourteenth Amendment** of 1868 prohibits **states** from denying civil rights and individual liberties to their residents. The Supreme Court is charged with interpreting the law, particularly as it applies to civil rights. Not until the **Gitlow Case** in 1925 did the Supreme Court begin to exercise this function with respect to state enforcement of the Bill of Rights. States are now expected to conform to the federal standard of civil rights. The amendment that is most closely identified with individual liberty in the United States is the **First Amendment**, which protects freedom of religion, speech, press, assembly, and petition. The First Amendment sets forth the principle of **separation of Church and State** with its "**free exercise**" and "**establishment**" clauses. These have led the Supreme Court to rule against such practices as school prayer (**Engle v. Vitale, 1962**) and Bible reading in public schools (**Abington Township v. Schempp, 1963**).

The **Fourth Amendment**, which outlawed *unreasonable searches and seizures*, mandates that warrants be granted only *upon probable cause*, and affirms the *right of the people to be secure in their persons*, is fundamental to the Court's interpretation of due process and the rights of the accused.

The **Fifth Amendment**, which calls for a grand jury, outlawed **double jeopardy** (trying a person who has been acquitted of a charge for a second time) and states that a person may not be compelled to be a witness against himself, is also the basis for Supreme Court rulings that protect the accused. *Cruel and unusual punishments* are banned by the **Eighth Amendment**. This clause has been invoked by opponents of capital punishment to justify their position, but the Supreme Court has ruled that the death penalty can be applied if states are judicious and use equal standards in sentencing to death those convicted of capital crimes. In the twentieth century, a major concern for litigation and review by the Supreme Court has been in the area of civil rights for minorities, particularly African-Americans.

When civil rights organizations such as the NAACP brought a series of cases before the courts under the *equal protection clause* of the **Fourteenth Amendment**, they began to enjoy some victories. Earlier when the Supreme Court enforced its *separate but equal* doctrine in the 1896 case **Plessy v. Ferguson**, it did not apply the equal protection standard and allowed segregation to be maintained.

The Court reversed itself in 1954 in the landmark case **Brown v. Board of Education**, which ruled that separate but equal was unconstitutional. This ruling led to an end to most *de jure* (legally enforced) segregation, but *de facto* (exists in fact) segregation persisted, largely due to housing patterns and racial and ethnic enclaves in urban neighborhoods.

Landmark Supreme Court Cases

In addition to the previously cited Supreme Court rulings in civil rights and individual liberties cases, the following landmark decisions are notable for their relevance to the concepts of civil rights and individual freedoms:

- **Dred Scott v. Sanford** (1857)—ruled that as a slave, Scott had no right to sue for his freedom and further that Congressional prohibitions against slavery in U.S. territories were unlawful.

- **Near v. Minnesota** (1931)—barred states from using the concept of prior restraint (outlawing something before it has taken place) to discourage the publication of objectionable material, except during wartime or in the cases of obscenity or incitement to violence.

- **West Virginia Board of Education v. Barnette** (1943)—overturned an earlier decision and ruled that compulsory saluting of the flag was unconstitutional.

- **Korematsu v. United States** (1944)—upheld the legality of the forced internment of persons of Japanese ancestry during World War II as a wartime necessity.

- **Mapp v. Ohio** (1961)—extended the Supreme Court's exclusionary rule, which bars, at trial, the introduction of evidence that has not been legally obtained to state courts as well as federal courts. The Court has modified this ruling, particularly with reference to drug cases, so that evidence that might not initially have been obtained legally, but which would eventually have turned up in lawful procedures, can be introduced.

- **Gideon v. Wainwright** (1963)—ruled that courts must provide legal counsel to poor defendants in all felony cases. A later ruling extended this right to all defendants facing possible prison sentences.

- **Escobedo v. Illinois** (1964)—extended the right to counsel to include consultation prior to interrogation by authorities.

- **Miranda v. Arizona** (1966)—mandated that all suspects be informed of their due process rights before questioning by police.

- **Tinker v. Des Moines School District** (1969)—defined the wearing of black armbands in school in protest against the Vietnam War as "symbolic speech" protected by the First Amendment.

- *New York Times* **v. United States** (1971)—allowed, under the First Amendment's freedom of the press protection, the publication of the controversial Pentagon Papers during the Vietnam War.

- **Roe v. Wade** (1973)—legalized abortion so long as a fetus is not viable (able to survive outside the womb).

- **Bakke v. Regents of the University of California** (1978)—declared the University's quota system to be unconstitutional while upholding the legitimacy of affirmative action policies in which institutions consider race and gender as factors when determining admissions.

- **Hazelwood School District v. Kuhlmeier** (1988)—ruled that freedom of the press does not extend to student publications that might be construed as sponsored by the school.

US Citizenship Rights

Citizens of the United States enjoy all of the freedoms, protections, and legal rights that the Constitution promises. Some of the freedoms and rights protected in the Bill of Rights include:

- Freedom of Religion

- Freedom of Assembly

- Right to Keep and Bear Arms

- Freedom of Speech

- Freedom of the Press

- Protection for Those Accused of Crimes

US Citizenship Privileges

- Citizenship allows people to vote and participate in the representative democracy by voting for people who reflect their positions or views on public policy matters.

- Citizens are entitled to an American passport, and they enjoy the protection of the American government if they are persecuted by a foreign government.

- Citizens cannot be deported to another country.

- Citizens may sponsor friends or family who wish to apply for citizenship.

- Citizens are eligible for many welfare benefits, like food stamps or medical aid.

- Citizens can hold certain jobs that require candidates to be at least naturalized U.S. citizens. Only citizens may run as candidates in local, state, and federal elections and hold positions in government.

- Citizens have the right to leave the United States and even live outside of it without abandoning their citizenship.

Key Responsibilities of a U.S. Citizen

One of the key roles of citizens in the United States is to participate in civic life. The Constitution, while it does not explicitly list responsibilities, does assume some civil duties that are inherent in the Constitution.

- Citizens are presumed to obey the laws of the land in letter and spirit.

- Citizens must remain loyal to the United States.

- Citizens have a responsibility to serve as impartial jurors when called.

- Citizens have a responsibility to serve in the armed forces when called upon to do so.

- Citizens should participate in public life and must vote responsibly. Through voting, people have a voice in the government. This civic duty requires that citizens be informed about public issues, be aware of how their political leaders and representatives fulfill their responsibilities, understand the different views of the parties and candidates, and cast votes in elections.

- Citizens should engage in civic activity and participate in civil institutions, organizations, or charities.

- Citizens must pay taxes.

What Is History?

5

What is **history**? Is it really just an old recitation of facts, stories of the past, or a variation of "his-story" that omits the experiences of half of the population, or "her-story?" Are there really "facts" to be learned—a one-way understanding of the past? Today's historians consider history to be much more complex—less "factual" and more interpretive—more understanding of differing perspectives and different "truths." In the past, history was taught as a series of dates, events, and activities of extraordinary individuals (in most cases, men). Teaching history this way did little to uncover the many facets of history and failed to develop students' understanding or use of the concepts that are fundamental toward understanding and analyzing historical events and phenomena.

History teachers today approach the past with a more open eye, realizing that the experiences of class, gender, race, ethnicity, and age affect not only our understanding of what happened in the past but also what the past was.

History may be defined as the study of the past through the use of material, oral, and written sources. It encompasses political, economic, social, and cultural aspects of the past. The term "history" is derived from the Greek word *historia* which means "information" or "an enquiry designed to elicit truth."

A primary focus in the study of history lies in trying to answer WHY something occurred. What were the reasons that an event happened? In the study of history, **causality** is the reason why something either changed or remained the same. Historians seek to define why and how a certain event happened—were the reasons evident or hidden? Theories of historical causation have dominated historical discourse since the time of Plato.

Historians use two types of sources: **primary sources** and **secondary sources.** Basically, the distinction between these two types of sources is the author's proximity to an event. Primary sources are documents, oral histories, or physical objects that were created during the period being studied or immediately after it. The idea is that the primary sources reflect an "insider's" understanding of an event, or "first-hand knowledge" of an event. Examples of primary sources are: original documents, diaries, personal narratives, speeches, government records, letters, interviews, autobiographies, pottery, buildings, clothing, novels, newspaper articles (written soon after an event), photographs, manuscripts, original theatrical or literary works, coins, stamps, or even tombstones.

Secondary sources are one step removed from an event, and they contain someone's impressions, judgments, and interpretations of primary material or an event. **Secondary sources** include, history textbooks, journal articles, and documentaries, books written about a period of time, encyclopedias, histories, and biographies.

Whether approaching either a primary or secondary source, historians must learn how to properly analyze a document. Historians should consider how, when, and where a document was created, as it might have a tremendous effect on what was actually recorded. As all sources have bias, historians need to try to uncover how bias has affected the source. They should consider how close in time and location a source was created to a certain event. What was the intention of a document? Was it meant for private or public consumption?

Because bias is present in all sources, some sources might be considered more reliable than others. In addition, of course, each historian might have a different opinion based on his or her own biases about what is "reliable" or not. This process can pose some thorny questions. Is an eyewitness to an event more or less reliable? Could eyewitnesses have been so consumed with emotion that their view or understanding of an event was skewed? Should the historian privy a source that was meant for public consumption or one that was more private? Which would be more truthful?

To make matters even more confusing, sometimes secondary sources are also primary sources. For instance, if you were writing a paper looking at HOW a particular author has written history, well, that author's history books would then become your primary sources. So, to a large degree, the designation of whether or not a source is primary or secondary is determined by HOW the author intends to use the source.

One tool that historians use when examining a period is its **chronology**. Chronology is the timeline of an event.

Historical context is the political, economic, social, and cultural setting for a particular idea or event. Historians must look at context in order to better understand something in history and to situate an event or situation in its wider meaning. By looking at its historical context, a historian can ascertain how unique or ordinary an event or situation was in comparison to others; historical context gives the historian clues to an event's or person's meaning.

Historians often may be focused on **conflict**, or the opposition of ideas, principles, values, or territorial claims. Conflict occurs when ideas or people oppose one another. Conflict may occur both within and between societies.

The role of **bias** in historical accounts must not be taken lightly. Not only does every writer have bias, or a prejudice or presupposition toward or against a person or idea, but every historian has as well. When historians look at primary source material, they must decide how the author viewed his material or situation. Moreover, when historians consider a source, they bring in their own biases or predispositions to value certain pieces of information over another. Because bias exists, whether or not historians acknowledge it, the focus of historians on certain events, peoples, or ideas taints their material. Indeed the very authenticity of "fact" remains rather problematic.

Periodization of history: Trying to make sense of the past as a whole can be quite difficult for historians unless they break it up into periods that seem to make more sense, that seem to have mark either periods of continuity or change. By and large, periodizing the past is a rather political event, where historians use their own biases or understandings to group the past into what makes sense to them.

Dividing history chronologically emphasizes certain stages of contact between and among civilizations. For the purposes of the FTCE, the makers of the test have divided world history into three major divisions: before 1500, 1500–1850, and 1850 to the present.

Approaches to the periodization of World History, as taught in U.S. classrooms, continues to privilege looking at the world through the lens of the West, from 1500 onward. As you can tell from the periodization below, dividing the nineteenth century and beyond, the Western experience is supposed to stand as the arbiter of the West. The problem of looking at developments in World History in a linear fashion, which in the end is supposed to explain the rise of the West, leads historians to miss a great many connections and understandings of the rest of the world. For historians that study "the rest of the world," an attempt to understand those societies on their own terms marks the newest trend in history, the "cutting edge" approach, so to speak. For instance, many of the Western Civilization classes that many of you took as undergraduates may have begun their exploration with Mesopotamia and Egypt—which, in the current understanding of a world bifurcated into East and West, would mean that Iraq and Egypt were Western. While undoubtedly these two civilizations did have influence on "the West," they also had significant influences on Africa, South Asia, the Middle East, and East Asia as well.

A better way, perhaps, to approach World History is to look at how the world is connected and disconnected across political, social, and cultural boundaries. By looking at how trade, for instance, promotes long-distance ties between and among cultures, so too do we see connections between scholars, religious leaders, and even militias. We might look too at what some of the big motivations were for historical change and continuities as we look for the transfer of ideas and peoples across great swathes of land. By examining how societies connect and diverge among and between each other, we might come closer toward understanding the history of the peoples of the world on a more realistic level.

For the purposes of the test, we will further divide these periods into additional eras, in order to help emphasize both continuity and change that occurred at the macro-level.

World History before 1500:

- Prehistory to 500 CE

- India and China: 3000 BCE to 500 CE

- Ancient Greece: 1900–133 BCE

- Rome and the Rise of Christianity: 600 BCE–500 CE

- Rise of Islam and the Islamic Empires: 600–1500 CE

- Early African Civilizations: 2000 BCE–1500 CE

- Asian World: 400–1500 CE

- Emerging Europe and the Byzantine Empire: 400–1300 CE

- Europe in the Middle Ages: 1000–1500 CE

- The Americas: 400–1500 CE

- Renaissance and Reformation: 1350–1600 CE

World History 1500–1850:

- Age of Exploration (1500–1800)

- Crisis and Absolutism in Europe (1550–1715)

- Muslim Empires (1350–1850)

- East Asian World (1400–1800)

- Revolution and Enlightenment (1550–1800)

- French Revolution and Napoleon (1789–1815)

- Industrialization and Nationalism (1880–1870)

World History 1850–Present:

- Mass Society and Democracy (1870–1914)

- Imperialism (1800–1914)

- World War I and Revolution (1914–1919)

- Peace and the Interwar Period (1920–1939)

- World War II (1939–1945)

- Cold War (1945–1970)

- Contemporary World (1970–Present)

Another way of framing World History is to organize the story around significant turning points or periods that marked changes in regional and cultural boundaries. This might mean looking at history according to when environments changed, new religions developed and spread, empires were formed, and new technologies were developed.

When we periodize World History by chronology, we attempt to figure out the ways that the world has had both shared and unshared experiences.

One way that history has been periodized is with dating. Western historians have used the birth of Christ as their reference point. BC stands for "Before Christ," and AD stands for *Anno Domini* or the Year of Our Lord. Historians today prefer to use a secular dating systme that uses BCE, Before Common Era, and CE, Common Era, instead.

Historians today should be more sensitive to periodization and should be more careful about referring to an era with a term that only makes sense according to one geographical area. For instance, the Victorian Era makes sense when looking at the reign of Queen Victoria in England. It would not be appropriate to label the same time period in China as "Victorian."

Time

One of the first problems one encounters in history is how to define "time." Time is the arena in which historical events occur, and needs a reference point. A society's notion of time is a socially constructed category that defines time according to a particular group's understanding of it. While American historians today use terms like BCE and CE, a 24-hour clock, and a 12-month calendar, notions of time have differed across the ages. In the past, people have used a variety of methods to refer to time: reigns of rulers, planting seasons, generations, the position of stars and planets, and the position of the moon.

Various methods of chronology have existed. Western historians since the European Renaissance have understood time as **linear**, with the belief that events build toward or away from a particular event. Christian tradition has used the birth of Jesus as their starting point in time; Muslims have used Muhammad's flight to Medina in 622 CE as the year 1 AH (*Anno Hijra*). Another way to view time is through a **nonlinear** calendar. The ancient Egyptians, for instance, used a dual calendar system: one built on a lunar calendar, and the other built on a solar calendar that divided the year into four seasons.

The Mayans also had a dual calendar: one based upon a ritual calendar of 260 days and another solar calendar of 365 days. The Mayan starting point for their calendar began with a point they determined to have been the creation of the world.

Other nonlinear calendars looked at time in a cyclical fashion. Indian astronomers measured the world in cycles based upon millions of years. In some Sub-Saharan communities, time was measured with reference to plagues or even according to generations.

The Chinese calendar melded both linear and nonlinear time into two concurrent calendars. One calendar defined the beginning of time when the sun, moon, and planets were perfectly aligned and developed according to cosmic cycles. These cosmic cycles used the span of dynasties to define time further. Each dynasty was defined both in accordance to its ruler and in accordance to its place in a cyclical notion of a dynasty of birth, maturity, and decline.

As one proponent of a certain calendar moved into additional territory, they often imposed their view of time on the conquered. For instance, in the nineteenth century, when European imperialism was in full swing, they brought their calendars with them as they went into other territories. Today, most historians use a linear calendar based upon the Christian calendar. As we stated earlier, however, the terms BCE and CE are considered preferable to BC and AD. Even clocks themselves were not regulated until World War I, when there was a need to devise a system of time that promoted coordinated military efforts.

COMPETENCY 4.1
Identify characteristics of prehistoric cultures and early civilizations (e.g., Mesopotamian, Egyptian, Indus Valley, Chinese).

The mere definitions of "history" versus "prehistory" are rather subjective and fluctuate from region to region. While historians traditionally have looked at written sources, and humans have been around before writing began, historians in the nineteenth century began to refer to the period of time before the acquisition of writing as "prehistory," and once a society began to write, it entered the "historic" phase. So, basically, the difference between history and prehistory rests with the presence or absence of writing. Because writing appears in different places at different times, some places might be in the prehistoric phase, while others are in the historic phase.

One question students might have is whether or not historians can actually study prehistory—doesn't it fall under the purview of the archaeologists? This debate, while by no means settled, has acknowledged that there is a perception that archaeologists study the ancient past by looking at non-written records and the historian focuses on the written. However, this division is not so simple, as many historians use archaeological sources for their work, and archaeologists sometimes use historical sources as well. One question remains, though: what sort of evidence can one use to understand a society before it began to leave written records? Historians of the prehistoric era rely upon archaeologists for their evidence and must wait for them to dig up tools, buildings, weapons, bones, and pottery shards.

Primarily historians of prehistory have to rely on their colleagues from another field, the archaeologists, to help them. It is through the careful examination of non-written records, pottery shards, and the like that we begin to understand a bit about what life was like in its very earliest incarnation. But, this version of history is a bit like a moving target, as every day, archaeologists uncover more and more new evidence about the past. So history constantly undergoes revision as we gather additional evidence, and what you learn today might be quite different from what your parents and grandparents learned.

Scientists estimate that Earth is approximately 4.5 billion years old. The appearance of the first humans is another contentious issue as there is a bit of debate about from whom and what humans descended. A creature known as *homo habilis* appeared on the scene about 2.5 million years ago and made hand axes from stones. When scientists declared *homo habilis* as the first "human," they had defined humans as toolmakers—a point that is now discredited. Later, anthropologists thought that *homo erectus* were the first humans because they stood up straight and used tools when they appeared on the scene about 1.5 million years ago. *Homo ergaster* later was believed to be the first human because archaeologists found evidence that they stacked the bones of the dead and must have had some sort of reverence for the dead.

Species that occurred earlier than those we class under the heading "hom" tend to get labeled with names that sound less than human. Current terminology favors the use of the word **australopithecines** (southern ape-like creatures). In 1974, archaeologists spotted the bones of an australopithecine in Ethiopia and called her "Lucy," after the Beatles song, *Lucy in the Sky with Diamonds*. Lucy had died over 3 million years ago. She stood about three feet tall, walked on two legs, and lived in family groups. Walking upright enabled Lucy and other australopithecines to travel distances more easily, to carry food and children, and to keep away from threatening animals. These australopithecines also had developed the opposable thumb, meaning that the tip of the thumb is able to cross the palm of the hand. The opposable thumb was crucial for tasks like picking up small objects and making tools. While Lucy was the first australopithecine discovered, recent digs have found evidence of creatures like Lucy as old as 6 million years.

Homo habilus, who appeared in Africa about 2.4 million years ago, began to eat more nutritious seasonal foods than the australopithecine that came before him. As a result, *Homo habilus* had greater intelligence and was able to locate different things to eat in different seasons. This proved to be a boon for him as he altered his movements to correspond to what food was available. *Homo habilus*, known as "handy man," developed tools with razor-sharp edges. These tools as used by the gatherers (largely women) could cut vines and the like, but they were also used to scavenge meat from the kills made by animal predators. They even developed something like large stone choppers for cracking open bones to get to the nutritious marrow inside. As they became more proficient at finding food, they would gather together and share their booty.

When *Homo erectus* made an appearance about 1.9 million years ago with a brain size one-third larger than *Homo habilus*, man learned how to control fire and could now cook his food and adjust to colder climates. Cooked meat, vegetables, and grains tasted infinitely better than the rare versions, and so man, when he could, ate more, thereby increasing his nutritional intake. Like *Homo habilus*, *Homo erectus* was also a scavenger, but he was a bit more clever at finding and stealing the kills of other predators. *Homo erectus* devised hand axes that were used not only to skin and butcher animals but also to be used as a weapon to throw and kill animals as much as 100 feet away. Historians portray *Homo erectus* as the first hunter, but it is more likely that he used his brain to trap large prey and then descend on them in moments of weakness. His larger brain, advanced use of tools such as the hand axe, and ability to hunt big-game resulted in a huge increase in his numbers. So, as *Homo erectus* ate more protein, and ate cooked food, he proliferated.

Scientists today argue that modern humans descended from just one group of *hominids* called *homo sapiens sapiens* (a sub-species of **homo sapiens**) and appeared in Africa and Southwest Asia between 150,000–200,000 years ago. The term *sapiens* means "wise." These hominids, and others like them, like *homo* **Neanderthals,** which looked like *homo sapiens* but had bigger brains, became extinct. There are many theories about the origin of humans and how they evolved and spread from one area to another. Most of the theories suggest that about 100,000 years ago, there were a variety of homids all over the world. For instance, *Homo sapiens* are largely believed to have lived in Africa and Southwest Asia, while *homo erectus* lived in Asia and *homo Neanderthalensis* lived in Europe. Something changed and these diverse groups became one group of *homo sapien sapiens.* Two of the big schools of thought suggest that either homids developed similarly at the same time in different locations, or that there is a single origin for humans.

One theory, the **Multiregional Continuity Model,** suggests that *homo sapiens* evolved from a group of *homo erectus* who left Africa and dispersed all over the world. Over time, the *homo* erectus changed in some ways, but retained common characteristics in other ways—creating the division of people into different races that we see today. Another theory, the current leading theory, is the **Out of Africa Model** that holds that modern humans developed only recently. This theory holds that although as *homo erectus* left Africa and did mingle with other populations, it was in Africa that *homo sapiens* developed and eventually took over, without interbreeding, all of the other homids.

Prehistory is defined primarily as the period before writing—which varies across the globe, based primarily on the tool-making technology prevalent in each area, the Stone Age, the Bronze Age, and the Iron Age.

Historians divide the **Stone Age**, or prehistory, into three periods: Paleolithic, Mesolithic, and Neolithic. The **Old Stone Age** or **Paleolithic** (Greek for "old stone") period occurred 2,5000,000 years ago in Europe, Asia, and Africa until 10,000 BCE with the emergence of the Neolithic Revolution. This period marks the period of the emergence of the first hominids *homo sapiens sapiens*. In the most advanced parts of the Middle East and Southeast Asia, it ended about 6000 BCE, but it lingered until 4000 BCE or later in Europe, the rest of Asia, and Africa. The Stone Age in the Americas began when human beings first arrived in the New World, some 30,000 years ago, and ended in some areas about 2500 BCE, at the earliest.

These Paleolithic peoples are characterized by six characteristics:

1. Hunter-Gatherer

2. Highly mobile, nomadic with a large territorial range

3. Crude tools

4. Work divided along gender lines

5. Art

6. Use of fire to provide warmth and light

Paleolithic peoples did not know how to grow crops or raise animals, and so they relied on hunting and gathering to take care of themselves. The lived in small bands of around 20 individuals and needed a rather large space to support their food needs. As a result, they were nomadic as they had no choice but to follow animal migrations and vegetation cycles. Paleolithic peoples did know how to make tools and weapons that could have made them effective hunters. Tools and weapons that they did use were ground stone tools like chipped pebbles, stone flakes, needles, and harpoons. Work was divided primarily along gendered lines, where the men focused on activities like hunting where upper body strength was important, and women focused on cooking and child bearing. During this time, Paleolithic peoples sought refuge in caves and other natural formations. We have found evidence of paintings of animals on the walls of caves during this period. Around 500,000 years ago, the people began to use fire to provide light and warmth in shelters and caves. Over time, people used the fire to improve techniques of making tools and weapons.

The **Mesolithic** ("Middle Stone Age") period occurred from 10,000 to 7,000 BCE. There are three major characteristics of human experience that happened during this period:

1. End of era marks the beginning of the Neolithic Revolution (turn to farming)

2. Change in tools to axes, spears, bows and arrows, boats, baskets, and ground stone tools

3. Beginning of pastoral societies

It was during the Mesolithic age that a period of climate change sparked the beginning of what is referred to as the **Neolithic Revolution**. Recent evidence has suggested that the **Neolithic Revolution**, rather than occurring in the later **Neolithic** age (New Stone Age), had actually begun to transpire much earlier, during the Mesolithic period. This revolution, perhaps one of the most significant turning points in all of history, was the shift from food-gathering to food-producing, or farming. This shift laid the foundations, ultimately, for the rise of civilizations. With the development of farming, humans began to turn away from a nomadic lifestyle and settle down in one place. Some say that

Archaeological and Historical Periods Chart

Period		Years

Stone Age	Before 10,000 BCE
	10,000–8000 BCE
	8000–5500 BCE
	5500–4000 BCE
	4000–3000 BCE
		Paleolithic (Old Stone Age)
		Mesolithic (Middle Stone Age)
		Neolithic (New Stone Age)
		   Prepottery
		   Pottery
		   Chalcolithic (Copper Age)

Bronze Age	3000–2800 BCE
	2800–2500 BCE
	2500–2200 BCE
	2200–2000 BCE
	2000–1800 BCE
	1800–1500 BCE
	1500–1400 BCE
	1400–1200 BCE
		Early Bronze Age (EB)
		   EB I
		   EB II
		   EB III
		   EB IV
		Middle Bronze Age (MB)
		   MB I
		   MB II
		Late Bronze Age (LB)
		   LB I
		   LB II

Iron Age	1200–1000 BCE 1000–600 BCE	Iron I Iron II
Babylonian and Persian Periods	586–332 BCE	
Hellenistic Period	332–37 BCE	
Roman Period	37 BCE–325 CE	

women initiated this change as they were the first farmers, the ones who figured out the life cycle of plants and who made it possible for families to support themselves on one piece of land. The cultivation of crops on a regular basis made possible the support of larger populations, at first small villages and eventually larger towns. Farming provided a steady source of food and changed the need for people to migrate from land to land to follow food cycles.

A simultaneous transformation happened with the domestication of animals, like horses, dogs, goats, and pigs. Settling down in one location had both its advantages and disadvantages. Farming and settled life brought a change in the way people related to each other, and also made people more susceptible to animal-borne diseases and the whims of nature. Food supplies became less reliable because people depended on a relatively small range of farmed foods, and their diet narrowed to what they could produce, rather than a wider variety of what they could gather. More problems arose, because as these food producers settled down, they had to protect their food sources and devote considerable time to clearing and cultivating their land. As food supplies stabilized, people stayed in one place, and they also began to create more stable housing. During this period, there were small, widely dispersed settlements but no cities.

On your exam, you will not have too many questions about this period before the Neolithic Revolution, but what you will need to focus on is when spoken language developed, when man found out how to control and use fire, and that man had learned how to make simple tools out of stone.

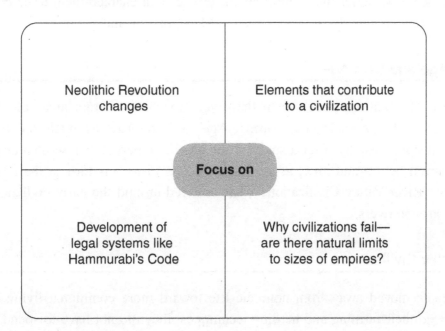

During the **Neolithic Period**, from 7000 BCE to 4000 BCE, humans further domesticated plants and animals as the end of the Neolithic Revolution occurred. These are the main characteristics of the Neolithic period:

1. Discovery of farming

2. Development of new technologies

3. Development of agriculture

4. Turn from nomadic way of living toward agricultural villages

5. Early cities and villages developed

6. Institutions like family, religion, and state governments began

7. Development of crafts, pottery, knitting, spinning, and weaving

8. End of the period saw development of Bronze Age tools.

During the Neolithic period, cities and villages began to develop as a division of labor began to occur. This led to the development of crafts, pottery, knitting, spinning, and weaving and a rise in trade among groups. Institutions also began to develop such as the family, religion, and state governments. Between 4000 and 3000 BCE, writing developed. With the existence of written records, we have the end of the Neolithic period and the emergence of societies that exhibit characteristics that enabled them to be considered civilizations. The first civilizations emerged in Mesopotamia and Egypt.

Bronze Age and Iron Age

Because of variations about when these ages reached different areas of the world, historians today do not tend to use "Bronze Age" or "Iron Age" as much to delineate the periods of history. Usually, after a study of the Neolithic period, whose own origins blur into the period before and after, according to locale, historians turn to the next period the idea of "River Valley Civilizations" that centered around the early civilizations that sprang up around rivers.

River Valley Civilizations

As people moved away from nomadic life toward more communal living in towns and advanced their farming and herding techniques, they did not have to spend as much time growing food. As a result, they were able to divide labor among people so that some could specialize in certain methods of production. With these developments, people then turned toward other types of production, like pottery and textiles, and in turn, **civilization**—the institutions of law, government, economic growth, military, and religion—emerged. More complex societies developed around river valleys—around 6000 BCE in the Fertile Crescent, 4800 BCE in the Nile Delta, in China, and 2500 BCE in India. All of these early communities had certain things in common that qualifies them as "early civilizations."

One of the main things that they had in common was that they developed along rivers. Why rivers? Not only do people need water for survival, but also the lands around rivers tend to be quite fertile and full of nutrients left over by floods. Rivers not only have fish, another source of food supply, but they also attract animals to them, thus providing people with another means of bolstering their food supply. Rivers also provided transportation.

Main Characteristics of River Valley Civilizations

1. **Cities or large dense settlements:** Early civilizations arose from cultures that had been able to transition from producing small amounts of food to becoming proficient enough in farming to be able to produce enough food surpluses to sustain large populations. As they were able to do so, urban centers began to develop.

2. **Separation of population into specialized occupational groups:** Because food was more readily available, people now were free to do things other than activities that revolved around finding enough food to eat. All of the early civilizations turned to specialization of labor due to the availability of surplus agricultural resources. People could now turn to crafts, artisans, metallurgy, forestry, merchants, etc.

3. **Social hierarchy including an elite exempt from subsistence labor:** Another byproduct of developing specialized occupational groups was social stratification in which an elite class of warriors, priests, nobles, and royalty developed whose domination of lower social classes elements freed them from having to engage in everyday subsistence labor. The elites justified their existence by providing services to the entire population in the form of military protection, religious direction, political representation, legal authority, and social order.

4. **Elite able to extract taxes and tribute from lower classes:** Ruling elites imposed various forms of tribute and taxes like poll taxes, property taxes, income taxes, export duties, and sales taxes on lower social classes in the interest of the state. These resources were used to benefit the common good, such as offerings to the gods or the construction of urban defenses.

5. **Monumental public buildings:** All civilizations used the advantage of their large populations to engage in the construction of monumental buildings for the state. These buildings ranged from defensive city walls in Babylon and China to beautiful temples and palaces. Monumental public buildings not only furnished security and improved the quality of life for its inhabitants, but the character of the achievement tended to reflect the aspirations of a civilization, not to mention its level of cultural development.

6. **Writing:** All great civilizations developed a system of writing and record keeping.

7. **Long distance trade** was central.

8. Establishment of **a rule of law**.

9. The formation of a **non-kin-based community** with a common sense of purpose.

Mesopotamia

By around 3000 BCE, the first urban-agricultural societies began to emerge in Meso-potamia, which literally means "the land between two rivers" and which geographically meant the fertile land between the Tigris and Euphrates rivers. A series of ancient civilizations sprang up along these rivers—the Sumerians, Akkadians, Babylonians, and the Persians.

The history and culture of Mesopotamian civilization is dependent on the ebb and flow of the Tigris and Euphrates Rivers. Thanks to the flash floods and torrential rains that could change the course of the Tigris and the Euphrates Rivers, life could be unstable as the rivers could destroy crops, livestock, and village homes. So, while the rivers constantly threatened the welfare of the towns, they were beneficial to them as they nourished the soil, enabling the people to produce a surplus of food.

As food production became more reliable and plentiful and could be produced by fewer people, some folks gave up farming and became craftsmen, laborers, merchants, and officials. Mesopotamian villages and towns eventually evolved into independent and nearly self-sufficient city-states, with little interest in unification with the other Mesopotamian city-states.

Sumerians

Basic Trademarks of Sumerians

> **Writing with cuneiforms**
>
> Math developments
>
> **Polytheistic and ziggurats**
>
> Epic poems—*Gilgamesh*

Two of the earliest groups in this region, the **Sumerians** and **Akkadians**, utilized the advantages that the rivers gave them. They built tremendous irrigation projects in an effort to control the water around them. Such projects like the building of canals, dikes, drainage ditches, and reservoirs not only helped people regulate water and control flooding, but these large projects required organization: people to assign jobs, allocate resources, and do the building. As a result, leaders emerged, government formed, and a civilization developed.

The most important of these peoples, the Sumerians who lived in southern Mesopotamia, were the first group to develop a system of writing. What began as a pictographic form of writing soon turned into **cuneiform** (wedge-shaped) writing. Unlike pictograms, cuneiform could convey concepts and sounds. The resulting writing system became so complicated that a new class of professional scribes was the only ones who could master it. Scribal schools began to flourish throughout Sumer and became centers of culture and learning. They also developed cylinder seals that people would use to "sign" documents or to show ownership.

With these developments in writing, Mesopotamians made great advancements in other methods of learning: mathematics, medicine, and religion. Their math system was based on the number 60 and it is because of their system that we still divide an hour into 60 minutes and a circle into 360 degrees. They also learned how to use geometry and to transform their knowledge to the construction of buildings and irrigation systems. Mesopotamians also understood multiplication and division and developed a calendar based upon lunar phases. They also made many scientific advances. They invented the wheel and plow and learned how to use bronze to produce stronger tools and weapons. In medicine, evil spirits were believed to cause sickness, and treatment was by magic, prescription, and even basic surgery.

The Sumerian religion was **polytheistic** with the creation of gods and goddesses who represented almost everything in the cosmos. Their gods took the form of man and used nature to punish society. Society itself sought to appease the gods through public, state-organized religion that focused on temples maintained by priests. These step-shaped large temples that contained, at the heart of them, a pyramid shaped structure called a **ziggurat.** They typically were built in the center of Sumerian cities and were focal points of Sumerian life and religion. The priests were powerful members of Sumerian society and controlled some of their early governments. Because the farmers had believed that their crops depended upon the gods being pleased with them, they sought the priests to act as intermediaries with the gods. The priests, from the ziggurat, managed the irrigation systems, demanded portions of each farmer's crops as a tax, and ran the ziggurat like a city hall. The priests began to lose power when the society needed a military to protect it against invaders. These military leaders, in time, became full-time rulers, passing on their power to their sons after them and creating a series of city-states under the rule of **dynasties**.

The Mesopotamians created myths to explain the origins of the universe and mankind. They produced the first epic poem, *The Epic of Gilgamesh*. The epic, written around 2700 BCE, tells us something about the organization of Sumerian society. The epic tells the tale of the ruler of Uruk, Gilgamesh, and his friend Enkidu and explains the creation of the universe. It also details how Uruk and Enkidu perform heroic acts but how Enkidu eventually offends the gods and dies. The tales explore morality, immortality, loyalty, and friendship.

Sumerian society was made up of nobles, free clients, commoners, and slaves. The king was supreme and kingship was hereditary. The nobility—the king, his family, the chief priests, and high palace officials—controlled most of the wealth in land and held most of the power. The commoners were free and had a political voice. The Sumerian slave population included foreigners, prisoners of war, criminals, and debtors. Sumerian women could pursue most of the occupations of city life and could even become priests.

The Sumerian civilization looked, on the surface, like it had a good set-up. The Sumerians organized a government of city-states and developed educational and religious systems, but it was fatally flawed in where it chose to locate itself. The river valley had neither geographic protection nor predictable river flooding and proved vulnerable to a series of invasions from the Babylonians, Hittites, and Assyrians. By 1700 BCE, the civilization had been overthrown, but its conquerors adapted many of their traditions and technologies.

Other Mesopotamian Regimes

North of Sumeria, another group, the **Akkadians**, led by **King Sargon I** about 2331 BCE, created a permanent army, attacked Sumer and all of northern Mesopotamia, in turn forming the world's first empire that stretched from the Mediterranean Sea to present-day Iran in the east. Sargon's empire would last about 140 years, until the advent of another empire that would come from Babylon. A group of Amorites, led by **Hammurabi**, united all of Mesopotamia under the **Babylonian Empire** in 1792 BCE. Hammurabi's greatest legacy was the code of laws that he put together known as the **Code of Hammurabi**. **Hammurabi's Code** created one of the world's earliest comprehensive law codes that, for the first time, was written down for all to see. It had two notable features: it instituted different laws and punishments for rich and poor and for men and women and was based on the idea that the punishment should fit the crime. The Code also set up an important idea in Mesopotamian society—that government had a responsibility for what occurred in society as, if all else failed, it ultimately had to answer to the victim of a crime.

In 1595 BCE, an Indo-European tribe that had settled in Asia Minor (now Turkey), sacked Babylon. The **Hittites** introduced iron tools into agriculture and war. Their success largely came through because they learned how to use iron in their weapons while their enemies used weapons made out of bronze, a much weaker element. The Hittites also used the horse-drawn chariot to beat their enemies. The Hittites remained a strong force in western Asia until about 1200 BCE and were ultimately defeated by the Lydians.

After the Hittite Empire fell, other groups emerged in the region, like the Assyrians, a powerful people who relied chiefly upon its military strength and established its capital at **Nineveh**. Its army contained war chariots, foot soldiers, and a cavalry. They were masters at siege warfare and used terror to control their enemies. The Assyrian system of government allowed kings to rule through local leaders who collected taxes, enforced laws, and raised troops. They constructed a system of roads that linked distant parts of their empire together.

The **Chaldeans** took advantage of a crumbling Assyria and took the old city of Babylon as their new capital. Their most famous ruler was **Nebuchadnessar II** who fought the

Egyptians and Jews, captured the Jewish capital of Jerusalem, and rebuilt Babylon into a city of splendor that featured the **Hanging Gardens of Babylon**. The Chaldeans made great advances in astronomy and charted the position of the stars as it related to political and weather events.

The **Phoenicians** built a wealthy trading society at the western end of the Fertile Crescent along the Mediterranean Sea in what today is Lebanon. The Phoenicians were great sailors who founded colonies along their large trade routes. One such colony was Carthage, which was to figure prominently later on. Their biggest legacy was the Phoenician alphabet, a writing system set up to help with trade. It was more flexible and easier to use than pictographs or cuneiforms. The **Phoenician alphabet** consisted of 22 letters, all of which were consonants. The Greeks would later take this alphabet and add vowels to it, and later it was modified further by the Romans into our modern alphabet.

The earliest Hebrews lived in the area between Mesopotamia and Egypt in the second millennium BCE. While the origin of the Jews is uncertain, they migrated from Egypt into the Sinai Peninsula and Palestine. They were originally a nomadic people, but as cities grew and prospered, some Hebrews migrated to these cities. In the power vacuum created by the fall of the Hittite and Egyptian states, a Hebrew state emerged. The Hebrews encountered the Philistines, another ancient people who settled in Canaan. The Philistines enjoyed a definite advantage over the Hebrews as they knew how to forge iron into swords and shields and used them in their ships and chariots. Over time, the Hebrews learned the secrets of smelting iron and could fight the Philistines on more equal terms.

The Hebrews instituted **monotheism**, the worship of one God, Yahweh. This put them squarely at odds with their neighbors who prayed to multiple gods. More detail on Judaism will be found in the next section.

Under Saul and David, the 12 tribes of Israel became united under a monarchy. David led the Jews to defeat the Philistines and to capture Jerusalem. There, King Solomon built a large temple in Jerusalem where it became the home of the Ark of the Covenant, which was considered the promise between God and the Hebrew people and demonstrated their unity. King Solomon eliminated the tribal division of Israel and instead placed it under 12 territorial districts. Upon Solomon's death, the kingdom was divided in two as the northern kingdom (Israel) was destroyed by the Assyrians in the eighth century BCE. The southern half became the center of Judaism with the capital in Jerusalem until the Babylonians destroyed it in 587 BCE. It was during this "Babylonian Captivity" that the exiles redefined their beliefs into the law of Yahweh—and became known as Jews. About 50 years after the fall of Judah, the Persian king Cyrus the Great conquered Babylon in 539 BCE and allowed 40,000 Jews to return to Jerusalem to rebuild Solomon's Temple, which had been destroyed by the Babylonians. The walls of Jerusalem were rebuilt in 445 BCE.

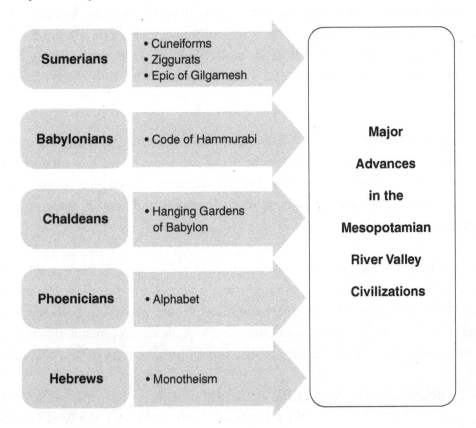

Sumerians
• Cuneiforms
• Ziggurats
• Epic of Gilgamesh

Babylonians
• Code of Hammurabi

Chaldeans
• Hanging Gardens of Babylon

Phoenicians
• Alphabet

Hebrews
• Monotheism

Major Advances in the Mesopotamian River Valley Civilizations

Egypt

Another river valley civilization, Egypt, shared many similarities with those of the Tigris-Euphrates Valley. The distance from Babylon in Mesopotamia to the Nile River Valley was about 750 miles—if one traveled by caravan, that is—this was close enough for the Egyptians and Mesopotamians to exchange some goods and customs, but it was far enough away that a distinct Egyptian civilization emerged, one that was deeply religious and united under a strong central authority, a divine king, the pharaoh. Egyptians settled along the Nile River, an area of extremely rich soil made so by the predictable floods of the river each year that gave them a very stable agricultural cycle and helped them to compile ample food surpluses.

The Egyptians recognized two sets of geographical divisions in their country: Upper (southern) Egypt consisted of the narrow valley of the Nile, and Lower (northern) Egypt consisted of the triangular Delta region. This might seem odd, that the south is considered "upper" and the north "lower," but the names are given according to the direction that the Nile flows. Protected by the desert and a marshy, harbor-less seacoast and endowed with predictable river flooding that deposited fertile soil along the river banks each year, Egypt took advantage of its natural isolation and self-sufficiency to create a unique culture that depended little on its neighbors. The cities along the Nile were part of a single state that was first unified by about 3000 BCE and then continued to be unified for the next 2,500 years.

The Egyptians established an effective government with a highly structured bureaucracy under the divine kings, the **pharaohs**. Egyptian society was less urban than Mesopotamian society and also less stratified. Peasants made up the majority of the population, slavery was limited, and women enjoyed more freedoms and legal protections than their Mesopotamian counterparts.

The stability that the pharaohs and the bureaucracy provided also enabled them to develop complex forms of art, religion, writing, and mathematics. The Egyptians spent considerable resources on preparing for the afterlife and glorifying both the living and dead pharaohs. To a large extent, these interests drove the developments of art, mathematics, science, and engineering with the construction of burial tombs for the pharaohs.

The civilization of the Nile Valley is usually broken up into five periods: the predynastic period 4000–3100 BCE, **Old Kingdom** (2650–2200 BCE), the **Middle Kingdom** (2050–1570 BCE), the **New Kingdom** (1570–1090 BCE), and the Third Intermediate Period (1090–332 BCE). The exam will focus on the Old, Middle, and New Kingdoms, and it is largely considered that under the New Kingdom, ancient Egypt reached its height.

In Mesopotamia, the king was considered to have been appointed by the gods; however, in Egypt, the pharaoh was considered to actually BE a god. It was the pharaoh, so believed the people, who actually made the Nile rise and fall each year, and with that, went the fortunes of the people. From his capital at Memphis, the god-king administered Egypt according to set principles called *ma'at,* order, justice, and truth and did so with the help of the huge bureaucracies that he created to run the government. The leader of the bureaucracy was the **vizier**, a hereditary position that enabled the vizier to control all of the Egyptian bureaucracy. The Egyptians believed that in return for the pharaohs building and maintaining temples, the gods oversaw the welfare of the state and thus ensured the continuing pharaonic rule. The pharaoh had a similar obligation to the people in that he was obligated to rule in a benign and beneficent manner and to safeguard the people's welfare.

The political unification of Egypt began during the period of the Old Kingdom—a period of prosperity and cultural growth. Because the pharaoh was thought to be a god, religion and government were closely intertwined in the Old Kingdom and Egypt was considered to be ruled by a **theocracy**.

The most dramatic symbols of the king's divinity were the **pyramids**. The pyramids were temples where the king would continue to be worshipped even after his death. They also illustrated the hierarchical structure of Egyptian society, of which the pharaoh was the capstone. Only princes, royal wives, and select officials were given the privilege of erecting a tomb beside the royal pyramids.

The pyramids played a political purpose as well. By carrying out an astonishingly large project focused on his person, the king made a statement about his power. The sheer size of the Great Pyramids at Giza demonstrated the pharaoh's ability to organize a vast labor force. Some suggest that the encampment of workers at Giza represented the largest gathering of human beings to that date.

As mentioned above, the pharaoh's obligation was to rule over Egypt carefully. The Old Kingdom saw a huge bureaucracy develop that extended from the village to the district to the central administration to keep track of land, labor, products and people, and, of course, the amount of taxes that everyone owed.

So, how did the Egyptians keep track of all of this? Well, they depended on scribes and a system of writing called **hieroglyphics**. A hallmark of the administrative class was literacy, and scribes were expected to not only know that but also a cursive script that developed around 2500 BC. The scribes worked on papyrus, made out of the papyrus reed that grew only in Egypt. Scribes also used their writing skills to develop literature, poetry, religious hymns, and instruction manuals.

Egyptian society was less urban than its Mesopotamian counterparts, but it was also less stratified to the degree that both men and women had remarkably equal legal rights. The social hierarchy demanded that the royal family ranked highest, followed by priests, administrators, regional governors, military commanders, and then free workers. The majority of the population was made up of peasants, and slavery was quite limited. Egyptian art and literature from this period display interest in maintaining social order and proper relations with the gods and instructing high officials in appropriate behavior.

The Egyptian religion embodied a complex vision of the afterlife and much of the kingdom's wealth went for these religious purposes: preparing for the afterlife and glorifying the divine pharaoh. Egyptians believed in the afterlife and they made extensive preparations for safe passage to the new world and a comfortable existence once they arrived there. The Egyptian **Book of the Dead,** present in many excavated tombs, contained rituals and spells to protect the journeying spirit. The final and most important challenge was the weighing of the deceased's heart to determine whether or not the person lived a good life.

To serve their religious needs, Egyptians developed technologies that enabled them to construct monumental tombs and temples, and their interesting mummification made them well schooled in chemistry and medicine. Originally, the Egyptians did not mummify their dead at all; they simply buried them in reed caskets in the sand. The searing hot sand caused the remains to dry quickly, preventing decomposition. But when they began constructing tombs and placed the bodies in wood casks, the sand could not get to the bodies and the bodies then started decomposing. So, the Egyptians developed an elaborate mummification process, the extent of which depended upon the wealth of the deceased. The first step in the mummification process was the embalming of the body. The dead body was embalmed with several preserving fluids. Then the major organs were removed, with the exception of the heart, and stored in stone jars laid out around the corpse.

The elite classes utilized the most expensive kind of mummification. The cadaver was immersed for long periods in dehydrating and preserving chemicals and eventually wrapped in linen. The mummy was then placed in one or more decorated wooden caskets and deposited in the tomb.

The wealthier you were, the more lavish your final resting place. Common people had to make do with simple pit graves or small mud brick chambers, and sometimes, they were just wrapped up in linen and buried in the sand. The kings erected pyramids filled with treasures and curses and other magical precautions to foil tomb robbers, all to no avail—for when archaeologists entered the tombs, they seldom discovered an undisturbed royal tomb.

Mummies attracted a great deal of attention again in the nineteenth century when amateurs and professionals went in search of the royal tombs. Mummies were found, and it became quite fashionable in Europe to seek the medicinal advantage that ground-up mummies provided.

The government of the Old Kingdom collapsed around 2100 BCE. For almost 200 years, a series of problems, invasions, famine, and civil war dominated the region until about 2055 BCE, when a new dynasty rose to power as the **Middle Kingdom** with their capital at Thebes. The Middle Kingdom prided itself on the great defense that it provided. However, it fell to invaders called the **Hyksos**, around 1650 BCE from Syria. The Hyksos, a Semitic people, had advanced military technologies at the time, including the long bow, armor, and horse-drawn chariots and brought bronze making to Egypt. They ruled for almost 100 years, but the Egyptians resented the appearance of these foreigners. It was a time though where trade developed with Mesopotamia and the Indus Valley, as well as their neighbors, the Kush from the southern kingdom of Nubia.

Some historians allege that climate change brought both the Old and the Middle Kingdoms down, for it altered the regular flood pattern of the Nile and caused the divine authority of the monarch to erode and brought civil war that destroyed the unity. The situation worsened when Egypt succumbed to invasions by the Hyksos, a Semitic people from the Syria-Palestine region. It was not until nobles from Thebes emerged to overthrow the Hyksos that Egypt was once again united and thus ushered in the New Kingdom phase from 1570–1075 BCE.

The New Kingdom rulers realized that they needed to build up their military to keep Egypt safe from invaders. They created Egypt's first permanent army with foot soldiers, archers, and charioteers. The pharaohs also felt that they needed to extend their rule south in order to have a land barrier from troops coming from further afield. With the expansion of Egyptian rule, trade also increased.

One of the best-known pharaohs was a woman who took power around 1500 BCE, **Queen Hatshepsut**, when her husband died and she proclaimed herself ruler in the name of her young son. She realized some of the difficulties of a woman ruling, so she dressed like a man, even wearing the false beard that male pharaohs wore. Unlike other rulers, she spent her 22-year reign focusing more on trade and trading expeditions than war. When Hatshepsut died, her stepson, **Thutmose III**, proved to be more interested in war than trade and is reported to have murdered his stepmother, taken over, and destroyed all paintings and statues of her.

Another important ruler from the New Kingdom was **Akhenaton** (originally named Amenhotep IV) who ruled from 1363–1347 BCE. Akhenaton proclaimed that all of Egypt should worship only one god, the sun god **Aten**. He banned the worship of other gods and even ordered all other gods' images destroyed.

Egypt's brief experiment with monotheism did not last, as Akhenaten's successor, Tutankhamon, restored the worship of Egypt's traditional gods and moved the kingdom's capital back to Thebes. Under Ramses the Great (**Ramses II**), the Egyptians settled a conflict with the Hittites (Rames married a Hittite princess), and he ruled for more than 60 years. The Egyptians regained Palestine but faced increasing invasions from the Kush and the Assyrians.

Religion retained its central place in New Kingdom society. The royal family in the New Kingdom built most of Egypt's magnificent temples, whose sculpted columns set a precedent for later Greek architecture. So intense were Egyptians' religious feelings that they threatened the stability of the New Kingdom in the fourteenth century BC when the pharaoh Akhenaten reformed the official religion and created the cult of Aten and attempted to impose monotheism on the Egyptian population. The principal gods of Ancient Egypt were Amon and Re. During the Old and Middle Kingdoms, the priests began to combine them into a cult of Amon Re. The cult of Osiris also became important.

From the end of the **New Kingdom** until 12 BCE, Egypt and the entire Near East were greatly influenced by two migrations of Indo-Europeans that disturbed and remolded existing states. While Mesopotamia became unified under the Hittites, Egypt was first influenced by Hyksos and then by the introduction of monotheism by the pharaoh **Akhenaten**.

	Main Achievement	Importance
Early Egypt	Unification	Created civilization that would endure for centuries
Old Kingdom	Bureaucracy	Provided a framework for ruling Egypt
Middle Kingdom	Stability	Economic prosperity
New Kingdom	Created Empire	Increased trade

India

Like Mesopotamia and Egypt, the **Indus Valley** developed a civilization along the banks of a river system, the Indus and Ganges Rivers. Unlike the Nile Valley and Middle Eastern civilizations, these Indian civilizations had a nearly continuous history stretching over many centuries into the present, aided partly because the huge mountains north and west of the Indus River prevented the numerous invasions that Mesopotamia encountered. However, thanks to the **Khyber Pass** through the Hindu Kush Mountains, these civilizations did have some trade contact with other lands, as material evidence points to trade contacts between Indus Valley cities and the resource rich areas to the north and to Mesopotamia to the west. The civilization likely collapsed as a result of ecological changes in the river valley and along the coast.

One of the earliest significant civilizations in India appeared about 2800 BCE, centered in the cities of **Harappa** and **Mohenjo-Daro** that archaeologists think were each home to more than 100,000 people. Both cities were located along the Indus River and they shared many of the characteristics of the other ancient river valley civilizations. Both cities display a striking uniformity of planning and construction, each including high brick walls and streets arranged in a rectangular grid, and had sophisticated drainage systems that carried waste under the streets and outside the city walls; moreover, excavated ruins reveal that that they were skilled builders and evidence from clay seals demonstrate the presence of a highly sophisticated written language (albeit, un-translated as of yet). Evidence exists that the Harrapans were centers of crafts and trade and conducted trade as far as Sumer. Among its important technologies, this civilization produced a writing system that remains un-deciphered. Archaeologists and historians have not conclusively agreed upon the reasons for its decline, but some assert that either they were overrun by conquerors from the north, the **Aryans**, the Indus River changed its course, over-farming of the land, or that their decline emanated as a result of internal dynamics around 1750 BCE.

Unlike the Harappans, the Aryan invaders left a treasure of literature and a huge cultural legacy, but virtually no architectural artifacts. In 1500 BCE, the Aryans, a Sanskrit-speaking people, crossed over the northwest mountain passes into the Indus River Valley and left an indelible imprint on society there. While they established a simple form of government and engaged in agriculture by using the iron plow to clear land along the Ganges River valley, their largest legacy was their sacred literature, the **Vedas,** four collections of prayers, magical spells, and instructions for performing rituals, all of which was to form the foundations for the Hindu religion. Much of what we know about the

Aryans comes from the **Rig-Veda**, their collection of 1,028 hymns that presents their history in religious terms. The Aryans were led by a war chief, or *raja*, who was responsible for protecting his people in exchange for payments of food or money.

The Aryans, a term from the Sanskrit for "noble," were taller, lighter skinned, and spoke a different language than the Indians that they found in the Indus Valley, who they referred to as *dasas* (dark). (*Dasas* eventually became the Aryan word for slave.) The Aryans were pastoral people who lacked a writing system and who counted their wealth in cows. The *dasas*, however, were town dwellers who lived in walled cities and had extensive trade networks as well as a writing system. When the Aryans first arrived in India, they were divided into three social classes: the **Brahmins** (priests), warriors, and peasants or traders. The class that an Aryan belonged to determined his or her role in society. Eventually, non-Aryan laborers or craftsmen formed a fourth group, the **shudras**. Over time, the Aryans developed the attitude that they should have limited contact with non-Aryans. So, to regulate those contacts, the Aryans made class restrictions more rigid, and dividing society along occupation and color lines became more apparent. The resulting system instituted four **Varnas** that ranked people at birth according to family occupation, color, and ritual purity: priests (**Brahmins**), warriors (**Kshatriyas**), landowners and merchants (**Vaishyas**), and peasants and laborers (**Shudras**). These groups were further subdivided by castes (**jati**) of people who lived, worked, ate, and married within their group. There were groups of people who were outside the **Varna** system who were referred to as the untouchables, who included those whose occupations, as butchers, gravediggers, trash collectors, etc., were believed to have made a person physically and spiritually unclean and thus had none of the protections of caste laws. The idea here was that even their touch would endanger the ritual purity of others. This system is known today as the caste system, a name that was given to it by the Portuguese who settled in India in the fifteenth century CE.

The Vedic religions evolved into Hinduism, the religion of hundreds of millions of people in South Asia today. Hinduism was not always called "Hinduism," however, as the name was given to the Indian people by the Muslim invaders in the eleventh century CE. Hinduism today is increasingly being referred to as **Sanatana Dharma**, meaning "eternal law." The process by which the Vedic religions were transformed into Hinduism largely remains hidden from us. What we do know, however, is that the Brahmins maintained their high social status and influence, and individuals were given more opportunities for direct contact with the gods.

Hinduism emphasized the worshipers' personal devotion to a particular deity, usually Vishnu, Shiva, or Devi (the Goddess). The popularity of the individual gods and goddesses largely reflected their pre-Aryan origins, as Devi and Shiva were more prominent in the southern Dravidian areas and Vishnu was more popular in the north. Vishnu, the preserver, is a benevolent deity who helps his devotees in times of need. Hindus believe that whenever demonic forces threaten the cosmic order, Vishnu will appear on Earth in one of a series of avatars, or incarnations. Shiva, on the other hand, represents both creation and destruction. Devi is also represented in two ways—either as a mother goddess who promotes fertility and procreation as the docile and loving wife, Parvati, or as the frightening deity known as either Kali or Durga, who lets loose a torrent of violence and destruction.

Despite the multiplicity of gods (over 330 million), languages, and cultural beliefs, there was unity in Hinduism. A worshipers' devotion to one god or goddess did not preclude a denial of other gods and goddesses as ultimately, all of the gods and goddess are believed to be manifestations of a single divine force. The capacity of the Hindu religion to assimilate a wide range of popular beliefs facilitated the spread of elements of a common Indian civilization across the subcontinent, and permitted regional differences that we see even today.

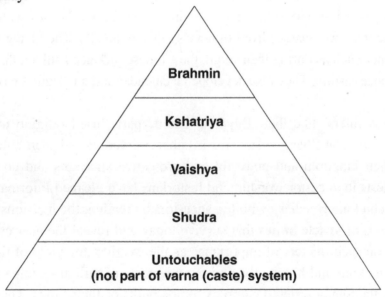

Early China

Even before the Sumerians settled in southern Mesopotamia, early Chinese cultures began farming settlements along the Huang He valley (known as the Yellow River Valley) sometime around the eighth millennium BCE, and like that of India, has had a nearly continuous existence. Also, like many of the other civilizations we have studied in this first unit, geography has heavily influenced its development. China's many rivers and mountains put China in isolation, and Chinese culture evolved with little outside influence.

In the North China Plain, as in the river-valley civilizations of Mesopotamia and Egypt, the presence of great, flood-prone rivers and the lack of dependable rainfall directed the formation of institutions capable of organizing and mandating large numbers of people to build and maintain irrigation systems. As in the other ancient river-valley civilizations, society became more complex as villages began to expand.

According to legend, the first Chinese dynasty, the **Xia** (Hsia) dynasty, emerged along the Huang He. While much of what we know about this dynasty might be legend, the formation of an authoritarian central government became a hallmark of Chinese civilization. The first historic dynasty, the **Shang**, controlled China for about 500 years from 1532–1027 BCE and was a central force in introducing irrigation and flood control systems in the Huang He valley. Unlike the cities of the Indus Valley or Fertile Crescent, the major Shang cities were constructed of wood and were highly stratified. The major Shang city, Anyang, had higher classes living within the city walls in timber framed houses with walls of clay and straw while the lower classes lived in hovels outside the city. The Shang did have other accomplishments, such as during their reign, the Chinese produced silk cloth, pottery called kaolin, and bronze casting. They also developed a calendar and an original written language.

The Chinese rulers, like their Egyptian counterparts, used religion to bolster their position in society. The Shang rulers, for instance, served as indispensable intermediaries between their kingdom and powerful and protective ancestors and gods. They were considered priests in ancestor worship and historians have gleaned information about the ruler's role as chief intermediary with the ancestors by reading the incisions etched on the tens of thousands of **oracle bones** that survive today and reveal the answer the ancestors gave the ruler on such matters of importance as the weather, the yield of the net harvest, the health of the king and his family, and the prospects of military campaigns. Also like the Egyptians, the Shang ordered complex tombs built for their kings. These burial sites were designed and built, and when the king was buried, people were sacrificed to be buried with the kings to assist them in their afterlife.

Also, like the Egyptians, the Shang engaged in massive building projects, which required them to be able to control large labor forces. The Shang, for instance, were known for surrounding their cities with tremendous earthen walls. These walls took a great number of men to build, likely over 10,000 over a long period of time. Also, like the Egyptians, the Shang depended upon the development of a large bureaucracy to enable him to rule from his capital, to recruit and manage the military and collect taxes.

The Shang had limited contact with the rest of the world, although it did engage in long-distance trade with Mesopotamia. They developed an ethnocentric attitude and considered Shang China to be the center of the world. The central role of the family played an important part in Shang society. Usually multiple generations would live in the same household in a **patriarchal** structure that gave the most power to the eldest living male. Even when family members died, they continued to play a central role in day-to-day life as one's ancestors were considered to be a family's intermediaries with the gods. So, ancestor worship and respect dominated family life.

Around 1100 BCE, the Shang were overthrown by the **Zhou.** The Zhou developed the concept of the ruler as the divine Son of Heaven who ruled in accord with the **Mandate of Heaven**. The basic idea of the Mandate was that if the gods were pleased with a ruler, wars would be won and harvests would be plentiful. However, if the opposite should happen, the people had a right to change the rulers. Carefully applying this Mandate of Heaven to their own ascension to rule, a new group on the scene, the Zhou, justified the removal of the Shang Dynasty.

The Zhou instituted a great deal of reforms and improvements. They started large water projects to control rivers and irrigation, established the manufacture and trade of silk, developed caravan routes across Central Asia, and established schools of ancient philosophy.

During the Zhou rule, trade and crafts increased, and social mobility and advancement occurred. There was a great deal of expansion, which increased the available land for cultivation. They established a decentralized system of government, dividing their territory into 200 domains. This was to prove their undoing. A feudal system developed in which land was given to trusted nobles who provided loyalty and military service to the king and protection to the people. At first, the local lords submitted to the control of the Zhou rulers; however, over time, local lords became less dependent on the king and later bound together and led to a period of **Warring States** in which the old aristocracy was undermined by competition between the states and advances in military technology. As a result, regional lords became powerful and fought each other from 403 to 221 BCE.

As part of their quest for power, these lords sought out the advice of teachers and advisers. **Confucius**, for instance, was one of the many teachers who answered the lords' pleas for advice and wisdom. The various philosophies that these teachers formulated became known as the **Hundred Schools of Thought**. Teachers tried to explain all things through the dual principles of yin and yang, as well as the five elements: water, fire, wood, metal, and earth. The ideas taught in the Hundred Schools of Thought influenced Chinese thought for centuries. **Kongfuzi**, known in the West by the Latin form of his name, Confucius, withdrew from public life after unsuccessful efforts to find employment. He gathered around himself a circle of students to whom he presented his wide-ranging ideas on morality, conduct, and government that were later written down by his followers in what we know today as the **Analects**.

Confucius taught that the family was important to the state and that the values of the family applied to national life, and only educated and virtuous people should enter government service. The perfect Confucian gentleman was a man of integrity, education, and culture who should use those qualities to serve his ruler. If Confucianism emphasized social engagement, its great rival, **Daoism**, taught that people should withdraw from the empty formalities and rigid hierarchy and distractions of Chinese society. For **Laozi**, who is credited with the foundational text of Daoism, the **Dao De Jing**, almost all purposeful actions are counterproductive.

COMPETENCY 4.2
Evaluate the influence of ancient civilizations (e.g., Greek, Roman, Indian, Chinese) on the evolution of modern civilization.

Greece—the Cradle of Western Civilization

Civilization in Europe was concentrated in the Aegean Sea and differed in several ways from the River Valley civilizations, no doubt due in large part because the Greek civilization had neither a river valley nor plains, nor even a contiguous body of land to unify them. What they did have was a number of small islands that, while beneficial in terms of trade, were unable to support large populations. Consequently, the city-states that dominated ancient Greece were constantly looking for new land, new colonies in the Mediterranean. Such quests undoubtedly led to a tremendous amount of tension and conflict both between and within the city-states as a result of the heated competition for limited resources. In their quest to gain territories and to establish spheres of influence and chiefly from the activities of Alexander the Great, whose conquests spread Greek culture from the Aegean to the Mediterranean to North Africa and then all the way to India, Greek influence dominated a significant part of the globe. The results of Greek culture flourished and propagated as their influence continued across both time and space, and today's world owes much to the Greeks.

Lord Byron, the English poet, declared that "We are all Greeks!" He was not far off, if we consider how much influence ancient Greece has had on modern civilization. Much of the reason behind why the ancient Greek language and culture has had such a global effect on modern civilization lay mostly in the sciences and the humanities. If one opens up almost any textbook in the humanities, you will see results of Greek scientific achievements. Among the more important contributions the Greeks have made were in the sciences, mathematics, philosophy, naturalistic art, literature, rhetoric, western-style warfare, architecture, religion, philosophy, government, the humanities, sports, politics, theater, and education.

So embedded are remnants of Greek culture in modern civilization that people give little thought to their Greek origins. For example, in the United States, newly minted medical doctors swear by the principles of human treatment in the Hippocratic Oath. They laid down the foundations for the way we approach studies of human behavior through the development of the disciplines of history and philosophy. We owe much of our understanding of more ancient civilizations through the writings of these ancient Greeks (and, thanks to the Muslims in the Middle East, the ideas of the ancient Greeks were preserved in their libraries when Europe eschewed that sort of learning and destroyed libraries). Greek philosophies of Aristotle, Plato, and Socrates continue to shape the ideas of generation after generation. In the field of sports, the ancient Greeks gave us the idea of athletic competitions, rewarding those who excelled on their own merit, rather than through family connections and corruption—they gave us the Olympics, where athletes then would compete in the nude, partly a symbolic gesture that all were equal in the eyes of the judges—no families could buy them off, as excellence would be apparent when stripped nude. Greek contribution to the theater is remarkable, not only for the dramatic literature that Greeks produced and the themes of their stories, but even the ways dramas are staged can be traced to the Greeks and in the designs of theaters themselves. The works of Greek writers are studied, read, acted, and produced today and are a cornerstone of liberal arts education in the United States. In literature, we still study the works from Greek tragedies like Sophocles, Euripides, Aeschylus, Greek epics (Homer), and Greek comedy (Aristophanes). One of the most well known is Homer, whose *Iliad* details the tale of the Greek expedition against the Trojans and *Odyssey,* which tells the adventures of Odysseus. They were important in defining Greek ideals. Homer's *Iliad* and *Odyssey,* where were the first epic poems, no doubt influenced Roman Virgil whose *Aeneid* borrowed from Homer.

The Greeks left their imprint on education, so much so that when the Romans conquered the Greeks, the Romans insisted on having Greek teachers for their children. The Greek educational system featured such things as educational competitions, mentor networks, setting styles of teaching and asking students questions (e.g., the Socratic method), and emphasizing that strength of body was as important as strength of mind, no doubt influencing the inclusion of physical education into school curriculum. Geometry, a cornerstone in modern civilization, also had its beginnings in Ancient Greece. Euclid, a mathematician, formed many geometric proofs and theories, as well as the discovery of pi. Greek architecture's form and substance has been a cornerstone of architecture throughout the world. Buildings in ancient Greece reflected their mathematical origins as buildings were believed to be the embodiment of perfect mathematical design: symmetrical, perfectly proportioned. Not only do we have many copies of buildings today that reflect Greek design, but on top of almost every column today, we have one of three Greek styles: Doric, used on plain capitals, Ionic, in which the capitals were fashioned after ram's horns, and Corinthian, which were made to mirror acanthus leaves.

Democracy is in large part a Greek invention. Modern democracies are based largely on the Athenian form of direct democracy where each citizen had a voice in government. Today we see how modern civilizations have used this philosophy as a basis for their own indirect democracies, where citizens elect officials who then make and enforce laws. One might also allege that it was Greek democracy that paved the way for some of the freedoms that western democracies so pride themselves on, like freedom of speech, freedom of the press, and freedom of movement, where citizens of democracies can think critically and speak out without fear of antagonizing and without adverse personal or political repercussions.

It is to the Romans that much of Greek influence was transmitted throughout the west. The scholarship of Alexandria so impressed the Romans when they came into contact with Hellenism that they constantly strove to emulate the Greeks—they hired Greek tutors for their children, sought to master rhetoric in Greek style, and even considered Greek an important language for them to learn. The Romans adopted much of the Greek culture that they encountered as they took over Greek lands. In addition to borrowing several Greek artistic and educational ideas, they also adopted many Greek religious customs, as a quick perusal of the Roman pantheon of gods and goddesses reveal that the Romans largely took the Greek gods and "Romanized" them for their own.

The study of Greek classics also was a cornerstone of the Renaissance period where Europeans turned toward the classics for inspiration and knowledge. Even Reformation leaders considered a study of Greek to be essential. Greek art reached levels of excellence that were not reproduced until, arguably, the Renaissance when master painters in Southern Europe looked to ancient Greece for theme, styles, and techniques.

Greek influence on modern culture though has not always been of a positive sort. Greek life was organized around the **polis**, the Hellenic city-state. Because geography of Greece almost dictated this type of ruling system in which there were hundreds of poleis, and each evoked a kind of loyalty and attachment by its citizens that made the idea of dissolving one's own polis into a larger unit unthinkable. The result was twofold: both constant war among states and extraordinary achievements in literature and art. So, the idea of unification bred both positive and negative results.

Because no one city-state could produce large numbers of men to fight on the battlefield, the Greeks constructed their society in a way that would make them more efficient than their foes. The institution of a slave economy freed up male citizens to, among other pursuits, make war. Although Greek slavery differed in some important aspects from the later Western version—Greek slavery was not based on race in the same way—it helped to expand their economy and territory and became an institution that the West would later emulate.

While we champion the Greek society for its development of democracy, we should note that not all people were able to participate in it. While Athenian citizenship was granted to adult males of native parentage, it also limited the freedom of women, immigrants, and slaves. These exclusions of parts of the population from enjoying the benefits of democracy set the precedent for many of modern civilization's views about freedoms, rights, and privileges in society. In terms of sexism, the Greeks gave women almost no political, social, or economic rights, perhaps making it harder for women today to be treated equally. Women, like slaves, lacked the right of political participation in the city-state, but freeborn women were citizens, enjoying the protection of the laws as well as having recourse to the courts in property disputes—but were not able to participate in the democracy. All women had to have male guardians to protect them physically and legally.

Men restricted women's freedom of movement partly to reduce uncertainty about the paternity of their children and to protect their daughters' honor. To preserve her reputation and ensure the paternity of her children, an upper-class woman was expected to avoid close contact with men other than family members or close friends. So even the design of the Athenian houses ensured limited exposure of women to non-relatives. Poorer women, however, had a bit more freedom, as they had to work and did so often as small-scale merchants and craft producers. While ostensibly women were allowed to inherit land and control their own dowry, in practice, a woman was not allowed to control the land she inherited. Often, female heirs would be forced to marry the dead man's closest male relative to produce sons so that her inheritance would go to a male heir.

Roman Empire

The Roman Empire, like its neighbors the Greeks, had a tremendous influence on modern civilization. However, much of what we term "Roman" may have indeed come from the Greeks as well as the Etruscans, those who lived in the area before them and from whom the Romans borrowed much of their religious and social institutions. In fact, one of the hallmarks of Roman civilization was its ability to assimilate ideas and institutions not only from the past but also from the areas that they conquered. They assimilated many of the customs of the ancient Etruscans, and then, like the Macedonians before them, also readily adopted the culture of Hellenic Greece. What emerged was a Greco-Roman culture that we find influences in art, law, architecture, language, government, and engineering.

From 1000 to 500 BCE, the Italian peninsula was dominated by three groups who inhabited the region and battled for its control: the Latins, Greeks, and Etruscans, and each seemed to influence the other. The Latins were members of an Indo-European tribe of farmers and shepherds who wandered into the region and settled on both sides of the Tiber River in a region they called Latium. They built the original settlement at Rome, a cluster of wooden huts atop one of the area's seven hills, Palatine Hill. Between 750 and 600 BCE, Greek settlers established about 50 colonies along the coastlines of Italy and Sicily. Links between these outposts, the Latins, and the Greek colonists created a cultural and political link with Greek civilization that existed for centuries. In about 616 BCE, the Etruscans emerged from northern Italy and brought their skill as metalworkers, jewelers, and engineers to the area. Romans borrowed much from the Etruscans, including their alphabet and number system, their type of government, gladiator games and chariot races, styles of sculpture and painting, and building techniques, including that of the arch.

Until 509 BCE when the Romans overthrew the last of the Etruscan kings, the Romans adopted Etruscan rituals believed to please the gods. Social life also seems to have borrowed much from the Etruscans. Rome had been composed of three tribes which were further divided into clans, which were composed of groups of families. In each of these divisions, which we have seen time and again throughout European history, was a class of nobles and a class of commoners. The nobles, referred to as **patricians**, occupied some important positions in society: they were landowners who were also advisors to the king. Society was a patriarchal one in which the father of the family was responsible for protection and was the priest of his home. It was a patron-client society in which patrons had clients who they protected and whose own position in society was bolstered by the number of clients one had.

Romans also borrowed some ideas of government that they later implemented in their system, and which has been emulated by other modern societies. The early Etruscan kings were not hereditary ones, but rather they were elected by the nobles. The Etruscan kings also had a council, or senate, that was composed of 30 senators. So, the concept of leaders having a group of people that gave them advice continued to be important throughout the civilizations that followed.

While we do see elements of continuity from their past, the Roman Republic could also be considered a departure from the common experiences of ancient civilizations. Having begun as a monarchy, Rome expelled its king and established an aristocratic republic somewhat like the Greek *poleis*. Rome though, unlike the Greek democrats, extended its citizenship to a large population, first throughout Italy and then across its entire empire. The Romans shared their citizenship with those elites that they conquered in order to guarantee loyalty and to strengthen Rome's grip on their territories. Roman policy of assimilation and toleration enabled it, like the Ottoman empire that followed it, to be successful in its early stages. Romans looked to Greece not only for fighting techniques but also for education and approaches to learning. Most upper-class Romans hired Greek tutors, and most educated Romans knew Latin as well as Greek.

The Romans became empire builders though almost by accident, and their imperialism, it could be argued, brought more harm than good. A conflict in southern Italy led to foreign involvement, first in Sicily and then in North Africa during the Punic Wars between Rome and Carthage. (Remember George Washington's admonition to "Beware of foreign entanglements" in his *Farewell Address*—it is from the Roman experience that he based his sage advice.)

In 509 BCE, the Romans overthrew the last of the Etruscan kings, as they were none too pleased to be ruled by the Etruscans, subjected to perceived tyranny of the king, and the nobles wanted more power and control of the government. They set up a new form of government called a republic, from the Latin *res publica* which means "public affairs." A republic is a form of government in which citizens vote on their leaders. In Rome, the only people who had voting rights were free-born male citizens.

The Roman government seemed to work well because it included a system of checks and balances in which each government constrained the actions of others, so that no one person would gain too much power.

In many ways, the Roman Empire remains the ideal upon which much of Western civilization, and certainly American civilization, has shaped itself. We need only to look at the architecture of the U.S. Capitol, the composition of the government, and the influence of Christianity in this country to see the Roman influence. Because so much of the United States has been constructed on Roman foundations, a fascination with why Rome fell has occupied historians and political pundits alike. In an effort to avoid repeating the mistakes of the past, our attention has become attuned to looking at the nature and extent of the empire in an increasingly global environment. Are we doomed to repeat the mistakes of the past? Are empires a thing of the past, or has the word "empire" just been replaced with the word "hegemony" (power) today?

Military victory brought economic and political change, a change in lifestyle, and, some alleged, general moral deterioration. In consolidating its power over huge territories, the Romans committed atrocities, enslaved whole peoples, and destroyed cities with little provocation. Roman gods were morphed into older Greek gods and given a name-change—for instance, Greek god Zeus became Juniper, Hera became Juno.

Also, as the military grew more powerful, foreign conquests created huge amounts of standing armies and veterans who needed to be occupied during times of peace. The trouble these groups tended to wrought in Rome prompted many to urge expansion just to keep the soldiers out of the affairs of Roman senators. As these military men grew powerful, turmoil between old and new elites loomed on the horizon. Military expansion produced another problem in that rural Roman society moved from one of independent farmers to one in which slave labor became the primary means of the rural economy. By the end of the first century BCE, the slave population comprised about 2–3 million slaves. Prisoners of war and conquered civilians comprised most of the slaves.

Legacy of the Romans

What is the legacy that Rome offers us? Do Roman ideas really form the foundation of Western society? The legacy of the Roman Empire can be seen today in language, law, government, architecture, urban and regional development, and in the Christian churches.

Rome's language, Latin, was the official language of the empire, and until the seventeenth century, both Latin and Greek were considered standard courses for all educated Europeans. The Latin language was predominant in the Roman Empire and became the basis for Spanish, French, Portuguese, Romanian, and Italian—the Romance Languages. These languages started out as frontier languages where peoples tried to blend their language with that of the new rulers, and the result was really just different versions of "bad Latin," that later established themselves as bona fide languages. Latin also exerted its influence in areas that did not speak any romance languages, largely as a result of the influence of the Roman Catholic Church. Until only 30 or so years ago, Latin served as the language of prayer in the Roman Catholic Church. Many English words, especially legal and medical terminology, have Latin roots.

Another legacy of the Roman Empire is the hundreds of towns that Rome founded and developed in the frontiers of their empire. These new towns served as their administrative centers and today provide the basic structure of cities around much of Europe and North Africa. Roman roads, 50,000 of them, connected the cities of the empire and formed the foundation for much of Europe's land transportation today. The Romans developed systems for water and sewage that made it possible for the cities to move further away from rivers and water and settle the interiors of countries. Their development of concrete facilitated not only the building of the aqueducts but also large buildings and structures. Roman development of a government financed and controlled system of connected roads also facilitated their expansion and today influences our state planning and even the construction of highway systems.

Roman art and architecture has left an enormous imprint on modern design. It is from the Romans that art embraced realistic representations of people and moved away from the idealized visions that the Greeks had provided us. These realistic representations were plastered all over Rome, not just in the form of majestic statues, but also in graffiti that adorned public buildings and became a form of criticism of public officials and societal issues and to which modern architecture is also inundated. The Roman legacy is found today in neoclassical architecture with the use of arches and vaults and in the Romanesque architectural style. The arch, in particular, because it is extremely efficient as a weight-bearing structure, is found on buildings and aqueducts. Many of the Roman buildings served as models for buildings in the United States. For instance, Thomas Jefferson used the Roman Parthenon as his inspiration for the University of Virginia's Rotunda, and the U.S. Capitol Building also reflects basic tenets of Roman architecture. We also see Roman inspiration in a basic component of modern urban civilization, the apartment.

Roman influence in science and engineering can also be felt today. While the Greeks had been more interested in new scientific research and were interested in knowledge for knowledge's sake, the Romans, ever more practical, were more interested in application of knowledge and in collecting and organizing information. **Galen,** a physician who lived in Rome in the 100s CE, wrote several volumes of medical knowledge; physicians up until the last century used his compendium of knowledge as a basic reference work. **Ptolemy** synthesized the knowledge of others into a single theory of astronomy that Earth was the center of the universe. Roman engineering made it possible for people to construct enormous buildings through their developments in human-powered cranes that could lift up heavy blocks of stone and put them into place. Bricks were laid in which no mortar was needed to hold the bricks together.

The Romans used their knowledge that they had gained from science and applied it in a practical way. They applied the knowledge that they gained from science to plan their cities, build water and sewage systems, and improve farming methods. They used their engineering to construct bridges and roads that still survive today. Their contributions to urban planning can be felt today in most European cities that have elements of a grid system of roads that were originally planned by Roman engineers.

Modern literature, drama, and history writing owe great debts to Roman authors. **Virgil**, **Livy**, **Plutarch**, and **Tacitus** not only gave us great themes for modern literature and theater, but Tacitus's history writing served as emulation for historians over the years. Modern literature and drama owe a great debt to Rome. For example, the technique of satire was developed from Roman authors.

Roman law inspired the formation and imposition of civil law, a form of law based on a written code of laws that we have today. The Romans, for instance, were the first to come up with the idea of "innocent until proven guilty" and that the burden of proof was on the accuser. They believed that people had rights guaranteed to them under the law. The civil law system was adopted by many countries in Europe after the empire fell. Centuries later, those nations carried their systems of laws to colonies in Africa, the Middle East, Asia, and the Americas. As a result, many countries in these regions have civil law systems that we have in place today. We also see the Roman legacy in the U.S. government today as it has formed the basis of our republican form of government. We even use some of the same terms in government that the Romans used, like Senate. They even had two chambers of government, the senate, and the assembly.

Contemporary indirect democracies also owe a lot to Rome for the development of the government form. The social and political structure of Rome was actually set up rather similarly to the Greeks—the Romans had **patricians** (land owning nobles), **plebeians** (all other free men), and slaves. Roman government was organized as a representative republic. The main governing body was made up of two distinct groups: the Senate, which comprised patrician families, and the Assembly, initially made up of patricians but later opened up to plebians.

Although the Romans tolerated Judaism, many Jews were discontented with Roman rule and hoped for a Messiah who would win their independence. In this setting, Jesus was born. His teachings, which formed the basis of the new religion of Christianity, spread among all people within the empire, not just Jews. The Romans persecuted the early Christians because the Christians refused to worship the emperor. Nevertheless, Christianity gained many followers and during the 300s CE, it became the official religion of the Roman Empire. As Roman rule became more decentralized and centers of Christianity sprang up in Byzantium and Alexandria, it greatly influenced the people there. The Roman Church used the Roman imperial administrative organization for its own uses and later became known as the Holy Roman Empire.

Classical Civilizations of India: Mauryan Empire and Gupta Dynasty

India's Mauryan and Gupta civilizations contributed to modern civilization primarily through their development of trade, religions, mathematics, and science. The Mauryan civilization arose around 321 BCE and lasted until approximately 180 BCE. The height of the civilization occurred during the reign of **Ashoka Maurya**. During his period, the Mauryan Empire became quite powerful due to its trade in silk, cotton, and elephants and its military prowess. While the Mauryans were able to extend their influence considerably through these activities, Ashoka's reaction to a rather violent military victory actually made him renounce such activities and convert to Buddhism. Concerned now more with nonviolence and moderation, the Mauryan Empire became more concerned during

Ashoka's rule with spreading his new religion. As a result, his conversion helped the religion spread beyond India and into many parts of Southeast Asia. Buddhism today is practiced by more than six percent of the world's population.

After Ashoka's death in 232 BCE, the Mauryan Empire began to decline and it was not until the appearance of the more decentralized and smaller **Gupta Empire** from 320 to 550 CE that considerable advances in the arts and sciences made their mark on the civilizations that followed. One tremendous influence that contemporary civilization has from the Gupta mathematicians was the concept of zero that they developed, without which modern mathematics would be impossible. They also came up with the concept of *pi* and a decimal system that used the numbers 1 through 9. The numbers we use today come from Hindu-Arabic numerals that Indian scholars created and the Arabs brought to Europe.

Math, of course, is the key to science and Gupta mathematical advances also influenced what was going on in science. Astronomy developments were reflected in the work of the most famous Indian astronomer, **Aryabhata**, who correctly argued that Earth rotates on its axis and revolves around the sun. Aryabhata also knew that Earth was a sphere and calculated its circumference pretty accurately.

The Gupta Empire also influenced modern medicine with several of their innovations and day-to-day practices. The Indians introduced the idea of inoculations, how to inject small amounts of viruses to protect people against disease which had a lasting effect on civilization, as now a simple inoculation could prevent a crippling or fatal disease. Indian doctors also left their imprint on surgery as Indian doctors made several advances in it, as well as in the way broken bones and wounds were treated.

During the Gupta Dynasty period, we also saw problems begin to erupt for women that resulted in women increasingly losing their rights, particularly after the issuance of **Manu's Laws**. During this period, Indian women lost the right to win or inherit property, participate in sacred rituals, and study religion and were forced to marry at quite young ages, as young as six or seven. This marked a tremendous change for women and one that contributed significantly to some of the problems modern women have had with regard to equal rights and protections across the globe.

Han China

The **Han Dynasty** in China lasted about 400 years, from 206 BCE to 220 CE. The Han Dynasty reached its height under the emperor **Wudi** who ruled from 141 to 87 BCE. Under his rule, China extended its control to the north and west of China and even took Manchuria, Korea, and Vietnam. To strengthen China, Wudi promoted economic growth, set up new roads and canals, and instituted monopolies on salt, iron, and alcohol. He also took land away from large landowners and limited the power of merchants. Under his rule, we see many developments that influenced the evolution of modern civilization.

The most significant developments, as usual, belong to the fields of science and technology. The most important Han invention was paper. The Han made paper out of grinding plant fibers like hemp into a paste. They then let the paste dry in sheaves and used these sheaves to create books, which were essentially long sheaves tied together into a scroll. Needless to say, the invention of paper affected almost every aspect of modern life today.

In farming, Han inventions included the iron plow and the wheelbarrow that enabled the Han to plow more land faster. Han invention extended also to the seismograph, which measured Earth tremors. Han emperors were particularly concerned with these, as earthquakes were considered signs of the heaven's disapproval with it. In medicine, the Han made advances in acupuncture to control pain and to cure disease.

Wudi developed a civil service system in which candidates had to pass an exam in the Confucian classics in order to obtain a job in the government. His bureaucracy of more than 130,000 people was designed so that only the best and the brightest would have jobs. Job applicants took formal exams in history, law, literature, and in the texts of Confucius. While the exams were theoretically open to all, in reality, only the wealthy could afford the tutoring to pass the difficult exams.

Some of the major accomplishments of the Han Dynasty include:

- Brought common written language throughout the empire

- Built roads and defensive walls

- Created a centralized, bureaucratic government

- Invented paper, which made books more readily available, spread education, and resulted in a better educated workforce

- Developed a plow, wheelbarrow, and collar harness and improved farming

- Increased population to 60 million

- Developed a strong military

- Secured caravan traffic across Central Asia

- Created the Silk Road

- Expanded trade networks that helped assimilate people of different cultures under Chinese rule.

- Converted to a Confucian state

- Facilitated an expansion of intellectual, literary, and artistic life

- Produced first dictionaries

- Introduced Buddhism into China

- Implemented a meritocracy

The Han dynasty ultimately collapsed because of the high taxes that it had to institute to keep the system going. The economic imbalance caused resentment and ultimately the end of the empire. Because a system of inheritance allowed for each son to acquire equal portions of his father's land, plots of land became smaller and smaller with each generation. As a result, it became difficult for owners of small plots to make a living and to pay their taxes. Large landowners did not have to pay taxes, so when their land owning increased, their tax decreased. As a result, the gap increased between rich and poor.

Comparisons

India and China actually have more in common with the Roman Empire than one would think at first glance. Both empires expanded significantly, maintained their larger territories, integrated the conquered territories into their own, used superior weapons and technologies, spread their dominant belief systems and languages to the newer regions, developed internal transportation and trade, and set up an extensive political system replete with a wide bureaucracy to unite their respective areas. Such accomplishments could not have happened had the empires not had policies of integration and assimilation in place as they grappled with how to unify their empire as it expanded further and further away from the center.

Despite the similarities, however, they each developed a bit differently than the other. We have already explored what happened in Rome, and now we will look at China and India and then make some comparisons between them.

If we look closely at both the Chinese and Roman Empires, we would see similarities that would help us understand some of the basic truths about empires.

- Both empires had relations with groups they considered to be "barbarians." Rome faced not only the barbarians from the north but also those from Central Asia. China faced the Xiongnu and, like Rome, settled the "barbarians" near their borders and enlisted them in their imperial armies. The result though was different for each, for while the Huns helped bring down the Roman Empire, the Chinese were able to absorb them.

- Both empires had to contend with new belief systems but had different results. Christianity did nothing to save the empire in Rome and arguably hastened its demise, but the Chinese were able to absorb Confucianism and Daoism into the culture in such a way as to use the new religions to help build a "national culture."

- Both empires ascribed divine attributes to the emperor and both had difficulty in establishing rules for imperial succession. Neither believed, however, that one family should rule forever. The Chinese believed that the Mandate of Heaven would pass from one family to the next.

- Both empires used marriages to confirm political alliances and both insisted on strict sexual morality.

- In both empires, the army was crucial in creating and sustaining the political structure in the face of domestic and foreign enemies. Both empires had to deal with errant and ambitious generals and feared having restless veterans with nothing to do.

- Both empires faced the challenges of overextension, and controlling the financial expenses associated with the empire. When losses happened, in China, they were explained that the ruler had lost the Mandate of Heaven and dynasties would fall.

- Both empires engaged in huge public works campaigns to improve their capital infrastructure. While Rome built roads, aqueducts, and towns, the Chinese built the Great Wall, the Grand Canal, roads, towns, and a succession of capital cities.

- In both empires, the benefits of imperial wealth tended to flow toward the center and to the elites in capital cities.

- Both empires did not treat their peasants nicely, bound them to the soil, and forced the sons of soldiers to become soldiers as well. The Chinese civil service examination provided some advancement within the imperial bureaucracy.

- Both empires experienced frequent revolts against the emperor and his policies. While slaves led these revolts in Rome, in China, the peasants led the rebellions.

- Peasants in both empires lived a miserable existence and sought to evade taxes and conscriptions by selling themselves or taking refuge on landed estates.

When we add India to the comparison, we find a few differences. China and Rome instituted bureaucracies and systems of administration that lasted a thousand years in China and hundreds of years in Rome. By contrast, India's states and empires seemed to be extensions of family lineages, like the Mauryan and Gupta empires, and so rather than building institutions to prop up the rulers, power was held in the ruler and his family, rather than in the institution of power.

India, unlike the Romans and the Chinese, had so many kingdoms and states that if people lost favor in one area, they would abscond to a neighboring country to fight against their former ruler. In India, because power and therefore loyalty was vested in people rather than institutions, loyalty was quite different. If someone felt the ruler did not meet their needs, they felt little reason to continue to support them.

While in Rome and China the government touched much of the population through taxes, military conscription, imperial service, and bureaucracies, India's contact with the people differed. In India, social systems already in place seemed to continue to work regardless of whatever regime was in power and family lineages, caste and jati systems, guilds, local government, and religious institutions continued to work, even if the government changed.

COMPETENCY 4.3

Identify the major contributions of African, Asian, and Mesoamerican societies before 1500 CE.

Africa

The most significant early civilization in Africa for the purposes of the FTCE was Egypt, which was discussed in an earlier competency above. This civilization was located in northern Africa, along the Mediterranean, north of the Sahara Desert. While geographically a part of Africa, contemporary studies of Egypt place it more within the context of the Middle East, rather than North Africa. As such, we will focus on the other civilizations in Africa for this competency.

In order to understand developments in Africa before 1500 CE, historians rely on secondary source literature from travelers and traders to the region, art, artifacts, and other nontraditional historical sources. The peoples of these areas left few written records, but we do know that there was enough contact with the Muslim world that trade and conversion to Islam had a significant impact on the societies there. The source of our knowledge of the area is the study of language, oral traditions, music and archeological discoveries, and travel accounts. The village was the essential unit of political and economic life in the regions, and the chief or the elders exercised political control. The societies were matrilineal, which means that women played a crucial rule.

There were a variety of kingdoms, empires, and small city-states that arose in Africa during this period. Three of the biggest issues in particular that affected the development of African Kingdoms were **ecological change**, the development of **long-distance commerce** (trade), and the spread of **Islam**.

Environmental change affected African society as it altered settlement choices and facilitated the decline of empires. The drying up of the Sahara, for instance, forced farmers to move away from what had once been lush green areas to other areas that did not suffer from such ecological change. As the Bantu-speaking people migrated, they took their customs and agricultural methods with them and influenced others. Some environmental changes even led to the downfall of empires. For instance, Aksum's decision to cut down forests led to soil erosion and therefore affected its ability to produce enough food to feed its people.

Trade determined the extent of contact with other civilizations in both East and West Africa. When societies begin to trade with one another, not only were goods and monies exchanged, but ideas, religions, and culture. Traders from Greece, India, and Southeast Asia landed on the East coast of Africa, and in exchange for their pottery, silk, cotton cloth, and wheat, they received luxury goods like ivory, gold, coconut oil, and slaves. Traders brought with them new food for crops, like rice and bananas, that changed the eating habits of the Africans.

Trade was profitable not only for those directly trading with one another but also for those who lived along trade routes. In West Africa, Muslim traders crossed the Sahara to exchange salt for gold, and those who lived in-between profited immensely by taxing all trade along the trade routes.

While contact with other cultures inevitably resulted in an exchange of goods and ideas, the success of the transmission of ideas and religion should be examined with a bit of skepticism. Indeed, the social and religious practices of the merchants themselves had less influence than the highly prized goods that they brought with them. As a result, despite conversions to Christianity or Islam, many Africans did not forget their old practices or faiths and simply incorporated the new ideas into their belief system. As a result, while Islam was brought to the area by the traders, the practice and interpretation of it bore little resemblance to the original. In many ways though, it simply attests to the flexibility of the new religions and the ability to assimilate into new cultures.

By far the most important foreign influence on Africa was Islam. A network of caravan routes connected the Mediterranean coast with Sudan and shipping routes between the African coast and Yemen brought Islam into West Africa and stimulated trade there. With greater contact with Muslim traders, Africans began to convert to Islam. Because two of the Pillars of Islam mandate the giving of *zakat*, or charity, to others and to complete the hajj, new travel routes from Africa to Mecca opened up. Leaders, like Mansa Musa, who were eager to demonstrate their religiosity made pilgrimages to Mecca and on the way distributed alms to people. Some of these alms-giving resulted in the creation of new centers of learning and hospice along the hajj routes. Another benefit to the hajj expeditions was the exchange of ideas and people between those who had previously had little contact with one another.

In the areas south of Egypt and in the upper reaches of the Nile, two important kingdoms developed. The **Kingdom of Kush** in the south of the ancient region known as

Kingdoms of Kush, Axum, and the Swahili Coast

Kush	Axum	Swahili Coast
• Trade	• Trade—ivory and gold	• Mix with Arab cuture and language
• Tax collection on trade that passed through	• Spread Christianity and Islam	• Trade of gold, slaves, ivory throughout the Indian Ocean
		• Influence of Islam

Nubia, emerged independently of Egypt by 700 BCE. The **Kushites**, known as intermediaries between Egypt and East Africa, eventually became a distinct empire.

Trade was really the most important contribution that these African empires developed. Nubian civilization was tremendously influenced by its interactions with its more complex and technologically advanced neighbors, the Egyptians. Much of their contact with one another centered on their trade relationship, for the Nubians supplied the Egyptians with a wide range of goods, from building materials, to slaves, to ivory and ebonywood. Not only did the Nubians have control of valuable resources like gold and precious stones, but they also, due to its location, served as middlemen for trade along the Upper Nile. Nubians profited by charging taxes on any goods that went through their land. By 1472 BCE, apparently the taxes became so high that Queen Hatshepsut of Egypt had five ships carried across the desert to avoid paying taxes!

During the New Kingdom period, the Egyptian government imposed Egyptian culture, language, and religion on the native population, and Nubian architecture came to be based on Egyptian models. But, in the eighth century BCE, the kingdom of Meroe emerged, and Nubia overtook their once-powerful neighbors and ruled all of Egypt for half a century. During this time, the Nubian rulers retained their Nubian names but imitated the style and traditions of the pharaohs. By the fourth century though, power shifted south to the competing state of Axum and sub-Saharan African cultural influences replaced Egyptian ones.

Axum, located in modern-day Ethiopia, built its power from its ability to trade, especially in ivory and gold. Its trading routes extended into the Mediterranean and to the Red Sea areas, establishing long contacts between its people and the religions of those areas. Two sets of mass conversions impacted the development of Axum and its peoples. In the fourth century, Axum converted to Christianity, and in the seventh century, it converted to Islam. From Axum, Christianity spread throughout Africa.

The peoples who lived on the **Swahili Coast of Africa** (East Africans), primarily Bantu-speaking peoples, also engaged in a significant amount of trade. In fact, the word for trader (or coaters) is "Swahili." The Swahili language today reflects some of the effects of the trade their peoples engaged in as the Swahili language is a mix of the original Bantu language with Arabic and Persian. Extensive trade of gold, slaves, rhinoceros horns, spices, and ivory with Muslims in exchange for cotton cloth, copper and brass, and iron tools began in the early tenth century and flourished. The wealth that this trade brought created powerful kingdoms along the coast, wealthy trading centers that became important cultural and political centuries, and the spread of Islam throughout the region as the ruling elites and merchant classes converted in order to facilitate some of their developing political and economic relationships. The trade linked the East African coast with India, China, and the Indies.

Western Africa

Three of the most important empires in Sub-Saharan Africa were the Soninke people of Ghana, Mali, and Songhai and like those empires above, trade, specifically the gold trade, dominated economic activity and significantly influenced the social, political, and religious activities of the people who lived there. As Islam spread across North Africa in the seventh and eighth centuries, the African kingdoms became an important cog in the wheel of the Mediterranean economy. As people from south of the Sahara began to trade their goods for salt, they began to encounter Islamic traders who became interested in the goods that the West African peoples had—namely gold.

Located where we find Ghana today, the Soninke people thrived, ruled by their war chief that they referred to as a *ghana*. Muslim traders who visited the area referred to the whole region as Ghana. By the 700s, the Soninke were growing rich from taxing the trans-Saharan trade routes, particularly from the gold and salt that came through their country, ideally located between black Africa and North Africa. Only the king had the right to own gold nuggets and so he limited the supply of gold in order to keep its price from falling. It was through traders that Ghana came into contact with Islam, primarily attracting the rulers. These rulers tried to spread Islam beyond their court but had a bit of difficulty in doing so. Many of the upper classes, convinced that they needed to embrace Islam in order to appease the king, did observe Islam along with their former beliefs.

Among the upper classes, Islam's growth encouraged the spread of literacy and the Arabic language, as to study the Qur'an, converts had to learn how to read and write Arabic. As literacy became more important, the ruling kings began to get assistance from a large bureaucracy composed of family members who filled needed posts.

By the thirteenth century, the Kingdom of Mali was established. By 1235, the Kingdom of Mali had formed a party as a result of a shift of trade routes and the decline of the Ghana empire due to its numerous wars with Muslim empires to the north. The Kingdom of Mali rose to power built on the same territory Ghana had ruled 150 years earlier. Mali's first great leader, Sundiata, took over the Kingdom of Ghana and unified the area. He helped create his capital of Niani as an important center of commerce and trade. After Sundiata's death in 1255, and influenced by Arab traders in the region, some of Mali's rulers became Muslims, built mosques, attended public prayers, and supported the preaching of Muslim religious leaders. The most famous of them was Sundiata's grand-nephew, Mansa Musa, whose rule, historians debate, may have happened during either 1307–1338 CE or 1312–1337 CE. Mansa Musa was a skilled military leader who did a good job controlling the gold and salt trade. He kept up a large army of over 100,000 men. As a devout Muslim, his hajj in Mecca in 1324–1325 CE attracted quite a bit of attention as he brought 60,000 people with him. The people that the pilgrims met along the way were quite impressed with the entourage's lavish clothing and gifts. In fact, those on the pilgrimage gave away so much gold along their trip that the price of gold tanked. No doubt lured by the prospect of more gold, Mansa Musa's group attracted many artists, scholars, and architects along the way who returned with him to Mali and engaged in numerous projects in his empire, turning Mali's Timbuktu into a tremendous center of education, religion, and culture.

The Empire of Songhai emerged as a breakaway kingdom from Mali as Mali declined after the death of Mansa Musa. During the fifteenth and sixteenth centuries, the Songhai Empire stood as one of the largest empires in the history of Africa. It had two important rulers. First, Sunni Ali, helped build the empire from a professional army that featured a riverboat fleet of war canoes and a mobile fighting force on horseback. In 1468, Sunni Ali captured Timbuktu. Sunni Ali's son lost power after a rebellion that was initiated by Muslims who were angry that he did not practice Islam faithfully. The leader of the revolt was a devout Muslim named Askia Mohammad. During his rule, he set up an efficient tax system, initiated political reform, and revitalized the area, turning it into a well-governed and thriving empire. He also created religious schools, mosques, and opened his court to scholars and poets from all over the Muslim world.

The Kingdom of Benin also proved to be of tremendous import for the region. In the 1480s, Portuguese trading ships began to sail into Benin where they traded with Benin merchants for pepper, ivory, leopard skins, and slaves. This initiated European influence in the region where they enslaved Africans, seized, and colonized the region. The coastal part was known as the "Slave coast."

Trading Empires of West Africa

Empire	Key Facts
Ghana	**Location:** • Near Niger and Senegal Rivers **Key cities:** • Koumbi Saleh (capital) **Trade:** • Controlled gold-salt trade routes **Religion:** • Local beliefs, some Muslim influences
Mali	**Location:** • Along upper Niger River **Key cities:** • Niani (capital), Timbuktu **Trade:** • Controlled gold-salt trade routes **Religion:** • Islam and local beliefs
Songhai	**Location:** • Near Niger River **Key cities:** • Gao (capital), Timbuktu **Key rulers:** • Sundiata; Mansa Musa **Trade:** Trans-Saharan trade • Controlled gold-salt trade routes **Religion:** • Islam, local beliefs

Common Characteristics of African Societies:

There are some common characteristics of the West African societies during this period:

- Each featured a trade-based economy and sought to control both salt imports from the north and gold purchases from the south.

- All of the governments in the region filled their coffers from taxes imposed on the buying and selling of salt, gold, and other goods.

- Islam, too, was a unifying theme, as the ability to communicate in Arabic furthered the Arabic-centered trade, provided administrators, and stimulated intellectual life. Islam, as a cosmopolitan religion, found adherents mostly in the cities, while the countryside retained their traditional beliefs and gods.

- Due to extensive trade successes, a plethora of cities rose in the region that became centers of learning, trade, and politics. Similarly, a cultural gulf developed between urban and rural areas, reflecting the economic and political separations that arose as well as economic and political power moved to these powerful cities.

By the end of the fourteenth century, far-sweeping changes had enveloped the area as it became primarily concerned with maintaining and expanding trade. Important new developments during the fifteenth century were the presence of ships along the Atlantic and Indian coasts carrying European traders and missionaries from Portugal, Holland, Spain, and England. Initially, Africans saw the Europeans as another set of traders and were eager to supply them with slaves, goods, and minerals. These European traders initially seemed content to establish trade and supply centers along the coast and made little effort to expand their influence. It would prove to be a temporary and illusory effort by the Africans to direct the nature and extent of the trade with their new partners.

Asian Societies

Chinese Societies

By 1500, China saw three important Chinese dynasties develop: the T'ang (618–907 CE), the Song (960–1279 CE), and the Ming (1368–1644). We can look at the achievements of this region and place them into four key themes:

1. Triumphs and problems with the rise and spread of Buddhism

2. Intellectual and cultural achievements during the Tang and Song Dynasties

3. Mongols and their achievements

4. Ming Dynasty and the closing of China to the West

Spread of Buddhism

The religion that had the greatest impact on China was Buddhism. Buddhism first came to China during the Han era, but few Chinese adopted the religion at that time. By the Tang Dynasty, Buddhism was well established in China, as many of the Tang rulers were Buddhists and supported the religion. The period of time from 400 to 845 CE is actually referred to as the Age of Buddhism. During this period, as Buddhism spread, the Buddhist monasteries became centers of learning and medicine.

In the mid 800s, the Age of Buddhism came to an end when the religion lost official favor as it incurred the wrath of the Tang emperor, Confucian scholars, and Daoists. The Tang emperor, Emperor Wuzong, seeing the growing power of Buddhist religious communities, saw them as a threat and launched a violent campaign against them, destroying temples and text, killing monks, and forcing 26,000 Buddhist monks and nuns to return to life outside the protection of the monasteries. Confucians saw the Buddhist dismissal of the pursuit of material accumulation as a drain on the treasury and the labor pool. The Daoists saw Buddhism as a rival religion that threatened to take over.

Sui Dynasty

The Sui Dynasty formed in 589 when a ruler named Wendi reunified China and worked hard to build a centralized government. He initiated a series of reforms designed to improve government organization through creating a new legal code, restoring order, and reforming the bureaucracy. He also created policies to provide all adult males with land and to ensure the availability of grain for the people. The major accomplishment though was the building of the **Grand Canal**, a 1,000-mile waterway that linked the Yellow River with the Yangzi. The Grand Canal produced many economic benefits, but at a terrific human cost. Built in seven years, over 5.5 million people between the ages of 15 and 55 were pressed into service. Because these people were taken from their homes and fields reluctantly, as many as 50,000 police supervised the construction. Those who did not or could not work were flogged and chained. The economic toll that it cost for families was enormous, as not only were their men taken away from the family fields, but every fifth family had to provide one person who would supply and prepare food for the workers! It should be noted that huge public works such as this often required then (and now!) this type of forced labor—it was not limited to the Chinese.

The Sui Empire ended when a Sui general seized power and started the Tang Dynasty.

Tang

The Tang Dynasty ruled China beginning in 618 CE and until 907 CE, when it collapsed under the weight of an empire that had stretched its limits so much that local warlords were able to seize power. The Tang emperors presided over one of the most celebrated periods in Chinese history. But, they were not Chinese! They were of Turkic descent and brought with them the military and cultural practices of the nomads of Central and Inner Asia.

How did China change over the course of Tang rule? As it gained more power, it became less welcome of outside ideas. In the beginning of the Tang Dynasty, they dominated East Asia, but later, all along its borders, powerful states had established themselves. The late Tang Dynasty was not as eager to adopt music, craft, and art styles from distant lands. Earlier, the Tang Dynasty promoted artistic creativity and economic expansion, poetry flourished, and China enjoyed a golden age that made it the most sophisticated country in the world. But, as a society begins to feel the tension from their border areas, societies tend to withdraw into themselves, as we will see time and again throughout world history.

The late Tang Dynasty was more oriented toward the civil arts, and more and more welcomed into their midst men of literary talent from undistinguished families. It was also a time in which the Buddhist religion spread rapidly. Confucianism, too, was much stronger at the end of the Tang Dynasty, thanks to the intellectual flowering of the ninth century. During the Tang Dynasty, new technologies contributed significantly to the intellectual flowering of the period. Movable type, porcelain, gunpowder, and mechanical clocks were introduced. The Tang Dynasty was the great age of Chinese Poetry and the Complete Tang Poems include more than 4,800 poems by 2,200 poets. Men who wanted to be recognized as members of the educated elite had to be able to recognize lines quoted from earlier poets' works and write technically proficient poems at social occasions. The skill in composing poetry was so highly respected that it was tested in civil service examinations.

The mid-Tang Dynasty saw several women rise to positions of great power through their hold on rulers. Empress Wu (c. 625–705) even took the throne herself. How did she do it? Like any woman who seized power during this time, she was referred to as an evil seductress and usurper, who took power through her wiles, rather than her political acumen. Wu had entered the emperor's palace in 651 as a lesser consort. One day, the empress had been playing with Wu's baby girl. Wu came in and reportedly smothered her baby to death and blamed it on the empress. The emperor believed Wu, deposed the empress, and placed Wu in her stead. Years later when the emperor suffered a stroke, Empress Wu ruled in his stead. Soon after Wu's son came of age and took the opposite stand from his mother on issues, he died mysteriously, and many suspected that she had poisoned him. The next heir tried to keep a lower profile, but he was accused of plotting a rebellion and was banished and forced to commit suicide. By 690, after many Tang princes tried to accede to the throne only to be stymied in one way or another by Wu, she finally, at age 65, forced the abdication of her son and declared herself emperor. Now, was she really as awful as histories allege? Confucian writers wrote terrible things about her, saying that she had caused "the hearts of fathers and of mothers everywhere not to value the birth of boys, but the birth of girls," and accused her of grotesque tortures and murders, including tossing the dismembered but still living bodies of enemies into wine vats and cauldrons. It is hard really to figure out, but what we will observe is that when another woman takes power in the late nineteenth century in China, she is accused of virtually the same sins as Empress Wu. Later, even Madame Mao is accused of similar atrocities in the twentieth century. The common thread to these three women is that, of course, they are women. One thing that did happen in China during the Tang period was a tradition that deformed women for centuries and was thought to be a sign of beauty and love, that of foot binding.

Song Dynasty

After the fall of the Tang, warlords from several different ethnic identities fought for control of northern China, some of them establishing short-lived dynasties. For some reason, enormous amounts of people began to flee southward toward the Yangtze River, perhaps fleeing northern, Central Asian aggressors. This led to the formation of new power centers far away from the center. In time, the Song dynasty brought political and economic prominence to southern China.

While great flowering did happen, as described below, the cost to the peasant was, as always, rather steep. A change in the tax system left many peasants struggling for survival, and many went from owning land to renting or even becoming landless. As a result, people who used to exert a degree of independence became subject to wealthier people who lived in towns or cities.

The Song period saw the flowering of the **scholar-official class** that was certified through highly competitive **civil service** exams. In contrast to the exams during the

Tang period, the Song Chinese scholar-official class was larger, better educated, and less aristocratic. The spread of printing had aided the expansion of the educated class. With the introduction of printing, the price of books lowered and more Song scholars could afford to buy books. The demand to buy books was fueled by the eagerness to compete in the civil service exams. The Song rulers looked to these exams as a way to identify capable men. The exams were given a measure of legitimacy as to increase confidence in the objectivity of the examiners. The names of test takers were replaced with numbers and clerks recopied each exam so that the handwriting could not be recognized.

While the Song examination system produced four to five times more *jinshi* (presented scholars–the highest examination degree) more than the Tang, it did not decrease the value of the degree, but rather encouraged more men to take the test. While early in the eleventh century fewer than 30,000 men took the initial exams, by the end of that century, nearly 80,000 took the test, and by the end of the dynasty, about 400,000 took the test. Because the number of available posts did not change, each candidate's chances of passing plummeted, reaching as low as 1 in 333 in some places. Men often took the exam several times and were, on average, about 30 years old when they passed.

There had remained a way that young men whose fathers or grandfathers had risen to high rank in the government could allow their sons to by-pass the exam and get a government post. More than 40 percent of the posts in the Song era were filled that way, but those who entered through privilege had to begin at the very bottom. Many would have to spend their entire careers in remote places just collecting taxes and hearing legal cases. Many, not eager to be sent to the back-water, chose to try the civil service exams.

The exam system was quite a long one. Members of the Song scholar-official class would rarely have spent their entire lives in their home counties. Many traveled considerable distances to study with well-known teachers. If they succeeded in the first stage of the exams, they had to travel to the capital for the next stage, held every three years.

In what ways was China by the mid-fourteenth century different from the China of the Sui Dynasty? China's population had nearly doubled! More of the population lived in the south, which had become the undisputed economic center of China. China had become a more commercialized society, with a higher proportion of its farmers engaged in producing for the market, rather than subsistence farming.

Yet some continuities remain. Leaders had looked to some means of improving their rule and staffing their administrations and they came up with the idea of a sort of meritocracy, based on the creation of a civil service exam, or *jinshi*. This exam opened government service to the best qualified individuals, for as long as you could pass the exam, you were hired. The problem was, of course, that the exam was tremendously difficult. So, the few that passed the exam were well qualified. The repercussions of establishing this exam was widespread, for anyone who wanted to have a position in government took this exam. Without a sufficient enough education, the exam would be impossible to pass. So, education, and the public's commitment to it, expanded significantly and became a defining element in this culture.

The Song Dynasty begins, as we see with a powerful neighbor to the north, but, as we shall see in the following sections, the balance of power continued to shift in favor of the north, despite a bigger population in the south.

Mongols

The Mongols were a nomadic people from Central Asia who raised sheep and horses and whose prowess on horses and with archery gave them an enormous advantage over other peoples in the area. For centuries, Mongols were divided into separate clans, each led by a **khan**, who was chosen to lead based on his military and leadership skills. At the end of the twelfth century, a powerful khan named **Temujin** began to conquer his rivals and unite various Mongol tribes. In 1206, he took the title **Genghis Khan,** which means "Universal Ruler." Genghis Khan used his military and organizational skills to unify the Mongol tribes and set the Mongols on a path to conquer an empire that ranged from the Pacific to Eastern Europe.

With a population of about two million and a highly mobile army of 130,000 cavalry, the Mongols forged their empire through superior military technology, innovative battle tactics, and what amounted to effective "PR," as tales of a few conquests so frightened their enemies that many cities just surrendered rather than have to face the Mongols on the battlefield. Certain military advancements made their jobs much easier. For instance, Mongol horsemen could travel up to 90 miles a day—existing for the most part on dried beef and yogurt; they developed saddles and stirrups that enabled them to fire arrows accurately from horseback and could fire up to a range of 300 yards; they developed the tactic of encircling their enemies; they organized their armies in groups of ten, and further divided them into light and heavy cavalries and scouting units, which made for more effective and consistent organization and command; they also mastered the use of spy networks to provide reconnaissance before battles. Communication within the empire worked quite well, despite illiteracy, as Genghis Khan established the first pony express and postal system.

Genghis Khan's empire was divided after his death into **hordes,** or small independent empires. The Kipchak Empire (**Golden Horde)** conquered modern-day Russia and parts of central Asia; the Empire of Persia included the lands west of the Hindu Kush and south of the Caucasus Mountains and Oxus River; the Empire of Chaghatai included China; the Kipchak Empire (Golden Horde) included Russia and parts of central Asia; the Empire of Chaghatai included central Asia, and the Empire of the Great Khan, included Tibet, the Gobi Desert, and China where **Kublai Khan**, **Genghis Khan's** grandson, established the **Yuan** Dynasty. The Yuan Dynasty had numerous achievements that certainly paved the way for tremendous successes for China:

- Peace and prosperity promoted population growth.

- The Grand Canal was extended to Beijing—a feat that enabled the growth of his capital city and facilitated the rice trade from South China into the area.

- Construction of a 1,100-mile-long paved road facilitated trade and communication north to south and linked China to India and Persia.

- Implementation of paper money further facilitated trade.

The Mongols also delved into India under **Timur the Lame, or Tamerlane** to destroy the Delhi Sultanate for a few years—it would be a descendant of Timur, Babar, who would found the Mughal Empire there.

In spite of their reputation, largely written by those they conquered as the Mongols were illiterate, the Mongols brought notable economic progress to much of the area under which they ruled. The empire largely was peaceful, as a vital component of the Mongol's rule was to encourage and protect trade along established trade routes. The period is referred to as the **Pax Mongolica.** It was a time of increased contact with Europe, and internal transportation and communication were improved. One of the trademarks of the *Pax Mongolica* was the spread and exchange of ideas made possible by the peace and owing no small measure to the tax breaks that the Mongols gave teachers and clerics within the empire.

Another reason for the Mongol success was their ability as "diffusers of culture" and their ability to syncretize their ideas with those of their new territories. However, in some areas, notably in China, the Mongols kept their people separate from those that they conquered. Kublai Khan would not allow the Chinese to learn the Mongol language or to intermarry. This would prove to be a problem later as the Chinese would kick the Mongols out in 1368.

Ming Dynasty

In 1368, under the leadership of a peasant named Zhu Yuanzhang and a rebel army, the last of the Mongol emperors was overthrown. Zhu took the name **Hongwu,** which means "vastly martial" and found the Ming Dynasty. With Hongwu and his Ming (which means "brilliant") Dynasty, power in China was once again given back to the native Chinese. During this time, peace prevailed, and Chinese culture grew and flourished. The Ming emperors were determined to eradicate anything from the Mongol past, so they did so by trying to reinvigorate Chinese culture and to recreate the splendors of past dynasties of the Han, Tang, and Song Dynasties. In order to do so, they advocated a strong centralized government based on Confucian principles. With more power in their hands, the emperors were able to push their own agenda onto the whole of China.

One such emperor-led initiative was launched by the emperor Yonglo in which he sent one of his eunuch generals, by the name of **Zeng He,** on world-wide expeditions with enormous fleets to sail throughout Southeast Asia and the Indian Ocean all the way to East Asia and beyond to explore and find new areas to trade. The Chinese felt that there was little of interest abroad, and for mysterious reasons, all of the great fleets of junks were ordered back to China in 1433, never to sail again.

Another characteristic of Ming civilization was that neo-Confucianism was restored as the government's official ideology. The Ming reinforced Confucian division of Chinese society into four classes: the land-owning gentry and scholar-bureaucrats who administered the empire in the name of the emperor, and both groups had a vested interest in preserving the status quo; peasants; artisans; and merchants. As part of this re-Chinafication process, the civil service exam was restored.

Japan

The effect of Chinese civilization on East Asia cannot be denied, and it was their form of government, if not directly controlling areas of East Asia, that certainly exerted their influence and inspired emulation. Japan, because it was relatively isolated from the rest of East Asia, had a history largely determined by their geography. As four main islands chock full of great agricultural soil, off the coast of mainland Asia and surrounded with mountains, Japan was not only able to protect itself from serious invasions, but its contact with foreigners, even with China, was relatively limited.

Early Japanese culture prior to 400 CE remains somewhat of an enigma. It is not until the fifth century that we see the emergence of an important family, called the **Yamato Clan**—this clan emerged as leaders in the fifth century and continues to rule to this day.

Shinto, "the way of the gods," became the religion in Japan where they worshiped the *kami,* which refers to the nature and its forces, both seen and unseen. The goal under Shinto is to become part of the *kami* by following certain rituals and customs. The religion also encourages obedience and proper behavior. The Yamato clan claimed that the emperor was a direct descendant of the sun goddess, one of the main forces in the Shinto religion.

Japan's tenuous relationship with China resulted in periods where contact with it resulted in Chinese influences making their way into Japan. In 522, Korean and Chinese Buddhist missionaries went to Japan and unwittingly ignited a fascination with all things Chinese. While Buddhism did spread quickly in Japan, many Japanese chose instead to blend elements of Buddhism into Shinto or just practice both simultaneously.

Another significant Chinese influence occurred when **Prince Shotoku** in the seventh century borrowed ideas for bureaucratic and legal reforms from the Tang Dynasty. While he didn't get to implement them, they were enacted after his death and referred to as the **Takia Reforms** (645 BCE). These reforms created a centralized government, with a bureaucracy based on the Chinese systems, and a tremendous land redistribution process began in which land was nationalized and then redistributed. Peasant farmers were given land in exchange for a payment of a land tax and rice; the aristocrats retained a large amount of tax-exempt land and control over government offices. The Japanese also created a law code modeled on the one in China. They also borrowed styles of art, medical practices, scientific developments, a system of weights and measures, a calendar, and concepts of government. Two thing though that the Japanese did resist were Confucianism and the civil service exam.

Feudal Japan

In 794, the capital was moved to **Heinan**, which remained the capital until 1869 and today is called Kyoto. During this period, Chinese influence began to wane and the power of the aristocratic families increased. One of those families, the **Fujiwara**, intermarried over and over again with the emperor's family and eventually began to exert real power over the country. While the emperor did continue to rule, he became more of a figurehead and the Fujiwara exerted control of the Japanese government from the early ninth to the mid-twelfth centuries. Under the Fujiwara and during the **Heian period,** Japanese society experienced a golden age. Certainly the period was a boon in terms of the literature produced by aristocratic women. The women of the Heian court enjoyed writing fictional prose. Noblewomen wrote and read in Japanese and because, unlike the men, they were discouraged from learning to read or write Chinese, it was they, rather than the men, whose writings more accurately reflect some of the pure Japanese ideas of the period. Heian women produced some of the best works of early Japanese literature. The greatest writer was **Lady Murasaki Shikibu** who wrote the world's first full-length novel, a tale called *The Tale of Genji*, which describes Heian court life in great detail.

Japanese feudalism developed around the same time as Western Europe, and there are some similar ideas; however, they did develop independently. With power moving toward these aristocratic families and away from the emperor, power was a bit decentralized—particularly the further one got from the capital. Over time, great warrior-landowners living distant from the capital started building up private armies for protection as well as control. Famers and small landowners began to beseech these private armies for protection and traded their land for it. As a result, these landowning heads of armies called *daimyos* became even more powerful and built up private armies; when law and order broke down, farmers and small landowners traded part of their land for protection, and the landowners became even more powerful. Called the daimyos, these lords were a bit like the feudal barons in England and France, and they won the loyalty of the lesser samurai.

In 1338, the Fujiwara were challenged by the Minamoto and after numerous battles and plotting, in 1192, the emperor made Yoritomo Minamoto the title of great general, or *shogun*. The shogun became, like the Fujiwara before them, the real rulers of the country and left the emperor in place as a figurehead only. The shogun, in effect, became a military dictator and had control over the military, military finances, the laws, courts, and appointments. In 1338, real power once again changed hands and the Ashikaga family seized the office of shogun and held it for over 200 years.

Japan's feudal structure looked something like this:

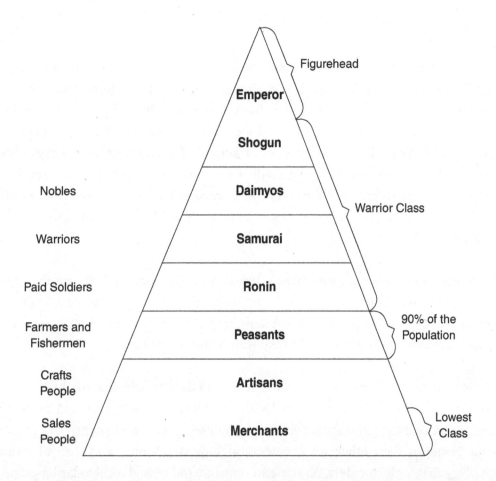

The daimyo were the huge landowners who acted more as the counterparts to the lords of medieval Europe. The daimyo were powerful samurai, who were like knights, only they were part warrior and part nobility. They in turn gave their land to lesser samurai, called **ronin**, who were basically "master-less" samurai who operated more as hired guns for whichever daimyo would pay them. Peasants and artisans worked in the fields and shops to support the samurai class. Just as in European feudalism, the hierarchy was bound together in a land-for-loyalty exchange.

The Samurai (meaning "one who serves") rested their claims to power on the possession of land and prowess with the sword. They followed a code of conduct, similar to the idea of chivalry in Europe—only the samurais were based on different values that reflected their society, called **Bushido,** or the "way of the warrior." The code stressed fidelity, politeness, bravery, virility, simplicity, and honor. If a Samurai failed to meet his obligations under the Code of Bushido, he was expected to commit **seppuku**, or ritual suicide.

Mesoamerica

Much of what we know about Mesoamerican civilization differs substantially from those civilizations that we have reviewed above. Rather than building their cities along river systems, the peoples of the Americas built their cities along the lakes or small rivers. They did not use metals in their tools, and they hardly used metal at all, except for artwork and jewelry. They did not use wheels or animals for transportation (largely because there were no such animals that they could use)—although llamas were used to carry small loads here and there. For the most part, transportation of people and goods was done by land or canoe. Writing systems, except for the Maya and possibly the Olmec, were unknown.

Mesoamerican civilization was largely based on a relationship between the gods and the environment. At Teotihuacan, people worshipped many gods and constructed enormous pyramids devoted to the Sun, the Moon, and to Quetzalcoatl. Human sacrifice was viewed as a sacred duty and essential to the well being of society.

The first distinct Mesoamerican culture was the **Olmecs,** which settled where we find Mexico today, and lived from 1200 to 1400 BCE. Olmec society centered on a priestly elite and peasant farmers and succeeded in producing a large food supply and great stone buildings. Some of their other achievements include developing a system of writing in hieroglyphics that, unfortunately, no one can translate today, and a calendar based on their observations of the heavens. Archaeologists believe that the Olmec, for some religious reasons, carved enormous heads weighing as much as 18 tons out of volcanic rock. This sort of large-scale art work that required the transport of such large rock over 80 miles away indicates that the Olmec must have had a rather sophisticated political and social organizational set-up and that they had a measure of technology that enabled them to carry out such transport. The Olmec civilization disappeared mysteriously around 200 CE.

The **Chavin** lived in the Andes from 900 to 300 BCE. The Chavin were a mostly agricultural society that had developed not only tools and weapons made of various metals, but they also used the llamas native to the area as beasts of burden.

Mayan

From about 300 BCE to 800 CE, the **Maya** peoples, whose descendants still dwell in the same area of the Yucatan peninsula of Mexico, Guatemala, and Belize, had to contend with a tropical climate and fragile soils. Mayan civilization developed around religious centers that became a collection of city-states that were ruled by one king. The Mayans who lived near cities manipulated their environment by draining swamps and building elevated fields and contributed significantly to the Amerindian civilization as they were able to produce enough food to feed their growing population. Their social structure was made up of priests, nobles, and warriors who did not work, a smaller merchant class, and the majority of the people were peasants or slaves.

The Golden Age of Mayan civilization was from 500 to about 850 CE. During that time, the Maya developed not only tremendous cities but also a complex calendar system. They also built impressive religious temples. Rulers served both political and priestly functions and participated in bloodletting rituals and hallucinogenic trances.

It was in **Tikal**, in today's Guatemala, that archaeologists excavated one of the Mayan cities. In the center, Tikal holds five temple pyramids, built about 200 feet high. (George Lucas used one of these as a setting in *Star Wars*). Tikal served as a spiritual and religious center that had enough housing and water cisterns to accommodate up to 50,000 people. At the height of its influence, archaeologists believe that Tikal contained about 1,000 square miles and 360,000 people—an incredible number of people in comparison to the other cities around the world.

The Mayans divided their cosmos into three parts: the heavens above, humans existing in the middle, and the underworld below. The Mayan creation story holds that the gods created humans out of maize and water. They also believed that the gods controlled agricultural cycles in exchange for sacrifices and bloodletting rituals. Much of their religious beliefs were concerned with the set up of time. If they failed to perform certain ceremonies at certain times, death would surely follow. This focus prompted the Mayans to become extremely particular about their calendar, which was based on a number structure of 20. The Mayans also created a system of time that was among the most accurate for its time. Mayan warfare also revolved around religious significance. A certain amount of days of religious ritual would precede a battle. One characteristic of Mayan warfare was that it was centered around the acquisition of slaves, rather than land. The slaves were used in large-scale building projects and in agricultural production. War and disagreements between the various city-states meant that they were often at war with one another and there were many people who were slaves or who became sacrifices.

For mysterious reasons, Mayan civilization collapsed beginning about 850 CE as the people began to abandon their cities. There has been quite a lot of speculation about why this occurred, and the leading reasons seem to be environmental degradation and overuse of land, political dissension, and unrest, natural disaster, and outside invaders.

The Aztecs

Yet another empire, the Aztec confederation that arrived in central Mexico in the mid-1200s was built on a policy of territorial expansion—and a state based on war, human sacrifice, and the veneration of women. Because war was used as a means to solidify their rule, Aztec rulers frequently went to war, promoting divine mandates, seizing land and peasants, and profiting in the spoils of war.

Despite the focus on war, women also held substantial power in Aztec society. Women dominated the household and markets, served as teachers and priestesses, and were seen as the founders of royal lineages. They built their capital at **Tenochtitlan,** which is modern-day Mexico City.

Despite having an empire that reached 12 million people at one point, the Aztecs did not use a bureaucratic form of government—by and large, they allowed people to govern themselves as long as they paid tribute. Roads were built to tie together their vast empire and to make it easier for them to collect taxes or tributes. Because of the improved road systems, under the Aztecs, we see transference of ideas and technology from both the conquerors as well as the conquered.

Farming was done on artificial islands called *Chinampas*. From the peoples they conquered, the Aztecs borrowed architectural techniques, the calendar, and a writing system, not to mention their social system, their religion, and many of their arts and crafts. The Aztec emperor held absolute power and was usually elected by the priestly and warrior elite. The emperor's word was law and he was treated like a god—as such he was considered head of state, commander in chief of the military, and head priest.

The Aztecs were polytheistic, and priests used a sophisticated calendar to determine the feast days of each god. Priests also sought to predict the future by reading signs and sometimes ordered human sacrifice to appease the gods. These sacrifices were most often social marginals of society or recent criminals and slaves. It is estimated that tens of thousands of men and women were killed annually—in 1487, for instance, 20,000 slaves were sacrificed on the steps of Aztec pyramids. Some historians contend that the most plausible reason for the use of human sacrifice was as an instrument of state terrorism. Aztec civili-

zation ended partly because of rebellions and partly due to the arrival of the Spanish conquistadors in 1519.

Andean Society

In the Andean regions of Peru, the Incas, an older civilization, flourished. Unlike the
Aztecs who practiced human sacrifice, the Inca method of control was not terrorism, but
rather imperial unification over the almost 2,000 miles of territory that it covered. Like
the Aztecs, the Inca emperor exercised total power, and he presided over a well-organized
empire. The Incas forced their conquered peoples to adopt the Inca religion, language,
and dress. The Incas built an excellent system of roads, a tremendously large-scale irrigation works, terraced hillsides to control erosion and could grow squash, potatoes, peanuts,
and other crops, had an effective bureaucracy, and enforced the worship of state approved
gods. Inca society was highly regimented, but the state took care of the poor and the aged.

Andean society divided itself into clans called *allyu*, which were expected to provide
labor and goods to their chiefs and to manage the exchange of goods across ecological
boundaries and linked together some 32 million people. Trade became the primary means
of interaction and unification among communities. Each community produced goods that
suited its locale: coastal regions produced maize, fish, and cotton; mountain valleys produced quinoa, potatoes, and tubers; higher elevations contributed wool and metal; and the
Amazonian region provided cocoa, medicines, and fruits. Communications between parts
of the empire were made possible by an elaborate network of roads and bridges. Because
the Incas lacked a written language, they kept records by using the *quipu*, a knotted string
in which the knots were tied in certain ways to mean certain ideas. The Inca also developed a sort of pony express system of communication in which stations were set up every
two miles and runners would deliver messages along the route. It proved to be an effective
means of communication for people who lacked a written language.

The Incan society was polytheistic and the emperor was considered the child of the
sun god, who was at the center of the state religion. Incan religion had a strong moral
aspect to it, as they emphasized rewards for good behavior and punishments for bad
behavior. Their emperors were mummified after the death and they were considered
the intermediaries between the gods and their people. With each new coronation of an
emperor, that usually took place after an all-out war between the various sons of the Incan
rulers, the mummies of previous rulers would be taken out of their palaces, placed atop
chairs, and paraded about to watch the new emperor being crowned. Incan rulers, because

they were considered gods, only married their sisters (with few exceptions), in order to keep their bloodlines pure. In order for an emperor to ensure his place in the afterlife, he had to secure new land, and so the empire was always in a state of expansion.

COMPETENCY 4.4

Identify the major contributions of the Middle Ages, the Renaissance, and the Reformation period to Western civilization.

What are the Middle Ages?

This is a period of time in European history from 476 CE when the Ostrogoth king forced the boy emperor Romulus Augustulus to abdicate, marking the end of the Roman Empire in the west until the Renaissance in the sixteenth century. Once regarded as a time of uninterrupted ignorance, superstition, and social oppression, the Middle Ages are now understood as a dynamic period during which the idea of Europe as a distinct cultural unit emerged. During late antiquity and the early Middle Ages, political, social, economic, and cultural structures were profoundly reorganized, as Roman imperial traditions gave way to those of the Germanic peoples who established kingdoms in the former Western Empire.

We can divide the period into three parts: Lower Middle Ages: 500–1000 CE; High Middle Ages: 1000–1250 CE; and Late Middle Ages: 1250–1500 CE. We will look at the major contributions that each period gave to Western civilization.

Lower Middle Ages: 500–1000 CE

Catholic Church

The fall of the Roman Empire left a vacuum in which the only force capable of providing a basis for social unity was the Roman Catholic Church. During this period, some contributions to Western civilization include:

Monasticism and Monasteries: Monks took on important roles during this time, primarily serving as protectors of a tremendous collection of learning—as monks tended to be one of the few members of European society who could read and write. Many monasteries contained **scriptorium** and libraries where they copied books and compiled **illuminated manuscripts** of various works, most notably religious texts, and preserved some of the books and texts from the ancient Greeks and Romans. The monasteries acted as schools for the upper classes and were sometimes inns, hospitals, or places of refuge in times of war. Monks, like St. Patrick and St. Boniface, also served as missionaries to the "barbarians" and spread the influence of the Catholic Church throughout Europe, eventually making it the major religion of the area. Monasteries also became important reservoirs for horticultural and agricultural skills. Monks were experts with herbs and cultivated their own grains, vegetables, and orchards. From their horticultural activities, the monks collected and developed many medicines. Many unique plants would be kept in monasteries and would become important later, during the Renaissance.

Integrated the Church in the Feudal System: The feudal system was certainly a trademark of medieval Europe, and the Church played an important role in it. The church controlled about one-third of all the lands in Western Europe tax-free, and the members of what the French would refer to as the "First Estate" had enormous amounts of wealth and power throughout the period. The bishops and the abbots played important roles in the feudal system. Some of their and the Church's excesses would be exactly what people would rebel against later, during the Reformation and the French Revolution. The Church demanded **tithe** from the people who lived in Christendom—a tax of one-tenth of one's assets that would be payable to the Church; even peasants had to pay **Peter's Pence**, about 1 penny per person.

Romanesque Architectural Style: The practice of using rounded arches, barrel vaults, thick walls, buildings with dark, simplistic interiors and small windows, usually at the top of a wall typified this architectural style found throughout Europe.

Carolingian Renaissance

Creation of schools: In an effort to reform the church, Charlemagne instituted clerical schools and created centers of learning that would become another hallmark of Western civilization with the unification of church and education. Students in these schools studied religion, music, grammar, and other subjects. Charlemagne invited scholars from all over Europe to come to Aachen to teach and study. The lasting contribution from this system might be the distribution of knowledge throughout Europe, not only because of this scholarly exchange but also because the scholars in their free time copied the ancient texts from Charlemagne's massive collection and sent the texts all over Europe. This enabled many valuable works from the ancient world to be preserved.

Carolingian miniscule: The creation of a script so that the Roman alphabet could be easily read and recognized using capital and small letters to distinguish one word from the next. The script was uniform and contained space between words—advancement that certainly became a standard in all of the languages of Western civilization.

Feudalism: the decentralized political, economic, military, and social system of personal ties and obligations that bound vassals to their lords. The nature of feudalism varied in different areas and changed over time. But at its base were serfs—peasants who were bound to the land. They worked on the demesne, or lord's property, three or four days a week in return for the right to work their own land. In difficult times, the nobles were supposed to provide for the serfs.

Manorialism: Introduction of this economic system in which large estates, granted by the king to nobles, usually encompassed one village populated by serfs and strove for self-sufficiency. By 800 CE, about 60% of Western Europe was enserfed—this meant that there was a contractual agreement between lords, who provided justice and protection, and serfs, who provided their labor for a fixed amount of time each year. Large manors might incorporate several villages. The lands surrounding the villages were usually divided into long strips, with common land in-between. Ownership was divided among the lord and his serfs (also called *villeins*). The Black Death effectively ended manorialism. A long-term effect of feudalism and manorialism was agricultural surpluses. With these surpluses, eventually some members of the society were relieved from agricultural production and could move into other specialized areas. As a result, we see the emergence of craftspeople and the growth of towns and cities. With increased crafts, Europeans began to look to trade more with others and these skilled craftspeople began to earn extra money—this led to the development of a banking system and eventually a "middle class."

Crusades: The increased authority of the papacy and the relative decline in the power of the emperor became clear in the unforeseen emergence of the Crusades as a major preoccupation of Europe. Gregory VII hoped to lead an army to defend Eastern Christians after their disastrous defeat by the Seljuq Turks at Manzikert (present Malazgirt, Turkey) in 1071. Faced with the loss of Asia Minor and the continued expansion of the Turks, the Byzantine emperor Alexius I Comnenus (1057–1118) appealed for help to Pope Urban II in 1095. Urban's celebrated call to the Crusade at Clermont (France) in 1095 was unexpectedly effective, placing him at the head of a large army of volunteers motivated by religious zeal and other more-mundane concerns.

Although the capture of Jerusalem (1099) and the establishment of a Latin kingdom in Palestine were offset by disasters and quarrels, the papacy gained greatly in prestige and strengthened its position in relation to the emperor and Germany, which avoided participation in this first of many Crusades because of the ongoing Investiture Controversy. For more than two centuries, the Crusades remained a powerful movement headed by the pope. Numerous Crusades were waged in the Holy Land, and the Crusading ideal was applied to military and religious campaigns in Spain and Eastern Europe. Later popes launched Crusades against heretics and opponents of papal authority and sanctioned the emergence of military orders. The Crusades thus reflected the widespread devotion to the church and to its leader, the pope.

Rise of European Monarchies

As feudalism created layers of conflicting laws, customs, and traditions, many of the feudal courts that were established under the purview of dukes and earls often issued judgments that were contrary to those of the monarchs, threatening their authority and rule. The kings of England, Spain, France, and Portugal decided to take action and did so by centralizing governmental offices and placing officials throughout the kingdom to represent royal interests and solidifying national boundaries. These efforts met with considerable obstacles, most notably internal dissension, riots, wars, and other difficulties.

High Middle Ages: 1000–1250

The High Middle Ages were marked by economic and territorial expansion, demographic and urban growth, the emergence of national identity, and the restructuring of secular and ecclesiastical institutions. It was the era of the Crusades, Gothic art and architecture, the papal monarchy, the birth of the university, the recovery of ancient Greek thought, and the soaring intellectual achievements of St. Thomas Aquinas (c. 1224–74). During this period, the principle of common law was established in England by Henry II. He also created the idea of a grand jury, trial by jury and wrote a charter extending certain promises to his barons.

Division into three social classes:

1. **Clergy:** In charge of spiritual matters to save souls

2. **Nobility:** Landowners whose job was to be there to protect their subjects

3. **Third Estate:** Everyone else—middle class, peasants, serfs, slaves

The Magna Carta

While earlier kings of England—Henry I, Stephen, and Henry II—had issued charters, making promises or concessions to their barons, they were not threatened and the agreements were broadly phrased. The steady growth of the administration during the 12th century weakened the barons' position vis-à-vis the crown. But the need for heavy taxation for the Third Crusade, and for the ransom of Richard I after his capture by the Holy Roman emperor Henry VI, increased his successor's difficulties. John's position was further weakened by a rival claim to the throne and the French attack upon John's Duchy of Normandy. In 1199, 1201, and 1205 John's barons had to be promised their "rights;" his financial exactions increased after his loss of Normandy (1204), and, during his quarrel (1208–13) with Pope Innocent III. It is, therefore, not surprising that after 1213 Stephen Langton, archbishop of Canterbury, directed baronial unrest into a demand for a solemn grant of liberties by the king. The document, known as the Articles of the Barons, was at last agreed upon and sealed by John on June 15, 1215, at Runnymede (beside the River Thames, between Windsor and Staines, now in the county of Surrey). During the next several days the document went through further modifications and refinements, and the final version of the Magna Carta was accepted by the king and the barons on June 19.

Although written in stages, the charter has been traditionally discussed as consisting of a preamble and 63 clauses. Roughly, its contents may be divided into nine groups. The first concerned the church, asserting that it was to be "free." A second group provided statements of feudal law of particular concern to those holding lands directly from the crown, and the third assured similar rights to subtenants. A fourth group of clauses referred to towns, trade, and merchants. A particularly large group was concerned with the reform of the law and of justice, and another with control of the behavior of royal officials. A seventh group concerned the royal forests, and another dealt with immediate issues, requiring, for instance, the dismissal of John's foreign mercenaries. The final clauses provided a form of security for the king's adherence to the charter, by which a council of 25 barons should have the ultimate right to levy war upon him should he seriously infringe it. The language found in the United States constitution as well state constitutions can be traced to the Magna Carta.

Development of Gothic Architectural Style

Set up the Gothic style of pointed arches, high narrow vaults, thinner walls than the earlier Romanesque style, contained flying buttresses, elaborate, ornate, airier interiors with stained glass windows. Over time, the Gothic cathedrals became more than places of worship as the Church sponsored artists and sculptors to decorate them with their work. Much of the development of artwork then is centered on religion during this period.

Town Growth

- A Middle class formed as a separate group

  - **Burghers** wealthy merchants who lived within a walled town

  - **Bourgeoisie**

- **Hanseatic League**

  - With increased trade, towns with a lot of wealthy merchants in them arose near the manors. The wealthy merchants, called **burghers**, became politically powerful and eventually wanted to unite with other towns to control trade. The **Hanseatic League** was an economic alliance in northern Europe of guilds and trading cities who controlled trade.

- **Crusades:** European attempts to take over the Holy Land from the eleventh to fourteenth centuries

  - Helped to renew interest in the "ancient world" during this period.

  - Expanded trade routes across the Mediterranean, through Anatolia, and the Levant.

  - Marked the souring of relations between Europe and the Byzantine Empire, particularly after the Crusaders attacked and sacked Constantinople, a Christian city.

- With more contact with people outside of Europe, ideas and thinking expanded and people actually began to question old ways of thinking—citing **reasoning.**

- The Church responded to this by clamping down against what it termed as **heresies.**

- **Scholasticism**

- As people began to expand their way of thinking, more institutions began to develop to explore ideas; these **universities** inspired a greater movement to study some of the ideas and advances made in the Muslim cultures, ideas from law, science, philosophy, and medicine. As more of the texts from the ancient world that had been housed in the Muslim world for centuries made their way to Europe, the ideas of Aristotle, Ptolemy, and other Greeks were brought back to Europe to be studied.

- **Technological Advances:** enabled increased productivity, increased population, and growth in towns

  - **Heavier plow**

  - **Horse collar**

  - **Weapons for those on horseback**: development of axes, pikes, lances, and two-edged swords longer than those used by men on foot

  - **Three-field system**: Change from the two-field system to the three-field system allowed for more productivity, and in turn, this enabled people to be better fed, and in turn allowed them to be healthier and learn better.

Late Middle Ages: 1250–1500

- **Banking:** Developments in banking during this period centered on the banking institutions that had developed a little earlier in Florence, inspired by the Church backing off of its prohibition against charging interest. By 1338, there were 80 banking houses in Florence alone that had operations throughout Europe that would prove to be an important component of Western civilization. The greatest danger to banking was the demands from monarchs to help them finance wars—something too difficult to refuse. Banks could and did charge enormous amounts of interests to these monarchs, but nothing really could be done if a monarch refused to pay back a loan.

- **Black Death:** The first round of the Black Death struck Europe from 1347–1349 and killed between one-third and one-half of Europe's population. The effect on the region was immense, physically, socially, psychologically, economically, and spiritually. It also helped usher both the Reformation and the Renaissance. Black Death contributed to the elimination of the feudal system because of a loss of labor force and enforcement measures.

- **Parliament:** The establishment of a Parliament, by 1400, in which there were two houses: House of Lords and a House of Commons

- **Guilds:** The establishment of guilds dominated the world of the artisans. It was a controlled membership system in which a person moved from apprentice to journeyman to master craftsman according to their proficiency in a certain trade. This resulted in not only quality-controlled merchandise and controlled prices but also the beginnings of unions.

- **Inquisition:** Under **Pope Innocent IV**, in 1252, heretics against religious dogma were rooted out and attacked, interrogated, tried, and executed. Between 1265 and 1273, **Thomas Aquinas** wrote *Summa Theologica,* in which he asserted that faith and reason were not in conflict but rather were gifts from God that could be used to enhance each other.

The Renaissance (1300–1600)

The Renaissance, which literally means "rebirth," emphasized new learning, including the rediscovery of much classical material, and new art styles. Italian city-states, such as Venice, Milan, Padua, Pisa, and especially Florence, were the home to many Renaissance developments, which were limited to the rich elite.

Crusades and New Trade Routes gave Europeans contact with more advanced civilizations, inspired new ways of thinking.

Because of scandals that occurred, the Church lost much of its power, and people began to doubt its ultimate authority

Conditions that led to the Renaissance

With increased trade, and growth of middle classes, new ways of thinking emerged that reflected more desires for worldly goods and less concern about life in the hereafter

Competition among wealthy patrons led to developments in education and art, since wealthy people battled each other through sponsorship of scholars and artists

Humanism

Humanism was a new philosophy that really defined the Renaissance. It consisted of four main aspects:

1. Admiration and emulation of the Ancient Greeks and Romans

2. Philosophy of enjoying this life, instead of just waiting for the next one

3. The glorification of humans and the belief that individuals can do anything

4. The belief that humans deserved to be the center of attention

Basically the idea found, as intellectuals delved more into the writings and ideas of the ancient Greeks and Romans, that they were struck with the ancients' complete lack of preoccupation with ideas of salvation and afterlife that had dominated medieval thoughts and had actually resulted in societies becoming less concerned with improving their living conditions. They had felt that life on Earth was just something to get through on the way to heaven, rather than, as the ancient Greeks and Romans thought, that life was important andshould be enjoyed and human accomplishments in the scholarly, artistic, and political realms should be celebrated. Although it was a movement chiefly found among intellectuals, it had a huge impact on the age. Though many believe that humanism replaced religion in the Renaissance, in reality, the two coexisted. Most humanists were actually religious, and the only difference between the beliefs of church and of the humanists was that the humanists believed that this life was important and should be enjoyed, while the church did not, and felt that people should focus on awaiting the afterlife instead.

One impact of Humanism that has in turn dominated Western ideas even today is the concern and focus on the individual and individuality and a subsequent lessening of the import or authority of institutions.

Main Humanists

- **Petrarch** (1304–1374) was the first humanist of the Renaissance who felt that only true examples of moral and proper behavior could come from the Ancients.

- **Boccaccio** (1313–1375) was a writer who became famous for a collection of short stories called *The Decameron* that is now thought of as the first prose masterpiece ever written in Italian and was written to amuse, not edify, the reader. In it, Boccaccio tells the story of a young group [?] of Florentines who went to a secluded villa to escape the plague and began telling stories. It was considered groundbreaking because of its frank treatment of relationships and its creation of ordinary, realistic characters.

- **Baldassare Castiglione** wrote *The Courtier* about conversations between men and women of the court of Count Urbino and became a manual of proper behavior for gentlemen and ladies for centuries to come.

- **Guarino da Verona** and **Vittorino da Feltre** were educators who turned the ideals of the humanists into a practical curriculum. They founded a school in which students learned Latin, Greek, mathematics, music, philosophy, and social graces.

Literature, Art, and Scholarship

Humanists, as both orators and poets, were inspired by and imitated works of the classical past. The literature was more secular and wide-ranging than that of the Middle Ages.

- **Dante** (1265–1321) was a Florentine writer whose *Divine Comedy*, describing a journey through hell, purgatory, and heaven, shows that reason can only take people so far and that God's grace and revelation must be used.

- **Petrarch** encouraged the study of ancient Rome, collected and preserved work of ancient writers, and produced much work in the classical literary style.

Artists also broke with the medieval past, in both technique and content. Renaissance art sometimes used religious topics but often dealt with secular themes or portraits of individuals. Oil paints, chiaroscuro, and linear perspectives produced works of energy in three dimensions. Paintings tended to have more detailed backgrounds, were more realistic, and were more geometrically precise. Subjects also tended to show more emotion than in the paintings of earlier artists.

- **Leonardo da Vinci** (1452–1519) produced numerous works, including *The Last Supper* and *Mona Lisa*.

- **Michelangelo** (1475–1564) produced masterpieces in architecture, sculpture (*David*), and painting (the Sistine Chapel ceiling). His work was a bridge to a new, non-Renaissance style called Mannerism.

- **Raphael** (1483–1520) Used his mastery of perspective and ancient styles to produce works of harmony, beauty, and serenity and convey a sense of peace; represented these skills in *The School of Athens*.

- **Titian** (1479–1576) was a painter who painted scenes of luxury in such a vivid, immediate way that his paintings seem real to the viewer.

Renaissance scholars were more practical and secular than medieval ones. Manuscript collections enabled scholars to study the primary sources and to reject all traditions that had been built up since classical times. Also, scholars participated in the lives of their cities as active politicians.

- **Leonardo Bruni** (1370–1444), a civic humanist, served as chancellor of Florence, where he used his rhetorical skills to rouse the citizens against external enemies.

- **Machiavelli** (1469–1527) wrote *The Prince*, which analyzed politics from the standpoint of expedience. His work, amoral in tone, describes how a political leader could obtain and hold power by acting only in his own self-interest.

The Reformation

The Reformation destroyed Western Europe's religious unity and introduced new ideas about the relationships between God, the individual, and society. Its course was greatly influenced by politics and led, in most areas, to the subjection of the church to the political rulers. It also divided the Western Church into two halves: Catholicism and Protestantism.

Long-Term Causes of the Reformation

- Growth in the power of the secular king and the decrease in the power of the Pope

- Popular discontent with the empty Church rituals

- Movement towards more personal ways of communicating with God

- Fiscal crisis in the Church that led to corruption and abuses of power

Short-Term Causes of the Reformation

- **John Wycliffe** and his supporters, the Lollards, argued for a simplification of Church doctrine and a lessening of priests' power and questioned the idea of transubstantiation.

- **Jan Hus** burned at the stake in 1415 after he argued that the priests weren't a holy group, questioned transubstantiation, and said that the priest and the people should all have both the wine and the bread.

His followers fought and won against the emperor, who let them to set up their own church (the Utraquist Church).

- **The Avignon Exile and Great Schism** both undermined the power and prestige of the Church and made many question the absolute power of the Papacy.

- **The Printing Press** enabled quick distribution of ideas from those dissatisfied with the church, and now people could read the Bible for themselves and make up their own minds about truths.

Martin Luther (1483–1546)

Martin Luther, to his personal distress, could not reconcile the problem of the sinfulness of the individual with the justice of God. "How could a sinful person attain the righteousness necessary to obtain salvation?" he wondered. During his studies of the Bible, especially of Romans 1:17, Luther came to believe that personal efforts—good works such as a Christian life and attention to the sacraments of the church—could not "earn" the sinner salvation, but that belief and faith were the only way to obtain grace. By 1515, Luther believed that "justification by faith alone" was the road to salvation. On October 31, 1517, Luther nailed **95 theses**, or statements, about indulgences, the cancellation of a sin in return for money, to the door of the Wittenberg church and challenged the practice of selling them. At this time, he was seeking to reform the church, not divide it.

In 1519, Luther presented various criticisms of the church and was driven to say that only the Bible, not religious traditions or papal statements, could determine correct religious practices and beliefs. In 1521, Pope Leo X excommunicated Luther for his beliefs. In 1521, Luther appeared in the city of Worms before a meeting (Diet) of the important figures of the Holy Roman Empire,. including the Emperor, Charles V. He was again condemned. At the Diet of Worms, Luther made his famous statement about his writings and the basis for them: "Here I stand. I can do no other." After this, Luther could not go back; the break with the pope was permanent. Frederick III of Saxony, the ruler of the territory in which Luther resided, protected Luther in Wartburg Castle for a year. Frederick never accepted Luther's beliefs but protected him because Luther was his subject. The weak political control of the Holy Roman Emperor contributed to Luther's success in avoiding the Pope's and the Emperor's penalties.

Other Reformers

- **Anabaptist** (derived from a Greek word meaning "to baptize again") is a name applied to people who rejected the validity of child baptism and believed that such children had to be re-baptized when they became adults. A prominent leader was Menno Simons (1496–1561). Anabaptists sought to return to the practices of the early Christian church, which was a voluntary association of believers with no connection to the state. Anabaptists adopted pacifism and avoided involvement with the state whenever possible.

- In 1536, **John Calvin** (1509–1564), a Frenchman, arrived in Geneva, a Swiss city-state which had adopted an anti-Catholic position. He left after his first efforts at reform failed. Upon his return in 1540, Geneva became the center of the Reformation. Calvin's *Institutes of the Christian Religion* (1536), a strictly logical analysis of Christianity, had a universal appeal. Calvin emphasized the doctrine of predestination (God knew who would obtain salvation before those people were born) and believed that church and state should be united. Calvinism triumphed as the majority religion in Scotland, under the leadership of John Knox (ca. 1514–1572), and in the United Provinces of the Netherlands. Puritans in England and New England also accepted Calvinism.

- **Reform in England:** England underwent reforms in a pattern different from the rest of Europe. Personal and political decisions by the rulers determined much of the course of the Reformation there, when in 1533, **Henry VIII** defied the pope and turned to Archbishop Thomas Cranmer to dissolve his marriage to **Catherine of Aragon**. Protestant beliefs and practices made little headway during Henry's reign, as he accepted transubstantiation, enforced celibacy among the clergy, and otherwise made the English church conform to most medieval practices. Under Henry VIII's son, Edward VI (1547–1553), who succeeded to the throne at age 10, the English church adopted Calvinism. Clergy were allowed to marry, communion by the laity expanded, and images were removed from churches. Doctrine included justification by

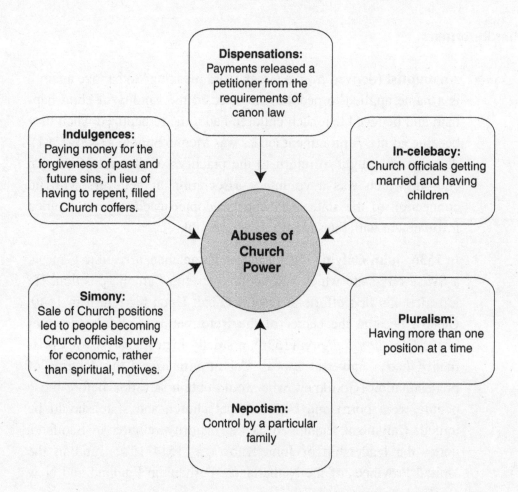

faith, the denial of transubstantiation, and only two sacraments. Some reformers wanted to purify (hence "Puritans") the church of its remaining Catholic aspects. The resulting church, Protestant in doctrine and practice but retaining most of the physical possessions, such as buildings, and many of the powers, such as church courts, of the medieval church, was called Anglican.

The Counter Reformation

The Counter Reformation brought changes to the portion of the Western church which retained its allegiance to the pope. **Ignatius of Loyola** (1491–1556), a former soldier, founded the Society of Jesus in 1540 to lead the attack on Protestantism. Jesuits became the leaders of the Counter Reformation. The Sack of Rome in 1527, when soldiers of the Holy Roman Emperor captured and looted Rome, was seen by many as a judgment of God against the lives of the Renaissance popes. In 1534, Paul III became pope and attacked abuses while reasserting papal leadership.

The Wars of Religion (1560–1648)

The period from approximately 1560 to 1648 witnessed continuing warfare, primarily between Protestants and Catholics. In the latter half of the sixteenth century, the fighting was along the Atlantic seaboard between Calvinists and Catholics; after 1600, the warfare spread to Germany, where Calvinists, Lutherans, and Catholics fought.

- **The Catholic Crusade:** The territories of **Charles V**, the Holy Roman Emperor, were divided in 1556 between Ferdinand, Charles's brother, and Philip II (1556–1598), Charles's son. Ferdinand received Austria, Hungary, Bohemia, and the title of Holy Roman Emperor. Philip received Spain, Milan, Naples, the Netherlands, and the New World. It was Philip, not the pope, who led the Catholic attack on Protestants. Spain dominated the Mediterranean following a series of wars led by Philip's half-brother, Don John, against Moslem (largely Turkish) forces. Don John secured the Mediterranean for Christian merchants with a naval victory over the Turks at Lepanto off the coast of Greece in 1571. Portugal was annexed by Spain in 1580 following the death of the king without a clear successor. This gave Philip the only other large navy of the day as well as Portuguese territories around the globe.

- **England and Spain:** England was ruled by two queens, **Mary I** (reigned 1553–1558), who married Philip II, and then **Elizabeth I** (reigned 1558–1603), while three successive kings of France from 1559 to 1589 were influenced by their mother, **Catherine de' Medici** (1519–1589). Mary I sought to make England Catholic. She executed many Protestants, earning the name "Bloody Mary" from opponents. Mary married Philip II, king of Spain, and organized her foreign policy around Spanish interests. They had no children. Elizabeth I, a Protestant, achieved a religious settlement between 1559 and 1563 that left England with a church governed by bishops and practicing Catholic rituals but maintaining a Calvinist doctrine. Catholics participated in several rebellions and plots. **Mary, Queen of Scots**, had fled to England from Scotland in 1568, after alienating the nobles there. In Catholic eyes, she was the legitimate queen of England. Several plots and rebellions to put Mary on the throne led to her execution in 1587. Elizabeth was formally excommunicated by the pope in 1570. In 1588, as part of his crusade and to stop England from supporting the rebels in the Netherlands, Philip II sent the Armada, a fleet of more than 125 ships, to convey troops from the Netherlands to England as part of a plan to make England Catholic. The Armada was defeated by a combination of superior English naval tactics and a wind that made it impossible for the Spanish to accomplish their goal. A peace treaty between Spain and England was signed in 1604, but England remained an opponent of Spain.

- **The Thirty Years' War:** Calvinism was spreading throughout Germany. The Peace of Augsburg (1555), which settled the disputes between Lutherans and Catholics, had no provision for Calvinists. Lutherans gained more territories through conversions and often took control of previous church-states—a violation of the Peace of Augsburg. A Protestant alliance under the leadership of the Calvinist ruler of the Palatinate opposed a Catholic League led by the ruler of Bavaria. Religious wars were common. The war brought great destruction to Germany, leading to a decline in population of perhaps one-third, or more, in some areas. Germany remained divided and without a strong government until the nineteenth century. After 1648, warfare, though often containing religious elements, would not be executed primarily for religious goals. The Catholic crusade to reunite Europe failed, largely due to the efforts of the Calvinists. The religious distribution of Europe has not changed significantly since 1648. Nobles, resisting the increasing power of the state, usually dominated the struggle. France, then Germany, fell apart due to the wars. France was reunited in the seventeenth century. Spain began a decline that ended its role as a great power of Europe.

COMPETENCY 4.5

Identify the social, cultural, political, and economic characteristics of African, Asian, and Eastern European societies from 1500 to 1900.

Africa

Social

All of the African societies had religious systems, and those that followed what we might term "African Traditional Religion" had the following components in common:

- Belief in a supreme God

- Belief in several divinities or lesser gods

- Belief in ancestors

- Belief in life after death

- Belief in reincarnation

- Belief in the power of the spoken word, like incantations and songs

- Belief in prayers

- Belief in sacrifice

- All had roles for priests, holy men, seers, and spirit mediums

Other religions, widely established elsewhere in the world, also found homes in Africa as Christianity, Islam, and Judaism flourished in different parts of the continent.

By far the biggest social impact in Africa during this period was the emergence of the slave trade, which depopulated tremendous areas throughout Africa. Typically the Atlantic slave trade sought men and the Eastern slave trade to the Islamic empires sought women. It is estimated that between 1500 and 1900, over 12 million Africans were taken just in the Atlantic slave trade alone, and perhaps as much as 50 million were taken altogether. The effects on the various societies were tremendous and are still being felt today as the continent still struggles to recover from the loss of almost 400 years of losing its strongest men and women. When many of the able-bodied people from ages 18–40 are removed from a civilization, it affects it in numerous directions—economically, socially, culturally, and politically.

Portugal was one of the first European countries to plunder the African continent in search of slaves. They first targeted Northern Mauritania in 1444 and eventually moved their way down the western coast of Africa. The Dutch, French, Spanish, and British soon followed in their footsteps.

Some of the ramifications of the slave trade were as follows:

- As the profit from Africans selling Africans into slavery was tremendous, many Africans engaged in the trade. Slavery itself was not a new concept in Africa, and most families actually had slaves in them. Because private land ownership was largely absent during this time, slaves were one of the few forms of wealth-producing property that Africans could possess. But slavery within African societies was different than the Atlantic Slave Trade experiences. In Africa, usually slaves were taken in times of war, they were allowed to marry and have children, and they were treated well within the household. In an effort to get more slaves to sell to the white slave sellers, more societies launched wars deeper and deeper within the African continent in order to meet the demand.

- The loss of so many able-bodied men from Africa made it rather easy for the continent to be colonized as Africa's ability to defend itself was compromised.

- Little development or modernization took place.

- In an effort to meet the demands of the slave trade, laws were changed that made crimes punishable by slavery.

- Populations in the cities decreased as people fled cities to avoid being captured. Without cities, civilization begins to suffer.

- Contact with the outside world became quite limited as slave-traders no longer brought with them new ideas or technologies.

- Racism took hold as blacks were thought to be less intelligent.

- Africa was seen as a cheap source of labor.

- Slave exports helped create a number of large and powerful kingdoms that relied on a constant warfare to generate the great numbers of human captives required for trade with the Europeans.

- The Yoruba kingdom of Oyo on the Guinea coast, founded sometime before 1500, used its rather large army and iron technology to capture tremendous numbers of slaves and sell them.

- In the nineteenth century, the kingdom of Dahomey, in what is now the Republic of Benin, became a major slave holder.

- The Kongo also became big slave exporters, starting their relationship with the Portuguese as early as 1483. The Kongo exported slaves and ivory in exchange for European luxury goods and guns. The Kongo developed in what would become a typical pattern for those African countries who engaged in the trade. Over time, as the Kongo sought to find more and more slaves to trade, the country focused itself on trying to find slaves, and as a result productive workers were removed from the area and an economy developed that was dependent upon slavery. Over time, the Kong became more dependent upon the Portuguese and was unable to provide basic necessities for it. Over time, Portuguese desire for slaves undermined the authority of the kings of the Kongo and the state gradually declined. Eventually war broke out and the kingdom was mostly destroyed.

- The Asante Kingdom on the Gold Coast of West Africa also became a major slave exporter in the eighteenth century.

Cultural

African music took a central role in almost all African societies. There was music for almost all occasions—work, naming ceremonies, marriages, funerals, etc.

African art was inspired by religion, kingship, and personal beautification. Traditionally art was made for the upper classes and royalty, but we see that in the 1500s–1900s, it becomes accessible to all. Some of the art forms included specialized wood, bronze, brass and stone sculptures, painting of homes, body adornments, charms, and amulets.

The cultural effects of the slave trade were also numerous:

- Areas hit hardest by the slave trade suffered from shortages of men.

- In areas where there were more women than men, women were thrust into roles previously occupied by the men. Because there were so few men, polygamy increased dramatically.

- Religious beliefs changed in Africa—introduction of Christianity and Islam to regions.

Political

In terms of political development throughout the African continent, we see a few major trends:

- The rise of empires and nation/states:
  - Ghana, Mali, and Songhai
  - Kanem, Bornu, and Hausa States
  - Ife, Oyo, Benin, Dahomey, Asante, and Kongo

Another political trend we see in Africa during this time is the appearance of European exploration that proved to be disastrous for the continent. Europeans came to Africa for the three G's: God, Government, and Glory. There were numerous effects from European exploration in Africa during this period:

- Trade in gold, ivory, and pepper certainly increased.

- Along the coast, Africans were kidnapped and sold into slavery, thus igniting the beginnings of the Trans-Atlantic slave trade.

- Forts and castles were constructed.

- Benin slipped into corruption and decay.

- South Africa and Mozambique began to have substantial European influence.

- The introduction of European weapons changed the balances of power that existed on the continent.

Economic

Throughout the continent, we see a few trends happening from 1500–1900. The pastoral economies, like those of the Fulani, Maasai, and Somali, are becoming more complex as three types of pastoral societies emerged: nomadic pastoralists, transhumant pastoralists, and agro-pastoralists (mixed farmers). As these agricultural economies expanded, famers successfully supplied the food needed for the population, and in time, surplus food enabled a market economy to develop.

Manufacturing also began to take off. Some of the main manufacturing that occurred were tanning from hides and skins, metallurgy, and textile manufacturing.

The slave trade shifted the existing trade routes within Africa, causing earlier, profitable trading patterns and routes to disappear.

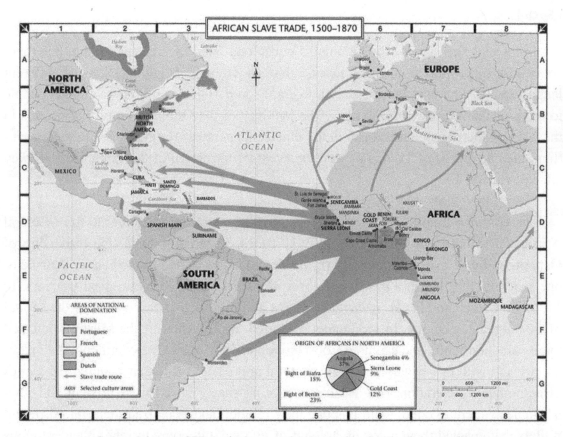

Source: Princeton QED (qed.princeton.edu) governed by Creative Commons license.

Asia

An important development during the early modern years was the development of the Gunpowder Empires. During this period, huge empires developed that were able to grow in part because of their adaptation of gunpowder to their armies. The Mongol invasions were significant because their knowledge of firepower and arms made those who were wiped out marginal. The Mongols also brought something called *yasa* law, secular law, and imposed it on the communities they conquered, and which the Ottomans later adopted as well. Both the Ottomans and Safavids also benefited from the introduction of gunpowder, guns, and canons and used them to gain a technological advantage over the Europeans. The Ottomans, Safavids, Mughals, and rulers of China and Japan were able to capitalize on that power, and so began a period of cultural efflorescence in which they were able to assume a great deal of political power, build opulent cities, and flourish in the arts.

Ottoman Empire

Social

The social structure of the Ottoman Empire consisted of a cosmopolitan, heterogeneous mix of peoples from many races, religions, ethnicities, and speakers of different languages. The Ottoman Empire sought to erase some of these differences and get people to think of themselves as "Ottoman." The inability of the Ottoman Empire to do this in the wake of increasing nationalism in the nineteenth century eventually led to its dismantling, the emergence of "Turkism," and the eventual formation of the Republic of Turkey after World War I.

The Ottoman Empire emerged from small tribal groups that had come from Central Asia and had been one of the Seljuk Turks tribes. Eventually, under the leadership of **Osman**, a *ghazi* warrior, little ouliks (princedoms) began to be grouped under the rule of one state and thus began a process of absorptions that attracted more ghazi warriors. In 1326, the Osman and his army captured Bursa and used it as a base to set up the capital of the burgeoning empire. In 1453 under **Mehmed the Conqueror**, the Muslims defeated the Byzantine Empire and captured Constantinople. They made Constantinople their capital city and with that began their multi-cultural approach to rule that featured the tactics of assimilation, toleration, and accommodation as they allowed the Christian and Jewish subjects there to continue to practice their religion and organized them into different **millets** that enabled them a certain amount of internal autonomy to retain their religious authorities, administer justice in matters of personal law (like marriage, inheritance, etc), and regulate their own economic, social, and legal affairs. Non-Muslims did have a degree of freedom in that they did not have to serve in the military. However, as Peoples of the Book, they were allowed to practice their own religion in freedom, but they did have to pay taxes (on the other hand, Muslims did not have to pay taxes, but they did have to serve in the military).

There were two main social groups in the Ottoman society: the ruling class and the subjects. Total loyalty and devotion to the sultan and the Ottoman State were the chief requirements for someone to belong to the ruling class. Since this was the only determining line between the ruling class and the subjects, there was a lot of mobility in the social structure. There were four main groups in the ruling class. First was the palace section, which provided leadership with the sultan at the head of the class. Then there was the military, the Janissaries, who protected the empire and expanded into new areas. Next was the treasury, in charge of taxes. Finally, there was the religious section with the **uleman** (religious scholars) who made sure that the Shari'ah, Muslim religious law, was followed, and formed mosques and schools. Ottoman subjects were largely divided according to occupation groups. The *askeri* or peasants farmed the land that was leased to them by the government; artisans crafted and were organized into craft guilds; merchants traded goods; and pastorals were divided into clans led by a bey, hereditary chief.

One issue that the Ottomans had to resolve was not only how to expand, but how to continue to expand and how to meld these areas into the Ottoman Empire. One tactic that they used was the slave system. The system, however, was quite unlike the slave system that we see in the Americas. The Ottoman slave system allowed for slaves to be educated and trained and to accumulate money and power. They found their slaves primarily in two places: the Balkans and the Caucuses. Through something called **devshirme** or "boy tax," boys periodically were taken from the Christian villages and moved to various parts of the Ottoman Empire where they would work in a variety of fields. In the sorting process, the Ottomans would use a science called **phrenology,** where they determined a boy's capabilities through an examination of the bumps on his head. The lucky few would be taken to Istanbul, converted to Islam, trained, educated, and then entered service as **Janissaries**, the military arm of the Ottoman Empire. Female slaves were brought to serve in domestic settings and they typically came from the Caucasus region. Some female slaves were brought into the Sultan's harem where they would undergo vigorous education, training in the hope of being married to an Ottoman official. Only very few were ever chosen to be the sexual partners of the Sultan.

Women did not have as much access to public power as men did; however, women in elite households, especially those in the Sultan's household, could be rather powerful political actors. Women could hold and inherit property, conduct business, run charitable foundations (control of *waqf*), and defend their interests in Islamic courts.

Cultural

Coffee houses were a center of male public life. They were places where they could drink coffee, naturally, but also they could trade news and public gossip as well as see entertainment by storytellers and musicians.

The **hamam** (bathhouse) also served a vital function in Ottoman society where ideas could be exchanged and alliances forged. Women in particular used the *hamam* as a place to arrange marriages, heal rifts between families, and conduct business.

Under **Suleiman the Magnificent**, from 1520–1566, Ottoman culture reached its zenith as he poured money into public construction, financing learning institutions and the arts. Architects, most notably **Sinan**, a Janissary of Armenian descent, built magnificent mosques and palaces, bridges, and other public buildings throughout Anatolia. During this time, there were great literary and artistic achievements that rivaled the achievements of the European Renaissance.

Political

As head of the Ottoman empire, the Sultan (which means "power holder") had immense power, issued all laws, and made all major decisions. He did, however, have numerous advisors—mostly gained from the Janissary training. Typically, the sons of the Sultan, until the reign of Suleiman the Magnificent, would be sent away at a young age to the provinces and given an area to rule. This period acted as a training ground for them, as they, with their mother's help, would have to amass a retinue of advisors and learn how to rule. There was no system of primogeniture like there was in Europe. Instead, the next sultan was chosen by his ability to eliminate all of his brothers—or fratricide. If a ruler had many offspring, it increased the number of candidates for power. So, questions arose about how to resolve succession issues: the rule of thumb became that those sons closest to the capital at the death of the ruler would win, or fratricide provided an option. The first ten Ottoman rulers were very capable because of their skill, military prowess, and they did not practice too much bloodletting. By 1617, the lust for fratricide began to wane and instead the siblings would be locked up in gilded cages instead of killing them.

Another important power-holder in the Ottoman Empire was the **valide-sultan**, or the Sultan's mother. She was in charge of reproductive politics as she decided who could be the sexual partners of the Sultan. She was in charge of the enormous budget that the Harem ran on, doled out all payments to the women of the Harem, and was in charge of the training of the next sultan.

The **Janissary Corps** was the Ottoman Sultan's standing army gleaned from the ranks of Balkan slaves gained through the **devshirme**, or "boy tax" on Balkan Christian communities every five years from boys ages 8–20. These boys were taught Turkish, converted to Islam, and given training in the bureaucracy, palace guard, or janissaries, depending on their abilities and the results of the phrenological exam The brightest ten percent of boys were given to the Palace School (the *college*) and trained for civil service in the bureaucracy. The others were initially sent to farms in the countryside and were trained for toughness. After completing a toughening up period on the farms, they were sent to be trained as Janissaries. They were allowed to collect wealth and power, and some attained the ranks of chief vizier, but they had three rules that changed over time: they were not supposed to marry, have any outside job, and their title and property was not to be passed on to their sons. All property was to revert to the Sultan upon the death of a Janissary. Over time, however, the strict discipline that had made the Janissaries an effective fighting force began to erode, and the earlier taboos against marriage and integration within the community began to wither away. By the second half of the Ottoman period, the *devshirme* also was ended, effectively preventing new recruits from Christian areas into the Janissary corps. Nepotism, and the admittance of family members into the Janissary corps, eroded the effectiveness of the institution, which became mired in political infighting. Over time, the Janissary Corps even became a threat to the Sultan, even killing one, as they rioted over any attempt to reform practices within their ranks. The Janissaries became a social class of their own as they began to take on outside jobs, mixed in with other members of the urban craftsmen, and acted as a bulwark against any social or political changes. In a mass attack led by a new military group privately funded by Sultan Mahmud II in 1826, the Janissaries were eliminated, hunted down and killed in an effort to save the empire from their reform-blocking ways.

The military was divided into two branches, the *sipahi* and the Janissaries. The sipahi were semi-feudal cavalry in which the officers were paid in land and given the right to revenues on the land, sort of like vassels; in exchange for rights of revenue the sipahi would provide a certain number of fighters. This did not bankrupt the empire and provided a good arrangement of cavalry. As new areas opened to Ottoman control, this system also provided for a basic administrative network. But, cavalry decreased in importance as gunpowder use increased.

A hallmark of Ottoman society was that it was a partial **meritocracy,** and so what mattered most was whether or not an individual had talent and therefore received preferential treatment. The early Ottomans drew significantly upon both Jewish and Christian talent, often raising them ahead of Muslim Turks due to their performance rather than their religion or connections.

A turning point in Ottoman history was the **Treaty of Karlowitz** where the Ottomans had to give up some claims to Hungary and Transylvania and which was thought by some to usher in the "decline."

Tanzimat or "restructuring" was the period in the nineteenth century where the Ottoman empire sought to give minorities more freedoms in an effort to keep them from wanting to break away from the Empire. Tanzimat ultimately did not work, as the Ottoman Empire fell victim to both European nationalism, as well as crafty European bankers all too willing to help finance Ottoman modernization efforts and who ultimately bankrupted the empire.

Economic

Artisans in urban areas were organized into **guilds** that helped to regulate membership and set standards of production that resulted in Ottoman goods being of high quality. Guilds also had social functions as well. They took care of sick or injured members and facilitated care of widows. In festivals, guilds would take part in grand processions that would demonstrate the mastery of their craft.

The role of **timar** in Ottoman society gave landed estates to the Ottoman ruling class. The timar were given for life (holders of a timar was called a **timariot**), but not for inheritance, and was given to those committed to Islam and the Sultan and well versed in the Turkish language and the culture of the Imperial court.

Highlights of Ottoman History

1071	Battle of Manzikert—Muslim victory over Byzantines encourages more Turkish settlement in Asia Minor
c. 1300	Foundation of the Ottoman Empire
c. 1326	Ottoman conquest of Bursa
1361	Ottoman conquest of Adrianople/Edirne
1402	Battle of Ankara—Tamarlane defeats Ottoman sultan Beyazid the Thunderbolt
1444–46, 1451–81	Reign of Mehmet the Conqueror
1453	Mehmet the Conqueror conquers then rebuilds Constantinople
1474–76	Mehmet codifies Ottoman dynastic law
1512–1522	Reign of Selim the Grim
1514	Battle of Chaldiran—sets border with Safavid Empire
1516–1517	Ottoman conquest of Syria, Egypt and the Hijaz (Mecca and Medina)
1520–1566	Reign of Suleiman the Lawgiver/Magnificent
1526	Battle of Mohacs—Ottoman defeat of the "flower of European knighthood"
1529	First unsuccessful Ottoman siege of Vienna
1551	World's first coffeehouse opens in Constantinople
1569	First capitulations (favorable trading status) awarded to French
1774	Treaty of Kucuk Kaynarca—first loss of Ottoman Muslim territory as Russia annexes Crimea
1826	Jannissaries annihilated in "the Auspicious Incident" by Mahmud II
1839	Tanzimat period begins; Noble Rescript of Gulhane gives equal citizenship to Muslim and non-Muslim
1856	Imperial Rescript institutes further legal and bureaucratic reforms
1875	Ottoman bankruptcy declared, European Great Powers control finances
1908	York Turk revolution
1909	Counterrevolution fails, triumvirate of Enver, Talat and Cevdet Pasas rules
1919	British occupy Constantinople

Three Pillars of Government

Men of the Sword	Men of the Pen	Men of the Turban
Defined Law and Order	Legal, economic, and tax collectors	Courts, schools, and mosques
Military	Intellectuals	Shari'a law
Soldiers	Kanun law	Religious scholars
Hierarchy: Grand Vizier Aga of Janissaries Imperial Barracks Pasha Sipahis Janissaries	**Hierarchy:** Grand Vizier Sublime Porte vali defender	**Hierarchy** Shaykh al Islam Suleymaniyya Mufti qadi

Safavid Empire

After the Mongols had raided northwestern Iran in 1220, the city of Ardabil was destroyed and subsequently revived. It had suffered from the worst of the Mongol onslaught and constant invasions from the east that made it break up into semi-feudal, warrior principalities. It was here that the Sufi order, called the **Safavids**, traces its origins. The empire was founded by **Safi al-Din**, a Sufi mystic, who died in 1334.

In 1500, 14-year-old **Isma'il**, with the aid of the Turkish-speaking military tribes, known for wearing red hats and called *kizilbash* (red-hats), and a small group of advisors took over Armenia and Azerbayjan, and he was proclaimed shah (king) in Tabriz. It is with him that the political and religious beginning of the Safavid Empire began. Isma'il claimed that not only was he related to 'Ali, the Sassanian kings, and Safi al-Din, but also that he was a direct descendent of the twelfth hidden imam. Therefore, he drew upon diverse claims of authority, to cover all the bases. He claimed that he was a pious person, a saint, and claimed semi-divine status and powers that held, at least until his defeat at Châldirân. Upon being crowned the shah, he then proclaimed Shi'ism as the official religion of the state.

Unfortunately for Isma'il, most of his subjects were Sunni. He thus had to enforce official Shi'ism violently, putting to death those who opposed him. Under this pressure, Safavid subjects either converted or pretended to convert. It is nearly impossible to determine exactly how many truly converted, because virtually the entire population claimed to have converted, out of fear of the consequences. Still, it is safe to say that the majority of the population was probably genuinely Shi'ite by the end of the Safavid period in the eighteenth century, and most Iranians today are Shi'ite, although small Sunni populations do exist in that country.

Social

As Shi'ism was the state religion, state clergy were extremely powerful and came to control vast lands that they used to create tax shelters that paid annuities and became a tremendous source of their power—power that they were able to capitalize on in the 1979 Iranian Revolution.

The empire itself was less ethnically diverse in comparison to the Safavid Empire, as a majority of the people who lived there were Persians; however, there were Arabs, Turks, and Armenians as well.

Much like the Janissaries, the Safavid government under the reign of Shah Abbas set up a slave army, called the **ghulam**.

The social structure placed the shah naturally at the top, then the bureaucracy and landed classes, and then the common people.

Cultural

During the reign of Shah Abbas, a Safavid culture emerged that drew from the best of the Ottoman, Persian, and Arab worlds. He also brought Chinese artisans into the empire and had them collaborate with Safavid artists, resulting in a spectacular achievement for the city of Isfahan as these decorations beautified the many mosques, palaces, and marketplaces. The resulting cultural mix blended the worldly and artistic features of Persian civilization with the religious elements of Shi'ism.

Iranian architecture was shaped by the building traditions of all of the diverse ethnic groups that lived in the empire. Seljuq ideas, from the eleventh and twelfth centuries, brought large vaulted spaces, the use of brick patterns as decoration, organizing public buildings around open spaces called midan's, which were large rectangular areas similar to European piazzas or town squares. They also introduced domed chambers into the mosques in Iran, and they were so popular that they dominated the skyline and became externalized as a symbol of royal power. They also established the use of the **iwan,** which is a vast vaulted space that is open at one end. The iwan was used for public audiences with rulers.

Poetry, a usual staple of Persian society, actually stagnated under the Safavids as the **ghazal** lacked the same degree of royal patronage as the other arts. The style of poetry was known as "Persian-Hindi" style, which eventually made its way to India as well.

Calligraphy assumed great importance as prescription against reproducing anything with a soul in it (humans, animals) turned people toward using the written word as a form of art. Most notably, calligraphy is used by taking either bits of the Qur'an or the *Shahnameh*.

Political

The first ruler of the Safavid empire was **Isma'il** who had proclaimed himself **shah**. He had complete control over his people and forced them to convert to Shi'ism. Any person who did not convert to Shi'ism was put to death. Isma'il destroyed the Sunni population of Baghdad in his confrontation with the Ottomans, sparking retribution from the Ottoman sultan at the time, the father of Suleiman the Magnificent, Selim the Grim who later ordered the execution of all Shi'a in the Ottoman Empire. Selim and Isma'il faced off at the **Battle of Châldirân** in 1514 in which the Ottomans decisively destroyed the Safavid empire thanks to the Ottoman advanced technology. The border created as a result of the conflict became the border between Turkey and Iran today. Shah Isma'il's loss initially troubled the Qizilbash and his supporters who had bestowed upon Isma'il semi-divine status. Shah Isma'il, in an effort to save face, declared that indeed he did still have God's blessings bestowed upon him, because any ordinary man in his position would have died in the battle, and God had saved him. His claim worked, and while he personally was said to "have never smiled again," his rule remained intact.

Shah Abbas (1587–1629) led the Safavid dynasty during one of its greatest periods. The Shah led many reform movements that strengthened and turned back the tide of incursions from the east and west. Fed up with the fractious Qizilbash, Abbas created his own new army, not unlike the Janissaries under the Ottomans, made up of converted Christians. Abbas seized Qizilbash lands and used the revenues to fund this gunpowder army. With this military reform came the recapture of Baghdad and the pacification of the eastern frontier. One of Abbas' greatest achievements was his new capital of Isfahan, which became the birthplace of a cultural explosion which coined the phrase "Isfahan is half the world." Abbas also set up an imperial bureaucracy who helped prolong the empire much farther than it would have lasted under Abbas' successors.

The Safavid government was a centralized one in which the **shah** made decisions, sometimes in consultation with his advisors who tended to be members of a nobility. The nobility tended to fill the administrative posts in the government. There was a wealthy merchant class as well, comprised mostly of ethnic Armenians, Georgians, and Indians, who gained a fair amount of power under Shah Abbas, who sought to increase the wealth of the empire through trade, and these groups benefited. There were healthy supplies of artisans, and the majority of the people in the empire were peasants.

The **Qizilbash** (you may see this also written as "Kizilbash") were the military force of the Safavid Empire until the reign of Shah Abbas. They were Shi'ites from the Eastern part of the Ottoman Empire and were of Turkish descent. They wore red headgear with 12 folds, and thus became known as the "redheads," or qizilbash.

Economic

Trade played a major factor in the economic set-up of the Safavid Empire where, notably, the Silk Road ran through the northern part of the Empire. Exports tended to be that of rugs and carpets, textiles, and silks.

Under the rule of Shah Abbas, traditional products became important to the economy. Shah Abbas encouraged the development of hand-woven Persian carpets that became an important industry for both import and export.

Shah Abbas also set up a state-run capitalism to fund his projects at home. His decision to move the capital inland to Isfahan in 1590 may have been because he was motivated by the city's economic potential with its river and fertile plains, as well as for security reasons, to make it less vulnerable to invasion.

The **bazaar** remained an important part of economic life throughout the period. Under Shah Abbas, a new "imperial bazaar" was established that housed imperial manufacturing like wholesale silk and fine textiles, goldsmiths, silversmiths, and jewelers.

Mughal Empire

As a land of Hindus ruled by a Muslim minority, the Mughal sultans of India differed substantially from the empires of the Ottomans and Safavids. While those empires were mostly, but not all, Muslim, the Mughals were in a different position, as they ruled over a land of "infidels." Muslims had to find a formula for Hindu-Muslim coexistence, and they emulated, to some degree, the Ottomans in their approach to tolerance.

The empire began with Babur, the founder of the Empire, who was the son of Tamerlane (Timur), a descendant of Ghengis Khan. At age 11 when the Timurid Empire split, Babur set his sights on Delhi. Invading from Central Asia, Babur took hold of Delhi after the Battle of Panipat in 1526, thus beginning a great empire that would not end until after the 1856 Mutiny in which the British ended their rule.

Social

The Mughal Empire was known for two things in terms of its rule: tolerance and syncretism. Akbar, in particular, sought to make sure that Hindus, the majority in India, were not discriminated against. He abolished the most discriminatory taxes on Hindus (the *jizya*) and filled his advisory councils with non-Hindus. He sought, in particular, a way to bridge the religious differences between Muslims and Hindus. He would invite both Hindu and Muslim scholars to his palace for weekly debates on religious topics. He even tried to institute a new religion that melded traits of both Hinduism and Islam into one "Din-il Ilahi" or **Divine Faith**.

Women's lives under Mughal rule improved. Men in the government, for instance, often relied upon their wives for political advice, and many rich or aristocratic women learned to read and write. Those women sometimes worked and received salaries and were also allowed to own land. However, the Mughals imposed several Islamic laws that restricted women, such as isolating women (purdah).

Cultural

Some cultural characteristics of Mughal India also reflected its syncretic ideology. Much of the art, particularly under Akbar, reflected designs that were mixtures of Persian and Indian themes. The architecture combined Persian and Islamic styles and consisted of domes, geometric patterns, and marble.

Fireworks were a common form of entertainment among the Mughals and were launched at many public festivals and state occasions.

Many of the hallmarks of Mughal culture revolved around "manly" exploits that had something to do with warfare. The attention and devotion, for instance, to archery and horseback riding reflected the ease of most of the empires that came out of Central Asia. Hunting, too, was a favorite pastime in which, Akbar, for instance, valued physical contact with the animals he was hunting (to be fair though, they were all placed within a fenced-off area) and chose to stab them with knives instead of with a bow and arrow. Many Mughal paintings use the hunting theme in them. Falconry, considered an early form of hunting, was considered a noble art by the Mughals, and the falconer was seen as a figure of authority, representing high birth and luxury. Chess, too, was considered a game that was prized for its strategy and continued throughout the Mughal era as a game for the educated and wealthy members of society. Polo, the sport of kings, was considered another war-training exercise that reflected a rider's adeptness on a horse.

The Mughal emperors kept specially trained pigeons that could tumble in the air, and these proved to be a favorite pastime for women. These "tumbler" pigeons could perform as many as 20 backward somersaults in mid-flight. Pachisi was another palace favorite. Gardens were very important because they came to represent the Islamic idea of paradise. Most popular were charbagh gardens, which were designed in four parts with a water feature at the center. The number four represents the four corners of the world and is thought of as prestigious in Islam.

The Mughal courts buzzed with artistic activity and emperors employed artists, poets, dancers, and musicians for their entertainment.

Political

The head of the Mughal Empire was the emperor. The Mughal Empire reached its apex during the rule of Akbar.

Akbar Babur's grandson, Akbar, ascended the throne at the age of 13 after his father slipped in the bathroom in an opium-induced stupor. Akbar, though illiterate, had a magnificent mind and was curious about what was around him. He loved animals and hunting. After securing his rule, he quickly launched into a great period of peace and solidified the empire. Akbar's main contribution was a policy of conquest and conciliation. He fervently believed in religious toleration and crafted his empire that way. He practiced what he preached, and one of the first things he did was to take four wives, one from each of the major religions. What began as a policy of conciliation turned into something much bigger with the cultural synthesis of all of the world's finest religions. He began a new religion, called **Din-i-ilahi**, which would incorporate both the common and best elements of the world's religions.

Akbar also appointed Hindu officials to government positions and tried to harmonize religious differences.

Akbar's son continued his policy of toleration and syncretism. This would prove to be both a boon and a blessing, as his interest in exploring new ideas would ultimately influence his son, **Jahangir**, who made a little mistake that was to cause India tremendous grief later—he allowed foreigners to begin trading.

Jahangir's son, **Shah Jahan,** was more orthodox than his father but less so than his son. While Shah Jahan was tolerant of Hindus, he also sought to quell future Hindu development by ordering all new Hindu temples destroyed. Under Shah Jahan, the empire begins to feel some of the pains of overexpansion.

Aurangzeb, perhaps the most educated of the Mughal emperors, was also its most conservative and intolerant. Unlike his great grandfather, Aurangzeb persecuted Hindus and put Islam above all other religions. His religious policies led to conflict within his large empire. Under Aurangzeb, the empire was at its largest but also its weakest.

There were various political and governmental structures in the Mughal government that largely drew on the power structure that had existed under the Delhi sultanate that had ruled before them. The principal officers of the central government were:

1. **Diwan**: The finance minister. The first of these dignitaries, the *diwan*, often called the **wazir** (the chief minister), supervised the assessment and collection of revenues and it was he who had to authorize any expenditure. All of the imperial orders were first recorded in his office before being issued, and the provincial governors, district *faujdars*, and leaders of expeditions came to him for instructions before assuming their duties.

2. **Mir bakhshi**: He was in charge of the War Department, army, inspecting soldiers, horses, and allocating expenses or defense.

3. **Mir saman**: Liaison between the merchants and the war department.

4. **Sadr:** The director of religious matters, charities, and endowments.

The chief *Qazi* or judge supervised other levels of judges, though most religious and caste groups kept their own legal systems.

Every important officer of state held a **mansab** or an official appointment of rank that required them to provide a certain number of fighters when and if needed. Akbar set up a ranking system for each official in the state. He had 33 grades of ranks, ranging from commanders of ten men to commanders of 10,000 men. There were three types of mansabs:

1. **Mansabdar**: they were in command of 10–400 men and horses.

2. **Amirs** (nobles): they were in command of 500–2500 men and horses.

3. **Umara-i-kabir**: these were in the higher category and were usually princes of the royal family in charge of thousands of men.

Originally each grade of mansab carried a specific rate of pay in return for the holder requiring a certain quota of horses, elephants, men, and carts. Mansabdars were either paid in cash or by temporarily giving them a *jagir* (the right to collect revenues). The system did work well in terms of organizing the empire, but it became rather burdensome on the state to have to pay each month. Akbar's grandson, Shah Jahan, introduced the practice of paying the mansabdars for 4 out of the 12 months each year.

The emperor usually was the one to appoint mansabdars, usually on the recommendation of military leaders, provincial governors, or court officials. The mansabdars might be comparable to the idea of a portable cadre of men in the civil service who serve in one area and are transferred every few years. Those young men who did not have mansabdars but were employed in the palace were called **ahadis** and were given a chance, through the meritocracy, to advance and eventually get a mansab.

Economic

While there was a rather small and extremely wealthy upper class, the majority of people did not share in such wealth. The land that peasants worked on to grow crops like rice, wheat, pulses, sugar cane, and cotton was taxed heavily. The zamindars typically collected one-third of the farmers' annual harvest.

Trade was a major source of income as the Mughals traded with Europe, Arabia, and Southeast Asia. The Mughals exported opium, spices, indigo, textiles, silk, and cotton. They typically imported gold and silver, horses, ivory, wine, and precious stones.

Revenue collection was based on the collection of taxes. Each of the important administrative and army positions were staffed by officers called *mansabdars*, each level of official having a separate zat (rank) and sawar (cavalry) ranking. Basically, the **mansabdar** system was set up by Akbar to replace the old land system called *iqta*. In it, Akbar divided his reign into different provinces (**subas**), districts, towns, and villages, and each level had its own governing, tax-collecting, judicial, and other appointees. Provincial administration was headed by a governor (the "holder" of a *suba*—a *subedar (dar* means "holder of"). So, the **mansab** were areas of control that gave people the right to collect taxes and control the land in exchange for providing an army of men and horses whenever required.

Another important position was that of the village accountant, or patwari. Throughout the Mughal period, the *patwari*, who was responsible for the maintenance of the financial records, was an employee of the village, not of the revenue administration. Under the Mughals, the **patwari** was considered an agent of the people, not the government (this changed under the British).

China

During this period, the Ming Dynasty ruled until 1644 when the Qing (or Manchu) Dynasty ruled until 1912.

Ming

The Ming had increasingly isolated themselves from Chinese life, ruling through eunuch servants and administrators. By closing itself off, it also chose not to develop a shipping industry and its navy effectively was inoperable. With no one to protect them, China suffered tremendously from pirates and smugglers on its eastern coast, and the government could not respond quickly or well. These problems continued when a series of famines struck China in the early seventeeth century and the government failed to organize effective relief efforts and the peasants revolted.

The Ming Dynasty closed China to foreigners. They were allowed in some restricted areas but were monitored closely. Chinese merchants were not encouraged to trade overseas. This resulted in a slow loss of the technical superiority that China seemed to possess earlier as by the end of the Ming Dynasty, China no longer could compete with Europe.

Social

Merchants were at the bottom of Ming society as they were seen as people who did not actually produce anything but profited off of the work of others. They were seen as supporting foreigners and almost engaging in robbery.

The Ming focused on eradicating anything foreign from Chinese society and a return to traditional values. The family was a central institution in Chinese society and renewed attention to it drove Ming social developments. Sons continued to be preferred over daughters and women's lives became centered around home activities, like raising children, maintaining the household, and controlling home expenses. Some women, however, did work as midwives, textile workers, and performers.

The patriarchal family took center stage in Chinese society. The Confucian ideal of filial piety was applied both to the patriarch of the family and to the emperor. The father was venerated as the head of the household, and all male ancestors were worshipped.

Cultural

Education was centered around preparation for the civil service exams. Local education flourished and enabled rural and urban poor a chance to take the exams.

Economic

They attempted to prop up their economy by changing paper money into a "single-whip" system based on silver currency. But, when the American silver flooded the market, it caused tremendous inflation in China.

Political

Qing

The Qing were not from China; they were from Manchuria and so not ethnically Chinese. The Qing chose to remain an ethnic elite and forbade interaction with the Chinese—

making it actually illegal for the Chinese to learn the Manchu language, to marry a Manchu, or to migrate to the Manchu homeland. Though they only comprised about three percent of the population in China, they were unable to run the government by themselves. Therefore, they chose to open up positions to only the best and the brightest of Chinese. The civil service exam became even more important, and it was opened to all in order to glean the best talent. Although the highest offices were reserved for the Manchu, it was Chinese officials who, in nonmilitary positions, presided, for the most part, over the Manchu outside of the capital. In many provincial government positions, a system of dual appointments was used—with the substantive work being done by the Chinese appointee and the Manchu there to ensure the Chinese loyalty to Qing rule. They also wisely realized that it would be senseless to impose a new system on the Chinese, so they retained many of the Ming institutions. For instance, the emperors continued to uphold Confucian court practices and presided over temple rituals.

Social

The Qing social hierarchy consisted of privileged classes, commoners, and the lowest of the low.

The privileged classes consisted of the emperor, scholar bureaucrats, and landowners.

There were three groups that comprised the commoner group: peasants (they were the most numerous), artisans and workers, and merchants (ranked at the bottom in terms of social rank, but in terms of wealth they were quite high).

The lowest of the low included actors, beggars, and prostitutes.

Cultural

The Manchu emperors supported Chinese literary and historical projects of enormous scope, and much of China's ancient literature was protected because of these Manchu projects.

A proliferation of books resulted from the invention of woodblock printing. By producing more books, it led to high literacy rates and a more educated and thoughtful people.

Traditional opera, drama, literature, and artistic techniques reached new heights. Of particular interest were themes devoted to Chinese historical topics and heroes.

Landscape painting practice of breaking and binding the feet of young girls produced women with deformed feet that could not support their weight. As a result, women were dependent upon help just to stand up. Such dependence was considered a virtue and one's marriage prospects were enhanced with bound feet.

Economic

During Quianlong's rule, the economy was doing so well that they cancelled tax collection four times!

Agricultural production increased during Quianlong's reign and New World crops made their way to China's shores. These new crops, like sweet potatoes, were quite effective and they, along with new techniques for irrigation and fertilizers, resulted in food surpluses, which resulted in a healthier population that increased substantially.

The Qing quest for political and social stability made them discourage technological innovation, as they feared that it would cause unsettling change and could incite riots. As a result, the more the Qing resisted foreign improvements, the more likely they were to lose the technological war between the two. Over the nineteenth century, the Chinese lost more and more ground to the Europeans whose Industrial Revolution catapulted them into a significantly advanced era. The Qing may have been right to be wary of the effect of foreign interaction, because as soon as they did open the gates, however minutely, the British began to ply the Chinese with opium and caused tremendous problems that eventually resulted in the **Opium War,** where Britain was angry that the Chinese did not want opium distributed on their soil. The Opium War with Britain lasted from 1838–1842, and the Chinese fell to the gun-powdered steamboats that the British used to attack the Grand Canal. As a result of a series of defeats, China had to enter into what is referred to as the "unequal treaties" in which they had to cede Hong Kong, open their ports to European commerce and residence, allow Christian missionaries on their soil, legalize the opium trade, and not issue any more tariffs on British imports to China. As a result, by 1900, 90 Chinese ports were under foreign control, foreign merchants were controlling China's economy, Christian missionaries were converting Chinese, and foreign gunboats were patrolling China's waters.

Eventually, the **Boxer Rebellion** was launched by an anti-foreign society called the Society of the Righteous and Harmonious Fists who tried to rid China of the "foreign devils." The rebellion was crushed.

Political

The basis for Manchu power was twofold: military strength and the corrupt, ineffective Ming government.

Under the Qing, strong and effective leadership kept tensions low. The emperors studied and understood Confucianism and patronized Confucian schools and academies, opened up a National library, and had an encyclopedia of Chinese history and thought written. Rulers did look after people's welfare and promoted agriculture.

The rule of **Quianlong** from 1736–1794 was long and brought global trade to China but at a heavy price.

Russia Under the Muscovites and the Romanovs (1613–1917)

Muscovy

Russia fell under Tatar rule in 1242 when they ruled a large part of Russia for two centuries, resulting in Russia becoming increasingly isolated for two centuries. In the fourteenth century, the Russian princes of Muscovy began to gain power as the Mongol power started to decline. In 1480, **Ivan III**, known as Ivan the Great, refused to pay tribute to the Mongols and declared Russia free of Mongol rule. He focused on expanding Muscovy territory and declared himself *tsar* (note that this can also be spelled czar—both are correct), the Russian word for emperor or Caesar. Ivan then went about legitimizing his rule—he married a Byzantine princess to give legitimacy to his connection to the Orthodox Church, acquired symbols of imperial rule—such as putting an imperial eagle onto his coat of arms and creating a genealogy that creatively traced his family's origins back to the Roman Caesars. He declared Moscow as the center of the Eastern Orthodox Church; Moscow was declared "the third Rome." He and his grandson, Ivan IV (Ivan the Terrible), both wielded absolute power in Russia. They used their power to expand Russia eastward. They did it by recruiting peasants and offering them freedom from their feudal lords if they agreed to settle in the east. The only issue was that they would have to settle it themselves. These peasant-soldiers became known as **Cossacks** and they expanded Russian territory from the sixteenth to eighteenth centuries into Siberia in the north and in the south all the way to the Caspian Sea.

By the mid 1500s, Ivan the Terrible had centralized power over the entire Russian sphere, was ruling ruthlessly, and was using the secret police against his own nobles. He regularly executed anyone who threatened his power, including his own son.

After Ivan IV's death in 1584, Russia's feudal lords battled over who should rule the empire. This is a period from 1604–1613 that historians have named the **Time of Troubles** as "pretenders" who took the throne would be killed one after the other. In 1613, **Mikhail Romanov** was elected tsar and thus entered the rule of the **Romanov Dynasty**.

Social

- Russian *boyars* (**nobles**) dominated society and always posed an underlying threat to those in power. Attempts were periodically made to limit their power.

- Ivan IV set up an advisory council of merchants and lower-level boyars in an attempt to lessen the power of the Boyars.

- Between 1484 and 1505, Novgorod was incorporated into a feudal system called *pomest'ia*. Ivan IV settled about 23,000 of his soldiers in Novgorod and gave them ample estates in return for military service. In contrast to what was accepted practice throughout Europe, he gave land to people not connected with the aristocracy: about 60% of his new estate holders were just regular soldiers. Land parcels on these lands were rented to serfs in return for their labor and service to the vassal. What soon transpired was that these peasants were turned into serfs who became tied to the land, unable to flee.

Cultural

- The Russian Orthodox Church dominated society.
- The adoption of Byzantine terms, rituals, title, and emblems provided legitimacy for their rule.
- Kinship and patronage dominated Muscovy life.

Political

- Rule was by the tsar, who was an autocrat.

- Russia expanded eastward and toward Siberia, much the same as other European conquerors in the new worlds, who felt that the lands were empty, their expansionary aims were beneficial to the natives, and that their work was ordained by God. With their more advanced technology of firearms, the Russians were able to conquer the native tribes of Siberia.

- Sub-units of the Muscovite state were the occasional royal councils, called **zemskie sobory**, central chancelleries, regional governorships, service people, and merchants.

- Under Ivan IV, a secret police, *oprichniki,* was created that was a force of 6,000 men who dressed in black and rode black horses, who rode through the empire punishing anyone who spoke out against the tsar or his policies.

- Ivan IV launched several killing sprees, perhaps influenced by his spiraling mental condition, against the people of Novgorod, who he suspected wanted to separate from Russia.

- Ivan IV's murder of his son, the sole heir to the crown, caused the **Time of Troubles** and left Russia without a monarch after the death of Ivan IV. This period is noted for being one of the reasons Russia lagged behind Western Europe.

Romanovs

Under Mikhail Romanov, Russia extended its empire to the Pacific. Romanov continued westernization. By the end of the seventeenth century, 20,000 Europeans lived in Russia, developing trade and manufacturing, practicing medicine, and smoking tobacco, while Russians began trimming their beards and wearing western clothing. In 1649, three monks were appointed to translate the Bible for the first time into Russian. The Raskolniki (Old Believers) refused to accept any Western innovations or liturgy in the Russian Orthodox Church and were severely persecuted as a result.

Peter I (reigned 1682–1725) was one of the most extraordinary people in Russian history. The driving ambitions of Peter the Great's life were to modernize Russia and to compete with the great powers of Europe on equal terms. By the end of Peter's reign, Russia produced more iron than England. Peter built up the army through conscription and a 25-year term of enlistment. He gave flintlocks and bayonets to his troops instead of the old muskets and pikes. Artillery was improved and discipline enforced. By the end of his reign, Russia had a standing army of 210,000, despite a population of only 13 million. The tsar ruled by decree (ukase). Government officials and nobles acted under government authority, but there was no representative body.

All landowners owed lifetime service to the state, either in the army, the civil service, or at court. In return for government service, they received land and serfs to work their fields. Conscription required each village to send recruits for the Russian army. By 1709, Russia manufactured most of its own weapons and had an effective artillery.

After a series of largely ineffective rulers, Catherine II "the Great," (reigned 1762–1796) continued the westernization process begun by Peter the Great. The three partitions of Poland, in 1772, 1793, and 1795, respectively, occurred under Catherine II's rule. Russia also annexed the Crimea and warred with Turkey during her reign.

COMPETENCY 4.6

Evaluate the significant scientific, intellectual, and philosophical contributions of the Age of Reason through the Age of Enlightenment.

The **Enlightenment** and the **Age of Reason** are two names given to the predominant intellectual movement of the eighteenth century that sought a distinct break with the past. It was an intellectual movement among the upper and middle class elites. It involved a new world view that explained the world and looked for answers in terms of reason rather than faith, and in terms of an optimistic, natural, humanistic approach rather than a fatalistic, supernatural one.

For the first time in human history, the eighteenth century saw the appearance of a secular worldview. This became known as the **Age of the Enlightenment**. In the past, some kind of a religious perspective had always been central to Western civilization. The philosophical starting point for the Enlightenment was the belief in the autonomy of man's intellect apart from God. The most basic assumption was faith in reason rather than faith in revelation.

The Enlightenment believed in the existence of God as a rational explanation of the universe and its form; "God" was a deistic Creator who made the universe and then was no longer involved in its mechanistic operation. That mechanistic operation was governed by "natural law." The intellectuals of the Enlightenment, called *philosophes*, began to question the traditions of society and to look at the universe in a scientific, critical light. During the Enlightenment, all the trademark aspects of European society were exposed to criticism and analysis through reason. No institution was spared, for even the church itself was attacked by the cynical philosophes. Though the Enlightenment began as a movement that only reached the intellectual elite of society, its repercussions would eventually reach and have a big impact on society as a whole.

The *philosophes* as a whole saw their societies emerging from the darkness of superstition, ignorance, and intolerance—much of what they associated with the Medieval Catholic Church and with Feudal monarchy. They believed that for man to continue to advance, people had to develop their powers of **reason** and leave behind emotion, superstitious belief, blind faith, autocratic and arbitrary rule in administration and government, and cultural heritage. They argued for the development of universal, cross-cultural, shared expressions of human action and thought and that if people started thinking similarly and sharing ideas and focusing on the merits of such, people's basic goodness would come out and then the world would be a better, more peaceful place, organized and tended to by ideas and the people who had them. The philosophes felt that society would gain and lose if it took up reason. They could lose the fanatical wars fought in the name of religion, the persecution of so-called heretics and other free spirits, the rule of absolute monarchs and privileged aristocrats, and the general ignorance and backwardness of a population that had been kept in the dark by worldly and spiritual authorities for too long. Other ills of society, like slavery, would be abolished, torture and cruel punishment removed from judicial systems, and freedom of conscience enhanced by the separation of churches and state. Progress was the banner under which societies would abandon their benighted old ways and usher in a liberated and altogether happier future.

Rationalists stressed deductive reasoning or mathematical logic as the basis for their epistemology (source of knowledge). They started with "self-evident truths," or postulates, from which they constructed a coherent and logical system of thought.

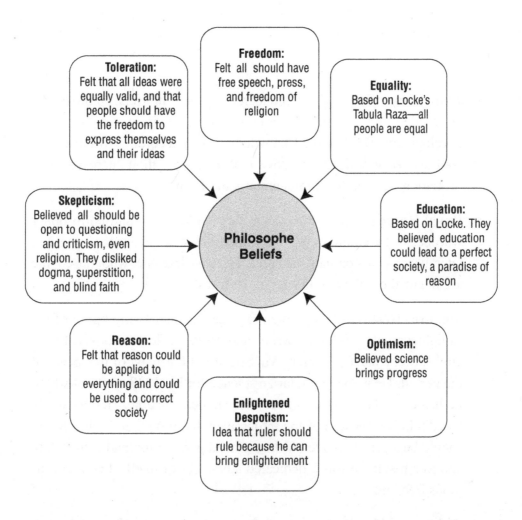

- **René Descartes** (1596–1650) sought a basis for logic and thought he found it in man's ability to think. "I think; therefore, I am" was his most famous statement.

- **Benedict de Spinoza** (1632–1677) developed a rational pantheism in which he equated God and nature. He denied all free will and ended up with an impersonal, mechanical universe.

- **Gottfried Wilhelm Leibniz** (1646–1716) worked on symbolic logic and calculus and invented a calculating machine. He, too, had a mechanistic world and lifeview and thought of God as a hypothetical abstraction rather than a persona.

Empiricists stressed inductive observation—the "scientific method"—as the basis for their epistemology.

- **John Locke** (1632–1704) pioneered in the empiricist approach to knowledge and stressed the importance of environment in human development. He classified knowledge as 1) according to reason, 2) contrary to reason, or 3) above reason. Locke thought reason and revelation were both complementary and from God.

- **David Hume** (1711–1776) was a Scottish historian and philosopher who began by emphasizing the limitations of human reasoning and later became a dogmatic skeptic. He was the one who raised the argument about the tree falling in the forest.

- **Voltaire** (1694–1778) was often regarded as the leading figure of the Enlightenment. A talented writer and social critic who poked fun at almost every facet of society, Voltaire stood for many of the ideals of the period. He helped popularize science for his 1738 work, in which he helped make Newton's discoveries understandable. He absolutely hated religion because of the intolerance that it bred and felt religion should be a private matter. Voltaire faced persecution and censorship, and as a result, he was a dedicated advocator of intellectual and religious freedom.

- **Diderot** (1713–1784) was most famous for his *Encyclopedia*, which classified all human knowledge from the most common to the most complex. The aim of the book was to "change the general way of thinking." Despite being banned throughout Europe, Diderot's masterpiece was still distributed and had a great impact on the intellectuals of Europe.

- **Baron de Montesquieu** (1689–1755) was a writer who believed that societies and political institutions could be studied scientifically, and that a balanced government with checks and balances would work.

The Enlightenment believed in a closed system of the universe in which the supernatural was not involved in human life, in contrast to the traditional view of an open system in which God, angels, and devils were very much a part of human life on Earth.

The "Counter-Enlightenment" is a comprehensive term encompassing diverse and disparate groups who disagreed with the fundamental assumptions of the Enlightenment and pointed out its weaknesses.

Roman Catholic Jansenism in France argued against the idea of an uninvolved or impersonal God. Hasidism in Eastern European Jewish communities, especially in the 1730s, stressed a joyous religious fervor in direct communion with God.

The Elite Culture of the Enlightenment

During the Enlightenment, a new form of elite culture took hold throughout Europe, crossing national and linguistic boundaries, united in their use of French, feelings of cosmopolitanism, and distinctly separate from the majority of people.

Europe's elite began to travel around the continent. They visited cultural centers and cities, as well as the ancient monuments of antiquity. Cities became ideal tourism spots for these elite, featuring new amenities like streetlights and public transportation, new public spaces that centered around a spread of ideas, like coffeehouses and public theaters, where people could meet and talk about ideas.

A **republic of letters** began to develop in which journals and newspapers circulated among the elite. Though the republic was limited to the educated, all classes and backgrounds could join in. The elite also met in salons and academies, both of which helped spread ideas and unite people. There, people could dispute their ideas and come up with new ones.

Also, during this time, publishing increased tremendously and people began to read more. Traveling libraries were developed, as were journals and, most importantly, newspapers. There were new employment opportunities in bookselling and publishing, as well as the smuggling of so-called bad books, which ranged from Voltaire to pornography (i.e., anything that was banned).

Art, Literature, and Music

The art of the Enlightenment consisted of two competing styles: **Rococo** and **Neoclassicism**. Rococo was the art of the nobility that emphasized the airy grace and refined pleasures of the salon and the boudoir, very pretty, using bright, swirling pastel colors, like Rubenism. It sought to make a break with the heavy, Baroque past and emphasized lightness and airy movement. Famous Rococo painters were Francois Boucher and Fragonard. **Neoclassicism**, on the other hand, favored line over color, and was all about drama, tension, emotion, content, and an imitation of ancient style. The *philosophes* loved the Neoclassicist works for they favored themes that the philosophes liked. One famous painter was Jacques Louis David.

Literature during the Enlightenment took center stage. The first modern **novel** was developed, by Samuel Richardson and Henry Fielding, both in England, and emerged as a new form of writing in which a story was told and characters were presented in a realistic social context filled with everyday problems. **Satire** was also perfected during the Enlightenment, by brilliant writers like Jonathan Swift and Voltaire. Also, during this time, **romantic poetry** was born. Before, poetry followed strict rules and was not very emotional, but in the Enlightenment, writers like William Wordsworth and Friedrich von Schiller took poetry into new directions—so new in fact that it turned into a new style, Romanticism. Johann von Goethe and his masterpiece, *Faust,* was a romantic poet who came to embody the entire period.

Music during the Enlightenment also shifted away from the dramatic organ and choral music of Bach and Handel and toward a lighter and more elegant work of Hayden, Mozart, and Beethoven. Particular attention was paid to the symphony and these composers left their indelible stamp on it.

COMPETENCY 4.7
Identify the causes, effects, events, and significant individuals associated with the Age of Exploration.

The Age of Exploration

Overseas exploration, begun in the fifteenth century, expanded. Governments supported such activity in order to gain wealth and to preempt other countries. We break down this age into three parts:

- Discovery: refers to the era's advances in geographical knowledge and technology

- Reconnaissance: preliminary exploration

- Expansion: migration of Europeans to other parts of the world

Causes

The reasons why the Age of Exploration happened when it did and where it did are quite varied and multifaceted. Scholars point to any number of reasons, none of them mutually exclusive.

While ideas about the Middle East, India, and China certainly had made their way to Europe before, the exploits of Christian Crusaders from the eleventh to thirteenth centuries enhanced curiosity about the region, its people, its scientific and technological advancements, spices, and other goods created an interest in developing more regular trade with the East. Trade opportunities, however, were stymied as Europeans, for ages, were limited largely to trade across land, and trade between Europe and Asia only occurred through middle men. These middle men varied; sometimes they were Ottomans, sometimes Mongols, and most recently Venetians. Each time a good passed through a foreign land, it was subject to taxes, and each time it passed through the hands of an individual trader, the price of the goods increased in order to allow for sufficient profit. By the time goods made their way to Europe, they had been taxed quite heavily. Europeans became anxious to find a way around the middle men and make their own deals in Asia and transport the goods themselves. Spain and Portugal, recognizing they both had easy access to the sea, set their sights on finding an easier and faster route to India.

The Renaissance, Reformation, and Age of Exploration happened around the same time, so many of the ideas of one impacted the other. The Renaissance prompted searches for new knowledge, and adventurism ignited dreams about the possibilities of what lay beyond the shores of the Atlantic and Mediterranean Seas. The Reformation infused a new spirit for missionaries, particularly those from Portugal and Spain, to find new souls to convert.

Political centralization in Spain, France, and England might also help explain their outward push as the government had more control of its resources to organize and develop incentives, funds, and opportunities for erstwhile traders to expand their markets, which had already been undergoing some expansion and organization since the founding of the Hanseatic League to help trade in northern Europe and the commercial revolution that made Europe eager for more markets for their products. Later, the Industrial Revolution would prompt Europe to look elsewhere for raw materials and a market for their finished goods. Portugal led the way in the initial stages of exploration primarily because it was strategically situated near the coast of Africa, had long-standing trade relations with Muslim nations, and was led by a royal family that supported exploration, **Prince Henry the Navigator**.

Prince Henry's contribution to the age was unbelievable. In 1415, he had joined in the Portuguese attack on Ceuta in North Africa. There they found lots of exotic spices and precious metals, along with new opportunities to spread Christianity. Prince Henry returned to Portugal intent on trying to expand Portugal's shipping reaches. Knowing the limits imposed by the current technology, he started a school devoted to navigation. Many of the advances occurred primarily as a result of Prince Henry's new school that contained a shipyard attached to the school as a ready experimental lab with which to facilitate nautical innovation. A maritime revolution that sparked advances in technology like the astrolabe, magnetic compass, and better maps, shipbuilding and the dominance of the *caraval*, and even the canon opened the minds of the Portuguese and Spanish to the possibilities of long-distance sea travel that had seemed rather risky and impossible earlier. The results took a while but ultimately worked. The Portuguese were able to take their ships further and further down the coastline of Africa, where they established trading posts along the way. It would be 20 years after Prince Henry's death that some of the dreams he had would be realized when Bartolomeu Dias passed the tip of Africa and 11 years later Vasco da Gama would sail to India.

While the above reasons account for why countries might be interested in exploration, there were also reasons why individuals might be interested in leaving the comforts of "civilization" to venture into the unknown. Some of the individual reasons for individual explorers to be interested in exploration may be summed up as the three G's: God, Gold, and Glory.

1. The crusading zeal that had inspired Europeans centuries before to look outward to other non-Christians, influenced the people of the sixteenth century who were out for more people to convert to Christianity. Realizing that they had already failed in their attempts to convert Muslims, they looked for new converts.

2. Economics and Politics: After the Reconquista, many men found that their economic and political choices were limited.

3. Quest for material profit

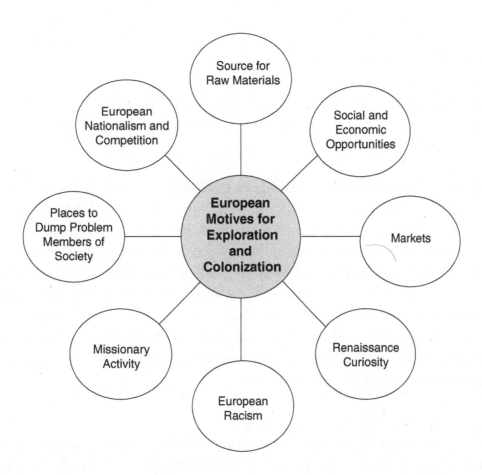

Effects

The effects of the Age of Exploration were also multi-variable, depending on time and place. Typically, historians have focused on the positive aspects of the age, without looking at what happened to the peoples that they conquered. So, we'll take a look first at some of the good things that happened as a result of exploration:

One unintended consequence was the transfer of horses to the Americas. During the conquistadors' expeditions into the Southwest, some horses escaped and formed large herds on the Great Plains. Within a few generations, Native Americans in the plains region became experts on horseback, expanding their hunting and trading capabilities and dramatically transforming Native American culture.

Another good result of exploration, at least in terms of the Europeans, was that European life expectancy increased back in Europe because of the availability of new foodstuffs that contained some essential vitamins that had been missing from the European diet. So, the population soared in Europe.

Another good result was the growth of foreign trade that helped, primarily England. England's biggest export, wool, had been taken up by other countries who were eager to tap into England's "monopoly."

Another mixed result was the **Columbian Exchange** that happened as a consequence of the Spanish and the Portuguese entry into the New World. New foods, resources, and animals were transferred between Europe and the Americas, resulting in massive changes for both regions. However, more dubious things exchanged as well with this new pattern of trade—an exchange of diseases, weapons, and people. War, slavery, and starvation claimed many lives, but disease, especially smallpox, had the most devastating effect. In Mexico, the native population plummeted from 25 million in 1519 to 2 million by 1600. European settlement physically displaced numerous tribes, setting in motion the sad fate of Native Americans throughout American history. The economy suffered because it could not meet the demand!

Some allege that the effects of exploration on the native peoples of the New World cannot be underestimated. In what really was genocide, the Native Americans suffered at the hands of each of the European groups who came to their lands. The biggest, and perhaps unplanned for, consequence was the diseases that spread,. The numbers of Indians who were dying from European diseases was so great that the Spanish and Portuguese had a problem with labor supply. Their solution to this problem was to bring their own labor with them—and thus began the **Atlantic Slave Trade**. The Europeans saw several advantages toward using African slaves for their labor. Most of the Africans had some immunity to the mosquitoes found in the Americas, and so they, unlike the Europeans, were resistant to the diseases that went along with mosquitoes. Africans also were well versed in farming, and so they had the skills to help cultivate crops. They also did not know the land where they were going to, so the slaves would have little chance or opportunity to flee—they would be stuck there. In 370 years, the Atlantic Slave Trade transported more than 9 million slaves, who made it to the shores (bear in mind that 20% of slaves died along the way) of the Americas. In what became referred to as the Triangular Trade System, Africans were sent to the Americas, merchants bought coffee, sugar, and tobacco, and then they sold the goods to Europe; another triangular trade had merchants selling Africans for sugar and then selling them to American rum producers.

With so much trade going on between Europe and the Americas, new ways of thinking about such trade developed. The English developed the ideas of mercantilism, which essentially was a system of economic regulations aimed at increasing the power of the state. Central to this idea was that a country needed to maintain a balance of trade with other countries. In order to do that, it needed raw materials and the colonies provided a great place for the acquisition of raw materials. So, another effect of the Age of Exploration was the development of colonies and **mercantilism**. Mercantilism was a system of economic regulations aimed at increasing the power of the state. Central to this idea was that a country needed to maintain a balance of trade with other countries. In order to do that, it needed raw materials and the colonies provided a great place for the acquisition of raw materials.

Main Events Early in the Age of Discovery

- In 1488, Portugal financed the voyage of Bartholomew Dias.

- In 1497, Vasco da Gama rounded the Cape of Good Hope, explored the east African kingdoms, and then went all the way to India where he established trade relations.

- In 1492, Columbus "discovered" the New World when he landed at Hispaniola and thought he had arrived in India. When he returned for a second trip, he brought an army for conquest.

- 1494: **Treaty of Tordesillas.** In an effort to settle a dispute between the Spanish and the Portuguese over who should get which territory, Pope Alexander VI (a Spaniard, actually), set up a Line of Demarcation that would separate the territories of the world between the two largest Catholic powers, the Spanish and the Portuguese. The Portuguese at the time were more concerned about preserving their spice trade in the east, and so they willingly gave the Spanish the New World territories, with the exception, as you can see from the map below, of what would be Brazil (this is why the Brazilians speak Portuguese and the rest of South America speaks Spanish).

Various limited liability companies were established to finance these explorations. The Dutch set up the Dutch East India Company.

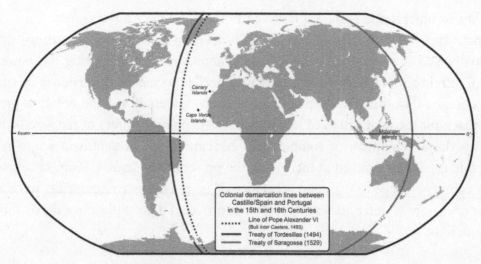

Source: Harper Atlas of World History. p. 139.

Fig. 5.2. The division of influence between Portugal and Spain by the Treaty of Tordesillas, 1494 and 1506.

Significant Individuals

Portugal

- Prince Henry the Navigator (1394–1460) supported exploration of the African coastline, largely in order to seek gold.

- Bartholomew Dias (1450–1500) rounded the southern tip of Africa in 1487.

- Vasco da Gama (1460–1524) reached India in 1498 and, after some fighting, soon established trading ports at Goa and Calicut.

- Albuquerque (1453–1515) helped establish an empire in the Spice Islands after 1510.

- Pedro Cabal (1467–1520) sighted Brazil and defeated Arabs in the Indian Ocean.

- Amerigo Vespucci: First to announce that the "New World" was not Asia, but rather a continent; cartographers began to call the New World "America" in honor of him.

Spain

- Christopher Columbus (1451–1506), seeking a new route to the (East) Indies, "discovered" the Americas in 1492.

- Ferdinand Magellan (1480–1521) circumnavigated the globe in 1521–1522.

- **Conquistadores**:

  - Conquests of the Aztecs by **Hernando Cortes** (1485–1547), and the Incas by **Francisco Pizarro** (ca. 1476–1541), enabled the Spanish to send much gold and silver back to Spain.

- **Vasco Núñez de Balboa** (1475–1517) crossed the Isthmus of Panama, first European to see the Pacific Ocean.

Other Countries

England

- In the 1490s, the Cabots, John (1450–1498) and Sebastian (ca. 1483–1557), explored North America.

- After 1570, various Englishmen, including Francis Drake (ca. 1540–1596) led English "sea dogs" against Spanish shipping around the world.

- **Sir Martin Frobisher** (1535–1594): northeastern Canadian coast

- **Sir Walter Raleigh** (1552–1618): Roanoke Settlement

France

- **Jacques Cartier** (1491–1557) explored parts of North America for France in 1534.

- **Samuel de Champlain** (1567–1635) and the French explored the St. Lawrence River, seeking furs to trade.

- **Giovanni da Verrazano** (1480–1527) explored northern Atlantic coast of modern-day U.S.

Dutch

The Dutch established settlements at New Amsterdam and in the Hudson River Valley. The Dutch founded trading centers in the East Indies, the West Indies, and southern Africa. Swedes settled on the Delaware River in 1638.

Missionaries: Francis Xavier

COMPETENCY 4.8

Assess the social, political, and economic effects of the Industrial Revolution.

Social Effects

There was an overall downfall in the socioeconomic and cultural situation of the people. Growth of cities was one of the major consequences of the Industrial Revolution. Many people were driven to the cities to look for work, in turn they ended up living in the cities that could not support them. With the new industrial age, a new quantitative and materialistic view of the world took place. This caused the need for people to consume as much as they could. This still happens today. Living on small wages required small children to work in factories for long days.

Political and Economic Effects

Twentieth-century English historian Arnold Toynbee came to refer to the period since 1750 as "the Industrial Revolution." The term was intended to describe a time of transition when machines began to significantly displace human and animal power in methods of producing and distributing goods, and an agricultural and commercial society converted into an industrial one.

These changes began slowly, almost imperceptibly, gaining momentum with each decade, so that by the middle of the nineteenth century, industrialism had swept across Europe west to east, from England to Eastern Europe. Few countries purposely avoided industrialization, because of its promised material improvement and national wealth. The economic changes that constitute the Industrial Revolution have done more than any other movement in Western civilization to revolutionize Western life.

Roots of the Industrial Revolution could be found in the following:

1. the Commercial Revolution (1500–1700), which spurred the great economic growth of Europe and brought about the Age of Discovery and Exploration, which in turn helped to solidify the economic doctrines of mercantilism;

2. the effect of the Scientific Revolution, which produced the first wave of mechanical inventions and technological advances;

3. the increase in population in Europe from 140 million people in 1750, to 266 million people by the mid-part of the nineteenth century (more producers, more consumers);

4. the political and social revolutions of the nineteenth century, which began the rise to power of the "middle class," and provided leadership for the economic revolution.

The revolution occurred first in the cotton and metallurgical industries, because those industries lent themselves to mechanization. A series of mechanical inventions (1733–1793) would enable the cotton industry to mass-produce quality goods. The need to replace wood as an energy source led to the use of coal, which increased coal mining, and resulted ultimately in the invention of the steam engine and the locomotive. The development of steam power allowed the cotton industry to expand and transformed the iron industry. The factory system, which had been created in response to the new energy sources and machinery, was perfected to increase manufactured goods.

The industrial revolution did necessarily improve people's socioeconomic and cultural situation. An outcome of the Industrial Revolution was the growth of cities, as the new factories acted as magnets, pulling people away from their rural roots and beginning the most massive population transfer in history. While ostensibly a good idea, **urbanization** had its drawbacks as too many people came to cities, which had neither the infrastructure nor the jobs to support them. Public sanitation and public health were woefully in short supply, and outbreaks of diseases such as typhoid and cholera broke out. Another effect of industrialization and the creation of factories was pollution. Chimneys, bridges, and factory smoke blocked out most of the light in towns, layers of smoke covered the streets, and burning coal produced a lot of dirty, black smoke that surely had an effect on the health of the people. Some attention to these conditions was accorded by Parliament in the form of Public Health Acts. These acts did improve conditions, though they were largely ineffective, for they did not grant local Boards of Health the powers to compel improvements. The result of these infrastructure problems like bad sewage, air and water pollution, and diseases resulted in higher infant mortality rates and shorter life expectancy in urban areas.

Urbanization brought people into already crowded environments. The sheer number of cities that grew was tremendous, and numbers of cities in Europe increased over 700% over 100 years. The cities themselves did not just develop willy nilly. Rather, they tended to develop in favorable locations, near resources such as coal, iron, water, and railroads. Rooms, for instance, were rented to whole families or perhaps even several families. If there were no more rooms to rent, then people wound up staying in lodging houses. All in all, the effect on family life was tremendous.

The emergence of the **factory system** not only changed how work was organized but also what work meant. No longer was skilled craftsmanship valued, but now the main motive was how to reduce work to its simplest, repetitive motions, in order to produce work faster, not necessarily better. So, the assembly line work revolutionized the work experience on an individual level and ultimately resulted in an almost dumbing down and de-skilling of the workforce.

Cities made the working class a powerful force by raising consciousness and enabling people to unite for political action and to remedy economic dissatisfaction.

The Industrial Revolution created a unique new category of people who were dependent on their job alone for income, a job from which they might be dismissed without cause. Until 1850, workers as a whole did not share in the general wealth produced by the Industrial Revolution. Conditions would improve as the century wore on, as union action combined with general prosperity and a developing social conscience to improve the working conditions, wages, and hours first of skilled labor, and later of unskilled labor.

A concerted effort to change fundamental values to one where **consumption** was encouraged, as it was the lifeblood of an industrialized and capitalistic society, took hold. Rather than practicing the good, old concepts of thrift and staying out of debt, the Industrial Revolution pushed people to consume! The economics of the society depended on people buying goods. If too few goods were purchased, then factory orders would fall and people would be laid off of work. A sure way to prevent any economic ruin was to convince people to be intensive and insatiable consumers, buying things they never even knew they needed. To encourage such consumption, the **advertising industry** was created, which sought to use any technique necessary to get people to feel they needed to purchase goods and to convince them that they should even throw away still functioning items in order to get the "latest, improved" models. Such technique worked and increased consumer demand. To keep up with and to keep track of such demand, there were improvements all along the supply chain, from transportation, warehousing, and shipping to record keeping, which led to bigger department stores, chain markets, and later mail-order catalogs, like the Sears catalog, to move goods rapidly from the shelves of stores to the hands of consumers.

One way to pay for all of these goods, especially when money was tight, sparked the development of credit services, credit and charge cards, lay-away plans, and even pay-over-time sorts of deals.

There were rises in the standards of living—however unequally applied. Consumption increased with a new materialistic view of the world. As the society became a one based on consumption, they needed more money in order to survive. Most families did not have enough money with just the parents working, so small children too were sent to work in factories. As people no longer lived on the farms where only certain types of food grew, in the cities, people had access to a variety of foods and so their diets improved as did their health.

A transportation revolution ensued in order to distribute the productivity of machinery and deliver raw materials to the eager factories. This led to the growth of canal systems, the construction of hard-surfaced "macadam" roads, the commercial use of the steamboat (demonstrated by Robert Fulton, 1765–1815), and the railway locomotive (made commercially successful by George Stephenson, 1781–1848). A subsequent revolution in agriculture made it possible for fewer people to feed the population, thus freeing people to work in factories, or in the new fields of communications, distribution of goods, or services like teaching, medicine, and entertainment.

The Industrial Revolution also brought changes in social hierarchies. The upper class started to consist more of very rich industrial and business families who then married into noble families to give themselves "old-world" authority as well. Upper middle classes consisted of lawyers and doctors (business people and professionals). Lower middle classes consisted of teachers, office workers, shop workers, and clerks. The lower classes were made up of factory workers and peasants.

Political Effects

The Industrial Revolution went hand in hand with the advent of imperialism. Industrial technology had consequences that not only supported and prompted Europeans to look beyond their borders but also facilitated it. The European countries that had already gone through industrialization had better and cheaper weapons and were able then to use their weapons, or the threat of them, to conquer people who did not have access to that same technology. In addition, countries needed a steady supply of raw goods as well as a market to sell the goods once they were manufactured. Colonies would prove wonderful opportunities to do both. The industrial imperialists turned to two areas of the world—Africa and Asia—where they saw big markets and with easy access to them.

The Industrial Revolution also led to the creation of new social and political ideologies. **Adam Smith** in his *Wealth of Nations* argued that economic prosperity for a country and fairness is actually best achieved through private ownership. Smith introduced the concept of the **invisible hand** that stated that if all individuals follow their own self-interests, it would be for the economic good of everyone, since everyone will do what they do best. He felt that individuals should own the means of production and sell their goods on an open and free market where demand, not the government, controlled prices and availability. When governments removed themselves completely from regulation, he called it the *Laissez Faire* economics. The industrialists embraced his ideas because for them, it assured them of more profit and less government regulation. Others were not so sure of his ideas and took quite different positions. **Jeremy Bentham** argued that the government should manage the economy and address social problems. **Malthus** argued that the reason for poverty is overpopulation and can be addressed by delayed marriages and abstinence instead of government involvement. **Robert Owen** and **Charles Fourier** also came up with socialist **utopian societies** without capitalists. **Karl Marx** pointed out that factory workers were exploited under capitalism not just because of individual malfeasance but because there were inherent flaws in the system. He noted that the working class could and would eventually revolt and take over the means of production. Once class structure was overturned and the instruments of power that conspired against the workers on behalf of the rich were overturned, then the workers' lives would improve. Marx's ideas sparked not only the foundation of **socialism** and **communism** but also movements that began to demand reform and improvement in the lives of workers. In fact, the hard working conditions and bad economic life led to various protests and riots by the workers and eventually led to the formation of trade unions and "benevolent societies" that tried to protect worker rights. Their efforts met with success when the Parliament passed the Factory Act of 1833, the Mines Act of 1842, and the repeal of the Corn Laws in 1846 that addressed the issues of abuse in the industrial sectors.

There were some good political effects of the Industrial Revolution as it resulted in the extension of the right to vote to the middle classes and then to all members of society; it helped push the idea of public education to meet the needs of an industrialized society; and it helped develop tools of mass media, beginning with print media. The **Chartist Movement** called for political reform, universal male suffrage, and other Parliamentary reforms, partly in an effort to give working men a voice in the government.

Economic Effects

The most obvious effect of the Industrial Revolution is that goods were produced more efficiently. This resulted in an increased supply of goods, and along with that the price of goods decreased. With the lowering of prices for goods, there was more consumer demand for goods. As a result, more factories were created to keep up with consumer demand.

The Industrial Revolution created a new type of wealth, no longer based on land, but now based upon the ownership of factories and machinery. The emergence of a new group of capitalists who financed and profited from industrialization began to emerge. These early entrepreneurs had to find two kinds of capital to finance their operations: long-term capital to expand present operations, and short-term capital to purchase raw materials, maintain inventories, and pay wages to their employees. While industrialists met their long-term capital needs through mortgages, short-term capital for raw materials and maintaining stock was accommodated by extending credit to the manufacturers by the producers or dealers. Often, a supplier of raw materials waited from 6 to 12 months for payment of his goods, after the manufacturer was paid for the finished product.

The payment of wages was not an easily solved problem but one which often was taken at the expense of the worker. Some employers staggered the days on which they paid their employees, while others paid them in script. Some paid a portion of their work force early in the day, allowing them to shop for household needs. When the money had circulated through the shopkeepers back to the employer, another portion of the work force was paid. All of these methods proved to be unacceptable. So, one outcome of this need to finance short-term capital came from new, private banks that catered to industrialists. Unfortunately, many of these banks failed as they were unable to meet the demands of the factory economy. A banking system was eventually set up to distribute capital to areas where it was needed, drawing it from areas where there was a surplus.

Industrialization brought about the rise of big business. With big business came the need to invest large amounts of money and the quandary of where to find it. Many businesses turned to selling stocks or shares of their business to investors. This added investment of capital enabled businesses to expand and delivered tremendous profits to investors and owners.

COMPETENCY 4.9
Identify the causes, effects, events, and significant individuals associated with the Age of Revolution.

Revolutions (1789–1848)

The Age of Revolution might be considered products of the Enlightenment, where the values of freedom, equality, and sovereignty created a shift in understandings about what the roles and functions of people, religion, and the state should be. No longer did people consider their rulers all-powerful beings who were given a Divine Right to rule. Now, with Enlightenment, people believed that just rule comes only from a ruler whose power came from their constituents. The tensions that this new way of thinking created resulted in a series of revolutions throughout the world:

- North America: Colonists sought freedom from Britain in the quest for enlightenment values of freedom, equality, and popular sovereignty.

- France: Inspired by events in North America, they abolished their monarchy, church, and aristocracy and established a republic built on equality and popular sovereignty

- Colonies in Latin America fought for their freedom against French and Spanish rule.

What is significant about this Age of Revolution is the seeming idea that these pressures for change existed throughout the world, each one inspiring the other to revolt. Challenges to governmental authorities inside one nation seem to provide inspiration across borders. The nineteenth century experienced such a wave with the American Revolution, the French Revolution, followed by the revolutions of 1830 and 1848 that then prompted revolutions in Latin America, central, southern, and eastern Europe, and even against Austria and Prussia, south of the equator, protests in Brazil sparked additional protests in Chile, etc.

The French Revolution I (1789–1799)

Radical ideas about society and government were developed during the eighteenth century in response to the success of the "scientific" and "intellectual" revolutions of the preceding two centuries. Armed with new scientific knowledge of the physical universe, as well as new views of the human capacity to detect "truth," social critics assailed existing modes of thought governing political, social, religious, and economic life. Ten years of upheaval in France (1789–1799) further shaped modern ideas and practices. Napoleon Bonaparte spread some of the revolutionary ideas about the administration of government as he conquered much of Europe. The modern world that came of age in the eighteenth century was characterized by rapid, revolutionary changes, which paved the way for economic modernization and political centralization throughout Europe.

Causes of the French Revolution

The rising expectations of "enlightened" society were demonstrated by the increased criticism directed toward government inefficiency and corruption and toward the privileged classes. The clergy (First Estate) and nobility (Second Estate), representing only two percent of the total population of 24 million, were the privileged classes and were essentially tax exempt. The remainder of the population (Third Estate) consisted of the middle class, urban workers, and the mass of peasants, who bore the entire burden of taxation and the imposition of feudal obligations. As economic conditions worsened in the eighteenth century, the French state became poorer, and totally dependent on the poorest and most depressed sections of the economy for support at the very time this tax base had become saturated.

Designed to represent the three estates of France, the Estates General had only met twice, once at its creation in 1302 and again in 1614. When the French *parlements* insisted that any new taxes must be approved by this body, King Louis XVI reluctantly ordered it to assemble at Versailles by May 1789. Election fever swept over France for the very first time. The election campaign took place in the midst of the worst subsistence crisis in eighteenth-century France, with widespread grain shortages, poor harvests, and inflated bread prices. Finally, on May 5, 1789, the Estates General met and argued over whether to vote by estate or individual. Each estate was ordered to meet separately and vote as a unit. The Third Estate refused and insisted that the entire assembly stay together.

Events

Phases of Revolution

The National Assembly (1789–1791): After a six-week deadlock over voting methods, representatives of the Third Estate declared themselves the true National Assembly of France (June 17). Defections from the First and Second Estates then caused the king to recognize the National Assembly (June 27) after dissolving the Estates General. At the same time, Louis XVI ordered troops to surround Versailles. The "Parisian" revolution began at this point. Angry because of food shortages, unemployment, high prices, and fear of military repression, the workers and tradespeople began to arm themselves.

The Legislative Assembly (1791–1792): While the National Assembly had been rather homogeneous in its composition, the new government began to fragment into competing political factions. The most important political clubs were republican groups such as the Jacobins (radical urban) and Girondins (moderate rural), while the *Sans-culottes* (working-class, extremely radical) were a separate faction with an economic agenda.

The National Convention (1792–1795): Meeting for the first time in September 1792, the Convention abolished monarchy and installed republicanism. Louis XVI was charged with treason, found guilty, and executed on January 21, 1793. Later the same year, the queen, Marie Antoinette, met the same fate. The most notorious event of the French Revolution was the famous "Reign of Terror" (1793–1794), the government's campaign against its internal enemies and counterrevolutionaries.

The Directory (1795–1799): The Constitution of 1795 restricted voting and office holding to property owners. The middle class was in control. It wanted peace in order to gain more wealth and to establish a society in which money and property would become the only requirements for prestige and power. Despite rising inflation and mass public dissatisfaction, the Directory government ignored a growing shift in public opinion. When elections in April 1797 produced a triumph for the royalist right, the results were annulled, and the Directory shed its last pretense of legitimacy. But the weak and corrupt Directory government managed to hang on for two more years because of great military success. French armies annexed the Austrian Netherlands, the left bank of the Rhine, Nice, and Savoy. The Dutch Republic was made a satellite state of France. The greatest military victories were won by Napoleon Bonaparte, who drove the Austrians out of northern Italy and forced them to sign the Treaty of Campo Formio (October 1797), in return for which the Directory government agreed to Bonaparte's scheme to conquer Egypt and threaten English interests in the East.

The French Revolution II: The Era of Napoleon (1799–1815)

Consulate Period, 1799–1804 (Enlightened Reform): The new government was installed on December 25, 1799, with a constitution that concentrated supreme power in the hands of Napoleon. His aim was to govern France by demanding obedience, rewarding ability, and organizing everything in orderly hierarchical fashion. Napoleon's domestic reforms and policies affected every aspect of society.

Empire Period, 1804–1814 (War and Defeat): After being made Consul for Life (1801), Napoleon felt that only through an empire could France retain its strong position in Europe. On December 2, 1804, Napoleon crowned himself emperor of France in Notre Dame Cathedral.

Militarism and Empire Building: Beginning in 1805, Napoleon engaged in constant warfare that placed French troops in enemy capitals from Lisbon and Madrid to Berlin and Moscow and temporarily gave Napoleon the largest empire since Roman times. Napoleon's Grand Empire consisted of an enlarged France, satellite kingdoms, and coerced allies. French-ruled peoples viewed Napoleon as a tyrant who repressed and exploited them for France's glory and advantage. Enlightened reformers believed Napoleon had betrayed the ideals of the Revolution.

The downfall of Napoleon resulted from his inability to conquer England, economic distress caused by the Continental System (boycott of British goods), the Peninsular War with Spain, the German War of Liberation, and the invasion of Russia. The actual defeat of Napoleon was the result of the Fourth Coalition and the Battle of Leipzig ("Battle of Nations"). Napoleon was exiled to the island of Elba as a sovereign with an income from France. After learning of allied disharmony at the Vienna peace talks, Napoleon left Elba and began the Hundred Days by seizing power from the restored French king, Louis XVIII. Napoleon's gamble ended at Waterloo in June 1815. He was exiled as a prisoner of war to the South Atlantic island of St. Helena, where he died in 1821.

The Post-War Settlement: The Congress of Vienna (1814–1815)

The **Congress of Vienna** met in 1814 and 1815 to redraw the map of Europe after the Napoleonic era and to provide some way of preserving the future peace of Europe. Europe was spared a general war throughout the remainder of the nineteenth century. But the failure of the statesmen who shaped the future in 1814–1815 to recognize the forces, such as nationalism and liberalism, unleashed by the French Revolution, only postponed the ultimate confrontation between two views of the world—change and accommodation, or maintaining the status quo.

The Vienna settlement was the work of the representatives of the four nations that had done the most to defeat Napoleon: England (Lord Castlereagh), Austria (Prince Klemens Von Metternich), Russia (Tsar Alexander I), and Prussia (Karl Von Hardenberg). Arrangements to guarantee the enforcement of the status quo as defined by the Vienna settlement included two provisions: The "Holy Alliance" of Tsar Alexander I of Russia, an idealistic and unpractical plan, existed only on paper. No one except Alexander took it seriously. But the "Quadruple Alliance" of Russia, Prussia, Austria, and England provided for concerted action to arrest any threat to the peace or balance of power.

From 1815 to 1822, European international relations were controlled by the series of meetings held by the great powers to monitor and defend the status quo: the Congress of Aix-la-Chapelle (1818), the Congress of Troppau (1820), the Congress of Laibach (1821), and the Congress of Verona (1822).

1848 Revolutions

The year 1848 is considered the watershed of the nineteenth century. The revolutionary disturbances of the first half of the nineteenth century reached a climax in a new wave of revolutions that extended from Scandinavia to southern Italy, and from France to central Europe. Only England and Russia avoided violent upheaval. The issues were substantially the same as they had been in 1789. What was new in 1848 was that these demands were far more widespread and irrepressible than ever. The accumulation of domestic economic and population crises seemed to build up enough pressure that contention spread easily and found long standing, highly repressive, and seemingly powerful governments become their target. Industrialization's exploitation of workers, the shifting of society away from skilled to unskilled labor increased people's irritation and angst. At the same time, advances in education and the appearance of liberal policies in the United States, England, Belgium, and Switzerland led to a gradual spread of reformist ideas and values, which contrasted sharply with the absolutist monarchies in power. This proved to be only fodder for those who remained under what they increasingly saw as untenable conditions. Generally speaking, the 1848 upheavals shared the strong influences of romanticism, nationalism, and liberalism, as well as a new factor of economic dislocation and instability.

While revolutions did occur one after the other, they also occurred for a variety of reasons and had different aims, from government to government. At first, these revolutions all appeared to be rather successful, but in the end, they all failed. The flurry of revolutions tended to occur in governments where there was widespread distrust and fear coupled with rising food prices and unemployment. In the end, the revolutions did not succeed, owing partly to divisions within the revolutionary ranks and also because the old governments refused to give in.

Causes

- Middle-class predominance within the unregulated economy continued to drive liberals to push for more government reform and civil liberty. They enlisted the help of the working classes to put more pressure on the government to change, and they demanded more rights.

- Financial crises caused by a downturn in the commercial and industrial economy prompted an economic slowdown.

- Businesses failed,

- Unemployment was widespread.

- Frustration among artisan and working classes as wages diminished.

- Living conditions deteriorated in the cities.

- Poor harvests, like the Irish potato blight and cereal harvest failures, caused severe food shortages and likewise an increase in the prices of basic necessities.

- Investment failures and financial crises resulted in workers being laid off and so urban and middle classes now found themselves in the same boat as the peasantry.

- Nationalism among European minorities sparked discontent and fervor in the Germanies, Italies, and Eastern Europe to overthrow the existing governments.

- Pre-1848 tensions seemed to exacerbate the situation.

- Industrialization and urbanization brought new economic challenges that rulers were not prepared to deal with.

- The population had doubled in the eighteenth century, causing widespread food shortages.

- Ideological challenges articulated some of these feelings of dissent as ideas of liberalism, nationalism, democracy, and socialism took hold.

- Repressive state measures sparked anger, rather than just fear, among the population.

Effects

Although none of the revolutions succeeded, they had a lasting impact on Europe.

- The widespread revolutions measured the failures of restoration, once again demonstrated the power of political ideas, and uncovered the effects of a generation of social change.

- Several gains, in fact, did endure: peasants in Prussia and Austria were emancipated, Piedmont and Prussia kept their new constitutions, and monarchs learned they needed to watch public opinion.

- Liberals learned that they needed educated, literate citizens in order to run a constitutional government. They saw that the masses might have their own demands that conflicted with their own. As a result, the educated liberals had to reevaluate their goals and how much they should buy into a system with which they disagreed. The left became quite bitter and hardened by the failures of 1848. They turned to more militant means to achieve their ends, even becoming willing to use terror, violence, and assassination to achieve it.

• The conservative elite began to realize that while using brute force is a good temporary measure to secure power, it was not a good, long-term response to revolutionary fervor, as it would only increase opposition and resentment.

• There was a realization that it would be better to have liberal concessions to keep radical voices marginalized so they would not gain more power.

• Everyone realized that revolutions needed power and armies to back them up but that, nevertheless, nationalism was a powerful new force in politics.

• More power was given to the Realism movement where art and literary forms of expression focused more on real life and portrayals of poverty, oppression, and injustice.

• Nationalist groups realized that there was indeed reason to fear both groups within their own country as well as outside of it. So, nationalist fervor continued to mount and created more fissures within the society and would weaken many of these new, tenuous governments.

France

France, already having had the experience of its earlier revolution behind it, certainly seemed that it could have the potential to be another lightning rod for revolutionaries. The 1848 revolutions started in France from disgruntled working classes and liberals who were upset with **King Louis Philippe**, who had ruled since 1830, and his minister **Francois Guizot** who refused to widen suffrage. Protesters had launched reform banquets to protest the King's refusal to grant any reforms and planned a large banquet to be held in Paris in late February 1848. The government banned the banquet, people decided to show up anyway, and guards fired on peaceful protesters. The National Guard, who was supposed to support the government, but who they themselves were politically disenfranchised, defected to the radicals' side. King Louis Philippe realized the position he was in, and after rioting in the streets, on February 24, he abdicated in favor of his grandson. A new provisional government was formed under a famous poet, **Alphonse de Lamartine,** who declared that France was now, again, a Republic. This new government though was dominated more by moderates than radicals, and while they did agree to universal male suffrage, the citizen's right to work, secular education, and an investigation of labor problems, workers were still not satisfied. The workers wanted social programs, a redistribution of wealth, and the implementation of "national workshops," which would provide work for the unemployed as relief programs. When the government disbanded the workshops, the workers agitated and started fighting in the streets. Government troops, under the direction of **General Cavaignac,** squashed the demonstrators in bloody battles referred to as the **June Days** and then established what would be a second French republic. Cavaignac restricted the press, suppressed the radicals, and instituted severe disciple on the workers. An election held in December resulted in another Bonaparte to the rescue, and **Louis Napoleon Bonaparte**, as the "law and order candidate," won 70% of the vote. Bonaparte purged the government of radical officials and replaced them with conservatives, disbanded the national Assembly and held a new election, and used force against anyone who disagreed with his policies—effectively, another dictator was in place.

Austria

The Austrian government, headed by Ferdinand I, was a rather conservative monarchy that had to control a heterogeneous population with about a dozen different language groups. The society was still reliant on the bondages of serfdom for its economic stability and having the majority of its population still tied to the land in this way while they could see that other countries were beginning to do away with it led to a generally dissatisfied populace growing more dissatisfied by the day. The February Revolution in France triggered outbursts in Vienna by mid-March when people campaigned for liberal reforms. The Austrian Empire responded by establishing a free press and national guard and even allowing Hungary to levy its own taxes and form its own army. Students in Vienna who had heard about the Hungarian concessions rose up and rioting broke out in Vienna. **Metternich** ended up resigning, the censorship that had long been a bane of intellectuals was ended, a constitution was promised, the Constituent Assembly met, serfdom was abolished, and universal male suffrage was bestowed upon the population.

The concessions given to Hungarian demands for autonomy created a "me too" atmosphere as the Czechs in Bohemia, the Croatians in Croatia, and the Romanians in Transylvania all campaigned for the same freedoms. The Hapsburgs ultimately defeated all of these smaller rebellions, in no small measure due to the support of the Russians and Tsar Nicholas who joined the Hapsburgs in defeating the Magyars in August 1849. In the end, the Hapsburgs regained power and used their armies to force all of the revolutionaries into submission.

Prussia

Frederick William IV of Prussia, an anti-liberal, and slightly crazy, monarch, upon hearing about the Viennese uprising, decided to allow some reform. He relaxed censorship and even called the **Landtag** (Parliament) in May 1848–May 1849. This attempt at loosening bonds did not really work out that well, and fighting broke out anyway. When Frederick William IV agreed to remove his troops from Berlin and allow an elected constitutional assembly, German liberals were overjoyed. However, such joy proved to be short-lived and riots broke out in Berlin. The **Frankfurt National Assembly,** comprised of 830 men, was one of three assemblies created as a way to reorganize that which was Prussia, its task was to unify Germany. The Frankfurt Assembly spent much of its time debating various plans for a unified Germany, but it also had to decide on immediate practical problems, such as the nature of the executive power and Germany's territory. Archduke John of Austria, a comparatively liberal uncle of the Austrian emperor Ferdinand, was appointed regent of Germany and head of the **assembly**'s executive power on June 29. Yet it soon became clear that the executive appointed by the **assembly** had no power except such as was granted to it by the governments of the individual states.

While the **Frankfurt National Assembly** attempted to take over the conduct of a war with Denmark, Prussia abruptly concluded the war. Prussia's **Frederick William IV** had lost all patience with the liberals and had turned increasingly toward ultraconservative advisers. In Austria the emperor Ferdinand had abdicated in favor of his nephew **Francis Joseph**, who likewise relied on conservative ministers.

The **Frankfurt National Assembly** adopted a proposed constitution for Germany on March 28, 1849. This document provided for universal suffrage, parliamentary government, and a hereditary emperor. Germany was to have a unified monetary and customs system but would maintain the internal autonomy of the constituent German states.

But in the meantime, Austria had proclaimed a new constitution (March 4, 1849), which mandated that either the entire Austrian Empire or none of it would enter the new Germany. This was a blow to those liberals who had hoped for a Germany that would include Austria, or at least its German-speaking provinces. The initiative thus passed to those who wanted to exclude Austria from a Germany that would be under the leadership of Prussia. Accordingly, when the election of an emperor took place in the **national assembly** on March 28, 290 votes were cast for **Frederick William** of Prussia against 248 abstentions. On April 3 the king received a deputation from the **assembly** that came to offer him the crown—he refused the offer—he was too deeply conservative to receive a German imperial crown from any hands except those of the other German princes. Prussia also rejected the proposed constitution.

Without the support of either Prussia or Austria, the **Frankfurt National Assembly** would not survive. By May, Gagern's ministry had broken up, and the majority of the deputies were ordered home by the governments of their respective states. The rump that remained was forced to move to Stuttgart and was finally dispersed on June 18 by Württemberg troops and police. The **Frankfurt National Assembly** and the revolutions of 1848 that had inspired it were over.

Italy

Like the other revolutions, the Italian revolution seemed successful, constitutions were received, but then they ultimately failed. Italian nationalists in Milan, Lombardi, and Venetia sought to end foreign domination of Italy. In the *Five Glorious Days of Milan*, the Austrians were forced to retreat and the Venetian republic was reestablished. The Piedmont also joined the war against Austria.

In the end, Austria's military force was more superior and they returned, beat Piedmont and its allies, and regained control. Sicily fell to Naples in May 1849, and Venetia fell to Austria in August 1849. Much of the reason why the Italian revolutions did not work out was that the rural populations did not support the revolt, and the revolutions had to be carried out by the urban middle classes. Goals, too, were uneven, and distrust among allies ran rampant. Many moderates so feared the radicals that the entire revolutionary structure collapsed. There was also a lack of a coherent leadership to speak with one voice—instead, the revolutionaries each put forth their own ideas, goals, and agendas, thus weakening the revolution with their differences.

COMPETENCY 4.10

Evaluate the impact of imperialism and nationalism on global social, political, geographic, and economic development.

The term **nationalism** is generally used to describe two phenomena: the attitude that members of a nation have when they care about their national identity and the actions that the members of a nation take when seeking to achieve or sustain self-determination. Nationalism has had an enormous influence on world history. The quest for national hegemony has inspired millennia of imperialism and colonization, while struggles for national liberation have resulted in many revolutions. In modern times, the nation-state has become the dominant form of societal organization. Historians use the term nationalism to refer to this historical transition and to the emergence and predominance of nationalist ideology. When nationalism turns ugly, the results are war, military conflict, and even genocide. Possibly the most dominant concept in world history is war. War is a constant. It can be said that in human history, there have been very few, if any, times when war was not being waged somewhere on the globe. In today's world of terrorism, the concepts of war and genocide are no longer found only within nation-states, making the elimination of war and genocide even more of a challenge.

Extent of Colonialism in 1939

	Great Britain	France	Belgium	Netherlands	Germany (1914)
Area in Square Miles	94,000	212,600	11,800	13,200	210,000
Population	45,500,100	42,000,000	8,300,000	8.500,000	67,500,000
Area of Colonies	13,100,000	4,300,000	940,000	790,000	1,100,000
Population of Colonies	470,000,000	65,000,000	13,000,000	66,000,000	13,000,000

Source: Mary Evelyn Townsend, *European Colonial Expansion Since 1871* (Chicago: J.P. Lippincott Company, 1941), p. 19.

Percentage of Territories Belonging to the European/U.S. Colonial Powers (1900)

Region	Percentage Controlled
Africa	90.4%
Polynesia	98.9%
Asia	56.5%
Australia	100.0%
Americas	27.2%

Source: A. Supan, *Die territoriale Entwicklung der Euroaischen Kolonien* (Gotha, 1906), p. 254

Impact of Imperialism on Global Social, Political, Geographic, and Economic Development

In 1900, the British ruled 400 million subjects and controlled a quarter of the globe; the French controlled 6 million square miles and 52 million subjects; Germany acquired 1 million square miles and 15 million people; and by 1914, most of the world was under formal European control. Such domination not only resulted in a remarkable transformation in the relationship between Europe and the wider world but also brought up the question of whether or not this was a good idea. There are two sides to this investigation: basically, was Western intervention a boon, bringing technological development, liberal politics, and social reform, or was it a bust, destroying the world for the sake of their own pockets and guilty pleasures, creating tremendous political instability, poverty, social divisiveness, and eroding the chances of these nations to thrive in the modern world as independent nations?

The impact of Western imperialism had and continues to have a dramatic, transforming, and disruptive impact on the societies of Africa, Asia, the Americas, and the Pacific. In fact, only a few non-industrialized regions were able to withstand the aggressive agendas of the West. Most significantly, it undermined civilizations, even putting an end to some of them. Indigenous civilizations of the Americas, like the Aztecs and Incans, were decimated and so seriously undermined that the region still feels the effects of it today. The forced migration that occurred through the African Slave trade radically changed the landscape not only of Africa but also the Americas. Lasting effects of racial oppression continue. The economic toll that the Western economic exploitation had world-wide as they plundered the colonial world was unequaled. The imposition of the West's "liberal" forms of government and reforms actually unraveled political and social structures in Africa and Asia to such an extent that it never recovered.

An important point to remember is the differences between **colonialism** and **imperialism**, and one is not necessarily interchangeable for the other. Colonialism is the official government rule of one state over the other; imperialism is when one country exerts cultural or economic influence over another without having governmental institutions act for them; in practical terms, it also is the perpetuation of the influence of a colonial empire over a country, even when it no longer has sovereignty over it. So, today, the United States exerts an imperial influence over much of the world, as its popular culture and economics influence a great percentage of it; however, the United States's role as a colonial enterprise is much more limited. Countries under imperial domination do retain a degree of autonomy and self-determination, while their counterparts under colonial control do not.

There were targeted differences between British and French colonialism that might explain some of their imperial control today. British colonialism was fueled by the search for more resources and new markets in order to increase their profits. There were two phases of British colonialism: the first phase concentrated on the New World, West Africa, and India, and the second phase included India, Australia, New Zealand, and parts of eastern and southern Africa. British efforts at colonialism largely found justification from Kipling's idea of **white man's burden,** in which they thought that native peoples were not capable of governing themselves, so it was the duty of the British to provide and maintain order.

French colonialism, on the other hand, was driven more by the state, church, and military than business interests, like the British. The first phase of French colonialism was focused on Canada, the Louisiana Territory, the Caribbean, and West Africa. During the second phase of French Colonialism, the empire grew to include North Africa and Indochina. The ideological justification for French colonialism was the *mission civilisatrice*, which, while a little similar to the English concept of white man's burden, actually had as a corollary goal, to spread French culture, language, and religion throughout the colonies, in an effort to "civilize" them. The French had two forms of colonial rule: indirect and direct. **Indirect rule** referred to the French practice of governing through native political structures and leaders and **direct rule** occurred when the French would impose new governments on indigenous populations.

Political Impact of Imperialism

Part of the political impacts of colonialism lies in the creation of new nations with new government structures ruled by a new group of people with vested interests in achieving and protecting their own ideas about how to govern and their personal property. In addition, many of the political systems have no historical precedent in the region or are weak, without effective support from the people.

Social Impact of Imperialism

The social impact of imperialism was complex, as people were exposed to empire in different ways. People who were embraced by the colonial regimes, sometimes local elites, sometimes educated middle classes who had a vested interest in making deals with the new power, were simultaneously viewed as "friends" by the colonizer and "collaborators" by those who were colonized.

Another social impact of imperialism is the social inequality bred by colonial policies. One example is that of the Aboriginal peoples in Canada who, prior to colonization, were actually healthier than Europeans. They had a more balanced diet and lifestyle, education took place in their communities, and people learned to live off of the land. Today, we can see that there were deleterious effects on the Aboriginal populations who are less healthy, less educated, and have less healthy lifestyles.

Geographic Impact of Imperialism

Colonizers tended to assume that because they may have had technological superiority over the places they colonized, they also came to believe that they had racial, cultural, and religious superiority as well. What resulted were these beliefs of environmental determinism that assumed that the reason why certain peoples were "behind" in terms of technology could be traced to climactic and racial reasons. What resulted was colonial behavior and thought that emanated from a physical mapping of the world, visually separating colonized and colonizer into "them" and "us."

An end geographical result of colonialism on geographical development was the imposition of borders that bore little resemblance to "natural" borders or to political borders that had existed prior to colonial rule. The carving up of the Ottoman Empire, the Middle East, and South Asia into areas designed to maximize benefits for the former colonizers rather than the inhabitants created numerous conflicts that are still being born out today. For example, the modern political boundaries in West Africa are based upon linguistic, political, and economic contrasts that resulted from colonial policies in the region, rather than "on the ground" realities. The use of techniques like partition as parting gifts to countries at the end of colonial rule fashioned new countries that had little bearing on the political realities of the area, and doomed them to a history of conflict not only within their borders but outside it as well.

Economic Impact of Imperialism

The economic consequences of empire varied depending on the nature and the extent of the imperial relationship. When imperialism involved demographic displacement, colonial peoples experienced catastrophic results with huge losses of people, lands, and resources that continue to be felt today. In other places, we see mixed results. In the early modern trading empires, certain colonial peoples benefited from the new trade relationships that were established with Europeans that changed or bolstered their positions within their own societies. Other societies, like China during the Opium Wars, wanted to restrict trade. Some consequences of imperialism were the transfers of tools and technologies and also the exchange of animals and plant species (along with diseases). For instance, Australia benefited from the introduction of sheep, and Native Americans made effective use of the horse.

Some of the disparity about the varied economic effects on post-colonial environments may also reflect the differences between empires. For instance, North American success stories may be attributed to a favorable legacy of growth-conducive institutions from England that helped secure and define property rights, thereby resulting in more favorable investment early-on. Also, the costs of achieving independence, in terms of the United States, was largely born by other countries, like the French, whereas in South America, the cost of freedom and revolution was borne solely upon those countries, making it more difficult for them post-independence to move into self-sustaining growth.

Despite certain incursions that limited colonial economic development, in some cases, the imperial hand both gave and took away. For instance, the British did take over trade that had been happening between India and Europe, but on the other hand, some indigenous enterprises did flourish. In West Africa, European sea trade enabled African farmers to field new crops based on Amazon staples, like cocoa, making the West Africans the main cultivators of that crop.

Because one of the purposes of colonies was to provide raw materials for the colonial government to be manufactured in the homeland and then resold at substantially higher prices, little effort was paid to improving manufacturing in the colonies. There were some exceptions, as when Korea was under Japanese rule and was the only colony that had imperial creation of heavy industrial enterprises built on their soil. The British though were not averse to Indian economic development if it increased their markets but refused to help in areas where they felt there was conflict with their own economic interests or political security.

Another aim of colonial economics was to control trade and to set up cash crop economies. In many cases, indigenous farmers were forced to change the crops that they were growing and upon which they used for subsistence and instead grow cash crops. The problem occurred during failed harvests, or when colonial powers manipulated the prices paid to these farmers, so much so that rather than growing their own food, people now had to pay for it. When harvests failed, and people received little to no money for their cash crops (like cotton and jute), they starved and there was widespread famine.

The implementation of European institutions on the colonies often resulted from a misguided attempt to interpret the existing indigenous system in terms that the Europeans could understand. Reform attempts, or attempts to organize indigenous economies, had unintended disastrous economic or social consequences. The best example of this case was the English complete misunderstanding of land policy in India where they interpreted *zamindar* rights to collect taxes and manage the land in the name of the Mughal Emperor, as landlord rights. The result was that millions of Indians were denied use of their land, forced to pay rent and taxes on their land even during times of famine, or risk being evicted. The British ideas of land ownership also created opportunities for Europeans to own huge swathes of fertile land, seized from those who could not afford the high rents, and to create an Indian economic elite with political power based on how much land a person controlled.

Colonial governments also had a rather mixed view on how it implemented economic and social reform. While Europe's mercantilist agenda in the Americas had encouraged slavery, it responded somewhat haphazardly when they took up the issue after their own abolitionist movements in the early nineteenth century. Europe, during the scramble to divide up Africa in the ninteenth century committed themselves to abolishing slavery on the continent. In actuality, however, it took decades before they enforced their prohibitions of slavery south of the Sahara.

It is also doubtful if there were any real economic benefits to the colonizers, as long-term effects destabilized their currencies, as was the case with Spain and the influx of bullion creating unmanageable inflation, or the destruction of regimes, as was the case of France whose exploit actually served to bring about the French Revolution as financial crises took hold. Even the benefits that Great Britain was assumed to have had, with the influx of cheap materials and the availability of captive markets, was not as much as had been thought, and may have resulted in a myopic and destructive view of the need to remain competitive outside their own colonial markets. Trade increases resulted more from domestic and European markets, rather than colonial trade. However, no doubt it did reap enormous help from the availability of raw materials from their colonies.

COMPETENCY 4.11
Analyze the causes and effects of political transformations and military conflicts in the twentieth century.

World War I

Causes

- There are many different interpretations about what caused the war, but the Treaty of Versailles, after the war, blamed it all on Germany.

- Direct cause of WWI: the **assassination of Archduke Franz Ferdinand** at Sarajevo on **28 June 1914**

- Intense nationalism—specifically Serbian nationalism

  - Germany: **Weltpolitik**—desire for world power status

  - France: Revenge over Alsace and Lorraine

  - British—fighting own imperialist issues and emergent nationalism in its colonies

- Alliance system and the rivalry between powers

  - Before 1914, Europe's main powers were divided into two armed camps by a series of alliances. These were the **Triple Alliance** of Germany, Austria-Hungary, and Italy (1882) and the **Triple Entente** of Britain, Russia, and France (1907)

  - Although these alliances were defensive in nature, they meant that any conflict between two countries involved the other country.

- **The main rivalries between the powers were:**

  - Germany and France over Alsace. This division made an alliance between both countries impossible.

  - Russia and Austria over the Balkans.

  - Britain and Germany over their navies and economic power.

- Crises before 1914 that exposed rivalries and rifts

  - **First Moroccan Crisis—1905 Kaiser Wilhelm II** visited the Morocco and denounced French influence there. This prompted outcry by both France and England, who was sensitive to other countries getting involved in their colonies. Brought an Anglo-French entente.

  - **Second Moroccan Crisis**—Germans sent gunboat to Morocco to protect German citizens there and said that France had ignored terms of Algeciras Conference. Germans agreed to leave Morocco in return for rights to the Congo.

  - **Annexation of Bosnia-Herzevinia** by Austria; angered Serbia and almost caused war to break out between supporters of each side.

- **Militarism:** The arms race was running amok, with military spending and sizes of armies doubling between 1870 and 1914.

	1910–1914 Increase in Defense Expenditures
France	10%
Britain	13%
Russia	39%
Germany	73%

- Economic rivalry

- Imperialism

- Germans trying to distract their population from problems and fears about Russians, so they wanted more colonies and territory in Europe.

- Growth of German power in Central Europe challenged Great Powers (France, Great Britain, and Russia).

- International competition among European powers for colonies and economic markets.

- Naval rivalry between Great Britain and Germany due to colonial rivalry.

- Breakdown of the European treaty system and the "Balance of Power."

- The Eastern Question—both Austria and Russia wanted control of the Balkan as the Ottoman Empire was losing its grip on the area. Russia encouraged Slav nationalism there, and Austria feared nationalism would spill over to their territory the Balkans.

- Domestic political factors—hopes among elites that a war would erase issue of socialism and would lose its favor among those groups clamoring for it.

Effects

Creation of New States After World War I

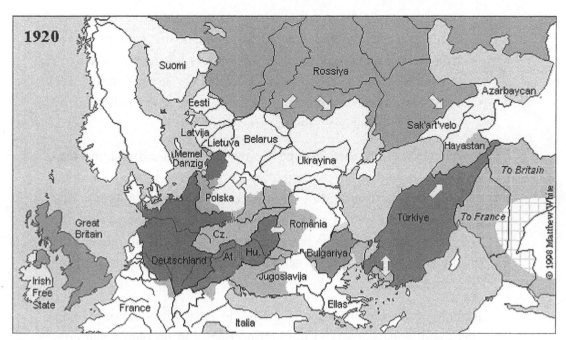

Source: htt://users.erols.com/mwhite28.post-ww1.htm. © Matthew White 1998

Political

- Socialist ideas experienced a boom in Europe, spreading from Germany and the Austrian Empire to Britain (1923) and France (1924).

- Republic became the most popular type of government to gain influence after the war in Europe. Before the war, Europe contained 19 monarchies and 3 republics, yet only a few years afterward, they had 13 monarchies, 14 republics, and 2 regencies.

- 1919 Treaty of Versailles had deleterious effects on the post-war environment as it caused hostilities and resentment that later paved the way for World War II.

- Germany was singled out for harsh treatment:

  - forced to sign a humiliating treaty accepting blame for causing the war and ordered to pay compensation for it;

  - size of the German state was reduced, while Italy and France was enlarged;

  - Weimar government not liked by most of the citizens and maintained little power in controlling the German state;

  - any German soldiers refused to give up fighting, even though Germany's military was ordered to be drastically reduced. Given such orders, numerous German ex-soldiers joined the Freikorps, an establishment of mercenaries available for street-fighting. The open hostility and simmering feelings of revenge exhibited by Germany foreshadowed the start of World War II

- Colonies who supported Europe during the war, like India and protectorates, like Egypt, thought they would be rewarded for their support. When Britain shot down one of Wilson's 14 Points that advocated the right of **self-determination** for all countries, the colonies rebelled. World War I also showed the vulnerabilities of the colonizer and massive nationalist movements started in many of the colonized states.

- Redraw of the boundaries of the Middle East, introduction of new states and leaders, sparked long-term crises and problems that continue today.

- Women acquired the right to vote throughout most of the countries in Europe.

- Status of working classes increased.

- United States's position in the world elevated.

- Break-up of the Ottoman Empire

- Rise of the Turkish Republic

- Increased involvement of government in society

- Increased propaganda

Economic

- Technology changed tremendously after the war, in part because of developments in mass production made during the war, like automobiles, airplanes, radios, and even certain chemicals.

- Tremendous war debt caused European governments to print more and more money, only to spur on uncontrollable inflation.

- Members of the middle class who had been living reasonably comfortably on investments began to experience a rocky financial period.

- German mark devalued tremendously. For instance, in 1923, in just three months, the mark jumped from 4.6 million marks to the dollar to 4.2 *trillion* marks to the dollar.

- War debt shifted world's financial center from England to the United States.

- Property damages were quite heavy in Europe, particularly France.

- War strained resources of each country to the maximum.

- Many social customs faded out, and society became more open (at least for a time).

- There was also a rapid development of new technology.

- There was a disruption of world trade.

Social

- Growing distrust with political and government officials over some of the horrors of the war and the reluctance that government officials had toward pursuing peace during the war.

- Tremendous sense of loss and anger in some part of Western Europe where one in four young men died in battle. The war killed 10–13 million people.

Russian Revolution of 1917

Causes

Economic

- Tsar's mismanagement

- Tremendous economic strains of World War I on the society

- So many men joined the army (15 million) that there were insufficient numbers to run the factories and farms, which led to widespread shortages of basic food, and working conditions in the factories deteriorated so badly that workers rioted and engaged in strikes to try to get better wages.

- Tsar responded to worker strikes with violence, which only caused more strikes, including strikes by transportation workers that further paralyzed the country.

- Prices soared as availability of goods plummeted.

- Famine threats to big cities

Political

- Dire economic situation was faced by the urban workers. Most worked eleven-hour days, and health and safety conditions were dismal.

- Upper classes and educated classes resented Tsar Nicholas's autocracy.

- Perception of government decadence and ineptness affected each level of society who saw the Romanov regime as corrupt.

- Irritation when Tsar Nicholas decided to take direct command of the army during World War I, leaving his German wife at the helm of the government (and she was under the sway of **Rasputin**).

- Army's morale was terrible. By October 1916, Russia had lost between 1.6 and 1.8 million soldiers, with an addition two million prisoners of war and one million who had gone missing. Mutinies occurred as soldiers lacked food, shoes, and weapons.

- Tsar Nicholas was blamed for the poor condition of the army as well as his handling of the War.

- Unwillingness of Tsar Nicholas to grant political reforms, his failure to let the Duma be effective, and his active attempt to diminish its power, caused all political opposition to become revolutionary.

- Rise of radical socialist political parties dedicated to overthrowing both Tsarism and (eventually) capitalism: Liberals—Kadets and Octoberists; Socialist Populists (the SRs); Marxists (Bolsheviks and Mensheviks).

Social

- Continuance of popular opposition to the Tsar and his policies due to discontent of peasants, worker, and minorities

- Centuries of oppression towards the lower classes, about 85% of whom were peasants who had been emancipated in 1861 by Tsar **Alexander II of Russia**, and had been given land to work on by the government, but the land was insufficient and peasants frequently rioted over their conditions and feelings of being "second-class subjects"

- Need for workers in the factories and lack of land for peasants resulted in many moving to the cities, which quickly became overrun and living conditions worsened.

- Vast discontent among Russian citizens

- Growing student and intelligentsia political radicalism, inspired by the West, who wanted quick change

- Failure of middle class to provide a base for liberal reforms to be enacted

Effects

- End of autocratic rule

- Establishment of a socialist/communist government

- Withdrawal of Russia from World War I

- Industrial growth and organization of economy on five-year plans

- Complete transformation of Russian society, government, and economy

- Formation of the Soviet Union

- Emergence of Russia as a world power

- Spread of communism throughout the world

- Criticism of imperialism, which lent a hand to nationalist movements in colonized countries

- Tremendous focus on education in the Soviet Union had an enormous impact on the population, which started the twentieth century as mainly illiterate into one of the world's most well-rounded educational systems

- Division of world into communist and capitalist camps—Cold War

World War II

Causes

Economic

- Great depression created environment for the emergence of the Nazi Party

Political

- Treaty of Versailles:

    - Germans unhappy with elements of the treaty that they considered to be humiliating and burdensome:

    - War Guilt Clause: they had to accept blame for starting the war.

    - Reparations: Germany had to pay tremendous costs for the war.

    - Disarmament: Germany only allowed to have a small army and six naval ships; no tanks, air force, or submarines allowed, and the Rhineland was to be demilitarized.

- Territorial Losses: Land taken away from Germany and given to other countries; no merger with Austria allowed.

- Hitler's Actions—He built up the military, ordered troops into the Rhineland, made alliances with Mussolini and Japan, and marched into Austria. He responded to world concern about his expansionist moves, and he replied that he had no more interest in expansion; however, he did when he demanded the Sudetenland and invaded first Czechoslovakia and then Poland.

- Failure of Appeasement: In order to make up for the harshness of the Treaty of Versailles, Neville Chamberlain thought that if they gave into Hitler's demands, he would be appeased. Hitler's response was to invade Czechoslovakia. Chamberlain acquiesced and said Britain would only step in if Hitler invaded Poland. Hitler invaded Poland.

- Failure of the League of Nations: Weak and ineffective and unable to stop war from happening because: not all countries had joined the League (chief among them, the United States, Germany, and Russia); the League had no power; the League had no army; the League was unable to act quickly because it only met four times a year and all decisions had to be agreed upon by all nations.

Social

- Emergence of fascism, which glorified the military, denounced international organization and cooperation, and considered war an accepted means for achieving national goals

Effect

- Massive human dislocations

- Extensive casualties

- Nuremberg war trials in which former Nazi leaders were tried for crimes against humanity carried out in the systematic murder of millions of Jews and others in the Holocaust

- Race for Space begins

- Early computer technology came out of World War II

- Emergence of third-world nationalist movements

- De-colonization of European empires

- Colonized countries, bolstered by weaknesses of England and France, galvanized to fight for independence

Political

- United States and USSR emerged as the two superpowers of the twentieth century.

- The bi-polarization of Europe and the beginning of the Cold War

- Division of Germany

  - Germany divided into four zones of occupation, each controlled by one of the victorious powers.

- Creation of the UN

- Japanese war trials

- Japan temporarily placed under United States rule; in ruins from extensive bombing and U.S. nuclear attack; military leaders tried and convicted of war crimes; emperor retains crown.

- England and France take a back seat to the United States and the USSR.

- Russian army built up to fight against Germans and by the end of the war, they occupied most of Eastern Europe.

Economic

- Creation of the International Monetary Fund (IMF) and General Agreement on Tariffs and Trade (GATT)

- England had been devastated by bombing and had to rely on aid from the United States.

- U.S. economy booms and actually have labor shortages, rather than any unemployment.

Social

- New technology developed during the war to fight diseases would sharply lower mortality rate and increase population growth.

- Technological developments during war had a significant impact— for instance, the English developed radar, which paved the way for television; progress in computers and electronics were important.

- Development of atomic bomb changed the nature of future wars.

- Women involved in workforce and this sparked changes.

COMPETENCY 4.12
Analyze major contemporary global political, social, economic, and geographic issues and trends.

Globalization has many definitions and many perspectives. The one thing to remember is that it is not a new concept—globalization has been happening for thousands of years. Basically, behind the definition of globalization is the notion that no one nation stands by itself, for the world really is one in which we see the interaction and integration of people, governments, and businesses with people of other nations through trade and investment. It challenges the idea that a state's influence stops at its borders, which really are just man-made designations of where a country should stop.

Today we see more examples of globalization than we may have seen previously, simply in its scope and diversity. In the past few decades, the flow of information and technology between and among peoples has spurred increases in cross-border trade, as goods and services are distributed more quickly than ever before. As a result, the world seems more connected in its day-to-day operations than previously. Such interaction has its effects on all aspects of life—environmental, cultural, political, economic, and social.

There are two principle drivers of globalization today: economic policies and technology. In terms of economic policies dictating the extent and direction of global interaction, we have seen that the adoption of free-market economic systems throughout the world has resulted in new international opportunities for trade and investment. Knocking down trade and political barriers has resulted in expansion of foreign markets and a re-honing of domestic ones. It is this constant integration with the world beyond one's borders that has made both countries and businesses realize that they need to have a carefully crafted international business and financial structure in place in order to meet needs. The other driver in globalization is technology, which has dramatically transformed the economic life of individuals, companies, and nations. These new tools make it easier to communicate worldwide, conduct international financial transactions with a flick of a switch, and collaborate with partners all over the world.

Globalization, however, is not without its detractors. Opponents of globalization have argued that the hold that multinational corporations now have over societies worldwide has been at the expense of local enterprise, development, culture, and the common people. Resistance to globalization has pushed such movements as "buy local," "sustainability efforts," and calls for increased attention to regulation of these megalith countries. Environmentalists express concern about the destruction of resources, like the rainforest, to meet the temporary needs of these corporations.

Below are some big issues that are happening today. The best way to become familiar with the latest on any of these issues is to pick up some copies of reputable, thoughtful newspapers and/or magazines and read about current thought and developments on any of the following topics. By no means is this an exhaustive list.

Political

- Clash of Civilizations: Inter-religious conflict, especially the tensions between Islam and Christianity

- Terrorism and the Rule of Law

- How can nations fit into an increasing global world that emphasizes internationalism?

- Role of the United Nations and NGOs

- Palestinian-Israeli Conflict

- Change in the world's power structure—emergence of China and India

- Widening of the gap between political views on the right and left and disappearance of true "left" with the fall of the Soviet Union

- "War on Terror"

- Wars in the Middle East

- "Axis of Evil" countries and the demonizing of others

- Controversies about genocide—who defines it, where is it happening, when should other countries intervene?

- Peace-keeping missions

Social

- Women, children, and family issues

- Sex trade

- Role of the media

- "Bread and Circuses" idea and the use of entertainment to turn people away from focusing on current problems

- Health crises and ethical questions of who should receive health care and who pays

Economic

- Current global economic crises and their causes and consequences

- Successes and stresses of global economic development

- Global poverty and hunger

- Reform of World Bank and the International Monetary Fund, focusing particularly on international coordination of macroeconomic policy

- Global economic imbalances and their affects on the U.S. Dollar

- Monetary integration in Europe and elsewhere

- Trade reform

- Development gap and ways of closing it

- Intellectual property rights in an increasingly technological and global world

Geographic

- Impact on environmental disasters like oil spills

- Impact of global climate change

- Mass migrations and demographic challenge

- Global environmental crisis

- Genetic engineering of food and the future

- Creation of sustainable societies

COMPETENCY 4.13
Identify major world religions and ideologies.

Judaism

From the South of Phoenicia arose a small kingdom of ancient Jews. These people, the Hebrews, were a nomadic clan who descended from the patriarch Abraham and migrated from Mesopotamia to Palestine. According to Hebrew scripture, they lived in Palestine until a drought forced them to move to Egypt where they were enslaved. **Moses** led the Hebrews out of slavery in Egypt around the first half of the thirteenth century BCE. After wandering the Sinai desert for many years, they re-entered the land of Palestine. By 1000 BCE, the Israelites under the leadership of Saul fought a war against the Philistines, divided into 12 tribes, and had established a monarchy to rule over the tribes. After Saul's death, **David** ruled from 1004–965 BCE where he carried on Saul's work, brought the Israelites together, defeated the Philistines again, took over Palestine, and made Jerusalem the capital. David united the Kingdom of Israel. His son, Solomon, built the temple of Jerusalem during his rule. After his death, the Hebrews broke into two halves: the northern kingdom (Israel) with a capital at Samaria and the southern kingdom called Judah with its capital of Jerusalem. With the Kingdom of Israel completely taken over by 722 BCE, many of the Israelites were dispersed to other parts of the Assyrian empire. The Jews, despite being taken over by various other polytheistic regimes, retained their faith. Judah survived under the Assyrians but was conquered by the Chaledans who destroyed Jerusalem in 586–587 BCE. Many Jews fled into exile during the **Babylonian Captivity**. The people of Judah became known as Jews.

The central tenant of Judaism that made it different from those religions that came before it was its belief in monotheism, which made people suspicious and nervous about this new religion in a polytheistic atmosphere. The Jews' only god was referred to as **Yahweh**. The proper worship of Yahwah was embodied in the Ten Commandments. The Hebrew Scripture is referred at the *Torah* or the *Tanakh*. It consists of 24 books that are divided into three sections: the Torah (Law), *Nev'im* (Prophets), and **Ketuvim** *(Writings)*. The term *Torah* also refers to the parchment scroll that includes the first five books of the *Tanakh* (Genesis, Exodus, Leviticus, Numbers, and Deuteronomy).

Judaism's basic beliefs are:

- There is one God who created the world. He is omnipotent, omniscient, and omnipresent.

- The single, all-powerful, all-seeing God chose the Hebrew people to be "His people." Yahweh entered into a covenant with the Hebrews in which he promised to take care of them in return for them obeying him fully. The covenant set out standards of behavior that the Jews were obliged to obey. The commandments that Yahweh gave the Jews are the structure of religious practice and daily life. If either a person or a community goes against Yahweh's commandments, then they and/or the community have committed a sin.

- Ethical conduct and treatment of others

- Group worship and prayer are essential elements of a Jewish life.

There are three basic branches of Jewish belief and practice:

Orthodox Judaism: This group conducts worship only in Hebrew and interprets Jewish law strictly and literally.

Reform Judaism: Originated in the eighteenth century in Europe as a part of an assimilationist policy where Jews attempted to fit in with other Europeans. It adopts a more liberal interpretation of legal and religious doctrines; dietary laws are not traditionally observed.

Conservative Judaism: Combines doctrinal reform with traditional observance.

Christianity

Christianity, one of three Abrahamic religions (the others being Judaism and Islam), began as a Jewish reform movement, which maintains that **Jesus of Nazareth** was the Messiah who appeared in the first century CE. The historical Jesus attracted followers during his three years of preaching, performing miracles, and teaching others about the Word of God in and around the area of Galilee and northwest Palestine. He welcomed n'ere-do-wells, other castoffs from society, and women into his band of cohorts and followers. He shocked contemporaries used to the trappings of society and catering to the wealthy when he reached out to outcasts, like the sick, poor, and social outcasts. He fought against what he saw as the corruption of Jewish society and the commodification of the temple. Jesus urged people to look beyond the material world, focus on the spiritual, and asserted that there would be a life after death in the Kingdom of Heaven that was far better than the material world. Jewish society did not embrace Jesus's teachings, and scoffed upon the idea that he was the Messiah, someone they expected would be rich, powerful, and would have an army to support him. Jesus's teachings struck fear not only in Jewish power-holders but also among the occupying Romans who saw him as a potentially political threat. Jesus was captured, tortured, and crucified. Christians believe that Jesus's miracle days were not over with his death as three days after his death, he rose from the dead, spent 40 days with his disciples, and then ascended into heaven.

Christians believe that Jesus is the Son of God who died on the cross to save mankind. The Christian scripture consists of two major parts: the Old Testament, basically Jewish scripture, and the New Testament, chief of which are the four Gospels. It is from the Gospels that the life and teachings of Jesus are revealed.

The basic tenants of Christianity are:

- There is one God who is omniscient.

- Jesus Christ is the Son of God and died for our sins.

- The doctrine of the Trinity—God the Father, God the Son, and God the Holy Spirit—all work together and separately to address the needs of mankind.

Unlike Judaism, Christians observe Sunday as the Sabbath day. This day was chosen as the "day God rested" after the creation of the world and to mark the day that Jesus rose from the dead.

There are differences in practice among Christians. Christians believe in sacraments—holy rituals that mark major developments in life. The Roman Catholic and Eastern Orthodox churches recognize seven sacraments: baptism, confirmation, penance, Holy Communion (Eucharist), marriage, ordination, and anointing of the sick. Protestant churches only recognize two sacraments: baptism and Holy Communion. Christians believe that God will judge them after they die and they will go to either heaven or hell. Roman Catholics and Eastern Orthodox churches believe in an in-between place called purgatory where sinners burn off their sins in a last-ditch effort to get into heaven.

Christians, like the Jews and Muslims, believe in the Ten Commandments of the Old Testament. In fact, Jesus's teachings did not contradict Jewish law and his first followers were mostly Jews. Christians also believe in the "New Commandment" or the "Golden Rule," to "do unto others as you would have them do unto you".

It was only after Jesus's death that proclamations that he was the Son of God began to make the rounds. Among those who worked to spread Jesus's message were 12 disciples that he called the **Apostles.** His apostles gathered after his death and decided to spread his teachings among the Jewish communities. It was Peter who was believed to be the "rock of the Church" upon which it was founded as the teachings of Jesus were spread throughout Palestine and Syria.

It was Saul of Tarsus (10–67 CE), later called Paul, who transformed Christianity into a small, Jewish reform movement, into a separate religion. Although Paul initially disdained the Christian movement, on a trip to Damascus, he had a conversion experience and converted. Paul believed that he was chosen by God to convert non-Jews, or Gentiles. Paul taught that Jesus had actually advocated a completely new way of believing in God and that rather than being a splinter movement off of Judaism, it was actually a whole new religion. Paul spread the new religion through his missionary work in the Eastern Mediterranean. His *Epistles* laid the basis for the religion's organization and sacraments. People were attracted to Christianity because it was open to all and held out a promise of salvation and forgiveness. Finding that some Jewish customs, like dietary restrictions, were prohibiting his work and people's reception to Christianity, he argued that in fact, it was not necessary to keep up older, Jewish traditions.

Christianity did spread throughout the Pax Romana. There were sporadic persecutions of Christians at the local level, but by and large, persecution by the Romans was rather rare. As it grew, however, it became more of a threat to those in control, particularly under the Emperor Diocletian.

The earliest Christian churches developed rituals to unite the communities. Two such rituals became sacraments: Baptism and the Eucharist. Baptism, the dunking into water of a new member of the faith, served as a common experience that all Christians underwent. Another ritual was that of the Eucharist that served to remind everyone of Jesus's last supper with his disciples. Christians ate bread and drank wine in memory of his death and Resurrection. By the year 100 CE, those priests who led these rituals were thought to have obtained spiritual authority from God and who were thought to continue the work of Jesus's apostles. As the church expanded, it set up an administrative structure. **Bishops** oversaw church affairs within a certain jurisdiction and had authority over all of the priests within the same area. By the 300s, the heads of the congregations in Rome, Jerusalem, Antioch, Alexandria, and Constantinople were called **patriarchs,** and they held authority over the bishops. The apostle Peter, to whom Jesus had referred to as the "rock" on which the Catholic Church would be built, was the Bishop of Rome. Later bishops of Rome claimed to be the heirs of Peter. These bishops said that Peter was the first **pope,** and all subsequent bishops of Rome were believed to be the Apostle Peter's spiritual heir.

Around 312 CE, a critical moment in Christianity occurred when the Roman emperor Constantine was fighting rivals for power, and on the day before the **Battle at Milvian Bridge,** he had a vision of a cross in the light of the sky that bore the inscription, "In this sign, conquer." Constantine ordered artisans to paint the Christian symbol on the shields of his soldiers, and their victory prompted Constantine to become a patron of Christianity. In 313 CE, Constantine issued the **Edict of Milan** that proclaimed Christianity legal within the Empire and promoted religious toleration for all in the Roman Empire. In 391 CE in Constantinople, Emperor Theodosius I moved away from the idea of religious toleration for all, and he proclaimed Christianity as the Empire's official, and only acceptable, religion.

Christianity continued unabated until 1054 when the Eastern Orthodox Church broke away from the Roman Catholic Church. More problems happened for the church in the sixteenth century when several reformers split away from the Church, igniting the Protestant Reformation.

Buddhism

Buddhism developed during the same period of religious questioning that shaped modern Jainism and Buddhism. The historical Buddha was born Prince Siddhartha Gautama to a wealthy Kshatriya family, near Kapilavastu, in the Himalayan foothills of a border region between India and Nepal in the 500s BCE. According to Buddhist tradition, five days after his birth, he was brought to the temple to have his astrological charts and body marks read. His parents were told that all signs pointed to the baby taking one of two paths: that if he stayed at home and was sheltered, he would become a world leader, and if he were left at home, he would become a spiritual leader of the world. His father, anxious that his son would fulfill the prophesies and become a world leader, sheltered him.

Buddhist sources say that he lived a sheltered life, free of hardship until the age of 29–30 when he ventured outside the palace four times. During these excursions, he saw an old man, a sick man, a dead man, and a wandering ascetic. Siddhartha felt that these events meant that there were four big phases in life that everyone would have to go through: old age, sickness, death, and that only living the life of a religious person was redeemable. He resolved to try to find a way to keep people from falling victim to age and sickness. So after, Siddhartha decided to spend his life searching for "truth."

For six years, he wandered through the forests of India searching for enlightenment. He tried many ways to become enlightened: starvation, studying with gurus, and other tactics—yet none worked. Out of frustration, he turned to meditation. He sat under a fig tree, determined not to arise until he found a way to end human suffering. After 49 days, he reached enlightenment and became from then on the **Buddha,** the Enlightened one. He henceforth resolved to spread the lessons he learned to others. He created an order of monks and taught how to escape from life's suffering through the "Middle Way"—that by living in moderation, once could avoid the extremes of either comfort or discomfort in the search for **nirvana**.

Buddha is said to have learned the **Four Noble Truths** that summarize his worldview:

- Suffering and sorrow are a part of human life and no one could escape it.

- Suffering is caused by peoples' selfish preoccupation with material goods and pleasure.

- Desire can be overcome, and when it is, it brings an end to suffering.

- Desires can be overcome by following the **Eightfold Path**, which is called the Middle Way between desires and self-denial.

The **Eightfold Path** is a series of steps that Buddhists believe leads to enlightenment, or nirvana:

1. Right views

2. Right attitude

3. Right speech

4. Right conduct

5. Right livelihood

6. Right effort

7. Right mindfulness

8. Right meditation

The **Three Jewels of Buddhism** form the core of Buddhist beliefs:

- The Buddha is the perfect model for humans.

- The dharma, or the Buddhist worldview and way of life

- The monastic community of Buddhist nuns and monks

Buddhists today recognize the importance of the Three Jewels of their faith by declaring, "I take refuge in the Buddha. I take refuge in the law. I take refuge in the community."

While Buddhism shares some key beliefs with Hinduism, such as the idea of nirvana and the belief in multiple gods, it rejects the Upanishads, the *varna* system and denies the existence of an individual soul. Because it rejected the caste system, it did attract many laborers and craftspeople who felt that Buddhism would uplift them from their position in society. However, despite this attraction, Buddhism actually did not prosper much in India, and instead gained a significant foothold in other parts of Asia. Some say Hinduism simply absorbed Buddhism and the Buddha came to be identified as one of the ten incarnations of the god Vishnu.

After the Buddha's death, his disciples gathered together to compile his teachings, but there were different opinions on the correct teachings and practices. Despite some shared beliefs, several different types of Buddhism emerged.

Theravada Buddhism, meaning the Way of the Elders, adheres most closely to earlier practices and the earliest Buddhist writings and today is practiced mostly in Sri Lanka, Thailand, and Burma. These writings are collectively called the **Pali Canon,** because they were written in the Pali language. Theravada Buddhism teaches that the best way to attain nirvana was to focus on the last of the Eightfold Path: meditation. It advocated that one should become a monk or a nun and spend as much time as one could in meditation. In practical terms, this was difficult for those who were not monks or nuns, particularly as they were then obligated to support those who chose the monastic life.

Mahayana Buddhism (Greater Vehicle) focuses on compassion for others over personal progresses toward enlightenment. This branch advocates bodhisattva, the idea of postponing enlightenment in order to help others. They believed that the Buddha was not merely a man, but rather the earthly expression of a human being. Unlike Theraveda Buddhism, Mahayana Buddhism asserts that one need not enter monastic life in order to attain nirvana—that everyone could do it.

Vajrayana Buddhism (Tantric Buddhism) is Tibetan Buddhism and shares many ideas with Mahayana Buddhism, believing that with the use of mantras, hand gestures, mandalas, and prayer wheels, one can tap into spiritual energy and achieve nirvana in a single lifetime.

Confucianism

The era between 600–300 BCE in China has been called the era of a **Hundred Schools** during which time, Chinese philosophers also were contemplating moral, political, and theological ideas. The most famous of these Chinese philosophers is **Confucius** (551–479 BCE) who lived during the time when the **Zhou Dynasty** was being torn apart by warring lords. Confucius thought that the turbulence in society was happening because of a disappearance of love and respect. He thought that by restoring respect for tradition, society would once again become stable and orderly. His Chinese name was **Kung Fu'tzu**. After Confucius's death, his sayings were compiled by disciples into a book called the *Analects*. The *Analects* form the foundation for the Chinese philosophy of Confucianism, which basically developed a code of ethics, morality, and way of life that should form the basis not only of a ruler's actions but also those of society in general. It remained a philosophy until about the first century CE when Buddhism entered China and began to take on aspects of a religion.

Confucius believed that a moral society was ruled by hierarchical relationships between family members. The main idea here is something called "filial piety." He believed that social order, harmony, and good government could be restored in China if Chinese society were organized around five basic relationships that were based upon the family: 1) ruler and subject, 2) father and son, 3) husband and wife, 4) older brother and younger brother, and 5) friend and friend. He thought that even rulers should practice these traits and in return, the subjects of a ruler would be loyal.

Confucius believed that questions about religion, afterlife, and spirits were beyond the capacity of human reason. His philosophy was of an ethical nature, and his teachings were essentially an ethical system for people to follow. Confucianism advocated that people should follow five key values that would enable one to practice the virtues of *Xiao*, filial piety, and *Wen*, civilization:

- **Ren**: reciprocal human feeling—the ultimate Confucian virtue

- **Yi**: righteousness

- **Li**: propriety and correct behavior

- **Zhi:** knowledge

- **Xin:** trustworthiness

For Confucius, finding the way (**dao**) was the most important aspect of life.

He believed that the best government was one filled with educated and conscientious people and that men of talent were better than those of birth. He defined the term "gentleman" to mean a man of moral cultivation, rather than noble birth. His idea of a meritocracy and for governments to select those of talent was later reflected in the institution of the Chinese civil service exam and the creation of **bureaucracy**. He felt that a man of government must exercise the following, "In his private conduct he was courteous, in serving his master he was punctilious, in exacting service from the people, he was just."

Confucius's teachings then attacked the importance society placed on class distinctions: the perfect person should see virtue above all else.

Much of the success of Confucius's ideas is due to his followers who focused on certain aspects of his teachings. **Mencius** advocated a benevolent government, asserted that human nature was fundamentally good, and spent most of his time trying to convince rulers to adopt his ideas. Xunzi stressed that all people are born selfish and that selfishness could only be overcome through education and ritual.

Islam

In the Arabic language, *islam* means "submission," which in a religious context means submission to God. A person who submits is called a *"Muslim"* (the prefix "mu" is "one who"), which is also the word for a follower of the religion of Islam. Western writers in the past have sometimes referred to Islam as "Mohammedism." This word can be offensive to many Muslims, because it insinuates the worship of the prophet Muhammad as a deity, which could not be further from the truth. Muhammad, Muslims believe, is the last prophet of God (Allah), and they seek to use his life as an example by which to live.

In 570 CE, Muhammad was born in Mecca, a trading crossroads and pilgrimage spot in Arabia. At the time, Arabia was a buffer zone between two great empires: the Byzantine Empire to the West, and the Sasanian Empire to the East. Being a buffer zone enabled the region to develop on its own and relatively free from interference from these two political giants. This proved to be a boon for Islam, as it encountered only local, rather than outside, interference. Moreover, Islam spread significantly, primarily because of its birth in a trading post among merchants who travelled far and wide and who could export the religion easily. Moreover, because traders came through who practiced a great many religious beliefs, the effect on early Islam was tremendous. Despite this, most of the people in the region were not Christians or Jews, and most practiced some form of polytheism.

Muhammad, whose name means "worthy of praise," was born in about 570 in Mecca. His father, Abdullah, died before Muhammad was born, and his mother, Amina, died when he was six years old. His uncle, Abu Talib, a caravan trader, raised him. Little is known about his early life, but he was not wealthy, and being raised in the household of a caravan trader did give Muhammad exposure to peoples of different beliefs.

When he was 25, he married Khadija, a wealthy widow who was about 15 years older than him. Being the husband of a wealthy woman had its advantages: the primary one being that it freed him from a life of work and enabled him to focus on spiritual endeavors. Muhammad frequently went outside Mecca to go on retreats in nearby caves.

In 610 CE, Muhammad went on another retreat. As he was meditating, he received a message from the Archangel Gabriel that told him to "Recite" (Qur'an—sometimes spelled Koran) everything he said. These revelations, which would continue over the next 23 years, from the Archangel Gabriel were believed to be God's message to humanity through his final prophet, Muhammad. Muslims believe that these revelations were corrections to previous Abrahamic revelations. Islam, like Christianity and Judaism, is an Abrahamic religion that practices monotheism.

As an Abrahamic religion, Islam sees its roots in the prophet Abraham. While the Jews recount that Abraham married Sarah, who bore Issac, who was the father to Jacob and Esau and from Jacob came the 12 tribes of Israel, the Muslims acknowledge that they spring from Abraham's relationship with Hagar who had Ishmael, from whom the 12 Arabian tribes emerged.

The Qur'an itself, with its beautiful poetic language and lofty expressions, is considered a miracle, something beyond Muhammad's education and experience, especially as he was illiterate. The revelations were ultimately recorded after Muhammad died under the second and third caliphs (successors). It contains 114 suras (chapters) and over 6,000 verses.

Muhammad was initially quite concerned that he was hearing voices, yet eventually he came to understand that he was hearing the voice of God (in Arabic, *Allah*). His revelations called on people to proclaim that one god had created the universe and everything in it. That god would judge them at the end of life, and those who had not sinned would go to paradise and the sinners would go to hell.

Significantly, Muslims believe that Gabriel delivered God's message to Muhammad and that Muhammad was simply God's messenger. Muslims do not believe that Muhammad himself was divine in any way. To believe that would be to contradict the single premise of Islam, that there is only one God. This makes Islam quite different from Christianity, which does believe in the divinity of Jesus. Another important concept of Islam is that Muhammad is the last prophet. The Qur'an names many Jewish and Christian prophets in it and accepts many of the Jewish and Christian traditions. The Qur'an in fact names 25 prophets, including Abraham, Moses, Jesus, and Muhammad. For Muslims, Muhammad is simply the last in a long line of prophets, which includes many Jewish and Christian prophets. But while the Qur'an says that the earlier prophets were true, it also says that their messages were corrupted over the years. Muslims believe that God's message to Muhammad restored the purity of the original messages, and because the Qur'an is believed to be God's final word, Muslims do not accept the existence of any prophets after Muhammad.

As a result, Muslims believe that although Muhammad received his revelations in the seventh century, Islam was actually the faith that was taught by the earlier prophets; it had just been corrupted over time. The Archangel's revelations just corrected the earlier, distorted messages.

Some of the differences between Christianity and Islam with regard to Jesus are the following: both agree that while Jesus's birth was miraculous and he performed miracles, they do not believe that he was killed on the cross but rather escaped execution. They do not believe that Jesus was the son of God but rather a prophet.

The basic tenant of Islam, that there is only one God (Allah), caused great consternation among the people of Mecca. Because Mecca earned a great deal of its money from pilgrimages, the focus on "one god" made the leaders of Mecca, a clan called the Quryash, quite nervous and upset. In addition, one of the primary traits of the culture was one of ancestor worship. Muhammad's teaching asserted that before his revelations was a time of ignorance, the Jahiliyya. All who lived in the Jahiliyya were not admitted into paradise. This greatly upset people who could not accept that all of their ancestors had been doomed. The two issues conflicted and created a mood ripe for Muslims to be persecuted.

Muslims believe that the Torah and the Bible are both the word of God, and that Jews and Christians are *Ahl al-Kitab,* or peoples of the book, and as such, are to be protected.

One of the miracles of Muhammad concerns his famous Night Journey, which occurred before the death of his wife, Khadija. Basically, Islam believes that the angel Gabriel came to Muhammad while he was sleeping near the Ka'ba one night, and escorted him first to Jerusalem, then through seven heavens—where he met Abraham, Moses, and Jesus—to the presence of God. This event later helped establish Jerusalem as the third-holiest city in Islam, after Mecca and Medina. During his journey, Muslims believe that Muhammad was told of several tenets of Islam that became some of the most basic acts of the religion, such as praying five times daily. People at first did not believe Muhammad's story, but one thing he said convinced them. He said that on his way back from his night journey, he saw a big caravan coming through. This caravan was not expected, and when it came to town on the day that Muhammad had said, people were convinced that he did indeed go on his night journey.

Muslims believe that there are Six Principles of faith:

- There is one God who does not make mistakes and is flawless.

- They believe in angels, who are God's servants.

- They believe in prophets who were sent by God and teach the guidance for God. They believe that Muhammad was God's last and final messenger.

- They believe in the Torah, the Bible, and the Qur'an.

- They believe in the day of judgment where all will be resurrected and judged.

- They believe that one should submit oneself in full acceptance of God's decisions.

There are FIVE pillars of Islam, which define what it means to be a Muslim and how one should practice Islam:

1. To be a Muslim, one does not need a long conversion process, but one simply has to say the **Shahada,** or bear witness that "there is no God but Allah, and that Muhammad is his Messenger." This declaration of the faith must be uttered publicly at least once in a Muslim's lifetime, although most Muslims recite it daily.

2. The **Salat** (Prayer): The Muslim holy day is Friday, when congregations gather just past noon in a **masjid,** or mosque in English, the Muslim place of worship. On Fridays, the **imam,** or prayer leader, gives a sermon (the **khutba)** and leads the congregation in prayer. Islam itself is a portable religion—one can take it anywhere and does not need either an *imam* or a *masjid* to pray. Muslims may pray anywhere—in the middle of an airport, a busy shopping mall, in school, in the street, etc. All they need to do is to find the direction of Mecca, the *qibla,* and pray toward it. They must observe the qibla in all cases though, by facing towards the Ka'ba in Mecca when praying. Prayers, for Sunni Muslims, must be performed five times daily—at dawn, noon, mid-afternoon, sunset, and nightfall. The prayers always contain verses from the Qur'an, and must be said in Arabic and after having washed themselves (in the absence of water, sand will do).

3. **Zakat** (alms): Muslims believe that all things belong to God, and that humans hold wealth in trust for him. For that reason, Muslims believe wealth should be distributed throughout the community of believers, or **umma. Zakat** is usually considered to be 2.5 per cent of a person's wealth every year, the proceeds of which are distributed to the less fortunate. Additional charity work is also encouraged, and many do things like provide *iftar* during Ramadan for the poor or less fortunate.

4. *Sawm* (Fasting): During the month of Ramadan, the ninth month in the lunar Islamic calendar, Muslims fast between dawn and dusk. They must abstain from food, liquid, and intimate contact during those hours of the day, in order to commemorate the month in which the revelations from the Archangel Gabriel began. Fasting is seen as a method of self-purification, by cutting oneself off from worldly comforts. The sick, elderly, children, travelers, and nursing or pregnant women do not have to fast during Ramadan. The end of Ramadan is celebrated by the *Eid al-Fitr*, one of the major festivals on the Muslim calendar.

5. *Hajj* (Pilgrimage to Mecca): All Muslims are required to make one pilgrimage to Mecca in their lifetime, provided they are physically and financially able to do so. The Hajj begins in the twelfth month of the Islamic lunar calendar, which means, like Ramadan, it does not correspond to a specific month in the solar calendar. Like Ramadan, the end of the Hajj is also celebrated with a festival, the *Eid al-Adha,* which is celebrated by all Muslims, whether or not they made the pilgrimage. Those who complete the *hajj* get the honorific *hajji* or *hajja* added to their name.

Islam advocates the following moral principles: to stay away from alcohol, pork, and gambling; to practice charity, patience, and humility; to forgive enemies; and to avoid greed, lying, and malice.

One thing that students often lose sight of is that Islam was considered a rather progressive religion at the time, appealing to women and minorities, in particular, because it treated them better than other religions at the time. Women were given the right to earn their own living, choose their own marriage partners, and to own and dispose of their personal property and earnings as they wished. At the time (and even in England until the late nineteenth century), female infanticide was quite common; Islam, however, preached that men and women were equally valued, and so it forbade female infanticide. While women were considered equally important in society, they do have equal rights and responsibilities; however, the roles of men and women may be different, but are seen as complementary and just as important as the other's.

Facing a tremendous amount of hostility from the **Quraysh** in Mecca, Muhammad received a welcome invitation from the leading families in Medina, a city to the north of Mecca, to come and arbitrate a dispute. Muhammad, known far and wide for his charisma and sense of fairness, was anxious to get his followers out of a touchy situation in

Mecca. In 622 CE, in a date known as the *hijra,* which is the beginning date of the Islamic calendar, Muhammad and his small band of followers fled over 200 miles to Medina. The flight to Medina marked a turning point in the history of Islam and saw the beginning of increased conversions to Islam. Those in Medina found his message appealing and many of the regions Bedouins joined him. In 630 CE, Muhammad and his followers fought the Meccans in order to reclaim the city for Muhammad and his followers. Muhammad died two years later, at the age of 62.

After the death of Muhammad in 632 BCE, there were tremendous questions about who would lead the small Muslim community after his death. Muhammad had not designated a successor. Abu Bakr, the oldest and most venerated of the Muslim community, was chosen, much to the consternation of those who instead had favored the nephew and son-in-law of Muhammad, 'Ali. The ascension of Abu-Bakr to the caliphate marked the beginning of the **Rashidun Caliphate** (or rather the **Rightly Guided Caliphs)**. The Rashidun Caliphates consisted of the first four successors to Muhammad who all had known him and had supported him and his mission. During this period, the Muslims extended their rule significantly. Under Abu Baker, the Muslim state controlled all of Arabia. Under Umar, the second caliph, the Muslims conquered Syria and lower Egypt, parts of the Byzantine Empire. Under Uthman and 'Ali, Islam expanded eastward and westward. By 750, Islam ruled from the Atlantic Ocean to the Indus River, about 4,000 miles.

After each death of one of the caliphs, supporters of 'Ali, the *Shi'a Ali* (the "Party of Ali" from whence Shi'ites emerged) campaigned for him to become the leader of the Muslims. Each time, however, he was not chosen. Finally, however, 'Ali was chosen after the assassination of Uthman. Upon his ascension, however, his right to rule was challenged by Mu'awiya, a governor of Syria. In 661 CE, 'Ali was assassinated in a mosque while praying. With his death, so died the elective system of choosing a caliph.

Mu'awiyya and his family known as the Umayyads came into power, where they set up a hereditary system of succession. Mu'awiyya moved the capital to Damascus. This created a bit of hostility among the Arabs who did not like the center being moved away from the beginnings of Islam. The Umayyads ruled more as "rulers" with the trappings of wealth and ceremony and a small minority, the **Shi'a 'Ali,** in particular, felt that they had departed from "traditional" Islam.

The **Shi'a 'Ali** felt that the caliph should be a relative to the Prophet in order to retain the charisma and legitimacy of Islam. Those who supported the Umayyad rule became known as the **Sunnis**. Civil war broke out, eventually leading to the death of Husayn, 'Ali's son and Muhammad's grandson.

Expansion

Because Islam spread so rapidly under both the Rashidun Caliphate (the rule of the four caliphs after the death of Muhammad in 632; means "rightly guided") and the Umayyad Caliphate, for the first hundred years or so, Muslims remained a minority in the lands that they ruled. They did not force conversion on the lands that they conquered, and so the Peoples of the Book were accorded dhimmi status, which permitted people to continue to practice their religion after paying a small poll tax. As time progressed, many people, for reasons explored in your textbook, began to convert, perhaps out of the desire to curry favor with the conquerors or to assume leadership positions. When adherents to these other faiths did convert to Islam, they brought with them many of their cultural traditions, and Islam was adaptable enough to incorporate these other traditions into the Muslim way of life.

Islam proved to be a religion that was quite conducive to rapid expansion for the following reasons:

- Islam was easy to learn and practice—one just needed to know the six basic principles and the five pillars.

- There was no priesthood, so one could practice it everywhere.

- It teaches equality, so many were attracted to it because it improved their status in society.

- Non-Muslims welcomed Muslim rule because they were not treated badly, nor were they forced to convert. Non-Muslims were considered, *Ahl al-Kitab* or **People of the Book**. They were allowed religious freedom but did pay additional taxes.

- It was easily portable because no equipment was needed. It easily spread along trade routes.

- The idea of jihad, included a defensive idea that said one should always strive to perfect oneself (lesser jihad), but also, when attacked or threatened, one was allowed and expected to defend oneself (greater jihad).

With expansion, the role of native Arabs in the Dar al-Islam (House of Islam) changed significantly during this time. During Muhammad's lifetime, virtually all Muslims had been Arabs from central or southern Arabia, and their cultural traditions and the way they practiced Islam reflected that. When the Umayyads moved the political capital to Damascus (located in today's Syria), warriors moved to new lands with their families that began to change.

Non-Arabs who converted to Islam became adoptive members of Arab kin groups and many non-Arabs began to marry Arabs. Over time, most of the non-Arab Muslims living west of Iran adopted the Arabic language.

By the time the Umayyad Caliphate fell to the Abbasids, dissent had begun to emerge from many of the non-Arab Muslims who claimed that they were not treated as favorably as Arab Muslims. Throwing their weight of support to the Abbasids, the new seat of the Caliphate was moved significantly eastward, to Baghdad. But, despite the cosmopolitan and scholarly attractions that Baghdad offered, regional centers of non-Arab Muslims sprang up all the way from Spain to modern-day Pakistan.

Regional centers began to spring up far away from the Abbasid stronghold in Baghdad. Regional empires sprang up in Spain, Egypt, and Iran that all developed a particular intellectual, religious, and artistic character within the overall unity of Islam. With an ever-increasing sense of regionalism also came the idea of becoming more in-tune with regional crises than those happening in Baghdad. For instance, those who lived in North Africa or Spain were not concerned at all about the onslaught of the Muslims; they were more worried about the Christians to the North. Egypt and Iran cared little about the confrontations between Spain and Christians like Charles "the Hammer" Martel. The Egyptians were increasingly concerned about the Crusaders, while Iran was more concerned with the Huns to the north.

It was during the rule of the Abbasids that Baghdad became the center of learning. Here is where any scholar of merit flocked to join the *Beit al Hikma* or the House of Wisdom. Generously funded by the Caliph, scholars made extraordinary accomplishments in science and mathematics, drawing on some of the teachings and work of the ancient Greeks. It was the Abbasid scholars who translated these works, and essentially preserved them so that they could be used later in the European Renaissance. Without the Abbasids, today we would have little knowledge of the great Greek masters and classical developments.

What is United States History?

Spanish and Portuguese Beginnings

The **Treaty of Tordesillas** (1494) drew a line dividing the land in the New World between Spain and Portugal. Lands east of the line were Portuguese. This is why Brazil became a Portuguese colony and Spain laid claim to the rest of the Americas. In order to conquer the Americas, Spain turned to a group of independent adventurers known as the "conquerors," or the **conquistadores**. The European diseases that the conquistadores and their army unwittingly carried along with them infected and then devastated the local Native American populations, who had no immunities against such diseases. Spain administered its new holdings as an autocratic, rigidly controlled empire in which everything was to benefit the parent country. The Spaniards developed a system of large manors or estates (*encomiendas*), with Indian slaves ruthlessly managed for the benefit of the conquistadores. The *encomienda* system was later replaced by the similar but somewhat milder hacienda system. As the Indian population died from overwork and European diseases, Spaniards began importing African slaves to supply their labor needs.

English and French Beginnings

In 1497, the Italian **John Cabot** (Giovanni Caboto, ca. 1450–1499), sailing under the sponsorship of the king of England in search of a Northwest Passage (a water route to the Orient through or around the North American continent), became the first European since the Vikings more than four centuries earlier to reach the mainland of North America, which he claimed for England. Beginning in 1534, **Jacques Cartier** (1491–1557), authorized by the king of France, mounted three expeditions to the area of the St. Lawrence River, which he believed might be the hoped-for Northwest Passage. He explored up the river as far as the site of Montreal.

When the English finally began colonization, commercial capitalism in England had advanced to the point that the English efforts were supported by private rather than government funds, allowing English colonists to enjoy greater freedom from government interference.

Impact on the Americas

The insatiable European appetite for expansion of its trade, search for new commodities, desire to build empires, and use of slave labor to extract the wealth from their new land greatly affected not only the lands where they were conquering but also many other areas of the world. Spain deliberately destroyed the native, wealthy, and perhaps rather oppressive empires in America, only to substitute their own brutal rule in their stead. As they expanded their areas of control, Spain forced elements of their own culture onto weakened populations, forcing new religion, new languages, new power structures, new political and sexual cultures, and new attitudes toward the role of women in society. Europeans took over areas perceived to be "stateless" where local rule was deemed illegitimate, and they ethnically cleansed the areas of the local inhabitants and set off economic and political changes that permeated indigenous societies throughout the continent.

Early Spanish exploration's impact on the Americas was that devastating. In the West Indies, a pattern would be set that would be followed throughout the conquistador period. Priests forced many of them to become Christians, or else perish at the hands of the army's sword. Native people were enslaved to toil in mines and on plantations. On the Taino Islands, for instance, when the Spanish arrived, there were between one and two million residents. Within 50 years, there were only 500 left. Following Portugal's example, the Spanish looked to Africa to find laborers, and from 1518 to the mid-1800s, the Spanish brought millions of slaves to the Americas.

While the Spanish did introduce new animals to the Americas, like horses, sheep, cattle, and pigs, the conquistadores destroyed at least two great civilizations, the Aztecs and the Incas. The effects on Mexico were devastating as it went from a population of 25 million people to 1 million in only 100 years.

Portuguese settled in Brazil, and their actions there affected people tremendously. The Portuguese, like the Spanish, forced people to give up their religion and convert to Christianity. They forced people to work on sugar plantations. So many people died there because of diseases that the Europeans brought with them and for which they had no immunity, that the Portuguese were left needing laborers to extract the resources from their newly conquered land. So, starting in the mid-1500s, they turned to West Africa, where they bought slaves and transported them to work in Brazil. This forced migration of Africans to Brazil changed the racial landscape of the Americas.

Europeans in North America took similar tactics against the native populations. They wiped out anywhere from 50–90% of their populations through war, exposure to disease and new germs, and slavery.

Economic Impact:

- There was rapid economic growth and an increase in business and trading.

- Vast amounts of gold and silver were swiped away and redistributed to Europe and across the globe.

- Prices of goods rose due to inflation and mercantilist economic policies.

- Capitalism emerged as the dominant economic system.

Social Impact:

- Rising middle class benefited from new economic and social opportunities.

- Power and wealth concentrated in the hands of a few white people of European descent.

- Strict economic and social hierarchy developed.

- Foundation laid for continued economic and social issues to develop.

- Millions of Africans were imported to the New World as slaves.

- Slave system altered how and where land was developed and destroyed lives.

- Native populations were roundly decimated. Anywhere from 2–20 million killed from disease and malnutrition, war, or forced labor. Blending of indigenous populations with Europeans and Africans resulted in new cultural and racial groups and a blending of cultures.

Political Impact:

- New forms of political systems and control were set up that placed the Native Americans on the outside or bottom of the system.

Cultural Impact:

- Christianity spread throughout the Americas.

- Christian missionaries worked to convert the native populations and set up schools.

- Catholic Church became dominant in many colonial regions.

- Christianity was blended with traditional beliefs and practices—syncretism.

- Animals from Europe brought to the Americas, like horses and cattle, changed both transportation and food sources.

- New plants and crops were exchanged.

COMPETENCY 5.2

Analyze the social, cultural, political, and economic development of the Americas during the colonial period.

The Colonial World

People came to the New World for a wide variety of reasons, some to make a profit for both themselves and whoever financed their trip, some out of a desire for religious freedom, and some for business reasons. By and large, the colonization of the Americas was born out of four major issues:

- the universal economic theory at the time, **mercantilism**, which held that colonies exist for the economic benefit of the mother country and are useless unless they help to achieve profit;

- the rivalry of three major nations—England, France, and Spain—that dictated and greatly influenced the nature and the development of each of the colonies,

- the geography, and

- the native population in the area.

While the European countries each had their individual approaches toward exploration and colonization, there were also some shared characteristics.

Spain's New World ventures focused primarily on South America, Central America, Mexico, and the American Southwest. For the Spanish conquistadores, the king remained the source of all authority. In fact, when disputes arose between explorers, or explorers wanted to gain some authority in the lands they conquered, they had to go back to the king in Spain to ask for his permission or help. The Spanish wanted, above all else, gold. They were a strongly Catholic regime who quickly brought in priests to convert the native peoples that they encountered. The Spanish wreaked havoc on indigenous societies, decimating all facets of their civilization, and were exceedingly cruel to their laborers.

France's experiences in the New World were more limited. They focused on North America; specifically their interests were in the fur trade as they plied their way into controlling the St. Lawrence and Mississippi River systems. Their relations, for the most part, were friendly with the Indians they encountered. Because their interests lay mainly in the fur trade, there was not as much opportunity for "settling down" and farming and building up industry. France never really sent many colonists to the New World, and it remained a rather limited enterprise. New France was strongly Catholic, and no Huguenots were allowed. The economic systems in place were joint stock companies. The French opened a lucrative trade in fur with the Native Americans. In 1608, Samuel de Champlain established a trading post in Quebec, from which the rest of what became New France eventually spread. French exploration and settlement spread through the Great Lakes region and the valleys of the Mississippi and Ohio rivers. French settlements in the Midwest were generally forts and trading posts serving the fur trade.

In 1609, Holland sent an Englishman named Henry Hudson to search for a Northwest Passage. In this endeavor, Hudson discovered the river that bears his name. Arrangements were made to trade with the Iroquois for furs. In 1624, Dutch trading outposts were established on Manhattan Island (New Amsterdam) and at the site of present-day Albany (Fort Orange). The Dutch were not interested in forming a colony in the New World; their interests remained purely economic. As traders, they were interested in procuring some of the resources from the country and the goods that the Native Americans were interested in; as such, their relations with the Native Americans were primarily good as they were their trade partners.

The English venture had slightly different beginnings, rooted in commercial capitalism in England, which had advanced to the point that the English efforts were supported by private rather than government funds, allowing English colonists to enjoy greater freedom from government interference. A capitalistic economy quickly emerged whereby small farmers, artisans, merchants, and aristocrats worked for profit. In time, some Americans created commercial monopolies that needed a constant source of dependent labor to augment their wealth. Five of the original 13 colonies had originated due to the financing of corporations: Virginia, Plymouth, Maryland, South Carolina, and North Carolina were corporate in origin.

Two groups of merchants gained charters from James I, Queen Elizabeth's successor. One group of merchants was based in London and received a charter to North America between what are now the Hudson and the Cape Fear rivers. The other was based in Plymouth and was granted the right to colonize in North America from the Potomac to the northern border of present-day Maine. They were called the Virginia Company of London and the Virginia Company of Plymouth, respectively. They were joint-stock companies that raised their capital by the sale of shares of stock. The Virginia Company of London settled Jamestown in 1607. It became the first permanent English settlement in North America. During the early years of Jamestown, the majority of the settlers died of starvation, various diseases, or hostile actions by Native Americans. The colony's survival remained in doubt for a number of years. Impressed by the potential profits from tobacco growing, King James I was determined to have Virginia for him. In 1624, he revoked the London Company's charter and made Virginia a royal colony. This pattern was followed throughout colonial history; both company colonies and proprietary colonies tended eventually to become royal colonies.

Many Englishmen came from England for religious reasons. For the most part, these fell into two groups, Puritans and Separatists. Though similar in many respects to the Puritans, the Separatists believed the Church of England was beyond saving and so felt they must separate from it. Led by William Bradford (1590–1657), a group of Separatists departed in 1620, having obtained from the London Company a charter to settle just south of the Hudson River. Driven by storms, their ship, the Mayflower, made landfall at Cape Cod in Massachusetts. This, however, put them outside the jurisdiction of any established government; and so before going ashore, they drew up and signed the *Mayflower* Compact, establishing a foundation for orderly government based on the consent of the governed. After a number of years of hard work, they were able to buy out the investors who had originally financed their voyage and thus gain greater autonomy.

The Puritans were far more numerous than the Separatists. Charles I determined in 1629 to persecute the Puritans aggressively and to rule without the Puritan-dominated Parliament. In 1629, they chartered a joint-stock company called the Massachusetts Bay Company. The charter neglected to specify where the company's headquarters should be located. Taking advantage of this unusual omission, the Puritans determined to make their headquarters in the colony itself, 3,000 miles from meddlesome royal officials.

Puritans saw their colony not as a place to do whatever might strike one's fancy, but as a place to serve God and build His kingdom. Dissidents would only be tolerated insofar as they did not interfere with the colony's mission. One such dissident was Roger Williams. When his activities became disruptive, he was asked to leave the colony. He fled to the wilderness around Narragansett Bay, bought land from the Indians, and founded the settlement of Providence (1636).

Another dissident was Anne Hutchinson, who openly taught things contrary to Puritan doctrine. She was banished from the colony. She also migrated to the area around

Narragansett Bay and with her followers founded Portsmouth (1638). In 1663, Charles II, having recently been restored to the throne, moved to reward eight of the noblemen who had helped him regain the crown by granting them a charter for all the lands lying south of Virginia and north of Spanish Florida. The new colony was called Carolina, after the king. In 1664, Charles gave his brother James, Duke of York, title to all the Dutch lands in America, provided James conquered them first. New Amsterdam fell almost without a shot and became New York.

North American Colonies

The colonies were generally divided into three regions: New England, Middle Atlantic, and Southern. Each region seemed to have a distinct culture and attitudes toward religion, politics, and economic interests. The geography of each region also contributed to their unique characteristics that reflected their origins.

New England Colonies

The New England colonies consisted of Massachusetts, Rhode Island, Connecticut, and New Hampshire and enjoyed a much more stable and well-ordered society than did the Chesapeake colonies. Puritans placed great importance on the family, which in their society was highly patriarchal. Puritans also placed great importance on the ability to read, since they believed everyone should be able to read the Bible. As a result, New England was ahead of the other colonies educationally and enjoyed extremely widespread literacy. Since New England's climate and soil were unsuited to large-scale farming, the region developed a prosperous economy based on small farming, home industry, fishing, and especially trade and a large shipbuilding industry. Boston became a major international port.

Southern and Chesapeake Colonies

Beginning around 1650, British authorities began to take more interest in regulating American trade for the benefit of the mother country. A key idea that underlay this policy was the concept of mercantilism. Each nation's goal was to export more than it imported (i.e., to have a "favorable balance of trade"). To achieve their goals, mercantilists believed economic activity should be regulated by the government. Colonies could fit into England's mercantilist scheme by providing staple crops, such as rice, tobacco, sugar, and indigo, and raw materials, such as timber, that England would otherwise have been forced to import from other countries. Parliament passed a series of Navigation Acts (1651, 1660, 1663, and 1673) to help accomplish these goals. On the bottom rung of Southern society were the black slaves. During the first half of the seventeenth century, blacks in the Chesapeake made up only a small percentage of the population and were treated more or less as indentured servants. Between 1640 and 1670, this gradually changed, and blacks came to be seen and treated as life-long chattel slaves whose status would be inherited by their children. By 1750, they composed 30 to 40 percent of the Chesapeake population. While North Carolina tended to follow Virginia in its economic and social development (although with fewer great planters and more small farmers), South Carolina developed a society even more dominated by large plantations and chattel slavery.

Tobacco, first planted by the Europeans in 1611, proved to be the commodity crop that the mercantilist enterprise had been searching for as Europeans on the continent clamored for it. As a result, in the 1620s, there was a tremendous boom in tobacco export, so much so that the colony quickly grew into a full-sized settlement that included men, women, and children. In fact, there was so much planting of the crop that the tobacco quickly exhausted the soil. As colonists expanded to sow more tobacco seed, the Powhatan tribe became so unsettled by the rapid expansion that on March 22, 1622, the Indians attacked and killed almost a quarter of the settlements. This did not sit well with King James I, who already was unhappy with the lack of profit that the Virginia Company was making, so he disbanded the company and made Virginia a royal colony. He started the headright system in 1617 as a means to get more Europeans to come to the New World and grow tobacco. The deal was that every new person would get 50 acres of land. Because not many people had the funds to pay for their trip over, wealthy planters would offer to pay people's way, provided they gave the land to the planter and agreed to work as an indentured servant for a period of time and at the end would be given a little plot of land of their own.

Middle Atlantic Colonies

Pennsylvania was founded as a refuge for Quakers. One of a number of radical religious sects that had sprung up about the time of the English Civil War, the Quakers held many controversial beliefs. They believed all persons had an "inner light," which allowed them to commune directly with God, and therefore they placed little importance on the Bible. They were also pacifists and declined to show customary deference to those who were considered to be their social superiors.

Delaware, though at first part of Pennsylvania, was granted a separate legislature by Penn, but until the American Revolution, Pennsylvania's proprietary governors also functioned as governors of Delaware. Eighteenth-century America's population continued to grow rapidly, both from natural increases due to prosperity and a healthy environment and from large-scale immigration, not only of English but also of other groups such as Scots-Irish and Germans.

By the end of the first century of European colonization in America, the colonists had accomplished quite a bit—they had created strong governments, had developed a wide variety of agricultural and industrial activities, and had established complex societies. By 1732, the colonies had created three types of governments:

- **Royal colonies,** where the English monarch controlled the colony and appointed governors and their councils to run it.

- **Proprietary colonies,** where landowners determined the direction of government.

- **Corporate colonies,** where corporations and their stockholders determined the direction of the government and economy.

By the mid-1700s, all 13 colonies had become royal colonies.

By the mid-1700s, economic activity was beginning a transformation as it had moved from one that was primarily focused on farming to one that included **household manufacturing** where families produced articles for their own use and some **commercial industries for profit**: fishing, lumbering, shipbuilding, flour milling, iron manufacturing. All of the industries were able to take advantage of the cheap and abundant natural resources and did not have to expend much capital.

By the end of the seventeenth century, the colonies already had become a diverse place with people of varying political, cultural, socio-economic, religious, and racial backgrounds. Such diversity was not without its problems, however, as some of these differences resulted in many conflicts over the decades. Some of these tensions existed primarily in the way that European colonists treated the varying nations of American Indians throughout North, Central, and South America. Unlike the English, the Spanish and French included Native Americans in the social and economic lives of their communities—admittedly, though, in a rather unequal manner. The English, on the other hand, did not even consider a syncretic approach to their American colonial experiment and purposefully excluded Indians from their social, economic, and political lives. The Quaker communities, on the other hand, exhibited tolerance.

Economic Changes During the Eighteenth Century

Compared to the economic environment in Europe, which was suffering the effects of war and inflation, the British colonists had a higher standard of living than their European counterparts. By the eighteenth century, colonists typically engaged in four types of work:

1. Agricultural: The main way they earned their livings was through farming. There were different types of farming—plantation farming was based upon commercial single-crop commodities; commercial farming was when people on smaller farms would raise crops, not for just their own sustenance, but to sell in the market; and self-sufficient family farming was where people grew crops to satisfy their own needs and use any surplus to buy goods or pay their taxes.

2. Craftsmen: Men would often work as craftsmen who had gone through some sort of training as an apprentice. Colonial craftsmen included blacksmiths, coopers, weavers, carpenters, and shipwrights.

3. Mercantilists: Trading was usually another option, where merchants would buy and sell goods they themselves did not make in order to make a profit.

4. Service provision: Other people offered services in communities, like butchers, market workers, doctors, and hair cutters.

Because of the emergence of more specialized industry, three types of classes characterized colonial society:

1. Rural landowners: Southern plantation owners who invested in land, slaves, buildings, lands, tools, and seeds

2. Merchants: traders and sellers of goods and services

3. Wage earners: wage earners who invested in industrial stock or various enterprises

Table 6.1
American Colonies

	Northern Colonies: Massachusetts Bay Colony; Rhode Island, Connecticut, New Hampshire, Maine	**Mid-Atlantic Colonies:** New York, New Jersey, Pennsylvania, Delaware
Type of Colonies	Small towns were the center of governments; typically started as royal colonies	Proprietary colonies established during the reign of Charles II (Restoration Colonies). Charles distributed land to his loyal followers and also used the colonies as a means to get rid of "problem" populations within England, like the Quakers
Economy	• Manufacturing, fishing, shipbuilding, lumbering, fur trading, commerce, small family run farms. • Most of the food was grown at home, that which was not was imported from England. • Self-sufficient farms. • Exported corn and wheat industry. • Profited from triangular trade with Africa and West Indies	• Part industrial, part agricultural; fur trade. • Farms were larger than those in New England. • Grew wheat, rye, and barley and was the "Bread Basket of the Colonies" • Raised livestock. • Factories produced iron, paper, and textiles. • Considerable trade with England.
Social Structure	Population largely homogenous, white, Puritans	Gentry Middling sort (farmers, shopkeepers, teachers)
Religious	People were considered, at least in the eyes of God, to be relatively equal. Pilgrims in Mass. sought religious freedom. Rhode Island passed laws of religious toleration. Religions: Puritans dominated New England	Quakers in Pennsylvania sought religious freedom—no army or war; greater toleration. Religions: Dutch Reformed and Presbyterian dominated
Motivations for Settling	Many sought to practice their own religion free of interference from government	Sought religious freedom (in Pennsylvania) and to make money. Many of those who came for the economic opportunities did not bring their families with them and so they eagerly worked hard
Who Settled	Primarily British Puritans	Dutch, English, Swedes, Germans, and French, so there was an emphasis on cultural diversity from the beginning. Many artisans and indentured servants came as well.

Table 6.1
American Colonies

	Chesapeake Colonies: Virginia and Maryland	Southern Colonies: North and South Carolinas, Georgia
Type of Colonies	• Virginia founded by the London Company for profit in 1607; later became a royal colony. • Maryland was a proprietary colony founded by the Calvert family.	• Restoration colonies • Georgia founded as a buffer between English colonies and Spanish Florida
Economy	• Single crop economies—money crops—rice, indigo, cotton, and tobacco. • Slaves formed a large part of the workforce on plantations. • Maintained close ties to England as South provided raw materials in exchange for European goods. • Had large debt to English merchants and bankers.	• Single Crop economies—money crops—rice, indigo, cotton, and tobacco • Slaves formed a large part of the workforce on plantations. • Maintained close ties to England as South provided raw materials in exchange for European goods. • Had large debt to English merchants and bankers.
Social Structure	Socially stratified— • Plantation owners at the top—wealthy owned many slaves and dominated economic, political, and social spheres • Small landowners (few owned slaves) • Tenant farmers: worked on others' land, paid rent, some worked as overseers • Slaves: Lowest	Socially stratified— • Plantation owners at the top– wealthy owned many slaves and dominated economic, political, and social spheres • Small landowners (few owned slaves) • Tenant farmers: worked on others' land, paid rent, some worked as overseers • Slaves: lowest
Religious	• Maryland passed laws of religious toleration. • Religion: Anglican (Church of England) dominated (except Maryland was Catholic)	• Religion: Anglican dominated
Motivations for Settling	• Mostly out to make maney • Mayland founded as haven for Catholics	• Mostly out to make money and as a long term venture, so they brought their families with them.
Who Settled	Primarily British: Adventurers and younger sons of aristocracy attracted to southern colonies; indentured servants worked on plantations to pay for their passage; criminals came to escape the death penalty (and chose colonies instead); as indentured servant numbers declined, slavery rose.	Primarily British: Adventurers and younger sons of aristocracy attracted to southern colonies; indentured servants worked on plantations to pay for their passage; criminals came to escape the death penalty (and chose colonies instead); as indentured servant numbers declined, slavery rose.

By the end of the eighteenth century, the gulf between the rich and poor had widened considerably. In Boston and Philadelphia, the top 10% owned over 60% of the wealth.

Colonial Societies During the Eighteenth Century

Most of colonial society could fit under one of these five societies:

1. **Colonial Farming Societies.** The bulk of the people who lived in the colonies lived on small, family-run, and self-sufficient farms. This included most who lived in the New England and Southern colonies, as well as many of those in the Middle Colonies.

2. **Urban Seaport Societies.** Big cities developed along the Atlantic Seaboard and became major seaports and commercial centers like Boston, New York, Newport, Philadelphia, and Charleston. Wealthy merchants and traders had become quite powerful.

3. **Frontier Societies.** As the next generation of colonists moved westward to find new, cheap land, they had to "rough it," living with bare necessities and creating their own environment. Much like the same issues that the first Europeans faced when they landed on American shores, these frontier societies had to create every element of their society. However, unlike the early colonists, the frontier societies did not have a strong community presence, due to how spread out everyone was and the lack of organized law and order, community institutions, or organized churches. As a result, the frontier lands were considered difficult places to live, and they increasingly faced conflict with those back East as they felt that they were not being treated equally by them. The Frontier societies protested that they were given inadequate protection from Indian attacks, did not have equal representation in government assemblies, and that the east purposely did not provide courts for the frontier. Some of these grievances could be traced to, according to the frontier societies, ethnic and economic differences between the two. The frontier population was decidedly "foreign"—meaning of German and Scots-Irish descent, and tended to consist of self-sufficient farmers or commercial farmers whose security was rather tenuous.

4. **Plantation/Slave Societies.** This was a highly stratified society in which social mobility did not really occur.

5. **Native American Societies.** European settlers engaged in a massive attempt to wipe the Indian peoples off of their lands. In 300 years, the Native American population declined from 10 million to just about 1 million. Many of those tribes that had close contact with Europeans suffered much the same fate as their South American counterparts as more than 50% caught diseases. As tribes were dispossessed of their lands, they moved westward in search of freedom.

Social Changes During the Eighteenth Century

Changes in colonial society occurred on a number of levels: population growth, ethnic diversity, increasing importance of cities, creation of urban elite, rising levels of consumption, and the growth of a stronger internal economy.

- Population changes abound during this period, as there were about 650,000 new immigrants, including about 325,000 slaves who came unwillingly. By the second half of the century, there were significant differences and stratification in terms of colonists' social and economic lives. There was enormous population growth, expanding from 300,000 people in 1700 to 2.5 million by 1775.

- The ethnic and linguistic composition of the immigrants also changed. Not only were more West Africans of various ethnic and linguistic groups coming as slaves, but there were changes among Europeans, too, as more Scots-Irish and German immigrants flocked to America.

- Cities now contained 20% of the population (ten percent higher than in 1700); there were four main cities in the colonies: Boston, New York, Philadelphia, and Charleston.

- Social and economic stratification intensified after 1750.

- Aristocratic plantation owners in the South had the most wealth and influence.

- Lawyers, merchants, officials, and clergymen dominated the North.

- Yeoman farmers constituted the majority of the population and they owned land.

- Lesser tradesman, manual workers, and hired hands who usually did not own land

- Indentured servants

- Slaves—about 20% of the population

- Emergence of movements such as the **Great Awakening**, which spread in the 1730s–1740s in the Southern and Middle Colonies, that was a reaction against established churches.

- Colonial press developed.

Figure 6.1
Population of the New England Colonies, 1620–1750

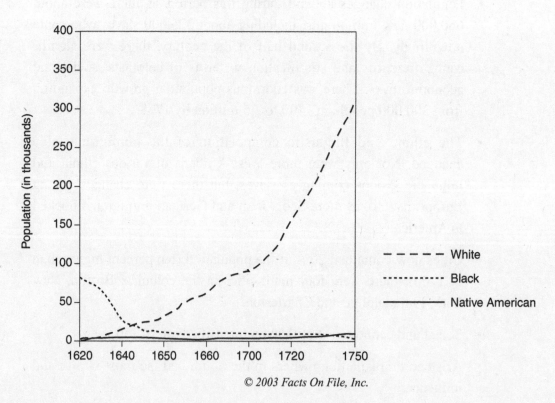

© 2003 Facts On File, Inc.

COMPETENCY 5.3

Identify the causes, significant individuals, and effects of the events associated with the Revolutionary era.

Albany Plan of Union

In 1754, representatives of seven colonies and 150 Indians met in Albany, New York to gain the allegiance of the Iroquois Confederacy and to provide a system for the collective defense of the colonies in the face of the coming war with France. After renewing the alliance with the Iroquois who promised to continue to protect the English from attacks by the French-supporting Hurons, Benjamin Franklin proposed the **Albany Plan of Union**, which provided for an inter-colonial government that would regulate dealings with the Native Americans, organize and run a colonial army, manage the public lands, legislate, and supervise the collection of taxes for a common defense fund. Not only did England reject the proposal because they felt that a union of the colonies would make them too unmanageable, but the colonies also failed to support it because they did not want to relinquish any of their powers, particularly the right to tax, to a grand council. Franklin's annoyance was reflected in the publishing of his cartoon in which he drew a snake broken into pieces with the inscription below, "Join or Die." The drawing was based on the popular belief that a snake that had been cut in half would come to life again if the pieces were joined before sunset.

Causes: Fear of what would happen if there were a war with France

Significant individuals: Benjamin Franklin

Effects: Provided an example of what would happen and issues that would arise in future inter-colonial gatherings like the First and Second Congress. Had it passed, it could have rendered the American Revolution unnecessary. This also proved to be the last attempt to devise an inter-colonial union.

Figure 6.2

JOIN, or DIE.

By Benjamin Franklin
Cartoon in the *Pennsylvania Gazette* May 9, 1754

The Seven Years War and the Treaty of Paris, 1763

The name "Seven Years' War" is a bit of a misnomer—it actually lasted nine years from July 1754 to 1763. Moreover, it also is called the **French and Indian War**, not because of war between the French and Indians, but rather because the French and Indians fought on the same side. The British refer to the war as the Seven Years War or **King George's War,** but the colonists called it the French and Indian War because that was who they were fighting. Nevertheless, the war was one of several skirmishes that happened all over the world (notably, India) out of fights for empire between the British and the French. Some historians have referred to this as the first world war.

There were three phases of fighting during the war:

- Phase 1: 1754–1756, characterized by limited nature of the war and it being confined to the North American continent.

- Phase 2: 1756–1757, when the war spread to the West Indies, India, and Europe. Still, much of the fighting continued to be in North America. **William Pitt**, the British Secretary of State, directed the war effort and issued orders to the colonists. He ordered British commanders to forcibly enlist colonists to serve and to seize needed supplies from them. These measures led to a struggle between the colonists and the British that hampered the war effort.

- Phase 3: 1758–1763: By 1758, some of the problems that had plagued the British started to resolve. Pitt relaxed some of his measures and gave more troops to the colonies, leading the British to regain some military successes. The Fall of Quebec in September 1759 helped the British to convince the French to surrender in 1760. Peace was not signed though until 1763.

Causes: While conflict and tensions between the French and English over colonial supremacy over North America had been going on for many decades, in the early 1750s, tensions came to a head as England and France both vied for land in the Ohio River Valley, near present-day Pittsburgh, PA. In 1754, English troops under the command of a rather inexperienced George Washington marched to oust the French by force. In a route called the Battle of Jumonville Glen, Washington and his troops massacred the French and Washington created a stockade that he named **Fort Necessity**, in anticipation of the French responding to his earlier attack. The French led a force of 600 troops against Washington, indeed forcing Washington to surrender the fort—Washington returned home to Virginia, where, oddly, he was considered a hero for his actions. Thus began the French and Indian War.

Effects: During the war, British-colonial tensions increased as anti-British feelings in the colonies found their voice. The different styles of fighting between the British and the colonial militias caused significant resentment on both sides. There had been disagreements with the British over what sort of tactics to use, and the colonial preference for guerilla tactics annoyed the British who preferred to march in formation. The colonial militias who helped fight for the British remained under their own command, despite British insistence that they remain under British authority.

Britain was also deeply in debt because of the war, and thought that Americans should share the cost of the war, so they imposed new taxes. The colonists did not want to pay any higher taxes to pay for the cost of the war. Britain felt that they had been fighting for the defense of the colonists and such ungrateful responses were unjustified, and they believed that the colonists should have to pay for their own defense. The new British king, **George III**, and his Prime Minister, **George Grenville**, also considered that the tax burden that the colonists had to bear was considerably less than that of taxpayers back in England, so they did not think that it was too harsh of a burden.

As a result of the British victory in the French and Indian War, France lost its foothold in the New World. The **Treaty of Paris 1763** made them relinquish their New World possessions, including Canada. They also agreed to get out and stay out of India, which made

Great Britain the supreme military power in that part of Asia. Spain also gained and lost in this treaty as they lost Florida to England, but gained all French land west of the Mississippi. In addition, as compensation for Spain's loss of Florida to England, Spain was awarded the Louisiana territory.

At the end of the war, Britain had mixed emotions about the war. While they were grateful that they now had a larger and safer empire, they also had accumulated significant debt. The colonists' protests against paying that debt resulted in significant feelings of contempt for the colonists. British attempts to force the colonists to pay for the war and to recoup their financial losses by issuing taxes wound up only sparking colonial anger and fueling revolutionary fervor. For the colonies, the war had united them against a common enemy for the first time. It also created long-standing anger against the British who were viewed as overly harsh and whose disdain for the colonists created even more resentment.

Another effect of the war was that the English raised the price of goods that they sold to the Indians and stopped paying rent on their western forts. In response, the Ottawa leader, Pontiac, united an unprecedented amount of tribes due to concern about the spread of colonists and their culture and attacked colonial outposts in the Ohio valley. The attacks and the wars are referred to as **Pontiac's Rebellion** or **Pontiac's Uprising**. Although the British ultimately prevailed, how they handled the conflict provoked an enormous amount of resentment among the colonists.

In response to Pontiac's Rebellion and the attacks, the British issued the **Proclamation of 1763** that drew a line west of the rivers running through the Appalachians and said that the colonists were not allowed to settle past that line, in order to avoid further conflicts with the Indians. While this improved relations between the British and the Native Americans, it worsened the relationship between the British and the colonists. The problem, though, is that the colonists had already expanded beyond the Ohio River Valley and had encroached on Indians' lands. Settlers were annoyed by the proclamation and viewed it as unwarranted British interference. It also can be viewed as the first in a series of new efforts by the British to control the colonists more tightly, the end of **salutary neglect**, and the beginning of the road to revolution.

It also led to France wanting its own measure of revenge against the British, so they helped the American colonies during the revolution.

Grenville Acts

From 1763–1765, Grenville led the charge to exact more taxes on the colonists. He put forth four pieces of legislation that would be sources of great discontent for the colonists: the **Sugar Act (1764)**, the **Currency Act (1764)**, the **Quartering Act (1765)**, and the **Stamp Act (1765)**.

Sugar Act

This established a series of new duties aimed at deterring molasses smugglers by *lowering* the duty on molasses, sugar, textiles, coffee, and indigo to come into the colonies from the West Indies to 3 pence. The problem was that while a tax had been in place since the Navigation Acts of 1733, people had been paying bribes of 1½ pence for years. Parliament thought that the colonists would not mind paying 3 pence in legal tax versus 1½ pence on bribes. Unlike previous taxes, this tax was enforced and smugglers were prosecuted (where people looked the other way before).

Causes: The British decided to raise taxes on the colonists to pay for the Seven Years War.

Significant individuals: George Grenville

Effects: American colonists did not think it was fair that they should be taxed in the same manner as those who lived in England, particularly as they had no representation in Parliament. Cries of **"no taxation without representation"** filled town halls and public gatherings.

Colonists were upset that any violators would be tried in vice-admiralty courts, where judges could issue verdicts and there would be no deliberation of a jury. Colonists felt this overstepped British authority over them and violated their rights as Englishmen.

Currency Act

This act effectively forbade the colonies from issuing money, as it ruled that colonial currency could not be used for trade.

Causes: British felt that the colonial currency fluctuated too much to the detriment of the British.

Effects: Colonists were angered that their money had no value.

Quartering Act

This act forced colonial assemblies to raise colonial taxes to provide housing and provisions, like bedding, cooking utensils, firewood, beer, cider, and candles for 10,000 new British troops in barracks near colonial centers. Colonists questioned why troops were being sent over now, after the cessation of war with France. This law was expanded in 1766 and required the assemblies to billet all British soldiers residing in their borders in taverns and unoccupied houses.

Causes: The British did have some concerns about protecting the colonists from attack, and this law enabled them to do so cheaply, with the colonies bearing the burden of their own protection. The British also had a practical means of trying to figure out what to do with all of the Seven Years War veterans and how to pay for them to come home. By having the soldiers continue to stay in the colonies under the fiscal responsibility of the colonial assemblies, the English public would be spared another tax burden.

Effects: The reaction of the colonists was largely negative for three reasons:

1. Colonists had a traditional fear of standing armies and believed it was fiscally irresponsible to have them. The colonists generally preferred to rely on militia units rather than formal armies. Militiamen could be called for service during a particular crisis and then disbanded when the fighting was concluded, without having to pay for long-term provisioning.

2. Colonial assemblies fretted about the cost of expenses for an army that they did not feel they particularly needed. The French were no longer a threat by the mid-1760s, and so many believed that Britain had ulterior motives for keeping a large contingent in the colonies. They opined that England may have considered that it would need an army to force unpopular policies and laws on the colonists.

3. Colonists questioned the real motivation for having the troops. Since the French and Indian War was over and the colonists no longer feared the French, they believed the troops were unnecessary. Many suspected that

the real reason for the troops were not to protect the colonists, but to control them and to quell any potential outrage over new taxation policies.

Stamp Act

This direct, internal tax was a broad-based tax that required the use of stamped paper for all legal document, licenses, diplomas, almanacs, pamphlets, newspapers, and playing cards. The presence of the stamp on the paper indicated that the tax had been paid in sterling, the "official" currency, and not colonial currency. Funds from the tax were to be used to help pay for the provisioning of British soldiers in the colonies. The taxes ranged from one shilling for a newspaper to ten pounds for a lawyer's license, and there was little one could do in the colonies in which they would not be forced to pay the tax and so, it affected almost everyone, but particularly the elite, who used more paper anyway, and the lawyers. Violators of the tax would be held in the vice-admiralty courts, which meant that the violators would not have a trial by jury.

Causes: The British were not really trying to oppress the colonists but were trying to find a way to pay for the British troops who were stationed there.

Effects: It made colonists realize that this revenue-raising tax was likely only the beginning and that many more taxes would follow, and it made them realize that the tradition of self-taxation was being unjustly taken away by Parliament. So, reaction to the tax was more forceful than any that preceded it.

The tax united some of the most powerful and articulate members of colonial society, lawyers, clergymen, journalists, and businessmen, who deluged the public with pamphlets and argument against the tax. James Otis's pamphlet, *The Rights of the British Colonies Asserted and Proved*, decried the unconstitutionality of the taxation without representation. He argued that as colonists did not elect members to Parliament, then Parliament had no right to tax them, and therefore, the colonists did not have to pay them. The British ignored the plea in the pamphlet, asserting that according to the principles of **virtual representation**, Parliament members represented all subjects of the Empire, regardless of who actually voted for them. As such, the colonists had no authority to challenge the Parliament.

The act spread opposition to it. In Boston and New York, mobs burned the customs officers in effigy, tore down a custom's house, and almost destroyed the governor's mansion. They sought to intimidate potential tax agents into not performing their duties—and it worked. By the time the law was to go into effect, no duty collectors were willing to perform their job. Patriotic societies, known as **Sons of Liberty**, were formed to organize colonial resistance to the taxes. Merchants agreed not to import any British goods, and the Sons of Liberty exerted pressure on them to abide by that decision. The boycott so affected British merchants that they put pressure on Parliament to repeal the act, and they did so in 1766. In addition, George III replaced Prime Minister Grenville with Lord Rockingham, who oversaw the appeal and also put forth the **Declaratory Act,** which, as a face-saving gesture, stated that the British government had a right to tax and legislate in the colonies.

Townshend Acts (1767)

After William Pitt replaced Lord Rockingham as prime minister, he became too ill to govern effectively, and Charles Townshend became the Minister of the Exchequer and the dominant figure in colonial affairs, determined to settle the issue of imperial finance. He drafted the **Townshend Acts,** external taxes that issued levies on all lead, paint, paper, glass, and tea that was not produced in North America and that the colonists were only allowed to buy from Great Britain. These were aimed to pay the salaries of all government officials stationed in the colonies. One tactic the colonists had used before when they were protesting taxes was to refuse to pay the officials—so, this tax aimed to remedy this situation. Anyone who refused to pay this was also sent to the vice-admiralty courts, which would also be paid for from the taxes created from the Townshend Acts. One of the Townshend Acts, the **New York Restraining Act**, suspended the New York legislature for failing to comply with the law requiring the colonists to provide for British troops.

Causes: Continued problem of trying to solve financial costs to the English of running the colonial administration and defense

Effects: Colonists protested that Parliament did have the right to regulate colonial trade but not to raise revenue. There were repeated calls for protest and unity among the colonies to repeal the measures. Rallies were held that sought the support of all people, not just the elites. As a result, the rallies were more unnerving for the British as they were significantly larger and more threatening. A second import boycott was led by the **Daughters of Liberty,** who encouraged women to take up the cause and make their own goods, rather than buy British-made goods. By 1770, the Townshend Duties were repealed, all except for the tea tax.

Boston Massacre

As part of the Townshend Acts, the British sent an overwhelming number of troops, 4,000 of them, to Boston, a city of only 16,000 people. They were sent in response to a request by English customs officials that they needed help enforcing customs duties collections. Tensions between the troops and the townspeople flared, even more so when the soldiers competed for second jobs with the colonists. On one occasion, on March 5, 1770, a riotous crowd of about 60 Bostonian laborers and seamen shouted insults and threw rock-filled snowballs at a detachment of soldiers who were guarding the customs house. The redcoats fired into the crowd, killing five townspeople and wounding six others. The angry citizens, led by Samuel Adams, demanded the removal of the British troops. In the trial that followed, in which John Adams defended the soldiers in court, the soldiers were found not-guilty.

Causes: Tensions between the troops stationed in Boston and beleaguered colonists prompted an attack by the colonists and the British fired on them.

Effects: The Lieutenant Governor ordered the withdrawal of troops and the colonists considered it a victory. The majority of colonists, including John Adams, considered the mob actions inflammatory and did not support the rabble rousers. The event, however, became used as propaganda, much like the picture below, in order to arouse public indignation against the British.

Paul Revere's print of "The Bloody Massacre perpetrated in King Street" in Boston, March 5, 1770 was advertised in Boston's newspapers. Termed the "Bloody Massacre," it sought to stir up colonial hatred of the British government.

Concerned about an uprising that could get out of control, the governor ordered the soldiers out of the city. News of the "massacre" spread throughout the colonies and aroused hatred everywhere.

Tea Act

The British granted concessions to the financially floundering East India Company who had a whopping 18 million pounds of unsold tea sitting in their warehouses in India, that allowed it to ship tea directly to the colonies rather than only by way of Britain. The result would be that East India Company tea, even with the tax, would be cheaper than smuggled Dutch tea. The colonists would thus, it was hoped, buy the tea, tax and all. The East India Company would be saved, and the Americans would be tacitly accepting Parliament's right to tax them. The net result would have been cheaper tea for the colonists; however, there was a proviso—only British agents could sell the tea, cutting out local North American merchants. Americans responded, rather unexpectedly, by vociferously opposing yet another tax upon them. Public anger about the tea created a tense situation at colonial ports. In New York and Philadelphia, the ship masters saw the potential for trouble and did not land; in Annapolis, angry mobs forced the ship owner to burn his ship and tea cargo. In Boston, the colonists did not allow the ships to unload their cargo and the governor would not allow the ships to leave the harbor.

Causes: The British sought to help out the East India Company and to test the colonists on the taxation issue.

Effects: This led to the Boston Tea Party.

Boston Tea Party

In Boston, pro-British Governor Thomas Hutchinson (1711–1780) forced a confrontation by ordering Royal Navy vessels to prevent the tea ships from leaving the harbor. After 20 days, this would, by law, result in the cargoes being sold at auction and the tax paid. During the night of December 16, 1773, about 50 Bostonians disguised as Mohawks boarded the ships sitting in Boston Harbor, loaded down with tea, and dumped 342 chests (worth 10,000 pounds) into the harbor.

Causes: Tea Tax and the influx of British Soldiers due to the Townshend Acts.

Significant Individuals: Samuel Adams incited mobs to roam Boston's streets in the evenings to threaten violence with regard to the Tea Tax.

Massachusetts Governor Thomas Hutchinson vowed not to capitulate in the face of public opposition as had happened in other colonies.

Effects: Other ports "restaged' the Tea Party in order to inflame public opinion and garner more support for those opposed to the British.

The British responded with the **Coercive Acts** (also called the **Intolerable Acts**).

Intolerable Acts (1774)

Parliament moved quickly to punish Massachusetts for the Boston Tea Party and to reassert its authority over the colonies. It passed a series of acts that the colonists called "intolerable"

- Boston Port Act: This bill closed the port of Boston to all but essential trade (firewood and food) until local citizens would agree to pay for the lost tea (they would not). They sought to set an example for the other colonies.

- Massachusetts Government Act: Tightened control over the Massachusetts government and its courts, destroyed all colonial power in the legislature, greatly increased the power of Massachusetts's royal governor at the expense of the legislature, and limited town meetings.

- Administration of Justice Act: Provided that royal officials accused of crimes in Massachusetts could be tried elsewhere, where chances of acquittal might be greater. Therefore, any soldier who killed colonists would be granted extraterritoriality.

- Quartering Act: This new act allowed the new governor, General Thomas Gage (1721–1787), to quarter his troops anywhere, including unoccupied private homes.

Causes: British desire to restore order in Massachusetts following the Boston Tea Party. Some in Parliament expressed concern over what the reaction to these acts would be, but such restraint was ignored.

Effects: Prompted feelings of sympathy among the other colonies and moderates for what was happening in Massachusetts, fostered unity among the colonies against British rule, and pushed many moderates into the radical camp. Most significantly, it spurred the summoning of the **First Continental Congress** in 1774.

First Continental Congress (September 5, 1774–October 26, 1774)

In response to the Intolerable Acts, all of the colonies except Georgia decided to meet for seven weeks in order to formulate a united protest of the Intolerable Acts. Their goals in the meeting were to enumerate American grievances, find a strategy to resist them, and to come up with a document that firmly outlined what the colonial relationship was with the royal government, without severing their ties to it. Many of the prominent figures of the era were in attendance: George Washington, Samuel Adams, John Adams, Patrick Henry, and John Jay.

The First Continental Congress agreed on the following:

- They decided that the colonists would obey Parliament only when they thought it was best for both sides—this as a major break with British tradition and proved to be a huge step towards independence. They also stated they would start a total economic boycott (non-importation, non-exportation, and non-consumption accords) and petition King George III with a *List of Grievances* at the same time. They formed the **Continental Association**, which would help organize this boycott.

- They recommended that elected committees called **committees of observation** be started to enforce the boycott and attack dissention and that would become *de facto* governments. They would endeavor to convince people that they had different interests than England, and as such, we not really "English," but "American." The committee men became leaders of the revolution and gained power as time went on.

- The colonies had the right to tax and legislate themselves.

The colonies had the right to mobilize a colonial militia and raised a defensive force of 20,000 **Minutemen** to be ready in minutes, just in case they needed them.

They established that if their complaints were addressed adequately, they would meet a second time.

Causes: Intolerable Acts

Significant individuals: George Washington, Samuel Adams, John Adams, Patrick Henry, and John Jay

Effects: The Committees of Observation expanded their powers and coordinated all acts of insubordination in the colonies. The British underestimated the First Continental Congress and decided to teach the colonists a military lesson. They sent troops to Massachusetts, which was officially declared to be in a state of rebellion. Orders were sent to General Gage to arrest the ringleaders of the resistance, or failing that, to provoke any sort of confrontation that would allow him to turn the British military loose on the colonists.

Battles of Lexington and Concord (April 19, 1775)

General Gage dispatched 800 of his British troops to confiscate weapons that they believed were held in Concord. **Paul Revere** heard about this and sounded his alarm for the militiamen to get ready. They confronted the British in Lexington and the militiamen suffered 18 casualties—8 colonists were dead and 10 were injured. The Minutemen retreated to the woods and the British went on to Concord. Then at Concord, the British were met with even more resistance from the Massachusetts milita and the British suffered many more casualties than did the colonists. The ability of the colonists to resist the British caused the Battle at Concord to be referred to as "the shot heard 'round the world." For the year following Concord, the Americans besieged Boston, where the British had retreated.

Second Continental Congress (May, 1775)

This meeting convened just weeks after the battles of Lexington and Concord when the Congress was called to prepare the colonies for war and ended up being the main inter-colonial government. Congress was divided into two main factions. One was composed mostly of New Englanders and leaned toward declaring independence from Britain. The other drew its strength primarily from the Middle Colonies and was not yet ready to go that far. Nonetheless, they authorized printing American paper money, created Washington's Continental

Army, and offered to end armed resistance if the King would withdraw troops and revoke the Intolerable Acts. In July, the King rejected the Olive Branch Petition and Parliament passed the Prohibition Act that outlawed British trade with the colonies and instructed the Royal Navy to seize any American ships that were engaged in trade.

Declaration of Independence

The Declaration of Independence was primarily the work of Thomas Jefferson (1743–1826) of Virginia. It was a restatement of political ideas by then commonplace in America and showed why the former colonists felt justified in separating from Great Britain. It was formally adopted by Congress on July 4, 1776 when 12 colonies, except for New York, voted for it.

The primary importance of the Declaration was its statement of principle (life, liberty, and pursuit of happiness) and the explanation that government was based on the consent of the people. After the Declaration was signed, there really was no turning back—because the delegates had committed treason. This Declaration stated that the colonies were free and independent entities, absolved of all allegiance to England. It made official what had already been happening and the revolution was in full swing.

Effects: Articulated the colonies' grievances against the Crown and recognized both individual liberty and the government's primary responsibility—to serve the people.

Treaty of Paris (September 3, 1783)

Benjamin Franklin, John Jay, and John Adams negotiated peace with the British in Paris. The resulting treaty formally recognized the independence of the United States. It stipulated the following:

1. Britain and the major European powers all recognized that the United States was an independent nation.

2. Boundaries were set: its western boundary was the Mississippi River; its southern boundary was set at 31° north latitude (the northern boundary of Florida); Britain retained Canada but had to surrender Florida to Spain

3. Private British creditors would be free to collect any debts owed by U.S. citizens.

4. Congress was to recommend that the states restore confiscated loyalist property.

5. American fishing rights were established along the Newfoundland banks.

In the Treaty of Versailles, signed at the same time, Britain made peace with France and Spain and the Spanish regained Florida. All land between the Appalachians and the Mississippi River was ceded to the new American republic—and Briain promised to withdraw its garrisons throughout the territory without attempting to secure the land rights of its Indian allies. Both treaties were vague in defining the boundaries between the United States and its British and Spanish neighbors, creating frequent territorial disputes over the next 30 years.

Effects: The new nation had accumulated massive debt during its War of Independence (some though had been taken on by France), more than $11 million in national debt and state debts of more than $65 million.

COMPETENCY 5.4
Identify the causes, significant individuals, and effects of the events associated with the Constitutional era and the early republic.

After the collapse of British authority in 1775, it became necessary to form new state governments. By the end of 1777, ten new state constitutions had been formed. Most state constitutions included bills of rights—lists of things the government was not supposed to do to the people.

In the summer of 1776, Congress appointed a committee to begin devising a framework for a national government. The end result preserved the sovereignty of the states and created a very weak national government. **The Articles of Confederation** provided for a unicameral Congress in which each state would have one vote, as had been the case in the Continental Congress. Executive authority under the articles would be vested in a committee of 13, with one member from each state. In order to amend the articles, the unanimous consent of all the states was required.

The Articles of Confederation government was empowered to make war, make treaties, determine the amount of troops and money each state should contribute to the war effort, settle disputes between states, admit new states to the Union, and borrow money. But it was not empowered to levy taxes, raise troops, or regulate commerce. Ratification of the Articles of Confederation was delayed by disagreements over the future status of the lands that lay to the west of the original 13 states. Maryland, which had no such claim, withheld ratification until, in 1781, Virginia agreed to surrender its western claims to the new national government.

The United States Constitution (1787–1789): Development and Ratification

As time went on, the inadequacy of the Articles of Confederation became increasingly apparent. It was decided in 1787 to call for a convention of all the states to meet in Philadelphia for the purpose of revising the Articles of Confederation. The men who met in Philadelphia in 1787 were remarkably able, highly educated, and exceptionally accomplished. For the most part, they were lawyers, merchants, and planters. Though representing individual states, most thought in national terms. George Washington was unanimously elected to preside, and the enormous respect that he commanded helped hold the convention together through difficult times.

The delegates shared a basic belief in the innate selfishness of man, which must somehow be kept from abusing the power of government. For this purpose, the document that they finally produced contained many checks and balances, designed to prevent the government, or any one branch of the government, from gaining too much power.

Benjamin Franklin played an important role in reconciling the often heated delegates and in making various suggestions that eventually helped the convention arrive at the "Great Compromise," proposed by Roger Sherman (1721–1793) and Oliver Ellsworth (1745–1807). The Great (or Connecticut) Compromise provided for a presidency, a Senate with all states represented equally (by two senators each), and a House of Representatives with representation according to population.

Another crisis involved North-South disagreement over the issue of slavery. Here also a compromise was reached. Slavery was neither endorsed nor condemned by the Constitution. Each slave was to count as three-fifths of a person for purposes of apportioning representation and direct taxation on the states (the Three-Fifths Compromise). The federal government was prohibited from stopping the importation of slaves prior to 1808.

The third major area of compromise was the nature of the presidency. The result was a strong presidency with control of foreign policy and the power to veto Congress's legislation. Should the president commit an actual crime, Congress would have the power to impeach him. Otherwise, the president would serve for a term of four years and be re-electable without limit. As a check to the possible excesses of democracy, the president was to be elected by an electoral college, in which each state would have the same number of electors as it did senators and representatives combined. The person with the second highest total in the electoral college would be vice president. If no one gained a majority in the electoral college, the president would be chosen by the House of Representatives.

The new Constitution was to take effect when nine states, through special state conventions, had ratified it. As the struggle over ratification got under way, those favoring the Constitution astutely named themselves Federalists (i.e., advocates of centralized power) and labeled their opponents Antifederalists. By June 21, 1788, the required nine states had ratified, but the crucial states of New York and Virginia still held out. Ultimately, the promise of the addition of a bill of rights helped win the final states. In March 1789, George Washington was inaugurated as the nation's first President.

Few Anti-federalists were elected to Congress, and many of the new legislators had served as delegates to the Philadelphia Convention two years before. George Washington received virtually all the votes of the presidential electors, and John Adams received the next highest number, thus becoming the vice-president. After a triumphant journey from Mount Vernon, Washington was inaugurated in New York City, the temporary seat of government (April 30, 1789).

Ten amendments were ratified by the states by the end of 1791 and became the Bill of Rights. The first nine spelled out specific guarantees of personal freedoms, and the Tenth Amendment reserved to the states all those powers not specifically withheld or granted to the federal government. The Judiciary Act of 1789 provided for a Supreme Court with six justices, and invested it with the power to rule on the constitutional validity of state laws. It was to be the interpreter of the "supreme law of the land." A system of district courts was set up to serve as courts of original jurisdiction, and three courts of appeal were established.

Congress established three departments of the executive branch—state, treasury, and war—as well as the offices of attorney general and postmaster general.

COMPETENCY 5.5

Evaluate the impact of westward expansion on the social, cultural, political, and economic development of the emerging nation.

In just a five year period, the United States increased its size by a third. It annexed Texas in 1845; received half of the Oregon territory from the British; as a result of the US-Mexico War had acquired California, Nevada, Utah, and parts of Arizona, Colorado, New Mexico, and Wyoming. But such rapid expansion was not without its issues and intensified conflicts between North and South over whether or not slavery should be allowed in the new territories. Decisions about how and when to broaden the US borders had been evolving since its origins. It had taken American colonists 150 years just to push as far west as the Appalachian mountains and another 50 years just to push the frontiers to the Mississippi River.

Deciding where the western borders of the United States would be proved to be a rather thorny issue that took place over the course of the nineteenth century when the concept of **Manifest Destiny** typified American ideas about the west. Before that, however, there needed to be an understanding or policy about how territories would become states. The **Northwest Ordinance of 1787** set up a three-step process for statehood that centered on the numbers of people settled and the establishment of a constitution: it stipulated that the first step would be to settle 5,000 male landowners and write a temporary constitution then it could have a territorial legislature to manage local issues; step two would be to settle 60,000 male landowners and write a state constitution; and the third step would be to have Congress approve the constitution and its statehood. Treatment toward the Native Americans who lived in much of this land was not really taken into consideration. The Native Americans protested, and war between the United States and various Native American tribes ensued.

Although the term "Manifest Destiny" was not actually coined until 1844, the belief that the American nation was destined to eventually expand all the way to the Pacific Ocean, and to possibly embrace Canada and Mexico, had been voiced for years by many who believed that American liberty and ideals should be shared with everyone possible, by force if necessary. The rising sense of nationalism that followed the War of 1812 was fed by the rapidly expanding population, the reform impulse of the 1830s, and the desire to acquire new markets and resources for the burgeoning economy of "Young America." The completion of America's continental borders from the Atlantic to the Pacific was facilitated by policy makers who tackled the situation through four means:

- Purchase

- Diplomacy

- Legal appropriation

- War

Americans did purchase a great part of the land. The **Louisiana Purchase of 1803**, bought right when Napoleon was gearing up for war in Europe and was reeling from revolution in Haiti, offered the whole kit and caboodle, not just New Orleans as was initially thought, for the handsome price of $15 million. Thomas Jefferson was a bit nervous about the legality of such a thing as there was nothing in the Constitution that mentioned purchasing land, but he did so anyway, lest Napoleon change his mind. The **Gadsden Purchase of 1853** enabled the United States to buy the 29,640 square-mile area that today forms southern Arizona and south-western New Mexico from Mexico for $10 million. It also bought **Alaska** from Russia for $7 million in 1867.

Americans also used diplomatic relations and war to negotiate for land in the West. After the War of 1812, the United States and Britain decided that they would both occupy Oregon. The **Adams-Onis Treaty of 1819** had not only gained Florida from Spain but also set the northern boundary of Spanish possessions near the present northern border of California. The territory north of that line and west of the vague boundaries of the Louisiana Territory had been claimed over the years by Spain, England, Russia, France, and the United States. By the 1820s, all of these claims had been yielded to Britain and the United States. The United States claimed all the way north to the 54°40′ parallel. Unable to settle the dispute, they had agreed on a joint occupation of the disputed land. In the 1830s, American missionaries followed the traders and trappers to the Oregon country. They began to publicize the richness and beauty of the land. The result was the "Oregon Fever" of the 1840s, as thousands of settlers trekked across the Great Plains and the Rocky Mountains to settle the new Shangri-la. In 1846, with the Oregon Treaty, the United States agreed to a compromise with Great Britain. By the terms of the treaty, they agreed that the US-Canada boundary east of the Rockies, the 49th parallel, was extended westward to the Pacific in return for the United States accepting Vancouver Island as a British territory.

Another result of the 1812 war was that it removed Great Britain as a potential ally of the Native Americans, so now the United States was free to appropriate lands from the Native Americans without thinking twice about it. When he was a general under President

Monroe, Andrew Jackson received permission to invade Spanish Florida in an "unofficial war" that resulted in Spain ceding Florida in the Adams-Onis 1819 treaty.

The United States also gained Texas and California through its war with Mexico. Texas had been a state in the Republic of Mexico since 1822, following the Mexican revolution against Spanish control. The new Mexican government invited immigration from the north by offering land grants to Stephen Austin (1793–1836) and other Americans. By 1835, approximately 35,000 "gringos" were homesteading on Texas land. The Mexican officials saw their power base eroding as the foreigners flooded in, so they moved to tighten control through restrictions on immigration and through tax increases. The Texans responded in 1836 by proclaiming independence and establishing a new republic. The ensuing war was short-lived. The Mexican dictator, Antonio López de Santa Anna (1794–1876), advanced north and annihilated the Texan garrisons at the Alamo and at Goliad. On April 23, 1836, Houston (1793–1863) defeated him at San Jacinto, and the Mexicans were forced to let Texas go its way.

Houston immediately asked the American government for recognition and annexation, but President Andrew Jackson feared the revival of the slavery issue. He also feared war with Mexico and so did nothing. When Van Buren followed suit, the new republic sought foreign recognition and support, which the European nations eagerly provided, hoping thereby to create a counterbalance to rising American power and influence in the Southwest. France and England both quickly concluded trade agreements with the Texans. After a great deal of maneuvering and politicking, Texas was admitted into the Union in 1845. Mexico protested the admission of Texas into the United States, a protest that the United States saw as an excuse to send troops into Texas.

The Mexican-American War lasted two years and ended with the signing of the **Treaty of Guadalupe-Hidalgo** on February 2, 1848. The United States had succeeded in winning the war and, with the Treaty of Guadalupe-Hidalgo, succeeded in fulfilling its Manifest Destiny. The treaty itself represented U.S. expansionist goals. Bankrupt from the war, Mexico agreed to $15 million as payment for the vast land. In addition, the United States agreed to forgive all Mexican debts. A few years later, it was discovered that the boundary information in the Treaty of Guadalupe-Hidalgo was inaccurate. Diplomatic tension followed. In 1853, the United States negotiated with Mexico to resolve the boundary dispute that resulted at the termination of the Mexican War and to purchase the land in question. In what became known as the **Gadsden Purchase**, the United States paid $10 million for a strip of territory south of the Gila River in what is now southwestern New Mexico and southern Arizona. The district of New Mexico had, like Texas, encouraged

American immigration. Soon that state was more American than Mexican. The Santa Fe Trail, running from Independence, Missouri, to the town of Santa Fe, created a prosperous trade in mules, gold, silver, and furs, which moved north in exchange for manufactured goods. American settlements sprung up all along the route.

The U.S. War with Mexico raised a number of thorny issues that would continue to plague the Americans for decades to come. Americans had precipitated this war for territorial gain, an issue that flatly contradicted what it had fought for just decades earlier. The war also gave practical battle experience and tactical experience to young officers and soldiers who, 15 years later, would form the nuclei of the Union and Confederate armies. It also gave the Americans the false understanding that war was short and quick, which doubtlessly affected the bravado with which they threw around the threat of war and fighting.

Advocates of the war cheered the victory of a new Protestant democratic civilization against a corrupt Catholic quasi-tyranny. They also championed it as the final piece in the puzzle of the United Status's quest for Manifest Destiny and spanning the country from shore to shore. Opponents of the war—and there were many, among them John Quincy Adams, Ralph Waldo Emerson, Henry David Thoreau, and the young Abraham Lincoln—regarded it as a blatant, cold-blooded act of robbery by which a large, powerful nation set out to steal half of the territory of a smaller, weaker, innocent neighbor. Conspiracy theorists opined that the war was a proslavery conspiracy designed to secure territories receptive to slavery and could easily tip the balance in favor of the slave states.

The issues revealed by the war and attempts to justify it only grew more complex and problematic over the next few years. It helped to frame the context of American public life for the next 20 years. The land-hunger that drove the Mexican War and inspired the Treaty of Guadalupe-Hidalgo spurred American settlements and diplomatic saber-rattling elsewhere on the continent, most notably in the Pacific Northwest. Under the slogan, "54°40' or fight," American claims to that region—not only present-day Washington, Idaho, Montana, and Oregon but also large parts of Canada—led to a series of diplomatic clashes with Great Britain. But the British were far stronger than the Mexicans were, and diplomacy averted a full-scale war between the United States and Britain.

Anti-expansionists

Not everyone appreciated the idea of the United States expanding from sea to sea. Many argued that it was unconstitutional, dangerous (as treaties with the Indians would be broken, giving rise to an increase of attacks in the West), could lead to war with Mexico, and would produce a nation too large to govern. Other protests revolved around the idea of slavery. Abolitionists worried that expansion would lead to more slavery, which would impede the new manufacturing industry.

Social

Expansion westward seemed perfectly natural to many Americans in the mid-nineteenth century. Many considered it their duty to extend their liberty to new realms, to spread their wonderful government from sea to shining sea. At the heart of Manifest Destiny was the pervasive belief in American cultural and racial superiority. Native Americans had long been perceived as inferior, and efforts to "civilize" them had been widespread since the days of John Smith and Miles Standish. With religious fervor spiking because of the Second Great Awakening, many sought to apply this movement to a need to spread the word of God to the Native Americans. Many settlers believed that God had shined his blessing on the American nation and it was the duty of Americans, as Christians, to spread the word of God to the Native Americans, who they considered heathens.

A utopian sense of purpose and opportunity also affected Americans who considered the opportunity to civilize the west and spread their government there would justify any misdeeds that had to happen along the way. The belief permeated society that by civilizing the "noble Savage," forcing them to become "humanized," "civilized," and "Christianized" by adopting the behaviors, dress, and beliefs of white, American society, then the Native Americans would be "saved." Those who stood in the way of such progress deserved to be eliminated. So, what was viewed as "progress" for the white man was considered a disaster for the Native American who suffered through physical, spiritual, and mental attacks and then displacement.

Opportunity also lured people to move westward. The government extolled the virtues of the West and arranged programs to sway people into leaving the East and moving to new land. News of gold and other valuable minerals being found in the West, coupled with government programs that could help them acquire and hold land, caught the public's attention and many Easterners flocked to the West. They left the comforts of the East, supported by their belief that as individuals, they had a right and duty to move westward and that by doing so, they were fulfilling a national duty of Manifest Destiny.

Economic

Economic motives were some of the chief motivators of westward expansion. The desire for more land brought aspiring homesteaders to the frontier. When gold was discovered in California in 1848, the number of migrants increased even more. Regional approval for westward expansion resulted from each believing that westward expansion could solve some of their problems. Northerners felt that the wide expanse of the west could resolve a pressing issue of urban over-population and economic instability. The South argued that expansion would free up a lot of land for agriculture and manufacturing, which would help the stability of the economy. Both regions realized that as the United States expanded, and hopefully would reach the Pacific Coast, the railroad would take a more central role in the U.S. economy. By extending the railroads, new trade could be created, not only in the United States, but also could provide access to the Pacific Ocean trade. Having more land also gave the United States more trading power with countries such as Asia, and the manufacturing that developed in the west made America more efficient and self-reliant. The settlers could obtain or make many goods that had previously been obtained only by trade with other countries.

Cultural

Expanding the boundaries of the United States was in many ways a cultural war as well. The desire of Southerners to find more lands suitable for cotton cultivation would eventually spread slavery to these regions. North of the Mason-Dixon Line, many citizens were deeply concerned about adding any more slave states. Manifest Destiny touched on issues of religion, money, race, patriotism, and morality. These clashed in the 1840s as a truly great drama of regional conflict began to unfold.

Political

While Manifest Destiny united many Americans with a shared belief that God had a grand mission for them, it also divided them. As the United States acquired more territory during the first part of the nineteenth century, the issue of slavery and where it would be permitted began to divide the country. Increasingly through this period, many Southerners and some Northerners wanted slavery to exist everywhere in the United States, including in the new territories added to the country. Many other Americans did not want slavery to expand at all, and some wanted slavery to be prohibited across the entire nation. Eventually these tensions would lead to the American Civil War.

COMPETENCY 5.6

Identify the social, cultural, political, and economic characteristics of the antebellum period.

Political

Between 1819 and 1860, critical issues emerged in the United States that would serve as both the foundation of crises that would explode in the United States in the 1850s and 1860s. The period immediately following the War of 1812 witnessed a high tide of nationalism and unity, but just underneath the surface lurked issues such as federal versus states rights, an issue that really had never been resolved. Attendant to that concern was another critical issue—this one pit the North against the South—the extension of slavery in the western territories. The Compromise of 1820 had settled this issue for nearly 30 years by drawing a dividing line across the Louisiana Purchase that prohibited slavery north of the line but permitted slavery south of it. As the nation expanded beyond the confines of the Louisiana Purchase territory, questions about whether or not slavery would be permitted in the western territories and who had the authority to make the decisions regarding slavery in the new territories became a simmering source of conflict—content for a while to embrace the temporary resolution of 1820.

But, the seizure of new territories from Mexico reignited the issue. California adopted a constitution that prohibited slavery and applied for statehood in 1849. Some members of Congress were unwilling to admit California as a free state and were concerned about other issues, such as the movement to end slavery in the District of Columbia and the emergence of personal liberty laws in the North that barred courts and police from returning runaways to the south. Furthermore, there were several other territories such as New Mexico, Oregon, and Utah, all of which had applied for statehood. The Union had 15 free and 15 slave states in 1849, but the admission of these Western states threatened to upset the balance. Southern representatives brought up the idea of secession while state legislatures in the North passed resolutions demanding that slavery be prohibited in the Western territories.

The Compromise of 1850 attempted to settle the problem by admitting California as a free state but allowing slavery in the rest of the area acquired from Mexico, and the abolition of the slave trade, but not slavery in the District of Columbia. The idea here that averted an immediate crisis was found with the introduction of **popular sovereignty** that allowed individuals living within a territory or state to decide for themselves, rather than Congress making the decision for them, whether or not they would allow slavery.

Enactment of the **Fugitive Slave Law** as part of the Compromise exacerbated sectional tensions. Northerners resented the new act that enabled Southerners to travel freely within the North and seize individuals who they claimed were fugitives, including some free African-Americans and a number of escaped slaves who had been living in the North for several months and in some cases, years. The South was angered by Northern attempts to prevent the Fugitive Slave Act from being enforced by the passage of state laws that barred the deportation of slaves, despite the federal act authorizing Southern agents to retrieve runaway slaves.

The question of slavery in the territories exploded once again when the senator from Illinois, Stephen A. Douglas, in an effort to get a transcontinental railroad built so that it would run through his home state, proposed that Kansas and Nebraska territories be opened to white settlement and that the status of slavery be decided according to the principle of popular sovereignty. Douglas reasoned that if territory north of the 36°30' line were admitted to the Union, it would strengthen his argument that the railroad should be built in the North. The resulting **Kansas-Nebraska Act of 1854** left the fate of slavery up to residents without specifying when and how they were to decide. The act also repealed the Missouri Compromise, further destabilizing the political situation. The Kansas-Nebraska Act convinced many Northerners that the South wanted to open all federal territories to slavery and brought into existence the Republican Party, committed to excluding slavery from the territories. In addition, many Northern states passed **personal liberty laws** that required a trial by jury for all who were accused of being fugitive slaves and guaranteed them the right to have an attorney. Southerners were naturally furious at this deliberate weakening of the Fugitive Slave Law.

Sectional conflict was intensified by the Supreme Court's Dred Scott decision, which declared that Congress could not exclude slavery from the western territories. Dred Scott, a Missouri slave, had sued his owner for his freedom after his owner took him to a free state. Scott won his case, but then lost on appeal, and so the case went to the Supreme Court in 1857. Normally, the Supreme Court stayed out of slavery controversies and let the state courts decide outcomes. But this time, the Supreme Court did take on the case and Scott lost. The Court stated that Scott was not a citizen, so he could not sue in federal courts. The Court also stated that residency in a free state did not make one free; moreover, the Court decided that Congress did not have the power to regulate slavery in the territories. This decision nullified the Missouri Compromise and the Kansas-Nebraska Act as well. The Dred Scott decision meant that slavery essentially could be anywhere in the United States and its territories, and it became a turning point in the impending crisis between North and South. The ruling did not prevent individual states from passing anti-slavery laws or measures enforcing them, but it did make it clear that the federal government could not act on or enforce such laws due to the designation of slaves as property. The ruling seemed to weaken the ability of any state to prohibit slavery since the federal government would not intervene and it caused outrage in the North, while Southerners considered it to be a major step forward since it upheld their argument that slaves were property.

The last incident that divided the Union and provoked the secession crisis was the election of Abraham Lincoln in the 1860 Presidential election. The deep divisions within the major parties and the United States led to the election of Lincoln, who received only 40% of the popular vote. Lincoln had engaged Stephen A. Douglas in a number of debates during the Illinois state race and, although he lost, he gained considerable attention. Lincoln had little political experience and was opposed to the expansion of slavery. The South viewed Lincoln as an abolitionist and a direct threat to the Southern way of life. Immediately following the election of Lincoln, South Carolina began to discuss secession from the Union. Southern states had long maintained that they had the right to nullify acts of Congress and even withdraw voluntarily from the Union without approval from the federal government if they had sufficient cause or grievances.

It did not take long for South Carolina to pass a bill of secession, and six other states followed its lead and voted themselves out of the Union. These six states were Mississippi, Florida, Alabama, Georgia, Louisiana, and Texas. These six states would form the Confederate States of America and Jefferson Davis was chosen to be the President of the "nation." As President Buchanan was leaving office, he told Congress that states did not have the right to secede but that the federal government did not have the right to use force to prevent them from doing so. Attempts to negotiate failed, and the situation was unresolved when Lincoln arrived for his inauguration. Lincoln made it clear that he considered secession to be insurrection and stated that the federal government should take all actions necessary, including force, to protect forts and property in the south and to put an end to insurrection.

Social and Cultural Characteristics

The white South's social structure was much more complex than the popular stereotype of proud aristocrats disdainful of honest work and ignorant, vicious, exploited poor whites. The old South's intricate social structure included many small slave-owners and relatively few large ones. Large slaveholders, the **planters** were extremely rare. In 1860 only 11,000 Southerners, three-quarters of one percent of the white population owned more than 50 slaves; a mere 2,358 owned as many as 100 slaves. However, although large slaveholders were few in number, they owned most of the South's slaves. Over half of all slaves lived on plantations with 20 or more slaves and a Slave ownership was relatively widespread. In the first half of the 19th century, one-third of all southern white families owned slaves, and a majority of white southern families owned slaves, had owned them, or expected to own them. These slave-owners were a diverse lot. A few were African American, mulatto, or Native American; one-tenth were women; and more than one in ten worked as artisans, businesspeople, or merchants rather than as farmers or planters. Few led lives of leisure or refinement.

The average slave-owner lived in a log cabin rather than a mansion and was a farmer rather than a planter. The average holding varied between four and six slaves, and most slaveholders possessed no more than five. White women in the South, despite the image of the hoop-skirted southern belle, suffered under heavier burdens than their northern counterparts. They married earlier, bore more children, and were more likely to die young. They lived in greater isolation, had less access to the company of other women, and lacked the satisfactions of voluntary associations and reform movements. Their education was briefer and much less likely to result in opportunities for independent careers.

The plantation legend was misleading in still other respects. Slavery was neither dying nor unprofitable. In 1860 the South was richer than any country in Europe except England, and it had achieved a level of wealth unmatched by Italy or Spain until the eve of World War II.

During the Antebelllum period, a wave of social reform swept the United States. Many of the reform movements that resulted grew out of the **Second Great Awakening**, which, like the original Great Awakening, was a period of revival that spread throughout the country and sparked an intense period of evangelicalism throughout the South and the

West. It preached religious conversion and that the Second Coming was near, and encouraged people to speed the process and fight evil present in the United States through social reform. A number of reform movements sprang up throughout the country targeting alcohol and poverty as social evils. Women, in particular, were drawn to this movement and were targeted as well, creating both the emergence of a movement called **true womanhood** and the suffrage movement.

Society in America was in flux in the early nineteenth century to begin with—not only was there a new nation going through all the pangs of emerging out of colonialism into full-fledged self-rule, but also tremendous sweeping movements of immigration, industrialization, urbanization, and westernization that all affected life at home. The composition of the population of the United States also was changing as immigrants from Ireland and Germany flooded the country, introducing new cultures to the mix. White, middle-class, native-born men left their home businesses and set off to work in new factories, stores, and offices. As this happened, middle-class women became more rooted in the home as the idea of **separate spheres**, where women were in charge of the private domain and men were in charge of the public domain, became the dominant ideology of the period. Working-class and farm women left their homes and communities to work in growing factories, thus bringing up a whole host of new problems that women faced as they worked in "the man's sphere." Changes did not just affect white women, but also slave women who found their lives and family life disrupted once again. The surge in demand for Deep South cotton combined with a stagnant economy in the northern part of the South prompted mass translocation of slaves from the Upper South to the Lower South, in the process ripping apart families and selling them to Southern cotton plantation owners hundreds of miles away.

In this rapidly changing society, Americans clung to what they thought would be an area of stability: the family. The belief that men and women belonged in separate, but complimentary, spheres took hold and it was considered that women, due to their gentle, sensitive, and emotional souls , belonged to the private sphere, in the home, where they would provide a haven for their husbands and children who were no doubt suffering from the rigors of industrialization and capitalism. What emerged was something referred to as the **cult of true womanhood** that defined how women, true women, were supposed to act and acknowledged that a true woman's goals should be twofold: marriage and motherhood. It focused on four attributes considered to be important: religious piety, moral purity, submissiveness, and domesticity. The ideology of **true womanhood** was perpetuated through print culture, religion, and discourse, which both empowered and confined women. It did expand access and elevate the importance of women's education, because it emphasized that women needed more schooling in order to raise their sons to be good citizens and to influence their husbands. This same reasoning though opened up one profession deemed suitable for females: teaching. By the 1840s, women had used this ideology to create a nascent women's rights movement.

Women in particular jumped on the bandwagon and embraced the idea of reforming different elements of society. For women revival meetings and reform societies offered them unique opportunities for participation in public life and politics. One area that women successfully targeted was the temperance movement that sought to reduce alcohol consumption. Inspired by religion, as well as the effects alcohol had on family life and the workplace, **Temperance Societies** sprang up that encouraged people to sign pledges not to drink and in some places, pushed for prohibition. The movement did result in a sharp decline in alcohol consumption. The group also targeted gambling, and by 1860, every state had laws that outlawed lotteries on the books. After an 1830 report on the prevalence of prostitution in New York City, women formed **The Female Moral Reform Society** in 1834 that sought to eliminate prostitution and to help rehabilitate those women who were caught in its web. Other reform societies emerged that targeted problems in penitentiaries, orphanages, and asylums, under the idea that society had an obligation to provide for those unable to take care of themselves.

Another movement that came out of a reform-minded culture was the creation of utopian groups. The **Shakers** split from the Quaker groups and built communes where they could share work and all of the good things that came out of it. They had some progressive ideas about life and granted near equal rights to women. However, their numbers never really took off as they also practiced celibacy. One experimental community was **Brook Farm,** which was dedicated to another group of reformists, mainly intellectuals who were writers and philosophers, called the **Transcendentalists,** who believed that humans shared aspects with God. This meant that ultimately, if guided properly, man could attain perfection. Some well-known Transcendentalists were **Nathanial Hawthorne, Ralph Waldo Emerson, Henry David Thoreau,** and **Elizabeth Peabody**.

Before the 1830s, abolition movements were dominated by free blacks, and gained only sporadic and few white supportors, save for a few movements, like the Quakers, who believed slavery should end as it was morally wrong, and the **American Colonization Society,** founded in 1816, that sought to transfer free slaves and ship them back to Africa. Prominent black support did come from free slaves such as **Frederick Douglass, Harriet Tubman, and Sojourner Truth**. When the white abolitionist movement took more shape in the 1830s, it split into two groups: the **immediatists,** who became the voice of the abolitionist movement and who advocated instant and complete emancipation, all at once, and the **gradualists,** who wanted a slower approach to the freedom of slaves as they feared that immediate emancipation would create social chaos.

Congress became concerned about the tactics of some immediatists like **William Lloyd Garrison**, whose writings in his newspaper the *Liberator* spurred Southern attacks on the paper and abolition movements. Congress adopted the **Gag Rule,** which limited public disapproval of slavery. What resulted from this and other attempts at stymieing free speech was that the abolition movement grew and became even more radicalized. With increased radicalization of the abolitionists combined with a similar entrenchment of the South on the issue, slavery began to take center stage, particularly in combination with Westward expansion and decisions about what to do about new states.

The South absolutely had a slave-holding culture attached to white Southerners. The bulk of Southern whites only had one to four slaves in their household—few, but nonetheless still participants in the slave culture. In comparison to the South at large, not that many had 50 or more slaves. Slave resistance also became more of an issue in the antebellum South. Some slaves chose indirect means of resistance, like slowing down their work pace or sabotaging work. The idea of an **Underground Railroad** also became an important cultural concern.

The culture of slavery resulted in the construction of Black Christianity of Baptists and Methodists with emotional worship services that featured "negro spirituals." Some languages developed that retained African roots like the **Gullah** language or **pidgin**. Nuclear family ties, as they became more fragile, also became more important. Even extended family ties took on greater roles. Music remained an important part in the slave's life.

Economic

There were several characteristics of the U.S. economy during the antebellum period that had an effect on later events.

1. The divisions between the North and South continued in that the South continued to be primarily agrarian and the North had moved more into manufacturing. The South continued to be rather slow to industrialize.

2. Economic power had shifted more from the upper South to the lower South as cotton became more important to the lower southern antebellum economy and upper Southern tobacco slid into a free-for-all. Since the 1793 invention of the cotton gin by Eli Whitney, in which seeds could be more easily removed from cotton, cotton cultivation spread everywhere throughout the South, wherever the soil and climate could support it. Initially there was tremendous demand for Southern cotton, both from the Northern mills and English textile mills, in full swing because of early industrializationA drawback to this added importance is that the South became dependent on the availability of cotton around the world, particularly in far flung parts of the British Empire. The availability of Indian cotton, in particular, influenced the price of American cotton. Any downswing in price resulted in an economic adjustment for the entire South. The idea that "**Cotton is King**" took hold, and by 1860, cotton production exploded in the South and comprised 57% of all U.S. exports.

   With the spread of cotton, however, also came the spread of slavery. From 1820–1840, around 2 million people from various places in Africa were moved or sold to others in the Gulf States region of the United States. The South itself had experienced a population boom of large-scale migration into the area.

   A series of panics about the state of the economy caused enormous financial pressures in the Union. The period 1819–1821 saw panic in the economic sectors that resulted in a lessening of demand in U.S. cotton due to British colonial presence in India. The drop in cotton prices due to lack of demand also affected land prices and precipitated almost a run on banks as banks had to call in loans to pay for depositors' desire to withdraw their funds. Many banks were unable to collect their loans quickly enough and then went bankrupt, leaving depositors without funds to pay the loans they owed. Another panic in 1837 that further reduced the British need for American cotton exacerbated the problems with the Southern cotton economy, lowering the price of cotton even further and causing additional economic fallout due to British reluctance to invest in America as well (it had its own colonies to worry about). Wheat crop failures also prevented balanced payments of goods. An additional panic in 1857, the year of the Sepoy Mutiny in India that preoccupied the British, resulted in an increasingly weak market. The end of the Crimean War reduced the demand for American grain. Farmers and manufacturers worried that they had exceeded the supply of products for which there was little American demand.

3. The banking system in effect was rather rudimentary and subject to tremendous periods of financial strain. The creation of a **Second Bank of the United States** after the expiration of the First Bank Charter in 1811 revealed problems with the nascent banking system. The U.S. government, embarrassed that it was unable to float loans or transfer funds across the country during the War of 1812, prompted the new bank's formation. This bank received a charter for 20 years and the Federal Government owned one-fifth of the stock and appointed one-fifth of the directors of the new bank.

4. The availability of transportation continued to be somewhat more limited in the South than in the North. The inadequacy of it posed even more problems for the Southerners in terms of getting their goods to the market or ports. During this period, there were calls for government-led internal improvements, such as the construction of canals and a national railroad.

5. The period also saw the emergence of more protective tariffs that sought to increase the appeal of American goods by increasing the duty for imported goods.

COMPETENCY 5.7

Identify the causes, significant individuals, and effects of the events associated with the American Civil War and Reconstruction eras.

Causes of the Civil War ("The War of Northern Aggression")

- **Growth of Sectionalism.** The differences between the Southern plantation cotton economy and the Northern industrial economy resulted in not only differences in income levels but also differences in economic attitudes that manifested themselves in considerations of race. For instance, the South, based on the advantages of agrarian life, was not as tuned in as the North, where different cultures and classes rubbed shoulders all day. The differences in the way of life— agrarian communities versus factories—further polarized the North and the South as the South remained almost completely agricultural, with an economy and a social order largely founded on slavery and the plantation system where the South derived its wealth. The North was not as reliant upon the South for its agricultural products, but it was able to develop more commercially and industrially in ways the South was not. In many ways, the North was more self-sufficient than the South. Over time, these tensions magnified.

- **Unfair taxation.** The development of the North and South into different types of economies caused some polarization. The South, had an agrarian economy that was dependent upon slave labor in order to realize profits. The Northern economy was based upon manufacturing. In the early days of the country the South preferred to trade with England rather than the North – it would send its cotton to English mills and would buy European goods in return. The North was irritated that its southern neighbors were eschewing their goods in favor of European ones. So, by the early 1800s, the Northern politicians made efforts to attack the foundations of the Southern economy (or so the South perceived it) through abolition movements, of course, but also through taxes. They pushed through heavy taxes on European goods so Southerners would be forced to buy goods from the North instead. The South perceived this as blatantly unfair and as a tax directed at them.

- **States versus federal rights.** Unresolved issues of state versus federal authority festered as Southern states argued that they should have the right to decide if they wanted to accept certain federal legislation. Not only was slavery an issue that they wanted to be able to bypass federal rules about import taxes that they felt jeopardized their well being. These states asserted that they had the right of **nullification** where they could rule federal acts as nullified. The federal government refused to allow nullification, and proponents of federal rights, primarily Northerners, argued that nullification was a dangerous precedent that would just make the country weaker and more open to take-over or dissolution.

- **Growing controversy between proslavery versus no-slavery proponents.** Each time the United States gained more territory, there were disagreements over whether or not the new state should allow slavery. The vociferousness of these disagreements was a little odd as the average U.S. citizen in BOTH the North and the South did not own slaves, but the politicians became interested in slaves and the concept of slavery. The North viewed it as a moral issue, and the South viewed slavery as an economic issue. Efforts to reach compromises resulted in legislation like the Fugitive Slave Act that allowed slaveholders to capture their slaves in free territory. The Kansas-Nebraska Act of 1854 created two new territories that allowed popular sovereignty to determine whether or not it would be a free state or a slave state. In Kansas, the violence of the proslavery forces from Missouri named "Border Ruffians" **exacerbated the conflict**, and the fighting caused it to be called **Bleeding Kansas**. The ruckus extended itself to the Senate floor where pro-slavery Senator Preston Brooks from South Carolina beat Senator Charles Sumner of the antislavery movement over the head.

- **Growth of the Abolitionist Movement.** Feelings in the North intensified with the passage of the Fugitive Slave Act, the Dred Scott Case, the publication of Harriet Beecher Stowe's *Uncle Tom's Cabin*, and John Brown's Raid. Religious and reform groups sprang up that targeted the immorality of slavery, and media campaigns as well as groups dedicated to rescuing slaves sprang up, to the consternation of the South.

- **The 1860 election of Abraham Lincoln.** The run-up to the election caused political rifts within the Whig party, which resulted in its dissolution and the Southern members joining the Democratic Party and the Northerners joining the Republic Party. In the razor-thin 1860 Presidential election. Abraham Lincoln defeated three candidates— Stephen A. Douglas (Northern Democrat), John C. Breckinridge (Southern Democrat), and John Bell of the Constitutional Union party. Before Lincoln was sworn in, South Carolina seceded from the Union and six other states joined it.

The Civil War and Reconstruction (1860–1877)

Hostilities Begin

On **December 20, 1860,** South Carolina passed a secession ordinance and shortly there-after, Mississippi, Florida, Alabama, Georgia, Louisiana, and Texas joined them. By **February 1861,** the **Confederate States of America** was formed in Alabama. In his inaugural address, Lincoln urged Southerners to reconsider their actions, but warned that the Union was perpetual, that states could not secede, and that he would therefore hold the federal forts and installations in the South. Only two remained in federal hands: Fort Pickens, off Pensacola, Florida; and **Fort Sumter**, in the harbor of Charleston, South Carolina. Lincoln soon received word from Major Robert Anderson, commander of the small garrison at Fort Sumter that supplies were running low. Desiring to send in the needed supplies, Lincoln informed the governor of South Carolina of his intention, but promised that no attempt would be made to send arms, ammunition, or reinforcements unless Southerners initiated hostilities.

Confederate General P.G.T. Beauregard, acting on orders from the Confederate President Davis, demanded Anderson's surrender. Anderson said he would surrender if not resupplied. Knowing supplies were on the way, the Confederates opened fire at 4:30 a.m. on **April 12, 1861**. The next day, the fort surrendered. The day following Sumter's surrender, Lincoln declared an insurrection and called for the states to provide 75,000 volunteers to put it down. In response to this, Virginia, Tennessee, North Carolina, and Arkansas declared their secession. The remaining slave states, Delaware, Kentucky, Maryland, and Missouri, wavered but stayed with the Union.

Advantages of the Confederacy and the Union

The North enjoyed at least five major advantages over the South. It had overwhelming preponderance in wealth and was vastly superior in industry, giving them vast resources to draw upon. The North also had an advantage of almost three to one in manpower; and over one-third of the South's population was composed of slaves, whom Southerners would not use as soldiers. Unlike the South, the North received large numbers of immigrants during the war. The North retained control of the U.S. Navy, and thus, would command the sea and be able to blockade the South. Finally, the North enjoyed a much superior system of railroads.

The South did, however, have several advantages. It was vast in size, making it difficult to conquer. Its troops would be fighting on their own ground, a fact that would give them the advantage of familiarity with the terrain, as well as the added motivation of defending their homes and families. Its armies would often have the opportunity of fighting on the defensive, a major advantage in the warfare of that day.

At the outset of the war, the South drew upon a number of highly qualified senior officers, men like **Robert E. Lee, Stonewall Jackson,** and **Jeb Stuart.** By contrast, the Union command structure was already set when the war began and thus was hampered by the lack of new ideas and initiatives (particularly as many of the great senior officers had joined the South). **Winfield Scott** came up with the **Anaconda Plan** to blockade Southern ports and cut off Southern trade along the Mississippi. Jefferson Davis had extensive military and political experience, while Lincoln was much superior to Davis as a war leader, showing firmness, flexibility, mental toughness, great political skill, and, eventually, an excellent grasp of strategy.

Progress of the War

At a creek called **Bull Run** near the town of Manassas Junction, Virginia, just southwest of Washington, D.C., the Union Army under General Scott met a Confederate force under Generals P.G.T. Beauregard and Joseph E. Johnston on July 21, 1861. In the **First Battle of Bull Run** (called First Manassas in the South), the Union army was forced to retreat in confusion back to Washington, alarming Union picnickers who had come to watch what they had thought would be an entertaining rout. The reaction among the Union officials was to embark on a series of commander changes throughout 1861–1862, hoping to turn back the Southern troops. Some victories, such as at the **Battle of Antietam**, the bloodiest battle in the Civil War where a total of 31,000 men perished from each side, gave the North a bit of confidence, but was not enough to make the North confident in its military leadership. Nevertheless, after claiming the Battle of Antietam a victory, Lincoln issued the **Emancipation Proclamation**, which took effect on **New Year's Day, 1863**, that freed all of the slaves in the areas of rebellion.

As the war dragged on, the greater population and material advantages of the North became a significant factor. The blockade and Union victories that gave them control of the Mississippi allowed Union forces to divide the South in half and to interrupt their trade and supply lines. The Union had a better Navy and in addition to blocking Southern ports, also shelled land forts and took part in joint Army and Navy actions. The one battle between the newly constructed Union ironclad, **The Monitor**, and the Confederate ironclad, **The Virginia**, demonstrated the superiority of the Union Navy even though neither side actually won the battle between the two ships.

Furthermore, several key Confederate officers, such as Stonewall Jackson and Johnston, were severely injured or killed. The replacement of the North's largely ineffective McClellan only made an impact when he was permanently removed from the command of the Army in favor of **Ulysses S. Grant**. After 1863, the Union was able to go on the offensive and invade the South. **Vicksburg** and **Gettysburg** were besieged and ultimately fell to the Union. Lincoln's **Gettysburg Address** stressed the honor of the dead on both sides and the need to bind up the wounds of a nation. This conciliatory attitude, as well as his determination to readmit the Southern states as quickly as possible, would be reflected in his **Ten Percent Plan**.

The final Union campaign consisted of a series of coordinated offensives in the South. Sherman's "March to the Sea" created a path of destruction and aroused bitter feelings in the South that would not end with the war. The final Confederate collapse was only a matter of time. Grant cut off all supplies to Lee and the Army of Northern Virginia, which had withdrawn to the area around Richmond, and on April 9, 1865, Lee surrendered at **Appomattox Court House**. Other Confederate armies still holding out in various parts of the South surrendered over the next few weeks. Lincoln did not live to receive news of the final surrenders. On April 14, 1865, he was shot in the back of the head while watching a play in Ford's Theater in Washington.

The Ordeal of Reconstruction

Reconstruction began well before the fighting of the Civil War came to an end. The North was concerned with four basic issues: who would the local rulers be for the South and what role would they have; should governmental control of the South be in the hands of the President or Congress; issues with the freedom of former slaves; and should they reestablish the old system that had been in place, or build something anew so that these problems would not happen again. There were two main views about these problems, one that rested with the executive branch, Lincoln, and another with the legislative, basically the Radical Republicans in Congress. Lincoln favored leniency and the Radical Republicans favored revenge.

To restore legal governments in the seceded states, Lincoln developed a policy called the **Ten Percent Plan** that made it relatively easy for Southern states to enter the collateral process. Lincoln's plan stipulated that Southerners, except for high-ranking rebel officials, could take an oath promising future loyalty to the Union and acknowledge the end of slavery. When the number of people who had taken this oath within any one state reached 10% of the number who had been registered to vote in 1860, a loyal state government could be formed. Tennessee, Arkansas, and Louisiana formed loyal governments under Lincoln's plan but were refused recognition by a Congress dominated by Radical Republicans.

Radical Republicans such as **Thaddeus Stevens** of Pennsylvania believed that Lincoln's plan did not adequately punish the South, restructure Southern society, or boost the political prospects of the Republican Party. Instead, the radicals in Congress drew up the more stringent **Wade-Davis Bill,** which required a majority of individuals who had been alive and registered to vote in 1860 to swear an "iron-clad" oath stating that they were loyal and had never been disloyal. Under these terms, no confederate state could have been readmitted unless African-Americans were given the vote. Until a majority of individuals took the oath, the state could not send representatives to Congress. Lincoln killed the bill with a "pocket veto," and the radicals were furious. When Lincoln was assassinated, the radicals rejoiced, believing that Vice President Andrew Johnson would be less generous to the South, or at least easier to control. However, Johnson, although having pledged earlier to be harsh with the South, changed his mind and embraced Lincoln's Ten Percent Plan to be more lenient with the Southern states. His plan was not totally magnanimous, however.

His plans for reconstruction waffled a bit. First he stated that certain Southerners, like officers, officials, and members of the planter class whose property was worth more than $20,000, were not allowed to take the oath of loyalty and had to apply personally to the president for a pardon. But this policy lacked teeth as Johnson proceeded to grant thousands of pardons, which then allowed the previous social and governmental power brokers in the South to remain there. After only eight months, Johnson declared that Reconstruction was over and former Confederates could return to Congress in December 1865. Congress, on the other hand, was agitated by Johnson's overtures to the South and decided to refuse to admit ex-Confederates to its ranks. Congress justified their position by arguing that the Constitution gave them, not the president, the power to admit new states.

Thirteenth and Fourteenth Amendments and Congressional Reconstruction

Tensions between Congress and Johnson continued to build, and Congress decided that it would go ahead and embark on their own reconstruction plans. The **Thirteenth**

Amendment, officially ending slavery, had already been passed. After Johnson's succession to the presidency, Congress passed a Civil Rights Act and extended the authority of the Freedman's Bureau. Johnson vetoed both bills, claiming they were unconstitutional, but Congress overrode the vetoes. Congress then approved the **Fourteenth Amendment** and sent it to the states for ratification in June 1866. The Fourteenth Amendment defined citizenship and forbade any states to deny various rights to citizens. Any state that denied the vote or other rights to eligible citizens, including African-Americans, would have their representation in Congress reduced. The Amendment also prohibited the paying of any Confederate debts and made former Confederates ineligible to hold public office. Johnson tried to block the Fourteenth Amendment throughout the country, urging Southern state legislatures to vote against it and organizing a National Union Convention in the North to do the same.

In response to Johnson's machinations, Congress embarked on some manipulating of their own with the passage of a series of Reconstruction Acts, which would give Union generals control of military districts in the South and supervision of elections. They also forced states to ratify the Fourteenth Amendment, to make changes to their state constitutions, and to submit them to Congress for approval. Johnson continued to work against Congressional policies so they fought back by passing the Tenure of Office Act that was passed over Johnson's veto. This act forbade Johnson from dismissing his cabinet members without permission of Congress. In particular, they limited Johnson's power over the army by forcing him to issue orders through Grant, who in turn was not allowed to be dismissed without Congressional approval. Congress also passed this measure in order to protect the Secretary of War, Edwin M. Stanton, who was the last radical Republican Cabinet Member still in office. In response, Johnson issued orders to commanders in the South that limited their powers, removed some of the best officers, and then, as a last straw, dismissed Stanton in order to test the constitutionality of the Tenure of Office Act. Before the matter could be taken up in court, Congress responded by impeaching Johnson but was one vote shy of removing him from office. Johnson remained in office but offered little resistance to the Radical Republicans during his last months in office.

The Election of 1868 and the Fifteenth Amendment

In 1868, the Republicans nominated for president Ulysses S. Grant, who had no political record and whose views—if any—on national issues were unknown. The narrow victory of even such a strong candidate as Grant prompted Republican leaders to decide that it would be politically expedient to give the vote to all blacks, in the North as well as the South. For this purpose, the Fifteenth Amendment was drawn up and submitted to the states. Ironically, the idea was so unpopular in the North that it won the necessary three-fourths approval only with its ratification by southern states. Though personally of unquestioned integrity, Grant naively placed his faith in a number of thoroughly dishonest men. His administration was rocked by one scandalous revelation of government corruption after another.

Many of the economic difficulties that the country faced during Grant's administration were caused by the necessary readjustments from a wartime economy back to a peacetime economy. The central economic question was deflation versus inflation, or more specifically, whether to retire the un-backed paper money, greenbacks, printed to meet the wartime emergency, or to print more.

Early in Grant's second term, the country was hit by an economic depression known as the **Panic of 1873**. Brought on by the over-expansive tendencies of railroad builders and businessmen during the immediate postwar boom, the Panic was triggered by economic downturns in Europe and more immediately, by the failure of Jay Cooke and Company, a major American financial firm.

The Panic led to clamor for the printing of more greenbacks. In 1874, Congress authorized a small new issue of greenbacks, but it was vetoed by Grant. Pro-inflation forces were further enraged when Congress demonetized silver in 1873, going to a straight gold standard. Silver was becoming more plentiful due to Western mining and was seen by some as a potential source of inflation. Pro-inflation forces referred to the demonetization of silver as the "Crime of '73." In the election of 1876, the Democrats campaigned against corruption and nominated New York Governor Samuel J. Tilden (1814–1886), who had broken the Tweed political machine of New York City. The Republicans passed over Grant and turned to Governor Rutherford B. Hayes of Ohio. Like Tilden, Hayes was decent, honest, in favor of hard money and civil service reform, and opposed to government regulation of the economy. Tilden won the popular vote and led in the electoral vote 184 to 165. However, 185 electoral votes were needed for election, and 20 votes, from the three Southern states still occupied by federal troops and run by Republican governments, were disputed. A deal was made whereby those 20 votes went to Hayes in return for removal of federal troops from the South. Reconstruction was over.

Consequences of Reconstruction

Reconstruction had effectively ended. The struggle between the President and the Congress and between the North and the South had finally ended, but the impact of both the war and the efforts to restore the Union would continue to exert an influence on the development of the United States. The Union had been preserved, but at what cost and to what extent was the nation that emerged after 1877 fundamentally different from the one that had gone to war in 1861?

The abolition of slavery led to real changes in the lives of former slaves, but it did not end their economic dependence on Southern whites nor did it end discrimination in the South. African-Americans after the Civil War were able to marry and divorce, and hundreds published letters and ads seeking loved ones from whom they had been separated as a result of the internal slave trade. African-Americans immediately began to form their own schools and churches. The restrictions that forbade slaves from learning to read and write in the old slave codes were now nullified, and former slaves emphasized the importance of education, especially for children. Former slaves also began to leave white churches and form their own church communities, which often had distinctive elements such as music or dance as part of the service. African-Americans also gained control over their time and their movements, but in terms of their economic status, little had changed. The failure of the government to provide former slaves with land or other economic opportunities meant that many blacks ended up renting land or sharecropping from their former masters. White southerners could no longer exercise complete control over former slaves—for instance, many African-American males refused to allow their wives to work for whites—but they could demand a large portion of their crop as rent payment. Whites could also charge African-Americans high prices for seed and other supplies that had to be purchased from stores owned by whites.

Despite these efforts by conservative southerners, the new Southern Republican party came to power in the constitutional conventions of 1868–1870, and as a result, the new Southern state constitutions were more democratic. Initially both blacks and Republicans were elected to serve in the new governments.

Reconstruction laws encouraged investment and industrialization though, while it helped in some areas, it also increased corruption. The question of land redistribution was very important to blacks but was not paid adequate attention by Republicans. The effects on the Southern economy were terrible. Government industrialization plans geared toward helping the South industrialize did not work well. High tax rates turned public opinion against reconstructionists whose governments had to raise taxes substantially to pay for the Civil War damage.

Reconstruction transformed Southern society and culture and increased divisions within the population. The first division was between those who supported and those who disagreed with Reconstruction. Opponents called Southerners who cooperated with reconstruction or who joined the Republican Party **scalawags,** and the Northerners who ran such programs were referred to as **carpetbaggers** and considered to be greedy, corrupt businessmen trying to take advantage of the South. The influx of these Northern "carpetbaggers" to the South resulted in the Republican Party gaining power in the South and passing some civil rights laws like ones that legalized interracial marriage and that allowed black students to attend schools. In many of the state senates, blacks gained positions of power.

The rapid cultural and economic changes that were occurring in the South resulted in racial tensions as former slaves also faced campaigns of terror and intimidation by white Southerners designed to keep them in their place in society, sabotage black civil rights, and persuade them not to try to exercise their right to vote. The **Ku Klux Klan** targeted all of those who supported Reconstruction—black and white. They often attacked and murdered scalawags and leaders of all races, community activists, and teachers. In response to the violence in the South, Congress passed the **Enforcement Acts** and an **Anti-Klan Law** in 1870–1871 that made actions against the civil rights of others to be criminal offenses. The laws did not have much impact, however, and Klan violence continued.

Eventually, the North lost interest in continuing their pursuit of enforcing the laws and measures designed to advance civil rights for blacks. Many of the civil rights laws were overturned and conditions worsened for blacks in the South. Congress passed the **Posse Comitatus Act** that prohibited federal authorities from exercising any power or control over local enforcement agencies, so that the interpretation of laws was left to individual Southern districts. In 1883, a rewrite of the Fourteenth Amendment declared that Congress only had the power to outlaw public rather than private discrimination. The **Plessy v. Ferguson** case ruled that state-mandated segregation was legal as long as there were "separate but equal" facilities. In response to this case, Southern states introduced **Jim Crow Laws** designed to segregate whites from African-Americans.

It was not just in the South that African-Americans encountered discrimination and hostility, although the worst abuses did take place in the South. All in all, reconstruction was a mixed bag, but in terms of achieving equality within the United States, it was clearly a failure.

COMPETENCY 5.8

Evaluate the impact of agrarianism, industrialization, urbanization, and reform movements on social, cultural, political, and economic development in the late nineteenth and early twentieth centuries.

Agrarianism

After the Civil War, despite the appearance of some cotton mills in the South and a few tobacco processing plants, the vast majority of Southerners remained farmers. In the post-war era, individual farmers had a difficult time in the South as many were forced to sell their land if they could not pay their debts. Wealthy landowners swooped in and took over farms. Landless farmers were forced into **sharecropping** in which people who were unable to pay their debts had to promise to pay it with their crops—the **crop lien** system was designed to keep the poor in constant debt as their crops would rarely be worth enough money, so they would borrow more money. Huge interest rates on their loans forced these sharecroppers to continually borrow more and more money and promise more and more crops, essentially keeping both black and white sharecroppers in a different type of slavery—one that lacked any sort of social safety net. Economic problems also intensified in both the South and the Midwest as Southern yeoman farmers were forced into growing cotton rather than their own food, making them at the mercy of cotton merchants and unable to sustain themselves. In the Midwest, dropping prices and rising technology resulted in increases in production that resulted in a tremendous over-supply of their products.

Farmers tried to deal with their mounting debts, and so they supported ways to increase the money supply, which they reasoned would make payments easier. They knew that it would cause inflation, which would make the farmers' debts worth less money, and they thought that the banks would not be as interested in pursuing them. The farmers advocated using silver, rather than gold, as the banking standard because they thought it would be advantageous for them to do so. With the support of Western miners along with the farmers in the South and Midwest, they felt that they could come out ahead.

The result of a lot of this economic and social pressure was that farmers decided to form agrarian cooperative organizations that would protect them from outside interests. In the 1870s, farmers in the Midwest, South, and Texas formed a network of **Granges** that not only addressed economic issues of farmers but also social and educational issues. The Grange Movement, which by 1875 had more than 1 million members, sought to allow farmers to buy machinery and sell crops as a group and therefore reap the benefits. They tried to lobby for legislation, notably what became referred to as the **Granger Laws** that sought to address some of the problems of railroad exploitation that farmers faced trying to get their goods to market. Eventually the Granger Laws were ruled unconstitutional and Congress passed the **Interstate Commerce Act of 1887** that sought to address the same issues. The Grange movement eventually died out due to lack of funds. They were replaced by **Farmers' Alliances** in the 1890s. One movement started in Texas, and then another formed in the Midwest—both alliances sought to group farmers together to combat the effects of railroad and industrial exploitation of farmers. The Farmers' Alliances were more political and less social than the Grange movements had been. They ran for political office, eventually controlling eight state legislatures and in the 1890s had 47 representatives in Congress. The Farmers' Alliances pushed the **Subtreasury Plan** to help farmers by having the federal government keep crops until prices rose and to finance low-interest loans to farmers.

Divisions within the Northern and Southern sections of the Farmers' Alliance prompted the formation of a third party in Omaha in 1882, the **People's Party,** which became the political arm of the Populist Party. The People's party put up a candidate for the 1892 election under a platform called the **Omaha Platform,** which called for government ownership of utilities, railroads, and the telegraph, government-sponsored farm loans, a graduated income tax, shorter workdays, direct election of U.S. senators, abolition of the National Bank, government-operated postal savings banks, restriction of undesirable immigration, abolition of the Pinkerton detective agency, generous coinage of silver, and a single term for the president and vice-president. Although its candidate lost, the party did receive a million votes and gained a few Congressional seats, enough to put their interests in the public spotlight.

Ten days after Cleveland took office in 1883, the country entered a four-year financial crisis. Several major corporations went bankrupt, 16,000 businesses disappeared, the stock market crashed, banks began to fail, and by 1895, unemployment reached a staggering 3 million. Populist cries to enlarge the money supply grew considerably, and progressive parties gained in popularity. By 1896, the Populists backed the Democratic candidate William Jennings Bryan against the Republican William McKinley. Bryan ran on his call for **free silver**. In a famous speech that he gave called the **Cross of Gold** speech, he argued that although increasing the money supply would be an inflationary move, it would loosen the Northern banking hold on the rest of the country and no longer would big business be able to "press down upon the brow of labor this crown of thorns" nor

Figure 6.4
Election of 1892
Electoral College Results

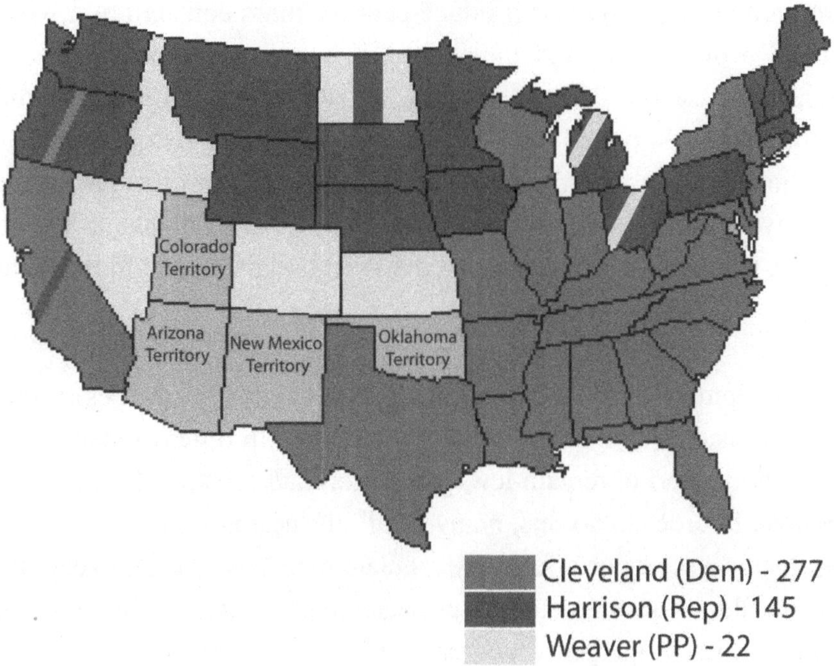

Cleveland (Dem) - 277
Harrison (Rep) - 145
Weaver (PP) - 22

"crucify mankind upon a cross of gold." Despite gaining a lot of political fervor during the election, Bryan lost, partly because the Populists were unable to court the interests of the urban classes and convince them of the benefits of a silver standard. McKinley, upon his election, quickly passed the **Gold Standard Act** that required all paper money be backed by gold—a rather fortuitous move because with the discovery of gold in Alaska, the economy improved.

Industrialization

Between 1860 and 1900, the United States moved from the fourth largest manufacturing nation to the world's leader through capital accumulation, natural resources, especially in iron, oil, and coal, and new inventions. Industrialization was also advanced by an abundance of labor supplemented by massive immigration, transport, and communications. The telephone was introduced by Alexander Graham Bell in 1876. The development of the modern steel industry introduced by Andrew Carnegie, the discovery of electrical energy by Thomas Edison, and George Westinghouse's discovery of how to use alternating current and transformers to transmit electricity over long distances further stimulated industrial growth. Henry Ford experimented with the internal combustion engine and figured out how to mass produce cars for mass consumption with the formation of the **Ford Motor Company** in 1903. A few individuals such as John D. Rockefeller, who came to control 95% of all U.S. oil refineries by 1877, became extremely wealthy, but the mass of workers who were employed by the rising number of factories had a difficult time earning enough to feed and clothe their families. The benefits of these new inventions were transmitted throughout the United States thanks to the efforts of the railroad industry, which not only opened up the West but also aided in the development of other industries.

With the development of more technologies that enabled businesses to produce better and faster, industry had to struggle more to make profits. In order to make sure they could sell their goods, prices had to remain low, production had to expand, and wages were kept as low as possible. In order to do this, many small businesses went out of business as they failed to meet loan payments or effectively regulate their business and keep production up to economies of scale. As a result, businesses began to consolidate in order to remain viable. More and more businesses merged which only led to greater economies of scale and led to corporate **consolidation**. Some of the consolidating techniques that companies used were:

- **Pools**—These were essentially "Gentlemen's Agreements" between companies that set limits on production and created an agreement to share profits. They did not last very long because they required companies to be honest with one another and proved to be rather detrimental to small businesses and farmers. The **Interstate Commerce Act of 1887** made these pools illegal among railroads.

- **Trusts**—Originated by John D. Rockefeller, trusts relied on the idea that one company could control another by forcing it to yield control of its stock to the bigger company's board of trustees. One type of trust was pioneered by Rockefeller when he used a method of **horizontal integration** to build Standard Oil. Horizontal integration created monopolies within a particular industry. Rockefeller used horizontal integration to take over oil refineries in the United States through either legally buying out smaller companies or destroying them through cut-throat competition or pooling agreements. Antitrust legislation later eliminated the use of horizontal integration.

- **Holding Companies**—This was when a corporation could hold enough stock in various companies to have a controlling interest in the production. This method of **vertical integration** allows other companies to survive, although it might buy out all of the factors in production. One example of this was Gustavus Swift who took over the stockyards, slaughterhouses, processing, and packaging plants in the meat industry but still allowed other companies to compete with it. Andrew Carnegie also did this with the steel industry.

Numerous problems arose because of the corporate consolidation of power. The banking system became more fragile as bigger businesses became their lifeblood. If a major business failed, bank failures soon followed. As a result, the United States suffered financial instability throughout the late nineteenth and early twentieth centuries. Monopolies also created a class of extremely powerful men who believed in **laissez-faire economics,** in which they believed not only that there was no room in the market for government intervention but also that **Social-Darwinism** supported their ideas—for only the fittest companies should and would survive in the market, and state intervention or regulation was futile. As conditions worsened for the "average worker" and small businessman, public resentment increased and the government did respond with various attempts at limiting the power of these strong businesses and powerful businessmen.

Conditions in factories were often appalling, and the rise of the Union movement was partly a response to the dangerous working conditions, low pay, and lack of job security. Mechanization of industry brought enormous changes for workers. No longer were workers their own bosses; they now had to report to others. Specialization and routinization of work in mass-production assembly lines resulted, over time, in a lessening of skill among workers. Efforts to increase worker efficiency led to more and more attempts to regulate and control worker's lives outside of work. Wages for male workers were lowered and jobs for men were eliminated as factory owners found out that they could employ women and children and pay them even lower wages. Pressure to speed up production at the expense of safety and health resulted in a more dangerous workplace.

Management used a series of tools at hand to force people to stay in their jobs without complaint. Should workers strike, businesses paid people called "scabs" to come in and take over their jobs. They launched all-out PR campaigns to discredit any striking workers. They also used Pinkerton agents to infiltrate unions and as guards to keep suspected unionists and strikers out of factories. Other techniques were employing lockouts, blacklisting of workers, yellow dog contracts that made, as a condition of employment, a worker agree not to join a union, court injunctions, and boasting of open shops, which did not make joining a union a condition of employment.

Workers, struck by the widespread misery that was infecting cities, sought to unite to seek changes. Labor unions formed to counter poor treatment of workers. Many in government, the courts, and business considered labor unions to be radical organizations and were not receptive to their demands. One of the first national labor unions was the **Knights of Labor**, founded in 1869 by a Philadelphia tailor, Uriah Stephens, and who led a series of strikes under the leadership of **Terrence Powderly** in the 1880s. The Knights organized skilled and unskilled workers to join it. The basic ideology of the Knights of Labor was that they wanted to get rid of capitalism and instead have a cooperative workers' alliance that would allow workers to work for themselves. The Knights advocated an eight-hour work day, abolition of child and prison labor, equal pay for men and women, safety codes in the workplace, prohibition of contract foreign labor, a federal income tax, government ownership of railroad and telegraph lines, and abolition of the National Bank. Originally disdainful of strikes as they favored arbitration, they increasingly advocated violence to meet their goals. As a result, the popularity of the Knights began to decline and unions became more associated with violence and political radicalism.

On May 1, 1886 in Chicago, several groups had gathered to campaign for an eight-hour workday. In the midst of the demonstrations an outbreak of police brutality was met with a bomb explosion that killed some police there. Many blamed the unions for the bomb, the unions blamed anarchists, and the arrest of eight immigrant radicals led many to associate anarchy with labor movements, discrediting the real goals that the labor movements advocated.

The formation in 1886 of the **American Federation of Labor** (AFL) led by **Samuel Gompers** sought to take the Labor Movement in a different direction. Gompers believed that it would be best to focus on issues of higher wages and shorter workdays. Gompers avoided the sort of rhetoric associated with the Knights of Labor that had attracted anarchists to it and instead included only skilled laborers. The AFL sought to avoid party politics and was formed as a confederation of trade unions that represented skilled workers in matters of national legislation. They maintained a national strike fund to support striking workers, engaged in a PR campaign that wrapped trade unions up in evangelical rhetoric and boasted of its moral imperatives, mediated disputes between labor and management, and pushed for closed shops that barred employment to non-union workers. Another organization soon emerged, the **Industrial Workers of the World,** referred to as the **Wobblies,** that sought to unite all workers and felt that the only way to make sure workers were treated fairly was to overthrow capitalism with violence.

Notably, there were two groups consistently excluded from union membership: women and immigrants. Unions felt that women, immigrants, and African-Americans would compete for jobs and would endanger workers' well being. In 1903, the **Women's Trade Union League** was founded and tied some of the travails of women in the workplace to the lack of suffrage.

Industrialization did have some good benefits to society as it spread technology and goods to formerly isolated communities. Income levels did rise as did employment levels, leading to growth in the commercial society. Higher life expectancies resulted from improved access to medical care and varied diets. Other changes to society happened thanks to the increase in commercialization of society (thanks to industrialization). Flush toilets, processed and preserved foods, ready-made clothing, department stores, print culture, and advertising all became familiar components of daily life thanks to industrialization. Despite the drawbacks, industrialization did enable the United States to emerge as a major power.

Urbanization

Rapid urbanization, the process by which an increasing portion of the population moved to the cities and suburbs as a result of industrialization, migration, and corporate incentives, became another hallmark of the era. Cities, where most factories were located, became dirtier and less healthy environments and became the new frontier. Cities became impersonal metropolises that were divided into business, residential, social, and ethnic centers, rather than the old types of cities where people tended to have merged sectors. The emergence of the Boston to Washington area as a series of cities that provide common needs—like centers of banking, commerce, media, academics, and immigration—functioned almost like one gigantic city, referred to in hindsight as a **megalopolis.**

Advances in **mass transportation** like railroads, streetcars, and subways not only facilitated transportation of goods but also people to cities. It enabled the expansion of the cities and the construction of newer neighborhoods as people could move between the inner core of the city and the outer core, or the suburbs. What resulted from this development was a sort of stratification of society as class distinctions began to emerge from where people lived, as opposed to just what occupation they held. Many immigrants who arrived after 1880 tended to be from other areas of Europe, Southern and Eastern Europe, and settled in the inner core of the cities. Many of the new immigrants began to settle in **ethnic neighborhoods** in **tenement housing**, which were multi-family urban houses (a simultaneous housing also developed that targeted wealthier urbanites, **row houses** which were single-family dwellings that shared walls with other houses). While some of these new neighborhoods experienced severe overcrowding and squalid conditions, they also provided opportunities for some—namely women, who were able to find work outside the home, albeit at reduced wages.

Increased urbanization also provided opportunities for some select men who sought to facilitate the needs of these new urban residents who were having trouble contending with problems of housing, transportation, water, and sanitation, in return for political favor. These **political bosses** did help the poor find homes and job, get citizenship and voting rights, and build parks, roads, and sewage lines. But, they did so through **graft** and **kickbacks** as they also expected "donations" for their work and political support when they needed it. The political bosses in turn built **political machines,** the most famous of which was **Boss Tweed of Tammany Hall in New York City**, that made sure communities received help and services that they otherwise would not have been able to accomplish. This might not have been a bad system had these bosses not resorted to criminal means to accomplish their goals. A whole host of problems developed that then inspired reform movements to try to tackle some of the growing problems of urban life.

Reform Movements

Middle class organizations, largely run by women, targeted the urban poor for their reform efforts. They sought to lobby local governments for building safety codes, better sanitation, and public schools. The **Settlement House Movement** focused on building community centers in slum neighborhoods to provide assistance for people who needed it. They engaged in activities like child care, English lessons, college courses, and cultural activities. **Jane Addams** was one of the most influential members of the movement and along with **Ellen Gates Starr** founded **Chicago's Hull House** to provide English lessons for immigrants, day care for working mothers, and playgrounds for children. She also cultivated notions of social responsibility for the urban poor and inspired the formation of other settlement houses so that by 1910, there were over 400 settlement houses nationwide.

Efforts also targeted the political realm, focusing on the evils of political machines and patronage. **Thomas Nast**, a political cartoonist, helped arouse public outrage against

Boss Tweed, who was eventually found guilty of corruption and sentenced to jail. After an all-out political brawl, the **Pendleton Service Act of 1883** created the bipartisan Civil Service Commission that made appointments to federal jobs a meritocracy awarded to candidates based on their performance on examination rather than through their political connections.

Women's suffrage became an important political issue during this period, led by **Susan B. Anthony** who sought to get Congress to amend the constitution and permit women to vote. By 1890, while suffrage had yet to make it to national consideration, the **American Woman Suffrage Association**, which had targeted state constitutions, had given women the right to vote on school issues. It was not until 1920 and the **Nineteenth Amendment** that women were given the right to vote.

COMPETENCY 5.9

Evaluate the impact of immigration on social, cultural, political, and economic development in the late nineteenth and early twentieth centuries.

Immigration had a tremendous effect on the cities during the Gilded Age of the late nineteenth and early twentieth centuries, as it proved to be one of the great ages of immigration in American history. Between 1870 and 1920, approximately 20 million Europeans arrived in the United States in search of a better life, trying to escape families, land shortages, and religious or political persecution. But in many ways, this immigration differed from previous immigrations in that the immigrants were refugees from the ailing empires of Austria-Hungary, Russia, Italy, and Germany. Greeks, Slavs, Armenians, and Jews rounded out the new group of immigrants that came to the US in the 1890s. One reason for this influx of immigration simply was because travel was easier. With the development of large ocean-going steamships and the time cut down to only three weeks for trans-Atlantic voyages, the appeal of making the move to America increased and the cost for such a trip dropped considerably. Moreover, the rise of American industries and the growth of the railroad system created thousands of jobs that acted as powerful inducements to those wanting to venture to the United States to try their luck.

Most of these "new" European immigrants settled in the Northeast, dominated by Irish and Italians, and the Midwest, dominated by Germans. While the West also experienced an influx of European immigrants, it mostly attracted immigrants from China.

Lured by the prospect of earning money by working on the expanding western railroad system, many Chinese immigrants settled in California.

Problems attendant to the numbers of new immigrants were that cities needed to have resources available to take care of them. The floods of immigrants that poured into the nation's largest cities wound up swamping the cities' resources of housing and employment. The living conditions in the urban areas where most immigrants settled were horrendous. The tenement buildings where they lived were crowded, lacked windows, did not have indoor plumbing or water, and sanitation was lacking. Cholera and typhoid diseases were prevalent due to the lack of adequate medical care, limited access to safe drinking water, horse manure and garbage piled up on the streets, and sewage flowing through open gutters. Massive fires that occurred in almost every major city provided another frequent issue that immigrants had to deal with. In 1871, for instance, a fire in Chicago that roared for 24 hours killed 300 people, made 100,000 homeless, destroyed 17,500 public buildings, and cost $200 million in damages. In San Francisco in 1906, a fire that lasted for four days killed 1,000 people, left 200,000 homeless, destroyed 28,000 public buildings, and left $500 million in damages. Crime in these areas intensified as gangs formed, political corruption ran amok, theft was prevalent, and alcoholism took a grip on many new immigrants depressed at what the "land of opportunity" actually provided them.

In response to growing alarm at urban immigrants' living and working conditions, social reformers began to organize public and private relief programs and to pursue attempts to establish legal standards for housing and working conditions. These scattered reform efforts were among the seeds of a much larger, more comprehensive series of reform movements that soon came to dominate American life. They chiefly targeted improving sanitation and health concerns. Moreover, an **Americanization Movement** designed to teach immigrants the skills they needed to assimilate into American culture dominated attempts by reform organizations seeking to help these new citizens. Some of these programs were government funded and taught immigrants citizenship skills, "American cooking," and social etiquette.

Not all immigration, however, was encouraged. In a twist of hypocritical thinking, although immigration was one of the primary forces that shaped the country, Americans were not overly enthused about immigration and did not hail its virtues. In fact, the emergence of a new idea called **nativism** became more prominent where there was overt favoritism towards native-born Americans. Immigrants became viewed as potential threats to the American way of life. Native-born Americans (and by this we mean "white"

Americans) feared that newcomers would not only do much better than they would, but might even do so well in the new world that native-born Americans would wind up getting excluded from reaping the benefits of any economic or social success. Anti-immigrant feeling was linked rather closely to religious, ethnic, and racial prejudices of the late nineteenth century. Americans seemed to fear that the "new immigrants" would not fit into the **melting pot** and take on the new blended identity of Americans in which merged people shed the languages and customs of their national origin to embrace their new American identity. Some though were worried that immigrants from despotic monarchies would dilute or pollute American democracy. They felt that these immigrants could not understand democracy and would take enormous educational resources away from native-born children and instead devote precious resources toward the futile democratic training of these immigrants. These fears had little basis in reality. Indeed, for millions of immigrant children, school became their primary contact with America, and they all too willingly shed their own identity in an effort to Americanize and fit in with their peers.

This also was the first great period of Asian immigration to America, mostly from China but with a trickle of immigrants from Japan and Korea as well. However, anti-Asian feeling in the western United States arose, likely born out of fears that native-born workers would lose their jobs to Chinese immigrants who willingly accepted lower wages. Such anti-Asian sentiment resulted in a series of acts that targeted these groups specifically. In 1882, Congress passed the **Chinese Exclusion Act** that banned entry for ten years to all Chinese except those who were more valued, like students, teachers, merchants, government officials, and tourists. In 1892, the ban was extended for another ten years. In 1902, the immigration of Chinese immigrants was restricted indefinitely and not repealed until 1943. In 1906, waves of anti-Chinese aggression that filled the streets became extended to Japanese residents and other Asian peoples. Attacks weren't limited to just physical assaults: local government entities began imposing their own measures designed to give Asian immigrants the message that they were unwelcome. The San Francisco local Board of Education segregated Japanese children by putting them in separate schools. Japan protested the treatment of its emigrants and President Theodore Roosevelt worked out a deal called the 1907–1908 **Gentlemen's Agreement** by which Japan agreed to limit the number of unskilled workers they sent to the United States for repeal of the San Francisco segregation order.

At the start of the 1920s, the United States started setting limits and quotas to restrict immigration. The **Quota Act of 1921** set immigration quotas based on national origins and discriminated against the "new immigrants" who came from southern and eastern Europe. The Act imposed a cap of 3% of the number of immigrants from any country living in the United States in 1890. These limits were set to reduce the "foreign influence" in the country. The **Immigration Act of 1924** further restricted immigration by reducing the 1921 cap from 3% to 2% The **National Origins Act of 1929** put quotas on immigration in proportion to the origins of Americans in 1920.

COMPETENCY 5.10

Identify the causes, significant individuals, and effects of the events associated with the World War I era.

American foreign policy continued to remain committed to the **Monroe Doctrine,** which asserted that America would intervene anywhere in the Western Hemisphere where it felt its interests or security was at stake. It resolved to stay out of Europe's disputes. When **Woodrow Wilson** won the presidency in 1912, he seemed to advocate what the public wanted with regard to the simmering tensions in Europe—the United States should just stay out if it.

When World War I broke out in Europe, Wilson issued a proclamation of American neutrality on August 4, 1914. But what did such neutrality really mean? Neutrality called for Americans to treat all of those fighting in the war fairly and without favoritism. Wilson had opined that America might be the new world arbiter of international disputes. Wilson urged Americans to be neutral in thought as well as in action. However, Americans, despite proclamations of neutrality as the best course for America, were really not neutral at all. America was a rather ethnically diverse country and people took sides according to their ethnic origins—German-Americans supported the Germans, British-Americans supported the British, and the Irish, as they did not like the British, supported the Germans as well. Economic ties with the British continued according to international law, which stated that neutral countries could trade with countries on both sides of the conflict and that any attempt to stop such trade was also legal and could be done through blockade. Wilson himself shared ideological similarities with the British and believed that the British were the ones best able to promote his brand of **Wilsonianism** that consisted of ideas of democracy, internationalism, American exceptionalism, and diplomacy. Moreover, a number of Wilson's advisors openly favored the Allies. A series of events occurred that made Wilson reconsider his position of neutrality:

Blockades made it difficult for America to continue to deal with both sides of the war. England was able to effectively stop American ships from trading with the Germans. The

British impounded and confiscated U.S. vessels, but in an effort not to anger U.S. merchants, paid for the confiscated merchandise. The Germans meanwhile attempted to counter the blockade with **submarines** or **U-boats**. By using the U-boats, the Germans had a problem in that they could not, as stipulated by international law, warn civilian vessels of an impending attack. Even though the Germans warned Wilson that they would attack any U.S. civilian ship as it might contain wartime materials, Wilson was adamant that the Germans respect international law.

Sinking of the Lusitania, May 7, 1915. In May 1915, the British passenger liner *Lusitania* on a voyage from New York to Liverpool was sunk by a German submarine, killing 1,198 passengers, among them 128 Americans. Unbeknownst to the passengers, the ship had been loaded up with hidden arms and munitions destined for the British war effort. The action provoked condemnation of the Germans by the Americans and for a while, the Germans responded by limiting their use of submarine warfare.

Secretary of State William Jennings Bryan, a pacifist, believed that Americans should be forbidden from traveling on belligerent ships and that contraband should not be allowed on passenger ships. Wilson disagreed and insisted that the Germans should stop their submarine warfare. Bryan resigned rather than insisting on questionable neutral rights and was replaced by Robert Lansing.

In 1916, the Germans sank another passenger liner, the *Arabic*. In response, Congress debated the **Gore-McLemore Resolution,** which attempted to do just what Bryan had advocated, but the resolution never passed. Wilson, in response, asked Congress to put the military into a state of preparedness for war, just in case it was needed.

After another U-boat attack on *The Sussex* on March 24, 1916, Wilson threatened Berlin with severing diplomatic relations and the Germans promised not to do it again.

Two incidents elevated tensions between the United States and Germany.

Germany announced on January 31, 1917 that it would sink all ships, belligerent or neutral, without warning in a large war zone off the coasts of the Allied nations in the eastern Atlantic and the Mediterranean. Wilson broke diplomatic relations with Germany on February 3, and the Germans responded by sinking several American ships during February and March.

The British intercepted a secret message from the German foreign secretary, Arthur Zimmerman, to the German minister in Mexico, and turned it over to the United States on February 24, 1917. The **Zimmerman Telegram** included a German proposal that, in the event of a war between the United States and Germany, Mexico should attack the United States. After the war, the territories lost in the Mexican-American War—Texas, New Mexico, and Arizona—would be returned to Mexico. The telegram also suggested that Germany would help Japan, too, if they went to war with America. When the telegram was released to the press on March 1, many Americans became convinced that war with Germany was necessary.

Wilson first asked Congress for "armed-neutrality," but anti-war Senators filibustered the plan and so Wilson called the Congress into a special session and declared war on Germany on **April 6.**

During the War

After the declaration of war, the United States realized that their 120,000-man army had little experience and was not ready for war. The government embarked on a series of measures to make sure that it would win the war. Congress passed the **Selective Service Act** that required all males between the ages of 21 and 30 to register. By the end of 1918, over 24 million American men had registered for the draft, 4.8 million had served in the war, 2 million had seen active combat, 400,000 African-Americans had served in segregated units, and 15,000 Native Americans had served as scouts, messengers, and snipers in non-segregated units. Most of those drafted were white, poorly educated Americans in their early twenties.

Government power expanded significantly during the time America was involved in the war. It took control of the telephone, telegraph, railroad, and added a new bureaucracy to handle it. It created the **War Industries Board** to liaison with big business to meet government needs. The Board coordinated all facets of the economy, both industrial and agricultural production, to guarantee and standardize the quality of goods. It created the **Food Administration** led by Herbert Hoover that promoted things like "victory gardens" as well as setting prices and regulating the distribution of food during the war. It also set up the **Railroad Administration and Fuel Administration** to regulate each industry and to ration gasoline throughout the country.

The government also took advantage of the wartime situation to put some restrictions on civil liberties during the war. Anyone who refused to support the war was targeted.

Unfortunately, some groups, particularly those of German descent, were also persecuted and even killed during anti-German hysteria that developed during the war. The Government chimed in on public fears by passing two acts, the **Espionage Act of 1917** and the **Sedition Act of 1918.** The Espionage Act of 1917 provided for fines and imprisonment for persons who made false statements that aided the enemy, incited rebellion in the military or obstructed recruitment or the draft. Printed matter advocating treason or insurrection could be excluded from the mails. The Sedition Act of May 1918 forbade any criticism of the government, flag, or uniform, even if there were not detrimental consequences, and expanded the mail exclusion. The laws were applied in ways that trampled on civil liberties. The Espionage Act was upheld by the Supreme Court in the case of *Schenck v. United States* in 1919. The opinion, written by Justice Oliver Wendell Holmes, Jr. (1841–1935), stated that Congress could limit free speech when the words represented a "clear and present danger," and that a person cannot cry "fire" in a crowded theater. The Sedition Act was similarly upheld in *Abrams v. United States* a few months later. Ultimately 2,168 persons were prosecuted under the laws, and 1,055 were convicted, of whom only ten were charged with actual sabotage.

World War I: The Military Campaign

The American force of about 14,500, which had arrived in France by September 1917, was assigned a quiet section of the line near Verdun. When the Germans mounted a major drive toward Paris in the spring of 1918, the Americans experienced their first important engagements. In June, they prevented the Germans from crossing the Marne at Chateau-Thierry and cleared the area of Belleau Woods. In July, eight American divisions aided French troops in attacking the German line between Reims and Soissons. The American First Army, with over half a million men under Pershing's immediate command, was assembled in August 1918, and began a major offensive at St. Mihiel on the southern part of the front on September 12. Following the successful operation, Pershing began a drive against the German defenses between Verdun and Sedan, an action called the Meuse-Argonne Offensive. He reached Sedan on November 7. During the same period, the English in the North and the French along the central front also broke through the German lines. The fighting ended with the armistice on November 11, 1918.

Wartime Social Trends

Large numbers of women, mostly white, were hired by factories and other enterprises in jobs never before open to them. When the war ended, almost all returned to traditional "women's jobs" or to homemaking. Returning veterans replaced them in the labor market. The labor shortage opened industrial jobs to Mexican-Americans and to African- Americans. **W.E.B. DuBois**, the most prominent African-American leader of the time, supported the war effort in the hope that the war would make the world safe for democracy and bring a better life for African-Americans in the United States. About half a million rural Southern African-Americans migrated to cities, mainly in the North and Midwest, to obtain employment in war and other industries, especially in steel and meatpacking. In 1917, there were race riots in 26 cities in the North and South, with the worst in East St. Louis, Illinois.

In December 1917, a constitutional amendment to prohibit the manufacture and sale of alcoholic beverages in the United States was passed by Congress and submitted to the states for ratification

Peacemaking (1918–1920)

From the time of the American entry into the war, Wilson had maintained that the war would make the world safe for democracy. He insisted that there should be peace without victory, meaning that the victors would not be vindictive toward the losers, so that a fair and stable international situation in the postwar world would ensure lasting peace. In an address to Congress on January 8, 1918, he presented his specific peace plan in the form of the **Fourteen Points**. The first five points called for open rather than secret peace treaties, freedom of the seas, free trade, arms reduction, and a fair adjustment of colonial claims. The next eight points were concerned with the national aspirations of various European peoples and the adjustment of boundaries. The fourteenth point, which he considered the most important and had espoused as early as 1916, called for a "general association of nations" to preserve the peace.

Wilson decided that he would lead the American delegation to the peace conference, which opened in Paris on January 12, 1919. In doing so, he became the first president to leave the country during his term of office. In the negotiations, which continued until May 1919, Wilson found it necessary to make many compromises in forging the text of the treaty. Following a protest by 39 senators in February 1919, Wilson obtained some changes in the **League of Nations** structure to exempt the Monroe Doctrine and domestic matters from League jurisdiction. Then, on July 26, 1919, he presented the treaty with the League within it to the Senate for ratification. Almost all of the 47 Democrats supported

Wilson and the treaty, but the 49 Republicans were divided. About a dozen were "irreconcilables" who thought that the United States should not be a member of the League under any circumstances. The remainder included 25 "strong" and 12 "mild" reservationists who would accept the treaty with some changes. The main objection centered on Article X of the League Covenant, where the reservationists wanted it understood that the United States would not go to war to defend a League member without the approval of Congress.

On September 3, 1919, Wilson set out on a national speaking tour to appeal to the people to support the treaty and the League and to influence their senators. He collapsed after a speech in Pueblo, Colorado, on September 25, and returned to Washington, where he suffered a severe stroke on October 2 which paralyzed his left side. He was seriously ill for several months and never fully recovered. The treaty failed to get a two-thirds majority either with or without the reservationists. Many people, including British and French leaders, urged Wilson to compromise with the reservationists, including the issue of Article X. Many historians think that Wilson's ill health impaired his judgment, and that he would have worked out a compromise had he not had the stroke. The Senate took up the treaty again in February 1920, and on March 19, it was again defeated both with and without the reservationists. The United States officially ended the war with Germany by a resolution of Congress signed on July 2, 1921, and a separate peace treaty was ratified on July 25. The United States did not join the League.

Domestic Problems and the End of the Wilson Administration

In January 1919, the Eighteenth Amendment to the Constitution prohibiting the manufacture, sale, transportation, or importation of intoxicating liquors was ratified by the states, and it became effective in January 1920. The Nineteenth Amendment providing for women's suffrage, which had been defeated in the Senate in 1918, was approved by Congress in 1919. It was ratified by the states in time for the election of 1920.

Americans feared the spread of the Russian Communist revolution to the United States, and many interpreted the widespread strikes of 1919 spurred by inflation as Communist-inspired and the beginning of the revolution. Bombs sent through the mail to prominent government and business leaders in April 1919 seemed to confirm their fears, although the origin of the bombs has never been determined. The anti-German hysteria of the war years was transformed into the anti-Communist and anti-foreign hysteria of 1919 and 1920, and continued in various forms through the 1920s.

Attorney General A. Mitchell Palmer, who aspired to the 1920 presidential nomination, was one of the targets of the anonymous bombers in the spring of 1919. In August 1919, he named J. Edgar Hoover (1895–1972) to head a new Intelligence Division in the Justice Department to collect information about radicals. After arresting nearly 5,000 people in late 1919 and early 1920, Palmer announced that huge Communist riots were planned for major cities on May Day (May 1, 1920). Police and troops were alerted, but the day passed with no radical activity. Palmer was discredited and the Red Scare subsided.

White hostility based on competition for lower-paying jobs and black encroachment into neighborhoods led to race riots in 25 cities in 1919, with hundreds killed or wounded and millions of dollars in property damage. The Chicago riot in July was the worst. Fear of returning African-American veterans in the South led to an increase of lynchings from 34 in 1917 to 60 in 1918 and 70 in 1919. Some of the victims were veterans still in uniform.

COMPETENCY 5.11

Identify social, cultural, political, and economic developments (e.g., Roaring Twenties, Harlem Renaissance, Great Depression, New Deal) between World War I and World War II.

The Inter-War period saw the United States retreat into isolation. The Senate refused to ratify the Versailles Peace Treaty and signed a separate peace with Germany and Japan. In another embarrassing move, the United States also refused to join the League of Nations—the same league whose creation came out of an idea proposed by the U.S. President, Woodrow Wilson. It sought to isolate itself a bit on the trade front, raising tariffs on imports. It also ended the concept of free and open access to immigration to the United States. Until 1914, more than 1.2 million people had immigrated to the United States. But once the 1920s immigration restrictions were in place, the overall total of immigrants per year was limited to about 160,000, and each country had a fixed number of immigrants. The United States turned inward, and such a move proved to be a bit of a good thing. The 1920s became known as the **Roaring Twenties,** a time where America was reveling in its prosperity, enjoying the fruits of its inventions like the electric motor, beginning its love affair with the automobile as by 1929, 1 out of every 5 residents owned a motor vehicle, and soon, the post-WWI United States was one of the richest nations in the world.

The Roaring Twenties (1920–1929)

Economic Developments

The economy remained the story of the 1920s, both for its highs and for its lows. Some of the big developments in the period were as follows:

- **Initial Recession Followed by Recovery**: Following the war, with demobilization and the return of the soldiers looking for jobs, the U.S. economy began to slide into a recession. By 1922, not only had the economy recovered, but it also began to grow and prosper. Recovery proved to be rapid, except for farmers who were finding it impossible to meet and beat worldwide competition.

- **Retreat from Regulation**: After the war, regulatory institutions were quickly dismantled and government, which had already been working with businesses through the War Industries Board during the war, became more **pro-business** than ever. Organized labor had rather limited success during this period as not only had public opinion turned against anyone who protested and their membership declined from 5 million to 3.5 million nation-wide, but also strikes over unfair wages or unsafe working conditions resulted in federal troops being called in to suppress the strikes. Women, blacks, African-Americans, and immigrant workers remained at the bottom of any scale.

- **Emergence of Welfare Capitalism:** Businesses, in an effort to keep unions out, developed **welfare capitalism** in order to persuade workers not to join unions and instead enjoy new benefits offered by their places of employment, like pension plans, profit sharing, stock purchase plans, and insurance. Welfare capitalism seemed to have worked as long as prosperity continued. As such, the 1920s prosperity wrought a fast erosion in union membership.

- **Corporate Consolidation:** Without regulation, more mega-companies formed during the 1920s with a trend toward corporate consolidation. In most fields, an oligopoly of two to four firms dominated. This is exemplified by the automobile industry, where Ford, General Motors, and Chrysler produced 83% of the vehicles in 1929. Government regulatory agencies such as the Federal Trade Commission and the Interstate Commerce Commission were passive and generally controlled by persons from the business world.

- **Lobbying:** Special interest groups began to band together to affect federal legislation.

- **Mass Consumption:** The speed with which materialism spread throughout the United States was breathtaking. Due to technological breakthroughs, especially the ability to electrically wire households (WWII 80% of American households had electricity), there were more and new products on the market, and people wanted them. Automobiles, washing machines, refrigerators, electric irons, electric and gas stoves, and other inventions made living much easier and improved the quality of life. Mass-produced articles like clothing and food became more affordable. As Americans craved these new goods, many sought to buy them on credit. A new type of credit called **installment credit** let purchasers spread payments out over time for some of these new household goods. These new household inventions resulted in new ways of thinking about domestic work, which was now cut down considerably with new products that could perform tasks in a fraction of the time it used to take.

- **Economic Polarization Among Various Classes Reached New Heights:** By 1929, the richest 1% in America held 45% of the wealth. This rising gap between the rich and the poor caused many to think that perhaps America was moving in the wrong direction.

- **Bank Consolidation:** There was also a trend toward bank consolidation. Because corporations were raising much of their money through the sale of stocks and bonds, the demand for business loans declined. Commercial banks then put more of their funds into real estate loans, loans to brokers against stocks and bonds, and the purchase of stocks and bonds themselves.

Political Developments

The Roaring Twenties saw three presidents—**Warren G. Harding**, **Calvin Coolidge**, and **Herbert Hoover**—all firmly pro-business Republicans who surrounded themselves with advisors who thought similarly.

Warren G. Harding: Harding, a handsome and amiable man of limited intellectual and organizational abilities, who had spent much of his life as the publisher of a newspaper in the small city of Marion, Ohio, was elected in 1920. He recognized his limitations and so decided to surround himself with a series of advisors that he trusted would help him but who proved to be riddled with corruption. While Harding appointed some outstanding persons to his cabinet, including Secretary of State Charles Evans Hughes, a former Supreme Court justice and presidential candidate; Secretary of the Treasury Andrew Mellon, a Pittsburgh aluminum and banking magnate and reportedly the richest man in America; and Secretary of Commerce Herbert Hoover, a dynamic multimillionaire mine owner famous for his wartime relief efforts, he also appointed less impressive cronies like Albert B. Fall as secretary of the interior and Harry M. Daugherty as attorney general. The Teapot Dome Scandal began when Secretary of the Interior Albert B. Fall in 1921 secured the transfer of several naval oil reserves to his jurisdiction. In 1922, he secretly leased government oil reserves at Teapot Dome in Wyoming to oilmen in return for $400,000 in bribes. Harding's Veteran's Bureau chief was caught stealing Bureau funds, and the Attorney General was found to have been engaging in influence peddling. Harding died in office and Vice President Calvin Coolidge became president upon his death in 1923.

Calvin Coolidge: Known as "Silent Cal," Coolidge really did not do much except to continue Harding's conservative economic policies, lowered income-tax rates, reduced debt, built roads, and sought to prohibit government interference with business. He ran in 1924 on the platform "Coolidge Prosperity" against the Progressive **Robert M. LaFollette** who had started his own party and who railed against monopolies, called for the nationalization of railroads and the direct election of the president.

Herbert Hoover: Coolidge did not seek another term, and the convention quickly nominated Herbert Hoover, the secretary of commerce, for president. The platform endorsed the policies of the Harding and Coolidge administrations. Hoover, an Iowa farm boy and an orphan, graduated from Stanford University with a degree in mining engineering. He became a multimillionaire from mining and other investments around the world. After serving as the director of the Food Administration under Wilson, he became Secretary of Commerce under Harding and Coolidge. He ran against the New York Governor Alfred E. Smith, a Catholic and an anti-prohibitionist, who controlled most of the non-Southern delegations. Southerners supported Hoover's nomination with the understanding that the platform would not advocate repeal of prohibition. Hoover believed that cooperation between business and government would enable the United States to abolish poverty through continued economic growth. The main thing that he ended up dealing with was the Depression.

Social Developments

With consumerism and modernization, there came a migration to the cities, where manufacturing jobs were more readily available. By 1920, for the first time, a majority of Americans (51%) lived in an urban area with a population of 2,500 or more. A new phenomenon of the 1920s was the tremendous growth of suburbs and satellite cities, which grew more rapidly than the central cities. Streetcars, commuter railroads, and automobiles contributed to the process, as well as the easy availability of financing for home construction. The suburbs had once been the domain of the wealthy, but the technology of the 1920s opened them to working-class families.

The principal driving force of the economy of the 1920s was the automobile. Automobile manufacturing stimulated supporting industries such as steel, rubber, and glass, as well as gasoline refining and highway construction. During the 1920s, the United States became a nation of paved roads. The Federal Highway Act of 1916 started the federal highway system and gave matching funds to the states for construction. The car made Americans take to the roads and allowed people to move further away from city centers, thus starting a whole new area of living called **suburbia**. By 1929, out of the 100 million people who lived in the United States, more than 23 million had cars.

Traditional American moral standards regarding premarital sex and marital fidelity were widely questioned for the first time during the 1920s. The automobile, by giving people mobility and privacy, was generally considered to have contributed to sexual license. Birth control, though illegal, was promoted by **Margaret Sanger** (1883–1966) and others and was widely accepted. When it became apparent that women did not vote as a block, political leaders gave little additional attention to the special concerns of women. Divorce laws were liberalized in many states at the insistence of women. Domestic service was the largest job category. Most other women workers were in traditional female occupations such as secretarial and clerical work, retail sales, teaching, and nursing. Rates of pay were below those for men. Most women still pursued the traditional role of housewife and mother, and society accepted that as the norm.

The migration of southern rural African-Americans to the cities continued, with about 1.5 million moving during the 1920s. By 1930, about 20% of American blacks lived in the North, with the largest concentrations in New York, Chicago, and Philadelphia. While they were generally better off economically in the cities than they had been as tenant farmers, they generally held low-paying jobs and were confined to tiny, segregated areas of the cities. A native of Jamaica, **Marcus Garvey** (1887–1940) founded the **Universal Negro Improvement Association**, advocating African-American racial pride and separatism rather than integration, and called for a return of African-Americans to Africa. In 1921, he proclaimed himself the provisional president of an African empire, and sold stock in the Black Star Steamship Line, which would take migrants to Africa. The line went bankrupt in 1923, and Garvey was convicted and imprisoned for mail fraud in the sale of the line's stock and then deported. His legacy was an emphasis on African-American pride and self-respect.

Increased life expectancy and a decreasing birth rate also posed some problems for Americans. Although they lived better and longer due to advances in nutrition and sanitation, they also had fewer children. With fewer children and people living longer than before, old age pensions became an important issue.

Cultural Developments

The 1920s witnessed the birth of new forms of mass culture and new opportunities for leisure time for Americans. As a result, there were new forms of entertainment and culture. The **movies** became an important part of American culture, first with silent film and then with sound with the first sound flick being *The Jazz Singer.* Sports also took center stage, especially baseball and players like Babe Ruth who was idolized by millions. Sports figures and movie stars became celebrities and idols to many.

Prohibition did not prevent people from going to **speakeasies** to drink alcohol. Prohibition did bring all sorts of problems to the country as some groups, like the mafia, found ways to continue the supply of alcohol to a population who still seemed to want it.

Many writers of the 1920s were disgusted with the hypocrisy and materialism of contemporary American society and were disillusioned by World War I. Often called the "Lost Generation," many of them, such as novelists Ernest Hemingway (1899–1961) and F. Scott Fitzgerald (1896–1940) and poets Ezra Pound (1885–1972) and T. S. Eliot (1888–1965), moved to Europe where they wrote about America from afar. Common themes from literature at the time reflected some of the anxiety about the changes that were happening: alienation, hypocrisy, conformity, etc. In their writings, they lambasted the narrow-minded, small-town values of pre-War America and waxed on about the evils associated with the materialistic business culture of the 1920s.

The twenties also inspired new styles from talented artists like **Georgia O'Keefe** in painting, **Aaron Copland** and **George Gershwin** in music, and **Frank Lloyd Wright** in architecture.

African-Americans flocked to Harlem where a movement sprang up in the largest black neighborhood of New York City. Theaters, cultural clubs, and newspapers celebrated black culture. Writers of the **Harlem Renaissance** like poets **Langston Hughes** and **Countee Cullen**, and ovelists **Zora Neale Hurston** explored the black experience in America. A major part of the Harlem Renaissance was the proliferation of **jazz,** which owed a lot to black culture and music and featured improvisation and free-spiritedness. Jazz became emblematic of the Roaring Twenties, so much so that the period is also referred to as the **Jazz Age**. Jazz became hugely popular in the cities, and its best known musician of the era was **Louis Armstrong**. Many whites were attracted to the vibrant movement and provided some financial support; however, this support was rather tepid as whites wanted to experience the carefree vivaciousness offered by the Renaissance and joined in celebrating the "African-ness" of American black culture, but they did not want to hear about real problems facing Black America.

The youth of the era, particularly urban, middle-class, college students, rejected the values that their parents had about sex, dress, public behavior, and religion. The generation flirted with all sorts of temptations that their parents had forbidden—they drank bootleg liquor, went to jazz clubs, dated, and partied throughout the night. Women too embraced this new era with gusto as they challenged ideas about how women should act in public. The **flapper** characterized the free spiritedness of the era and welcomed in a whole new world for women who now had obtained the right to vote. Flappers illustrated a marked change from women in the past—no longer corseted and shrouded in long, heavy, drab dresses, these women sported makeup (previously associated with only prostitutes and actresses) highlighted by their red-ruby lips, wore short dresses, flesh colored silk stockings, bobbed hair, and strings of pearls. They broke all sorts of ideas about how women should behave in public: they drank, smoked, and danced provocatively.

There were conservative backlashes though to the freedoms offered by the Roaring Twenties. People who dwelled in rural areas, in particular, felt threatened by the changes happening in society. The return of the **Ku Klux Klan**, this time to the Midwest where it soon spread to the South, grew to more than 5 million members and targeted not only blacks, but Catholics, Jews, immigrants, and anyone who deviated from their understanding of acceptable behavior and native, white, Protestant supremacy. They used vigilante justice, terror, and political pressure to achieve their aims.

While the KKK may have taken fears about "the other" to the extreme, there were other examples of racism deemed more "socially acceptable" and government approved. As mentioned earlier, immigrants became specifically targeted by the government, which started passing immigration quotas for certain immigrants. The **Sacco-Vanzetti Case** illustrated the growing concern about immigrants. Sacco and Vanzetti were two Italian immigrant anarchists who were arrested on charges of murder. Despite there being no real evidence tying them to the crime, they were convicted and executed in 1927.

Religious fundamentalism grew in the 1920s, perhaps out of sincere alarm at the flapper movement and general *carpe diem* attitude of the *bon vivants* of the day. The clash between religion and science led to the **Scopes Monkey Trial,** which dealt with a teacher, John Thomas Scopes, who broke a 1925 Tennessee law that forbade teachers from teaching evolution. The attorneys for the case, **Clarence Darrow,** the civil liberties lawyer, for the defense and **William Jennings Bryan** for the prosecution, battled in a courtroom some of the conflicts that were happening throughout the country: how to reconcile tradition with progress. Scopes wound up being convicted and had to pay a small fine, but Bryan, who in his arguments posited that the Bible was error-free but found himself not really knowing what was in it, looked foolish and he, along with the fundamentalist movement and the entire South, became targets of ridicule in the press.

The Great Depression and the New Deal (1929–1941)

Political and Economic Developments

Reasons for the Depression

Stock prices increased throughout the decade. The boom in prices and volume of sales was especially active after 1925 and was intensive during 1928–1929. Nine million Americans were invested in the market—many seeking quick profits had borrowed money to buy stocks on margin. These margin buyers had bought stock by putting 10% down and borrowing 90% of it through a broker's loan using the stock that they were buying as collateral. All was good, as long as prices continued to rise. But, careful investors, realizing that stocks were overpriced and becoming concerned about the health of the market, began to sell to take their profits. During October 1929, prices declined as more stock was sold. On **Black Thursday**, October 24, 1929, almost 13 million shares were traded, a large number for that time, and prices fell precipitously. As normally happened, when the price of a stock fell more than 10%, the lender sold the stock for whatever it would bring and thus further depressed prices. When this process started in late October, the forced sales brought great losses to the banks and businesses that had financed the broker's loans, as well as to the investors. Investment banks tried to boost the market by buying, but on October 29, **Black Tuesday**, the market fell about 40 points, with 16.5 million shares traded. Prices continued to drop all the way through mid-November when stocks eventually lost more than 70% of their value.

While the **Stock Market Crash of 1929** certainly took its toll on the American economy, a crash in the market should not necessarily result in a depression. There were contributing factors that led to it:

- *Overproduction/Underconsumption*: In order to continue to finance their businesses and having to expand and produce under ideas of **economies of scale,** companies expanded to such a degree that they had to keep producing more and cutting wages in order to keep their profits up. By cutting wages, however, they reduced people's ability to buy goods. As a result, companies had a hard time unloading their merchandise and created large inventories. By 1929, not only could those at the lower end of the economic scale not buy goods, but those at the upper end had cut back on purchases as well.

- *Corporate Debt*: Companies, in their efforts to expand quickly and due to their problems getting rid of merchandise, were forced to get loans to keep themselves afloat. In many cases, they lied or exaggerated their assets to banks who wound up being left empty-handed when corporations defaulted on their loans.

- *Bank Failures*: Throughout the 1930s, over 9,000 banks failed and the lack of insurance on bank deposits meant that people lost their money when a bank failed. Banks that did survive were unwilling to lend, and as a result, the economic situation worsened and a potential means of recovery was eliminated.

- *Lack of Recovery in Farming*: The farm economy, which involved almost 25% of the population, had been depressed throughout the decade as they never recovered from the post-war recession, continued to see a decline in prices, faced a return of foreign competition, and were often unable to repay their debts.

- *International Trade Difficulties*: European economies, already burdened with WWI debt repayments, were unable to buy U.S goods that already had high tariffs on them.

- *Government Policies*: Government policies, with their hands-off approach to regulation of industry, did little but to encourage easy credit with discounted rates that proved to be harmful to the economy.

During the early months of the depression, most people thought it was just an adjustment in the business cycle that would soon be over. As time went on, the worst depression in American history set in, reaching its bottom point in early 1932. As banks crashed and drought conditions affected the Midwest, people lost their money, jobs, and then homes. The homeless built shantytowns that they referred to as **Hoovervilles** in all of the major cities. As farm prices dropped even lower and drought conditions turned the Great Plains area into a giant **Dustbowl**, many left their farms and homes to move westward, in search of a better life.

Hoover's Depression Policies

At first, Hoover was encouraged by his Secretary of the Treasury, **Andrew Mellon,** not to embark on any federal relief programs as it would undermine the American ideal of **rugged individualism.** Later, as it became more apparent that this was not just a momentary dip in the economy, he embarked on attempts to get companies to voluntarily promise not to lower wages anymore and to maintain employment. He also asked state and local governments to step in and provide relief efforts. His plan did not work as businesses did not cooperate, and local and state governments could not keep up with the demand for aid. Eventually he tried some other ideas in an effort to boost the economy.

The Agricultural Marketing Act: Passed in June 1929, before the market crash, this law, proposed by the president, created the Federal Farm Board. It had a revolving fund of $500 million to lend agricultural cooperatives to buy commodities, such as wheat and cotton, and hold them for higher prices.

The Hawley-Smoot Tariff: This law, passed in June 1930, raised duties on both agricultural and manufactured imports to extremely high rates in order to protect American trade. It had the reverse effect and worsened the economy as it completely killed off any foreign trade.

The Reconstruction Finance Corporation (RFC): Chartered by Congress in 1932, the RFC loaned money to railroads, banks, and other financial institutions. It prevented the failure of basic firms, on which many other elements of the economy depended, but was criticized by some as relief for the rich.

The Federal Home Loan Bank Act: This law, passed in July 1932, created home-loan banks, to make loans to building and loan associations, savings banks, and insurance companies to help them avoid foreclosures on homes.

Election of 1932

The Republicans re-nominated Hoover while the Democrats nominated Franklin D. Roosevelt, governor of New York. Not only was Hoover reeling from the problems associated with the Depression, but another event also plagued him. In June 1932, just when Congress was getting ready to deliberate about a bill that would give WWI veterans an early payment of benefits, a bonus, 10,000 impoverished WWI veterans and their families marched on Washington in support of the bill. When the bill was defeated, about 3,000 of these "bonus marchers" stayed in Washington to protest. They set up camp in Anacostia Flats in the southeast portion of the city in the Hoovervilles there, and some squatted in empty government buildings throughout the summer. In July, Hoover ordered the army to remove the bonus marchers, but **General Douglas MacArthur** went overboard. He used the army to march on the veterans. Armed with tear gas, bayonets, and tanks, they attacked the protesters, burned down their makeshift shacks, and in the process killed 100 people, including two babies who suffocated from exposure to the tear gas. The attack on the veterans resulted in widespread condemnation of the administration and seemed to symbolize Hoover's response to any crisis: odd and ineffective. It also killed any chance he may have had for reelection.

Roosevelt, on the other hand, appeared to be a shining light in the midst of turmoil and uncertainty. He seemed prepared and eager to attack some of the problems that the country faced. In order to find a good platform, Roosevelt gathered a "Brain Trust" of lawyers and university professors. Together, they decided that the way to end the depression was that government had to regulate business and restore purchasing power to the masses by cutting production. They believed this would lead to rising prices and rising wages and made sense according to the economic principle of **economics of scarcity**. Roosevelt also believed in direct unemployment relief and repealing prohibition. So, although he called for a cut in spending, Roosevelt communicated optimism and easily defeated Hoover, with over 57% of the popular vote.

The First New Deal

In February 1933, before Roosevelt took office, Congress passed the Twenty-First Amendment to repeal prohibition and sent it to the states. In March, the new Congress legalized light beer. The amendment was ratified by the states and took effect in December 1933. When Roosevelt was inaugurated on March 4, 1933, the American economic system seemed to be on the verge of collapse. Roosevelt assured the nation that "the only thing we have to fear is fear itself," called for a special session of Congress to convene on March 9, and asked for "broad executive powers to wage war against the emergency." Two days later, he closed all banks and forbade the export of gold or the redemption of currency in gold.

The special session of Congress, from March 9 to June 16, 1933, passed a great body of legislation that has left a lasting mark on the nation. The period has been referred to ever since as the "**Hundred Days**." Historians have divided Roosevelt's legislation into the **First New Deal (1933–1935)** and a new wave of programs beginning in 1935 called the **Second New Deal**.

Name of Policy, Agency, or Act	Abbrev.	Year Enacted	Problem to Solve	Significance
Agricultural Adjustment Act	AAA	1933	Farmers still having difficulty.	Protected farmers from price drops by providing crop subsidies in exchange for an agreement to reduce production by up to one-half. The money to pay for the subsidies came from a tax on the processing of the commodities. Farm prices increased, but tenants and sharecroppers were hurt when owners took land out of cultivation. Was a public relations disaster for the New Deal as so many in the country were going hungry at the time. The law was repealed in January 1936 on the grounds that the processing tax was not constitutional.
Beer-Wine Revenue		1933		After the repeal of Prohibition with the Twenty-First Amendment, Congress imposed new taxes on the sale of wines/beers.

Name of Policy, Agency, or Act	Abbrev.	Year Enacted	Problem to Solve	Significance
Civilian Conservation Corps	CCC	1933	Unemployment rate was 25% in 1933, which meant that 16 million Americans were jobless.	Between 1933–1941 sent over 3 million young men ages 18–25 to work camps to perform reforestation and conservation tasks all over the country. Planted nearly 3 billion trees to reforest America. Removed surplus of workers from cities, provided healthy conditions for boys, gave each boy $30 a month of which $25 was required to be sent home to their families.
Civil Works Administration	CWA	1933	Unemployment still high.	Provided public works jobs at $15/week to four million unemployed workers to take on temporary and makeshift jobs like sweeping streets. Brought much criticism, and the experiment was terminated in April 1934.
Commodity Credit Corporation		1933		Established by the AAA to make loans to corn and cotton farmers against their crops so that they could hold them for higher prices.
Emergency Banking Relief Act		1933	Lack of confidence in the banking system.	First day of the special session of Congress passed this act, which provided for de facto 100% deposit insurance. It also put unsound banks under the purview of the Treasury Department and granted special government seals to those who were deemed sound. The bill was passed before a four-day Bank Holiday that Roosevelt instituted in order to give his plan time to work. In his first **Fireside Chat**, he told everyone that it was safe to put their money back into reopened banks. To everyone's relief, when the banks reopened for business on March 13, depositors stood in line to redeposit money. This resulted in a tremendous boost on the stock market as the exchange recorded the largest one-day percentage price increase ever. This ended the run on banks.
Emergency Farm Mortgage Act		1933	Stop farm foreclosures from taking place.	Provided funds to protect famers in danger of foreclosure.
Frazier-Lemke Farm Bankruptcy Act		1934		Allowed farmers to defer foreclosure on their land while they obtained new financing, and helped them to recover property already lost through easy financing.

Name of Policy, Agency, or Act	Abbrev.	Year Enacted	Problem to Solve	Significance
Federal Emergency Relief Act	FERA	1933	Millions of Americans had been unemployed for years, and local relief agencies could no longer help them.	Distributed $500 million to state and local relief agencies to provide relief to citizens in their communities. Constructed over 5,000 public buildings and 7,000 bridges, organized adult literacy programs, financed college education for poor students, and set up day-care centers for low-income families.
Federal Farm Act Credit				Consolidated all farm credit programs into the Farm Credit Administration to make low-interest loans for farm mortgages and other agricultural purposes.
Federal Housing Act	FHA	1934		Insured long-term, low-interest mortgages for home construction and repair.
Glass-Steagall Act (also called, the Banking Act of 1933)	FDIC	1933	Concern about bank failures and lack of public confidence in the banking system.	Created federally insured bank deposits ($2,500 per investor at first) to prevent bank failures. Established the Federal Deposit Insurance Corporation (FDIC) to insure individual deposits in commercial banks, and separated commercial banking from the more speculative activity of investment banking.
Home Owners Loan Corporation		1933	Prevent home foreclosures.	Gave authority to borrow money to refinance home mortgages and prevent foreclosures. Lent more than three billion dollars to more than one million home owners.
National Industrial Recovery Act	NIRA	1933	American factories had decreased their production levels and factories were stagnant. The goal was to increase the productivity of industry but at the same time protect it from overproduction and unstable prices.	This law was viewed as the cornerstone of the recovery program. It sought to stabilize the economy by preventing extreme competition, labor-management conflicts, and overproduction. A board composed of industrial and labor leaders in each industry or business drew up a code for that industry, which set minimum prices, minimum wages, maximum work hours, production limits, and quotas. Created National Recovery Administration (NRA) to regulate business through the establishment of fair competition, production codes, limiting production, instituting minimum wages, and to permit collective bargaining of workers and the right of them to join unions. Granted immunity from antitrust prosecutions for major industries.

Name of Policy, Agency, or Act	Abbrev.	Year Enacted	Problem to Solve	Significance
Public Works Administration	PWA	1933		Received $3.3 billion appropriation from Congress for public works projects. Under Secretary of Interior **Harold Ickes** spent $4 billion on construction of 35,000 projects like dams, bridges, office buildings, highways, schools, and hospitals.
Securities and Exchange Commission	SEC	1934		Regulated stock market and restricted margin buying. Set up commission to supervise stock exchanges and punish fraud in securities trading.
Tennessee Valley Authority	TVA	1933	Unemployment in the TVA region and attempted to revitalize the economy there.	Roosevelt's first major experiment in regional public planning. Federal government built a series of 20 dams in 40,000 square miles to prevent flooding, soil erosion, improve navigation, and generate and sell hydroelectric power. It also manufactured nitrates for fertilizer, conducted demonstration projects for farmers, engaged in reforestation, restocked bodies of water with fish, and provided jobs, all in an effort to rehabilitate the area and enrich the land. First public competition with private power industries. One problem is that it unintentionally flooded some farmland.
Truth in Securities Act		1933	Designed to eliminate fraud in the stock market.	Declared that companies that deceived their stockholders could be sued. Required that full information about stocks and bonds be provided by brokers and others to potential purchasers.

The economy improved but did not recover. The GNP, money supply, salaries, wages, and farm income rose. Unemployment dropped from about 25% of nonfarm workers in 1933 to about 20.1%, or 10.6 million, in 1935.

Many people began to complain about Roosevelt's policies. Conservatives felt that there was too much regulation, taxation, and government spending. They opposed the higher tax rates and complained that relief programs stymied American self-interests in lifting themselves up and thwarted their individualism. Leftists complained that the AAA policy of letting food go to waste when people were starving was immoral. They also felt that government policies were still geared too much toward helping business rather than punishing them for the greed that got the country in this position.

The Second New Deal

Roosevelt launched a second series of legislative initiatives aimed at continuing to tackle the problems of the economy and to make more inroads into recovery.

Name of Policy, Agency, or Act	Abbrev.	Year Enacted	Problem to Solve	Significance
National Youth Administration	NYA	1935		Established as part of the WPA to provide part-time employment to more than two million college and high school students and youth not in school but who lacked jobs.
Rural Electrification Administration	REA	1935	Rural areas of the United States lacked access to electricity as only 1 in 10 in the rural areas had it.	Encouraged farmers to join cooperatives to bring electricity to farms in rural areas not served by private companies. Used money to run power lines, wire home and barns, and to lend to rural cooperatives to build power plants. Despite its efforts, by 1940, only 40% of American farms were electrified.
Social Security Act		1935	No safeguards to protect the elderly.	Established a retirement plan for persons over age 65, which was to be funded by a tax on wages paid equally by employee and employer. The first benefits, ranging from $10 to $85 per month, were paid in 1942. Another provision of the act had the effect of forcing the states to initiate unemployment insurance programs. It also provided aid to blind, deaf, disabled, and dependent children as well as those injured in industrial accidents.
Soil Conservation Act		1936	Stop erosion from the drought created in the Dustbowl area.	Encouraged farmers to change farming practices to reduce run-off and soil erosion. Subsidized farmers to stop producing soil-depleting crops.
Works Progress Administration	WPA	1935	Unemployment still as high as in 1934, 10 million Americans still unemployed.	Created as a result of the **Emergency Relief Appropriations Act of April 1935.** Funds of 4.8 billion used to employ 8.5 million workers in construction and other jobs, but more importantly provided work in arts, theater, and literary projects. The WPA employed people from the relief rolls for 30 hours of work a week at pay double the relief payment but less than private employment. Was able to stimulate local economies and beautify cities.
Wagner Act	NLRB	1935		Allowed workers to join unions and outlawed union-busting tactics by management.

The Last Years of the New Deal

Frustrated by a conservative Supreme Court that had overturned much of his New Deal legislation, Roosevelt, in February 1937, proposed to Congress the **Judicial Reorganization Bill**, which would allow the president to name a new federal judge for each judge who did not retire by the age of 70 1/2. The appointments would be limited to a maximum of 50, with no more than six added to the Supreme Court. He also tried to increase the size of the court from 9 to 15 judges, but the Congress rejected the measure. The president was astonished by the wave of opposition from Democrats and Republicans alike, but he uncharacteristically refused to compromise. In doing so, he not only lost the bill but also control of the Democratic Congress, which he had dominated since 1933. Nonetheless, the Court changed its position, as Chief Justice Charles Evans Hughes and Justice Owen Roberts began to vote with the more liberal members.

Most economic indicators rose sharply between 1935 and 1937. Roosevelt decided that the recovery was sufficient to warrant a reduction in relief programs and a move toward a balanced budget. The budget for fiscal year 1938 was reduced from $8.5 billion to $6.8 billion, with the WPA experiencing the largest cut. During the winter of 1937–1938, the economy slipped rapidly and unemployment rose to 12.5%. In April 1938, Roosevelt requested and received from Congress an emergency appropriation of about $3 billion for the WPA, as well as increases for public works and other programs. In July 1938, the economy began to recover, and it regained the 1937 levels in 1939.

Social Dimensions of the New Deal Era

Unemployment for African-Americans was much higher than for the general population, as they were pushed deeper into poverty and segregation, and before 1933, they were often excluded from state and local relief efforts. Racism itself made their lives more difficult. The **Scottsboro Trial** in 1931 revealed the uneven hand of justice as after nine black teens were arrested for throwing white homeless men off of a train, they were then accused and convicted by a white jury of rape. Although the Supreme Court intervened, they were still imprisoned. Organizations like the **Brotherhood of Sleeping Car Porters** and the militant **Harlem Tenants League** fought for civil rights and attacked discrimination.

With Roosevelt's election, African-Americans generally switched over to the Democratic side, mainly because of the relief programs. More African-Americans were appointed to government positions by Roosevelt than ever before, but the number was still small. Despite some of these advances, Roosevelt seems to have given little thought to the special problems of African-Americans, and he was afraid to endorse legislation such as an anti-lynching bill for fear of alienating the Southern wing of the Democratic Party.

Black protest at the apparent unequal treatment in welfare programs that often wound up excluding blacks from receiving aid finally reached a head. In 1941, in a **March on Washington Movement**, the leader of the porters union planned a huge march. Afraid that the march would lead to riots, FDR promised to outlaw discrimination in war industries in exchange for a cancellation of the march. In **Executive Order No. 9902** on June 25, 1941, in exchange for the cancellation of the march, FDR established the Fair Employment Practices Committee (FEPS).

Native Americans also suffered from the unequal distribution of federal aid during the Great Depression. In 1929, a Supreme Court ruling stated that landless tribes could not receive federal aid. These Native Americans had to wait until 1931 when John Collier, the commissioner of the Bureau of Indian Affairs, persuaded Congress to repeal the Dawes Act of 1887 by passing the **Indian Reorganization Act of 1934.** The law restored tribal ownership of lands, recognized tribal constitutions and government, and provided loans to tribes for economic development.

Mexican-Americans too were not allowed to receive aid as no government programs addressed the needs of migratory farm workers. It was not until 1937 when the government set up the Farm Securities Administration that any aid to those in migratory labor camps was received.

Labor Unions

Labor unions lost members and influence during the 1920s and early 1930s. The National Industrial Recovery Act gave them new hope when it guaranteed the right to unionize, and during 1933, about 1.5 million new members joined unions. The passage of the **National Labor Relations, or Wagner, Act in 1935** resulted in a massive growth of union membership, but at the expense of bitter conflict within the labor movement. The American Federation of Labor was made up primarily of craft unions. Some leaders wanted to unionize the mass-production industries, such as automobiles and rubber, with industrial unions. In November 1935, John L. Lewis and others established the Committee for Industrial Organization to unionize basic industries, presumably within the AFL.

President William Green of the AFL ordered the CIO to disband in January 1936. When the rebels refused, they were expelled by the AFL in March 1937. The insurgents then reorganized the CIO as the independent **Congress of Industrial Organizations**. During its organizational period, the CIO sought to initiate several industrial unions, particularly in the steel, auto, rubber, and radio industries. In late 1936 and early 1937, it used a tactic called the sit-down strike, with the strikers occupying the workplace to prevent any production. By the end of 1941, the CIO was larger than the AFL. Union members comprised about 11.5% of the work force in 1933 and 28.2% in 1941.

COMPETENCY 5.12

Identify the causes, significant individuals, and effects of the events associated with the World War II era.

Belief that the United States should stay out of foreign wars and problems resurrected itself in the 1920s and 1930s. A Gallup poll in April 1937 showed that almost two-thirds of those responding thought that American entry into World War I had been a mistake and many resolved that the United States should not become embroiled in international war again. When the **Nye Commission**, led by Senator Gerald Nye, issued their report in 1936 that revealed American arms manufacturers had lobbied intensely for WWI, had bribed officials then, and were currently supplying Fascist governments with weapons, the public sentiment declared that involvement in European wars was destructive in many ways for America. As tensions gathered in Europe, Congress passed a series of **Neutrality Acts** that reflected the anti-war supporters that had gripped the nation.

The Neutrality Acts:

The Johnson Act of 1934: This law prohibited any nation in default on World War I payments from selling securities to any American citizen or corporation.

The Neutrality Acts of 1935: On outbreak of war between foreign nations, all exports of American arms and munitions to them would be embargoed for six months. In addition, American ships were prohibited from carrying arms to any belligerent, and the president was to warn American citizens not to travel on belligerent ships.

The Neutrality Acts of 1936: The laws gave the president authority to determine when a state of war existed, and prohibited any loans or credits to belligerents.

The Neutrality Acts of 1937: The laws gave the president authority to determine if a civil war was a threat to world peace and if it was covered by the Neutrality Acts. It also prohibited all arms sales to belligerents, and allowed the **cash-and-carry** sale of nonmilitary goods to belligerents.

The Neutrality Act of 1939: Roosevelt officially proclaimed the neutrality of the United States on September 5, 1939. The Democratic Congress, in a vote that followed party lines, passed a new Neutrality Act in November. It allowed the cash-and-carry sale of arms and short-term loans to belligerents, but forbade American ships to trade with belligerents or Americans to travel on belligerent ships.

The American Response to the War in Europe

All the while the United States was proclaiming its neutrality; it simultaneously began to develop contingency and preparatory plans just in case they would be needed. After all, American neutrality before WWI did not weather the whole war. In August 1939, Roosevelt created the **War Resources Board** to develop a plan for industrial mobilization in the event of war. The next month, he established the **Office of Emergency Management** in the White House to centralize mobilization activities.

There was an unusually high level of public interest in what was happening in Europe, and more Americans than ever spoke out on foreign policy, mainly due to the accessibility of information via the radio and the ethnic origins of many recent immigrants. Almost all Americans recognized Germany as a threat. They were divided on whether to aid Britain or to concentrate on the defense of America. The **Committee to Defend America by Aiding the Allies** was formed in May 1940, and the **America First Committee**, which opposed involvement, was incorporated in September 1940. Gradually, however, especially with the fall of France in June 1940, Americans began to change their minds and more talk about America entering the war heightened concerns.

In April 1940, Roosevelt declared that Greenland, a possession of conquered Denmark, was covered by the Monroe Doctrine, and he supplied military assistance to set up a coastal patrol there. In May 1940, Roosevelt appointed a **Council of National Defense**, chaired by William S. Knudson (1879–1948), the president of General Motors, to direct defense production and to build 50,000 planes. The **Office of Production Management** was created to allocate scarce materials, and the **Office of Price Administration** was established to prevent inflation and protect consumers.

Congress approved the nation's first peacetime draft, the **Selective Service and Training Act**, in September 1940. Roosevelt determined that to aid Britain in every way possible was the best way to avoid war with Germany. In September 1940, as Britain ran out of money to buy new war supplies from the United States, Roosevelt signed a **Destroyers for Bases Agreement** to give Britain 50 old American destroyers in return for a 99-year lease on air and naval bases in British territories in Newfoundland, Bermuda, and the Caribbean.

Roosevelt had become so concerned about U.S. involvement in the war that after Hitler had invaded France in 1940, and a takeover of England was in the cards, Roosevelt decided to run for an unprecedented third term, breaking a tradition that had existed since George Washington. He won.

American Involvement with the European War

Roosevelt turned the United States into an "arsenal of democracy" with the **Lend-Lease Act.** The act was pro-active in its objective, much like, as Roosevelt opined, "helping to put out the fire in your neighbor's house before your own house caught fire and burned down." This act allowed the United States to lend armaments to Britain, who no longer could afford to buy them, in exchange for goods and services after the war. It was signed on March 11, 1941. In effect, the Lend-Lease Act ended the pretense of American neutrality. In April 1941, Roosevelt started the American Neutrality Patrol. The American navy would search out but not attack German submarines in the western half of the Atlantic and warn British vessels of their location. Also in April, U.S. forces occupied Greenland. Germany, cognizant that America really was no longer neutral, had its U-boats torpedo the merchant ship the SS Robin Moor that flew under a U.S. flag, outside of the war zone. Reportedly after the ship sank, the German crew pulled up to the captain's lifeboat, gave him four tins of bread and two tins of butter, and explained that the ship had been sunk because she was carrying supplies to Germany's enemy. In May, the president declared a state of unlimited national emergency.

Germany invaded Russia in June 1941. American marines occupied Iceland, a Danish possession, in July 1941 to protect it from seizure by Germany. The American navy began to convoy American and Icelandic ships between the United States and Iceland. On August 9, 1941, Roosevelt and Winston Churchill met on a battleship in Newfoundland and issued the **Atlantic Charter** that outlined their wartime goals, which included disarmament, self-determination, freedom of the seas, and guarantees of each nation's security, despite the fact that the United States was not yet in the war.

The American destroyer *Greer* was shot at (but missed) by a German submarine near Iceland on September 4, 1941. The United States then entered into an undeclared naval war on Germany as Roosevelt ordered the American military forces to shoot on sight any German or Italian vessel in the patrol zone. In addition, American ships began to escort British merchant ships across the Atlantic. The American destroyer *Kearny* was fired on by a submarine on October 16, and the destroyer *Reuben James* was sunk on October 30, with 115 lives lost. In November, Congress eliminated the cash-and-carry policy and allowed the United States to ship munitions to Britain on armed merchant ships. In November, the United States extended lend-lease assistance to the Russians.

Considering all of the activity that was happening between the United States and Germany in the European theater, it strikes one as odd that the direct attack on American soil happened, not from Germany, but from Japan.

The Road to Pearl Harbor and War

After the **Tripartite Pact** that resulted in an alliance between Japan, Germany, and Italy was conducted in September 1940, the United States had to reconsider its dealings with Japan. It embargoed all aviation gasoline, fuel, and metal with Japan. This posed a great threat to Japan who relied on foreign imports and who needed the oil for its war machine. A year later, as Japan occupied French Indochina and seemed an unstoppable force in the Pacific, the United States ended trade altogether with Japan. In October 1941, a new military cabinet headed by General Hideki Tojo took control of Japan. The Japanese secretly decided to make a final effort to negotiate with the United States and to go to war if no solution was found by November 25. A new round of talks followed in Washington, but neither side would make a substantive change in its position, and on November 26, Hull repeated the American demand that the Japanese remove all their forces from China and Indochina immediately.

The Japanese gave final approval on December 1 for an attack on the United States. They planned a major offensive to take the Dutch East Indies, Malaya, and the Philippines in order to obtain the oil, metals, and other raw materials they needed. At the same time, they would attack Pearl Harbor in Hawaii to destroy the American Pacific fleet to keep it from interfering with their plans. The United States meanwhile had broken the Japanese diplomatic codes and knew that trouble was imminent—they just did not know where the attack would occur. Between December 1 and December 6, 1941, it became clear to administration leaders that Japanese task forces were being ordered into battle.

American commanders in the Pacific were warned of possible aggressive action there, but not forcefully.

At 7:55 a.m. on Sunday, December 7, 1941, the first wave of Japanese carrier-based planes attacked the American fleet in Pearl Harbor. A second wave followed at 8:50 a.m. The United States suffered the loss of two battleships sunk, six damaged and out of action, three cruisers and three destroyers sunk or damaged, and a number of lesser vessels destroyed or damaged. All of the 150 aircraft at Pearl Harbor were destroyed on the ground. Worst of all, 2,323 American servicemen were killed and about 1,100 wounded. The Japanese lost 29 planes, five midget submarines, and one fleet submarine.

On December 8, 1941, Roosevelt asked Congress for and received, albeit with one dissenting vote, a declaration of war on Japan. Three days later, on December 11, Germany and Italy declared war on the United States. Great Britain and the United States then established the Combined Chiefs of Staff, headquartered in Washington, to direct Anglo-American military operations. On January 1, 1942, representatives of 26 nations met in Washington, D.C., and signed the **Declaration of the United Nations**, pledging themselves to the principles of the Atlantic Charter and promising not to make a separate peace with their common enemies.

The Home Front

As had happened during other periods of crisis, the federal government acquired and exercised more power, and during the war, the size of the government more than tripled. It established a few key agencies that enabled it to mobilize men and war supplies more effectively.

War Production Board (WPD)—The WPD was established in 1942 to convert the economy from a civilian basis to a wartime economy. The WPD allowed the government to mobilize industry toward the war effort in return for guaranteeing them lucrative profits. The board regulated the use of raw materials. It helped to allocate scarce materials, limit the manufacture of civilian goods so that more military goods could be produced, and was in charge of handing out military production contracts.

National War Labor Board—Created out of the **Labor Disputes Act of 1943**, not only mediated labor-management disputes, but controlled the government takeover of businesses deemed necessary to national security.

Office of Price Administration—Created in 1942, the OPA imposed price controls to stem inflation. It also established **rationing** on almost all consumer goods through local **War Price and Rationing Boards**.

Office of War Mobilization—Coordinated efforts of government agencies, private industry, and military.

Office of Scientific Research and Development—Spent over $1 billion on improving radar, building rockets and aircraft, and making new drugs for soldiers.

Office of War Information (1942)—established to encourage support on the home front by putting out propaganda pieces about the war. Hollywood joined in and created numerous films to boost the morale of troops overseas and to shore up stateside support.

Social Changes at Home

The war brought numerous changes on the Home Front, as it affected almost every aspect of daily life, creating new tensions and exacerbating old ones, providing new opportunities for some and closing the door to others.

One effect that the war had was the migration of Americans to centers of war production. As jobs opened up and new industries developed that were geared to the war effort, people flocked to them. Many moved to the West coast, where new factories opened up to meet war needs. As a result, many left rural areas in the South and moved to the cities in the North and West. In the war-industry cities, housing shortages exacerbated already fragile cities that were suffering from overcrowding. Urban slums grew and conflict between older residents and newcomers resulted in a proliferation of gang-related troubles. Race riots also became more frequent as more African-Americans entered new cities where only few had existed previously. For instance, in 1943 alone, more than 700,000 blacks moved from the South to the West, of which 120,000 moved to Los Angeles.

The war also brought significant changes to the roles of women and the family in American society. More than six million women entered the paid labor force to meet war-industry needs; about one million worked in the aerospace industry alone and over 300,000 enlisted in the armed forces. By 1945, women constituted over one-third of all employed workers. Images of **Rosie the Riveter** plastered throughout American society exemplified the millions of women who joined the workforce in previously male-dominated occupations. Considered to be vital to the nation's war effort, these women were considered temporary workers who did not have to be paid the same as male workers. Moreover, the women were expected to maintain their home responsibilities as well. This proved to be a bit difficult as women were forced to leave their children, oftentimes young children, at home alone while they worked their shifts in the factories. The result was a breakdown in the family and a rise in juvenile delinquency. During this period, perhaps as a result of the wartime strains, marriages, births, and divorces soared.

African-Americans struggled in the war both to fight against America's enemies as well as to fight for equality at home. A planned march on Washington at a time when Roosevelt was worried it would provide fodder for the Axis Powers was canceled when he signed an executive order that created the **Fair Employment Practices Committee** and prohibited discrimination in defense industries and government agencies. In addition, the NAACP and the Congress of Racial Equality campaigned for civil rights for African-Americans during the war. Once the war began, labor shortages forced factory owners to employ African-Americans, so much so that participation in defense industry jumped from 3% to 9% of workers. In addition, more than a million African-Americans served in the Armed forces, but unfortunately usually in segregated units that were commanded by white officers. Few of these would see combat service, with the exception of the **Tuskegee Airmen,** and most of these units were in supply and transportation divisions. The U.S. army would not be desegregated until 1948. Despite these difficulties, African-Americans were given greater opportunities and political power because of their experiences during the war.

Government attacks on civil liberties during the war resulted in the abhorrent treatment of Japanese-Americans during it. Following the attacks on Pearl Harbor, prejudice and attacks on Japanese-Americans erupted. The U.S. government exacerbated the situation by viewing all people of Japanese descent as potential enemy agents. They uprooted over 112,000 Japanese Americans, over two-thirds of whom had been born in the United States and had U.S. citizenship, and placed them in internment camps in the West and Southwest, far away from the Pacific Ocean where there was a fear that a Japanese invasion would take place. None of those who were interned were ever convicted of any collusion with Japan. Most of those who were interned lost their homes and their possessions. The Supreme Court upheld the evacuation and internment of these Americans, building on an earlier case in 1919, **Schenck v. United States,** which stated that a citizen's civil liberties could be restricted during times of war. It was affirmed in **Korematsu v. United States** (1944), which stated that even though compulsory evacuation of large groups from their homes was abhorrent, when U.S. shores were threatened by hostile forces, "the power to protect citizens must be commensurate with the threatened danger."

As the war inched its way to a conclusion, the Allies met to discuss what the fate would be in Europe. They embarked on a series of key conferences to hash out what the post-war world would look like.

The first meeting occurred in **Teheran** from November 28 until December 1, 1943 where Roosevelt, Stalin, and Churchill met to discuss war strategy and the opening of a second front, as well as what the fate would be of Eastern Europe after the war. Stalin left the conference upset with what he saw as lackluster seriousness in fighting Germany. A decision was made at the conference to invade France, and the Soviets agreed to help in the war against Japan as soon as Germany was defeated.

The **Yalta Conference** was the second meeting attended personally by Stalin, Churchill, and Roosevelt. It lasted from February 4–11, 1945. A plan to divide Germany into zones of occupation, which had been devised in 1943 by a committee under British Deputy Prime Minister Clement Attlee, was formally accepted with the addition of a fourth zone taken from the British and American zones for the French to occupy. Berlin, which lay within the Russian Zone, was divided into four zones of occupation also.

The third summit meeting of the Big Three took place at **Potsdam** outside Berlin after the end of the European war but while the Pacific war was still going on. The conference began July 17, 1945, with Stalin, Churchill, and the new American President Harry Truman attending. The meeting did not go very well as the United States and the Soviet Union strongly disagreed over what would happen in Germany and Eastern Europe. However, they did agree that Germany should be disarmed, its war industries dismantled, all Nazis should be removed from government, and that war crimes trials would be held. A Potsdam Declaration, aimed at Japan, called for immediate Japanese surrender and hinted at the consequences that would ensue if it were not forthcoming. While at the conference, American leaders received the news of the successful testing of the first atomic bomb in the New Mexico desert, but the Japanese were given no clear warning that such a destructive weapon might be used against them.

On August 6, 1945, the bomb was dropped by a single plane on Hiroshima, and an entire city disappeared, with the instantaneous loss of 70,000 lives. In time, many other persons died from radiation poisoning and other effects. Since no surrender was received, a second bomb was dropped on Nagasaki, obliterating that city. Even the most fanatical of the Japanese leaders saw what was happening, and surrender came quickly. The only departure from unconditional surrender was to allow the Japanese to retain their emperor

(Hirohito, 1901–1989), but only with the proviso that he would be subject in every respect to the orders of the occupation commander. The formal surrender took place September 2, 1945, in Tokyo Bay on the deck of the battleship *Missouri*, and the occupation of Japan began under the immediate control of the American commander General Douglas MacArthur (1880–1964).

COMPETENCY 5.13

Identify the causes, significant individuals, and effects of the events associated with domestic and foreign affairs during the Cold War era.

The Emergence of the Cold War and Containment

Much of the rivalry that developed between the USSR and the United States developed for a few reasons and became the "third-world war" of the twentieth century:

Power Vacuum: Following the collapse of Germany and Japan and Europe's preoccupation with rebuilding its countries, there was a vacuum of power and questions remained about how and where rebuilding would occur and who would have what role in the old Axis countries.

Decolonization: With the disintegration of the British and French empires outside of Europe, the United States and the USSR competed to gain both military bases and markets in the new countries.

Failure of Diplomacy: As both the United States and the USSR always thought they each had the "right" ideology, there was little regard toward appeasing the other.

U.S. Strategic and Economic needs: The United States wanted to continue expanding its markets through an activist foreign policy.

Truman's Tough Style: Truman's diplomatic style was not appreciated. When Roosevelt died in April 1945, the Soviet Union knew little about Truman, other than that he said to the press in June 1941 when the United States was debating which side of the war it would join: "If we see Germany is winning we ought to help Russia and if Russia is winning we ought to help Germany and that way let them kill as many as possible. . . ." In April 1945 when the Soviet Foreign Minister V. M. Molotov met with Truman for the first time at a brief meeting at the White House on the way to attend the UN conference in San Francisco, Truman reportedly gave Molotov a tongue-lashing and Molotov stormed out of the meeting. Hostility between the two intensified at the conference when the Soviets thought the United States would form a bloc of anti-Soviet nations. In retaliation, Truman ended the lend-lease program to the Soviets and condemned the Soviets for taking over Eastern European countries. Truman's advisor, Secretary of State Byrnes, advocated a "get tough" stance with the Soviets and urged Truman to wield the news of the U.S. atomic bomb over the Russians at the Potsdam conference in order to frighten them into compliance with the U.S. agenda. The Soviets understood what Truman was doing and were annoyed.

Atomic Diplomacy: The USSR's annoyance at the United States trying to scare them into concessions because of their monopoly on the atomic bomb festered. When Truman refused to give the bomb over to an international institution unless all of the world's fissionable materials were also given to an agency, the Soviets surmised that the United States would continue to force their agenda onto the world unless another country developed a weapon as well. The Soviets reinvigorated their campaign to develop an atomic bomb.

U.S. Suspicion of Soviet Intentions: The United States obsessed over what the USSR had the potential to do, not what the reality was. The United States despaired and then geared up for a fight whenever the USSR sought interests in another country. U.S. concerns began when the communist government took over Poland and then Hungary and Czechoslovakia, areas that had been under its control during the end of WWII. The U.S. reaction was that the Soviet Union was trying to take over the world, and the result was a prolonged **cold war** in which both sides used mythological overtones of good versus evil to portray their conflict.

The failure of the Western Powers and the Soviet Union to come to any agreement at Postdam on which areas of influence each would possess or what new political alliances would form, led the United States and the West to give up on the idea that communism and democracy could co-exist in the same space. Instead, the United States turned to the idea that if they could not co-exist or eliminate communism, then they needed to **contain** it. The containment idea was spelled out by **George Kennan** on February 22, 1946, in his capacity as the American *chargé d'affaires* in Moscow. Kennan sent a confidential cable to the State Department referred to as the "Long Telegram." In it, Kennan outlined Soviet policy and intimated that the USSR was on a quest to obliterate the West, as evidenced by a recent speech from Stalin, who indicated that wars between communist and capitalist countries were inevitable and would lead to the destruction ofCapitalism. In March, Churchill's "**Iron Curtain**" speech solidified opposition to Soviet encroachments in Europe.

As would be the case throughout the **Cold War,** competition between the two countries would be played out in others. In 1947, civil war in Greece created a dynamic where the west was on one side and the Soviets were on another. When Great Britain notified the United States that it could no longer support the Greek government in its war against the communist insurgents, Truman asked Congress for $400 million in military and economic aid for Greece as well as neighboring Turkey, which was also in danger. In what became known as the **Truman Doctrine**, he argued that while the United States would not initiate a war with the Soviet Union, it would support all free peoples in countries that were resisting communism.

After Truman's speech, George Kennan wrote an anonymous article in *Foreign Affairs* (he signed it "Mr. X") in which he articulated the policy of **containment**. He argued that the spread of communism beyond the Soviet Union's buffer zone, even if should happen as a result of free, democratic elections, was unacceptable, a threat to U.S. national security and needed to be contained, even if it meant using force.

As part of this containment policy, the United States decided to invest in areas that might be at risk for a Soviet takeover. Chief among the targets was Europe. Secretary of State **George C. Marshall** (1880–1959) proposed in June 1947 that the United States provide economic aid to help rebuild Europe. The following March, Congress passed the European Recovery Program, popularly known as the **Marshall Plan**, which provided more than $12 billion in aid to Europe over the next three years. Although money was offered to Eastern Europe and the Soviet Union, they did not take it.

After the United States, France, and Great Britain announced plans to create a West German Republic out of their German zones, the Soviet Union in June 1948 blocked surface access to Berlin. The United States then instituted the **Berlin Airlift** to transport supplies to the city until the Soviets lifted their blockade in May 1949. The crisis in Berlin prompted the formation in April 1949 of **NATO (North Atlantic Treaty Organization)** which was signed by the United States, Canada, Great Britain, and nine European nations. The signatories pledged that an attack against one would be considered an attack against all. The Soviets formed the **Warsaw Treaty Organization** in 1955 to counteract NATO. Shortly after the creation of NATO, the Soviets exploded their first atomic bomb in 1949. This prompted the creation of the **National Security Council** and the **Central Intelligence Agency**.

If the U.S. problems with the Soviet Union in Europe were not enough, it received a shock when Chiang Kai-shek's Nationalist government, to whom the United States had given more than $2 billion in aid between 1945 and 1948, lost out against **Mao Zedong's** communist insurgents. Once Mao took office, the United States refused to enter into any diplomatic relations with him, effectively pushing Mao into dealing with the Soviet Union and Stalin, whom Mao already did not like. It would not be until 1979 that the United States would formally recognize the People's Republic of China.

The conflict with communism resulted in mass hysteria in the United States and the start of a second **Red Scare**, just as Americans had faced after WWI. In order to counteract charges that liberal Democrats were soft on communists, the Truman Administration set up **Loyalty Boards** to investigate the loyalty of all three million federal government workers in an effort to locate any security risks. Federal administrators—not judges— ran the hearings without having to bother with rules of evidence, testifying under oath, and with no penalty for perjury. These Boards kept trial-like transcripts, however, and regularly leaked their results to the press. For many citizens, persons named as suspected members of the Communist Party were considered guilty of treason. Unlike a court system, however, the Loyalty Boards could not imprison people; they could only fire them. But, anyone who was fired was **blacklisted**. To make matters worse, the Truman Justice Department compiled lists of organizations that opposed American foreign policy. Since American foreign policy was essentially anti-communist, any one or any group who opposed U.S. actions was considered communists. The Attorney General's office circulated membership lists of such disfavored groups.

This bred a whole atmosphere of fear within American society. Anyone who was found to have a weakness, be it previous associations with "known communists," alcoholics, or homosexuals, was dismissed from the government without a hearing. **Alger Hiss,** a former State Department diplomat who served as Roosevelt's advisor at Yalta, was accused of disloyalty by Whittaker Chambers, a confessed Soviet spy, who asserted Hiss had given him classified documents. Hiss sued Chambers for libel and was even defended by Truman. Ultimately, however, he was convicted, not of espionage, but of perjury in 1950. Democrats, many of whom supported Hiss, were seen as being soft on communism. After Hiss, Americans began to fear that there were enemies in the United States, just waiting to get them and destroy the country.

The House of Representatives created the **House Un-American Activities Committee** and launched an investigation into purported communist influence in the movie business. They targeted writers, directors, actors, and studio executives, brought them in to testify, and then inquired whether they "were now or had ever been a member of the

Communist Party." The movie industry, worried about what effect this would have on their own profits, launched their own communist hunt and brought in ex-FBI agents to clean up the studios. Agents made lists of anyone who had suspicious political beliefs and many of these individuals were blacklisted and did not work for the studios again. Some writers, however, worked under known *nom de plumes* and were able to continue to work, albeit quietly. The agents recorded anyone thought to possess suspicious political beliefs on a blacklist.

In 1950, Julius and Ethel Rosenberg and Harry Gold were charged with giving atomic secrets to the Soviet Union. The Rosenbergs were convicted and executed in 1953. By 1950, after the double shock of the Soviets exploding the atomic bomb and the Chinese takeover by the Communist Party, the Truman government decided that it needed to take the worldwide lead in resisting communism. In April, 1950, it issued a report, **NSC-68**, that stated the United States should take a lead in stopping communism wherever it occurred, without respect to its strategic or economic value to the United States. This led to a major expansion of American military power along with increased defense spending. It also directly dictated the U.S. response to communism, played a role in its participation in the Korean and Viet Nam wars and explained how the United States would view any country who tried to gain its independence from colonial powers if they turned to the Soviet Union for help.

Senator McCarthy began to deliver speeches about the Communist influence that had wormed its way through the U.S. government. In a speech in February 1950, he declared that he had a list of more than 200 communists who were currently in the State Department. He continued to lead a campaign of innuendo that destroyed the lives of many thousands of innocent people. He held years of hearings in an effort to root out communists. Those who were subpoenaed were forced to confess to associations with communists. Industries created blacklists that prevented these people from working. When McCarthy accused the Army of harboring communists and started a televised series of **Army-McCarthy Hearings**, McCarthy had pushed too far. The Army fought back, with the help of **Edward R. Murrow**'s television show, and McCarthy was made to look foolish. In 1954, he was censured by the Senate for his activities. Finally, the public turned against him, and the era of McCarthyism ended.

Efforts to contain the spread of communism led the United States into the **Korean War**. On June 25, 1950, North Korea invaded South Korea. President Truman committed U.S. forces commanded by General MacArthur, but under United Nations auspices. By

October, the UN forces (mostly American) had driven north of the 38th parallel, which divided North and South Korea. Chinese troops attacked MacArthur's forces on November 26, pushing them south of the 38th parallel, but by spring 1951, the UN forces had recovered their offensive. In June 1953, an armistice was signed, leaving Korea divided along virtually the same boundary that had existed prior to the war.

Cold War under Eisenhower

The Eisenhower administration basically kept Truman's policies toward the communists, but instead of calling the policy "containment," they called it liberation. Attendant to that idea was the threat that perhaps the United States would free Eastern Europe from Soviet control. Eisenhower's policy was termed New Look and characterized the plan that should there be war, it would not be conventional, but rather massive retaliation with nuclear weapons. The fear of massive retaliation was supposed to be a deterrent for any Soviet action that would put such an attack in motion. Dulles allowed confrontations with the Soviets to be taken to the edge of war, an approach called brinksmanship. Dulles and the Eisenhower administration popularized the domino theory that if one nation would fall to communism, then nations around it would also fall like dominos.

There was, however, a fatal flaw in Eisenhower's doctrine of massive retaliation, as it left the United States without any other option than nuclear war to combat Soviet aggression. In 1956 when the Soviet Union put down a democratic uprising in Hungary, the United States could not provide the asked-for assistance, as Eisenhower knew that such a move would turn the Cold War into a nuclear war over an inconsequential issue. So, he realized that in addition to his liberation and massive retaliation policies, he also needed to work quietly in a more indirect manner in order to control the communist menace. He used the CIA, headed by Dulles' brother, Allen Dulles, to plant fake stories in newspapers, train foreign military officials, and launch a variety of covert operations to subvert any governments around the world considered "too friendly" to the communists. The Eisenhower administration also tried to spread American culture and thereby discontent in the USSR through the United States Information Agency, which funded the Voice of America. There was also Radio Free Europe and Radio Liberty, funded by the CIA, which sent anti-Soviet messages around the world.

With this atmosphere and Eisenhower's policies, Cold War tensions remained high throughout the decade. With the death of Joseph Stalin in 1953, there was some hope that relations between the United States and USSR would improve. However, this was short lived. While initially Nikita Khrushchev offered the idea of peaceful coexistence among nations with different philosophies of government and economics, he became more aggressive with Eastern bloc countries who wanted to use the idea of "peaceful coexistence" to break free of Soviet control. When the Soviets crushed these rebellions, relations between the United States and USSR worsened. Soviet advances in science, like the explosion of the hydrogen bomb, development of the first Inter-Continental Ballistic Missile (ICBM), and launching Sputnik into space, created enormous anxiety within the administration as well as a determination to win the space race with the creation of NASA (National Aeronautics and Space Administration).

Some other big events under the Eisenhower Administration that affected the Cold War included:

- **Khrushchev's Ultimatum** (1958): The USSR employed their own feeble attempt at brinksmanship when they expressed anger about the bombers that the United States had in West Germany. The Soviets announced that unless talks began immediately on German reunification and disarmament, they would recognize East German control of all of Berlin. The United States did not do anything in response, and the Soviets backed down.

- **U-2 Incident** (1960): In 1960, the Soviet Union shot down an American **U-2 spy plane.** Eisenhower and the U.S. government initially denied that the United States was flying any U-2 missions over the Soviet Union. However, when the USSR produced the captured American pilot who was still alive, the United States had to admit it. However, Eisenhower refused to apologize or promise to suspend future spy missions against the USSR.

- In 1957, in order to protect American oil interests in the Middle East, Eisenhower announced the **Eisenhower Doctrine**, which stated that the United States would provide military and economic assistance to any Middle Eastern countries who resisted communist insurgents. This resulted in a variety of actions in the Middle East.

- While earlier than the official Eisenhower Doctrine, the United States ordered a CIA-orchestrated coup over Mohammed Mossadeq in Iran, which resulted in the re-installation of Mohammed Reza Pahlavi as Shah. This would prove to be an enormous long-term mistake that severely damaged the U.S. reputation in the region, and is referred to over and over again today as one of the reasons for the anti-American movement in the Middle East.

- **Suez Crisis**: Another tool the United States used during the Cold War was to offer foreign aid in order to get countries to comply with what it wanted and to turn away from the Soviet Union. In the case of Egypt, however, when funding for **Gamal 'Abd al-Nasser**'s hallmark Aswan Dam project that was supposed to provide electricity and additional farming land in Upper Egypt fell through, Nasser turned to the Soviets for aid and then seized the British-controlled Suez Canal—which had fallen under British control after Egypt's declaration of bankruptcy. Great Britain and France asked Eisenhower for military assistance to retake the canal, but Eisenhower refused. This forced the two powers to join with **Israel** and invade the **Suez** in 1956. Fearing that such an invasion would force the Egyptians into the arms of the Soviets, Eisenhower condemned the attack on Egypt and exerted heavy diplomatic and economic pressure on the aggressors. Unable to sustain the action in the face of U.S. disapproval and financial pressures, they all withdrew, Egypt retook the Canal, and the Soviets built the Aswan Dam.

- American Intervention in the Third World: With the fall of Britain and France's colonial empires, many of the new countries were reluctant to become pawns in the Cold War and were more intent on cementing their own nationalist struggles for power and doing what they needed to do as "new" nations, free of colonial control. The United States tried to expand its influence in these areas in controversial ways:

  - *Guatemala*: In 1951, leftist leader **Guzmán** was elected President, and once he decided to expropriate all of United Fruit's (big U.S. company) unused land, the United Fruit officials claimed he was a communist, which led to the generation of a CIA plot to overthrow him. In 1954, CIA-supported troops drove him from power, and the new pro-U.S. regime returned the land before a huge civil war erupted. The coup drew enormous amounts of criticism around the world and severely damaged U.S.-Latin America relations.

- *Cuba*: In 1959, the **Cuban Revolution** erupted–Batista was ousted, and **Fidel Castro** took control. From the start, Castro was anti-American and confiscated a lot of U.S. business interests there. Washington responded by cutting purchases of Cuban sugar. Castro responded to that by nationalizing all of the U.S. companies there, asking the Soviets for loans and to pick up the trade slack left by the Americans. Eisenhower broke off diplomatic relations with Cuba.

- *Indochina*: Vietnamese nationalists under the leadership of Ho Chi Minh had sought independence from France. Ho Chi Minh turned to the Soviet Union in the 1950s after U.S. officials had rebuffed his earlier requests for help in securing independence. The USSR supplied money and arms to Ho Chi Minh, which forced Eisenhower to support the other side–this time, the French colonial regime, in order to contain the USSR. It poured in money in an attempt to control communism and that laid the foundation for U.S. troop involvement in the Vietnam War

Cold War in the 1960s

Under Eisenhower, the Central Intelligence Agency had begun training some 2,000 Cuban exiles for an invasion of Cuba to overthrow Fidel Castro, the left-leaning revolutionary who had taken power in 1959. On April 19, 1961, this force invaded at the **Bay of Pigs** but was pinned down and forced to surrender. Some 1,200 men were captured and Kennedy was left with an embarrassing situation and irate Soviets who had been antagonized.

In August 1961, Khrushchev closed the border between East and West Berlin and ordered the erection of the Berlin Wall. The Soviet Union began the testing of nuclear weapons in September 1961. Kennedy then authorized resumption of underground testing by the United States.

By 1961, both the Soviet Union and the United States had invested huge amounts of money in nuclear weapons, both as an attempt to maintain parity with each other's stockpiles, but also because they believed that such stockpiles served as a means of deterrence. With ever-expanding nuclear stockpiles, both realized it was not good enough to have the weapons, but they needed to be put in places where they could actually be launched. The United States put missiles in Turkey and the Soviets put missiles in Cuba. When U.S. spy planes and satellite pictures revealed the Soviet military bases and missiles in Cuba, Kennedy used brinksmanship to confront the crisis. He instituted a naval quarantine of Cuba, went on national TV and issued an ultimatum for missiles to be removed. Krushchev denounced the blockade and readied Soviet missiles for launch. The U.S. forces were placed on highest alert and were ready to "push the button." Kennedy and Krushchev reached a secret agreement: the Soviet Union would remove missiles if the U.S. agreed not to attack Cuba and removed missiles from Turkey. As the American public did not know about the missiles in Turkey, when the crisis was averted, it was assumed that it was because Kennedy had forced the Soviets to back down and that the United States had won. Recent scholarship has suggested otherwise and holds that it was Krushchev who actually was the hero in the crisis.

Krushchev and Kennedy were startled by how close they came to nuclear war and they set up a hotline between the two nations. This marked a shift in Cold War policy, away from direct confrontation and toward negotiation, in a new phase called **détente**, which, however, was not articulated as such until the Nixon administration. In 1963, both nations agreed to a treaty banning atomic tests in the atmosphere and the oceans.

It was also in the early 1960s that American containment policy shifted from heavy reliance on nuclear weapons to more conventional notions of warfare in pursuit of a more **"flexible response"** to the spread of communism. Kennedy and his Defense Secretary, **Robert S. McNamara,** crafted the flexible response doctrine that would enable the United States to combat Soviet forces around the world through a variety of means, money, troops, CIA coups, or, as a last resort, nuclear weapons.

Kennedy first applied his new doctrine to **Vietnam**, where U.S. funding of **Ngo Dinh Diem**'s corrupt South Vietnamese regime offended most South Vietnamese. The United States realized that money alone would not solve the issue, so, in an effort to prevent communist-backed insurgents from taking control of South Vietnam, Kennedy decided to send 15,000 troops to Saigon as **"military advisors."** With that, the United States became more deeply embroiled in the conflict, which turned into a costly mistake that two more U.S. presidents and the United States would have to deal with. In 1965, President Johnson committed more combat troops to Vietnam and announced that it was his intention to defend South Vietnam "whatever the cost or whatever the challenge."

The United States ultimately fought a bloody and costly war in Vietnam that poisoned U.S. politics and wreaked havoc with its economy. The Nixon administration inherited the conflict in 1969 and it was not until 1973 under the guise of a peace agreement that the United States left South Vietnam in what many regarded as a "loss" for the United States.

Cold War and Détente in the 1970s and 1980s

Nixon's approach to the Cold War was reflected in two ideologies that he had. Together Nixon and Kissinger came up with the term **détente,** which called for countries to respect each other's differences and to cooperate more closely with one another. Détente ushered in a relaxation of tensions that would last until the Soviet Union's invasion of Afghanistan in 1979. Moreover, Nixon issued his **Nixon Doctrine,** which announced that the United States would withdraw from its overseas troop commitments and instead rely on alliances with local governments to check the spread of Communism.

As proof in the thaw of tensions between communists and the United States, Nixon travelled to Communist China, a country which the United States had earlier refused to recognize. Nixon's trip eased tensions with China and opened the door to trade relations with it. It also enabled him to play his friendship with the Chinese off of the Soviet Union—as China and the Soviet Union, the world's two largest and most powerful communist countries, hated one another.

By the end of the 1970s, however, the chance for an extended thaw utterly vanished when the 1979 Soviet invasion of Afghanistan significantly soured U.S.-Soviet relations. Seeking to place a greater emphasis on human rights in his foreign policy, Carter angrily denounced the incursion and boycotted the 1980 Olympics.

With the election of Ronald Reagan, who spoke of waging war with the Communists wherever they may be, relations with the Soviet Union worsened considerably. In order to back up his threat, he dramatically increased military spending in the early 1980s. He backed up his military spending with harsh rhetoric when he called the Soviet Union, **"the evil empire."**

With the ascension in 1985 of **Mikhail Gorbachev** as head of the Soviet Union, change was in the air. Gorbachev believed that if the USSR were to survive, he needed to engage in a series of reforms, or opening. His package of liberal reforms was referred to as **perestroika,** and he embarked on an opening of relations with the West, a policy called

glasnost. By the time Reagan left the White House, tensions between the Soviet Union and the United States were quite warm. Despite improved East-West relations, however, Gorbachev's reforms were unable to prevent the collapse of a system that had grown rigid and unworkable. By most measures, the Soviet economy had failed to grow at all since the late 1970s, and much of the country's populace had grown weary of the aged Communist hierarchy. In 1989, the spontaneous destruction of the Berlin Wall signaled the end of Soviet domination in Eastern Europe, and two years later, the Soviet government itself fell from power. Thus marked the end of the Cold War, a period that had lasted for 46 years.

COMPETENCY 5.14

Identify the causes, significant individuals, and effects of the events associated with movements for equality, civil rights, and civil liberties in the nineteenth and twentieth centuries.

Civil Rights

Civil rights are those legal claims that individuals have to protect themselves from discrimination at the hands of both the government and other citizens. They include the right to vote, equality before the law, and access to public facilities. **Individual** or **civil liberties** protect the sanctity of the person from arbitrary governmental interference. In this category belong the fundamental freedoms of speech, religion, press, and rights such as **due process** (government must act fairly and follow established procedures, as in legal proceedings).

1877–1900: Reconstruction and Its Failures

The campaign for civil rights began long before the age where many think it originated, between the 1950s and 1970s. It actually had begun nearly a century earlier, during Reconstruction in the 1860s and 1870s. After the Civil War, Congress realized that it had a lot to do to protect former slaves. As one freedman, Houston Hartsfield Holloway, noted, "For we colored people did not know how to be free and the white people did not know how to have a free colored person about them." It passed a series of civil rights laws, and the states ratified three amendments to the Constitution to protect former slaves. But, it did not work. A combination of events resulted in many of the former slaves being unable to take advantage of their newfound freedom and most being held in a sort of economic bondage as sharecroppers who worked for under-handed white landowners and **Jim Crow** laws that kept them in inferior positions throughout the South.

Emancipation Proclamation, 1863: Lincoln's proclamation freed African-Americans in rebel states.

Thirteenth Amendment: emancipated all U.S. slaves wherever they were.

Civil Rights Act of 1866: enabled blacks to file lawsuits against whites and sit on juries. To safeguard these rights permanently, states ratified the **Fourteenth Amendment** and enfranchised black men with the **Fifteenth Amendment**.

Ku Klux Klan Act of 1871: outlawed racial terrorism.

Civil Rights Act of 1875: prohibited racial discrimination in most public places but was declared unconstitutional by a Southern-backed Supreme Court in 1883.

Fourteenth Amendment, defined citizenship; however, the Supreme Court held that it did not protect blacks from discrimination by privately owned businesses, and that they would have to seek equal protection from the states, not the federal government.

Black Codes and **Jim Crow** laws: Local statutes that "kept blacks in their place" and made loitering, unemployment, indebtedness, voting, and having sex with white women illegal offense for blacks. As a result, racism became legal. These codes gave impetus to groups like the KKK to terrorize blacks. This was exacerbated after the Supreme Court's 1896 decision in **Plessy v. Ferguson** that set up the "separate but equal" premise that would be used to make life difficult for blacks.

Radical Republicans also tried to use the **Freedmen's Bureau** to redistribute confiscated Southern plantation lands to blacks in order to put them on more equal footing with white farmers. In addition to these measures, Congress sent federal troops into the South to help blacks register to vote.

Significant Individuals: 1877–1900

Ignored for the most part by white progressives after the Civil War, blacks realized that they needed to better articulate their needs and provide a vision for their struggle. There were two approaches, characterized by **Booker T. Washington** and **W.E.B. DuBois**.

Booker T. Washington, a former slave, represented a rural point of view that embraced ideas of accommodation, rather than aggression. Harboring no illusions that white society would accept blacks any time soon, he urged blacks to strive for economic independence. He reasoned that the best way to do that was through self-help and hard work. To that end, he founded a vocational and technical college in Alabama for blacks, called the **Tuskegee Institute**. Washington argued in his "Atlanta Exposition," a famous speech that he delivered in Atlanta, Georgia in 1895, that social equality and political rights would come only if blacks first became self-reliant and improved their financial footing. In time, he believed, white Americans would eventually respect them. He pleaded for **accommodation** and he refused to press for immediate equal rights, believing pragmatically that it was too soon to do so. He did push for an end to segregation and supported organizations bent on securing political rights for more blacks.

W.E.B. DuBois: The other point of view, which tended to represent a more urban view, was that accommodation would doom blacks to poverty and second-class citizenship. Dubois felt that blacks should not have to tolerate white domination and should immediately fight for their social and political rights. He called on blacks to develop a **black consciousness** that would be distinct from that of whites and would emanate from an understanding of black history, art, music, and religion. In 1905, DuBois founded the **Niagara Movement,** which called for federal legislation to protect racial equality and for full rights of citizenship. Two years later, in conjunction with white liberals, DuBois headed the **National Association for the Advancement of Colored People (NAACP) that** advocated an end to discrimination. His quest proved to be so strenuous that he eventually left the United States and moved to Africa.

1900–1950: Early Twentieth Century Roots of the Civil Rights Era

National Business League (NBL): founded in 1900 by Booker T. Washington in the spirit of accommodation and his belief that blacks should "pull themselves up by their own bootstraps" through manual education and black capitalism. The NBL was meant to encourage blacks to accept segregation, to start their own businesses, and to frequent those establishments owned by blacks.

- **NAACP**: Formed in 1909 by W.E.B. DuBois and other bi-racial activists sought to educate whites on the need for racial equality while also trying to gain more political and legal rights for blacks. It tackled the Supreme Court's "separate but equal ruling," and launched desegregation suits in many different states. The NAACP also worked for anti-lynching laws, as lynchings, public whippings, tarring, and feathering and other KKK inspired tortures had reached an all-time high in the mid-1920s, and the urgency of the NAACP's intervention rose as well.

- **Harlem Renaissance**: Considered the first important movement of black artists and writers in the United States , black artists and writers flocked to the largest black neighborhood of New York City to promote W.E.B. DuBois' idea of cultivating "black consciousness" in order to achieve equality. Middle-class black artists and intellectuals flocked to the area and to some of the writing centers that DuBois started. These writers, like Zora Neal Hurston, Langston Hughes, Claude McKay, and Countee Cullen, sought to develop an appreciation and recognition of black culture. They also pushed the idea of the "New Negro," which would be someone who would provide a new vision of the Black American, not one viewed as inherently inferior or conform to degrading black stereotypes, and one independent of white stereotypes, one who was militant, self-assertive, and proud of his race.

- **Universal Negro Improvement Association (UNIA)**: Started in Jamaica by Marcus Garvey in 1914 to help blacks achieve economic independence in the United States and around the world. It also encouraged blacks to go back and settle in their ancestral homes in Africa.

- *Missouri ex rel. Gaines v. Canada,* 1938: The Supreme Court ruled that states that provide a school for white students need to provide an in-state school for blacks as well. They ordered that the University of Missouri had to build an entirely new law school for blacks or simply integrate them into the existing all-white school. This case marked the beginning of the Supreme Court's reconsideration of the "separate but equal" standard; however, it did not strike down segregation as it stated that if there were just one school available, then members of both races could attend it.

- **Tuskegee Airmen:** An elite all-black bomber unit in World War II who challenged stereotypes that black men lacked intelligence, skill, courage, and patriotism.

- **Congress of Racial Equality (CORE)**: launched peaceful protests in order to gain sympathy from white Americans

- **Executive Order 8802**: FDR's hand was forced, in an effort to prevent a march on Washington, which would be embarrassing for the United States and give a boost to the Axis powers, to pass a civil rights measure that outlawed racial discrimination in the federal government and in war factories. Roosevelt also established the **Fair Employment Practices Committee** to execute the order. As a result, more than 200,000 blacks found work in defense-related industries during the war. This also set the trend of Democrats having the support of blacks in elections, which would end up being significant in the quest for civil rights legislation in the 1960s.

- **President's Committee on Civil Rights:** Truman established this committee in 1946 to push for anti-lynching laws in the South and tried to register more black voters. Although symbolically powerful, the committee had little practical influence.

- *Morgan v. Virginia* **(1946) :** Eleven years before Rosa Parks would refuse to move to the back of the bus, 27-year-old Irene Morgan was jailed for refusing to give up her seat on a bus to a white person. Thurgood Marshall, as chief counsel for the NAACP at the time and who took up Morgan's case, chose to argue the case, not under the Equal Protection clause of the Fourteenth Amendment, but rather under the Interstate Commerce clause in the Constitution. The Supreme Court ruled that segregated interstate buses were illegal as they put an "undue burden on interstate trade and transport." This struck down laws requiring segregation, but only in instances where interstate transportation was concerned.

- **Executive Order 9981:** Truman ordered the desegregation of the armed forces in 1948.

- *Sweatt v. Painter* **(1950):** Heman Marion Sweatt filed this lawsuit when he was denied admittance into the University of Texas Law School in 1946 because he was an African-American. Thurgood Marshall and the NAACP took his case. As the case went through the court system, Texas built an all-black law school in a different part of the state, thinking this satisfied the requirements of *Mis-*

souri ex rel. Gaines v. Canada. But, the Supreme Court ruled that the new school was not really an equivalent to the University of Texas because, as in the cases of graduate schools, there is something more important in the school than just four walls. In this case, the Supreme Court stated, quantitative differences in facilities and intangible factors, such as its isolation from most of the future lawyers with whom its graduates would interact, made the two schools incomparable. So, the Equal Protection Clause of the Fourteeth Amendment mandated that Sweatt be admitted to the previously all-white university law school. This decision made it clear that segregation was doomed.

- *McLaurin v. Oklahoma State Regents* (1950): Another Thurgood Marshall-argued case that resulted in the Supreme Court decision that stated that an institution of higher learning could not provide different treatment to a student based on his race. Marshall had argued that segregated cafeterias, libraries, and seats in classrooms placed a "bade of inferiority" on black students.

Significant Individuals: 1900–1950

Marcus Garvey: A native of Jamaica, Garvey moved to Harlem and founded the U.S. chapter of the UNIA, advocated African-American racial pride and separatism rather than integration, and called for a return of African-Americans to Africa. In 1921, he proclaimed himself the provisional president of an African empire and sold stock in the Black Star Steamship Line that would take migrants to Africa. The line went bankrupt in 1923, and Garvey was convicted and imprisoned for mail fraud in the sale of the line's stock and then deported. His legacy was an emphasis on African-American pride and self-respect.

A. Philip Randolph: President of the National Negro Congress who threatened FDR with a march on Washington if the federal government did not pass civil rights legislation.

Thurgood Marshall : During this period, the future first African-American on the Supreme Court was the chief counsel of the NAACP. Marshall presented case after case to the Supreme Court in attempts to tear down segregation statues. His landmark victories helped chip away at segregation.

1950–1968: Civil Rights Era

The NAACP had been fighting throughout the 1940s and 1950s to attack segregation. Their efforts, slowly chipping away at the policy through the efforts of chief counsel, Thurgood Marshall, would finally result in a tremendous verdict in ***Brown v. Board of Education of Topeka (1954)*** that would result in an overturning of *Plessy v. Ferguson (1896),* which had set up the "separate but equal" standard. This in turn would give momentum to a vibrant Civil Rights Movement.

Brown v. Board of Education of Topeka (1954): The Supreme Court agreed to hear five cases regarding public school desegregation and filed under the collective name of "Brown" on the behalf of Linda Brown, a black school-aged child. The NAACP, led by Thurgood Marshall, used sociological and psychological research to argue that school segregation created feelings of inferiority among the students and thereby provided an inherently unequal education that denied kids equal protection under the law. The Supreme Court, after six months of deliberation, returned a unanimous decision that "separate educational facilities are inherently unequal" and ordered schools to desegregate. As no time frame was issued, Southern states plod slowly ahead on any desegregation. In 1955, the Supreme Court ruled in ***Brown v. Board II*** that they needed to desegregate "with all deliberate speed," so Southern schools resisted.

Reaction to the Brown decision was problematic. Southern states chose to make schools private and have students pay tuition in order to avoid desegregation. Some states closed schools rather than desegregate. President Eisenhower did not support the decision, calling Chief Justice Earl Warren's appointment the worst mistake he ever made. Eisenhower opposed rapid change and objected to compulsory federal segregation laws. Federal agencies hindered desegregation, the FBI was obstructionist, and the Departments of Agriculture and House permitted segregation in their policies. Southern congressmen signed the **Southern Manifesto** that called *Brown* a "clear abuse of judicial power." In **Little Rock, Arkansas,** in 1957, the governor of Arkansas called in the National Guard to prevent students from enrolling in a Little Rock high school. Mobs joined in and the situation was dangerous. Eisenhower did not want to get involved, but he did not want the publicity of mobs running amok in the streets of Little Rock. So, he reluctantly was forced to send in 10,000 National Guardsmen and 1,000 army paratroopers to ensure the students' safety, enforce the desegregation order, and enable African-Americans to enroll in the local high school. In response, schools there, and in Virginia, which was facing a similar court order, were closed for the following two years to avoid desegregation. The school closings created a crisis in the South with groups organizing **Save Our Schools** (S.O.S.) campaigns who wanted schools to remain open and traditionalists who did not.

Blacks responded to both the momentum that the *Brown* decision gave them as well as to the alarming white response by engaging in their own activism. The first major mass black activist movements came with bus boycotts.

On December 11, 1955, in Montgomery, Alabama, **Rosa Parks**, a black woman, refused to give up her seat on a city bus to a white and was arrested. Under the leadership of **Martin Luther King, Jr.**, an African-American pastor, they formed the **Montgomery Improvement Association** and African-Americans of Montgomery organized a bus boycott that lasted for a year, until in December 1956, the Supreme Court refused to review a lower court ruling that stated that separate but equal was no longer legal.

Sit-ins began to characterize the next phase in the Civil Rights Movement. Blacks started a campaign of sit-ins, peaceful, massive, and non-violent protest, which was met with violent reaction by Southern whites who attacked the non-violent protesters on a regular basis.

On February 1, 1960, upon being denied service, four African-American students staged a sit-in in the "white's only" section of a Woolworth lunch counter in Greensboro, North Carolina. Even though they were refused service, the four men remained sitting at the counter until the store closed. The next day, the four men returned along with over two dozen others and sat down and remained quietly at the counter until the store closed. More and more students flocked to Woolworths throughout the day and each day thereafter, numbering in the hundreds. By the end of the week, hundreds of black students and even several white students were waiting patiently for service in Woolworth's, with several hundred more at other restaurants in Greensboro. Although the students temporarily disbanded to negotiate a settlement, the Greensboro sit-in resumed the following spring when local business leaders refused to cave in to the protesters' demands. Blacks continued to boycott segregationist stores such as Woolworth's until the desperate merchants finally conceded that summer and desegregated the lunch counter.

The sit-in movement quickly spread throughout North Carolina and into Virginia and South Carolina. The sit-in movement consisted largely of black college students who were young, well educated, and upwardly mobile but were upset because, despite their education, there were little opportunities for them to enter the job force. While the sit-in movement itself was spontaneous, as it became more successful, civil rights leaders started to organize the protests and eventually, the sit-ins inspired thousands elsewhere in the South and led to the formation of the **Student Nonviolent Coordinating Committee**.

Student Nonviolent Coordination Committee (SNCC) formed when other groups tried to organize the students and the students decided that they wanted to remain independent. The SNCC formed their own organization, attempted to orchestrate more sit-ins, but when that idea failed, they decided to take their operations to rural areas where they would work to organize rural voting efforts for blacks. Their organization grew over time, from 40 workers in 1960 to 1,000 workers in 1964. Their numbers swelled largely because they were able to keep a clean reputation, free of violence (although this was not always successful). They set up a **Voter Education Project** and remained rather aloof from the more flashy civil rights leaders like Martin Luther King, Jr., who they saw swooping into an area, grabbing headlines, and swiftly leaving again. They also grew more distrustful of the federal government and its inability or refusal to help protect the SNCC from violence. The SNCC, perhaps because of the above, gradually became more radical and started to demand changes in the federal system. The SNCC drew criticism from other civil rights activists because they feared that the provocative sit-ins would destroy all of the work they had done over the years. Many all-black schools punished and expelled SNCC members. Despite the disapproval from black sources, many whites who had read about the sit-ins and the harassments that the protesters had to go through, wound up supporting and sympathizing with the students.

Congress of Racial Equality: Led by James Farmer, CORE, originally a mainly white, middle-class group, underwent a membership change and more blacks joined it. Like the SNCC, CORE focused on helping local people in the Deep South. While the SNCC concentrated on efforts in Alabama and Mississippi, CORE focused on Louisiana.

- **Freedom Rides (1961):** CORE organized a biracial **Freedom Ride** of seven black and six white people who boarded interstate buses to travel through the South in an effort to desegregate bus terminals, as was required by federal law. They hoped that media attention and the likely arrests and public harassment that followed would force President Kennedy and his brother, the Attorney General, to intervene. In May 1961, blacks and whites boarded buses in Washington, D.C., and traveled across the South to New Orleans to test federal enforcement of regulations prohibiting discrimination. They faced only mild opposition until they met a mob of white supremacists ten days later in Alabama. The mob, likely composed of KKK members, fire-bombed the bus and assaulted the Freedom Riders on board, nearly killing two of them. Once they arrived in Birmingham, another mob attacked them while police just watched nearby. Wounded and unsuccessful, the riders returned to the North and let the SNCC Freedom Riders take over. These new riders encountered severe opposition in Montgomery, Alabama, where yet another mob carrying iron pipes attacked the students. Police eventually arrested the SNCC Freedom Riders on charges of disturbing the peace. The Freedom Riders were put in small, windowless jail cells and were mistreated. Just as the protesters had hoped, the mob violence and police inaction in Birmingham and Montgomery outraged President Kennedy and were a major embarrassment for the U.S. government. In response, Kennedy sent 400 federal agents to prevent further violence in Montgomery and pushed the **Interstate Commerce Commission** to clarify its regulations regarding segregation on interstate buses. The success of the CORE and SNCC Freedom Rides prompted chapter organizations to sponsor their own rides in the Deep South throughout the 1960s.

- **Birmingham, Alabama** (1963): In April, 1963, Martin Luther King, Jr., and the SCLC helped launch a series of nonviolent demonstrations in Birmingham, considered the most segregated city in America, to desegregate public facilities in the city. The activists organized boycotts and sit-ins to goad white residents and city officials into reacting. Birmingham was committed to its policy of segregation. The Police Commissioner, Eugene "Bull" Connor, personally supervised effort to break up the marches by using police dogs, tear gas, clubs, electric cattle prods, and fire hoses to break up the demonstrations. The attacks on the demonstrators were televised and raised concerns about the issue far outside of the South. Demonstrations in other cities across the country were held in support of the Birmingham demonstrators. Alas, Birmingham remained unmoved. King, in a bold and perhaps reckless move, allowed hundreds of high school children to join the marches, calling it a **children's crusade**. Connor ordered the police to treat the children just like the grown-up marchers. The police department had a difficult time using violence against the little children. King himself was arrested again, and in jail, he took the opportunity to write his influential "Letter from Birmingham Jail," in which he explained the Civil Rights Movement to his many critics. The letter was published and circulated throughout the country. The violence in Birmingham prompted Robert Kennedy and the Justice Department to negotiate a settlement between the SCLC and city officials. The SCLC eventually agreed to end the boycotts and protests, but only after local merchants promised to hire more blacks and the city promised to enforce desegregation. Segregationists, however, protested the agreement and initiated a new wave of violence, forcing Kennedy to send 3,000 army troops to restore order in the city. The events that took place in Birmingham and the resulting agreements changed the Civil Rights Movement in two major ways. First, they mobilized the moderate majority of Northern and Southern whites against segregation. Second, the Birmingham campaign marked the first time poorer Southern blacks began demanding equality alongside the lawyers, ministers, and students. The majority of blacks wanted immediate access to better jobs, housing, and education and wanted the country in general to be desegregated.

- **March on Washington (1963):** The SCLC, NAACP, SNCC, and CORE organized the largest political rally in American history to help convince Congress to pass the president's new civil rights bill. On August 28, 1963, more than 250,000 blacks and whites marched down the Mall in Washington, D.C. and gathered peacefully in front of the Lincoln Memorial for the **March on Washington**. There, Martin Luther King, Jr. delivered his famous **"I have a dream" speech**, which with surging, sermonic declarations outlined the visions of the Civil Rights Movement and called for racial equality. The march marked one of the last moments of harmony that the Civil Rights Movement had.

- **Civil Rights Act of 1964**: The 1964 Civil Rights Act outlawed racial discrimination by employers and unions, created the Equal Employment Opportunity Commission to enforce the law, and eliminated the remaining restrictions on black voting. This is widely considered to be the most comprehensive piece of civil rights legislation and is the basis of all discrimination suits today. The law prohibited discrimination in employment as well as in public facilities. It also created the

Equal Opportunity Commission to enforce these new laws and gave more power to the president to prosecute violators. Civil rights leaders hailed the passage of the act as the most important victory over racism since the civil rights bills passed by Radical Republicans during Reconstruction. One interesting aspect of the Civil Rights Act of 1964 was that it outlawed not only racial discrimination but also discrimination on the basis of color, nationality, religion, and gender. Conservative Southerners had actually had gender equality written into the document in the hope that it would kill the bill before it even got out of committee. However, conservatives lost their gamble, and the act passed with the gender provisions, boosting the growing **feminist movement** and protecting millions of working women.

Mississippi Freedom Summer (1964): The SNCC decided to begin working in Mississippi where white and black college students worked together to integrate Southern communities. Their goals for the summer were to expand black voter registration in the state, to organize a legally constituted "Freedom Democratic Party" that would challenge the whites-only Mississippi Democratic party, to establish "freedom schools" to teach reading and math to black children, and to open community centers where indigent blacks could obtain legal and medical assistance The SNCC wisely believed that if black students were beaten or killed in demonstrations, it would mean little to the North. But, if Northern kids were hurt or killed, then the cause would be better publicized and they could gain more Northern support. In Philadelphia, Mississippi, three workers, one black and two white, were killed. While six white men were accused of the murders, no one was tried for murder in state court. The men were tried for civil rights violations in federal court, and the county sheriff and two deputies were found guilty and sentenced to jail. Violence erupted against the participants and local blacks on a massive scale—homes were bombed and burned.

Twenty-Fourth Amendment (1964): The Twenty-fourth Amendment to the U.S. Constitution outlawed federal poll taxes as a requirement to vote in federal elections. This helped both poor whites and blacks in the South.

March on Selma: The last great effort by the NCC was to organize the march on Selma in 1965. As had happened earlier, the NAACP and the SCLC came in and took over the effort. The violence the marchers encountered exceeded all that had gone before. Sherriff Jim Clark and the Alabama State Patrol led brutal attacks against the marchers. Two Northern whites were murdered while participating in the march. The events were captured on national TV and helped convince Congress to pass the **1965 Voting Rights Act**. While the march was successful, it did split the Civil Rights Movement apart.

- **Voting Rights Act of 1965**: This law focused on those states that denied blacks the right to vote, despite being given suffrage by the Fifteenth Amendment. It banned literacy tests as a prerequisite for voting and sent thousands of federal voting officials into the South to supervise black voter registration. As a result, the black voter registration rate jumped dramatically, in some places from less than 10% to more than 50%.

- **Emergence of the Militant Movement**: With the increasing violence civil rights that activists were facing, the outrage grew in the black community and so did the perception that perhaps nonviolent protest was not so effective after all. **Malcolm X,** a minister of the **Nation of Islam,** urged blacks to claim their rights "by any means necessary." Slowly the SNCC and CORE also changed their ideas about integration and embraced a more separatist radical program of **Black Power**. Stokely Carmichael, in 1966, called for the Civil Rights Movements to be "black-staffed, black-controlled, and black-financed." He argued that blacks needed to help their own communities and not rely on white aid. He argued that integration only siphoned the top black leaders into the white system, so perhaps it was not such a good idea. Later, he moved on to the Black Panthers, self-styled urban revolutionaries based in Oakland, California. Other leaders such as H. Rap Brown also called for Black Power. On April 4, 1968, Martin Luther King, Jr. was assassinated in Memphis by James Earl Ray. Riots in more than 100 cities followed.

- **Watts Riots** (1965): In August 1965, in the Watts district of Los Angeles, riots break out in which 34 people were killed and 1,000 wounded. Media could not understand why blacks were doing this as they had just received the long-awaited civil rights acts. Rioters responded that these acts were wonderful; however, they did little to help the condition of the people living in the inner cities. After the riots, MLK moved to Chicago to get blacks in the city there to join nonviolent protest. It did not work out well as when blacks and whites confronted each other, violence was barely avoided.

- **Black Panthers**: Formed by Bobby Seals, Eldridge Cleaver, and Huey Newton and became a para-military unit that would act as a police force in the ghettoes. Confrontation between the Panthers and the police led to shootouts and the disappearance of the SNCC and CORE influence and authority.

- **End of an Era**: The Civil Rights Movement reached an impasse in 1968 when the movement realized that many problems remained but it would require an overhaul of the entire American society to fix it—something most were not willing to do. Riots continued across the nation. When King was assassinated, riots in more than 60 cities broke out with scores killed and thousands injured.

Significant Individuals: 1950–1968

- **Martin Luther King, Jr.**—As President of the Montgomery Improvement Association, King had led the year-long bus boycott, and his galvanizing speeches put him on the national stage as a voice of the Civil Rights Movement. King had based his arguments on the belief that people did have a duty to obey moral laws, even if they conflicted with man-made laws. He adopted a strategy of nonviolence (perhaps inspired by Gandhi) and argued that violence should never be used to support moral law. He believed that the best way to attack segregation and racism was by using **creative tension,** which makes people think about the concepts. He used mass movements to develop creative tension and get media attention. For the most part, King was able to open doors for AfricanAmericans to mainstream society. Peaceful massive resistance characterized the movement in its early stages.

Women's Rights Movement

Causes

- Passage of the Fifteenth Amendment ensured voting rights for all citizens of the United States, regardless of race or color; however, women's right to vote was not mentioned. To test the issue, Susan B. Anthony voted in 1872 for Ulysses S. Grant, only to be arrested a few weeks later and convicted of illegal voting. Anthony was inspired to draft what became the Nineteenth Amendment, known as the Susan B. Anthony Amendment.

The major issues in the Women's Rights Movement can be separated largely into "pre-suffrage" and "post-suffrage."

Timeline of Women's Suffrage in the United States

Women Lose the Right to Vote at the Beginning of the United States

1637   Anne Hutchinson convicted of sedition and expelled from the Massachusetts colony for her religious ideas and outspoken behavior.

1776   In March, Abigail Adams wrote to her husband, John Adams, who was meeting with Thomas Jefferson about the Declaration of Independence and asked him "In the new code of laws which I suppose it will be necessary for you to make I desire you would **remember the ladies**, and be more generous and favourable to them than your ancestors. If particular care and attention is not paid [us], we are determined to foment a rebellion, and will not hold ourselves bound by any laws in which we have no voice." Adams replied with humor that the men will fight the **"despotism of the petticoat."** But alas, the Declaration's wording specifies that "all *men* are created equal."

1777–1807   **Women lost the right to vote** in all states. The states of New York, Massachusetts, New Hampshire, and New Jersey, which had previously allowed women to vote, rescinded those rights: New York (1777), Massachusetts (1780), New Hampshire (1784), and New Jersey (1807).

1787   U.S. Constitutional Convention placed voting qualifications in the hands of the states.

1820–1880   development of **the Cult of Domesticity** idea. Newspapers, public documents, novels, literature, and art of the time revealed stereotypical notions about women's and men's roles in society.

1821   Emma Hart Willard founded the Troy Female Seminary in New York—the first school to offer girls classical and scientific studies at the collegiate level.

1829   Englishwoman Frances Wright traveled the United States on a paid lecture tour and addressed audiences of both men and women. She attacked organized religion for the secondary place it assigned women and advocated the empowerment of women through divorce and birth control.

Women's Movement and Abolitionist Movement Combine

1830s   Formation of female anti-slavery associations.

1833   Oberlin College became the first coeducational college in the United States. Early graduates included Lucy Stone and Antoinette Brown.

1836   Grimké sisters, Angelina and Sarah, began their public speaking careers that tied the anti-slavery movement to the Women's Rights Movement. Angelina appealed to Southern women to speak out against slavery. Sarah was eventually silenced by male abolitionists who considered her public speaking a liability.

1837   The "Pastoral Letter of the General Association of Massachusetts to the Congregational Churches Under Their Care" was promulgated against women speaking in public against slavery; it was mainly directed against the Grimke sisters. The first **National Female Anti-Slavery Society Convention** met in New York City. Eighty-one delegates from twelve states attended. Mary Lyon founded **Mount Holyoke College** in Massachusetts, eventually the first four-year all-women's college in the United States. Other colleges followed: **Vassar** (1861), **Wellesley,** and **Smith Colleges** (1875).

1838   Sarah Grimké published *Letters on the Equality of the Sexes and the Condition of Women.*

1839   Mississippi passed the first Married Woman's Property Act.

1840   World Anti-Slavery Convention in London. Lucretia Mott, Elizabeth Cady Stanton, and other women were barred from participating on account of their sex. This snub led them to decide to hold a women's rights convention when they returned to America.

Women Organize and Target Suffrage

1844	Female textile workers in Massachusetts organized the first permanent labor association for working women, the **Lowell Female Labor Reform Association,** and demanded a ten-hour workday.
1848	July 19–20, 300 attended the first **Women's Rights Convention in Seneca Falls, New York**. Equal suffrage was proposed by Elizabeth Cady Stanton. After two days of discussion and debate, 68 women and 32 men signed a Declaration of Sentiments, which outlined the main issues and goals for the emerging women's movement. A set of 12 resolutions was adopted calling for equal treatment of women and men under the law and voting rights for women. The New York State Legislature gave women the right to retain possession of property that they owned prior to their marriage.
1849	Harriet Tubman escaped from slavery, and over the next ten years she led many slaves to freedom by the Underground Railroad. Elizabeth Blackwell graduated from Geneva College with the first medical degree awarded to a woman.
1850	A women's rights convention was held in April in Salem, Ohio and men were not allowed to speak at it. The first national women's rights convention was held in October in Worcester, Massachusetts and attracted more than 1,000 participants. This marked the beginning of annual women's rights conventions that were held from 1850–1861.
1851	**Amelia Bloomer** launched the dress reform movement with the publication of a description of a loose-fitting skirt worn over pantaloons. It became known as the **Bloomer costume.** Suffragists later distanced themselves from it as they feared it would detract attention away from suffrage. Former slave **Sojourner Truth** delivered her *Ain't I a Woman?* speech before a captivated audience at a women's rights convention in Akron, Ohio.
1854	The Massachusetts legislature granted property rights to women.
1855	Prominent suffragists Lucy Stone and Henry Blackwell married and excluded the vow of obedience from the ceremony and included a protest against unfair marriage laws.

1859	Vulcanization of rubber provided couples with reliable condoms for the first time. The birth rate in the United States continued its downward trend so that by the late 1900s, women raised an average of only two to three children, a marked difference from the 5–6 children they raised in 1800.
1863	Stanton and Anthony formed the **Women's Loyal National League** and gathered 300,000 signatures on a petition that demanded the abolition of slavery.
1865–1870	Southern white women created Confederate memorial societies to help preserve the memory of the "Lost Cause." This activity propelled many white Southern women into the public sphere for the first time. During this same period, newly emancipated Southern black women formed thousands of organizations aimed at "uplifting the race."
1866	Susan B. Anthony and Elizabeth Cady Stanton formed the **American Equal Rights Association**, founded to push for universal suffrage and civil rights for all Americans, irrespective of race, color, or sex. Lucretia Mott was elected president.
1867	Fourteenth amendment passed Congress, defining citizens as "male;" this was the first use of the word "male" in the Constitution. Kansas held a state referendum on whether or not to give the right to vote to blacks and/or women. Despite Stone, Anthony, and Stanton's campaign all over the state, suffrage for both blacks and women lost.

Suffrage Movement Divides Over Black vs. Women's Suffrage

1868	Fourteenth amendment ratified which extends to all citizens the protections of the Constitution against unjust state laws. This Amendment was the first to define "citizens" and "voters" as "male." Fifteenth amendment passed Congress, giving the vote to black men. Women petitioned to be included but were turned down. In New Jersey, 172 women attempted to vote; their ballots were ignored. Stanton and Anthony launched their women's rights newspaper, *The Revolution*, in New York City. Anthony organized the **Working Women's Association**, which encouraged women to unionize themselves to work collectively for higher wages and shorter hours.

1869   Frederick Douglass and others backed down from women's suffrage to concentrate on fight for black male suffrage. In May, the women's rights movement split over disagreements over the Fourteenth and Fifteenth Amendments. The more radical, New York-based National Woman Suffrage Association formed in May with Elizabeth Cady Stanton as president. The primary goal of the NWSA was an amendment to the Constitution giving women the right to vote. In November, a more conservative organization, American Woman Suffrage Association based in Boston, was founded by Lucy Stone, Henry Blackwell, and Julia Ward, with Henry Ward Beecher as president. On December 10, the Wyoming territory passed the first women's suffrage law since 1807.

Civil Disobedience and State Suffrage

1870   Fifteenth Amendment that granted suffrage to former male African-American slaves, but not to women, was ratified without the support of the NWSA who opposed the amendment because of its omission of women's suffrage. Frederick Douglass broke with the organization as a result. Utah territory granted women's suffrage.

1870–1875   Several women—including Virginia Louisa Minor, Victoria Woodhull, and Myra Bradwell—attempted to use the Fourteenth Amendment in the courts to secure the vote (Minor and Woodhull) or the right to practice law (Bradwell). They all were unsuccessful.

1871   The Anti-Suffrage Society was formed.

1872   Susan B. Anthony and supporters arrested for attempting to vote for Ulysses S. Grant in the presidential election. Anthony's sisters and 11 other women held for $500 bail. Anthony herself was held for $1,000 bail. At the same time, Sojourner Truth appeared at a polling booth in Battle Creek, Michigan, demanding a ballot; she was turned away.

1874   In *Myner v. Happerstett*, the U.S. Supreme Court decided that citizenship does not give women the right to vote and that women's political rights are under the jurisdiction of each individual state. The **Woman's Christian Temperance Union** (WCTU) was founded and later became an important force in the fight for women's suffrage. One of the most vehement opponents to women's enfranchisement was the liquor lobby, which feared women might prohibit the sale of liquor if they gained the right to vote.

1878   A Woman Suffrage Amendment was introduced in the U. S. Congress. The wording was the same one used in 1919.

1882   The House and Senate appointed Select Committees on Woman Suffrage, both reporting favorably.

1884   Belva Lockwood ran for president.

1886   Suffrage amendment reached the US Senate floor, and it was defeated two to one.

1890   The NWSA and the AWSA were reunited to form NAWSA–National American Woman Suffrage Association under the direction of Elizabeth Cady Stanton. The focus turned to working state by state to obtain voting rights for women. **Jane Addams** and **Ellen Gates Starr** founded **Hull House,** a settlement house project in Chicago's 19th Ward. Within one year, there were more than a hundred settlement houses—largely operated by women— throughout the United States. The settlement house movement and the Progressive campaign propelled thousands of college-educated white women and a number of women of color into lifetime careers in social work and made women an important voice to be reckoned with in American politics. Wyoming joined the union as the first state with voting rights for women.

1893   After a vigorous campaign led by Carrie Chapman Catt, Colorado men voted for women's suffrage. Other states soon followed suit: 1896: Utah and Idaho; 1910: Washington; 1911: California; 1912: Oregon, Kansas, and Arizona; 1913: Alaska and Illinois; 1914: Montana and Nevada; 1917: New York; 1918: Michigan, South Dakota, and Oklahoma.

1895   Elizabeth Cady Stanton publisheed **The Woman's Bible,** which caused NAWSA to distance itself from the "too-radical" Stanton and they refused to let her speak at any meetings.

1896   The **National Association of Colored Women** was formed, bringing together more than 100 black women's clubs and included Mary Church Terrell, Ida B. Wells-Barnett, Margaret Murray Washington, Fanny Jackson Coppin, Frances Ellen Watkins Harper, Charlotte Forten Grimké, and Harriet Tubman.

Suffrage Comes to Fruition

1903	The **National Women's Trade Union League** (WTUL) was established to advocate for improved wages and working conditions for women.
1907	Harriet Stanton Blatch, Elizabeth's daughter, formed the Equality League of Self Supporting Women, which became the Women's Political Union in 1910. She introduced the English suffragists' tactics of parades, street speakers, and pickets.
1911	In New York City, 3,000 marched for suffrage. The **National Association Opposed to Woman Suffrage** (NAOWS) was organized and supporters included distillers and brewers, urban political machines, Southern congressmen, and corporate capitalists—like railroad magnates and meat-packers—who supported the "antis" by contributing to their "war chests."
1912	Teddy Roosevelt's Progressive Party included woman suffrage in their platform.
1913	A women's suffrage parade on the eve of Wilson's inauguration was attacked by a mob. Hundreds of women were injured, but no arrests were made. **Alice Paul** and **Lucy Burns** formed the **Congressional Union** to work toward the passage of a federal amendment to give women the vote. The group was later renamed the **National Women's Party (NWP)** and used civil disobedience like hunger strikes and picketing the White House to publicize the suffrage cause.
1916	Alice Paul and others broke away from NASWA and formed the National Woman's Party. **Margaret Sanger** opened the first U.S. birth-control clinic in Brooklyn, New York. Although the clinic was shut down ten days later and Sanger was arrested, she eventually won support through the courts and opened another clinic in New York City in 1923.
1917	Beginning in January, NWP posted silent "Sentinels of Liberty" at the White House. In June, the arrests began. Nearly 500 women were arrested, 168 women serveed jail time, and some were brutalized by their jailers. Alice Paul and other suffragists were arrested and jailed for "obstructing traffic." When they went on a hunger strike to protest their arrest and treatment, they were force-fed. Women won the right to vote in North Dakota, Ohio, Indiana, Rhode Island, Nebraska, Michigan, New York,

and Arkansas. North Dakota, Indiana, Nebraska, and Michigan granted presidential suffrage; Arkansas granted primary suffrage. New York, South Dakota, and Oklahoma state constitutions granted suffrage.

1918   The jailed suffragists were released from prison. Appellate court ruled that all the arrests were illegal. President Wilson declared support for suffrage. Suffrage Amendment passed U.S. House with exactly a two-thirds vote but lost by two votes in the Senate.

1919   In January, the NWP lit and guarded a "Watchfire for Freedom." It was maintained until the Suffrage Amendment passed U.S. Senate in June. The battle for ratification by at least 36 states began.

1920   The **Nineteenth Amendment**, called the **Susan B. Anthony Amendment**, was ratified by Tennessee on August 18. It became law on August 26. Its victory accomplished, NAWSA ceased to exist, but its organization became the nucleus of the **League of Women Voters**.

1923   The National Woman's Party first proposed the **Equal Rights Amendment** to eliminate discrimination on the basis of sex. It has never been ratified.

Post-Suffrage – Women's Movement and Equal Rights

Birth Control, Equal Pay, and Feminism

1921   **Margaret Sanger** founded the **American Birth Control League**, which evolved into the **Planned Parenthood Federation of America** in 1942.

1935   **Mary McLeod Bethune** organized the **National Council of Negro Women,** a coalition of black women's groups that lobbied against job discrimination, racism, and sexism.

1936   The federal law prohibiting the dissemination of contraceptive information through the mail was modified and birth control information was no longer classified as obscene.

1960   The Food and Drug Administration approved **birth control pills**.

1961   President Kennedy established the **President's Commission on the Status of Women** and appointed Eleanor Roosevelt as chairwoman. The report recommended instituting fair hiring practices, equal pay, paid maternity leave, and affordable child care.

1963   **Betty Friedan** published **The Feminine Mystique**, which articulated the dissatisfaction felt by middle-class American housewives with the narrow role imposed on them by society. Congress passed the **Equal Pay Act**, making it illegal for employers to pay a woman less than what a man would receive for the same job.

1964   **Title VII of the Civil Rights Act** barred discrimination in employment on the basis of race and sex. At the same time, it established the **Equal Employment Opportunity Commission (EEOC)** to investigate complaints and impose penalties.

1966   The **National Organization for Women (NOW)** was founded by a group of feminists including Betty Friedan. NOW promoted child care, abortion rights, and the ERA.

1969   California became the first state to adopt a **"no fault" divorce law**, which allowed couples to divorce by mutual consent.

1971   *Ms. Magazine* was first published as a sample insert in *New York* magazine; 300,000 copies were sold out in eight days. The first regular issue was published in July.

1972   The **Equal Rights Amendment (ERA)** was passed by Congress and sent to the states for ratification. Originally drafted by Alice Paul in 1923, the amendment read: "Equality of rights under the law shall not be denied or abridged by the United States or by any State on account of sex." The amendment died in 1982 when it failed to achieve ratification by a minimum of 38 states. **Title IX of the Education Amendments** banned sex discrimination in schools. As a result of Title IX, the enrollment of women in athletics programs and professional schools increased dramatically.

1973   **Roe v. Wade** established a woman's right to legal abortion, overriding the anti-abortion laws of many states.

1978   The **Pregnancy Discrimination Act** banned employment discrimination against pregnant women. Under the Act, a woman cannot be fired or denied a job or a promotion because she is or may become pregnant, nor can she be forced to take a pregnancy leave if she is willing and able to work.

1981	**Sandra Day O'Connor** was the first woman to serve on the Supreme Court.
1994	The **Violence Against Women Act** tightened federal penalties for sex offenders, funded services for victims of rape and domestic violence, and provided for special training of police officers.
1996	In *United States v. Virginia*, the Supreme Court ruled that the all-male Virginia Military School had to admit women in order to continue to receive public funding. It held that creating a separate, all-female school would not suffice.
2006	The Supreme Court upheld the ban on the "partial-birth" abortion procedure. The ruling, 5–4, which upholds the **Partial-Birth Abortion Ban Act**, a federal law passed in 2003, was the first to ban a specific type of abortion procedure. Writing in the majority opinion, Justice Anthony Kennedy said, "The act expresses respect for the dignity of human life." Justice Ruth Bader Ginsburg, who dissented, called the decision "alarming" and said it was "so at odds with our jurisprudence" that it "should not have staying power."
2008	**Hillary Clinton** ran as the Democratic nominee for President, the first woman to be nominated by a major political party. Although she lost, President Obama appointed her Secretary of State.

COMPETENCY 5.15

Identify the causes, significant individuals, and effects of the events associated with contemporary domestic and foreign affairs.

Domestic Issues

In 2010, the chief domestic issues that the United States is facing are the economy, financial reform, housing reform, environmental disasters such as the oil spill in the Gulf of Mexico, and health care reform.

Current issues:

Abortion: Debate centers on the immorality of abortion versus the immorality of not providing for unwanted children. The idea of a "woman's right to choose" has sparked controversy and discussion. Currently some religious groups and the Republican Party have adopted a virulent anti-abortion/"pro-life" stance; however, there are Republicans who favor "pro-choice" just as there are Democrats who support the "pro-life" position.

College Costs: Rising college costs and the inability of middle-class Americans to pay for them has ignited discussion about where this will eventually lead. With the current state of the economy and the inability of new graduates to find jobs that pay enough for them to pay off college loans, the nation is facing the prospect of a declining percentage of college graduates among its adult population.

Credit Crisis: Tied to the economic downfall that the country is facing, the idea of who to give credit to, how much, and what will go into making those decisions remains a chief concern among government, financial, and consumer advocate institutions. **President George W. Bush's** administration pushed through the Temporary Aid to Reform P (TARP) just before leaving office in 2009. TARP saved many large banks, but **President Barack Obama** is facing an increasingly angry public as the unemployment continues and Americans are unable to solve their personal credit crises because the banks have tightened credit.

Energy: Since the 1973–1974 Arab oil embargo, production of alternative sources of energy has increased, albeit slowly. With conflict continuing to broil between the United States and oil producing countries, the United States has become more concerned about finding alternative sources of oil and energy. Before the Gulf oil spill, many were pushing for an extension of off-shore drilling rights. It remains to be seen what long-term effect the spill will have on energy policy.

Same-Sex Marriage: States have begun to pass legislation allowing for marriage or civil unions between two people of the same sex. Debate continues to rage that crosses traditional Republican/Democrat lines about the legality and morality of it.

Gun Control: Concerns about the proliferation of guns, easy access to buying them at gun shows, permits to conceal these weapons, which should not be permitted to buy them, and training associated with gun ownership continue to be questions that are debated, particularly in the West.

Health Care: Escalating health care costs, reluctance of insurance companies to cover procedures, and the lack of health care for everyone was a primary focus for President Obama. Debate raged over whether or not his plan would worsen the system, make things better, or did not go far enough, consuming American society during the first year and a half of his administration.

Immigration: After Arizona passed anti-immigration laws, in the spring of 2010, that made many, including the federal government, uncomfortable, immigration remains an issue in the United States. The same sort of fears expressed during the height of the immigration boom in the late nineteenth and early twentieth centuries continue to reveal themselves.

Poverty in the United States: The gap between rich and poor continues to widen. All of the issues attendant to the poor—housing, health care, and schooling, for example—will receive new focus. Faith-based initiatives were highlighted as a way to address growing poverty.

Public Education: A multi-state effort to reform education under the umbrella of so-called Common Core State Standards set out to encourage a higher degree of critical thinking in the classroom. But the new standards also stirred debate. Battle lines were drawn over issues ranging from teacher accountability to concerns over student performance on a new series of Common Core assessments.

Social Security: The availability of Social Security for future generations remains in doubt as the Social Security Administration began collecting less in taxes than it paid in benefits.

Stem Cell Research: Conservatives and liberals continue to debate the viability, morality, and the ethical questions associated with using stem cells for research and/or medical treatment.

Foreign Issues

Afghanistan: President Obama announced his intention to direct an "orderly withdrawal" from Afghanistan, which had been a haven for terrorist activity.

China: A trade imbalance with China continued to concern economists.

Climate Change: Coming up with a world-wide agreement on whether or not climate change is occurring and what we should do about it remains a topic of discussion and sometimes pointed exchange. The Obama administration has opened the door to wide-ranging discussions about global warming and climate change.

Colombia: The U.S. position on the War on Drugs seems to have taken a bit of a backseat to law enforcement's focus on the War on Terrorism.

Cuba: With the rise of Fidel's brother, Raul Castro, debate about whether or not to resume trade and diplomatic relations between the United States and Cuba still occurs.

Darfur: The role of the United States toward helping victims of genocide in areas not obviously of high economic or military interest to the United States has been a concern among activists.

Development: Policy about when and how to help out which foreign countries, particularly in a time of economic difficulty in the United States, which has its own infrastructure issues, remains a concern among foreign aid workers.

European Union: U.S.-EU collaboration embraces four broad tenets: promoting peace and stability, democracy and development around the world; responding to global challenges; contributing to the expansion of world trade and closer economic relations; and building bridges across the Atlantic.

Guantanamo: Issues of when and how to close the Guantanamo Bay detention camp and the U.S. treatment of prisoners there ignited debate.

Iran: In February 2014, the U.S. joined with five other world powers in reaching agreement with Iran on a timetable and framework for ending the conflict over Iran's nuclear program.

Iraq: Eight years after invading Iraq under the erroneous belief that its dictator, Saddam Hussein, was hiding weapons of mass destruction, the United States announced the end of its mission in Iraq, formally completing its troop withdrawal in December 2011.

Israel: The U.S.-Israel relationship continues to be dominated by the broad issues of Arab-Israeli and Palestinian-Israeli peace. According to a U.S. State Department Bureau of Near Eastern Affairs fact sheet, U.S. efforts to reach a Middle East peace settlement hinge on UN Security Council Resolutions 242 and 338 and "have been based on the premise that as Israel takes calculated risks for peace, the United States will help minimize those risks."

North Korea: North Korea has nuclear capabilities; therefore the United States has approached it differently, for example, than it has nations that are believed to be seeking nuclear capabilities. North Korea has also isolated itself, diplomatically and economically, from most of the world, with the exception of China.

Osama bin Laden: A Saudi militant who founded al-Qaeda, which trains and funds terrorist missions, bin Laden was the mastermind of a series of terrorist attacks against the United States and other Western powers, including the 2000 suicide bombing of the U.S. warship *Cole* in the Yemeni port of Aden and the Sept. 11, 2001, attacks on the World Trade Center in New York City and the Pentagon near Washington, D.C., as well as an airliner that crashed near Shanksville, Pennsylvania, when passengers attempted to wrest control of the plane from the terrorists. Bin Laden was killed on May 2, 2011, in his secure compound in Abbottabad, Pakistan, when a small U.S. force raided it.

Pakistan: Growing anti-Americanism and political instability there has made Pakistan a growing area of concern for the U.S. military.

Russia: Relations with Russia have waxed and waned over the years. The recent exchange of spies between the two countries may have an effect on relations in the future.

War on Terror: This continues to dominate U.S. foreign, and even domestic, policy, as not only is the United States embarking on military intervention abroad, but also has employed reactive policies whenever there is a terrorist attack or foiled attack. For instance, in reaction to the "shoe bomber," Americans now have to take their shoes off and run them through the detectors at airports.

COMPETENCY 5.16
Identify key individuals, events, and issues related to Florida history.

Indians

The first Floridians were Indians. At the time of the Spanish invasion, there were a number of tribes living there. In North Florida, the **Apalachee** lived in the Tallahassee Hills beginning around 1000 CE. Prior to European contact, there were probably at least 50,000–60,000 Apalachees who lived in widely dispersed villages. They were considered, among other Indian tribes, to be an advanced civilization, as they were prosperous, well-organized, and fierce warriors. In order to make themselves seem more fierce when they were fighting, they would paint their bodies with red ochre and put feathers in their hair. Their civilization seemed more developed than the others, as they had ball games, ceremonial mounts, and a rigid feudal system. After the Spanish arrival in 1528 led by the explorer Pánfilo de Narváez and later Hernando de Soto, the Apalachee attacked the Europeans. The advanced weapons that the Europeans overwhelmed the Apalachee, and they suffered from losses and contagious diseases. The Apalachee rulers, finally understanding the Spanish demands for conversion to Catholicism, did convert between 1633 and 1635. Alas, it was not enough to keep the peace with Europeans, and in the early 1700s, the British attacked them, killed, and enslaved many. Some of the Apalachee migrated north to Creek territory, and others moved, in 1763, to Louisiana.

The **Timucuans** lived between the Aucilla River and the Atlantic Ocean down to the Tampa Bay. They were farmers who lived in independent villages who survived on farming and hunting small game. The typical Timucuan villages had groups of small huts protected by a circular wall of tree trunks. They practiced a rigid feudal system, and each Indian's occupation was determined by birth. Males typically were warriors and hunters, although potters and canoe makers also had high status. Women and children did most of the planting and harvesting of food. From 1649 through 1656, the Timucuan suffered both from attacks by the English and other Indians troops as well as being ravaged by smallpox. Some scholars think that the few remaining Timucuans merged with the Seminole tribe.

The **Calusa**, a name which means "fierce people," lived on the southwest coast of Florida and controlled most of southern Florida. They were good sailors with a tremendous reputation of being good warriors. They typically were quite tall, averaging about four inches taller than the Europeans who arrived there, well built and sported long hair. Their villages were typically built on stilts and had roofs but no walls. Their houses were made of huge mounds of shells, and they dug deep moats around their villages to protect them from invaders. They did not farm but were fantastic at fishing. They are known as the "Shell Indians" because they used shells to do just about everything: tools, utensils, hunting, fishing, jewelry, and ornaments. It is suspected that the Calusa died out after being raided and sold as slaves by enemy tribes from Georgia and South Carolina, and the remaining ones were victims of smallpox and measles brought to them by the Spanish.

The **Tocobaga** Indians lived in small villages at the northern end of Tampa Bay from 900 to the 1500s. Each village was situated around a public area that was used as a meeting place. The houses were generally round and built with wooden poles that were topped with a roof made up of palm thatches. They used mounts in their villages and would typically build the chief's home and a temple atop them. Their main source of food was shellfish, manatees, and small game. They died out about a hundred years after Pánfilo de Narváez, a Spanish explorer, arrived there in 1528, due to both Spanish attacks and disease.

The **Tequesta** settled in South Florida near Biscayne Bay in the present-day Miami area. Like the other tribes in South Florida, the Tequesta were hunters and gatherers. The men often ventured out to the ocean in canoes to catch their food: sharks, sailfish, porpoises, sting rays, and sea cows. Women and children would focus their attention on gathering food in shallow waters, like clams, conchs, oysters, and turtle eggs. While they also gathered nuts and berries and had some small game, their food supply was more difficult to obtain and may be one reason why they never really expanded much. Like the other Indian tribes, their encounters with the Europeans spelled their doom.

Florida of the Conquistadores

The Spanish, in a quest for God, Gold, and Glory, ventured into the Americas.

Ponce de Leon is considered to be the European founder of Florida. In late March 1513, he landed near present-day St. Augustine and was so impressed with the flowers he saw there that he named it *La Florida*: land of the flowers. He continued up the coast of Florida until he reached the Calusa Indians, and frightened by them, he and his men returned to their ships and set sail. Eight years later, he returned with 500 men to build a colony. Upon landing, however, he and his men were again attacked by the Calusa, and de Leon was mortally wounded with an arrow to his thigh.

In April of 1528, another attempt was made by the Spanish to tame Florida. **Pánfilo de Narváez** arrived near Tampa Bay with a large army. A tremendous flaw in communication left de Narváez and his 300 soldiers and 40 horses stranded. His ship, which contained all of his food and supplies, landed somewhere differently from where they were told to land. Narváez and his men waited and waited for the ship and for an entire year, the ship's captain went up and down the coast searching for Narváez. Meanwhile, Narváez and his men were getting nervous, hungry, and sick and had been attacked by the Apalachee over and over again. After about a month of waiting, he and his men went to a bay on the Gulf, built five barges out of pine trees, and used their shirts to make sails. In September 1528, Narváez and approximately 240 men set sail towards a Spanish settlement in Mexico on home-made barges. Unfortunately, a violent storm capsized their barges, and many, including Narváez, died. About 100 made it to an island off of Texas. By spring, Narváez's provost, Nuñez de Cabeza de Vaca, and the few men who were still alive set off to walk to Mexico City. Seven years later, four of them, including de Vaca, eventually arrived there.

Hernando de Soto was given "La Florida" by Carlos V in 1536. De Soto, deeply in debt when he left Spain in 1538, thought he would regain his fortune by finding gold in "La Florida." His expedition, unlike the ones before him, was relatively well stocked with priests, women, horses, mules, war dogs, and pigs. On May 25, they made landfall in the Tampa Bay area and found a survivor from Narváez's expedition. **Juan Ortiz** had been living as an Indian since he was left behind and was able to work as both a guide and a translator for de Soto. As de Soto's expedition moved inland, however, they encountered resistance and fought with the natives. His brutal treatment of those he met, enslaving, mutilating, and executing those in his path, proved to be his undoing as the Indians began to fight back. By the spring of 1540, de Soto and his army, never finding the gold they were seeking, left and went to explore Georgia, North and South Carolina, Tennessee, and Alabama. In 1542, as he headed across the Mississippi River into Arkansas, he became ill and died of a fever.

Florida of the French

The French Protestants, called **Huguenots**, sought to establish France as a mercantile power. Many of them were merchants and sailors. Their leader, Admiral Gaspard de Coligny, convinced Charles IX that France's future success as a nation depended upon competing with Spain and Portugal for American colonies.

In 1562, **Jean Ribault** was sent from France to Florida in order to explore the area and begin a new colony. Ribault sailed with three ships that carried 100 Huguenots. He landed at St. Johns River and built a stone monument to mark his visit and claim it for France. Afterwards, he continued North where the Huguenots built a fort and named it Charlesfort, in honor of their king. Before long, the supplies began to dwindle, so Ribault sailed back to France. When he arrived, religious conflict had broken out so he went to England to ask Queen Elizabeth to fund his trip. She had him arrested for establishing a French colony in Spanish territory. He was put in a London prison. During this time, Ribault's lieutenant, **Rene Laudonnière**, was sent to rescue Charlesfort in South Carolina. He led an expedition of 304 Huguenot colonists who established a colony called Fort Caroline in present-day Jacksonville. Initially, he established good relations with the Timucuan Indians. Soon, however, supplies ran short and the French colony was unable to get food from the natives. Some of the colonists no longer believed in Laudonnière's leadership. They stole boats and sailed south to become pirates and raid Spanish treasure ships. Most of the colonists at Fort Caroline decided to go home to France. The French colony was in trouble. Ribault, newly released from prison, planned to rescue and take control of Fort Caroline. Meanwhile, a Spanish explorer named **Pedro Menendez de Aviles** arrived in Florida. Menendez was ordered to get rid of the French, so he built his own fort at St. Augustine, marched on Fort Caroline, and later killed Ribaut. Laudonnière, who was wounded in the attack, managed to escape to France.

Florida of the Spanish

Pedro Menendez de Aviles was sent to drive out the French colonists, given 11 ships, and took over 2,000 sailors, soldiers, and their families to Florida. As mentioned above, he built the fort at St. Augustine and defeated the French at Fort Caroline. He built watchtowers and forts to keep track of impending European vessels, and, as Florida's first Spanish Colonial Governor charged with making sure that all of Florida stayed under Spain's control, he established outposts up and down the coast and built more watchtowers at Cape Canaveral and Biscayne Bay. Menendez then sent two ships of settlers to what is now Parris Island, South Carolina. In 1569, more settlers arrived there and the town began to bloom. They named their town Santa Elena, and it became the capital of Spanish Florida. Unlike those who had come before him, Menendez sought to have a good relationship with the Indians. He signed a treaty with the Calusa Indians to trade gold for food and other supplies his troops needed to survive. As part of the desire for "God, Gold, and Glory," Menendez focused on converting the Native Americans to Catholicism. All of the ships coming from Spain, on his orders, contained priests who, in many cases became missionaries. Menendez went back to Spain to collect more settlers, but he died on September 17, 1574, before he could return to Florida.

Spanish Colonial System: Florida was part of the huge and complex Spanish empire, and was a Royal colony, like all Spanish colonies. As such, it was the lawful property of the Crown, and all appointments and decisions were made by the King and his advisors. The Spanish Empire was divided into two districts, New Spain and Peru. Florida was a province of New Spain. The colony was headed by a **governor** who was responsible for the welfare of all of the colonists. He had a variety of jobs that he had to perform. He served as general of the army and his primary duty in that regard was to protect St. Augustine. As the chief politician, he was required to administer the law, act as chief justice of the court, and settle little disputes. As a businessman, he was in charge of the colony's budget. As the chief in charge of the missionary effort, he was diplomat to the Indians, welfare director for the poor, construction engineer for the colony's defense, and religious leader. Florida governors served for five years if they came from Europe and three if they came from another colony. Governors were required to post one-half of their earnings in bonds to pay for any heavy fines they may accrue. Near the end of their term of office, the Spanish Crown would send undercover agents to evaluate the governor and his colony.

Threat from the British: Spanish Florida's greatest threat came from England who had begun to invade Florida's mission system as early as 1658. St. Augustine was raided in 1665 and 1668. Governor James Moore of South Carolina attacked the Spanish in 1722 with an army of about 1200 militia. More attacks followed as the Spanish mission system completely deteriorated. In 1740, Georgia's Governor James Oglethorpe organized a huge colonial militia to destroy St. Augustine, but the mission failed.

Florida: The British Period

In 1763, with the Treaty of Paris that marked the end of the French and Indian War, France gave up its land in North America and Spain gave Florida to the British. The British then divided Florida into two territories: East Florida and West Florida.

East Florida, bordered by the Apalachicola River, the Gulf of Mexico, and the Atlantic Ocean, chose St. Augustine as its capital. The first governor of East Florida, James Grant, remained on good terms with the Seminole Indians and had a flourishing trade with them. He also encouraged settlers in the other British colonies to come to Florida and settle there. Advertisements in London promised 20,000-acre lots to any group who wanted to settle in Florida. The rule was that individual holders could have 100 acres each. Former British soldiers were given 100 acres of land, and each of their family members was given 50 acres. Along with the British came slavery, and it was the slaves who largely built the colony. They cleared land, built homes, and introduced crops to the area like citrus fruit, sugar cane, rice, cotton, and indigo. Western Florida had Pensacola as its capital and consisted of the land between the Mississippi River and the Apalachicola River (in modern-day terms, that included Alabama, Mississippi, and Louisiana). It had some disadvantages as it was filled with pine trees and sand and was not as good for farming.

During the American Revolution, Florida remained loyal to the British, and even invited Loyalists to come live there when things became a little tense in the Northern colonies. In 1779 while the British were preoccupied with the American Revolution, Spain invaded Florida and regained control over it, and after the revolution, the entire Floridian area was given to Spain.

The Seminole Wars and Transfer to the United States

Following the War of 1812 between the United States and Britain, American slave owners came to Florida in search of runaway African slaves and Indians. These Indians, known as the **Seminole**, and the runaway slaves had been trading weapons with the British throughout the early 1800s and had supported Britain during the War of 1812. From 1817–1818, the U.S. Army invaded Spanish Florida and fought against the Seminole and their African-American allies. Collectively, these battles came to be known as the **First Seminole War.**

Americans reacted to these confrontations by sending Andrew Jackson to Florida with an army of about 3,000 men. Jackson was successful in his attacks and left many dead and dying Seminole behind in their destroyed villages. He went on to attack Spanish settlements and captured Spanish forts at St. Marks and Pensacola. Spaniards began to realize that they could no longer keep their territory. They had been unable to bring settlers to Florida, and it was beginning to be a drain. Meanwhile, Spain knew that the United States was interested in the region because it would benefit their attempt to use the Mississippi River as a major trading location. Spain negotiated a treaty signed by John Quincy Adams (U.S. Secretary of State) and Luis de Onis (Spain's Minister) in 1819. The **Adams-Onis Treaty** gave Florida to the United States and nullified the $5,000,000 debt Spain owed to the United States. Florida now belonged to the United States.

Andrew Jackson, in charge of setting up Florida's government, quickly divided Florida into two parts called counties. The area that had been West Florida became Escambia County, and what was once East Florida became St. Johns County. Jackson established county courts and mayors in the cities of St. Augustine (East Florida) and Pensacola (West Florida). Afterwards, Jackson left Florida and empowered **William Pope DuVal** to lead Florida as governor. Florida became an official territory on March 30, 1822.

As settlement increased, pressure grew on the U.S. government to remove the Native Americans from their lands in Florida. To the chagrin of Georgia landowners, the Seminole harbored and integrated runaway black slaves, and clashes between whites and Native Americans grew with the influx of new settlers.

Northern settlers were invading Tallahassee, a Seminole settlement. These settlers often clashed with the Seminole. In an effort to end these conflicts, the governor asked the Seminole to move. The Seminole refused. In 1823, it became necessary for the governor to offer the Seminole a treaty, which was called the **Treaty of Moultrie Creek**. This treaty required the Seminole to give up their land and move south. It also made them agree to discontinue hiding runaway slaves. The Seminole were given four million acres of land in the area south of present-day Ocala. The area that they were given was called a **reservation.** This reservation, however, did not meet their needs.

In 1829, President Jackson worked to have the **Indian Removal Act** made into a law. The Seminole were offered lands west of the Mississippi. Their leaders went to look at it, were persuaded to sign a treaty, did so, and then went back home and said they had been tricked. They refused to leave.

A warrior named **Osceola** led the Seminole in a surprise attack against the Americans. At the Dade Massacre, Osceola and his men killed over 100 Americans. The United States sent in more troops, and fighting between the two went on until 1842, with the Seminole getting pushed further and further south. Osceola died on August 14, 1842, by which time the United States had spent between $20–$40 million on the war.

On March 3, 1845, Florida became the twenty-seventh state of the United States of America.

Florida in the Civil War

In 1845 when Florida became a state, the population was approximately 140,000. Of these, 63,000 were African-Americans, most of whom were slaves. Florida also had its share of free blacks who were descendents of Spanish citizens of African ancestry. When Florida became a state, it was a slave state.

Following Abraham Lincoln's election in 1860, Florida joined other Southern states in seceding from the Union. Secession took place January 10, 1861, and after less than a month as an independent republic, Florida became one of the founding members of the Confederate States of America. Because Florida was an important supply route for the Confederate Army, Union forces operated a blockade around the entire state. Union troops occupied major ports such as Cedar Key, Jacksonville, Key West, and Pensacola.

Two major battles and several smaller skirmishes took place in Florida.

Fort Pickens: Beginning in early January of 1861, right after Florida joined the other Confederate states and seceded from the Union, Confederate soldiers demanded that the Union soldiers stationed at **Fort Pickens** surrender now that Florida was a Confederate state. The Union soldiers refused to leave the fort, and a battle between the two lasted until the early part of 1862. Finally, the Confederate troops withdrew and the Union occupied Pensacola for the rest of the war.

Tampa Bay: A standoff between a Union gunboat and the Osceola Confederate rangers in June 1862 resulted in the Union soldiers withdrawing.

On February 20, 1864, the largest Civil War battle in Florida occurred near Lake City. It was called the **Battle of Olustee,** and it took the Confederacy six hours to win it. The Union Army sought to cut off Confederate supply lines. Confederate troops under the command of General Joseph Finegan blocked the Union advance and sent them back toward Jacksonville. Almost 3,000 of the 11,100 who fought the battle were killed.

Battle of Natural Bridge, March 4, 1865: Another large battle in Florida took place near Tallahassee that resulted in Tallahassee being the only Confederate capital east of the Mississippi River that was not seized by Union troops. Major General John Newton landed U.S. Navy ships at the mouth of St. Marks River. They had trouble getting up the river, so the soldiers marched northeast to Tallahassee. A small Confederate militia group burned a bridge in their path so that the Union soldiers could not cross the river. The Union soldiers pressed on, and the two groups met at the Natural Bridge, a place where the river goes underground for a short distance. The Confederates were able to protect the natural crossing and push the Union soldiers back. The Union soldiers quickly retreated to their ships.

An estimated 16,000 Floridians fought in the Civil War. Most were in the Confederacy, but approximately 2,000 joined the Union army. Some Floridians didn't want to fight for either side, so they hid out in the woods and swamps to avoid being drafted. The Floridian soldiers were organized into 11 regiments of infantry, two cavalry, and numerous small units. Florida employed some groups dubbed the **Cow Cavalry** to protect the small towns and cattle ranches in the inner part of Florida. Numerous small battles occurred, and the Cow Cavalry met challenges. The group also helped keep the Confederate army supplied with food from Florida With the war nearing its end, the Florida governor, Governor Milton, who had earlier declared that he would prefer death over having to rejoin the Union, saw the writing on the wall and killed himself with a gunshot. Florida was ordered to surrender just a few weeks later, on April 26th. On May 10, 1865, Union Brigadier General Edward McCook and his staff entered Tallahassee and established federal control and authority over Florida and on May 20, the formal transfer of power began and slaves were freed in Florida.

Florida under Reconstruction

After meeting the requirements of Reconstruction, including ratifying amendments to the U.S. Constitution, Florida was readmitted to the United States on July 25, 1868.

Florida had not suffered much damage during the war, and with the expansion of the railroads, it became a popular tourist destination as railroads expanded into the area. Railroad magnate **Henry Plant** built a luxury hotel in Tampa, which later became the campus for the University of Tampa. **Henry Flagler** built the **Florida East Coast Railway** from Jacksonville to Key West and constructed numerous luxury hotels along the route, including in the cities of Saint Augustine, Ormond Beach, and West Palm Beach.

In February 1888, Florida had a special tourist: **President Grover Cleveland**, his wife, and some members of his staff. He visited the Subtropical Exposition in Jacksonville where he gave a speech supporting tourism to the state; then he took a train to Saint Augustine, meeting Henry Flagler, and then continued by train to Titusville, where he boarded a steamboat and visited Rock Ledge. On his return trip, he visited Sanford and Winter Park.

Florida during the Booming Years

The 1920s were a prosperous time for much of the nation. Florida's new railroads opened up large areas to development, spurring a **Florida land boom**. Investors of all kinds, mostly from outside Florida, raced to buy and sell rapidly appreciating land in new communities such as Miami and Palm Beach. Most of the people who bought land in Florida did so without stepping foot in the state, by hiring people to speculate and buy the land for them. By 1925, the market ran out of buyers to pay the high prices, and soon the boom became a bust. The **1926 Miami hurricane** further depressed the real estate market.

Florida also was able to take advantage of the railroads to boost its **citrus industry**. Citrus fruits became the staple of the economy there.

Florida in the Great Depression and the New Deal

The Great Depression arrived in 1929, but by that time, economic decay already consumed much of Florida. In 1931, the Florida State Legislature created a **State Racing Commission,** which legalized betting at both horse and dog racing tracks. When people won money from betting, a tax was taken out of the money. This new tax aided the state, but not as much as the legislature had hoped, as it was the depression after all.

Roosevelt's New Deal helped Florida when the Civilian Conservation Corps, or CCC, employed about 40,000 boys and cut down millions of trees to build fire lines. They also planted 13 million trees, created many of the state parks and wildlife preserves, built federal buildings and schools, and rebuilt the Overseas Railroad connecting Miami to Key West. This line would serve to bring tourism to Key West.

Florida's first theme parks emerged in the1930s and included **Cypress Gardens** (1936) near Winter Haven and **Marineland** (1938) near Saint Augustine.

Florida during WWII

The military was able to take advantage of Florida's warm climate and vacant land and throughout the 1930s built 172 military installations there, including 40 airfields. Two of the larger bases were Camp Blanding and the Jacksonville Naval Air Station.

By 1942, America's training facilities in Florida were so overcrowded that they had to take over many hotels and motels throughout Florida. Some places were used as barracks and others as makeshift hospitals for injured military personnel sent home from overseas.

Off the coast of Florida, German U-Boats sank over 24 ships, so many that burning ships could be seen from many areas along the coast. In late February 1942, German spies came on shore near Jacksonville with a plan to blow up railroad lines, but they were caught before they had a chance to accomplish their mission.

After this incident, the **Civil Air Patrol** was organized in March 1942, to protect the coasts of Florida. Dubbed the "Mosquito Fleet," they helped protect the coastlines of Florida and eliminated the threat from submarines.

Florida and Space

Because of Florida's low latitude, it was chosen in 1949 as a test site for the country's nascent missile program. **Patrick Air Force Base** and the **Cape Canaveral** launch site began to take shape in the 1950s. By the early 1960s, the space race was in full swing and generated a huge boom in the communities around Cape Canaveral. That area is now known as the Space Coast and features the **Kennedy Space Center**. It is also a major center of the aerospace industry. To date, all manned orbital space flights launched by the United States have been launched from Kennedy Space Center.

On July 24, 1950, a small rocket launched from Cape Canaveral inaugurated the U.S. space program. Fully engaged in a space race with the Soviet Union, Cape Canaveral became a centerpiece not only in the science program but also as a part of foreign policy. A side effect of the space program was the boom it brought to the economy with all of the businesses that opened up, like Pan American World Airways, the Radio Corporation of America, TransWorld Airlines, General Electric, and the Martin-Marietta Company, all of whom opened branches near the Cape.

In 1958, the **National Aeronautics and Space Administration**, NASA, was created to conduct space operations.

Kennedy's 1961 pledge that the United States would "put a man on the moon" before the end of the decade fueled interest and funding to NASA's space program. On February 20, 1962, **John Glenn** became the first American to go into orbit.

In 1963, NASA acquired almost 90,000 acres on Merritt Island near the Cape which became the headquarters of the American space industry. In that complex, the astronauts were trained and the space rockets were built. When President Kennedy was assassinated later in the year, the Cape's name was changed to Cape Kennedy, but it was later changed back to Cape Canaveral. However, the complex was renamed the Kennedy Space Center.

The space program continued to expand with the Apollo Program. The Apollo Program finally fulfilled the promise made by Kennedy when, on July 20, 1969, **Neil**

Armstrong stepped on the surface of the moon and said, "That's one small step for man, one giant leap for mankind." Visits to the moon continued as NASA continued to redesign itself and its mission.

The space shuttle program began in the 1970s, flourished in the 1980s, and made Florida once again the center of attention as this new spacecraft concept made space travel less of a dream and more of a reality. Attending launches became an exciting experience for Floridians and other Americans. Throughout the state, people could stand outside their homes and watch the shuttle go into space.

Florida, Disney, and Tourism

Walt Disney chose central Florida as the site of his planned **Walt Disney World Resort** in the 1960s and began purchasing land.

In 1971, the first component of the resort, the Magic Kingdom, opened and began the dramatic transformation of the Orlando area into a resort destination with a wide variety of theme parks. Besides Disney World, the Orlando area today features the Universal Orlando Resort, Sea World, and Wet'n Wild. The economic windfall that came with Disney created many side industries and made tourism one of the top industries in the state.

CHAPTER 7

What Is Social Science?

Identify social science disciplines (e.g., anthropology, psychology, sociology).

The social sciences emerged as a separate field in the middle of the nineteenth century, and is now counted as one of three types of science, among the natural sciences and formal sciences. Social science is a collection of disciplines that concern themselves with study human aspects of the world and draw upon empirical, quantitative, and qualitative methods to understand it. While each of the sciences explores one line of inquiry with regard to humans each also borrows or acquires knowledge from another field. In this respect, one of the disciplines cannot be completely studied in isolation.

- **Anthropology** has been called "the most scientific of the humanities, and the most humanistic of the sciences." Anthropology is a science of the entire panorama of humankind, from human origins to contemporary life. Anthropology's holistic perspective requires that anthropologists study all facets of society and culture, including tools, techniques, traditions, language, beliefs, kinships, values, social institutions, economic mechanisms, cravings for beauty and art, and struggles for prestige. It describes the impact of humans on other humans. There are four major fields within the discipline:

archaeological, biological, linguistic, and sociocultural anthropology. Anthropologists not only conduct field-based research, but they also use archival investigations and laboratory analyses.

- **Civics** is the branch of political science that examines civic affairs and the rights and duties of citizenship. It focuses on the role of citizens in a government.

- **Economics** is the social science that studies how people choose to use limited or scarce resources to obtain maximum satisfaction of unlimited wants. It looks at the production, distribution, and consumption of goods and services. Macroeconomics is the study of the economy as a whole. Some of the topics considered include inflation, unemployment, and economic growth. Microeconomics is the study of the individual parts, like households, business firms, and government agencies, that make up the economy and particularly emphasizes both how these units make decisions and the consequences of these decisions.

- **Education** is the social science field that is concerned with the pedagogy of teaching and learning.

- **Geography** is the study of the earth's surface, including such aspects as its climate, topography, vegetation, and population. It is a spatial discipline, one in which geographers preoccupy themselves with how to organize space. There are four main branches of geography: human, physical, regional, and topical/systematic. Geographers may specialize in a variety of subfields that break off of the four branches of geography, but all of them have as their focus the spatial perspective. **Population geography** is a form of geography that deals with the relationships between geography and population patterns, including birth and death rates. **Political geography** deals with the effect of geography on politics, especially on national boundaries and relations between states. **Economic geography** is a study of the interaction between the earth's landscape and the economic activity of the human population.

- **History**, derived from the Greek word *historia,* which means "information" or "an enquiry designed to elicit truth," is the study of political, economic, social, and cultural aspects of the past through the use of material, oral, and written sources. One line of inquiry that historians follow is to examine how the past affects our views of the present. Likewise, historians today acknowledge that the experiences of class, gender, race, ethnicity, and age affect not only our understanding of what happened in the past but also what the past was. Historians use almost all of the social science fields to round out their understanding of what happened in the past and how we should interpret it today.

- **Political science** is the study of the principles of government, the manner in which government conducts itself, how we identify ourselves as citizens of a particular nation, how we participate in our political structure and how it affects us, and what motivates us to affiliate ourselves with certain points of view or parties. They reveal the relationships underlying political events and conditions.

- **Sociology** is the study of human interaction, specifically how groups influence individual values, norms, and sanctions. Because individuals belong to multiple groups, each whose values, behaviors, and sanctions are not static and are socially constructed, sociologists examine the rules and processes that bind and separate these individuals and groups. Sociologists then study a range of human social relationships, social interaction, and culture, from how two people interact, to how nations and corporations interact with one another. They are especially interested in customs, traditions, and values that emerge from group experience and in the way the groups are affected by the customs, traditions, and values. Sociologists tend to draw heavily from the other social science disciplines of anthropology and psychology.

- **Psychology** is the scientific and systematic study of mental processes and/or behavior. Psychologists study directly observable behavior that may include talking, eating, and acting a certain way. They also study things that cannot be so readily observed, like dreams, thinking, emotions, and the way physiology impacts behavior. There are a variety of subfields in psychology that include specialties in these areas: clinical, counseling, school, industrial-organizational, experimental, social, developmental, and psychometric.

COMPETENCY 6.2

Identify social science concepts (e.g., culture, class, technology, race, gender).

Organizing the social studies curriculum in a way that as a social studies teacher K–12 can make understandable to their students and easier for them to teach would require using concepts and themes as a way to organize the content that you will need to teach. A **concept** in and of itself is abstract, a product gleaned from analysis and a synthesis of facts and experiences, rather than a simple, straightforward definition that can be memorized. Concepts are also dynamic constructs; they can expand as students grow and incorporate new experiences into their existing conceptual frameworks.

There are several ways to approach how to organize and identify key social studies concepts. The National Council for the Social Studies calls the main concepts "thematic strands" and suggests that these concepts, which may be found at *http://www.socialstudies.org/standards/strands#I,* are the following:

- Culture

- Time, Continuity, and Change

- People, Places, and Environments

- Individuals, Groups, and Institutions

- Power, Authority, and Governance

- Production, Distribution, and Consumption

- Science, Technology, and Society

- Global Connections

- Civic Ideals and Practices

The problem with such an approach is that it looks at social studies concepts as ideas that do not have wider explanations or theories and does not use multiple social science disciplines to further develop an idea. So, when you look at continuity and change, you also should look at wider ideas like reform, revolution, and progress.

Another way to organize social studies concepts is by discipline and to look at some of the major ideas on which each discipline tends to focus. Below, you will find brief, simplistic definitions of some of the major social science concepts arranged by discipline.

History

Arts and Ideas: Societies have used various forms of art, like dance, music, visual arts, literature, and theater, to express their beliefs, identity, and philosophical ideas. Art and ideas unite and motivate societies and may reflect conflict, or good attributes, and can define and divide a society.

Belief Systems: Religious, political, and philosophical systems have not only helped organize societies but also shaped the way societies act and react to both internal and external situations. Students will typically explore how religious beliefs have informed art, war, legal systems, and have shaped political, cultural, and social identities.

Change: the basic alterations in things, events, and ideas.

Conflict: a clash of ideas, interests, beliefs, agendas, objectives, or wills that results from forces that have incompatible ideas.

Choice: the ability, right, or power to select from a range of alternatives.

Continuity: how things remain the same.

Culture: the patterns of civilization, achievements, and customs of the people of a particular time and place and how they transmit these ideas to succeeding generations.

Diversity: Understanding, respecting others and oneself, and learning how to relate to those qualities and conditions that are different than our own. It celebrates differentiation in kind and degree within language, cognitive style, disability, gender, education, socioeconomic class, geographic background, language, physical appearance, religion, sexual orientation, and other human characteristics and traits.

Empathy: One's ability to understand others by thinking of how one would act if they were in the same situation.

Identity: the state or condition of being a certain thing. Identity plays a central role in history in terms of cultural, social, and political identity. To a large degree, identity may be constituted both internally and externally. Identity, or the perception of self and nation, plays a significant part in the formation and interpretation of history.

Interdependence: Reliance upon others in mutually beneficial interactions and exchanges.

Imperialism: The system and pursuit of empire through a process of accumulation and acquisition of land, resources, labor and profits that relies upon an ideology that suggests certain people need domination or assistance in becoming civilized.

Migration: The voluntary and involuntary transport of peoples, goods, and ideas from one place to another. Migration has transformed and defined empires and nations altering the social, political, and cultural landscape.

Movement of People and Goods: The constant exchange of people, ideas, products, technologies, and institutions from one region or civilization to another that has existed throughout history.

Nation-state: A political entity that provides a sovereign territory for a specific nation in which people are tied together through their citizenship (which might be linked to common language, ethnicity, race, ancestry, culture, etc.).

Nationalism: It has a wide variety of definitions. At its most basic, it means the common identity for groups of humans. Nationalism may reflect the feelings of pride in and devotion to one's country. It also could mean the desire of a people to control their own government, free from foreign interference or rule.

Science and Technology: Technological development from the creation of tools and fire to space exploration has shaped not only a country's military but also how it relates to their environment and belief systems.

Society: The complex pattern of political, economic, cultural, and social relationships bind people to a society. The establishment of social classes affects not only the customs and norms of a society but also the way it organizes itself politically, militarily, and economically.

Urbanization: Movement of people from rural to urban areas.

Geography

The six essential elements of geography:

The World in Spatial Terms—Geography maps the relationships between people, places, and environments by structuring the knowledge of them into real and mental maps and then conducting a spatial analysis of that information. So, maps become a primary tool that geographers use in order to present, acquire, process, and decipher information in spatial terms.

Places and Regions—Place and region are basic units of geography. Geographers examine the physical and human characteristics of places to understand how places work. They also trace peoples' perceptions of areas, how people create their own mental regions that come from their own view of the world, and how these perceptions or biases are created and organized.

Physical Systems—Physical processes shape Earth's surface and interact with plant and animal life to create, sustain, and modify ecosystems. This element of geography looks at environmental phenomena and the interaction through ecosystems, renewable resources, and the water cycle.

Human Systems—People are central to geography in that human activities help shape Earth's surface, human settlements and structures are part of Earth's surface, and humans compete for control of Earth's surface. This element looks at characteristics, distribution, and migration of human populations. It also tries to find patterns—in culture, economic interdependence, human settlement, conflict, and cooperation—and how these influence people's relationship with each other and the earth.

Environment and Society—Humans modify the earth's environment through their actions. Such actions happen largely as a consequence of the way people value or devalue the earth's resources.

The Uses of Geography—Geography informs people about the relationships they have between place and environments over time. This element explores how humans modify the physical environment, how physical systems affect human systems, and how the changes occur in the meaning, use, distribution, and importance of resources.

Environment—The surroundings, including natural elements and elements created by humans.

Geography and Environment—The elements undoubtedly influence the way and extent to which a society develops. People's attempts to modify their environment and adapt both themselves and the environment to meet their needs shapes the course of human history. The geography and environment of a people impact their political, cultural, economic, social, and religious beliefs and the way that they organize themselves.

Economics

Needs and Wants: Refers to the often confused goods and services that are essential such as food, clothing, and shelter that people need to survive, versus the good and services that people would like to have to improve their lives, like education, fancy clothing, health care, gym memberships, and entertainment.

Economic Systems: The way that a society allocates available resources and creates new ones shape the development of economic systems. Economic systems, from the simple bartering system to the more complex development of global capitalism, have shaped political and social systems. The development, exchange, and expansion of goods, markets, products, and ideas influence historical events both within and between societies.

Factors of Production: Resources that are necessary for production, like land, labor, capital, and enterprise.

Scarcity: Economic conflict when people have unlimited wants and needs but limited resources.

Science and technology: The tools and methods used by people to get what they need and want.

Civics

Justice: The fair, equal, proportional, or appropriate treatment rendered to individuals in interpersonal, societal, or government interactions.

Citizenship: Membership in a community (neighborhood, school, region, state, nation, or world) gained by meeting the legal requirements of national, state, or local governments with its accompanying rights, responsibilities, and dispositions.

Political Systems such as monarchies, dictatorships, and democracies address certain basic questions of government such as: What should a government have the power to do? What should a government not have the power to do? A political system also provides for ways that parts of that system interrelate and combine to perform specific functions of government.

Power: The ability of people to compel or influence the actions of others. "Legitimate power is called authority."

Government: Organization, agency, and institutions through which a political unit exercises authority, controls and administers public policy, directs and controls the actions of its members, and develops and maintains law-making and law enforcement.

Government and Civics: The way that societies are governed and the authority by which to govern remains a central theme of historical inquiry.

Civic Values: Those principles that serve as the foundation for our democratic form of government. These values include justice, honesty, self-discipline, due process, equality, majority rule with respect for minority rights, and respect for self, others, and property.

Human Rights: Those basic political, economic, and social rights that all human beings are entitled to, such as the right to life, liberty, and the security of person, and a standard of living that is adequate for the health and well-being of himself and of his family.

COMPETENCY 6.3

Analyze the interrelationships between social science disciplines.

See Competency 5.1 for discussion and analysis of social science disciplines.

COMPETENCY 6.4

Interpret tabular and graphic representations of information related to the social sciences.

A **table** is both a visual representation of a way to arrange data so it can be easily studied and compared with other information. In the social sciences, tables can be used to illustrate research and data analysis. Tables can differ significantly in variety, structure, flexibility, notation, representation, and use. There is always a title of the table that tells you what the subject is—this should give you a frame of reference for the information you are studying. A table contains an ordered arrangement of rows and columns, and one of them, at least, should have a row and/or column devoted to the **header**, which displays the names of what you are examining. Make sure on the exam that you identify the header so you can better interpret and understand the information you are being asked to analyze. The information in a table, usually statistics, is organized in rows and columns, usually two or more of each. The columns run vertically, and the rows are in the horizontal position.

The table below (Table 7.1) is a partial display of a complex table of population data from the United States Census Bureau. Of import in reading the title is the parenthetic notation "numbers in thousands," and the reference numbers in superscript. Any analysis of the data would require the discussion of the numbers in the context of thousands. For instance, the total number of people under discussion, both men and women, is 299,106,000 or two hundred ninety-nine million, one-hundred and six thousand people. In addition, analysis of the table information would take into account the inclusion of armed forces personnel and their families on post, whether oversees or state-side (see footnote 1) and, definition of Hispanic explained in the second footnote.

Table 7.1
Population by Sex, Age, Hispanic Origin, and Race: 2008
(Numbers in thousands. Civilian non-institutionalized population[1])

					Hispanic origin and race[2]						
						Non-Hispanic					
	Total		Hispanic		Total		White alone		All other races	
Sex and age	Number	Percent	Number	Percent	Number	Percent	Number	Percent	Number	Percent
Both sexes	299,106	100.0	46,026	100.0	253,079	100.0	196,768	100.0	56,312	100.0
.Under 5 years	20,902	7.0	5,014	10.9	15,888	6.3	11,210	5.7	4,678	8.3
.5 to 9 years	20,018	6.7	4,336	9.4	15,682	6.2	11,283	5.7	4,400	7.8
.10 to 14 years	20,038	6.7	3,986	8.7	16,052	6.3	11,641	5.9	4,410	7.8
.15 to 19 years	21,314	7.1	3,799	8.3	17,515	6.9	12,813	6.5	4,702	8.3
.20 to 24 years	20,529	6.9	3,617	7.9	16,912	6.7	12,742	6.5	4,170	7.4
.25 to 29 years	21,057	7.0	4,275	9.3	16,782	6.6	12,544	6.4	4,238	7.5
.30 to 34 years	19,089	6.4	3,861	8.4	15,227	6.0	11,307	5.7	3,920	7.0
.35 to 44 years	42,132	14.1	6,904	15.0	35,228	13.9	27,046	13.7	8,182	14.5
.45 to 54 years	43,935	14.7	4,887	10.6	39,048	15.4	31,331	15.9	7,717	13.7
.55 to 64 years	33,302	11.1	2,792	6.1	30,510	12.1	25,409	12.9	5,101	9.1
.65 to 74 years	19,588	6.5	1,530	3.3	18,058	7.1	15,226	7.7	2,832	5.0
.75 to 84 years	12,913	4.3	791	1.7	12,122	4.8	10,616	5.4	1,505	2.7
.85 years and over	4,289	1.4	234	0.5	4,055	1.6	3,600	1.8	455	0.8

[1] Plus armed forces living off post or with their families on post.

[2] Hispanic refers to people whose origin is Mexican, Puerto Rican, Cuban, Spanish-speaking Central or South American countries, or other Hispanic/Latino, regardless of race.

Source: U.S. Census Bureau, Current Population Survey, Annual Social and Economic Supplement, 2008. Internet release date: September 2009.

Information graphics or **infographics** are graphic visual representations of information, data, or knowledge. These graphics present complex information quickly and compactly. You might see them used in subway maps, (as in the London Underground map displayed below), journalism, signs, education, and technical manuals. These are usually good ways to communicate difficult concepts that people would become lost in if they were written out in text format.

Figure 7.1
London Underground Map

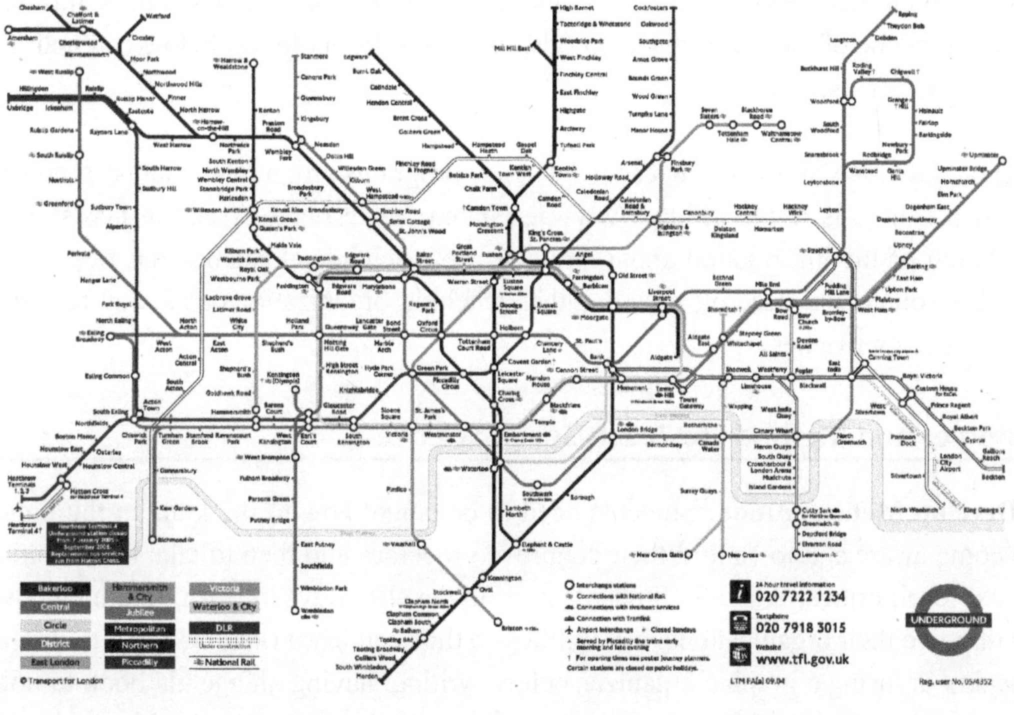

COMPETENCY 6.5
Identify appropriate strategies, methods, tools, and technologies for the teaching of social science.

Considering the breadth of state social studies standards that students are expected to know each year, teaching social science today mandates that teachers avoid teaching the subject as "just another long parade of facts." Teachers must carefully plan and assess lessons in order to provide learning experiences that result in meaningful learning by having students relate the facts and concepts that they learn to their understanding about how the world works. Content, therefore, should be integrative and lessons should enable students to learn actively. Students have to make connections to the material and between the material that they are taught, not only in one year, but in year after year. The goal of Florida's social science curriculum is to enable students to acquire the knowledge, skill, and judgment to learn independently; to engage students as citizen actors so that they can engage in civic life in an intelligent and responsible manner, and to make decisions about local, national, and international issues; to appreciate and use historical and cultural resources historic sites, museums, parks, libraries, and multimedia information sources to enrich their lives and expand their understanding of the social sciences throughout their lives. Some of the strategies, methods, tools, and technologies below can help in the teaching of social science.

There are a few strategies that social science programs around the country tend to use. One such source is found at http://www.tea.state.tx.us/resources/ssced/instass/strategies. htm. Much of the information about strategies to teach social science has been gleaned from that source and used by social studies teaching organizations as a way to organize pedagogical approaches.

Strategies and Methods to Teach Social Science

Develop Metacognition: Students need to be taught how to think about thinking and to become aware and to control their cognitive processes and then to take that thinking to the next level: critical thinking. Students need to develop ways to learn, find methods that help improve their organizational capabilities so they can learn (i.e., having a folder to put all papers in, using a graphic organizer before writing, having an agenda book to note all of their assignments in). There are a variety of ways to develop metacognition in students:

- *Share and model self-monitoring processes:* Show a piece of work and let them see how to make it better.

- *Explain strategies that a student can use:* Detail, out loud, how one might solve a problem, organize an essay, or prepare for a test.

- *Clarify why particular strategies are helpful and useful:* Help students develop their **conditional knowledge** by letting them know what works, when, and why.

- *Clarify and model when particular strategies are appropriate:* Show kids how you learn something and then learn something together. It helps to verbalize what you are thinking and how to solve a problem. Students benefit by seeing you make errors along the way, test a hypothesis that may and may not work out, and suggest improvements for the next time you might encounter something similar.

Help students to come up with their own plan to use metacogntion to ask and answer the following questions:

- What do I already know or understand about this subject, topic, or issue?

- Do I understand what I am supposed to know?

- Do I know where I can find some information to add to my knowledge?

- How much time will it take me to learn this new knowledge?

- What are some strategies and tactics that I can use to learn more about this?

- Did I understand what I just heard, read, or saw?

- How will I know if I am learning this new knowledge too quickly, too slowly, or just right?

- How can I spot a mistake if I make one?

- How should I revise my plan to learn this new knowledge if what I am doing is not working?

Activate Prior Knowledge: Learning happens when new information is added to old information and ideas. Some ways to activate prior knowledge are :

- *Brainstorming:* This can be done in a collective way or individually.

- *Cognitive Mapping:* The students have learned a great deal about their local environment by experiencing it. They can be led to use that knowledge to help them understand the places and events of the past.

Collaborative Processes: Having students work together to solve a problem, present an idea, or develop a project are skills that are helpful in a democracy. Collaborative work can help students retain information better and teaches them how to work with others.

- **Use cross-age or cross-ability pairings:** Sometimes the best way for students to learn something is to have to teach it.

Inquiry Teaching: Teach students how to use the scientific method of inquiry by having them ask and answer key issues. Teaching inquiry basically involves the following steps: identify and clarify an issue; propose a hypothesis; locate, collect, and organize the data or evidence information they receive; evaluate, interpret and analyze the data; then, finally, draw inferences and conclusions about it and use this information to make generalizations. This way, students generate their own knowledge

- **Use collaborate, substantive, and reflective discussions**

- **Cooperative learning structures**

- **Engage in problem solving and decision making**

- **Use case studies**

- **Use Storypath Method:** Uses the basic components of a setting, characters, and a plot—a story—to organize the social studies curriculum and integrates language arts with social studies.

- **Use spatial dynamics in the classroom:** Use models to replicate what students are studying.

- **WebQuests**

- **Virtual Museums**

Problem Solving: Students use facts, concepts, and generalizations in the process to finding solutions to problems.

Direct Instruction: Provide instruction direction, like in a lecture, explaining a new skill, providing baseline information, or modeling a thinking process.

Visual Strategies: Use visual aids to facilitate understanding.

- May use PowerPoints, photographs, graphs, tables, charts, or multi-media to convey a topic or idea.

Teaching Facts, Concepts, and Generalizations: Social studies instruction requires the teaching of facts, concepts, and generalizations. Because one depends upon the other, they cannot be taught in isolation. Concepts rely on facts, but facts are meaningless unless they relate to concepts and generalizations. Generalizations organize and summarize information obtained from an analysis of facts. While a generalization contains a broad assertion, a fact is only a truth about a particular incident. There are two ways to teach generalizations.

- Inductive/Discovery Approach: Students look at a set of materials, but then with a teacher, they examine key points and discuss the data and the patterns, similarities, and differences that they find. Then they draw conclusions, summarize their findings, and infer generalizations from it.

- Deductive/Expository Approach: Students are presented with a hypothesis or generalization and have to find evidence to support it. The concepts of the generalization are clarified. The teacher then provides instruction and assistance to students to verify the generalization. Then the students create or find new generalizations.

Concept: Concepts are the categories we use to organize information. They are the building blocks between facts and generalizations. Students should be taught how to move from lots of facts, to concepts, and then to generalizations.

Community-Based Instruction: Using real-life situations and setting to explain a concept or enrich curriculum.

- Field Trips

- Field Studies

- Mentoring/Apprenticeships

- Service Learning

Role Play and Simulations: These help students make events from the past, present, or hypothetical come alive. Simulations help them engage in problem solving in real-word contexts. Role play helps students see situations from multiple perspectives

Discussion Formats: Use dialogue to facilitate conversation about an issue.

- Debates

- Seminars

- Colloquium

- Use Graphic Organizers

Tools and Technologies to Teach Social Sciences

Fortunately for social studies teachers, many aspects of the social studies curriculum lend themselves quite well toward the integration of technology in the classroom. Using Florida State Standards as your guide, you can use some of the following applications of technology in your classroom to make it come alive for the students:

- Spreadsheet software like Microsoft Excel

  - Research and compare different information.

- Graphic Design software, like PrintShop

  - Have students make or design posters. They can use images gleaned from Google images. (Of course, students should learn that they need to provide citation of all images used.)

- Blogs: Students can use blogs, like those found on blogger.com, to create an electronic journal.

- Glogs: Students can use glogs to display group work on the web.

- Wikis: Teachers can use wikis, like those found on wetpaint.com or PBworks, as places for students to create three-dimensional research papers.

- Web pages: Teachers can use web pages to organize and display information.

- Presentation software: Teachers can use **PowerPoint** effectively (not a lot of words on a slide and good use of graphics and images) to bolster lectures, and students can learn how to use them to consolidate and present their own research papers. **Prezi** offers another type of presentation tool to excite student learning.

- Game technology: Teachers may use games, either on CDs or the Internet, to either help students role-play or to teach an important point in a visual and interactive manner.

- Graphic organizing software: This helps produce concept maps, like *Inspriation,*

- Use a publishing program to have students put their work in a desktop publishing finished piece.

- Use photographs, maps, and images from the computer to provide visual representations of topics or ideas that can be explored either individually, in groups, or in class-wide settings.

- Use tools like Google Earth to answer questions about geography, mapping, and history.

- Use digital story telling software like *Comic Life* to present ideas.

- Use social networking and web bookmarking tools to organize information such at *Diigo* and *delicious.*

- Internet projects where students learn how to sift through the information on the internet, how to verify information, how to cite information gleaned from it, and how to access databases of journals and newspapers.

- Use WebQuests of internet-based activities by giving students a task, scenario, or problem to solve.

COMPETENCY 6.6
Evaluate examples of primary (e.g., letters, photographs, political cartoons) and secondary (e.g., historical texts, encyclopedias) sources.

Historians use two types of sources: primary sources and secondary sources. Basically, the distinction between these two types of sources is the author's proximity to an event. Primary sources are documents, oral histories, or physical objects that were created during the period being studied or immediately after it. The idea is that the primary sources reflect an "insider's" understanding of an event, or "first-hand knowledge" of an event. Examples of primary sources are: original documents, diaries, personal narratives, speeches, government records, letters, interviews, autobiographies, pottery, buildings, clothing, novels, newspaper articles (written soon after an event), photographs, manuscripts, original theatrical or literary works, coins, stamps, or even tombstones.

Secondary sources are one step removed from an event, and they contain someone's impressions, judgments, and interpretations of primary material or an event. Secondary sources include: history textbooks, journal articles, documentaries, books written about a period of time, encyclopedias, histories, and biographies.

Whether approaching either a primary or secondary source, historians must learn how to properly analyze a document. Historians should consider how, when, and where a document was created, as it might have a tremendous effect on what was actually recorded. As all sources have bias, historians need to try to uncover how bias has affected the source. They should consider how close in time and location a source was created to a certain event. What was the intention of a document? Was it meant for private or public consumption?

Because bias is present in all sources, some sources might be considered more reliable than others. In addition , of course, each historian might have a different opinion based on his or her own biases about what is "reliable" or not. This process can pose some thorny questions. Is an eyewitness to an event more or less reliable? Could eyewitnesses have been so consumed with emotion that their view or understanding of an event was skewed? Should the historian privy a source that was meant for public consumption or one that was more private? Which would be more truthful?

To make matters even more confusing, sometimes secondary sources are also primary sources. For instance, if you were writing a paper looking at HOW a particular author has written history, well that author's history books would then become your primary sources. So, to a large degree, the designation of whether or not a source is primary or secondary is determined by HOW the author intends to use the source.

Practice Test 1

FTCE: Social Science 6–12

This test is also on CD-ROM in our special interactive TestWare® for the FTCE Social Science 6-12. It is highly recommended that you first take this exam on computer. You will then have the additional study features and benefits of enforced timed conditions and instantaneous, accurate scoring. See page 7 for instructions on how to get the most out of our FTCE book and software.

ANSWER SHEET FOR PRACTICE TEST 1

1. (A) (B) (C) (D)
2. (A) (B) (C) (D)
3. (A) (B) (C) (D)
4. (A) (B) (C) (D)
5. (A) (B) (C) (D)
6. (A) (B) (C) (D)
7. (A) (B) (C) (D)
8. (A) (B) (C) (D)
9. (A) (B) (C) (D)
10. (A) (B) (C) (D)
11. (A) (B) (C) (D)
12. (A) (B) (C) (D)
13. (A) (B) (C) (D)
14. (A) (B) (C) (D)
15. (A) (B) (C) (D)
16. (A) (B) (C) (D)
17. (A) (B) (C) (D)
18. (A) (B) (C) (D)
19. (A) (B) (C) (D)
20. (A) (B) (C) (D)
21. (A) (B) (C) (D)
22. (A) (B) (C) (D)
23. (A) (B) (C) (D)
24. (A) (B) (C) (D)
25. (A) (B) (C) (D)
26. (A) (B) (C) (D)
27. (A) (B) (C) (D)
28. (A) (B) (C) (D)
29. (A) (B) (C) (D)
30. (A) (B) (C) (D)

31. (A) (B) (C) (D)
32. (A) (B) (C) (D)
33. (A) (B) (C) (D)
34. (A) (B) (C) (D)
35. (A) (B) (C) (D)
36. (A) (B) (C) (D)
37. (A) (B) (C) (D)
38. (A) (B) (C) (D)
39. (A) (B) (C) (D)
40. (A) (B) (C) (D)
41. (A) (B) (C) (D)
42. (A) (B) (C) (D)
43. (A) (B) (C) (D)
44. (A) (B) (C) (D)
45. (A) (B) (C) (D)
46. (A) (B) (C) (D)
47. (A) (B) (C) (D)
48. (A) (B) (C) (D)
49. (A) (B) (C) (D)
50. (A) (B) (C) (D)
51. (A) (B) (C) (D)
52. (A) (B) (C) (D)
53. (A) (B) (C) (D)
54. (A) (B) (C) (D)
55. (A) (B) (C) (D)
56. (A) (B) (C) (D)
57. (A) (B) (C) (D)
58. (A) (B) (C) (D)
59. (A) (B) (C) (D)
60. (A) (B) (C) (D)

61. (A) (B) (C) (D)
62. (A) (B) (C) (D)
63. (A) (B) (C) (D)
64. (A) (B) (C) (D)
65. (A) (B) (C) (D)
66. (A) (B) (C) (D)
67. (A) (B) (C) (D)
68. (A) (B) (C) (D)
69. (A) (B) (C) (D)
70. (A) (B) (C) (D)
71. (A) (B) (C) (D)
72. (A) (B) (C) (D)
73. (A) (B) (C) (D)
74. (A) (B) (C) (D)
75. (A) (B) (C) (D)
76. (A) (B) (C) (D)
77. (A) (B) (C) (D)
78. (A) (B) (C) (D)
79. (A) (B) (C) (D)
80. (A) (B) (C) (D)
81. (A) (B) (C) (D)
82. (A) (B) (C) (D)
83. (A) (B) (C) (D)
84. (A) (B) (C) (D)
85. (A) (B) (C) (D)
86. (A) (B) (C) (D)
87. (A) (B) (C) (D)
88. (A) (B) (C) (D)
89. (A) (B) (C) (D)
90. (A) (B) (C) (D)

91. (A) (B) (C) (D)
92. (A) (B) (C) (D)
93. (A) (B) (C) (D)
94. (A) (B) (C) (D)
95. (A) (B) (C) (D)
96. (A) (B) (C) (D)
97. (A) (B) (C) (D)
98. (A) (B) (C) (D)
99. (A) (B) (C) (D)
100. (A) (B) (C) (D)
101. (A) (B) (C) (D)
102. (A) (B) (C) (D)
103. (A) (B) (C) (D)
104. (A) (B) (C) (D)
105. (A) (B) (C) (D)
106. (A) (B) (C) (D)
107. (A) (B) (C) (D)
108. (A) (B) (C) (D)
109. (A) (B) (C) (D)
110. (A) (B) (C) (D)
111. (A) (B) (C) (D)
112. (A) (B) (C) (D)
113. (A) (B) (C) (D)
114. (A) (B) (C) (D)
115. (A) (B) (C) (D)
116. (A) (B) (C) (D)
117. (A) (B) (C) (D)
118. (A) (B) (C) (D)
119. (A) (B) (C) (D)
120. (A) (B) (C) (D)

PRACTICE TEST 1

1. The two components of a climate graph are

   A. the amount of rainfall and temperature of an area.

   B. temperature highs and lows for a specific time of year.

   C. the amount of rain expected in the tourist seasons.

   D. future rainfall and temperature changes caused by global warming.

2. Which of the following regions is most threatened by desertification?

   A. South America

   B. Australia

   C. Europe

   D. Africa

3. A market economy relies on _____ to allocate resources.

   A. government

   B. good planning

   C. market forces

   D. small businesses

4. A demand deposit at a commercial bank is

   A. an asset to a bank and a liability to the Fed.

   B. a liability to the depositor and an asset to the bank.

   C. a liability to both the depositor and the bank.

   D. an asset to the depositor and a liability to the bank.

5. The purpose of the Truman Doctrine was to

   A. aid the economic recovery of war-torn Europe.

   B. prevent European meddling in the affairs of South American countries.

   C. aid countries that were the targets of Communist expansionism.

   D. expand the Monroe Doctrine to include Eastern Asia.

6. The Soviet leader whose policies of *glasnost* and *perestroika* encouraged the fall of communism in the Eastern bloc was

   A. Brezhnev.

   B. Khrushchev.

   C. Stalin.

   D. Gorbachev.

7. Which of the following statements best describes conditions in Africa before the European Age of Exploration?

   A. African cultures did not have the capacity to make iron before the first century C.E.

   B. Ghana was central to the trans-Saharan trade in gold and salt.

   C. Axum participated in the Indian Ocean trade, which stopped when it was conquered by Muslims.

   D. Zimbabwe flourished with the Arab trading ports along the east coast of Africa declined.

8. What form of government ruled Russia prior to the Revolution of 1917?

   A. Democracy

   B. Autocracy

   C. Monarchy

   D. Oligarchy

9. Renaissance Humanism was a threat to the Church because it

   A. espoused atheism.

   B. denounced scholasticism.

   C. denounced neo-Platonism.

   D. emphasized a return to the original sources of Christianity.

10. Which of these empires or kingdoms was NOT part of the Islamic world?

   A. Axum

   B. The Mongols

   C. The Mughals

   D. Ghana

11. In medieval European university, what language was used to study classical texts?

    A. Latin

    B. Greek

    C. Hebrew

    D. Aramaic

12. In the 1940s, the Việt Minh took over the Vietnamese government from whom?

    A. The French

    B. Emperor Bao Dai

    C. Prime Minister Ngo Dinh Diem

    D. Khai Dinh

13. Which of the following is true regarding the role of women in World War II?

    A. American women fought in combat.

    B. Japanese women were encouraged to serve in the armed forces.

    C. Chinese women and Soviet women served in the armed forces in combat.

    D. British women fought in combat.

14. What word below best describes *apartheid*?

    A. Desegregation

    B. Equality

    C. Segregation

    D. Violence

15. Germany's invasion of which country prompted the British and French to declare war, starting World War II?

    A. The Rhineland

    B. Poland

    C. Sudetenland

    D. Austria

16. Which of the following terms is closely related to *autocracy*?

    A. Democracy

    B. Capitalism

    C. Despotism

    D. Theocracy

17. Article 1 of the U.S. Constitution creates

    A. a bicameral legislature.

    B. a unicameral legislature.

    C. the presidency.

    D. the judicial branch.

18. Which statement best describes the foreign policy of the United States during the Cold War?

    A. The United States had a policy of noninvolvement in Latin America.

    B. The United States supported coups against the governments of Iran and Guatemala in this period.

    C. The United States had few investments in Latin America during this time.

    D. The United States refused to support abusive regimes in Latin America, the Middle East, and the Philippines.

19. Which historical movement was Immanuel Kant a part of?

    A. The Enlightenment

    B. The Scientific Revolution

    C. The Renaissance

    D. The Protestant Reformation

20. Which of the following statements about the Han Dynasty is true?

    A. The boundaries established by the Qin and maintained by the Han have more or less defined the nation of China up to the present day.

    B. The Han Dynasty ended before the birth of Christ.

    C. The Han relied on Buddhism as the philosophical basis for government.

    D. China was relatively unsophisticated during the Han Dynasty with little poetry or writings.

21. All of the following were aspects of Britain's policy of indirect rule in colonial Africa EXCEPT

    A. subsidizing primary education for Africans.

    B. the expectation of eventual self-government.

    C. decentralized administration.

    D. uniform government policy throughout the colonized territories.

22. Adolf Hitler became chancellor of Germany in 1933. What was one of his first official acts?

    A. He began secretly building up Germany's army and weapons.

    B. He established government policies to ease the effects of the Great Depression.

    C. He established alliances with Italy and Czechoslovakia.

    D. He met with France and Britain to work out treaties.

23. Paleolithic peoples are characterized by which of the following?

    I. Hunter-gatherer

    II. Highly nomadic

    III. Artist

    IV. Work with crude tools

    V. Grow crops

    A. I only

    B. I and II only

    C. I, III, IV, and V only

    D. I, II, III, and IV only

24. In 1831, Nat Turner organized and led a slave insurrection in Southhampton County, Virginia, that resulted in

    A. the gradual and compensated emancipation of the majority of slaves in Virginia.

    B. the immediate emancipation and eventual transportation of Nat Turner and his followers to Santo Domingo.

    C. Congress passing a stringent fugitive slave law.

    D. the southern states expanding their militia system and strengthening the slave codes.

25. In its decision in the case of *Plessy v. Ferguson,* the Supreme Court held that

    A. separate facilities for different races were inherently unequal and therefore unconstitutional.

    B. no slave could be a citizen of the United States.

    C. separate but equal facilities for different races were constitutional.

    D. imposition of a literacy test imposed an unconstitutional barrier to the right to vote.

26. All of the following statements about the Civilian Conservation Corps are true EXCEPT

    A. its members lived in camps, wore uniforms, and were under semi-military discipline.

    B. it engaged in such projects as preventing soil erosion and impounding lakes.

    C. it eventually came to employ over one-third of the American work force.

    D. it provided that some of the workers' pay should be sent home to their families.

27. All of the following describe the long-term cause of the Reformation EXCEPT

    I.   popular discontent with the empty Church rituals.

    II. movement towards more personal ways of communicating with God.

    III. Jan Hus was burned at the stake in 1415 after he argued that priests were not a holy group.

    IV growth in the power of the secular king and the decrease in the power of the Pope.

    V.   fiscal crisis in the Church that led to corruption and abuses of power.

  A.   I, II, and III only

  B.   II, III, and IV only

  C.   III, IV, and V only

  D.   I, II, IV, and V only

28. One of the major effects of the Industrial Revolution of the late nineteenth century in the United States was an

  A.   increased emphasis on worker health and safety issues.

  B.   increased emphasis on speed rather than quality of work.

  C.   increased emphasis on high-quality, error-free work.

  D.   increase in the number of small industrial facilities, which could operate more efficiently than larger, more costly industrial plants.

29. Which of the following statements is NOT true of *Homo erectus?*

  A.   It had the capacity to make fire.

  B.   It depended on gathering for survival and also hunting or scavenging.

  C.   It was the first hominid to leave Africa.

  D.   Its oldest fossils are found in Australia.

30. What is considered the cradle of Western civilization?

  A.   The Holy Roman Empire

  B.   Ancient Greece

  C.   Christianity

  D.   The Enlightenment and the Age of Reason

31. Which of the following would be considered a primary source in researching the factors that influenced U.S. involvement in the Korean War?

    I.   The personal correspondence of a military man stationed with the 5th Regimental Combat Team (RCT) in Korea.

    II. A biography of Harry S. Truman by David McCullough, published in 1993.

    III. A journal article about the beginning of the Korean War by a noted scholar.

    IV. An interview with Secretary of Defense George Marshall.

    A.   I and II only

    B.   II and IV only

    C.   II and III only

    D.   I and IV only

32. The first religious development to have an impact throughout colonial America was the

    A.   establishment of religious toleration in Maryland.

    B.   spread of Quaker ideas from Pennsylvania.

    C.   Parsons' Cause.

    D.   Great Awakening.

33. All of the following were weaknesses of the Articles of Confederation government EXCEPT that it lacked

    A.   the power to levy taxes.

    B.   the power to regulate commerce.

    C.   the power to borrow money.

    D.   a strong executive.

34. What is true regarding the Marshall Plan?

    A.   It ended the Cold War.

    B.   It granted British control over Palestine after World War I.

    C.   It ended the conflict in Korea.

    D.   It gave Western Europe billions to rebuild after World War II.

35. Which of the following is NOT an example of a scarce resource?

    A. Oil

    B. Coal

    C. Clean water

    D. Carbon dioxide

36. The economy experiences an increase in the price level, a decrease in real domestic output, and increased unemployment. Which of the following is the most likely cause?

    A. Increased productivity

    B. Increased input prices

    C. Reduced government regulations

    D. Increased exports

37. What are considered the factors of production in economics?

    A. Location, location, location

    B. Land, labor, capital, and entrepreneurship

    C. Land, money, and labor

    D. Money, motivation, and action

38. Which is NOT an example of how environmental concerns can become economic priorities?

    A. Recycling

    B. Reforestation

    C. Greenhouse effect

    D. Coal-generated electricity to replace imported oil

39. The economic indicator that measures the price change over time, using a fixed market basket of typical goods and services, is the

    A. producer price index.

    B. consumer sentiment index.

    C. GDP.

    D. CPI.

40. What is the definition of *sociology*?

    A.   The science of humankind

    B.   The study of how individuals become members of groups and move between groups, and how being in different groups affects individuals and the groups in which they participate

    C.   The study of the earth and its features

    D.   The study of the interpretation of the past and how it affects our view of the present

41. The research method which involves a social scientist living among and interacting with the people being studied is known as

    A.   strategic engagement.

    B.   experimentation.

    C.   content analysis.

    D.   participant observation.

42. According to the table below, what can you infer from the data about children from single-parent families in Florida?

Florida Children from Single-Parent Families, 2008

Scale: 5%–80%

Ethnic Group		
Non-Hispanic White	28%	
Black or African American	61%	
American Indian	S	
Asian and Pacific Islander	17%	
Hispanic or Latino	37%	
Total	36%	

Source: Data estimate has been suppressed. Estimates from the American Community Survey (ACS) are suppressed when the total confidence interval (upper bound minus lower bound) of the percent estimate is 10 percentage points or greater.

    A.   In 2008, most children from single-parent families were Hispanic or Latino.

    B.   The proportion of American Indian children from single-parent families is the lowest.

    C.   The percentage of children from Asian single-parent families is higher than the percentage of non-Hispanic white children from single-parent families.

    D.   The percentage of African-American children from single-parent families represents the largest group of children from single-parent families.

43. Miss Bailey teaches sixth-grade social studies with 25 students of various achievement levels. She is starting a unit on the history of their local community and wants to stimulate the students' thinking. She also wants to encourage students to develop a project as a result of their study. Which type of project would encourage the highest level of thinking by the students?

    A. Giving students a list of questions about people, dates, and events, then having them put the answers on a poster, with appropriate pictures, to display in class

    B. Giving students questions to use to interview older members of the community, then having them write articles based on the interviews and publish them in a booklet

    C. Discussing the influence of the past on the present community, then asking students to project what the community might be like in 100 years

    D. Using archived newspapers to collect data, then having them draw a timeline that includes the major events of the community from its beginning to the current date

44. Longitude and latitude are examples of which theme of geography?

    A. Location

    B. Place

    C. Region

    D. Movement

45. Economics is a science that deals with which of the following?

    A. Money and its uses

    B. Scarce resources and their allocation

    C. The examination of balancing scarce resources with unlimited wants

    D. Market and planned economies

46. In the first two decades under the United States Constitution, the main factor that separated Federalists from Republicans was whether they

    A. accepted the Constitution or opposed it

    B. favored the French Revolution or opposed it.

    C. leaned more toward states' rights or national sovereignty.

    D. had been patriots or loyalists during the American War of Independence.

47. Which of the following documents embodies the ideals of individual freedom so commonly associated with the United States?

    A.   The Declaration of Independence

    B.   The Constitution

    C.   The Articles of Confederation

    D.   Both the Declaration of Independence and the Constitution

48. The term *periodization* is used

    A.   to track economic trends.

    B.   to place an historical event into a chronological context.

    C.   in political science to study elections.

    D.   in geography to study time zones.

49. The religion that most influenced the development of sub-Saharan Africa before the Age of Exploration was

    A.   Christianity.

    B.   Hinduism.

    C.   Judaism.

    D.   Islam.

50. The Monroe Doctrine stated that the United States

    A.   was not concerned with the type of government other countries might have.

    B.   was concerned only with the type of government that the countries of the Western Hemisphere might have.

    C.   would not tolerate any new European colonization in the New World.

    D.   claimed the Western Hemisphere as its exclusive zone of influence.

Directions for questions 51 and 52: Place the following events in chronological order.

I.   President Andrew Johnson is impeached.

II. Abraham Lincoln issues the Emancipation Proclamation.

III. James Buchanan is elected president.

IV. General William Tecumseh Sherman achieves victory in Atlanta.

51. What are the first and last events in chronological order?

A. III and I

B. II and I

C. IV and I

D. I and IV

52. What are the middle two events in chronological order?

A. III and I

B. II and IV

C. IV and I

D. I and IV

53. The purpose of grandfather clauses and literacy tests, used in the southern states in the late 1800s and early 1900s, was to prevent

A. illiterate white people from voting.

B. recent immigrants from voting.

C. black people from running for public office.

D. black people from voting.

54. What change to European governments came to characterize the time period 1750–1800 as the Age of Revolution?

A. Many nations became either absolutist states or constitutionalist states.

B. Democratic governments evolved into socialist governments.

C. Aristocracies were overthrown by peasants.

D. Monarchies returned to power in most European nation-states.

55. What was the net result of the Eighteenth Amendment?

    A. All Americans were eligible to vote.

    B. Prohibition created major organized-crime activity in the United States.

    C. The Great Depression was eased.

    D. Presidents were limited to two terms of four years each.

56. What led to a large wave of Cuban immigration into southern Florida in the 1950s?

    A. The Cuban Missile Crisis

    B. The Cuban Revolution of 1959

    C. The Korean War

    D. The opening of Cape Canaveral

57. The concept of culture includes all of the following EXCEPT

    A. personal values.

    B. religious beliefs.

    C. styles of dress.

    D. individual intelligence.

58. Which of the following is NOT an example of a social network?

    A. A church congregation

    B. A university

    C. A family

    D. A party planner

59. The Himalayan mountain range runs through which of the following Asian countries?

    I. China

    II. Nepal

    III. India

    IV. Bangladesh

    A. I and II only.

    B. II and III only.

    C. I, II, and III only.

    D. I, III, and IV only.

Questions 60-64 are based on the following scenario.

Phyllis Johnson is a junior high school social studies teacher who has chosen human diversity as the topic for a lesson unit. She has decided to approach the topic by asking students to engage in introspective activities. On the day she introduces the topic to the class, she asks the students to make a list of the things they like about themselves. Then, she asks them to write two paragraphs in class describing their personal strengths in terms of (a) their classroom behavior and (b) their behavior or relationships with others outside class.

60. By asking her students to think about their own characteristics, Ms. Johnson is promoting her students' cognitive development by helping them to

  A. activate prior knowledge as a basis for understanding new concepts.

  B. demonstrate their ability to write personal narratives.

  C. practice their grammar and sentence structure.

  D. develop positive self-esteem by identifying their assets and skills.

61. When Ms. Johnson asks the students to write about their behavior in class and their behavior or relationships outside class, she is taking into consideration aspects of human development by

  A. stressing that some students are concrete thinkers in adolescence, according to Piaget.

  B. noting that most adolescents are thinking at the stage of formal operations, according to Piaget.

  C. observing that students' cognitive functioning is a product of both their innate intellectual characteristics and their environment.

  D. pinpointing that adolescent students tend to be socially unaware and cognitively insensitive to the thoughts of others.

62. The next lesson in Ms. Johnson's unit on diversity is a library project. In order to determine what kind of project students will undertake, Ms. Johnson leads the class through a brainstorming activity, allowing the students to generate a list of possible topics for the library project. By doing this, Ms. Johnson

  A. can determine the students' interests.

  B. gives everyone a chance to participate in class.

C.   demonstrates an approach for solving problems creatively.

D.   avoids giving everyone in class the same assignment.

63.   Students decide that they would like to read about an American they admire. Asking the students to work together in pairs, so that they can work together in the library, Ms. Johnson decides that this approach will allow students to be most productive and will ensure that learning preferences and learner characteristics are compatible for each pair of students. In choosing this approach, Ms. Johnson

A.   avoids having students form their own groups of working with someone she or he likes.

B.   takes advantage of the information she has about students' individual learning styles so as to maximize student learning effectiveness and efficiency.

C.   avoids randomly assigning students to pairs.

D.   risks having incompatible students working together in pairs.

64.   Before the class goes to the library, Ms. Johnson asks the students to predict how they will find the information they will need for the assignment. By doing this, Ms. Johnson is

A.   engaging the students in hypothetical thinking and inductive reasoning.

B.   saving time so the students will be able to go straight to work once they get to the library.

C.   helping her students acquire good self-management skills.

D.   assisting the librarian by covering important information in class.

65.   The main branches of geography include which of the following?

I.   Human

II.   Regional

III.   Physical

IV.   Population

A.   I only

B.   I and II

C.   I, II, and III only

D.   I, II, III, and IV

66. Geographers use _____ to analyze how places relate, including movements such as travel, migration, and the transmission of information.

A.   space-time interaction

B.   spatial interaction

C.   informatics

D.   spectrometers

67. Which of the following is a valid difference between the urban patterns of the United States and those of Latin America?

A.   Unlike U.S. cities, Latin American cities have ghettos.

B.   U.S cities follow a sector pattern, whereas Latin American cities follow concentric zones.

C.   Gentrification is more present in Latin American cities.

D.   Unlike U.S. cities, Latin American cities show patterns of wealthy residents emanating from the city's central business district.

68. An *oligopoly* is

A.   a market form in which a market or industry is dominated by a small number of sellers.

B   a government with a king or queen.

C.   a market form with a large number of sellers guaranteeing the lowest price.

D.   great for consumers.

69. Which of the following was an almost perfect crop for the lower South because it was easy to grow and well-suited to the region's climate and soil?

A.   Corn

B.   Cotton

C.   Wheat

D.   Rice

70. *Human geography* is best defined as the study of

   A.   where and why human activities are located.

   B.   where and why natural forces occur as they do.

   C.   populations and birth rates.

   D.   human conflicts.

71. Quotas, license fees, and subsidies are part of

   A.   a market economy.

   B.   a communist society.

   C.   the free enterprise system.

   D.   a planned economy.

72. In the 1790s political conflict between Thomas Jefferson and Alexander Hamilton, Jefferson would have been more likely to

   A.   take a narrow view of the Constitution.

   B.   favor Britain over France in the European wars.

   C.   favor the establishment of a national bank.

   D.   win the cooperation of presidents George Washington and John Adams.

73. Which of the following is an example of *monopolistic competition*?

   A.   The film industry

   B.   Agriculture

   C.   Public education

   D.   The automotive industry

74. The Federalist Papers were signed by "Publius." General consensus says the papers were written by

   A.   Alexander Hamilton, James Madison, and John Jay.

   B.   Thomas Jefferson, Alexander Hamilton, and George Washington.

   C.   James Madison, George Washington, and John Calhoun.

   D.   Alexander Hamilton, James Madison, and three others.

75. The architectural feature below is characteristic of which of the following cultures?

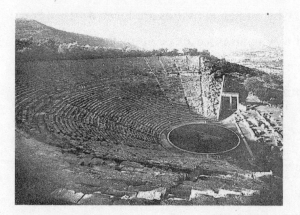

    A.   Germanic

    B.   Greek

    C.   Persian

    D.   Chinese

76. Which of the following best defines the term *prehistoric*?

    A.   Prior to the use of fire

    B.   Prior to the use of tools

    C.   Prior to the appearance of the written word

    D.   During the age of the dinosaur

77. Which of the following issues did NOT cause conflict among the framers of the Constitution?

    A.   Slavery

    B.   Power of the president

    C.   Large versus small states

    D.   Checks and balances

78. How are local governments chartered?

   A.   Local governments are chartered according to their state's constitution.

   B.   Local governments apply to the federal government for a charter.

   C.   States are divided into counties, and local governments are authorized by the counties.

   D.   Local governments simply write a constitution and notify the next largest government entity of their existence.

79. Which of the following phrases best exemplifies the definition of *continentality*?

   A.   The temperature in Tampa, Florida, was a scorching 86 degrees yesterday.

   B.   Clearwater Beach, Florida, is cooler than metropolitan Orlando, Florida, because it lies next to the Gulf of Mexico.

   C.   Tampa, Florida, is hotter than Atlanta, Georgia, because it is closer to the equator.

   D.   Summer rains typically move from west to east.

80. A climate graph has what two components?

   A.   Amount of rainfall and temperature of an area

   B.   Temperature highs and lows for a specific time of year

   C.   Amount of rain expected in the tourist seasons

   D.   Future rainfall and temperature changes due to global warming

81. What caused the many small Maya village populations and city-states to emerge?

   A.   Sophisticated, organized government

   B.   Improved farming practices

   C.   Climate changes

   D.   Advanced architectural designs

82. The term *socialization* is used by sociologists, social psychologists, and educators to refer to

    A.   the process of learning one's culture and how to live within it.

    B.   finding a date at a party.

    C.   the ability of people to find friendships or relationships.

    D.   humankind's unique pattern of marriage compared to other mammals.

Questions 83 and 84 refer to the following graph:

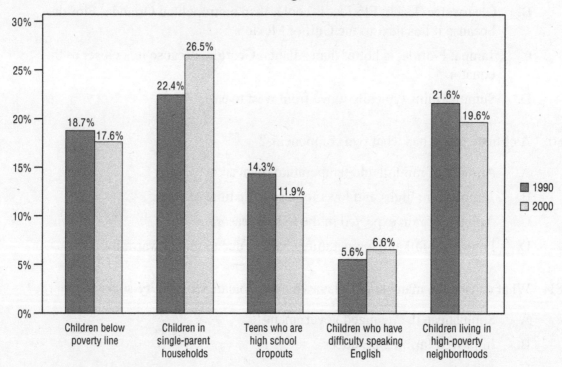

83. According to the graph, from 1990 to 2000, which of the following was true?

    A.   The number of teens who dropped out of high school increased.

    B.   The number of children who have difficulty speaking English increased.

    C.   The number of children living below the poverty line increased.

    D.   The number of children living in high-poverty neighborhoods increased.

84. According to the graph, the number of children who have difficulty speaking English increased from 1990 to 2000 from 5.6 percent to 6.6 percent. Which of the following can be inferred from the graph?

    A.   The percentage of children living below poverty is related to the percentage of children living in high-poverty neighborhoods.

    B.   Teens who are high school dropouts are most likely from single-parent households.

    C.   Children living in single-parent households are the same children who have difficulty speaking English.

    D.   A large percentage of children living in high-poverty neighborhoods live in single-parent households.

85. The first permanent European settlement in North America was

    A.   New Orleans, in what is now Louisiana.

    B.   Santa Fe, in what is now New Mexico.

    C.   St. Augustine, in what is now Florida.

    D.   Jamestown, in what is now Virginia.

86. What event made President Kennedy a national hero in 1962 due to the way in which people believed he successfully stood up to the Russians?

    A.   The Berlin Blockade

    B.   The Berlin Wall Crisis

    C.   The Pueblo Incident

    D.   The Cuban Missile Crisis

87. All of the following were characteristic of the 1920s EXCEPT

    A.   voting rights for women.

    B.   prohibition and bootlegging.

    C.   consumerism and easy credit.

    D.   union growth.

88. The term *Trail of Tears* refers to the

    A.   Mormon migration from Nauvoo, Illinois, to what is now Utah.

    B.   forced migration of the Cherokee tribe from the southern Appalachians to what is now Oklahoma.

    C.   westward migration along the Oregon Trail.

    D.   migration into Kentucky along the Wilderness Road.

89. What did the Civil Rights Act of 1964 accomplish?

    A.   It prohibited discrimination for reason of color, race, religion, or national origin in places of public accommodation covered by interstate commerce.

    B.   It desegregated public schools for the first time.

    C.   It ensured equal voting rights.

    D.   It dealt with housing and real estate discrimination.

90. Which of the following statements is NOT true of Africa?

    A.   Mount Kilimanjaro remains capped with snow year-round.

    B.   The Sahara is the largest and the hottest desert on the earth.

    C.   Africa has primarily two languages with many dialects.

    D.   Africa has rain forests.

91. Which of the following are broad subtopics of political science in the United States?

    I.   Political theory

    II. American government and politics

    III. International relations

    IV. Comparative government and politics

    A.   I and II only

    B.   II and III only

    C.   I, II, and IV only

    D.   I, II, III, and IV

92. What effect did the discovery of the New World have on the European economy in the sixteenth century?

    A.   It caused inflation due to the increased amount of precious metals in Europe.

    B.   It strengthened the craft guilds by stimulating trade.

    C.   It discouraged governments from interfering with the ventures of entrepreneurs.

    D.   It had no noticeable economic effect.

93. The Paleolithic, Mesolithic, and Neolithic periods are part of

    A.   the Copper Age.

    B.   the Bronze Age.

    C.   the Iron Age.

    D.   the Stone Age.

94. All of the following are true about World War I EXCEPT

    A.   at the end of the war most empires in Europe were dissolved.

    B.   European power declined.

    C.   ethnic tensions in the Balkans remained.

    D.   Ottoman Empire territories gained independence.

95. Which of the following is NOT true of the Cuban Missile Crisis?

    A.   It was a major incident during the Cold War.

    B.   The crisis began in 1961.

    C.   Russians refer to the event as the "Caribbean Crisis."

    D.   It would never have led to a war.

96. Which of the following was NOT an objective of the First Continental Congress?

    A.   To remain a part of Britain

    B.   To commission the building of a Continental army

    C.   To compose a statement of colonial rights

    D.   To provide a plan that would convince Britain to restore certain rights

97. Which of the following statements about the French and Indian War is NOT true?

    A. It is also known as the Thirty Years' War.

    B. George Washington fought to help the British.

    C. Native Americans fought with the British against British colonists and French troops.

    D. The war was part of a larger conflict that involved several European countries but was fought only in France.

98. Which of the following statements is true?

    A. There are at least 6,000 different languages spoken in the world.

    B. Poverty cannot realistically be called a culture.

    C. The earth's surface is 50 percent water.

    D. The Amazon is the world's longest river.

99. Which of the following is NOT used by geographers to determine absolute location?

    A. Equator

    B. Distance from the ocean

    C. Longitude

    D. Latitude

100. Prices tend to be inflated during wartime because

    A. guns cost more than butter.

    B. there is competition for fully employed resources.

    C. the Consumer Price Index is calculated differently in wartime.

    D. the cost of government is not included in the CPI.

101. What was the overall U.S. unemployment rate during the worst periods of the Great Depression?

    A. 10%

    B. 25%

    C. 40%

    D. 60%

102. Which is the best way to describe the GNP?

    A. Total goods and services

    B. Total national production

    C. Greater national production

    D. Government natural production

103. A headline reads: "Auto sales decline and the steel industry suffers a slump; unemployment rises." This type of unemployment can best be characterized in economic terms as

    A. frictional.

    B. structural.

    C. total unemployment.

    D. cyclical.

104. The principle of *popular sovereignty* was

    A. applied as part of the Missouri Compromise.

    B. a central feature of the Kansas-Nebraska Act.

    C. a policy favored by the Whig party during the late 1840s and early 1850s.

    D. successful in solving the impasse over the status of slavery in the Territories.

105. During the Congressional campaigns in 1994, when Republicans took control of both houses of Congress, Newt Gingrich and 300 Republican House candidates dramatically pledged to pass

    A. health care reform.

    B. a Contract with America.

    C. increased funding for education.

    D. new civil rights measures.

106. Which of the following is the BEST choice as the major cause of the Great Depression?

    A.   Military unrest in Europe

    B.   The Cold War

    C.   Extensive stock market speculation

    D.   Weak unions

107. Which of the following is NOT a correct statement regarding the Vietnam War?

    A.   More than 58,000 Americans were killed.

    B.   The war is considered the longest military conflict in U.S. history, lasting from 1959 to 1975.

    C.   The United States fought the North Vietnamese with no assistance from allies.

    D.   More than 3 million Vietnamese were killed.

108. What were the approximate dates of the Progressive Era?

    A.   1890 to 1917

    B.   1920 to 1929

    C.   1868 to 1900

    D.   1939 to 1945

109. Which of the following states was NOT one of the first seven states to secede from the Union just before the Civil War began?

    A.   Florida

    B.   Alabama

    C.   North Carolina

    D.   Texas

110. Which of the following statements is true of the Kansas-Nebraska Act?

    A.   It led to the disintegration of the Democratic party.

    B.   It was a measure that the South had been demanding for decades.

    C.   It led directly to the formation of the Republican party.

    D.   It maintained the tenuous sectional peace created by the Compromise of 1850.

111. A U.S. senator gets an item inserted into the federal budget, which allocates $6 million for building a ski lift at a resort in his home state. This is known as

    A.   a filibuster.

    B.   pork barrel legislation.

    C.   logrolling.

    D.   senatorial courtesy.

112. Which country was NOT a participant in the Potsdam Declaration setting the terms for how World War II peace settlements would be administered?

    A.   United States

    B.   Britain

    C.   China

    D.   France

113. What did the Manhattan Project accomplish?

    A.   It developed ideas for the Second Industrial Revolution.

    B.   It developed the airplane.

    C.   It developed the first nuclear weapon during World War II.

    D.   It developed the Sherman tank.

114. Frederick Douglass spoke in favor of all of the following EXCEPT

    A.   women's suffrage.

    B.   supporting civil rights.

    C.   sending freedmen to Africa.

    D.   ending slavery.

115. Following the terrorist attacks of September 11, 2001, Congress passed the Patriot Act, which

    A.   was supported for its fairness.

    B.   allowed for widespread deportation.

    C.   amended immigration laws in an attempt to successfully identify terrorists.

    D.   encouraged militias.

116. The policy promoted by Theodore Roosevelt and most blatantly pursued in Central America was the

    A. New Deal.

    B. Big Stick.

    C. Fair Deal.

    D. Good Neighbor.

117. Which of the following reasons was the immediate cause of the United States entering into World War II?

    A. Nazi Germany sunk American supply ships.

    B. Japan attacked the U.S. naval base at Pearl Harbor.

    C. Italy and Germany declared war on the United States.

    D. The Archduke of Austria was assassinated.

118. Which of the following best characterizes the methods of the Reverend Dr. Martin Luther King, Jr.?

    A. Nonviolent defiance of segregation

    B. A series of petitions to Congress calling for correction of racial abuses

    C. Armed violence against police and troops

    D. A series of speaking engagements in Northern cities in hopes of pressuring Congress to take action

119. An example of a country with a planned economy is

    A. Germany.

    B. France.

    C. China.

    D. Australia.

120. Who was the first president of the Confederacy?

    A. Abraham Lincoln

    B. James Buchanan

    C. Robert E. Lee

    D. Jefferson Davis

PRACTICE TEST 1 ANSWER KEY

Question	Answer	Field
1	A	Geography
2	B	Geography
3	C	Economics
4	D	Economics
5	C	Political Science
6	D	World History
7	B	World History
8	B	World History
9	D	World History
10	A	World History
11	A	World History
12	B	World History
13	C	World History
14	C	World History
15	B	World History
16	C	Political Science
17	A	Political Science
18	B	Political Science
19	A	World History
20	A	World History
21	D	World History
22	A	World History
23	D	World History
24	D	U.S. History

Question	Answer	Field
25	C	U.S. History
26	C	U.S. History
27	D	World History
28	B	World History
29	D	World History
30	B	World History
31	D	U.S. History
32	D	U.S. History
33	C	Political Science
34	D	U.S. History
35	D	Economics
36	B	Economics
37	B	Economics
38	D	Economics
39	D	Economics
40	B	Social Science
41	D	Social Science
42	D	Social Science
43	C	Social Science
44	A	Geography
45	C	Economics
46	B	Political Science
47	D	Political Science
48	B	World History
49	D	World History
50	C	Political Science

Question	Answer	Field
51	A	U.S. History
52	B	U.S. History
53	D	U.S. History
54	A	World History
55	B	Political Science
56	B	U.S. History
57	D	Social Science
58	D	Social Science
59	C	World History
60	A	Social Science
61	C	Social Science
62	C	Social Science
63	B	Social Science
64	A	Social Science
65	C	Geography
66	B	Geography
67	D	World History
68	A	Economics
69	B	Geography
70	A	Geography
71	D	Economics
72	A	Political Science
73	A	Economics
74	A	Political Science
75	B	World History
76	C	World History

Question	Answer	Field
77	D	Political Science
78	A	Political Science
79	B	Geography
80	A	Geography
81	B	World History
82	A	Social Science
83	B	Social Science
84	A	Social Science
85	C	U.S. History
86	D	U.S. History
87	D	U.S. History
88	B	U.S. History
89	A	U.S. History
90	C	World History
91	D	Political Science
92	A	World History
93	D	World History
94	D	World History
95	D	U.S. History
96	B	U.S. History
97	A	U.S. History
98	A	World History
99	B	Geography
100	B	Economics
101	B	Economics
102	A	Economics

Question	Answer	Field
103	D	Economics
104	B	Political Science
105	B	Political Science
106	C	U.S. History
107	C	U.S. History
108	A	U.S. History
109	C	U.S. History
110	C	U.S. History
111	B	Political Science
112	D	World History
113	C	U.S. History
114	C	U.S. History
115	C	U.S. History
116	B	Political Science
117	B	U.S. History
118	A	U.S. History
119	C	Economics
120	D	Political Science

PRACTICE TEST 1 PROGRESS CHART

Knowledge of Economics   ——/16

3	4	35	36	37	38	39	45	68	71	73

100	101	102	103	119

Knowledge of Geography   ——/10

1	2	44	65	66	69	70	79	80	99

Knowledge of Political Science   ——/19

5	16	17	18	33	46	47	50	55	72	74

77	78	91	104	105	111	116	120

Knowledge of Social Science   ——/14

40	41	42	43	57	58	60	61	62	63	64

82	83	84

Knowledge of U.S. History   ——/28

24	25	26	31	32	34	51	52	53	56	85

86	87	88	89	95	96	97	106	107	108	109

110	113	114	115	117	118

Knowledge of World History   ——/33

6	7	8	9	10	11	12	13	14	15	19

20	21	22	23	27	28	29	30	48	49	54

59	67	75	76	81	90	92	93	94	98	112

DETAILED EXPLANATIONS FOR PRACTICE TEST 1

1. **A**

    Climate can be displayed on a graph. A climate graph contains two pieces of information about an area: the amount of rainfall and the temperature. The temperature is shown as a line, and the rainfall is displayed as bars. The numbers shown on the graph are usually averages calculated over a number of years.

2. **B**

    Desertification is the spread of desert-like conditions into more arable regions as a result of human overuse and, perhaps, environmental shifts. According to deBlij and Murphy's research, South America, choice (A) is at a 20 percent risk; Europe (C), 9 percent; and Africa (D), 57 percent; by contrast, Australia (B) is at an 83 percent risk.

3. **C**

    In a market economy, in which everyone is free to make choices about what they purchase, market forces dictate the allocation of resources.

4. **D**

    By definition, a deposit at a bank is placed on the bank's books as a liability, as this is money that is owed by the bank to the depositor. The deposit is an asset to the depositor, as it represents value owned by the depositor.

5. **C**

    The purpose of the Truman Doctrine was to aid countries that were the targets of Communist expansionism.

6. **D**

    Gorbachev retreated from the Brezhnev Doctrine and allowed Eastern bloc nations the freedom of self-determination.

7. **B**

    Gold from Ghana was the basis of Mediterranean trade with the east. Iron-making arose in Africa as early as the first millennium B.C.E.

8. **B**

The February Revolution of 1917 led directly to the fall of the autocracy of Tsar Nicholas II of Russia, the last tsar of Russia, and sought to establish in its place a democratic Republic.

9. **D**

Renaissance Humanism was a threat to the Church because it emphasized a return to the original sources of Christianity—the Bible and the writings of the Fathers of the Church. In that light, the humanists tended to ignore or denounce the proceedings of Church councils and pontiffs during the Middle Ages.

10. **A**

Axum was a Christian kingdom of North Africa and because it often took in Islamic refugees during the early period of Islam, Muslims never attempted to conquer it.

11. **A**

Most of the classical texts were in Latin, which at the time, was the written language of educated people; therefore, it was used in the university.

12. **B**

On August 25, 1945, Emperor Bao Dai abdicated when the communist Viêt Minh, led by Ho Chi Minh, seized power. He then lived in exile in Hong Kong.

13. **C**

Chinese and Soviet women engaged in combat during World War II.

14. **C**

Apartheid is an Afrikaans word meaning "separateness." It was a legal system whereby people were classified into racial groups: white, black, Indian, and colored. They had separate geographic areas for each racial group. Apartheid laws were part of South Africa's legal framework from 1948 to 1994.

15. **B**

While Europe watched as Germany invaded the Rhineland, Austria, and the Sudetenland, it would not tolerate Hitler's invasion of Poland.

16. **C**

Another related term for *autocracy*, more commonly used in the past, is *despotism*, or rule by a despot.

17. **A**.

Our federal system of government includes a bicameral legislature—the Senate and the House of Representatives—established in Article 1 of the Constitution.

18. **B**

The United States supported the revolution that placed Reza Pahlavi in power as Shah of Iran. The U.S. also supported the revolution of Armas in Guatemala. U.S. investments in Latin America prompted involvement in Guatemala and other countries.

19. **A**

Immanuel Kant is regarded as one of the most influential thinkers of modern Europe and the last major philosopher of the Enlightenment.

20. **A**

The Han Dynasty, under whose rule China was reunited, is divided into two major periods: the Western or Former Han (206 BCE – 9 CE) and the Eastern or Later Han (25–220 CE). The boundaries established by the Qin and maintained by the Han have more or less defined the nation of China up to the present day. The Western Han capital, Chang'an in present-day Shaanxi Province, was a monumental urban center laid out on a north-south axis with palaces, residential wards, and two bustling market areas. It was one of the two largest cities in the ancient world (Rome was the other).

21. **D**

The British policy of indirect rule in Africa was designed to reduce tensions and minimize financial costs. It included flexibility and a minimum of direct British intervention. For this reason, the British tried to adapt their colonial policies to fit the wide variety of native systems in and between countries, and they did not want a tribal uniform policy, which would have been more rigid. Instead they modified the role of traditional rulers in local areas and relied on a decentralized administration, option choice (C). The goal for these colonies was eventual self-rule, option choice (B), and for this reason they supported basic primary education for Africans which would equip them for this eventuality.

22. **A**

Following his ascension to chancellor in January 1933, Adolf Hitler almost immediately began secretly building up Germany's army and weapons stockpile. In 1934, he increased the size of the army, commissioned the construction of warships, and created a German air force. Compulsory military service was also introduced.

23. **D**

Paleolithic peoples did not know how to grow crops or raise animals, so they relied on hunting and gathering for their needs. They were nomadic since they had little choice but to follow animal migrations and vegetation cycles. Paleolithic peoples did know how to make tools and weapons. Work was divided primarily along gender lines, where men hunted and women cooked.

24. **D**

The Nat Turner insurrection surprised the planters. After the uprising, the slave states reacted by expanding their militia systems, passing new slave codes, strengthening existing slave codes, and severely restricting the activities of slaves.

25. **C**

In *Plessy v. Ferguson* (1896), the Supreme Court upheld separate but equal facilities. It overturned this ruling with *Brown v. Topeka Board of Education* (1954). The ruling that no slave could be a citizen of the United States was the 1857 case, *Dred Scott v. Sanford.* Various Supreme Court decisions in the 1950s, 1960s, and 1970s dealt with literacy tests and affirmative action.

26. **C.**

The Civilian Conservation Corps never employed anywhere near one-third of the U.S. work force, but it was part of FDR's New Deal. Its workers did live in camps under semi-military discipline and worked on such projects as preventing soil erosion. It did provide that some of the workers' pay be sent home to help their families.

27. **D**

The burning of Jan Hus at the stake was essentially a short-term cause of the Reformation.

28. **B**

There were many major changes resulting from the rapid industrial development in the United States from 1860 through 1900. The most significant, however, was the attention to speed. First, there was a shift to building larger and larger industrial facilities to accommodate the new machine technologies coming into existence. Small factories could not absorb the cost of much of the machinery and did not produce enough to make the machinery profitable. So, contrary to choice (D), there was an increase in large industrial plants and a relative decline in small factories.

29. **D**

The oldest fossils are found in Africa, not Australia.

30. **B**

Greece was the most sophisticated society of the ancient world and predates the Roman Empire and Christianity.

31. **D**

Both the personal correspondence of a military man stationed with the 5th RCT in Korea and an interview with Secretary of Defense George Marshall are primary sources, as they involve correspondence or testimony from individuals who were actually involved with the Korean War.

32. **D**

The Great Awakening was the first religious development to have an impact throughout colonial America.

33. **C**

The Articles of Confederation government did have the power to borrow money and that is how it financed most of what it did. It did not, however, have the power to levy taxes or regulate commerce, and it lacked a strong executive.

34. **D**

After World War II, the European Recovery Plan, better known as the Marshall Plan, put more than $13 billion into Western Europe's economies to help rebuild Europe. It was also designed to help prevent the spread of communism.

35. **D**

    Answers options (A), (B), and (C) are considered scarce. Scarcity is based on the idea that a limited supply of goods or services comes up against an ever-increasing demand for it and that, as a result, every effort must be made to ensure its proper utilization and distribution so as to avoid inefficiency. Most goods and services can be defined as scarce since individuals desire more of them than they already possess (scarcity is maintained by demand). Carbon dioxide, however, is not scarce.

36. **B**

    When there is a supply shock, there is an unexpected increase in input prices, price levels rise, and GDP and employment decline.

37. **B**

    Land, labor, capital, and entrepreneurship are the factors of production.

38. **D**

    Given the fact that burning coal pollutes more than oil, this is an example of where economic and political priorities trump the environmental concerns. Relying less on oil as a fuel is a political concern since the United States imports the bulk of its oil from Canada, Mexico, and Saudi Arabia. The fact that the United States relies on foreign sources is problematic given that the United States is number one in oil consumption, outranking China almost 3 to 1.

39. **D**

    The consumer price index (CPI) measures the price change in a fixed basket of goods and services.

40. **B**

    Sociology, simply defined, is the study of how individuals become members of groups and move between groups, and how being in different groups affects individuals and the groups in which they participate.

41. **D**

    Participant observation involves a researcher interacting with and observing the personal lives of the research subjects.

42. **D**

   According to the graph, single-parent African-American families made up the largest percentage of single-parent families in Florida in 2008.

43. **C**

   The question asks for work on the analysis, synthesis, or evaluation level. It asks the students to analyze how past causes have produced current effects, then to predict what future effects might be based on what they have learned about cause-effect relationships. It requires students to put together information in a new way.

44. **A**

   Longitude and latitude are part of the location theme of geography.

45. **C**

   This answer is the simple definition of *economics*. Economics is the social science that examines how people choose to use limited or scarce resources to obtain maximum satisfaction of unlimited wants.

46. **B**

   Though many factors might contribute to an individual's choice of party and the party's stand on such issues as states' rights, the chief factor during this period was acceptance or rejection of the French Revolution—Jefferson and his supporters saw it as good, Hamilton and the Federalists did not.

47. **D**

   Both the Declaration of Independence and the Constitution outline the principles of freedom on which the United States was founded. The Articles of Confederation, choice (C) was the Second Continental Congress's first, but failed, attempt to define the new nation's federal government.

48. **B**

   Periodization is a term used in history to study events in context. An example given, in the review of this book, is the erroneous use of the term *Victorian era* to discuss an event in China.

49. **D**

Islam spread in Africa starting in the seventh century, and influenced the cultures of Ghana, Mali, and other African states. Sub-Saharan Africa was primarily influenced by Islam.

50. **C**

The Monroe Doctrine held that the United States would not tolerate any new European colonization in the New World. The U.S. did desire to see republican governments instituted in countries all over the world, but would intervene only to prevent new, not to remove, existing European colonization in the New World.

51. **A**

The chronological order of events is III, II, IV, I. James Buchanan was elected president in 1857, prior to Abraham Lincoln, who issued the Emancipation Proclamation in 1863. General Sherman's defeat of Atlanta occurred in 1864, near the end of the Civil War. Andrew Johnson became president after Lincoln's assassination but was impeached in 1868.

52. **B**

Abraham Lincoln issued the Emancipation Proclamation in 1863 before General Sherman's defeat of Atlanta occurred in 1864, near the end of the Civil War.

53. **D**

Before the Civil War most black people in the South were slaves. They were not citizens and had no civil or political rights. After the war, the Fourteenth and Fifteenth Amendments were added to the Constitution. The Fourteenth Amendment extended citizenship to blacks. The Fifteenth Amendment states that the "right of citizens of the United States to vote shall not be denied or abridged by the United States or by any state on account of race, color, or previous condition of servitude." Contrary to what one might assume, blacks did not immediately gain full voting rights. During the 1870s the Supreme Court held that the Fifteenth Amendment did not automatically confer the right to vote on anybody. States could not pass laws to prevent anyone from voting on the basis of race, but they could restrict persons from voting on other grounds. This interpretation of the Fifteenth Amendment allowed southern states to use several effective techniques to exclude blacks from voting.

54. **A**

   The Age of Revolution was the time period about (1750–1800) during which most European countries changed their government to absolutist states or constitutionalist states. The Age of Revolution specifically includes the American Revolution and the French Revolution.

55. **B**

   The Eighteenth Amendment made the sale of alcohol illegal, which led to a burgeoning bootlegging industry in which the Mafia played a major role. The amendment was repealed by the Twenty-first Amendment in 1933.

56. **B**

   The Cuban Revolution of 1959 led to a large wave of Cuban immigration into southern Florida, which transformed Miami into a major center of commerce, finance, and transportation.

57. **D.**

   Culture consists of the shared products of human interaction, both material and nonmaterial. An individual's intelligence is the result of personal development and genetic inheritance. Because intelligence may vary greatly among individuals, it is not shared among members of a society.

58. **D**

   Virtually any group can be considered a social network, but a party planner is not a group.

59 **C**

   The Himalayan mountain range, the highest in the world, runs 1,500 miles from the northernmost tip of India, through Nepal, and along the southwest border of China. The Himalayas include Mt. Everest (also known as Mt. Qomolongma), the tallest mountain in the world, and India's tallest mountain, Nanda Devi, which rises 25,645 feet. Bangladesh is almost completely surrounded by the northeastern border of India, facing the Bay of Bengal. It does have a small border with Burma on its southeast side.

60. **A**

   Introspective activities help students to connect new information to previously learned information, an important cognitive process.

61. **C**

One of the central tenets of human development is the constant interaction and precarious balance of nurture and nature.

62. **C**

Although brainstorming activities benefit learning by determining students' interests and giving everyone a chance to participate, these are merely benefits, not the real purpose of the activity.

63. **B**

This is the best rationale for the teacher choosing her action. Options (A), (C), and (D) are basically restatements of the idea that the teacher forms the groups instead of the students. This was specified in the context of the question.

64. **A**

Engaging the students in hypothetical thinking and inductive reasoning recognizes the cognitive principle underlying the teacher's assignment.

65. **C**

Geography can be divided into four main branches; human, the study of humans and the cultures they create; physical, which focuses on the physical environment of earth; regional, which focuses on areas of earth that are similar; and topical or systemic, which considers systematic studies of climate, landforms, economics, and culture. Population geography is not usually considered one of the four main branches, but is a subfield that deals with the relationships between geography and population patterns.

66. **B**

The answer is choice (B), spatial interaction which is the transportation supply and demand relationship that is often expressed over a geographical space. Spatial interactions usually include a variety of movements such as travel, migration, transmission of information, journeys to work or shopping, retailing activities, or freight distribution.

67. **D**

In Latin American and western European cities, the wealthy cluster nearer the central business districts and push outward from the focal point of the city, whereas in the United States the wealthy often live in suburbs outside the central cities. (A) is incorrect because many U.S. cities have ghettos. (B) is incorrect because many Latin American cities also show sector and concentric patterns. (C) is incorrect because U.S. cities show an equal if not greater influence of gentrifiers compared with Latin American cities.

68. **A**

An oligopoly is a market form in which a market or industry is dominated by a small number of sellers.

69. **B**

The perfect crop was cotton, especially for the lower South. It was easy to grow and its demands were met by the region's climate and soil. Between the cotton South and the wheat North, there was a middle ground in which the main crop was corn.

70. **A**

Human geography is the study of people's patterns and their processes in relation to the earth's patterns and processes. (B) is too narrow in that it does not include human processes. (C) and (D) are also too narrow, although all are a part of human geography.

71. **D**

Government intervention such as establishing quotas, collecting license fees, and providing subsidies is a sign of a planned economy. Taxes, however, are not normally considered a part of government intervention.

72. **A**

Jefferson would have been more likely to take a narrow view of the Constitution, Hamilton a broad and permissive one. Hamilton, rather than Jefferson, favored Britain over France, favored the establishment of a national bank, and won the cooperation of presidents Washington and Adams.

73. **A**

In a market structure in which several or many sellers each produce similar, but slightly differentiated products, monopolistic competition is a very common market form. Each producer can set its price and quantity without affecting the marketplace as a whole.

74. **A**

Alexander Hamilton wrote 52 of the papers; James Madison, 28; and John Jay, the remaining five. Thomas Jefferson and George Washington were not involved. John Calhoun, a U.S. senator and eventually vice president, was not born until 1782, and thus was only a child when the Federalist Papers were published.

75. **B**

Of the cultures listed, only the Greeks developed round open-air theaters. The one in the photograph was built toward the end of the Classical Age c. 350 B.C.E.

76. **C**

Merriam-Webster's Collegiate Dictionary defines *prehistoric* as "of, relating to, or existing in the times antedating the written word."

77. **D**

While the framers of the Constitution grappled with the issues of slavery, presidential power, and the role of large versus small states, among others, they all agreed that the new nation needed a system of checks and balances.

78. **A**

A local government is chartered according to its state's constitution. Just as the policies enacted by the state government must not conflict with Federal law, a local government is subject to the legal environment created by the state's constitution and statutes.

79. **B**

Continentality is the degree to which a location's distance from the sea affects the fluctuation in its temperature. Land heats and cools faster than the sea. Therefore, coastal areas have a lower temperature range than inland areas do. On the coast, winters are mild and summers are cool. In inland areas, temperatures are high in the summer and low in the winter. Clearwater Beach is on the Gulf of Mexico whereas Orlando is not on the coast; consequently, Clearwater Beach is subject to continentality.

80. **A.**

A climate graph contains two pieces of information: the amount of rainfall and the temperature of an area. The temperature is shown as a line, and the rainfall is displayed using bars. The figures are usually calculated as an average over a number of years.

81. **B**

As farming practices improved, the many small Maya villages could support larger populations and that allowed city-states to emerge. City-states such as Tikal had populations of nearly 40,000 people!

82. **A**

The term *socialization* refers to the process of learning one's culture and how to live within it.

83. **B**

In 1990, 5.6% of the children had difficulty speaking English; by 2000, the percentage had increased to 6.6%.

84. **A**

It can be inferred that the children living below poverty are a large percentage of those children living in high poverty neighborhoods where 20% of more of the population is below poverty.

85. **C**

In 1562, French Huguenots established a short-lived colony at Port Royal, South Carolina, and two years later, at Ft. Caroline, Florida. In response to these attempted French colonies, the Spanish established an outpost in 1565 in present-day Florida. This Spanish settlement, St. Augustine, became the first European town in the present-day United States. The first permanent English settlement in North America was Jamestown, founded in 1607.

86. **D**

The Cuban Missile Crisis was the ultimate test of John Kennedy's administration.

87. **D**

Women were granted the right to vote in 1920 by the Nineteenth Amendment. With new forms of credit and advertising, combined with increases in wages and productivity, consumerism became the new American ethic. Prohibition came with the passage of the Eighteenth Amendment in 1919.

88. **B**.

The term *Trail of Tears* is used to describe the forced relocation of the Cherokee tribe from the southern Appalachians to what is now Oklahoma.

89. **A**.

The Civil Rights Act of 1964 prohibited discrimination for reason of color, race, religion, or national origin in places of public accommodation covered by interstate commerce, that is, restaurants, hotels, motels, and theaters. Besides dealing with the desegregation of public schools, the act, in Title VII, forbade discrimination in employment. Title VII also prohibited discrimination on the basis of sex. In 1965, the Voting Rights Act was passed, placing federal observers at polls to ensure equal voting rights. The Civil Rights Act of 1968 dealt with housing and real estate discrimination.

90. **C**.

The people of the continent of Africa speak hundreds of languages, and if dialects spoken by various ethnic groups are also included, the number is even higher.

91. **D**.

At the present time, the study of politics in the United States is concerned with political theory, American government and politics, comparative government and politics, and international relations.

92. **A**.

The discovery of the New World led to conquests of native peoples from whom large amounts of gold and silver were taken and sent to Europe. With more money in circulation, the value of the currency declines; between 1500 and 1600, the prices of most goods rose about 300 percent.

93. **D.**

   Throughout the immense time span of the Stone Age, vast changes occurred in climate and in other conditions affecting human culture. Humans themselves evolved into their modern form during the latter part of it. The Stone Age has been divided accordingly into three periods: the Paleolithic, Mesolithic, and Neolithic.

94. **D**

   At the end of World War I, the Ottoman territories were under British control.

95. **D.**

   This crisis is generally regarded as the moment when the Cold War came closest to escalating into a nuclear war.

96. **B.**

   The members of the First Continental Congress sought a peaceful resolution of their differences with Britain. They wanted to establish their rights and have them recognized by the government in England. Military conflict was not on their minds at this time.

97. **A**

   The French and Indian War, or the Seven Years' War, occurred prior to the Revolutionary War.

98. **A.**

   The world has about 200 nations across which more than 6,000 distinct languages are spoken.

99. **B.**

   Distance from the ocean is not a part of pinpointing an absolute location on the global grid, whereas the other answer choices are all components in the determination of latitudinal–longitudinal intersection.

100. **B.**

   During wartime, the economy works to produce more materials for defense than in peacetime, which bids up prices. Choice (C) is false. Choice (D) is true, but if the government were included, it would probably cause more inflation.

101. B

The national unemployment rate soared to approximately 25 percent of the work force in early 1933. This meant that approximately 13 million workers were unemployed. While 25 percent was the national unemployment rate, in some cities, the number of unemployed approached 90 percent. This was at a time when there were no welfare benefits or unemployment funds in most areas of the country.

102. A

GNP is the gross national product and is defined as the total goods and services produced by the nation in a given year. Choice (B) is only partially correct because services are not specified. The others are not correct.

103. D

A decrease in aggregate demand results in a change in aggregate supply quantity. If consumption of autos declines, then the quantity of steel supplied, as an intermediate good, would also decline. If output declines, then jobs and income must also decline.

104. B

The principle of popular sovereignty was a central feature of the Kansas-Nebraska Act. A favorite policy of Democrats during the late 1840s and early 1850s, it proved a failure in solving the impasse over the status of slavery in the territories.

105. B

On September 27, 1994, at the Capitol Building, Newt Gingrich and Republican House candidates pledged to pass a Contract with America, which called for legislation to lower taxes, increase defense spending, and pass a balanced budget amendment to the Constitution.

106. C

The stock market crash, which was precipitated by extensive speculation, was one major cause of the Great Depression.

107. C

The U.S. military had assistance from many allies during the Vietnam War, including troops from Australia, Korea, and the Philippines, among others.

108. **A**

In the late nineteenth century, wealthy families like the Carnegies, Mellons, Rockefellers, and Morgans began building mansions on the edges of the cities. Housing developments of similar-looking single- or multiple-family dwellings, built by speculators, also sprouted on the edges of cities. These often catered to a new middle class of white-collar employees in business and industry. By 1900 more than a third of urban dwellers owned their own homes, one of the highest rates in the world at the time. This "progress" led the period from 1890 to 1917 to be labeled the Progressive Era.

109. **C**

Lincoln's election was the signal for the secession of South Carolina on December 20, 1860, and that state was followed out of the Union by six other states: Mississippi, Florida, Alabama, Georgia, Louisiana, and Texas.

110. **C**

The Republican Party came into being primarily out of the controversy stirred up by the Kansas-Nebraska Act. It did not cause the disintegration of the Democratic Party.

111. **B**

Special spending projects sponsored by members of Congress for their home states or districts are known as *pork barrel legislation.*

112. **D**

On July 26, 1945, the United States, Britain, and China released the Potsdam Declaration, announcing the terms for Japan's surrender, with the warning, "We will not deviate from them. There are no alternatives. We shall brook no delay." As the warning was being issued, the U-235 core of the "Little Boy" atomic bomb was being delivered to Tinian, a U.S.-controlled island in the Pacific.

113. **C**

The Manhattan Project was the project to develop the first atomic bomb during World War II by the United States, the United Kingdom, and Canada. Formally designated as the Manhattan Engineering District (MED), it refers specifically to the period of the project from 1941 to 1946.

114. **C**

Frederick Douglass was one of the best-known abolitionists. He did not advocate returning freedmen to Africa—rather it was Marcus Garvey who was a major proponent of the Back to Africa Movement.

115. **C**

The Patriot Act gave broad powers to the federal government for its work to counter terrorism.

116. **B**

Teddy Roosevelt's most memorable line was also the underpinning of his foreign policy strategy in Central America: "Speak softly but carry a big stick." The thrust of this policy was that the United States would not waste a lot of energy on words in settling issues in Central America; instead, there would be a focus on action.

117. **B**

Many factors contributed to the U.S. decision to enter World War II, including the fact that Nazi Germany was sinking American supply ships because the United States was providing financial and military support to the Allied troops (England, France, China, and Russia). The immediate cause, however, was Japan's attack on the U.S. naval base at Pearl Harbor, Hawaii, without a declaration of war or any warning that hostilities were being commenced. The day after the attack, December 7, 1941, President Franklin Roosevelt went before the U.S. Congress and asked for a formal declaration of war with Japan in retaliation. President Roosevelt never asked Congress to declare war with Italy or Germany. Instead, three days after December 7, Italy and Germany declared war on the United States.

118. **A**

Dr. King's methods were characterized by nonviolent defiance of segregation. While King and/or his supporters might make speeches or send petitions, civil disobedience gave his movement its urgency.

119. **C**

The economies of Germany, France, and Australia are much like that of the United States. China has planned much of its economy and the leaders of the communist party in China direct economic policy.

120. **D**

The Confederacy's first and only president, Jefferson Davis, was determined to oust the Federals.

Practice Test 2

FTCE: Social Science 6–12

This test is also on CD-ROM in our special interactive TestWare® for the FTCE Social Science 6-12. It is highly recommended that you first take this exam on computer. You will then have the additional study features and benefits of enforced timed conditions and instantaneous, accurate scoring. See page 7 for instructions on how to get the most out of our FTCE book and software.

ANSWER SHEET FOR PRACTICE TEST 2

1. Ⓐ Ⓑ Ⓒ Ⓓ
2. Ⓐ Ⓑ Ⓒ Ⓓ
3. Ⓐ Ⓑ Ⓒ Ⓓ
4. Ⓐ Ⓑ Ⓒ Ⓓ
5. Ⓐ Ⓑ Ⓒ Ⓓ
6. Ⓐ Ⓑ Ⓒ Ⓓ
7. Ⓐ Ⓑ Ⓒ Ⓓ
8. Ⓐ Ⓑ Ⓒ Ⓓ
9. Ⓐ Ⓑ Ⓒ Ⓓ
10. Ⓐ Ⓑ Ⓒ Ⓓ
11. Ⓐ Ⓑ Ⓒ Ⓓ
12. Ⓐ Ⓑ Ⓒ Ⓓ
13. Ⓐ Ⓑ Ⓒ Ⓓ
14. Ⓐ Ⓑ Ⓒ Ⓓ
15. Ⓐ Ⓑ Ⓒ Ⓓ
16. Ⓐ Ⓑ Ⓒ Ⓓ
17. Ⓐ Ⓑ Ⓒ Ⓓ
18. Ⓐ Ⓑ Ⓒ Ⓓ
19. Ⓐ Ⓑ Ⓒ Ⓓ
20. Ⓐ Ⓑ Ⓒ Ⓓ
21. Ⓐ Ⓑ Ⓒ Ⓓ
22. Ⓐ Ⓑ Ⓒ Ⓓ
23. Ⓐ Ⓑ Ⓒ Ⓓ
24. Ⓐ Ⓑ Ⓒ Ⓓ
25. Ⓐ Ⓑ Ⓒ Ⓓ
26. Ⓐ Ⓑ Ⓒ Ⓓ
27. Ⓐ Ⓑ Ⓒ Ⓓ
28. Ⓐ Ⓑ Ⓒ Ⓓ
29. Ⓐ Ⓑ Ⓒ Ⓓ
30. Ⓐ Ⓑ Ⓒ Ⓓ

31. Ⓐ Ⓑ Ⓒ Ⓓ
32. Ⓐ Ⓑ Ⓒ Ⓓ
33. Ⓐ Ⓑ Ⓒ Ⓓ
34. Ⓐ Ⓑ Ⓒ Ⓓ
35. Ⓐ Ⓑ Ⓒ Ⓓ
36. Ⓐ Ⓑ Ⓒ Ⓓ
37. Ⓐ Ⓑ Ⓒ Ⓓ
38. Ⓐ Ⓑ Ⓒ Ⓓ
39. Ⓐ Ⓑ Ⓒ Ⓓ
40. Ⓐ Ⓑ Ⓒ Ⓓ
41. Ⓐ Ⓑ Ⓒ Ⓓ
42. Ⓐ Ⓑ Ⓒ Ⓓ
43. Ⓐ Ⓑ Ⓒ Ⓓ
44. Ⓐ Ⓑ Ⓒ Ⓓ
45. Ⓐ Ⓑ Ⓒ Ⓓ
46. Ⓐ Ⓑ Ⓒ Ⓓ
47. Ⓐ Ⓑ Ⓒ Ⓓ
48. Ⓐ Ⓑ Ⓒ Ⓓ
49. Ⓐ Ⓑ Ⓒ Ⓓ
50. Ⓐ Ⓑ Ⓒ Ⓓ
51. Ⓐ Ⓑ Ⓒ Ⓓ
52. Ⓐ Ⓑ Ⓒ Ⓓ
53. Ⓐ Ⓑ Ⓒ Ⓓ
54. Ⓐ Ⓑ Ⓒ Ⓓ
55. Ⓐ Ⓑ Ⓒ Ⓓ
56. Ⓐ Ⓑ Ⓒ Ⓓ
57. Ⓐ Ⓑ Ⓒ Ⓓ
58. Ⓐ Ⓑ Ⓒ Ⓓ
59. Ⓐ Ⓑ Ⓒ Ⓓ
60. Ⓐ Ⓑ Ⓒ Ⓓ

61. Ⓐ Ⓑ Ⓒ Ⓓ
62. Ⓐ Ⓑ Ⓒ Ⓓ
63. Ⓐ Ⓑ Ⓒ Ⓓ
64. Ⓐ Ⓑ Ⓒ Ⓓ
65. Ⓐ Ⓑ Ⓒ Ⓓ
66. Ⓐ Ⓑ Ⓒ Ⓓ
67. Ⓐ Ⓑ Ⓒ Ⓓ
68. Ⓐ Ⓑ Ⓒ Ⓓ
69. Ⓐ Ⓑ Ⓒ Ⓓ
70. Ⓐ Ⓑ Ⓒ Ⓓ
71. Ⓐ Ⓑ Ⓒ Ⓓ
72. Ⓐ Ⓑ Ⓒ Ⓓ
73. Ⓐ Ⓑ Ⓒ Ⓓ
74. Ⓐ Ⓑ Ⓒ Ⓓ
75. Ⓐ Ⓑ Ⓒ Ⓓ
76. Ⓐ Ⓑ Ⓒ Ⓓ
77. Ⓐ Ⓑ Ⓒ Ⓓ
78. Ⓐ Ⓑ Ⓒ Ⓓ
79. Ⓐ Ⓑ Ⓒ Ⓓ
80. Ⓐ Ⓑ Ⓒ Ⓓ
81. Ⓐ Ⓑ Ⓒ Ⓓ
82. Ⓐ Ⓑ Ⓒ Ⓓ
83. Ⓐ Ⓑ Ⓒ Ⓓ
84. Ⓐ Ⓑ Ⓒ Ⓓ
85. Ⓐ Ⓑ Ⓒ Ⓓ
86. Ⓐ Ⓑ Ⓒ Ⓓ
87. Ⓐ Ⓑ Ⓒ Ⓓ
88. Ⓐ Ⓑ Ⓒ Ⓓ
89. Ⓐ Ⓑ Ⓒ Ⓓ
90. Ⓐ Ⓑ Ⓒ Ⓓ

91. Ⓐ Ⓑ Ⓒ Ⓓ
92. Ⓐ Ⓑ Ⓒ Ⓓ
93. Ⓐ Ⓑ Ⓒ Ⓓ
94. Ⓐ Ⓑ Ⓒ Ⓓ
95. Ⓐ Ⓑ Ⓒ Ⓓ
96. Ⓐ Ⓑ Ⓒ Ⓓ
97. Ⓐ Ⓑ Ⓒ Ⓓ
98. Ⓐ Ⓑ Ⓒ Ⓓ
99. Ⓐ Ⓑ Ⓒ Ⓓ
100. Ⓐ Ⓑ Ⓒ Ⓓ
101. Ⓐ Ⓑ Ⓒ Ⓓ
102. Ⓐ Ⓑ Ⓒ Ⓓ
103. Ⓐ Ⓑ Ⓒ Ⓓ
104. Ⓐ Ⓑ Ⓒ Ⓓ
105. Ⓐ Ⓑ Ⓒ Ⓓ
106. Ⓐ Ⓑ Ⓒ Ⓓ
107. Ⓐ Ⓑ Ⓒ Ⓓ
108. Ⓐ Ⓑ Ⓒ Ⓓ
109. Ⓐ Ⓑ Ⓒ Ⓓ
110. Ⓐ Ⓑ Ⓒ Ⓓ
111. Ⓐ Ⓑ Ⓒ Ⓓ
112. Ⓐ Ⓑ Ⓒ Ⓓ
113. Ⓐ Ⓑ Ⓒ Ⓓ
114. Ⓐ Ⓑ Ⓒ Ⓓ
115. Ⓐ Ⓑ Ⓒ Ⓓ
116. Ⓐ Ⓑ Ⓒ Ⓓ
117. Ⓐ Ⓑ Ⓒ Ⓓ
118. Ⓐ Ⓑ Ⓒ Ⓓ
119. Ⓐ Ⓑ Ⓒ Ⓓ
120. Ⓐ Ⓑ Ⓒ Ⓓ

PRACTICE TEST 2

1. Economics focuses on three basic questions. Which of the following is NOT one of them?

   A. What to produce?

   B. For whom to produce?

   C. How to produce?

   D. Who profits from the sale of goods and services?

2. *Plate tectonics* is a set of related concepts that describe how the earth's crust works. Which of the following statements is true?

   A. Plates that get pushed under one another create volcanoes.

   B. Plates bumping together cause volcanoes.

   C. Plate movement influences hurricanes.

   D. Plates don't move. They are stationary elements of the Earth.

3. In the United States, which of the following powers is reserved only for the states?

   A. Raise and maintain an army and navy

   B. Grant copyrights and patents

   C. Ratify proposed amendments to the Constitution

   D. Regulate naturalization and immigration

4. The principle of "popular sovereignty" was

   A. applied as part of the Missouri Compromise.

   B. a central feature of the Kansas-Nebraska Act.

   C. a policy favored by the Whig party during the late 1840s and early 1850s.

   D. successful in solving the impasse over the status of slavery in the Territories.

5. Which of the following was the most important factor in John F. Kennedy's 1960 presidential election victory over Richard Nixon?

    A. Americans' deep and growing dissatisfaction with the Eisenhower Administration

    B. Kennedy's better showing in nationally televised debates

    C. Kennedy's long record of administrative experience as governor of Massachusetts

    D. Nixon's failure to serve in the armed forces during the Second World War.

6. Which of the following series is in correct chronological order?

    A. French and Indian War, Revolutionary War, War of 1812

    B. Revolutionary War, War of 1812, French and Indian War

    C. War of 1812, French and Indian War, Revolutionary War

    D. War of 1812, Revolutionary War, French and Indian War

7. Ms. Alvarez has collected a variety of print and media resources for the students to use in their research. Which of the following would probably be the best way to motivate students to research the questions they have prepared?

    A. The teacher should assign two to three questions to each student so that all the questions are covered.

    B. The teacher should allow students to select the questions they would like to research.

    C. The teacher should select three key questions and assign them to all the students.

    D. The teacher should assign one topic to each student, then provide the students with additional information.

8. What concepts are always present in cooperative learning?

    I.   Team rewards

    II. Individual accountability

    III. Equal opportunities

    IV. Rule

    V.   Specific tasks

    A. I, III, and IV only

    B. I, II, and III only

    C. II, IV, and V only

    D. II, III, and V only

9. Which of the following types of pollution or atmospheric phenomena are correctly matched with their underlying causes?

    I.   Global warming—carbon dioxide and methane

    II. Acid rain—sulfur dioxide and nitrogen dioxide

    III. Ozone depletion—chlorofluorocarbons and sunlight

    IV. Aurora borealis—solar flares and magnetism

    A. I and II only

    B. II and III only

    C. I and IV only

    D. I, II, III, and IV

Question 10 is based on the following passage:

Mrs. Walker is thinking about developing a tenth-grade world history unit. The unit needs to emphasize Virgil's attempt to connect the origins of Rome to the events that followed the destruction of Troy by the Greeks. She wants the unit to be challenging, and yet the students must be able to handle the work. She is aware that this is the semester the students will take their first college entrance exam. The information from a cooperative learning workshop taken during the summer should be included in the unit.

10. In planning for the unit, what information about students is NOT needed?

    A. Individual learning style

    B. Student's cultural background

    C. Student's grades in previous history courses

    D. Student's daily class schedule

11. Which of the following is an example of monopolistic competition?

    A. The film industry

    B. Agriculture

    C. Public education

    D. The automotive industry

12. Kevin has lost his job in an automobile plant because the company began using robots for welding on the assembly line. Kevin plans to go to technical school to learn how to repair microcomputers. The type of unemployment Kevin is faced with is

    A. structural.

    B. educational.

    C. cyclical.

    D. natural.

13. What four religions were founded in the region now known as India?

    A. Hinduism, Buddhism, Jainism, and Sikhism

    B. Islam, Hinduism, Buddhism, and Sikhism

    C. Christianity, Buddhism, Baha'i Faith, and Jainism

    D. Hinduism, Buddhism, Taoism, and Sikhism

14. What was the focus of Mayan cities?

    A. Ceremonial centers

    B. Governmental headquarters

    C. Central marketplaces

    D. Festivals and celebrations

15. Resources that are readily abundant are considered

    A. free goods.

    B. worthless.

    C. priceless.

    D. scarce.

16. In a monopoly

    A. consumers can be sure they are paying a fair price.

    B. the firm is equal to an industry.

    C. there are multiple sellers protected by government regulation.

    D. competition drives down prices.

17. During the first two decades under the United States Constitution, the main factor that separated the two political parties, the Federalists and the Republicans, was whether they

    A. accepted the Constitution or opposed it

    B. favored the French Revolution or opposed it.

    C. leaned more toward states' rights or national sovereignty.

    D. had been patriots or loyalists during the American War of Independence.

18. The underlying issue that led to the outbreak of war between the United States and Japan in 1941 was

    A. Japanese aid to the Germans in their war against Britain.

    B. U.S. desire to annex various pacific islands held by Japan.

    C. Japanese desire to annex large portions of China.

    D. American resentment of Japanese trading policies and trade surpluses.

19. Which of the following was NOT included in the basic beliefs most of the Founders held that led them to view political parties as dangerous to stable government?

    A. Parties created and exploited conflicts that undermined consensus on public policy.

    B. Parties were instruments by which a small and narrow interest could impose its will on society.

    C. Parties provide only a general understanding of where the candidate stands.

    D. Parties stifled independent thought and behavior.

20. Which of the following statements is NOT true of the Silk Road?

    A. The Silk Road was a trade route that existed for the purpose of trading in silk and many other commodities.

    B. The Silk Road followed a single route, allowing for much more security and larger trading posts.

    C. The movement of people along the Silk Road correlates with the movement of religion and development of languages.

    D. Gold and ivory and even exotic animals and plants were traded on the Silk Road.

21. What are civil liberties?

    A. Fundamental individual rights given to all citizens by law

    B. Human rights

    C. Natural rights

    D. Both B and C

22. The Inductive/Discovery Approach is one of two ways to teach

    A. generalizations and facts in social science.

    B. theoretical precepts.

    C. historical events.

    D. the economic theories of supply and demand.

23. Why did the framers of the Constitution design the system of checks and balances?

    A. To maintain parity of power between the branches of government

    B. To minimize foreign intervention

    C. To help maintain the financial stability of the new government

    D. To set the foundation for a national bank

24. Which of the following topics does NOT fall within the scope of study in political science?

    A. Structure of government

    B. Political institutions

    C. Politics

    D. Social diversity

25. Which of the following criteria is NOT a requirement to be the president of the United States?

    A. Over 35 years old

    B. Natural-born U.S. citizen

    C. U.S. resident for at least 14 years

    D. Military service

26. For what length of term are federal judges appointed?

    A. 6 years

    B. 1 year, renewable annually

    C. Life

    D. 10 years

Use the following graphs to answer questions 27 and 28.

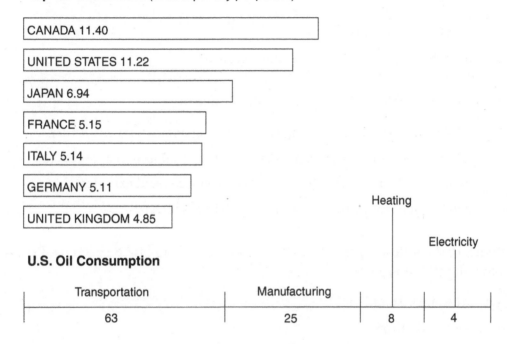

Top Oil Consumers *(in liters per day per person)*

CANADA 11.40

UNITED STATES 11.22

JAPAN 6.94

FRANCE 5.15

ITALY 5.14

GERMANY 5.11

UNITED KINGDOM 4.85

U.S. Oil Consumption

Transportation	Manufacturing	Heating	Electricity
63	25	8	4

27. Which is NOT a conclusion that can be drawn from the graphs?

    A.   Transportation takes up too high a portion of U.S. oil usage.

    B.   U.S. per capita consumption is over twice that of most European nations.

    C.   North American oil demands are the highest.

    D.   Manufacturing is a major consumer of oil.

28. Which would be LEAST likely to explain the statistics above?

    A.   The area size of a nation has a relationship to oil usage.

    B.   The European nations consume large quantities of oil.

    C.   The larger the population, the greater the usage.

    D.   Japan is the largest industrial power in Asia.

29. The major responsibility of the Federal Reserve Board is to

    A. implement monetary policy.

    B. control government spending.

    C. regulate commodity prices.

    D. help the president run the executive branch.

30. Another way to define GDP is as the market value of

    A. all final goods and services produced in an economy in a given year.

    B. all final and intermediate goods and services produced in a given year.

    C. national income earned by consumers, producers, and exporters.

    D. national income earned by producers and consumers.

31. Which of the following founders was one of the authors of the Federalist Papers and wrote the Bill of Rights?

    A. Alexander Hamilton

    B. James Madison

    C. John Jay

    D. Thomas Jefferson

32. *Ethnography* is the

    A. study of the cultures of prehistoric peoples.

    B. systematic description of a human society.

    C. the interpretive explanation of human behavior.

    D. the study of human groups, with a particular emphasis on social culture.

33. Which of the following is NOT an example of a social issue?

    A. How to address poverty

    B. Whether birth control is taught in schools

    C. Whether evolution is taught in schools

    D. How to balance a checkbook

34. Actions taken by the United States in response to Iraq's invasion of Kuwait in August 1990 included all of the following EXCEPT

    A. U.N. coordination.

    B. imposition of economic sanctions.

    C. declaration of a world war.

    D. protection of Saudi Arabia.

35. The Bill of Rights

    I. delegated to the federal government all the rights not given to the states.

    II. guaranteed a right to freedom of speech, press, and religion.

    III. established a viable two-party political system.

    A. I only

    B. II only

    C. III only

    D. I, II, and III

36. What is considered the first important movement of black artists and writers?

    A. Roaring Twenties

    B. Harlem Renaissance

    C. Lost Generation

    D. Jazz Age

37. What was the result of the Eighteenth Amendment?

    A. All Americans became eligible to vote.

    B. Prohibition heightened criminal activity.

    C. The Great Depression was eased.

    D. Presidents were limited to two terms of four years each.

38. Which of the following statements about Florida since World War II is true?

    A. Florida's economy has become more diverse.

    B. The citrus industry continues to decline.

    C. The university and community college system has expanded slowly.

    D. High-technology industries have avoided Florida.

39. McCarthyism in the 1950s was an attempt to reveal

   A.   communist infiltration in the United States government.

   B.   corruption in the Roosevelt administration.

   C.   misuse of corporate funds for political purposes.

   D.   the dangers of nuclear energy.

40. Which of the following associations is accurate?

   A.   Franklin D. Roosevelt and the New Deal

   B.   Adolf Hitler and economic prosperity

   C.   Black codes and freedom for slaves

   D.   Charles de Gaulle and the Tehran Conference

41. In 1492, Christopher Columbus's voyage took nearly 40 days to cross the Atlantic Ocean, a trip that would take a modern ship less than one week. This difference best reflects the geographic concept of

   A.   distance decay.

   B.   uneven development.

   C.   stimulus diffusion.

   D.   space-time compression.

42. Which of the following New Deal programs was designed to reduce unemployment?

   I.   The Public Works Administration

   II.   National Industrial Recovery Act

   III. Glass-Steagall Act

   IV. The Works Project Administration

   V.   Social Security Act

   A.   I, III, and V only

   B.   II and V only

   C.   III, IV, and V only

   D.   I and IV only

43. Which of the following is NOT true of both the ancient Egyptians and the Maya?

    A. Both built enormous pyramids.

    B. Both were agricultural societies.

    C. Both had an elaborate system of writing.

    D. Both cultures had indigenous beasts of burden.

44. Which European country colonized the largest amount of land in Africa?

    A. Germany

    B. France

    C. Britain

    D. Belgium

45. Which of the following best defines realism in the context of international relations?

    A. Nations cooperate for the sake of their common interests.

    B. Nation-states are the basic governmental unit and there is no authority above individual nations.

    C. Real authority is found in the United Nations.

    D. People are the real authority for all governments.

46. *Government by the many* is called

    A. democracy.

    B. oligarchy.

    C. monarchy.

    D. liberalism.

47. An example of relative location is

    A. regional geography.

    B. 28 North Main Street in Williamsport, Pennsylvania.

    C. the corner of 57th and 5th in Manhattan.

    D. the house across from the Mayfair Shops on Florida Ave, in Miami.

48. Which of the following represents monetary policy geared to increase the supply of money?

    A. The purchase of bonds by the Federal Reserve Bank

    B. The sale of bonds by the central bank

    C. An increase in reserve requirements

    D. An increase in the discount rate

49. If people start eating more fish and chicken to reduce their intake of cholesterol, and the importation of Canadian pork is restricted due to a steroid problem, what will happen to meat prices in the U.S.?

    A. The prices of chicken, pork, and fish will go down.

    B. The prices of chicken, pork, fish, and beef will go up.

    C. There will be no substantial effect on prices.

    D. The price of pork will go down, while the prices of chicken and fish will go up.

50. Which is NOT a method used to encourage expansion during a recession?

    A. Political crisis, such as war

    B. Increased government spending

    C. Increased taxation

    D. Deregulation of industry

51. Which of the following statements best represents the message of this political cartoon?

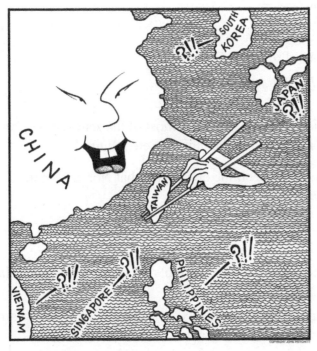

A. China has attempted to dominate many countries, but poses the most immediate threat to Taiwan.

B. China and Taiwan are enemies, but the status of other nearby nations is in question.

C. China and Taiwan are close allies, while other nearby countries resist Chinese domination.

D. China's status is threatened by Taiwan.

52. The period early in the development of human cultures, before the use of metals, is called the

A. Ancient Times.

B. Stone Age.

C. Horse Age.

D. Bronze Age.

53. Which of the following is NOT considered one of the three pillars of Western culture?

    A. Roman law

    B. Greek philosophy

    C. Catholic and Protestant Christianity

    D. Homer's *The Iliad*

54. During the period of Reconstruction, most of the states of the former Confederacy, in order to regain admission to the Union, were required to

    A. grant Black people all the civil rights that Northern states had granted them before the war.

    B. ratify the Fourteenth Amendment.

    C. ratify the Sixteenth Amendment.

    D. provide free land and farming tools for the recently freed slaves.

55. Which of the following regions was most heavily represented among immigrants to the United States during the years from 1865 to 1890?

    A. Northern and Western Europe

    B. Southern and Eastern Europe

    C. Asia

    D. Africa

56. Which of the following best describes the Vietnam War?

    A. South Vietnam invaded Laos with the help of the Soviet Union.

    B. Following the negotiation of the Paris Peace Accords, North Vietnam invaded South Vietnam and captured Saigon.

    C. Viet Cong from the south launched a guerilla war against the north.

    D. The Gulf of Tonkin Resolution was a declaration of war on Vietnam by the United States.

57. In the early years of self-government the United States implemented a national government based on the Articles of Confederation. What were some of the key weaknesses?

      I.   The inability to levy taxes, draft troops, regulate interstate and foreign trade

      II. The lack of a powerful or effective chief executive and a national court system

      III. The rule that amendments must be approved by unanimous consent

      IV. The inability of the government to make the states enforce legislation that they did not support

      V. States had no rights to raise militia

   A.   I, III, IV and V

   B.   II and V only

   C.   III, IV, and V

   D.   I, II, III, and IV

58. The primary American objection to the Stamp Act was that

   A.   it was an internal tax, whereas Americans were prepared to accept only external taxes.

   B.   it was the first tax of any kind ever imposed by Britain on the colonies.

   C.   the proposed tax rates were so high that they would have crippled the colonial economy.

   D.   it had not been approved by the colonists through their representatives.

59. Which of the following best describes *shifting cultivation*?

   A.   Primarily a subsistence practice, it involves a farmer using a plot and then abandoning it for return at a later time.

   B.   Usually a commercial agriculture endeavor, it involves rotating one crop type on a plot for another in a sequential pattern.

   C.   It is the movement of pastoral nomads from one food source to another.

   D.   Only used in wetlands, it is the use of pyramid-style farms for rice farming.

60. What was unique about the Hammurabi Code?

    A. It was the earliest-known example of a ruler proclaiming publicly to his people an entire body of laws.

    B. It was written in books that citizens could reference.

    C. It established a court system.

    D. It was the first body of laws based on the principle of human rights.

61. Which of the following individuals would NOT be considered a participant in the Protestant Reformation?

    A. Martin Luther

    B. John Calvin

    C. Jan Hus

    D. René Descartes

62. Which is NOT one of the four basic economic activities of capitalism?

    A. Production

    B. Distribution

    C. Manufacturing

    D. Labor

63. One of the chief crops in Central America is

    A. wheat.

    B. barley.

    C. bananas.

    D. rice.

64. Which of the following factors is NOT generally accepted as a reason for the fall of the Roman Empire?

    A. Decline in morals and values

    B. Public health and environmental issues

    C. Political corruption and no clear process by which to choose a new emperor

    D. Lack of an education system

Question 65 is based on the following:

The sixth-grade students in Ms. Alvarez's class are studying Native Americans. Ms. Alvarez wants to strengthen her students' ability to work independently. She also wants to provide opportunities for the students to use a variety of print and media resources during this unit of study. Ms. Alvarez plans to begin the unit by leading the class in a brainstorming session to formulate questions to guide their research about Native Americans.

65. Which of the following criteria should guide Ms. Alvarez as she leads the brainstorming session?

    A.   The questions should emphasize the factual content presented in the available print materials.

    B.   The questions should emphasize higher order thinking skills, such as comparison, analysis, and evaluation.

    C.   The questions should reflect the interest of the students.

    D.   The questions should include all of the sixth-grade objectives for this unit.

66. There are two categories of maps—reference maps and thematic maps. An atlas is an example of a

    A.   reference map.

    B.   thematic map.

    C.   physical map.

    D.   population map.

67. Which of the following is NOT an assumption of the Production Possibilities Frontier Curve model?

    A.   Society is capable of producing only two goods, e.g. guns and butter.

    B.   At a given point in time, society has a fixed quantity of resources.

    C.   All resources are used in their most productive manner.

    D.   Demand for goods increases as the price and supply increase.

68. Which of the following best describes productive or technical efficiency?

    I.   Producing the types and quantity of goods and services that most satisfies its people

    II. Not using more resources than necessary

    III. Using resources that are best suited

    IV. An equal distribution of scarce resources

    V. Using technology that minimizes cost

  A. I, IV, and V

  B. II, III, and V

  C. I and IV only

  D. I, II, and V

69. Which of the following places is least influenced by conflicts related to multilingualism?

  A. Nigeria

  B. Venezuela

  C. Quebec

  D. Cyprus

70. Which of the following are components of human systems in geography?

    I.   War

    II. Immigration

    III. Beach erosion

    IV. Movement from the Northeast to the Southwest

    V. College students on spring break

  A. II and IV

  B. III, IV, and V

  C. I, II and III

  D. I, II, IV, and V

71. Air conditioning is an example of humans

    A. adapting to their environment.

    B. modifying their environment.

    C. depending on their environment.

    D. destroying their environment.

72. Who wrote the Bill of Rights?

    A. Alexander Hamilton

    B. Thomas Jefferson

    C. George Washington

    D. James Madison

73. How does the Constitution provide for political parties?

    A. Political parties are considered viable if they are on ballots in two-thirds of the states.

    B. The United States' bicameral system is set up for two parties.

    C. Political parties are not mentioned in the Constitution.

    D. Political parties are mentioned as an area of state authority.

74. Which of the following actions are primarily the responsibilities of the states?

    A. Ensuring public safety, administering and certifying elections, and recording birth and death certificates

    B. Regulating interstate commerce as well as television and radio

    C. Regulating immigration and naturalization

    D. Providing for national defense and creating money

75. The modern democratic state in which the people do NOT take a direct role in legislating or governing, but elect representatives to express their views and wants is called a

    A. republic.

    B. liberalist state.

    C. constitutional monarchy.

    D. totalitarian state.

76. Which amendment to the Bill of Rights states in part that "Congress shall make no law respecting an establishment of religion?"

    A. Amendment 14

    B. Amendment 5

    C. Amendment 1

    D. Amendment 10

77. Reaganomics is most closely associated with

    A. the "trickle-down" theory.

    B. the "controlled growth" theory.

    C. the "bubble up" theory.

    D. New Deal reform economics.

78. Which of the following best describes a major difference between a state government and the federal government?

    A. State governments have more responsibility for public education than the federal government.

    B. State governments are more dependent upon the personal income tax for revenue than the federal government.

    C. State governments are more dependent upon the system of checks and balances than the federal government.

    D. State governments are subject to term limits, where as federal government representatives serve unlimited terms.

79. Primaries are used in the United States to determine presidential candidates. Who decides the rules of the primaries?

    A. The Congress

    B. The state chief of elections

    C. The national committees of each party

    D. State legislatures

80. The civilization known for its massive pyramids of the Sun and Moon was the

    A. Aztec

    B. Maya

    C. Teotihuacan

    D. Monte Alban

81. Which nation was the first to declare war in World War I?

    A. Germany

    B. Russia

    C. Austria-Hungary

    D. France

82. Toussaint L'Ouverture led a slave revolt that eventually established an independent

    A. Colombia.

    B. Mexico.

    C. Argentina.

    D. Haiti.

83. Which of the following structures is the earliest built?

    A. The pyramids in Mesoamerica

    B. The Acropolis in Athens

    C. The pyramids in Egypt

    D. The lion gate in Mycenae

84. Put the following in chronological order.

    I.   The Han Dynasty

    II. The fall of the Roman Empire

    III. The first Olympic Games

    A. III, II, then I

    B. I, II, then III

    C. II, I, then III

    D. III, I, then II

85. Which of the following was NOT a result of the Industrial Revolution?

    A. Important developments in transportation, including the steam locomotive, steamship, automobile, airplane

    B. Important developments in communications, including the telegraph and radio

    C. Agricultural improvements that made possible the provision of food for a larger nonagricultural population

    D. The replacement of science in industry with the production line

86. Which of the following people from the Renaissance is out of place?

    A. William Shakespeare

    B. Geoffrey Chaucer

    C. Giovanni Boccaccio

    D. Galileo Galilei

87. Which of the following would be considered the key influence on the development of the nation-state?

    A. World War I

    B. Peace of Westphalia

    C. The Thirty Years' War

    D. The Trojan War

88. Which of the following do historians generally consider the earliest cause of World War II?

    A. The Treaty of Versailles

    B. The rise of Adolf Hitler to power

    C. The alliance of Adolf Hitler and Benito Mussolini

    D. Japan's success in China

89. On what date was Florida first admitted to the United States?

    A. July 4, 1843

    B. March 3, 1845

    C. July 4, 1845

    D. March 3, 1843

90. The Presidential Succession Act of 1947 established the line of succession for the president of the United States. Who succeeds the president if the president and vice president are killed at the same time?

    A. Speaker of the House

    B. President pro tempore of the Senate

    C. Secretary of State

    D. Secretary of the Treasury

91. Which of the following saw their roles change most in the period between 600 and 1450?

    A. Islamic women

    B. European women

    C. African women

    D. Latin American women

92. The Vedic religions evolved into which one of the following religions?

    A. Buddhism

    B. Hinduism

    C. Calvinism

    D. Aryanism

93. Which one of the following countries was among the last to give women the vote?

    A. Great Britain

    B. France

    C. Russia

    D. Norway

94. Why did apartheid in South Africa end during the 1990s?

    A. The African National Congress demanded that it end.

    B. Whites realized how discriminatory the policy really was.

    C. South Africa's leaders decided the policy was harming the economy and international reputation.

    D. Its goals had been long met and were no longer useful.

95. Which religion had its greatest impact on China?

    A. Hinduism

    B. Buddhism

    C. Christianity

    D. Islam

96. If the federal government wants to influence state governments in an area that the Constitution establishes as a responsibility of the states, what action can it legally take?

    A. The federal government can use executive privilege.

    B. The federal political leaders can pressure state leaders.

    C. The federal government can threaten to withhold money for projects administered by the states unless states comply.

    D. The states can ignore the federal government.

97. When colonial Massachusetts Governor Thomas Hutchinson attempted to force the sale of taxed tea in Boston in 1773, Bostonians reacted with the

    A. Boston Massacre.

    B. Boston Tea Party.

    C. Declaration of Independence.

    D. Articles of Confederation.

98. When did the young United States decide to form a militia?

    A. After the First Continental Congress

    B. After the Second Continental Congress

    C. After Great Britain's retaliation for the Boston Tea Party

    D. After passage of the Stamp Act

99. The Twenty-sixth Amendment was passed during the Vietnam era. What did it accomplish?

    A. The amendment established age 18 as the legal drinking age throughout the United States.

    B. The amendment ended the draft.

    C. The amendment established age 18 as the legal voting age throughout the United States.

    D. The amendment gave women the right to vote.

100. The Truman Doctrine was issued in response to the threat of

    A. Communist expansion in Greece and Turkey.

    B. threat presented by the Red Army in Central Europe.

    C. Communist North Korean invasion of South Korea.

    D. Communist threat to South Vietnam.

101. Ellis Island was the main entry facility for immigrants entering the United States in the late nineteenth- and early twentieth-centuries. Which of the following statements about Ellis Island is true?

    A. It is within the boundaries of Massachusetts.

    B. Twelve million immigrants were inspected there.

    C. It was one of only 10 processing stations opened by the federal government.

    D. About one-third of all immigrants were denied admission to the United States and sent back to their countries of origin.

102. All of the following inventions or processes were significant parts of the Industrial Revolution EXCEPT the

    A. steam engine.

    B. Bessemer process.

    C. electric motor.

    D. spinning jenny.

103. Which of the following best describes the agreement that ended the 1962 Cuban Missile Crisis?

    A.   The Soviet Union agreed not to station troops in Cuba, and the United States agreed not to invade Cuba.

    B.   The Soviet Union agreed to withdraw its missiles from Cuba, and the United States agreed not to invade Cuba.

    C.   The Soviet Union agreed not to invade Turkey, and the United States agreed not to invade Cuba.

    D.   The Soviet Union agreed to withdraw its missiles from Cuba, and the United States agreed not to invade Turkey.

104. The Watergate scandal led to Richard Nixon's downfall primarily because

    A.   of his failed trip to China.

    B.   of his Vietnam War policies.

    C.   of his role in directing the cover-up of the break-in of the Democratic National Committee offices.

    D.   of his involvement with organized crime.

105. The "War on Poverty" was an attempt by

    A.   President Johnson to end hunger and economic despair in America.

    B.   President Kennedy to organize the Peace Corps.

    C.   George Marshall to feed the people of Europe after World War II.

    D.   President Eisenhower to reduce the number of people on public assistance.

106. Which scholar below may be best associated with human development?

    A.   Jean Piaget

    B.   Albert Einstein

    C.   John Stewart Gardner

    D.   John Dewey

107. Which of the following is NOT a characteristic of human populations?

    A. Death

    B. Marriage and divorce

    C. Athletic interests

    D. Migration

108. Cultural anthropologists systematically compare similar cultures. What is this process called?

    A. Social networking

    B. Cultural mapping

    C. Ethnology

    D. Mixed method analysis

109. Which of the following is most closely associated with social psychologists?

    A. Quantitative research

    B. Qualitative research

    C. Talk therapy

    D. Group therapy

110. The term *multicultural diversity* generally does NOT include

    A. race.

    B. culture.

    C. ethnicity.

    D. class.

111. In psychology, *perception* is

    A. the process of attaining awareness or understanding of sensory information.

    B. reality.

    C. one's point of view.

    D. a social issue.

112. *Deviant behavior* is the term used by sociologists to describe behaviors which the dominant group defines as

    A. violating basic norms.

    B. uncommonly brave or heroic.

    C. the standard for others to follow.

    D. very rare or unusual.

113. Mr. Robert's eighth grade social studies class has developed a research project to survey student use of various types of video games. They designed a questionnaire and then administered it to all sixth-, seventh-, and eighth-grade students on their campus. The students plan to analyze their data, and then develop a presentation to show at the next parent-teacher meeting. Which types of computer software would be helpful during this class project?

    I. Word processing

    II. Database

    III. Simulation

    IV. Graph/chart

    A. I, II, and IV only

    B. I and III only

    C. III and IV only

    D. I, II, III, and IV

Use the table below to answer questions 114 and 115.

Population of the United States by Sex, Age, Hispanic Origin, and Race: 2008 (Numbers in thousands. Civilian non-institutionalized population[1])

Sex and age	Hispanic		White alone		All other races	
	Number	Percent	Number	Percent	Number	Percent
Male	**23,652**	**100.0**	**96,613**	**100.0**	**26,591**	**100.0**
Under 5 years	2,563	10.8	5,742	5.9	2,390	9.0
5 to 9 years	2,216	9.4	5,774	6.0	2,243	8.4
10 to 14 years	2,036	8.6	5,997	6.2	2,217	8.3
15 to 19 years	1,943	8.2	6,538	6.8	2,343	8.8
20 to 24 years	1,899	8.0	6,480	6.7	2,005	7.5
25 to 29 years	2,413	10.2	6,286	6.5	2,022	7.6
30 to 34 years	2,030	8.6	5,657	5.9	1,802	6.8
35 to 44 years	3,638	15.4	13,469	13.9	3,773	14.2
45 to 54 years	2,478	10.5	15,505	16.0	3,556	13.4
55 to 64 years	1,342	5.7	12,452	12.9	2,285	8.6
65 to 74 years	665	2.8	7,062	7.3	1,250	4.7
75 to 84 years	344	1.5	4,431	4.6	530	2.0
85 years and over	85	0.4	1,220	1.3	174	0.7
Female	**22,374**	**100.0**	**100,155**	**100.0**	**29,721**	**100.0**
Under 5 years	2,451	11.0	5,468	5.5	2,288	7.7
5 to 9 years	2,120	9.5	5,508	5.5	2,156	7.3
10 to 14 years	1,950	8.7	5,645	5.6	2,193	7.4
15 to 19 years	1,856	8.3	6,276	6.3	2,359	7.9
20 to 24 years	1,717	7.7	6,262	6.3	2,166	7.3
25 to 29 years	1,863	8.3	6,258	6.2	2,217	7.5
30 to 34 years	1,831	8.2	5,651	5.6	2,118	7.1
35 to 44 years	3,266	14.6	13,577	13.6	4,409	14.8
45 to 54 years	2,410	10.8	15,826	15.8	4,160	14.0
55 to 64 years	1,450	6.5	12,957	12.9	2,816	9.5
65 to 74 years	865	3.9	8,164	8.2	1,582	5.3
75 to 84 years	447	2.0	6,185	6.2	975	3.3
85 years and over	149	0.7	2,380	2.4	281	0.9

[1]Plus armed forces living off-post or with their families on-post.

[2]Hispanic refers to people whose origin is Mexican, Puerto Rican, Cuban, Spanish-speaking Central or South American countries, or other Hispanic/Latino, regardless of race.

SOURCE: U.S. Census Bureau, Current Population Survey, Annual Social and Economic Supplement, 2008. Internet release date: September 2009

114. How many Hispanic women are between the ages of 20 and 29 years old?

    A. 3,580

    B. 1,717,000

    C. 3,580,000

    D. Data not available in this table.

115. What percentage of the population are African-American males between the ages of 5 and 19?

    A. 25.5%

    B. 8.8%

    C. Data not available in this table.

    D. 17.1%

116. Which of the following fields of study is NOT included in the broad field of social science?

    A. Political Science

    B. History

    C. Sociology

    D. Archeology

117. A person who believed in Manifest Destiny in the 1800s would most likely want to

    A. preserve the environment.

    B. respect the rights of others.

    C. rule foreign countries.

    D. acquire more land and power.

118. The top official in the Department of Justice is the

    A.   Secretary of State.

    B.   Attorney General.

    C.   Chief Justice.

    D.   Solicitor-General.

119. President Franklin D. Roosevelt's programs of relief designed to end the Great Depression were called

    A.   the Great Society.

    B.   Fireside Chats.

    C.   the New Deal.

    D.   the Fourteen Points.

120. In the American system of government, *checks and balances*

    A.   regulate the amount of control each branch of government wields.

    B.   make each branch of government independent.

    C.   give the president control.

    D.   give the supreme court control.

PRACTICE TEST 2 ANSWER KEY

Question	Answer	Field
1	D	Economics
2	A	Geography
3	C	Political Science
4	B	U.S. History
5	B	U.S. History
6	A	U.S. History
7	B	Social Science
8	B	Social Science
9	D	Geography
10	D	World History
11	A	Economics
12	A	Economics
13	A	World History
14	A	World History
15	A	Economics
16	B	Economics
17	B	U.S. History
18	C	World History
19	C	Political Science
20	B	World History
21	A	Political Science
22	A	Social Science
23	A	Political Science
24	D	Political Science

Question	Answer	Field
25	D	Political Science
26	C	Political Science
27	A	Economics
28	C	Economics
29	A	Economics
30	A	Economics
31	B	U.S. History
32	B	Social Science
33	D	Social Science
34	C	U.S. History
35	C	Political Science
36	B	U.S. History
37	B	Political Science
38	A	Economics
39	A	U.S. History
40	A	U.S. History
41	D	Geography
42	D	U.S. History
43	D	World History
44	C	World History
45	B	Political Science
46	A	Political Science
47	D	Geography
48	A	Economics
49	B	Economics
50	C	Economics

Question	Answer	Field
51	A	World History
52	B	World History
53	D	World History
54	B	U.S. History
55	A	U.S. History
56	B	World History
57	D	U.S. History
58	D	U.S. History
59	A	Geography
60	A	World History
61	D	World History
62	D	Economics
63	C	Economics
64	D	World History
65	C	Social Science
66	A	Geography
67	D	Economics
68	B	Economics
69	B	Economics
70	D	Geography
71	B	Geography
72	D	U.S. History
73	C	Political Science
74	A	Political Science
75	A	Political Science
76	C	Political Science

Question	Answer	Field
77	A	U.S. History
78	A	Political Science
79	C	Political Science
80	C	World History
81	C	World History
82	D	World History
83	C	World History
84	A	World History
85	D	World History
86	D	World History
87	B	Political Science
88	A	World History
89	B	U.S. History
90	A	Political Science
91	A	World History
92	B	World History
93	B	World History
94	C	World History
95	B	World History
96	C	Political Science
97	B	U.S. History
98	B	U.S. History
99	C	Political Science
100	A	World History
101	B	U.S. History
102	C	World History

Question	Answer	Field
103	B	World History
104	C	U.S. History
105	A	U.S. History
106	A	Social Science
107	C	Social Science
108	C	Social Science
109	A	Social Science
110	D	Social Science
111	A	Social Science
112	A	Social Science
113	A	Social Science
114	C	Social Science
115	C	Social Science
116	D	Social Science
117	D	Social Science
118	B	Political Science
119	C	U.S. History
120	A	Political Science

PRACTICE TEST 2 PROGRESS CHART

Knowledge of Economics   ——/18

1	11	12	15	16	27	28	29	30	38	48

49	50	62	63	67	68	69

Knowledge of Geography   ——/8

2	9	41	47	59	66	70	71

Knowledge of Political Science   ——/23

3	19	21	23	24	25	26	35	37	45	46

73	74	75	76	78	79	87	90	96	99	118

120

Knowledge of Social Science   ——/18

7	8	22	32	33	65	106	107	108	109	110

111	112	113	114	115	116	117

Knowledge of U.S. History   ——/23

4	5	6	17	31	34	36	39	40	42	54

55	57	58	72	77	89	97	98	101	104	105

119

Knowledge of World History   ——/30

10	13	14	18	20	43	44	51	52	53	56

60	61	64	80	81	82	83	84	85	86	88

91	92	93	94	95	100	102	103

DETAILED EXPLANATIONS FOR PRACTICE TEST 2

1. **D**

   Answer choices (A), (B), and (C) are the three basic questions that economics seeks to answer.

2. **A**

   Volcanoes are created when an ocean plate subducts, or moves beneath, a continental plate. Plates bumping together cause mountains to form. Plate tectonics has nothing to do with hurricanes.

3. **C**

   Only states can approve a proposed constitutional amendment. This requires an approval of a three-fourths majority of the states to be ratified.

4. **B**

   The principle of popular sovereignty was a central feature of the Kansas-Nebraska Act. A favorite policy of Democrats during the late 1840s and early 1850s, it proved a failure in solving the impasse over the status of slavery in the territories.

5. **B**

   Kennedy came off looking better in the televised debates. Americans were perhaps somewhat bored with Eisenhower, though not deeply dissatisfied; there were no revelations of corruption on Nixon's part; Kennedy had never been governor; and Nixon, like Kennedy had served in the Navy during World War II.

6. **A**

   The French and Indian War, or the Seven Years' War, occurred prior to the Revolutionary War. The War of 1812 occurred several decades after the Revolution that created the United States.

7. **B**

    Choice is an important element in motivating students to learn. Answer choice (A) is contradictory to the stated purpose of the activity. The students proposed the questions, so covering all the questions should not be a problem. Answer choice (C) is incorrect because the students have chosen what they consider to be key questions; the teacher should select different or additional key questions. And answer choice (D) is a possibility, but only if there is a specific reason why all the students should not research all the questions.

8. **B**

    Team reward, individual accountability, and equal opportunities for success are always present in cooperative learning. Rules and specific tasks may be part of the instructions given for cooperative learning groups, but are not required in cooperative learning situations.

9. **D**

    All are correctly matched.

10. **D**

    A student's daily class schedule is an external factor.

11. **A**

    In a market structure in which several or many sellers each produce similar, but slightly differentiated products, monopolistic competition is a very common market form. Each producer can set its price and quantity without affecting the marketplace as a whole.

12. **A**

    Structural unemployment, by definition, is the result of a mismatch of skills or location. This is a mismatch of job skills, as the robot has replaced the worker.

13. **A**

    Hinduism, Buddhism, Jainism, and Sikhism, the four major world religions founded in the region that is today's India, are spread throughout the subcontinent.

14. **A**

   The cities the Mayas built were ceremonial centers. A priestly class lived in the cities, but for the most part the Maya population lived in small farming villages. The priestly class would carry out daily religious duties, particularly sacrifices, and the peasants would periodically gather for religious ceremonies and festivals.

15. **A**

   Free goods are goods that are not scarce, which eliminates answer (D). Since people are able to use the free goods, the goods are not worthless. Free goods are not priceless, however, due to their abundance. Scarcity drives up prices.

16. **B**

   In a monopoly, one firm controls an entire industry, so the firm is the industry. Consumers (A) are at the mercy of the monopoly and there is no competition (D) because there are not multiple sellers (C).

17. **B**

   Though many factors might contribute to an individual's choice of party and the party's stand on such issues as states' rights, the chief factor during this period was acceptance or rejection of the French Revolution—Jefferson and his supporters saw it as good, Hamilton and the Federalists did not.

18. **C**

   The basic issue in the coming of war between the U.S. and Japan in 1941 was Japan's desire to annex large portions of China. The Japanese were not yet aiding the Germans in their war against Britain.

19. **C**

   The antiparty feeling was rooted in three basic beliefs: First, the Founders thought parties created and exploited conflicts that undermined consensus; second, they thought parties were instruments by which a small and narrow interest could impose its will on society; and third, they believed parties stifled independent thought and behavior. It is not surprising that the Constitution doesn't mention political parties, but it created a system in which parties, or something like them, was inevitable. When the Founders establish popular elections, they needed some kind of agency to organize and mobilize supporters of the candidates.

20. **B**

The Silk Road did not follow a single route. Crossing Central Asia, it branched out in several directions, passing through different oasis settlements.

21. **A**

The critical word in this question is *civil*, which refers to the law. Human rights (B) include civil liberties, but the term implies other rights not yet recognized by law. Natural rights (C) derive from natural law, not civil law.

22. **A**

Social studies instruction requires the teaching of facts, concepts, and generalizations and because one depends upon the other, they cannot be taught in isolation. Concepts rely on facts, but facts are meaningless unless they relate to concepts and generalizations. Generalizations organize and summarize information obtained from an analysis of facts. While a generalization contains a broad assertion, a fact is a truth about a particular incident.

23. **A**

The three-branch system of government created a system of checks and balances that would prevent any one branch from becoming too powerful, thus protecting the people from an oppressive government.

24. **D**

Social diversity is not a specific topic of study in political science. Political science does study and analyze the structure of government and other political institutions, and politics in general.

25. **D**

Answer choices (A), (B), and (C) are the requirements listed in the Constitution. Military service (D) is not required, although many presidents and presidential candidates have served in the United States military.

26. **C**

Federal judges are appointed for life by the president.

27. **A**

The facts from the graph may be used to try to prove the need to cut transportation oil consumption, but the graph itself makes no conclusions.

28. **C**

This cannot be a conclusion from the graphs, which are per person. Also, Canada, ranking second, has the smallest population on the list.

29. **A**

The Federal Reserve Board is a government agency consisting of seven members appointed for 14-year terms by the president, with the consent of the Senate. This board is at the head of the Federal Reserve System, which is comprised of member banks across the country. The primary function of the Federal Reserve Board is to implement monetary policy.

30. **A**

GDP is the total dollar value of all finished goods and services sold in the product market. This is done so that there is no double-counting.

31. **B**

James Madison was one of the authors of the Federalist Papers and wrote the initial draft of the Bill of Rights in 1789.

32. **B**

Ethnography is the systematic description of a human society, usually based on first-hand fieldwork. All generalizations about human behavior are based on the descriptive evidence of ethnography.

33. **D**

Choices (A), (B), and (C) are social issues considered being outside the control of a single individual and impact society-at-large and that can separate people in a community. Balancing a checkbook, while part of the larger issue of financial literacy, is not one that is divisive.

34. **C**

Operation Desert Shield became Operation Desert Storm on January 16, 1991. Immediate steps were taken to coordinate efforts with the U.N., protect Saudi Arabia, and impose economic sanctions.

35. **C**

The Bill of Rights guaranteed freedom of religion, speech, and press, and trial by jury.

36. **B**

The Harlem Renaissance is considered the first important movement of black artists and writers in the United States. Centered in the Harlem neighborhood of New York, the movement dispersed to other urban areas during the 1920s and promoted the publication of more black writers than ever before.

37. **B**

The Eighteenth Amendment made the sale of alcohol illegal. The amendment was repealed by the Twenty-first Amendment in 1933.

38. **A**

Since World War II, Florida's economy has become more diverse, with tourism, cattle ranching, and citrus groves, along with a host of new industries. Several major U.S. corporations have moved their headquarters to Florida.

39. **A**

In February 1950, Republican senator Joseph R. McCarthy of Wisconsin claimed that he had a list of Communists and Communist sympathizers in the U.S. Department of State.

40. **A**

Franklin D. Roosevelt was the architect of the New Deal, a plan to bring the United States out of the Great Depression, so answer choice (A) is most accurate. Adolf Hitler rose to power largely due to the economic misery that enveloped post-World War I Germany (B). Black codes were laws passed by southern states to tie slaves to the land. With regard to choice (D), Charles de Gaulle, president of France during the late 1950s and most of the 1960s, was not at the Tehran Conference; Roosevelt, Winston Churchill, and Josef Stalin were (C).

41. **D**

Space-time compression is defined as the decreasing effect of distance on the speed of human travel across space, in movement of people and communications. Choice (A) is the decreasing impact a phenomenon has on something as the distance from its origin increases. (B) refers to the negative impact of globalization in causing a growing divide between countries in the periphery and those in the core. Choice (C) is diffusion of an innovation that takes a newer form in the new place to match cultural customs.

42. **D**

Both the Public Works Administration (PWA) and the Works Project Administration (WPA) were instituted to reduce unemployment during the Great Depression and were part of the New Deal programs.

43. **D**

The Maya had no beasts of burden before the arrival of the Spaniards. Cattle, sheep, goats, and camels arrived in Africa through the migration of Asiatic peoples, who introduced the horse to Africa.

44. **C**

Britain added 4.25 million square miles of territory to its empire.

45. **B**

Realism has been one of the dominant forces guiding international relations theory and influencing foreign policy, especially since the end of World War II. Realism is an international theory that holds that nation-states are the basic governmental unit and there is no authority above individual nations.

46. **A**

Government by the many is what we have in the United States: a constitutional democracy.

47. **D**

Relative location implies a relationship between a specific location (the house) and the relative location (the Mayfair Shops).

48. **A**

When the Fed purchases bonds, it pays for them with money which increases money supply. Choices (B), (C), and (D) are contractionary moves by the Fed.

49. **B**

Choice (B) is the correct answer. The price of chicken and fish would be bid up by increased demand. The price of pork would go up due to controlled supply, and the price of beef would go up because it is a substitute for pork.

50. **C**

This is the most counterproductive to economic growth because it takes money out of spending circulation and reduces sales.

51. **A**

Taiwan declared itself the Republic of China following the flight of the Nationalists there after World War II. The government of Taiwan regards itself as the legitimate government of China, while the mainland Chinese, known as the People's Republic of China, regard themselves as the legitimate government.

52. **B**

The Stone Age is the time early in the development of human cultures, before the use of metals, when tools and weapons were made of stone. The dates of the Stone Age vary considerably for different parts of the world. In Europe, Asia, and Africa it began about 2 million years ago.

53. **D**

The *Iliad* by Homer is an epic poem recounting the Trojan War. It is considered a great work of literature, but is not one of the three pillars of Western culture. Rather, the three pillars, or foundations, of Western culture are ancient Greece (concretely Greek philosophy), the Roman Empire (specifically Roman law), and Catholic and Protestant Christianity. Broadly, these foundations are referred to as Greco-Roman and Judeo-Christian roots.

54. **B**

Southern states were required to ratify the Fourteenth Amendment. Actually, Black people had not always been granted full civil rights even in Northern states before the Civil War and after.

55. **A**

The Old Immigration, made up of those from Northern and Western Europe, still predominated after the Civil War until about 1890. Hereafter, the New Immigration, composed primarily of those from Southern and Eastern Europe, was most prevalent.

56. **B**

The United States never declared war on Vietnam, but opposed the Communist regime in North Vietnam. The Gulf of Tonkin Resolution authorized the use of force against the North Vietcong, but did not declare war.

57. **D**

Under the Articles of Confederation the United States government was weak and ineffective; more like a confederation of sovereign states, rather than a united country. Key weaknesses of the Articles included: its inability to levy taxes, draft troops, regulate interstate and foreign trade, its lack of a powerful or effective chief executive and a national court system, its rule that amendments must be approved by unanimous consent, and the inability of the government to make the states enforce legislation that they did not support. Options I through IV correctly identify key weaknesses and option V was never an issue under the Articles, therefore, only (D) can be correct.

58. **D**

Americans' primary objection to the Stamp Act was its purpose of raising revenue from the Americans without the consent of their representatives.

59. **A**

Shifting cultivation is primarily associated with subsistence farming, although it is also used by commercial farming systems. Essentially, it is farming a plot of land and then shifting to another plot the following year to allow the fertility of the soil in the farmed plot to regenerate. Answer choice (B) is incorrect because shifting cultivation is primarily a subsistence practice. Further, the rotation of crop types in a pattern on the same piece of land is known as crop rotation, not shifting cultivation. Option (C) describes pastoral nomadism; option (D) is intensive subsistence terrace farming often found in China.

60. **A**

It is critical to understand the importance of the Hammurabi Code. This code of laws is the earliest-known example of a ruler proclaiming publicly to his people an entire body of laws, arranged in orderly groups, so that all men might read and know what was required of them. The code was carved upon a black stone monument, eight feet high, and clearly intended to be reared in public view.

61. **D**

René Descartes, answer choice (D), was a mathematician and philosopher of the Age of Reason, an era that came after the Protestant Reformation. Martin Luther (A) was a leading voice of the Reformation who built upon work done by John Calvin (B) and Jan Hus (C). Many other reformers joined the cause as well.

62. **D**

Labor is a factor in creating all of the others, which are the basic activities.

63. **C**

Choice (C) is the correct answer. Some of Central America's chief crops are bananas, coffee, and corn.

64. **D**

Some generally accepted reasons for the fall of the Roman Empire are: decline in morals and values; public health and environmental issues; political corruption and no clear way to choose a new emperor; unemployment brought on by the advent of wealthy farm owners; inflation caused by the lack of the flow of gold used for coins; urban decay; inferior technology; military spending; and the return home of soldiers to stop a civil war in Italy.

65. **C**

The use of instructional strategies that make learning relevant to individual student interests is a powerful motivating force that facilitates learning and independent thinking. Choices (A) and (B) are both important factors to consider during a brainstorming session of this type, but both of these factors should influence the teacher only after the student interests have been included. Choice (D) indicates a misunderstanding of the situation described. The students are setting the objectives for the unit as they brainstorm questions.

66. **A**

Reference maps show the locations of places, and boundaries of countries, states, counties, and towns. Atlases or road maps are examples of reference maps. Choice (B) is incorrect because thematic maps show a particular topic such as population density, distribution of world religions, or physical, social, economic, political, agricultural, or economic features. Choice (C) is incorrect because a physical map is a thematic map that shows the topography of the land including land features and elevations. Choice (D) is incorrect because population maps are thematic maps that are used to show where people live in a particular region.

67. **D**

Answer choices (A), (B), and (C) are all assumptions that the model takes as a given to illustrate the axiom that economic choices we make result in trade-offs that can be measured. The Production Possibilities Frontier Curve is just one of the models which inform the realities that govern behavior in a free market system. As trade-offs are measured, we realize that various combinations of goods and services can be produced, but at a cost to production of an alternative good or service. Option (D) is not part of the model.

68. **B**

A society achieves productive/technical efficiency when it is producing the greatest quantity of goods and services possible from its resources at a minimum cost, thus using fewer resources and increasing production quantities. In turn, scarcity is reduced. Failure to do so is also a waste of resources which includes options II, III, and V. Option I is a function of allocative efficiency.

69. **B**

Nigeria, choice (A), has hundreds of local languages, which is one of the centrifugal forces challenging its unity. A major factor influencing the conflict over control of Quebec, choice (C) is the division between French- and English-speaking Canadians, because Quebec is where most French-speaking Canadians are clustered. The political conflict in Cyprus, choice (D), is highly related to the division between Greek speakers and Turkish speakers on the small island. By contrast, Venezuela (B) is considered by many to be as near to monolingual as a country can get in today's society. Spanish is spoken by a high percentage of Venezuela's population.

70. **D**

People are central to geography and make up the component of human systems. While human actions can have an effect on beach erosion, it is not a component of human systems.

71. **B**

Humans have learned to use technology like air conditioning to modify their environment. Though some may view air conditioning as a contributor to the destruction of the environment, (B) is still the *best* answer.

72. **D**

Initially drafted by James Madison in 1789, the Bill of Rights was written at a time when ideological conflict between Federalists and anti-Federalists, dating from the Philadelphia Convention in 1787, threatened the Constitution's ratification. The Bill of Rights was largely a response to the Constitution's influential opponents, including prominent Founders, who argued that it failed to protect the basic principles of human liberty.

73. **C**

The Constitution does not mention political parties. In fact, "factions" with "jealousies and false alarms" were feared to cause damage to the country. Political parties were thought of as searching for profit, not providing for the common good.

74. **A**

Option choices (B), (C), and (D) list activities that happen across state borders, so they are federal responsibilities. The actions in option choice (A) are local responsibilities.

75. **A**

The United States is a republic. The modern democratic state is usually a republic, in which the people do not take a direct role in legislating or governing, but elect representatives to express their views and wants. A democratic government exists when these representatives are freely chosen by the people, whose demands are then recognized by the duly elected government.

76. **C**

    Most people remember Article 1 of the Bill of Rights as the "free speech" article. It states: "Congress shall make no law respecting an establishment of religion, or prohibiting the free exercise thereof; or abridging the freedom of speech or of the press; or the right of the people peaceably to assemble, and to petition the government for a redress of grievances."

77. **A**

    Reaganomics was the term coined for President Ronald Reagan's supply-side economic policies. Reagan believed that the way to repair the shattered economy that he inherited from the Carter administration, was to cut federal spending on domestic programs while at the same time cutting taxes for the wealthy and for corporations, thereby allowing money to "trickle down."

78. **A**

    The responsibility for public education belongs to the state governments. The federal government has often passed legislation to regulate and provide funds for public education, but the main responsibility for establishing and regulating education resides with the state governments.

79. **C**

    The Democratic National Committee and the Republican National Committee decide how their respective party will conduct its primaries; each party has its own rules.

80. **C**

    Teotihuacan flourished from 300–800 C.E. and influenced other Mesoamerican cultures.

81. **C**

    Austria-Hungary declared war on Serbia, thus beginning World War I.

82. **D**

    The only successful slave revolt in history was led by Toussaint L'Ouverture at the French colony of Saint Dominguez on Hispaniola, which later became Haiti.

83. **C**

    The Egyptian pyramids were mostly built in the fourth dynasty of Egyptian antiquity, in approximately 3200 B.C.E. The pyramids of Mesoamerica were the last of the structures to be built.

84. **A**

    Greece was founded around 776 B.C.E., and Rome, around 753 B.C.E. The Han Dynasty spanned 206 B.C.E. to 220 C.E.

85. **D**

    Since the production line is an example of the application of science to industry rather than a replacement for science, (D) is the correct answer.

86. **D**

    Galileo Galilei was an astronomer and physicist. William Shakespeare (A), Geoffrey Chaucer (B), and Giovanni Boccaccio (C) were all writers known for great works of literature.

87. **B**

    The history of international relations is often traced back to the Peace of Westphalia of 1648, where the modern state system was developed. Prior to this, the European medieval organization of political authority was based on a vaguely hierarchical religious order. Westphalia instituted the legal concept of sovereignty.

88. **A**

    The Treaty of Versailles (A), signed in 1919, is cited as the earliest cause of World War II. The atmosphere in Europe and the attitude toward Germany in the period just after World War I was very anti-German. President Woodrow Wilson wanted a secure peace based on his Fourteen Points, because he wanted a peace that would be based on justice, that would have liberal principles at its core, and that would be maintained by a new international organization (The League of Nations). While Wilson agreed that Germany needed to be punished for starting the war, he wanted the punishment to be fair. However, Europe took the punishment to the extreme, setting the stage for the next conflict, World War II.

89. **B**

    Florida became the 27th state on March 3, 1845.

90. **A**

The succession after the vice president is speaker of the House, president pro tempore of the Senate, secretary of state, and then secretary of the treasury.

91. **A**

The role of Islamic women changed the most as they could take part in local trade and run small businesses, none of the other women could participate as publically.

92. **B**

Hinduism, the name given to the Sanatana Dharma by Muslim invaders, is the result of the evolution of Vedic religions.

93. **B**

France and Italy gave women the vote in 1945.

94. **C**

By the 1990s economic problems, internal unrest, and international opinions placed extreme pressure on the South African government to abandon the policy of apartheid.

95. **B**

Buddhism first came to China during the Han era, but few Chinese adopted the religion at that time. By the Tang Dynasty, Buddhism was well established as many of the Tang rulers were Buddhists and supported the religion.

96. **C**

The federal government has what is called "the power of the purse" which is the Constitutional power given to Congress to raise and spend money. With that power, Congress can compel states to act or not to act in a given area. Recent examples include money allocated for maintenance of the federal highway system which was tied to states changing the speed limit within their jurisdiction and the requirement of states to meet minimum education standards to receive federal education allocations.

97. **B**

The Bostonians reacted by throwing the tea into the harbor rather than allow the tax to be paid on it.

98. **B**

The members of the First Continental Congress had no desire to break away from Great Britain. By the time the Second Continental Congress met, however, military conflict seemed imminent.

99. **C**

The Twenty-sixth Amendment was proposed by Congress on March 23, 1971, upon passage by the House of Representatives, the Senate having previously passed an identical resolution on March 10, 1971. It states:

Section. 1. The right of citizens of the United States, who are eighteen years of age or older, to vote shall not be denied or abridged by the United States or by any State on account of age.

Section. 2. The Congress shall have power to enforce this article by appropriate legislation.

100. **A**

The Truman Doctrine was issued in response to the threat of Communist expansion in Greece and Turkey.

101. **B**

Twelve million immigrants were processed at Ellis Island before its closure on November 12, 1954. Ellis Island, located at the mouth of the Hudson River in New York Harbor, was one of 30 processing stations opened by the federal government. It was the major processing station for third-class/steerage immigrants entering the United States in 1892; it processed 70 percent of all immigrants at the time.

102. **C**

The electric motor was developed after the Industrial Revolution; the electricity was often produced by a steam engine.

103. **B**

The agreement ending the Cuban Missile Crisis called for the Soviet Union to withdraw its missiles from Cuba while the United States agreed not to overthrow Castro's regime there.

104. **C**

The *Watergate Scandal* is a general term that describes a web of political scandals from June 1972 to April 1974. All of the scandals relate to the burglary of the national headquarters of the Democratic Committee which was housed in the Watergate office complex in Washington, D.C. President Nixon, facing impeachment for his involvement in covering up White House involvement with the entire Watergate Affair, was forced to resign.

105. **A**

In his 1964 State of the Union message, President Lyndon Johnson called for a "War on Poverty." The Economic Opportunity Act of 1964 established the Office of Economic Opportunity to carry out antipoverty programs.

106. **A**

Jean Piaget's stage theory of development continues to influence teaching methodology.

107. **C**

Though many people enjoy and participate in sports and other physical activities, interest in athletics is not considered a characteristic of human populations.

108. **C**

Ethnology is a branch of anthropology that analyzes and studies the similarities and difference among cultures.

109. **A**

Social psychologists are devoted to quantitative, or empirical, research, which provides numerical data that can be analyzed and compared. Qualitative research provides verbal (word-based) rather than numerical data. Social psychology is not associated with talk or group therapy. Its focus is research.

110. **D**

Class is not generally included when discussing multicultural diversity. The term multicultural diversity refers to the state of racial, cultural, and ethnic diversity within the demographics of a specified place, usually at the scale of an organization such as a school, business, neighborhood, city, or nation.

111. **A**

In psychology and the cognitive sciences, perception is the process of attaining awareness or understanding of sensory information. It is a task far more complex than was imagined in the 1950s and 1960s, when it was proclaimed that building perceiving machines would take about a decade. But, needless to say, that is still very far from reality.

112. **A**

Deviance refers to those behaviors that a group stigmatizes because they are seen as violating basic norms. Rape, child abuse, and incest are examples of behaviors which are seen as deviant by many groups in the United States. Acts that are rare or unusual (D) are not considered deviant if they involve praiseworthy or inoffensive behaviors.

113. **A**

This question asks for an evaluation of which software programs will help the students achieve their goals of analyzing data and presenting the results. Item I, word processing, would be used in developing and printing the questionnaire, as well as writing a report on the results. Item II, a database, would be used to sort and print out information in various categories so students could organize and analyze their data. Item III, a simulation, would not be appropriate here because the students' basic purpose is to collect data and analyze it. The project does not call for a program to simulate a situation or event. Item IV, graph or chart, would be very useful in analyzing information and presenting it to others.

114. **C**

The question requires you to add the numbers of Hispanic women in each of the age brackets (20 to 24 and 25 to 29) together to get the answer: $1,717 + 1,863 = 3,580$. And, since all the amounts in the table are shown as thousands your answer must be 3,580,000. All of the other options are incorrect.

115. **C**

The tabular information in the "All other races" column does not break out the data by African-American, Asian, or any other races, therefore the data is not available. This table's *main purpose* is to display the population by Sex, Age, and Hispanic Origin and Race. However, race is constructed as white and other. Any analysis would need to account for the limits of any discussion of race other than white, since Hispanic is not a race; rather it is an ethnic identification. Many people who self-identify as Hispanic also identify as white. This table does account for that phenomena since it has the category, "White alone."

116. **D**

Archeology is the study of past human societies through the recovery of materials, e.g., artifacts, architecture and landscape. Archeology employs many forms of scientific analysis such as carbon dating and as such is considered a "hard" science. All the other options are social science fields.

117. **D**

People who believed in Manifest Destiny believed the United States had a right and duty to settle the entire North American continent.

118. **B**

The attorney general is the cabinet official in charge of the Justice Department.

119. **C**

Answer option (A) refers to President Lyndon Johnson's legislative War on Poverty which was patterned after Roosevelt's New Deal but Johnson's legislation was enacted in the 1960s. While Roosevelt did have "Fireside Chats," option choice (B), that was not the name given to his legislative priorities. The New Deal, option (C), was a collection of programs and legislation designed by Roosevelt's "brain trust" to bring the country out of economic crisis. The way to end the depression was that government had to regulate business and restore purchasing power to the masses by cutting production. Roosevelt and his "brain trust" believed this would lead to rising prices and rising wages which made sense according to the **economics of scarcity**. Roosevelt also believed in direct unemployment relief and repealing prohibition, Answer option (D) is the document created by President Wilson to put an end to World War I.

120. **A**

Answer choice (A) is correct; checks and balances provide each branch of government with the ability to limit the actions of the other branches. (B) is not correct because the founders wanted each branch interdependent. Choices (C) and (D) are also incorrect because they deal with only one branch of the government.

Index

NOTES

NOTES

NOTES

NOTES

NOTES

NOTES

NOTES

NOTES

NOTES

Installing REA's TestWare®

System Requirements

Microsoft Windows XP or later; Internet Explorer 6.0 or higher; 64 MB available RAM.

Installation

1. Insert the FTCE Social Science 6-12 TestWare® CD into the CD-ROM drive.

2. If the installation doesn't begin automatically, from the Start Menu choose the RUN command. When the RUN dialog box appears, type d:\setup (where d is the letter of your CD-ROM drive) at the prompt and click OK.

3. The installation process will begin. A dialog box proposing the directory "C:\Program Files\REA\FTCE_SS" will appear. If the name and location are suitable, click OK. If you wish to specify a different name or location, type it in and click OK.

4. Start the FTCE Social Science 6-12 TestWare® application by double-clicking on the icon.

REA's TestWare® is **EASY** to **LEARN AND USE**. To achieve maximum benefits, we recommend that you take a few minutes to go through the on-screen tutorial on your computer. The "screen buttons" are also explained here to familiarize you with the program.

Technical Support

REA's TestWare® is backed by customer and technical support. For questions about **installation or operation of your software**, contact us at:

> **Research & Education Association**
> **Phone: (732) 819-8880 (9 a.m. to 5 p.m. ET, Monday–Friday)**
> **Fax: (732) 819-8808**
> **Website: *www.rea.com***
> **E-mail: info@rea.com**

NOTE: In order for the TestWare® to function properly, please install and run the application under the same computer administrator-level user account. Installing the TestWare® as one user and running it as another could cause file-access path conflicts.